INTERNATIONAL LIBRARY OF SOCIOLOGY AND SOCIAL RECONSTRUCTION

Founded by Karl Mannheim

Editor : W. J. H. Sprott

A catalogue of the books available in the INTERNATIONAL LIBRARY OF SOCIOLOGY AND SOCIAL RECONSTRUCTION, and new books in preparation for the Library, will be found at the end of this volume.

HUMAN BEHAVIOR

and

SOCIAL PROCESSES

An Interactionist Approach

ARNOLD M. ROSE, EDITOR

UNIVERSITY OF MINNESOTA

LONDON

ROUTLEDGE & KEGAN PAUL

*First published in Great Britain in 1962
by Routledge & Kegan Paul Ltd
Broadway House, 68–74, Carter Lane,
London E.C.4*

*Printed in Great Britain by photolithography
Unwin Brothers Limited, Woking and London*

SBN 7100 3413 X

Foreword

WHEN ONE CONSIDERS how important symbolic interaction theory has been to social psychology, how great has been
the number of students who have been exposed to its teachings
over the years, and how abundant have been the scholarly contributions made to it, it is indeed surprising that so little should
have been done up to now to consolidate our knowledge of this
body of theory. Here is a singular lag which Arnold Rose and
his collaborators have sought to correct. They have given us in
this book the fullest available account of the theory of symbolic
interaction. They have provided us with more of its facets,
nuances, and implications than we have had before. Especially
have they demonstrated the utility of the theory for research.
This book shows that interaction theory can provide us with a
body of significant testable propositions regarding the relationship of self and society.

This book is significant, then, because of its subject matter. It
is important also because it is well done. And it is well done in
part because the contributors are all highly competent. Besides,
Professor Rose has exercised his editorial powers freely. He com-
missioned most of the chapters expressly for this book and provided common instructions to the authors. The result is a
symposium with unusual coherence.

Human Behavior and Social Processes meets a long-standing
need, and merits the attention of teachers of social psychology.

M. F. NIMKOFF

Preface

SOME SCIENTIFIC THEORIES are systematically stated and empirically buttressed by their innovators. Others grow crescively, with an idea here, a magnificent but partial formulation there, a little study here, a program of specialized studies there. The interactionist theory in sociology and social psychology belongs in the latter category: it had its predecessors in certain ideas of William James and James Mark Baldwin; it was developed in various ways by John Dewey, Charles Horton Cooley, William I. Thomas, Florian Znaniecki, Robert E. Park, and especially George Herbert Mead. Significant contributions were made by Ernest W. Burgess, Herbert Blumer, Everett C. Hughes, and Louis Wirth. Empirical researches supporting the theory were conducted by these and many others. Perhaps half the sociologists of the United States were nurtured, directly or indirectly, on its conceptions and approaches to research.

But nowhere within the confines of one volume has there been a systematic formulation of interaction theory, or a summary of empirical support for it, or even a collection of related contributions by several exponents.[1] For a theory which emphasizes the significance of self-consciousness, it has been unusually devoid of self-consciousness, as expressed by the writers most closely associated with its development. It does not even properly have a name, the term "interactionist" being a latter-day appellation

[1] There are, of course, excellent summaries of *symbolic* interaction theory and knowledge, in the narrow sense, but not of interactionism as a whole. Notable among the former are: Alfred R. Lindesmith and Anselm L. Strauss, *Social Psychology* (New York: The Dryden Press, 1956); Robert E. L. Faris, *Social Psychology* (New York: The Ronald Press Company, 1952); Walter Coutu, *Emergent Human Nature* (New York: Alfred A. Knopf, 1949); and Tamotsu Shibutani, *Society and Personality* (Englewood Cliffs, N.J.: Prentice-Hall, Inc., 1961).

used by only some writers. Some refer to it by the names of its leading discoverers. Some call it "action theory," following the terminology of the German sociologist, Max Weber, who independently developed a theory that is, in many significant respects, strikingly similar to the more comprehensive American-developed theory that we are considering. Some psychologists call it "role theory," although most of them are familiar with only a portion of the theory.[2] Others refer to it as the "Chicago tradition" after the fact that most of the early contributors to the theory were associated with the University of Chicago.[3]

Interactionist theory has had considerable impact on sociological research and thought, as the separate chapters of this volume will testify. Its influence has extended to a number of psychologists, psychiatrists, social workers, and others. The influence continues through the years. But the lack of systematic formulation and of "self-consciousness" renders the research contributions and extensions of the theory somewhat disparate; there is no adequate *cumulation* of theory and confirmation. One of the purposes of the present volume is to fill this gap.

There are two major strains in interactionist theory, separable although highly interrelated. One is through the study of the socialization of the child, and may be considered social-psychological in focus. This is sometimes called "symbolic interaction theory," and we shall use this appellation to distinguish the first strain from the second. The second strain is through the study of social organizations and social processes and may be considered

[2] The "translator" of interactionist theory for the psychologist is Theodore Newcomb who incorporated a partial statement of it in his *Social Psychology* (New York: The Dryden Press, 1950). While Newcomb acknowledged his sources and laid no claim to originality, some psychologists today refer to "Newcomb's role theory" while having reference to a portion of interactionist theory.

[3] Of the innovators mentioned in the first paragraph, Dewey, Thomas, Park, Mead, Burgess, Blumer, Hughes, and Wirth were at the University of Chicago for many years. The term "Chicago tradition" in sociology is also sometimes used to refer to approaches to the fields of human ecology and urban sociology developed by Robert Park and Ernest Burgess. In this volume we shall have practically no interest in the latter fields. It is a datum of interest to the sociologist of knowledge that only those who had little or no direct contact with the University of Chicago's sociology department think of it as being primarily associated with ecological theory and research. Actually the Chicago sociologists always regarded ecology as a minor sub-field of sociology.

primarily sociological in focus. The distinction between social psychology and sociology is neither clear nor always legitimate. Cooley and Mead implied this in insisting that the socialized individual and the society are two aspects of the same thing. Nevertheless, it is heuristically convenient to distinguish the behavior of the socialized individual from the social structure, social psychology from sociology.

There are several characteristics of interactionist theory of a methodological nature that are manifested in the contributions to this volume but are not explicitly discussed. They will only be mentioned here; more thorough study needs to be accorded to the relationships between theories and the methodology for their verification. The first characteristic to be noted is the tendency to select behaviors, influences, structures, and variables for study on the level of common experience with them. That is, empirical research tends to use observations from a selected portion of "everyday" life; abstraction is left for conceptualization, analysis, and generalization. Thus, the research technique tends to be observation in some form, rather than — say — experimentation under artificially controlled conditions. The methods of observation are manifold, ranging from raw impressions to highly systematic measurement, from the use of haphazard samples to the employment of sophisticated *post hoc* experimental designs, from concentrating on "objects" that are seen to statements that are heard or read. This emphasis upon observation distinguishes the researches of the interactionists from those of most psychologists.

A second characteristic rests on the assumption that human behavior and social life are continually in flux. There is no abstract separation of social structure and social change, although one researcher may wish to concentrate on the structural aspects of a dynamic situation while another may wish to concentrate on its changing features. Social life is assumed to be "in process" never "in equilibrium." The integration that is found in the individual or in society is assumed to be based on ever changing relationships, not on inherent tendencies of a homeostatic character. This emphasis on process distinguishes the thought and researches of the interactionists from those of most followers of "functional" theory in sociology (although in practically every other respect the two are very similar or identical).

A third characteristic rests on the assumption that all social objects of study (behaviors, influences, and the like) are "interpreted" by the individual and have social meaning. That is, they are never seen as physical "stimuli" but as "definitions of the situation." This arises from the assumption that man lives in a symbolic environment which mediates the relation of the physical environment to him. (This point will be explained further in the text.) When he is acting as a socialized creature (although it is recognized that man does not always act as a socialized creature), man is believed to *select* and *interpret* the environment toward which he is "responding." This assumption of the symbolic character of man's environment is largely what distinguishes the interactionists from most followers of "positivist" or "behaviorist" theory in sociology and psychology.

In contributing to a volume on interactionist theory and research, most of the authors of this volume do not thereby refuse to recognize inadequacies and gaps in the theory. The editor will use himself as an example in stating that most interactionists find many significant weaknesses in the theory: (1) There is a neglect of biogenic and psychogenic influences on behavior, and sometimes even a tendency to assume that these do not exist. It is legitimate to exclude biogenic and psychogenic influences for theoretical purposes, but not to minimize these influences when examining empirical data. Further, interactionist theory must assume important psychogenic influences at least in early infancy and in certain aspects of collective behavior. (2) There is a neglect of unconscious processes in behavior, and sometimes even a tendency to assume that these do not occur. While eschewing most aspects of psychoanalysis, several authors of this volume implicitly or explicitly accept Freud's theory of unconscious motivation. (3) There is a neglect of power relationships between persons or groups, and while these are generally assumed to exist, they are seldom given due weight. A few of the authors of this volume have found it necessary to bring political factors into their analysis. Thus, it seems that some contemporary interactionists are beginning to fill at least these gaps in their theoretical tradition.

In presenting a volume on interactionist theory and research, we are not declaring a faith or hoping to build a cult. We are rather systematizing what we believe we have already accomplished, taking stock of our strengths and weaknesses, correcting and extending our own intellectual tradition, and communicating to those who may not be already fully aware of what interactionist theory consists of. We follow our methodological assumption that everything is in process, including our own ideas and procedures. It may very well be that future developments in sociology and social psychology will find us narrowing the gap between interactionism, functionalism, positivism, and other theoretical orientations as they are actually used in our field. In presenting this volume, we do not pretend to follow exactly in the footsteps of our founding fathers, merely carrying on an intellectual tradition which they started. Nor do we pretend to be the only interactionists; the volume could only be so large and another collection of authors could have done as well or better.

In presenting this volume, we do believe that every serious student and investigator of human behavior should be familiar with interactionist theory and research. We have tried to present our materials in such a way that they will be intelligible and useful to psychologists as well as sociologists and to sociologists in the functionalist, historical, and positivist traditions as well as to sociologists in the interactionist tradition. But we are aware that, such being the nature of attachments and commitments to the theoretical tradition that one has been trained in (this itself as interactionist observation), most of the teachers who will want their students to read this volume will be in the interactionist tradition. While the volume is useful in several courses in sociology, it is most usable as a text in courses in social psychology. We hope its broad scope will not deter teachers of social psychology from so using it: interactionists generally consider social psychology as basic to the rest of sociology, and in these days when the boundary lines between fields are recognized to be matters of convenience rather than realities inherent in the subject matter, there is a certain advantage in considering the concrete contributions of social psychology in the study of the other specialized areas of sociology.

Although this volume is the joint product of many authors, it is believed to have a high degree of coherence not always found in symposia. This is due (1) to the common theoretical tradition which informs the work of all the authors; (2) to the fact that most of the contributions were planned and written specifically for this volume rather than being collected from the already published literature (only nine of the contributions have been previously published, in whole or in part, and these have been carefully selected as fitting into the plan of the volume rather than because of their publication in either prominent or obscure journals); (3) to the common instructions provided the authors before they began their writing. Still, there is no denying that this volume does not have the degree of integration typically found in the work of a single author. We hope this may have some advantages: it permits the cream of ideas and analyses to be skimmed from the work of many able authors; it permits the instructor who uses the book as a text to provide some of his own integration and his own creative contributions.

We launch this work in the hope that it will stimulate research as well as pertinent teaching in social psychology. The interactionist tradition has too often been thought of as long on theory and short on empirical investigation. The selected researches included in the volume provide diverse models for further investigation; most of the authors have sought to couch their theoretical analyses in terms of propositions susceptible to empirical verification. Students in the third or fourth years of the undergraduate college, or in graduate departments of sociology, ought to begin learning not solely in terms of "what is known" but also in terms of "how do we know it" and "how can we find out more about it." We hope that no one considers the contents of this book dogmatic; we trust that the book can be supplanted within a few years.

This volume has benefited from the editorial help of Irwin Deutscher, Meyer Nimkoff, Caroline Rose, and Sheldon Stryker. The editor alone must take responsibility for the organization of the volume, the selection of the authors, critical suggestions leading to revision of the contributions, and the headnotes to each contribution.

University of Minnesota   ARNOLD M. ROSE
June 1961

Contents

xiii

Contents

PART THREE
Studies in Social Process

Contents

Part One

THEORY FOR
SOCIAL PSYCHOLOGY

A Systematic Summary
of Symbolic Interaction Theory

ARNOLD M. ROSE

UNIVERSITY OF MINNESOTA

Symbolic interactionist theory, which guides many of the expositions and studies presented in this volume, had its American origin around the turn of the century in the writings of C. H. Cooley, John Dewey, J. M. Baldwin, W. I. Thomas and others. Much of the theory had an independent origin in Germany in the writings of Georg Simmel and Max Weber. Its most comprehensive formulation to date is the posthumously published volume by George Herbert Mead, Mind, Self, and Society *(1934). Perhaps because of the complex and unintegrated character of these writings, and their failure to use truly operational language, the theory has not had the understanding and testing which it merits. This first chapter attempts to restate the theory in simple, systematic, and researchable form.*

Because of its diversified origins, interactionist theory cannot claim complete agreement in concepts, premises, and propositions among all those who consider themselves its adherents. Thus, the author has to take responsibility for the specific formulation offered, and agree that at a few points he has made state-

ments for which equivalents are not to be found in the writings of the leading exponents of symbolic interaction theory.

Much of existing psychological theory is grounded on assumptions about vertebrate behavior in general and has sought confirmation in research on animals other than man — whether these be the rats studied by the behaviorists or the apes studied by the Gestaltists.* The result is that we know a good deal about man's behavior insofar as the principles governing his behavior are also applicable to other animals. When psychologists of the behaviorist and Gestaltist schools have studied man's behavior, they have either limited their study to those aspects of man's behavior which he shares with the other animals, or they have substituted middle-range theories in the place of large-scale theories. The frustration-aggression theory of the Yale neo-behaviorists, and the group-influence theory of the "group dynamics" Gestaltists are examples of such middle-range theories. Insofar as these excellent researches and theories can be linked up to large frameworks of theory they make no reference to man's distinctive characteristics which make his behavior different from that of the other vertebrates.

It would seem valuable to have a social psychological framework of theory — as distinct from a general psychological theory — grounded on assumptions about man's distinctive characteristics and on researches dealing with man himself. This would not be in opposition to the behaviorist and Gestaltist theories, but supplementary to them. Both psychoanalytic and symbolic interactionist theories seek to do this. The present essay seeks to set forth symbolic interactionist theory in a systematic fashion as grounded on man's distinctive characteristics. The attempt is made to state the theory in terms that will fit the frame of reference of the behaviorist or Gestaltist so as to make it more generally understandable. (It is not suggested that the theory is reducible to behaviorist or Gestaltist propositions.) Only assumptions, definitions, and general propositions are presented;

* This statement has benefited from the criticisms of Herbert Blumer, Caroline Rose, Gregory Stone, and Sheldon Stryker, but they did not always agree with the author or with one another.

specific hypotheses deduced[1] from the theory are set forth in other contributions to this book.

ASSUMPTION 1. *Man lives in a symbolic environment as well as a physical environment* and can be "stimulated" to act by symbols as well as by physical stimuli. A *symbol* is defined as a stimulus that has a learned meaning and value for people, and man's response to a symbol is in terms of its meaning and value rather than in terms of its physical stimulation of his sense organs.[2] To offer a simple example: a "chair" is not merely a collection of visual, aural, and tactile stimuli, but it "means" an object on which people may sit; and if one sits on it, it will "respond" by holding him up; and it has a value for that purpose. A *meaning* is equivalent to a "true" dictionary definition, referring to the way in which people actually use a term in their behavior. A *value* is the learned attraction or repulsion they feel toward the meaning. A symbol is *an incipient or telescoped act*, in which the later stages — involving elements of both meaning and value — are implied in the first stage. Thus, the symbol "chair" implies the physical comfort, the opportunity to do certain things which can best be done while sitting, and other similar "outcomes" of sitting in a chair. It should be understood, as Mead points out, that "language does not simply symbolize a situation or object which is already there in advance; it makes possible the existence or the appearance of that situation or object, for it is a part of the mechanism whereby that situation or object is created." (5, p. 180)

Practically all the symbols a man learns he learns through communication (interaction) with other people, and therefore

---

[1] The term "deduced" is used here in a hopeful, rather than a rigorous, sense. Ideally, the specific hypotheses ought to be logically deducible from the theory. Actually, the theory has not yet been elaborated to the point where the hypotheses used in research are rigorously deducible, and the most we can say is that they are logically consistent with the theory. Similarly, the general propositions ought to be deduced, but in fact they are merely logically consistent. (General propositions differ from hypotheses in that they are too broad to be empirically testable.)

[2] A symbol stimulates the sense organs too, of course, and in this sense it is also physical. But it becomes incorporated into behavior in a different way than does what we are labeling physical stimuli, which have a direct effect on behavior through the physical stimulation of the sense organs.

most symbols can be thought of as common or shared meanings and values.[3] The mutually shared character of the meanings and values of objects and acts give them *"consensual validation,"* to use a term of Harry Stack Sullivan (although it must be recognized that the consensus is practically never complete). "Meaning is not to be conceived as a state of consciousness," says Mead, ". . . the response of one organism [or object] to the gesture of another in any given social act is the meaning of that gesture, and also is in a sense responsible for the appearance or coming into being of the new object — or new content of an old object — to which the gesture refers through the outcome of the given social act in which it is an early phase."

Man has a distinctive capacity for symbolic communication because he alone among the animals (*a*) has a vocal apparatus which can make a large number and wide range of different sounds, and (*b*) has a nervous system which can store up the meanings and values of millions of symbols. Not all symbols are words or combinations of words that are transmitted through hearing — symbols are also transmitted through sight, such as gestures, motions, objects. But for most individuals and for men

[3] Common values may be considered in two categories: (1) *norms,* which are direct guides to actual positive or negative actions; (2) *ideals,* which are what the individual says or believes he would like to do, and which may coincide sometimes with the norms but at other times have only an indirect and remote relationship to actual behavior. Values have degree; and strong common norms have the character of mobilizing collective sanctions when they are breached. Even when ideals do not coincide with norms, they provide guides to behavior in the sense of being remote goals which are to be reached indirectly. When considering the values from a subjective aspect — that is, from the standpoint of the individual — we call them *attitudes.* Attitudes thus also may be considered to have two categories, the normative and the idealistic, and the difficulty of distinguishing between these two is one of the main sources of difficulty in using attitude research to predict behavior. Some sociologists and psychologists use the term "values" in the same, more restrictive, sense in which I use the term "ideals." Talcott Parsons, for example, says: "By the values of the society is meant conceptions of the desirable type of society, not of other things the valuations of which may or may not be shared by its members." (3) Everyday usage of the term "values," as well as the usage of most economists and some sociologists and psychologists, is the broader meaning which I use here. In any case, a term is needed to cover the valuational aspects of both what people say they would like to do and what people actually do, and "values" is as good a term for this as any.

as a species, sound symbols precede sight symbols. In other words, man is distinctive in having language, which is based (in the "necessary" not the "sufficient" sense of causation) on certain anatomical and physiological characteristics such as a complex brain and a vocal apparatus, and this permits him to live in a symbolic environment as well as a physical environment.

ASSUMPTION 2. *Through symbols, man has the capacity to stimulate others in ways other than those in which he is himself stimulated.* In using symbols, man can evoke the same meaning and value within himself that he evokes in another person but which he does not necessarily accept for himself. We may oversimplify and say that a man communicates to another in order to evoke meanings and values in the other that he "intends" to evoke.[4] Studies indicate that communication among other animals is based on observation of the body movements or sounds of another, and *invariably* evokes the same body response in the observer as in the stimulator. Following Mead, we may say that man's communication can involve *role-taking* — "taking the role of the other" (also called *"empathy"*) — as well as more spontaneous expression that happens to evoke in the other a feeling tone and body response which are present in himself. The learned symbols which require role-taking for their communication Mead called *significant symbols*, as distinguished from *natural signs*, which instinctively evoke the same body responses and feeling tones in the observer as in the original expresser. An animal expresses natural signs whether another animal is around or not, but the human individual does not express significant symbols unless another person is around to observe them (except when he wishes to designate a meaning or value to himself or to a spiritual force imagined to be present); yet both signs and symbols are means of communication.

In communication by natural signs, the communicator *controls* the behavior of the attender, whether by intention or not, for the body of the attender invariably responds in a specific way to the impact of stimuli on his sense organs. In communication

---

[4] This is oversimplified in many respects, among which we may note: (a) that the meaning evoked is seldom absolutely identical for two persons, but is merely similar; (b) that the meaning evoked is not necessarily the one intended by the evoker; (c) that the meaning may be only partial and anticipatory of communication of further meanings.

by significant symbols, on the other hand, the communicator may *influence* the behavior of the attender, but he cannot control it, for the symbol communicates by its content of meaning and value for the attender. While the communicator emits the sound or the visible gesture, it is the attender who ascribes the meaning and value to the sound or sight. Thus the symbolic communication is a social process, in which the communicator and the attender both contribute to the content of the communication as it impinges on the nervous system and behavior of the attender. This is true even when the attender appears to be perfectly passive, and it does not become more true when the attender responds with a new communication directed to the original communicator.

For example, a bee that has discovered a source of honey wriggles in a kind of rhythmic dance. Other bees, observing this, tend to follow the wriggling bee to its discovery and so aid in carrying the honey to the hive, but each bee discovering a source of honey will wriggle whether other bees are around to observe it or not. The tension in the body of one animal, usually occurring in the presence of presumed danger, will transmit itself to observing animals of the same species; and we note in man also the tendency for emotion expressed in the manner or voice of one individual to be transmitted to other individuals. These are examples of natural-sign communication, and may have had the original biological function of alerting the observing individual, or otherwise preparing him to act quickly in response to dangers in the environment or to attack from the emotion-emitting individual. Communication by means of significant symbols, on the other hand, involves words or gestures intended to convey meaning from the communicator to the observer. It is not the noise of the words or the physical movement of the gesture itself which communicates, but the meaning for which the noise or physical movement stands as a symbol. Both the communicator and the observer have had to learn the meaning of the words or gestures in order to communicate symbolically, but the communication by natural signs takes place instinctively and spontaneously.

Role-taking is involved in all communication by means of significant symbols; it means that the individual communicator imagines — evokes within himself — how the recipient of his communication understands that communication.[5] Man can take the role not only of a single "other," but also of a *"generalized other"* — in which he evokes within himself simultaneously the diverse behaviors of a number of persons acting in concert in a team, a group, a society.

ASSUMPTION 3. *Through communication of symbols, man can learn huge numbers of meanings and values — and hence ways of acting — from other men.* Thus, it is assumed that most of the modern adult's behavior is learned behavior, and specifically learned in symbolic communication rather than through individual trial and error, conditioning, or any other purely psychogenic process. Man's helplessness at birth — his "need" to learn from others — as well as the relatively lengthy proportion of his life in which he is immature are biological facts which also aid this learning process. It is to be noted that this social learning process, while slow in the young infant, becomes extremely rapid. Through tests with readings or lectures using new material, it has been found that a normal, alert person can learn over a hundred new meanings within the space of an hour, and that most of this new learning can be retained for weeks without reinforcement. In most human learning involving trial and error (except for learning manual skills), it has been found that only one failure is enough to inhibit the false response, and usually one success is enough to fix the correct response — unlike trial-and-error learning among other animals, where many failures and successes are necessary to fix the new correct response.

All this is another way of saying that man can have a *culture* — an elaborate set of meanings and values — shared by members of a society, which guides much of his behavior.

GENERAL PROPOSITION (DEDUCTION) 1. *Through the learning of a culture* (and subcultures, which are the specialized cultures found in particular segments of society), *men are able to predict*

[5] There is a methodological implication here that the investigator should view the world through the eyes of the actor and not assume that what he — the investigator — observes is identical with what the actor observes in the same situation. Mead was emphatic in distinguishing between his own concept of "empathy" and Charles H. Cooley's concept of "sympathy" — defined as the process in which one imagines himself in the same situation as another.

each other's behavior most of the time and gauge their own behavior to the predicted behavior of others. This general proposition is deduced from the previous assumptions about role-taking with common symbols, as the predictions are based on *expectations* for behavior implied in the common meanings and values. A society can be said to exist only when this proposition is true. In this sense and only in this sense, society is more than a collection of individuals: it is a collection of individuals with a culture, which has been learned by symbolic communication from other individuals back through time, so that the members can gauge their behavior to each other and to the society as a whole.[6]

There is thus no need to posit a "group mind" or "folk soul" to explain concerted behavior or social integration, as some psychologists (like William McDougall and Wilhelm Wundt and others) have done. There is also no need to posit a "tendency" for society to have functional integration as some sociologists and anthropologists of the functionalist school have done.

ASSUMPTION 4. *The symbols* — and the meanings and values to which they refer — *do not occur only in isolated bits, but often in clusters, sometimes large and complex.* The evocation of a lead meaning or value of a cluster will allow fairly accurate prediction of the rest of the meanings and values that can be expected to follow in the same cluster. Different terms have been used to refer to these clusters, but we shall use the following two terms: (1) The term *role* will be used to refer to a cluster of related meanings and values that guide and direct an individual's behavior in a given social setting; common roles are those of a father, a physician, a colleague, a friend, a service club member, a pedestrian. A person plays one of these roles in each social relationship he enters. A person is thus likely to play many roles in the course of a day, and role-playing constitutes much of his behavior. (2) The term *structure* will be used to refer to a cluster of related meanings and values that govern a given social setting, including the relationships of all the individual roles that are expected parts of it. Structures may be fairly small or temporary ones, such as a conference committee, or a large and "permanent" one, such as a state or a society. A structure and the roles that

[6] Whether this be in cooperation or in conflict is unimportant in this context.

are related in it are two aspects of the same thing, one looked at from the standpoint of the individual, the other looked at from the standpoint of the social setting.

GENERAL PROPOSITION (DEDUCTION) 2. *The individual defines (has a meaning for) himself as well as other objects, actions, and characteristics.* The definition of himself as a specific role-player in a given relationship is what Mead calls a *"me."* William James observed that each of us has as many selves as there are groups to which we belong; or — in Mead's terminology — we have a defined "me" corresponding to each of our roles (i.e., "me" and role are the same thing, the first viewed from the subjective aspect and the second viewed by another person or persons). Some roles may have more positive value associated with them than do others; the "groups" or relationships in which we play these more highly valued roles are called reference groups.[7] An individual's various "me's" are seen by him not only as discrete objects; he may perceive all of them at once and in a hierarchy according to the degree of positive attitude he holds toward them. This perception of himself as a whole Mead called the

[7] I would prefer calling them "reference relationships" rather than "reference groups," since the term "group" usually refers to a number of individuals, whereas a "relationship" can be to only one other person or to oneself alone. Also, the term "group" is sometimes confused with a collectivity or agglomeration of individuals in which no relationship is involved, such as all people aged 10–20, an audience in a darkened theater, or the observers of a given advertisement. A *relationship* occurs when — and only when — role-taking is involved among the persons in the group.

While I have said that a reference relationship is one which is valued highly, the term is obviously relative; except for the very lowest one, every reference relationship is higher than some other one. We must think of reference relationships as forming a continuum from high to low with some of the low ones possibly even having a negative value. *Negative reference relationships* seem typically to occur when a person is forced into having the relationship against his personal values, and is obliged to act in accord with the expectations for one in the relationship, as in the case of a Negro who hates being a Negro but is obliged by his Negroness to act in accord with the expectations for Negroes' behavior.

Mead used the terms "significant other" and "significant others," but these do not allow for the "other" to be oneself, nor do they imply that there are *degrees* of significance. The concept of "reference relationship" seems best because it permits the "other" to be a single individual, a group, or even oneself in the case of a narcissistic individual. It also permits one to have degrees of "reference" or "significance" in the relationship, even down to a negative value.

"*I*," or "self-conception."[8] Once defined, the self-conception takes on characteristics and attributes which are not necessarily part of its constituent roles. That is, the self-conception acquires a purely personal aspect once the individual establishes a relationship to himself. Mead distinguished the "I" and "me" as follows: "The 'I' is the response of the organism to the attitudes of the others; the 'me' is the organized set of attitudes of others which one himself assumes. The attitudes of the others constitute the organized 'me,' and then one reacts toward that as an 'I.'" In sum, the individual has parts of himself which are reflections of his relationships with others, and which others can take the role of and predict fairly accurately how the individual is going to behave in the relationship. There is another part of the individual — his self-conception — the attitudes of which may be, in part, assigned by the individual to himself and which are not necessarily expected in the culture. This personal self-conception may be conformist as well as deviant, and while it is always subject to change, it is often stable enough for another person to predict fairly accurately what behavior the individual will engage in even aside from the cultural expectations for his roles. The "I," while personal, is by no means independent of cultural expectations, since it is built on the individual's "me's," and since the individual always sees himself in relation to the community.

ASSUMPTION 5. *Thinking is the process by which possible symbolic solutions and other future courses of action are examined, assessed for their relative advantages and disadvantages in terms of the values of the individual, and one of them chosen for action.* Thinking is strictly a symbolic process because the alternatives assessed are certain relevant meanings, and the assessment is made in terms of the individual's values. In thinking, the individual takes his own role to imagine himself in various possible relevant situations. Thinking is a kind of substitute for trial-and-error behavior (which most animal species engage in) in that possible future behaviors are imagined (as "trials") and are accepted or rejected (as "successes" or "errors"). Thought can lead to learning, not through hedonistic rejection of errors or reinforce-

---

8 It is not clear whether Mead equated the "self-conception" with the "I" or the "me," but the author of this article finds it more consistent and otherwise preferable to equate the conception of self with the "I."

ment of successful trials, but through drawing out deductively the implications of empirical data already known. Thinking is generally more efficient than actual trial-and-error behavior in that (*a*) imaginative trials usually occur more rapidly than behavioral trials, (*b*) the individual can select the best solution (or future course of action) known to him rather than merely the first successful solution, and (*c*) he takes less risk in experimenting with trials that are likely to be dangerous. Through thinking, man brings the imagined or expected future into the present, so that present behavior can be a response to future expected stimuli, and courses of action can be laid out for quite some time into the future. For example, a college freshman, in choosing a future occupation, engages in immediate behavior intended to get him into that occupation and lays out future actions for himself that will probably get him into that occupation. In much the same way that the future is brought into the present during the process of thinking, so is the past. The individual imagines the past symbolically — not only his own past experience but the past experiences of anyone he knows about, including people who lived thousands of years ago. Present and future courses of action may be selected in terms of what the individual knows, or thinks he knows, about the past.

The presentation of symbolic interaction theory thus far has been analytic in terms of its major concepts and their assumed interrelationships. The presentation can also be genetic — that is, in terms of the process of socialization of the individual child. This approach will now be presented in brief form.

ASSUMPTION 1. *Society — a network of interacting individuals — with its culture — the related meanings and values by means of which individuals interact — precedes any existing individual.* The implication of this assumption is that the individual is expected to learn the requirements for behavior found in the culture and to conform to them most of the time. Robert E. Park put this in epigrammatic form: "Man is not born human. It is only slowly and laboriously, in fruitful contact, cooperation, and conflict with his fellows, that he attains the distinctive qualities of human nature," (2, p. 9) in which the word "human" stands for conforming to expected patterns of man's behavior.

While this statement puts the cultural expectations foremost, it does not mean a cultural determinism for several reasons: (*a*) Some of the interaction between individuals is on a non-cultural or natural-sign level, so that some learned behavior is universally human and independent of specific cultures. (*b*) Most cultural expectations are for ranges of behavior rather than for specific behaviors. The expectations that people will wear clothes, for example, sets limits for permissible coverings for the human body, but leaves room for considerable choice within those limits. (*c*) Most cultural expectations are for certain roles, rather than for all individuals, and for certain situations, rather than all situations, and the individual has some "freedom of choice" among the roles and situations he will enter. Different occupations, for example, require different clothing, and the process of entering a given occupation is not completely culturally determined. (*d*) Some cultural expectations are for variation rather than conformity. The scientist and the fashion designer, for example, are culturally expected to be innovators in certain ways, and their innovations are not predictable from the culture. (*e*) The cultural *meanings* indicate possibilities for behavior, not requirements or "pressures" for a certain kind of behavior (as the cultural *values* do). The fact that a chair is an object to be sat on, for example, does not mean that the chair is only to be used for sitting or that one must always sit when a chair is available. (*f*) The culture, especially our culture, is often internally inconsistent, and one may move from one culture or subculture to another, so that there are conflicting cultural expectations for an individual. This does not mean solely that the individual has a choice between the two conflicting patterns of behavior he is exposed to, or can make a synthesis of them, but also that he can — within the limits permitted by the culture — define for himself somewhat new patterns suggested by the variation among the old ones. (*g*) To extend the last point somewhat, whenever the individual is "blocked" in carrying on behavior expected within the society, he has some possibility of innovating — within the limits of cultural tolerance — to devise new behavior patterns that will take him around the block. The self — Mead's "I" — is a creative self (the nature of thinking in symbolic interaction theory has already been indicated). (*h*) Finally, the symbolic interactionist does not exclude the influence of biogenic and psychogenic factors in behavior, even though he does not incorporate them into his theory.

These eight important qualifications to a cultural determinism do not nullify the importance of the basic assumption that all men are born into an on-going society and are socialized in some significant degree into behavior which meets the expectations of its culture.

ASSUMPTION 2. *The process by which socialization takes place can be thought of as occurring in three stages.* (*a*) The first stage, in the young infant, is learning through some psychogenic process — such as conditioning, trial and error, or any process found also among the other animals — so that the infant is "habituated" to a certain sequence of behaviors and events. (*b*) When a blockage arises in this habit — for example, the mother does not appear when the infant is hungry — the image of the incompleted act arises in the mind of the infant. By designating the image with a word or words (perhaps not at first part of the common language but later so modified), he is in the future capable of calling up the image mentally even when he is not blocked. The image in our example is that of the mother feeding him, and through numerous similar events he is able to differentiate "mother" as an object designated by a symbol.

The world of the infant is at first a motley confusion of sights, sounds, and smells. He becomes able to differentiate a portion of this world only when he is able to designate it to himself by means of a symbol. Initially, the infant acts in a random fashion, and a socialized other responds to the random gestures in a meaningful way, thus giving a social definition to the random gesture of the infant. Once the infant understands the meaning of its gesture (e.g., a cry, a wave of the arm), through a combination of his imagining the completion of his act and of others' defining by their behavior the completion of the act for him, that gesture has become a symbol for him. Socialized others complete the act which the infant's gesture suggests to them, and thus make a meaningful symbol out of the gesture for him. The symbol may remain fixed in meaning and value or take on increments of meaning and value, depending on subsequent experiences. (*c*) As the infant acquires a number of meanings, he uses them to designate to others as well as to himself what is in his mind. In the increasing communication, very slowly at first but with growing frequency, he learns new meanings (and later values) through purely symbolic communication from others. The new meaning is transmitted through combinations of, and analogies with, existing meanings. This is not to say that there is no further psychogenic learning, but as the fund of vocabulary increases, the child is able to learn by means of symbolic communication with ever increasing rapidity. The amount of such learning can increase throughout life, although typically the child reaches a level of socialization after a while and so does not try to learn much more, or there is not much more to be learned unless he moves into another culture or subculture. The *rate* of such learning reaches an insurmountable level which is a function of the intelligence and time limitations available to the child. Except for rare spurts, probably no child actually learns as rapidly as he is capable of learning once he achieves an adequate vocabulary, so intelligence limits are never a barrier to socialization except for the feeble-minded child. There are, however, emotional and external barriers to socialization (4).

ASSUMPTION 3. *The socialization is not only into the general culture but also into various subcultures.* A society not only has a culture expected to be learned by all, but also distinctive groups with their own subcultures. By his interactions within these groups, the child learns their subcultures at the same time as he learns the general culture. Through adult life, he may change his group affiliations and so continue to be socialized into subcultures, even though he may already be adequately socialized in terms of the general culture. Some group affiliations are typically dropped as the individual matures, whereas others are characteristically retained. Socialization continues throughout life in another sense: the society and its groups are constantly creating new meanings and values (the individual himself contributes to these innovations) and their members usually learn the new, as well as sometimes learning to use the old no longer. This is a social change.

ASSUMPTION 4. *While "old" groups, cultural expectations, and personal meanings and values may be dropped, in the sense that they become markedly lower on the reference relationship scale, they are not lost or forgotten.* Symbolic interaction theory shares with psychoanalytic theory the assumption that man never forgets anything.[9] But this memory is not simply a retention of discrete "old" items; there is an *integration* of newly acquired meanings and values with existing ones, a continuing modification. In this integrative sense, man's behavior is a product of his life history, of all his experience, both social and individual, both direct and vicarious through communication with others. The long-neglected concept of the nineteenth-century psychologist J. F. Herbart — "apperceptive mass" — would be valuable here if it is understood that it applies to all behavior and not merely to perception.

The integrated, cumulative, and evaluated character of experience — symbolic learning — in symbolic interaction theory gives it certain aspects which are not found in other theories. We may consider the following characteristics of human experience as deductions from symbolic interactionist assumptions on a genetic level. In the first place, the relation of experience and behavior is seen as highly complex. While it is feasible to conceive of developing an automatic machine that can learn as an animal does, without symbolic learning — the "mechanical mouse" that learns to run a maze as efficiently as a live mouse — it is as yet beyond knowledge how to invent a machine that can learn and behave symbolically. It is not inconceivable theoretically to invent such a social machine, but the necessary knowledge is not nearly at hand, and the anthropomorphic machines optimistically or fearfully promised by certain scientists and engineers are a function of their behaviorist theories of man's psychology more than are a function of their present knowledge.

Second, a *group* composed of individuals learning by means of symbols, according to symbolic interaction theory, has a culture with a history. Thus there is no pure (i.e., uncultured) group that can serve as a universal control group in group-dynamics experiments. When Bales (1) sought to measure the characteristics of such a "universal control group" he soon found the characteristics of the group changing and he had to collect new individuals periodically. Symbolic interactionists would interpret

[9] Mead would recognize that it is possible for a person not to recall something he once knew. That is, he cannot guide himself by the recollection because it is not a specific object for him. In the text we are pointing to the fact that the unremembered object still influences his behavior because it has been incorporated into the meanings of other objects.

this to be partly a result of the individuals' getting to know each other and acting partly in terms of their increasingly informed expectations for each other's behavior. But, since each individual's behavior is a function of his cultural and subcultural experience in one degree or another, and since therefore he "knows" the other individuals as co-members of the society or subsocieties, they cannot form a "pure" group even before they come to know each other as individuals.

Third, because a person can never "unlearn" something — although he can drastically modify the learning ("relearn" it) — and because the conception of self is the most important meaning for man's behavior, a conception of self once learned affects an individual's behavior throughout his life. If an individual, for example, once conceives of himself as an alcoholic, a drug addict, a criminal, or whatever, he will never completely eliminate that self-conception, and — even if he were to be "cured" by learning new self-conceptions — a temptation to take a drink or drugs or steal something will have a challenging meaning for such an individual which it does not have for another individual who has never defined himself as an alcoholic, a drug addict, or criminal. The psychogenic "habit" may be broken, but the self-conception is never forgotten, and the ensuing behavior is an outcome of a struggle between an old self-conception and newer ones.

The symbolic interaction theory of human behavior has been stated above in outline form, without all the nuances and qualifications which its proponents would add. Mead's posthumously published *Mind, Self, and Society* is a far more complete and satisfactory, although in some ways obscure, statement of the theory. Yet the very starkness and simplicity of our statement has advantages for comprehension by those trained to think in other theoretical frameworks. Subsequent chapters in this work will develop selected aspects of the theory or will illustrate uses of the theory in empirical research.

References

1. Bales, Robert F. *Interaction Process Analysis.* Reading, Mass.: Addison-Wesley Publishing Company, Inc., 1950.

2. Park, Robert E. *Principles of Human Behavior*. Chicago: The Zalaz Corporation, 1915.

3. Parsons, Talcott. "Toward a Healthy Maturity," *Journal of Health and Human Behavior*, Vol. 1 (Fall 1960), pp. 163–173.

4. Rose, Arnold M. "Incomplete Socialization," *Sociology and Social Research*, Vol. 44 (March–April 1960), pp. 244–250.

5. Strauss, Anselm (ed.). *The Social Psychology of George H. Mead*. Chicago: The University of Chicago Press, 1956.

2

Role-Taking:
Process Versus Conformity

RALPH H. TURNER

UNIVERSITY OF CALIFORNIA, LOS ANGELES

Because role-taking is the central process in interactionist social psychology, it deserves detailed analysis in this volume. Professor Turner explores certain continuities in Meadian role theory through further refinement and clarification of the concept "role-taking." In pursuit of this goal, he reveals some of the weaknesses in the concept of social role as it has come to be traditionally employed.

Only a cursory glance at sociological journals is necessary to document both the great importance and the divers applications of "role theory" in current thought and research. First gaining currency as G. H. Mead's (17) "taking the role of the other," and adopted by psychologists reflecting Kurt Lewin's Gestalt approach (22), role theory was made to serve rather different purposes by three popular developments. Ralph Linton (16, pp. 113–131) employed the concept "role" to allow for variability within culture; Jacob Moreno (20) made staged "role-playing" the basis of psychodramatic therapy and research; and investigators bent on uncovering strains in organizational functioning chose "role conflict" as their orienting concept.

Simultaneously, several important criticisms have emerged. The charge has been made that the referents for the term "role" are so heterogeneous as to defy rigorous study and coherent theory formation. Some critics have minimized the importance of roles, suggesting that they are superficially adopted and abandoned without important implications for the actor's personality (14). Role theory has been repudiated as a system of rigid cultural and mechanical determinism (1, pp. 81–82). Role theory often appears to be entirely negative, to consist of elaborate generalizations about the malfunctioning of roles in role conflict, role strain, and so on, but to lack any theory of how roles function normally. Finally, role theory is sometimes redundant, merely substituting the term "role" for "social norm" or "culture" without introducing any novel dynamic principle.

All of these criticisms have some merit, but we believe that their validity arises from the dominance of the Linton concept of role and the employment of an oversimplified model of role functioning in many current organizational studies. Role-conflict theory should be firmly grounded in a sophisticated conception of normal role-playing and role-taking as processes. Such a conception is found or implied in the earlier Meadian theory. This essay will call attention to some pertinent aspects of the theory in order to show that there is more to it than simply an extension of normative or cultural deterministic theory and that the concept of role does add novel elements to the conception of social interaction.

Basic Elements in Role-Taking

The Role-Making Process. An initial distinction must be made between taking the existence of distinct and identifiable roles as the starting point in role theory, and postulating a tendency to create and modify conceptions of self- and other-roles as the orienting process in interactive behavior. The latter approach has less interest in determining the exact roles in a group and the specific content of each role than in observing the basic tendency for actors to behave *as if* there were roles. Role in the latter sense is a sort of ideal conception which constrains people to render any action situation into more or less explicit collections of interacting roles. But the relation of the actor to the roles which he comfortably assumes may be like that of the naive debater to the set of assumptions from which he confidently assumes that his explicit arguments are deducible, but which he can neither specify nor defend fully when challenged. Roles "exist" in varying degrees of concreteness and consistency, while the individual confidently frames his behavior as if they had unequivocal existence and clarity. The result is that in attempting from time to time to make aspects of the roles explicit he is creating and modifying roles as well as merely bringing them to light; the process is not only role-taking but *role-making*.

Military and bureaucratic behavior had best be viewed not as the ideal-typical case for role theory, but as a distorted instance of the broader class of role-taking phenomena. The formal regulation system restricts the free operation of the role-making process, limiting its repertoire and making role boundaries rigid. As the context approaches one in which behavior is completely prescribed and all misperformance is institutionally punished, the process of role-taking–role-making becomes increasingly an inconsequential part of the interaction that occurs.

Free from formal regulation, the self- and other-role perspective in any situation may occasionally shift. Roles resemble poles on axes, each axis constituting a dimension in space. In factor analysis, an infinite number of placements of the axes will meet equally well the logical requirements of the data. Similarly, from the point of view of the role-making process an actor has an infinite number of definitions of the boundaries between roles which will serve equally well the logical requirements of role-taking. But the placement of any one of these boundaries, whether for a fleeting instant or for a longer period, limits or determines the identification of other roles. It is this tendency to shape the phenomenal world into roles which is the key to role-taking as a core process in interaction.

Role-Taking: Process Versus Conformity

"Self-Roles" and "Other-Roles." Within the ideal framework which guides the role-taking process, every role is a way of relating to other-roles in a situation. A role cannot exist without one or more relevant other-roles toward which it is oriented. The role of "father" makes no sense without the role of child; it can be defined as a pattern of behavior only in relation to the pattern of behavior of a child. The role of the compromiser can exist only to the extent that others in a group are playing the role of antagonists. The role of hero is distinguished from the role of the foolhardy only by the role of the actor's real or imaginary audience.

This principle of role reciprocity provides a generalized explanation for changed behavior. A change in one's own role reflects a changed assessment or perception of the role of relevant others. Interaction is always a *tentative* process, a process of continuously testing the conception one has of the role of the other. The response of the other serves to reinforce or to challenge this conception. The product of the testing process is the stabilization or the modification of one's own role.

The idea of role-taking shifts emphasis away from the simple process of enacting a prescribed role to devising a performance on the basis of an imputed other-role. The actor is not the occupant of a position for which there is a neat set of rules — a culture or set of norms — but a person who must act in the perspective supplied in part by his relationship to others whose actions reflect roles that he must identify. Since the role of alter can only be inferred rather than directly known by ego, testing inferences about the role of alter is a continuing element in interaction. Hence the tentative character of the individual's own role definition and performance is never wholly suspended.

Linton's famous statement of status and role probably established the conception of role as a cultural given in contrast to Mead's treatment of role chiefly as the perspective or vantage point of the relevant other. Linton moved the emphasis from taking the role of the other to enacting the role prescribed for the self. In so doing, he disregarded the peculiar conception of interaction which revolves about the improvising character of the "I," the more rigid social categorization of the "me" than of the "I," and the continuing dialectic between "I" and "me" (17).

Roles as Meaningful Groupings of Behavior. Role-taking and role-making always constitute the grouping of behavior into units. The isolated action becomes a datum for role analysis only when it is interpreted as the manifestation of a configuration. The individual acts as if he were expressing some role through his behavior and may assign a higher degree of reality to the assumed role than to his specific actions. The role becomes the point of reference for placing interpretations on specific actions, for anticipating that one line of action will follow upon another, and for making evaluations of individual actions. For example, the lie which is an expression of the role of friend is an altogether different thing from the same lie taken as a manifestation of the role of confidence man. Different actions may be viewed as the same or equivalent; identical actions may be viewed as quite different: placement of the actions in a role context determines such judgments.

The grouping aspect of role-taking is perhaps most clearly indicated in the judgments people make of the *consistency* of one another's behavior. Such judgments often violate logical criteria for consistency. ' But the folk basis for these judgments is the subsumability of a person's behavior under a single role. The parent who on one occasion treats his child with gentleness and on another spanks him is unlikely to be adjudged inconsistent because both types of behavior, under appropriate circumstances, are supposed to be reasonable manifestations of the same parental role. A more devastating extension of the judgment of inconsistency is that the behavior doesn't make sense, that it is unintelligible. Behavior is said to make sense when a series of actions is interpretable as indicating that the actor has in mind some role which guides his behavior.

The socially structured world of experience has many dimensions of classification. The role dimension refers to types of actors. It is the nature of the role that it is capable of being enacted by different actors, but remains recognizable in spite of individual idiosyncrasies. While people tend to be given stable classification according to the major roles they play, the specific referent for the term "role" is a type of actor rather than a type of person. Such a distinction allows for the contingency that one individual may adopt even conflicting roles on occasion, and that otherwise quite different people may play the same role. There is a kind of structure represented in this conception of role — and implied, we believe, in the work of G. H. Mead — that falls between the rigidity of role as a set of prescriptions inherent in a position and Kingsley Davis' view of role as the actual behavior of the occupant of a status (8, pp. 89–91). Role refers to a pattern which can be regarded as the consistent behavior of a single type of actor. The behavior of the occupant of a given status is a unique constellation, its components tied together only by their emanation from a single individual who is oriented to a single status during the period of his action. But the folk judgment of consistency requires that some more general principle be invoked. The principle must either be one which is already recognized in the group or one which is capable of representation to a relevant group. The unique behavior of the occupant of a given position may or may not constitute a role, either to him or to relevant others, depending upon whether a principle is employed in light of which the behavior seems consistent.

A point of view in important respects similar to this one but also in important respects dissimilar is represented in Merton's statement on *role-sets* (18). The occupant of an organizational position is said to have a distinct role for each type of relevant other with whom he interacts in that position. The cluster of roles which he assumes by virtue of occupying the position is his "role-set." The key importance of self–other interaction in role theory is thus acknowledged. But limitation of the concept "role" to a single reciprocity provides less scope for what we regard as the other important feature of the role-taking process, namely, the process of discovering and creating "consistent" wholes out of behavior. The problem of the school teacher–mother which arises out of the need to compromise two roles because of simultaneous involvement in both is in important respects different from that of the school teacher who must devise and enact her role in simultaneous relationship to students, parents, and principal. In the latter instance there is no question of abandoning one relationship, and the essence of the role is devising a pattern which will cope effectively with the different types of relevant others while at the same time meeting some recognizable criteria of consistency. Except in special instances, these are not experienced as separate roles by their enactors or those to whom they are relevant other-roles.

Role-taking as a process of devising and discovering consistent patterns of action which can be identified with types of actors suggests a theorem regarding role-conflict situations which should be worthy of empirical test. Whenever the social structure is such that many individuals characteristically act from the per- spective of two given roles simultaneously, there tends to emerge a single role which encompasses the action. The single role may result from a merger process, each role absorbing the other, or from the development and recognition of a third role which is specifically the pattern viewed as consistent when both roles might be applicable. The parent and spouse roles illustrate the former tendency. In popular usage the sharp distinctions are not ordinarily made between parent and spouse behavior that sociologists invoke in the name of logical, as distinct from folk, consistency. The politician role exemplifies the second tendency, providing a distinct perspective from which the individual may act who otherwise would be acting simultaneously as a party functionary and as a government official. What would constitute a role conflict from the latter point of view is susceptible of treatment as a consistent pattern from the point of view of the politician role.

THE CHARACTER OF ROLES AS UNITS

Two lines of further clarification are required in order to give substance to the view enunciated here. First, the character of the reciprocities among roles must be specified in greater detail. How do self and other interact? How does the role of alter affect that of ego? Second, the character of the grouping principle that creates boundaries between roles requires further explora- tion. There is an apparent paradox in saying on the one hand that a fixed set of roles does not exist and on the other hand that people make judgments of consistency and inconsistency on the basis of their success in bringing a succession of actions into the sphere of a single role. Since the second area of elaboration con- cerns the relation of role-taking as process to the kind of investigation which centers on social structure rather than the individual actor, we shall examine it first.

Roles in Organization and Culture. The normal role-taking process, as we have suggested, is a tentative process in which roles are identified and given content on shifting axes as interaction proceeds. Both the identification of the roles and their content undergo cumulative revision, becoming relatively fixed for a period of time only as they provide a stable framework for interaction. The usual procedures of formal organization lessen the tentative character of interaction, making each functionary's performance less dependent upon his conception of the roles of relevant others, and minimizing the Gestalt-making process by substituting role prescriptions. The effort is normally only partially successful, as indicated by the abundant literature on informal organization within formal structures.

Studies of informal groups suggest that role differentiation develops around the axes of group functioning, such as the axes of securing agreement, acceptance of responsibility, guarding of group norms, etc. (3). Interaction in such a context permits role-taking in its "purest" form to occur. Interaction involving organizational or status roles is more complex, producing a compromise between the role-taking process and the simple conformity behavior demanded by organizational prescriptions.

The manner in which formal designations "cramp" role-taking can perhaps best be seen in relation to the reciprocity of self–other roles. In actual interaction the identification of a role is not merely a function of the behavior of the actor but of the manifested other-role. The role of leader, for example, incorporates a complex of actions which are supposed to be reflections of certain competencies and sentiments. But if the relevant others fail to reciprocate, or if they are already reciprocating to another person in the role of leader, the identical behavior serves to label the actor as "dissenter" and "trouble-maker" rather than "leader." Such labeling by the relevant others eventually forces redefinition on the would-be leader, who must then either continue in the dissenter role or change his behavior. Organizational definitions, however, seek to attach the informal leader–follower roles to specific positions whose occupants can be formally named. Part of the formalization procedure is the specification of ritual forms of behavior by which each participant acknowledges the nature of the reciprocity. The formalization is supposed to keep the officially designated followers adhering to the follower role, even when the leader fails to enact his leader role, and similarly to prohibit erosion of the leader role in case of non-reciprocation.

The effectiveness of such formalization efforts in limiting the normal range of role-taking adjustments is quite varied. The parent may maintain the exemplar role in the face of his child's non-reciprocation, or he may abandon it to enact a role on the axis of his child's pattern of behavior. The corporation official may continue to act with dignity as if his orders were being obeyed, or he may abandon responsibility and adopt a comprehensive pattern attuned to impotency. But the formal role itself, considered apart from the effective incorporation of the informal role, is merely a skeleton consisting of rules which are intended to invoke the appropriate informal roles. The formalized roles are to the full roles as detonators to explosives — merely devices to set them in motion.

The Framework of Role Differentiation... The unity of a role cannot consist simply in the bracketing of a set of specific behaviors, since the same behavior can be indicative of different roles under different circumstances. The unifying element is to be found *in some assignment of purpose or sentiment to the actor*. Various actions by an individual are classified as intentional and unintentional on the basis of a role designation. The administrator, for example, must make decisions which necessarily help some and hurt others. But the hurt done to some is defined as inadvertent insofar as the role is viewed as that of the impartial or responsible administrator. The individual who plays a nurturant, comfort-giving role necessarily establishes a relationship in which he is superordinated to the comfort-receiver, but the superordination is inadvertent. Since the role definition itself directs perception selectively, the superordination or the administrative harm may not be noticed by the actor or by relevant others. Role-taking involves selective perception of the actions of another and a great deal of selective emphasis, organized about some purpose or sentiment attributed to the other.

Role-Taking: Process Versus Conformity

Not all combinations of behavior are susceptible of being classed into a single role. Since, as we indicated at the start, the role-taker acts as if roles were real and objective entities, there must be criteria by which the actor assures hi. .self that what he has in mind is truly a role. Such verification derives from two sources, the "internal" validation of the interaction itself, and the external validation supplied by what G. H. Mead called "the generalized other."

Internal validation lies in the successful anticipation of the behavior of relevant others within the range necessary for the enactment of one's own role. This in turn depends upon the existence of roles which provide a pattern for interacting with an individual exhibiting the peculiar selection of behavior whose coherency as a role is subject to verification. The internal criterion means that a given constellation of behavior is judged to constitute a role on the basis of its relation to other roles.

The internal criterion can easily suggest that we have let a system of fixed roles in through the back door unless two important observations are made. First, there is not just one role which enables an individual to interact in what is adjudged a consistent way with any given other-role. Roles are often comprehensive alternative ways of dealing with a given other-role. The range of possibilities is further enhanced by the fact that normal interaction is to a large extent limited in intimacy, intensity, and duration, so that only a small segment of each role is activated. We propose as a reasonable hypothesis that the narrower the segment of a role activated the wider the range of other-roles with which it may deal and which may deal with it.

Second, in light of our statement that role-making is a Gestalt-making process, what cannot be conceived as constituting a role when related to a single relevant other-role may be so conceived when viewed as interacting with two or more different other-roles. The total role of the school superintendent in the study by Gross and associates (12) would not produce the requisite predictability in the responding teacher role, and therefore would have to be treated as incoherent behavior when viewed from its relation to the teacher role alone. But when seen as a way of maximizing predictability simultaneously in the relevant other-roles of school board member, teacher, and parent, the behavior

becomes increasingly susceptible of interpretation as the manifestation of a single role. What is inconsistent behavior viewed
in relation to only a single type of relevant other is perfectly
coherent in relation to a system of others.

The internal criterion insures that there is constant modification
of the content of specific roles, occasional rejection of the identification of a role, and sometimes the "discovery" or creation of
a new role. Such modification takes place in the continued interplay between the somewhat vague and always incomplete ideal
conceptions of roles and the experience of their overt enactment
by self and other. Since each interaction is in some respects
unique, each interaction incorporates some improvisation on the
theme supplied by self-role and other-role. The very act of
expressing a role in a novel item of role behavior enables the
actor to see the role in a slightly different light. Similarly, the
uniqueness in alter's behavior and the unique situation in which
alter's behavior must be anticipated or interpreted serve to cast
his role slightly differently. Internal testing includes experiencing
in varying degrees the sentiments or purposes which provide the
role's coherence. Differing degrees of involvement in the role
at the time of its enactment, and differing relations vis-à-vis alter,
allow the role to be understood in different ways, and each such
experience leaves its residual effect upon the self- and other-role
conceptions of the participants.

What we have called the *external validation* of a role is based
upon ascertaining whether the behavior is judged to constitute
a role by others whose judgments are felt to have some claim to
correctness or legitimacy. The simplest form of such a criterion
is discovery of a name in common use for the role. If the pattern
of behavior can be readily assigned a name, it acquires *ipso facto*
the exteriority and constraint of Durkheim's "collective representations" (9). Naming does not assure that there will be agreement on the content of the role; it merely insures that people
will do their disagreeing as if there were something real about
which to disagree.

Major norms and values serve as criteria of role coherency
since they are ordinarily applied with the implicit assumption
that no person can really both support and disparage any major
norm or value. There is probably considerable popular agree-

ment on the existence and character of a role of murderer, which incorporates a much more comprehensive pattern of behavior than just the act of killing or actions which are functionally connected with murder. The role is a more or less imaginary constellation of actions and sentiments and goals which describe an actor whose relation to the major sacred norms of society is consistent in the simplest way — by being comprehensively negative. Because most individuals have no opportunity to test their conception of the role of murderer by internal criteria, such roles remain relatively impervious to the lack of empirical confirmation, and can serve as sufficient other-roles for the highly segmented self-roles which the ordinary citizen has an opportunity to enact in relation to the murderer.

Role validation is also anchored in the membership of recognized groups and the occupancy of formalized positions. People easily form conceptions of the American Legionnaire, the Jew, the Oriental, etc., incorporating the sentiment and goals distinctively ascribed to members of the group. The greater tangibility of formal statuses and organizational positions as compared with informal roles means further that there is a tendency to merge the latter with the former. Informal roles are often named by borrowing from formal statuses with which they are associated, as in references to a "fatherly" role or a "judicious" role.

Finally, external verification includes a sense of what goes together and what does not, based upon experience in seeing given sets of attitudes, goals, and specific actions carried out by the same individuals. The sense derives on the one hand from what has actually been rendered customary by the prevailing social structure and on the other from the example of key individuals whom the individual takes as role models. Some of the divisions of task and sentiment imposed by the culture follow lines which increase efficiency in society, but others arise from accidental circumstances or perpetuate divisions which no longer have functional implications. Acceptance of the role behavior of an individual model as a standard may lead to the inclusion of much otherwise extraneous behavior within a role and to the judgment that kinds of actions which, by other criteria are contradictory, are actually not inconsistent.

Each of the several criteria, both internal and external, must operate in relation to the others. Under conditions of perfect harmony, the various criteria converge to identify the same units as roles and to identify their content similarly. But under the normal loose operation of society various criteria are partially consistent and partially at odds. Since working human motivations do not divide as neatly as society's major norms would have them, there is often a penumbra on the boundaries of those roles which are oriented to the mores when both the external normative and the internal interactive criteria are brought into play. The formal rules which are invoked when roles are named from organizational positions and statuses do not necessarily fit entirely the sentiment which is experienced when the role is played or taken in actual interaction. These discrepancies which arise from the operation of multiple criteria for role units insure that the framework of roles will operate as a hazily conceived ideal framework for behavior rather than as an unequivocal set of formulas. In a sense, role conceptions are creative compromises, and an important phase of role theory should concern itself with how they are achieved.

THE NATURE OF ROLE INTERACTION

Two facets of the role-taking process have been stressed in this statement, namely, the process of grouping behavior into "consistent" units which correspond to generalizable types of actors, and the process of organizing behavior vis-à-vis relevant others. We have elaborated somewhat the character and bases for the Gestalt-forming aspect of role-taking. There remains for further clarification the nature of relationships between self- and other-roles.

Dynamics of Self and Other. The customary use of the concept of role in sociological and related literature today depicts the dynamic relationship between roles as primarily *conformity*. There are three key terms in this popular model, namely, *conformity, expectation,* and *approval*. A component of each role is a set of expectations regarding the behavior of individuals in relevant other-roles. When ego takes the role of alter the aspect of alter's role to which he is crucially sensitive is the set of expectations with respect to his (ego's) role. Ego takes the role of alter in order to conform to alter's expectations. Lack of conformity must be explained by erroneous role-taking, or by deficiencies in empathic ability or opportunities to perceive and judge the role of the other. The confirmation that role-taking and role-playing have proceeded correctly according to the conformity principle is the registration of approval.

We suggest that the foregoing model is not in itself incorrect; it is merely of insufficient generality. It describes only one of several ways in which the role-taking and role-playing process may occur, only one of several kinds of dynamic relations which may exist between self- and other-roles. Instead, we propose that the relations between self- and other-roles are interactive in a full sense, the dynamic principles being of several sorts, depending upon the objectives of the role-players and upon the character of their relationships with one another. Furthermore, the enactment of a given role often involves the simultaneous role-taking relationship with several different other-roles, and the dynamic relationship between each self- and other-role may be of a different sort.

In some athletic events such as the game of baseball the roles are highly standardized and the allowance for improvisation is at a minimum, so that the assumption that each role incorporates clear expectations for each other-role is quite valid. But in most situations what the role-player expects from the relevant other on the basis of the latter's role is not likely to be a specific action but some behavior which will be susceptible to interpretation as directed toward the ends associated with the other-role, expressive of the sentiment which dominates the role in question, or as consistent with the values attached to the role. A group torn by internal dissension may turn to someone who it is hoped will enact the role of compromiser. In doing so they have an expectation which identifies the general purpose and sentiment which will guide his actions and some general conception of the kind of behavior which will contribute to the achievement of compromise and which will not. But they do not have any exact notion of what the specific steps will be.

The articulation of behavior between roles may be described better by the term "preparedness" than by the term "expectation." The crucial consideration is that ego's role *prepares* him for a loosely definable *range* of responses from alter on the basis of the latter's role. The potential responses of alter, then, divide into those which are readily interpretable upon the basis of the assumed self- and other-roles and those which seem not to make sense from this vantage point. A response which fell outside of the preparedness range would be one of two kinds. It might be a response which was initially perceived as irrelevant, that is, not interpretable as the expression of any role in the context of the present focus of interaction. Or it might be a response which seemed to indicate a different role from that which had been attributed to alter.

The more or less definite expectations for ego's role which are part of alter's role, the preferences, the conceptions of legitimate and illegitimate behavior, and the evaluations, all directed toward ego's role, are a part but not the whole of alter's role. Role-taking may or may not concentrate on these aspects, and when it does it has been referred to as reflexive role-taking (25). Role-taking is always incomplete, with differential sensitivity to various aspects of the other-role. Only under special circumstances is the sensitization likely to be exclusively to the reflexive aspect. Such sensitization goes along with a conformity relationship, but not necessarily with approval in the simple sense.

The most general purpose associated with sensitization to the reflexive aspects of the other-role is to validate a self-image. The object is to present the self in a fashion which will conform to the relevant other's conception of the role by which the actor seeks to be identified. The role may, however, be one of which the relevant other approves or disapproves or toward which he is neutral. The young "tough" may be unsure that he has sufficiently exemplified the desired self-image until he provokes a vigorous condemnation from the teacher. The individualist may be dissatisfied until he provokes disagreement from a conventional person.

Elsewhere the kinds of dynamic relationship between roles have been discussed under the headings of role standpoint and reflexive versus non-reflexive role-taking (25). But the most general form of self–other relationship is that in which the relationship is a means to the accomplishment of either some shared goal or separate individual goals. Under such circumstances, the role relationship will be pragmatic, the two roles (or the same role enacted by two interacting individuals) being viewed as an efficient division of labor. In role-taking the salient aspects of the other-role will be their instrumental features, and the self-role will be enacted in such a fashion as to combine effectively with the instrumental features of the other-role to accomplish the intended purpose. Conformity to alter's expectations may enter as a partial determinant in this truly interactive relation but principally because it is an adjunct to the efficient accomplishment of the objective. The conformity principle may also come to be dominant because the effects of the role interaction in the promotion of the group goal are not readily apparent, as in a standby military organization or in an educational organization where no real tests of the effectiveness of the educational process are available. But conformity remains a special instance of the more general interactive principle rather than the general principle itself.

The Normative Component of Role-Taking. Roles are often identified as sets of norms applicable to an actor playing a recognizable part. Since norms are at least partially equatable with expectations, such a conception may convey the same simple conformity formula with which we have just dealt. However, there is an essentially normative element in the concept of role which derives from the fact that a minimum of predictability is the precondition of interaction. This interdependency has been well described by Waller and Hill (28, pp. 328–332) by reference to the "interlocking habit systems" which develop between marriage partners. To the extent to which one member patterns his behavior to fit with the past regularities of behavior in the other, the former's behavior becomes inappropriate when the latter makes unanticipated alterations in his behavior. The inappropriateness invokes indignation against the innovator and the charge that he had no right to alter his behavior. Thus, although no norm originally existed and no explicit commitment had been made, a norm has in fact developed because of the damage which one person's unpredictable behavior does to the other. The prediction is of two sorts, prediction of the role to be played and prediction that behavior will continue to exemplify the same role once it is established in interaction. It is the latter which is most fundamental. The basic normative element in role-taking-and-playing is the requirement that the actor be consistent — that his behavior remain within the confines of a single role. So long as it remains within the role, the other will be generally prepared to cope with the behavior, whether he approves of it or not.

In institutional contexts, the additional normative element that designates a priori what role each individual must play is introduced to insure the required division of labor and to minimize the costs of exploratory role-setting behavior. But the norm of consistency is the more fundamental since it applies to role-taking in both informal and formalized settings, while the norm which assigns roles to persons applies chiefly in the latter.

The norm of consistency is mitigated in operation by an implicit presumption that actors are adhering to the norm. Indications that an actor is from an out-group, special symbols of deviant identity, or glaring evidences of "inconsistency," cause the assumption to be questioned. But in the absence of such cues, the initial presumption that each actor must be adhering to *some* role creates a strong bias in favor of finding a set of interpretations of his behavior which will allow it to be seen as pertaining to a single role. The bias may go as far as the synthesizing of a partially new role for one of the actors. Once the actor's role has been identified, either on the basis of indications of his position, placing oneself in his situation, or bits of his behavior, there is a further presumption that his subsequent behavior represents the same role. The flexibility with which most actions can be interpreted, emphasized, and de-emphasized, affords considerable scope for the role-taker to find confirmation of his preconceptions.

The normative principle of consistency, then, works both in the direction of enforcing a pattern onto behavior and in the direction of allowing a range of actions to be subsumed under a given role. The following hypotheses are suggested. The restricting impact of the consistency norm on behavior tends to be greater under conditions of dominance, whether authoritarian or instrumental, when participants are sensitized to interpret deviations from standard roles as symbolic denials of the dominance—

submission relationship. The restricting effect tends to be greater when there is relatively little basis for faith in the role enactor's possession of the appropriate role sentiment. Such faith in turn arises out of prior experience with the other's role performance or out of esteem accorded the other by persons whose judgments are respected.

Many studies of role conflict proceed as if the dynamics of adjustment lie primarily in a choice of which set of expectations to honor in the face of an urgent desire to adhere to two or more incompatible sets. If the view is accepted that conformity is but one type of working adjustment to the other-role, then role conflict should be seen in the light of attempts to establish some kind of working relationship with the roles of relevant others. In its most general sense, role conflict exists when there is no immediately apparent way of simultaneously coping effectively with two different relevant other-roles, whether coping is by conformity to expectation or by some other type of response. The problem of a man whose friend has committed a serious crime need not be primarily or exclusively how to conform to the expectations both of his friend and of the police. The problem is to cope with the roles of each, conformity to expectation being but one of the alternatives before him. The definition of modern woman's problem as primarily how to conform simultaneously to the conflicting expectations of those with traditional and egalitarian views of her role reveals the same limited conception. The problem is more fundamentally how to engage in effective interaction with men, some of whom have modern and some traditional and some mixed conceptions of the masculine role, and with women who may have the same or different conceptions of the feminine role.

SUMMARY AND IMPLICATIONS

Role theory, originally depicting a tentative and creative interaction process, has come increasingly to be employed as a refinement of conformity theory. In consequence, the theory has become relatively sterile except with respect to the consequences of role conflict and other forms of deviation from the conventional model of role behavior. Role taking, however, suggests a process whereby actors attempt to organize their interaction so that the behavior of each can be viewed as the expression of a consistent orientation which takes its meaning (or consistency) from its character as a way of coping with one or more other actors enacting similarly consistent orientations. Conformity to perceived expectations is but one special way in which an actor's role-playing may be related to the role of relevant others. From this viewpoint, role behavior in formal organizations becomes a working compromise between the formalized role prescriptions and the more flexible operation of the role-taking process. Role conflict is the attempt to devise an orientation from which the actor can cope effectively with multiple other-roles which apparently cannot be dealt with in a "consistent" fashion.

The conception of role relations as fully interactive rather than merely conforming harmonizes with current trends in sociology and anthropology to subordinate normative to functional processes in accounting for societal integration. Emphasis on the binding power of the mores and folkways or on the blind adherence to custom corresponds with a society populated by people playing roles principally as sets of expectations with which they must comply. On the other hand, a functional view emphasizes the interdependence of activities in accounting for cultural persistence and social stability. The interactive consequence of role relationships provides the social-psychological mechanism through which the functional principle of social stability operates.

References

1. Allport, Gordon. *Becoming.* New Haven: Yale University Press, 1955.
2. Bates, Frederick L. "Position, Role, and Status: A Reformulation of Concepts," *Social Forces,* Vol. 34 (May 1956), pp. 313–321.
3. Benne, Kenneth D., and Paul Sheats. "Functional Roles of Group Members," *Journal of Social Issues,* Vol. 4 (May 1948), pp. 41–49.
4. Blumer, Herbert. "Psychological Import of the Human Group," in Muzafer Sherif and M. O. Wilson (eds.), *Group Relations at the Crossroads.* New York: Harper & Brothers, 1953, pp. 185–202.

5. Brim, Orville G., Jr. "Family Structure and Sex-Role Learning by Children," *Sociometry*, Vol. 21 (March 1958), pp. 1–18.

6. Cottrell, Leonard S., Jr. "The Analysis of Situational Fields in Social Psychology," *American Sociological Review*, Vol. 7 (June 1942), pp. 370–382.

7. Coutu, Walter. *Emergent Human Nature*. New York: Alfred A. Knopf, 1949.

8. Davis, Kingsley. *Human Society*. New York: The Macmillan Company, 1948.

9. Durkheim, Émile. *Sociology and Philosophy*. London: Cohen and West, 1953.

10. Faris, Ellsworth. *The Nature of Human Nature*. New York: McGraw-Hill Book Company, Inc., 1937.

11. Faris, Robert E. L. *Social Psychology*. New York: The Ronald Press Company, 1952.

12. Gross, Neal, Ward S. Mason, and Alexander W. McEachern. *Explorations in Role Analysis*. New York: John Wiley & Sons, 1958.

13. Kirkpatrick, Clifford. "The Measurement of Ethical Consistency in Marriage," *International Journal of Ethics*, Vol. 46 (July 1936), pp. 444–460.

14. Kluckhohn, Clyde, and Henry A. Murray. "Personality Formation: The Determinants," in Clyde Kluckhohn, Henry A. Murray, and David Schneider (eds.), *Personality in Nature, Society, and Culture*. New York: Alfred A. Knopf, 1953, pp. 53–67.

15. Lindesmith, Alfred R., and Anselm L. Strauss. *Social Psychology*. New York: The Dryden Press, 1956.

16. Linton, Ralph. *The Study of Man*. New York: Appleton-Century Co., 1936.

17. Mead, George H. *Mind, Self, and Society*, ed. by Charles W. Morris. Chicago: The University of Chicago Press, 1935.

18. Merton, Robert K. "Role Set: Problems in Sociological Theory," *British Journal of Sociology*, Vol. 8 (June 1957), pp. 106–120.

19. Miyamoto, S. Frank, and Sanford M. Dornbusch. "A Test of Interactionist Hypotheses of Self-Conception," *American Journal of Sociology*, Vol. 61 (March 1956), pp. 399–403.

20. Moreno, Jacob. *Who Shall Survive?* Washington, D.C.: Nervous and Mental Disease Monograph, No. 58, 1934.

21. Neiman, Lionel J., and James W. Hughes. "The Problem of the

Concept of Role: A Resurvey of the Literature," *Social Forces,* Vol. 30 (December 1951), pp. 141–149.

22. Newcomb, Theodore. *Social Psychology.* New York: The Dryden Press, 1950.

23. Parsons, Talcott, Robert F. Bales, and others. *Family, Socialization and Interaction Process.* Glencoe, Ill.: The Free Press, 1955.

24. Sarbin, Theodore R. "Role Theory," in Gardner Lindzey (ed.), *Handbook of Social Psychology,* Vol. I. Reading, Mass.: Addison-Wesley Publishing Company, Inc., 1954, pp. 223–258.

25. Turner, Ralph H. "Role Taking, Role Standpoint, and Reference Group Behavior," *American Journal of Sociology,* Vol. 61 (January 1956), pp. 316–328.

26. Videbeck, Richard. "Dynamic Properties of the Concept Role," *Midwest Sociologist,* Vol. 20 (May 1958), pp. 104–108.

27. Videbeck, Richard, and Alan P. Bates. "An Experimental Study of Conformity to Role Expectations," *Sociometry,* Vol. 22 (March 1959), pp. 1–11.

28. Waller, Willard, and Reuben Hill. *The Family: A Dynamic Interpretation.* New York: The Dryden Press, 1951.

3

Conditions of Accurate Role-Taking:
A Test of Mead's Theory

SHELDON STRYKER

INDIANA UNIVERSITY

A theoretical orientation such as symbolic interactionism requires not only logical conceptual refinements of the type offered by Turner in the preceding chapter, but also deliberate empirical testing. Since role-taking is the basic social process according to interactionist theory, Professor Stryker focuses on the important question of the differential extent to which the actor can accurately take the role of relevant others. He has ingeniously formulated and tested certain hypotheses about the conditions of accurate role-taking and concludes that, although Mead's theory exhibits an essential soundness, it needs to be qualified to take into account variations in the degree of rationality, utility, and organization in different sets of role relationships.

The work of George Herbert Mead has long been a potent stimulus for sociologists interested in social psychology.* However,

* This essay is a somewhat revised version of (20) and is reprinted with the permission of The University of Chicago Press. The study on which it is based was originally prepared as a Ph.D. thesis under the direction of Professor Arnold M. Rose at the University of Minnesota (19).

while Mead's theory has been extended, little has been done to test or refine his premises.[1] Thus, as it stands, Mead's theory has perhaps as much honorific as scientific status in social psychology. The intention of this research is to draw from Mead a set of propositions integral to his theory; to develop the research tools for taking the theory out of the realm of speculation; to derive from the propositions specific testable hypotheses; and to test these hypotheses.

No single study can test all the implications of a theory as complex as Mead's; one must take much of it for granted, testing only specified aspects. We are concerned with the process termed "taking the role of the other," or, briefly, "role-taking."[2] Four propositions underlie the hypotheses and methods of this study.

A. *Social activities are imbedded in a structure of roles.* Social activities are inevitably "self–other" patterns involving the relationship of one person to at least one other; for every role there is at least one counter or supporting role.

B. *To engage in social activity, a person must take the role of the other(s) implicated with him in that activity.* To play a role, Person A must incorporate into his "self" the role of Person B. A must anticipate or predict the response of B, since that response is the basis for A's further activity.[3]

C. *A significant segment of the role of the other which one must take consists of attitudes.* For Mead, "taking the role of the other" is not fundamentally different from "taking the attitude of the other." An attitude is simply an early stage of activity, including role activity (12, pp. 6, 11, 159–160, 254 ff.).

D. *Ability to take the role or attitude of the other is predicated upon a common universe of discourse.* "[A] universe of discourse

1 Found especially in Mead (12). For possible exceptions to this appraisal see Sullivan (22), Foote (5), and Sarbin (15).

2 We shall not try to present Mead's entire theory or to justify extensively the specific formulation of the propositions drawn from it. For the former see Mead (12); for the latter see Stryker (19). Here we are concerned with *conditions* of role-taking accuracy. For a report of findings with regard to *consequences* of such accuracy in adult offspring–parent relationships, see Stryker (21).

3 See Mead's account of the significance of the conversation of gestures (12, pp. 14, 63, 167, 179, 253–254). That role-taking involves anticipating the response of another is seen in Mead's account of the requirements for participation in an organized game, and of intelligence (12, pp. 141, 151, 242–243, 253–254).

is always implied as the context in terms of which . . . significant gestures or symbols do in fact have significance. . . . A universe of discourse is simply a system of common or social meanings." (12, pp. 89–90)

The present study investigates role-taking among married adults and their parents, using a married couple and the parents of one, but not both. Use of family units was based upon three considerations: the necessity of controlling, as far as possible, opportunity for knowledge of and intimacy with the other whose role was to be taken; the desirability also that subjects should have had some minimal opportunity to learn appropriate role responses; and the decision to focus upon comparatively unspecialized and "whole" relationships.

The hypotheses are derived from Proposition D, but presume A and B as well. From Proposition D it follows that circumstances permitting the development of shared meanings will make for accurate role-taking. Without, for the moment, attempting to justify those hypotheses whose relation to the propositions is not apparent, it can be expected that role-taking will be more accurate in (1) persons of blood relationship than in persons of in-law relationship; (2) persons of the same sex than in persons of opposite sex; (3) females in relation to males than in males in relation to females; (4) females in relation to blood relatives than in males in relation to blood relatives; (5) males in relation to in-laws than in females in relation to in-laws; (6) persons of similar occupations than in persons of different occupations; (7) persons of similar educational background than in persons of different education; (8) persons of similar religious orientation than in persons of different orientation; (9) persons of similar community background than in persons of different background; (10) persons close in age than in persons distant in age; (11) persons having frequent contact with each other than in persons having infrequent contact; (12) persons of relatively equal status than in persons of unequal status. It can further be expected that accurate role-taking will (13) vary with the significance of the role area for the relationship; (14) vary with the significance of the other for the role-taker; (15) be independent of sympathy with the views of the person whose role is taken.

Many of the hypotheses seem clearly implied by the propositions. Hypotheses 3–5 and 12–15 require some justification, since hitherto undiscussed reasoning separates them from the propositions.

Hypothesis 3. The confused character of expectations impinging on females in our society has been noted (9, 14). Further, the folk dictum that this is a man's world is in many ways correct. Thus, experiences of males are more likely to be meaningful to females than are experiences of females to males. We may expect that there will be greater opportunity for females to share systems of symbolic meaning deriving from the male than for males to share such systems deriving from the female (1).

Hypothesis 4. Females are less emancipated from and closer to their families than are males (10, 18). There is thus greater opportunity for females to hold systems of shared meanings with members of their own families.

Hypothesis 5. This hypothesis is based on the observation that in our society in-laws tend to pose problems chiefly to women (2, p. 7; 11, pp. 285–295). It follows that there will be a greater sharing of a universe of discourse between males and in-laws than between females and in-laws.

Hypothesis 12. Unequal status presents barriers to the sharing of perspectives which equal status does not. This reasoning provides the link between Proposition D and the hypothesis.

Hypotheses 13 and 14. Taft, in a thorough review of research on accuracy of judgments of others, notes that accuracy varies, among other things, with that which is judged and the person who is judged (23). It is certain that not all areas of interaction are equally significant in a relationship or all persons equally significant with respect to a given area of interaction. It may be expected that opportunity to develop shared systems of meaning will vary with differential significance, both of area and of persons.

Hypothesis 15. This hypothesis is implied only negatively, in that the propositions speak of role-taking without the emotional involvement usually considered an aspect of sympathy. In Mead's theory, social behavior is predicated upon the role-players' accurate estimate of one another's future activities. Whether one is sympathetic or not is irrelevant: the efficient policeman must base his actions on his predictions of the responses of the criminal (12, pp. 303–304).

Perhaps the basic reason why few have tested Mead's theory is the difficulty of defining its variables operationally. The first need is for an adequate measure of accuracy in taking the role of another.

The measure used here derives from Proposition B, in terms of which accurate role-taking is equated with accurate prediction,[4] and from Proposition C. In the present study, subjects were required to predict the responses of another to statements of attitudes — that is, to ascribe the attitudes of others.[5] The criterion of accuracy was the actual set of responses of the other. Thus, a married couple and the parents of one spouse were asked to respond to a set of statements about attitudes. Each offspring was asked to indicate how he felt about the items and how he thought each of his parents felt about them. Similarly, each parent was asked for his own response and to ascribe the response of each offspring. The responses were in terms of one of four categories: Strongly Agree, Agree, Disagree, or Strongly Disagree. Our index of accuracy consists of the number of correct predictions A makes of B's responses, expressed as a percentage of total predictions of B's responses.[6]

The hypotheses and the design of the study stem from an interest in testing implications drawn from Mead's theory. Given this interest, we have employed a conception of role-taking as a person's anticipation of the responses of others implicated with him in an on-going social situation. Accurate role-taking has been operationally defined as the correct prediction of the responses of others. Role-taking, so conceived, is obviously related to such concepts as empathy, insight, social sensitivity, and so on,

---

[4] Not to equate role-taking with the predictive procedures of science, a logically different process.

[5] Hereafter, role-taking and attitude ascription are synonyms. The relevance of Proposition C at this point is apparent.

[6] This general approach to role-taking is not new. What appears to be novel here is (*a*) the scoring technique, which avoids some of the problems of techniques previously used, and (*b*) the use of the technique to test hypotheses drawn from a significant and complex body of theory.

studies of which have used similar measurement procedures. These concepts are not, however, synonyms; and the similarity of measurement procedures should not be taken to imply identical conceptualization or theoretical concern.[7]

A self-administered interview schedule provided the data necessary to test the hypotheses. It consisted of a series of face-sheet questions, an ascription scale, a dependence index, and an adjustment index.

The *ascription* technique required attitude statements to which offspring and parents could respond for themselves and for one another. It was adapted from a scale measuring family ideology on an autocratic–democratic continuum (8). As modified for present purposes, the scale consisted of twenty items. Four response categories were used, after extensive pretesting designed to provide items to which responses would be relatively stable

[7] There is considerable confusion in the literature with regard to the concepts role-taking, empathy, sympathy, identification, insight, social sensitivity, etc. These are sometimes seen as independent, sometimes as overlapping, and sometimes as essentially identical. We cannot attempt, here, to distinguish systematically among these concepts: Dymond (4) provides an extensive review of this literature, offering necessary distinctions. Suffice it to say that, for us, role-taking is anticipatory behavior; and that the emotional unity, participation in emotional life of others, "feeling-with" quality, and fellow-feeling that sometimes (although not always) are incorporated into these other concepts are not seen as part of the role-taking concept.
It is true that there may be diverse sources of accuracy when role-taking scores are based on correctness in prediction. From the standpoint of Mead's theory, which postulates that one's behavior is predicated on the symbolic anticipation of responses of others, the "impurity" of our role-taking index is of little consequence. This theory, as it has thus far been developed, does not require distinguishing the various possible bases of accuracy. The problem of "impurities" in studies of empathy, insight, etc., has been attacked by Hastorf and Bender (7), Cronbach (3), and Gage and Cronbach (6). Hastorf and Bender suggest that "projection" can be screened out by subtracting from an accuracy score a second score based on the coincidence of ascriber's own responses and his predictions for another. This technique is unable, however, to distinguish between correct ascriptions based on knowledge and correct ascriptions based on projection when, in fact, ascriber and other respond identically to an item. The technique has the same difficulty with correct predictions when ascriber and other disagree with respect to an item (6). Cronbach (3) develops a model which distinguishes four components of accuracy scores. The model is, however, premised on a research design which requires judges to predict responses of (the same) multiple others, rather than on a design strictly analogous to ours.

both when a subject answered for himself and when he predicted another's answer.[8] After experimentation with four-, five-, and three-category response systems, it was decided to use the four-category system *and* to consider as identical the categories Strongly Agree and Agree on the one hand and Strongly Disagree and Disagree on the other.

These decisions were reached through the following considerations. In the pretest stage, an arbitrary criterion was set up permitting a 10 per cent shift in responses to items. When five- and three-category systems were used and any change in response was considered a shift, subjects altered responses on approximately one-fourth of the items. There seemed to be no appropriate rationale for combining neutral and either affirmative or negative responses (16). Since respondents to attitude statements avoid extreme categories, it seemed best not to use an agree–disagree dichotomy, in spite of the intention to dichotomize in scoring. When shifts *within* the agree and disagree categories were ignored, the number of shifts fell close to the criterion.[9]

We have not dealt with the validity or reliability of these twenty items taken as a unitary scale, since this report makes no assumption about these matters. Some data on conventional questions of validity and reliability are available (19).

The *dependence* index was based on ten items referring to a superordinate–subordinate dimension included in the schedule (for example: "Asks my advice more than I ask his"; "If we differ, I can generally convince him that I'm right"). Subjects labeled each as true or false of the others to whom they ascribed attitudes. Index scores were then computed by subtracting the number of items marked in a manner indicating subordination from the number marked so as to indicate superordination.[10]

The larger study on which this report is based used an index measuring the adjustment of all offspring and parents which incorporated items tapping various dimensions: affection, intimacy, tension, and sympathy (ego-involvement). Only the sympathy

[8] The ascription technique necessitates the demand for *item* stability rather than conventional test–retest *total score* reliability.
[9] 10.4 per cent for own responses and 12.8 per cent for predicted responses.
[10] For data relating to the validity of this index, see Stryker (19, pp. 66–69).

dimension is pertinent here.[11] The index of sympathy consisted of ten items, which subjects labeled as true or false in relation to the others for whom they ascribed attitudes (sample items: "I find myself imitating him often"; "He does many things I would not do"). Scoring proceeded in a manner directly analogous to that for the dependence index.

The universe from which the sample of family units was drawn was defined as follows: An offspring pair with only one living parent was unacceptable. All were white residents of Bloomington, Indiana. Offspring and parents maintained separate residence. The maximum age of parents was seventy.

Ideally, families would have been drawn at random from the total number meeting the specifications. But the writer was unable to conceive of any means within the limits of the resources of the study by which a comprehensive listing could be made.[12] The procedure was as follows: a roster of 133 potentially eligible families was compiled by consulting ministers of local churches and a "New Citizens" column in the local newspaper, which reported names and addresses of grandparents as well as parents of newborn infants. Forty-six of the 133 units completed the schedules. Of the remainder, 35 did not actually meet specifications; in 25, no person in the unit completed a schedule; in 27, completed schedules were obtained from one or more but not all four. All subjects were reached in their homes between June and October 1954.

Two instances illustrating how the data were analyzed will be presented, then a table summarizing the results of the analyses. The summary table provides the basis for a reconsideration of the theory from which the hypotheses were derived.

Each subject ascribed the attitudes of two others; for example,

11 For an account of the derivation, reliability, and validity of the complete index, see Stryker (18).

12 Another consequence of our procedure will be noted later, with some implications of these defects. The following may be pertinent: nonrespondents and respondents did not differ on any characteristic for which information was available; the study revealed no relationship between accuracy scores and a variety of demographic and social variables — age, years married, number of children, education, etc.; random sampling is assumed to be less important in a study of social *process* such as this than in one involving description of *content*.

the son ascribed the responses of either his father and mother **or** of his father- and mother-in-law. Thus, the 184 subjects may be categorized in terms of four attributes: sex, generation, relationship with the other whose attitudes are ascribed (own relative or in-law), and sex of that other. There are, consequently, 16 categories, each containing the responses of 23 persons. These categories and the notations for them are as follows:

1. Son ascribing to father: S–F
2. Son ascribing to mother: S–M
3. Son ascribing to father-in-law: S–IF
4. Son ascribing to mother-in-law: S–IM
5. Daughter ascribing to father: D–F
6. Daughter ascribing to mother: D–M
7. Daughter ascribing to father-in-law: D–IF
8. Daughter ascribing to mother-in-law: D–IM
9. Father ascribing to son: F–S
10. Father ascribing to daughter: F–D
11. Father ascribing to son-in-law: F–IS
12. Father ascribing to daughter-in-law: F–ID
13. Mother ascribing to son: M–S
14. Mother ascribing to daughter: M–D
15. Mother ascribing to son-in-law: M–IS
16. Mother ascribing to daughter-in-law: M–ID

These categories may be grouped and analyzed in a number of ways: (1) by the sex of the person whose attitudes are ascribed; (2) by the sex of the ascriber; (3) by the relationship of the ascriber to the object of ascription; (4) by the generation of the ascriber; (5) by the linkage — same or cross-sex — involved in the relationship. These *modes of analysis* have been labeled as follows:

1. "Ascription, female other" and "ascription, male other"
2. "Female ascription" and "male ascription"
3. "Ascription, own" and "ascription, in-law"
4. "Offspring ascription" and "parent ascription"
5. "Ascription, same sex" and "ascription, cross-sex"

The specific statistical technique selected to test the hypotheses was the analysis of variance.[13]

---

[13] We obtained responses from four members of the same family unit. In

To turn to the illustrative instances of tests of the hypotheses. Hypothesis 1 stated: *role-taking will be more accurate for persons of blood relationship than for persons of in-law relationship.*[14] Table 1 presents the test of Hypothesis 1 when the persons whose attitudes are ascribed are female. Here it is the relationship variable, contrasting the four own-relative with the four in-law categories, which is pertinent. The mean ascription scores for these two groupings are 62.85 and 57.17, respectively. The *F*-ratio for the relationship variable is significant beyond the .01 level.[15]

Hypothesis 6 states: *role-taking will be more accurate for persons of similar occupations than for persons of different occupations.* Subjects were placed in one of the following categories: professional, business, white collar, blue collar, student, housewife. Wives listing an occupation other than housewife were placed in the category appropriate to their response; the others were placed in their husbands' categories. A student was classed as either professional or business.

The test of Hypothesis 6 proceeded by contrasting those relationships in which occupations are on the same level with those on different levels. The expectation is that the former will be

---

consequence, a pair of offspring will have ascribed the attitudes of the same parent; the same offspring will have ascribed the attitudes of two parents; and parent and offspring will have ascribed each other's responses. Thus, in any given mode of analysis, the data in various pairs of cells in the analysis will not be statistically independent. This is in violation of an assumption underlying the analysis of variance, namely, that the observations be randomly drawn, independent samples. There is, of course, no reason why data cannot be grouped as has been done. The problem emerges when reference is made to the *F*-distribution as a test of statistical significance. In what follows we do, in fact, refer to the *F*-distribution. Given violation of assumptions, one must either use informal tools to assess his data or formal statistical criteria in spite of violation of assumptions. It seems better to impose upon oneself the discipline of formal statistical tools. An important question here is the kind of inference to be drawn on the basis of technically inappropriate statistical tools. We move from the statistical tests to a general consideration of Mead's theory; our interest is in suggesting modifications of the theory which could be subjected to further test. The use of our data and the procedures for this purpose appear to be warranted.

[14] More precisely, the hypothesis tested is the null hypothesis, rejection of which by inference supports the positively stated hypothesis.

[15] The *F*-ratios for the first-order interactions are also significant. It would appear that the observed relationship difference depends on the generation and sex of the ascriber.

TABLE 1

Ascription, Female Other

Ascriber–Other Pair	Mean Ascription Score	N	Mean Scores, Contrasting Combined Categories	
			VARIABLE	MEAN
Son:				
S–M	53.91	23		
S–IM	62.60	23	*Generation:*	
			Offspring	60.58
Daughter:			Parent	59.43
D–M	68.00	23		
D–IM	57.83	23	*Sex:*	
			Male	58.84
Father:			Female	61.17
F–D	62.57	23		
F–ID	56.30	23	*Relationship:*	
			Own	62.85
Mother:			In-law	57.17
M–D	66.91	23		
M–ID	51.96	23		

Completed Analysis of Variance

Source	Sum of Squares	df	Mean Square	F
Generation	60.99	1	60.99	....
Sex	248.21	1	248.21	1.14
Relationship	1,537.38	1	1,537.38	7.08
Interaction:				
Gen. x Sex	248.89	1	248.89	1.15
Gen. x Rel.	1,120.20	1	1,120.20	5.05
Sex x Rel.	2,184.54	1	2,184.54	10.05
Gen. x Sex x Rel.	241.67	1	241.67	1.11
Within groups	38,245.91	176	217.31	....
Total	43,887.79	183	....	....

$$F_{95}(1,176) = 3.90$$
$$F_{99}(1,176) = 6.79$$

more accurate in their ascription. As seen in Table 2, the hypothesis holds when the object of ascription is female. The F-ratio testing the weighted mean difference of 5.57 between the rows is significant beyond the .05 level.

All hypotheses were tested by using one of the two designs of the illustrative cases. There were fifteen hypotheses, each tested with from one to ten of the modes of analysis. Further, three

TABLE 2

Ascription, Female Other, by Occupational Similarity or Difference

OCCUPATIONAL LEVEL	ASCRIBER–OTHER RELATIONSHIPS								
	S-M	S-IM	F-D	F-ID	D-M	D-IM	M-D	M-ID	Row
Same:									
Mean score	54.38	66.50	60.00	67.50	76.40	58.33	52.50	68.90	64.50
N	8	10	6	10	10	6	6	10	66
Different:									
Mean score	53.67	59.61	55.00	58.46	61.54	57.65	51.77	65.38	57.50
N	15	13	17	13	13	17	17	13	118

COMPLETED ANALYSIS OF VARIANCE

Source	Sum of Squares	df	Mean Square	F
Columns	4,801.70	7	685.96	3.19
Rows	1,233.61	1	1,233.61	5.74
Interaction	899.83	7	128.55	......
Within groups	36,098.44	168	214.87	......

Weighted mean difference, rows = 5.57

$$F_{.95}(1,168) = 3.90$$
$$F_{.95}(7,168) = 2.06$$

were tested with two different sets of data. Consequently, there were 147 individual tests of the hypotheses. Table 3 summarizes the results of these 147 tests, giving equal weight to each.

Listed horizontally in Table 3 (by number used earlier) are the fifteen hypotheses. Listed vertically are the ten modes of analysis. Each cross-classification cell represents one mode of analysis for one of the hypotheses. Separate columns are provided when different sets of data applied to the same hypothesis.

A plus mark in a cell indicates that, for this mode of analysis, a finding resulted which supported the hypothesis significant beyond the .05 level (an exception to this use of the plus sign is for Hypothesis 15, where negative statistical results implied support for the hypothesis). A minus mark indicates a statistically significant finding contradictory to the hypothesis. An "I" means that a given mode of analysis was irrelevant for the hypothesis. Cells with no entry are cases in which the findings were not statistically significant.

Beneath each column are two numbers. The uppermost is the number of times a hypothesis was tested and was supported by statistically significant findings. The lower number is the frequency with which a hypothesis was tested and failed to hold.

To the right of each row is a second pair of numbers. The first is the number of times a mode of analysis was relevant to the hypotheses and produced statistically significant results supporting these. The second is the number of times a mode of analysis was relevant but failed to support the hypotheses.

Of the 147 tests, 57, or 39 per cent, produced results clearly supporting the theory; 90, or 61 per cent, did not. Only one test produced a statistically significant finding contradictory to the hypotheses. Two other facts, not appearing in the table, are pertinent: of the 90 instances in which clear support for the theory was not forthcoming, 11 produced results significant between the .10 and .05 levels in a direction favorable to the hypotheses; and with few exceptions — concentrated in the cases of the age-difference hypothesis — mean scores for contrasted sets of categories differed in the direction predicted by the hypotheses.

Having summarized findings, we now ask: upon what criteria can the judgment of over-all soundness of a theory be made?

TABLE 3

Summary of Findings: Hypotheses by Modes of Analysis*

Modes of Analysis	Hypotheses (by Numbers Previously Used)								
	1	2	3	4	5	6	7	8 a	8 b
Ascription, female other ..	+	I	I	I	I	+	+		+
Ascription, male other		I	I	I	I	+			
Female ascription	+		I	I	I	+	+		
Male ascription			I	I	I	+			
Ascription, own	I	+	I	+	I	+			
Ascription, in-law	I		I	I		+	+		+
Offspring ascription			I	I	I	+		+	+
Parent ascription	+		I	I	I	+	+		
Ascription, same sex	+	I	I	I	I	+			
Ascription, cross-sex		I		I	I	+	+	+	
N, hypothesis relevant, holds	4	1	0	1	0	10	5	2	3
N, hypothesis relevant, fails ......,............	4	5	1	0	1	0	5	8	7

* Key: + = Statistically significant finding supporting hypothesis (except for Hypothesis 15, where negative statistical results imply support for the hypothesis); − = Statistically significant finding contradictory to hypothesis; I = Mode of analysis irrelevant to hypothesis; Blank = Statistically nonsignificant finding.

Certainly one criterion is the frequency with which it allows correct predictions of empirically observable events. But, outside the limiting case of the crucial experiment, is this a demand for perfect prediction? It is not reasonable to hold social-psychological theory to this standard of perfection. Even presuming a theory to exhaust relevant variables, our concepts are too loose, our established knowledge too meager, our logic too crude, our measurements too imprecise, our observations too error-ridden, to expect perfect prediction.

This, however, raises the further question of the minimal degree of success required. One can use a statistical criterion: if the .05 level is used in tests of hypotheses, it may be expected that in five out of one hundred cases significant results will appear on the basis of chance. Success beyond this ratio would then be greater than chance expectation; the larger the ratio, the greater the degree of permissible confidence in the theory which provided

TABLE 3

(*Cont'd.*)

Hypotheses (by Numbers Previously Used)									N, Hypothesis Relevant, Holds	N, Hypothesis Relevant, Fails
9 a	b	10	11 a	b	12	13	14	15		
		−	+	+				+	7	7
+					+			+	4	10
			+	+	+			+	7	8
+							+	+	4	11
+			+	+	+		+	+	9	6
								+	4	11
								+	4	11
								+	4	11
+	+							+	5	9
			+	+	+	+	+	+	9	6
1	4	0	4	4	2	3	3	10	57	
9	6	10	6	6	8	7	7	0		90

the hypotheses. Also relevant are the frequency of findings approximating satisfactory levels of significance and the degree to which the general tendency of the data is compatible with the hypotheses, regardless of levels of statistical significance.

To turn to a second criterion useful in assessing a theory: is there an alternative explanation which could better account for the findings?

Table 3 shows the frequency with which each mode of analysis either produces or fails to produce findings supporting the hypotheses. There is a greater tendency for the "ascription, female other" mode of analysis to hold in contrast to the "ascription, male other"; the same is true for "female ascription" in contrast to "male ascription," "ascription, own" in contrast to "ascription, in-law," and "ascription, cross-sex" in contrast to "ascription, same sex."

One alternative explanation is that role-taking ability is a function of intelligence. This does not seem likely for two reasons. It is the same subjects, ascribing for different persons, who are included in the "ascription female other" and "ascription, male other" modes of analysis, as well as in the "ascription, cross-sex" and "ascription, same sex" modes. Yet the hypotheses are differentially successful in the first of these pairs in contrast to the second. Moreover, if education is taken as a rough index of intelligence, our data indicate no consistent differences, by educational level, in role-taking accuracy.

A second alternative is that accurate ascription is a function of length of acquaintance. This supposition would do less well in predicting the findings than did Mead's theory. Length of acquaintance could not explain the relative superiority of females over males in ascribing to their own relatives. Too, daughters ascribing attitudes to their in-laws have been married longer than sons doing the same;[16] yet sons are somewhat better in-law ascribers than are daughters, and parents ascribe somewhat better to sons-in-law than to daughters-in-law. Further, S–IM is superior to S–M ascription and M–IS to M–S. These facts deny the significance of length of acquaintance beyond some minimum necessary to establish patterned relationships.

A third possibility is that accurate ascription is a function of similarity, per se, of role-taker and other, apart from the relevance of similarity for the creation of a common universe of discourse. Theory based on this assumption would fail wherever Mead's theory fails. Furthermore, this notion runs afoul of the fact that the "ascription, cross-sex" mode of analysis produced significant results more often than did "ascription, same sex." Moreover, predictions made through Mead's theory supported by the data could not be made through a simple similarity theory — superior ascription by females to own relatives and the superiority of females to males in cross-sex ascription, for example.[17]

A third criterion of judgment is the degree of modification necessary to align the theory with empirical observations. Why

[16] The mean number of years married for daughters ascribing to in-laws is 6.09; for sons, 4.70. This difference is not statistically significant.
[17] Considering another type of similarity, agreement with the views of another is highly related to accurate ascription. When, however, variations in agreement could be statistically controlled, those sets of data which produced significant findings when agreement was not controlled continued to do so; those data which did not produce significant results originally still did not do so. It appears that differences in accuracy predicted by the hypotheses are superimposed upon the differences due to attitudinal agreement or disagreement.

were not predictions more successful? The answer involves the kind and extent of modification necessary to reconcile the theory with the findings. To anticipate the conclusion: necessary alteration, although serious, does not require discarding the broad outline of Mead's theory.

In the light of the data and reasoning here presented, Mead's theory does exhibit an essential soundness.

Mead was philosopher as well as social psychologist and his philosophy had a bearing on his social psychology. He was a pragmatist; he saw mental activity as problem-solving, knowledge as instrumental, and the test of knowledge as experience. His analysis of the "act," the point at which his philosophy and social psychology are articulated most closely, follows these characteristic patterns. In brief, an act refers to purposive behavior which began in an impulse requiring some adjustment to appropriate objects in the external world (13, pp. 3–25). A social act is one in which the appropriate object is another individual or, more precisely, another organism of the same form as that which has the impulse (13, p. 7). The attitudes of others constitute a stimulus, adjustment to which involves role-taking. Role-taking is necessitated by the pertinence of others to one's own ends.

An act may be reflective or non-reflective. Mead is concerned primarily with those acts in which a "blocked impulse requires the reflective process to set up hypotheses in order to guide action." (17, p. 72) In short, he conceptualized the act, individual and social, on the model of research procedure.

Mead also sought a universal community, in which all men are united within a common universe of discourse and take the role of an all-inclusive "generalized other" (12, Sect. IV).

To return to Mead's social psychology: for him, the basic datum of social psychology is "intelligent" and purposeful activity as it takes place in the form of the social act. His concern is with such problems as "how to bridge the gap between impulse and rationality; how the organism acquires the capacity of self-consciousness, reflective thinking, abstract reasoning, and purposive behavior; and how man as a rational animal arose." (17, p. 71)

Certain consequences for Mead's theory flow from these philosophical dispositions and from the kinds of problems set for social psychology. Mead's social psychology is highly rational-istic. As ideal types, various modes of orientation may enter the concrete act — traditional, affective, evaluative, and rational. It is clear that Mead focuses on the last to the virtual exclusion of the other three: behaviors involving absolute ends, affect, or tra-dition remain, by and large, outside his view.

Mead's social psychology is also highly utilitarian. A social act begins with a problem and proceeds to the resolution of that problem. Role-taking is necessary, since others are implicated in the ends of the individual. Thus persons act in social situations with specific ends in view. Or, rephrased, social situations in-volve well-structured, clearly defined goals.

Furthermore, in Mead's social psychology, social life is seen as highly organized. In stressing the "generalized other" and a universe of discourse, and in the ideal of a universe of discourse coterminous with humanity, Mead uses a model of social life in which the rules of the game are well defined, roles are precisely appropriate and neatly articulated, and goals are specific, con-sciously held, and ·unanimously accepted.

If these comments are sound, a key to the cases in which pre-diction failed is provided. For, considering the setting of this study, the family departs relatively far from the model from which Mead's analyses develop. The argument is not that the American family is unorganized or that familial behavior is devoid of rational and utilitarian elements. It is rather that, compared with many other social situations, the family is relatively less organized, family activity less purely rational and utilitarian. In these terms, the successful predictions may be seen as a function of the degree to which concrete family relationships approach the model on which the theory is based; the failures, a function of the degree to which concrete family relationships depart from it.

A glance through recent textbooks on the family will reveal these propositions: the American family is a rapidly changing institution; no clear institutional pattern has yet emerged to re-place the older pattern of well-defined relationships, explicit ex-pectations, and integrated activities; as a primary group it is held together by bonds of sentiment, emotion, and custom rather than utilitarian necessity; non-rational and irrational elements are decisive in establishing the relationships that grow up between family members; emotional life within the family is intense as compared with that in extra-family relationships. These propositions do not fully describe the American family; again, it is a matter of their relative applicability to the family as compared with other social units.

It is suggested that a qualification be incorporated into the body of theory deriving from Mead to take into account differentials in the degree of rationality, utilitarianism, and organization in various sets of social relationships. For Mead these are implicitly assumed *constants* of social situations; we are proposing that they be treated as explicit *variables* in the theory, variations among which would be pertinent to predictions. The expectation is that, to the degree that these characteristics are present in social relationships, observations of role-taking will more completely support hypotheses based on Mead's theory.

The present study does not provide the data necessary to test this interpretation of the failure of the hypotheses. There is, however, some evidence which does lend it plausibility in the differential success of the hypotheses in the various modes of analysis. There was, it will be recalled, a greater tendency for the hypotheses to hold when objects of ascription were female rather than male; when ascribers were female rather than male; when objects of ascription were own relatives rather than in-laws; and when ascriber and object were of opposite sexes rather than same sex. The relevance of these differentials may be seen by contrasting features of family life for the various pairs of relationships involved in the modes of analysis.

A greater proportion of a female's life is family-related; her interests and activities tend to be family-centered in a way in which a male's activities and interests are not. She is more dependent upon family relationships in both a psychological and an economic sense. For her, more than for a male, the family represents a means through which directly utilitarian, as well as other, satisfactions are achieved. What Waller called the "principle of least interest" applies to her (24, pp. 190–192). More irrevocably committed to her family than is a male, she must arrive at some *modus vivendi* in relation to others in the family.

Her attitudes are generally more relevant to the actual organization of family life.

If these observations are sound, the greater success of the hypotheses when the role-taker is female and when the object of ascription is female can be explained in a manner supporting our critique and suggested modification of Mead's theory. For the female, accurate knowledge of attitudes of relatives is essential to immediate life-experiences. In short, her approach to family life is likely to be more rational and utilitarian than that of the male.

We are less prepared to elaborate upon the significance of the greater success of the "ascription, own" and "ascription, cross-sex" as compared with the "ascription, in-law" and "ascription, same sex" modes of analysis. It may be that a greater degree of rationality is possible in cross-sex familial relationships than in the same sex. It is possible that this assertion would hold for blood in contrast to in-law relations, in which strong stereotypes may interfere with rational appraisal. A possible further bar to rationality in in-law relationships is that the explicit recognition of differences might strain already tenuous bonds. If differences remain below the' threshold of awareness, areas of potential conflict where conflict is especially dangerous are avoided. The implication is that bonds between blood relatives can better stand the strain of recognized differences.

References

1. Brown, J. D. "An Experiment in Role-Taking," *American Sociological Review*, Vol. 17 (1952), pp. 587–597.
2. Cavan, Ruth S., Ernest W. Burgess, and Robert Havighurst. "The Family in Later Years." Preliminary report, Committee on Dynamics of Family Interaction, National Conference on Family Life, n.d.
3. Cronbach, L. J. "Processes Affecting Scores on 'Understanding of Others' and 'Assumed Similarity,'" *Psychological Bulletin*, Vol. 52 (1955), pp. 177–193.
4. Dymond, R. F. *Empathic Ability: An Exploratory Study.* Unpublished Ph.D. dissertation, Cornell University, 1949.
5. Foote, Nelson N. "Identification as the Basis for a Theory of

Conditions of Accurate Role-Taking

Motivation," *American Sociological Review*, Vol. 16 (1951), pp. 14–21.

6. Gage, N. L., and L. J. Cronbach. "Conceptual and Methodological Problems in Interpersonal Perception," *Psychological Review*, Vol. 62 (1955), pp. 411–422.

7. Hastorf, A. H., and I. E. Bender. "A Caution Respecting Measurement of Empathic Ability," *Journal of Abnormal and Social Psychology*, Vol. 47 (1952), pp. 574–576.

8. Huffman, P. E. "Authoritarian Personality and Family Ideology." Unpublished Master's thesis, Western Reserve University, 1950.

9. Komarovsky, Mirra. "Cultural Contradictions and Sex Roles," *American Journal of Sociology*, Vol. 52 (1946), pp. 184–189.

10. Komarovsky, Mirra. "Functional Analysis of Sex Roles," *American Sociological Review*, Vol. 15 (1950), pp. 508–516.

11. Landis, Judson T., and Mary G. Landis. *Building a Successful Marriage.* Englewood Cliffs, N.J.: Prentice-Hall, Inc., 1948.

12. Mead, George H. *Mind, Self, and Society*, ed. by Charles W. Morris. Chicago: The University of Chicago Press, 1934.

13. Mead, George H. *The Philosophy of the Act*, ed. by Charles W. Morris. Chicago: The University of Chicago Press, 1938.

14. Rose, Arnold M. "The Adequacy of Women's Expectations for Adult Roles," *Social Forces*, Vol. 30 (1951), pp. 69–77.

15. Sarbin, Theodore R. "Contributions to Role-Taking Theory. I. Hypnotic Behavior," *Psychological Review*, Vol. 57 (1950), pp. 225–270.

16. Schuessler, Karl F. "Item Selection in Scale Analysis," *American Sociological Review*, Vol. 17 (1952), pp. 183–192.

17. Strong, S. M. "A Note on George H. Mead's *The Philosophy of the Act*," *American Journal of Sociology*, Vol. 45 (1939), pp. 71–76.

18. Stryker, Sheldon. "The Adjustment of Married Offspring to Their Parents," *American Sociological Review*, Vol. 20 (1955), pp. 149–154.

19. Stryker, Sheldon. "Attitude Ascription in Adult Married Offspring–Parent Relationships: A Study of the Social-Psychological Theory of G. H. Mead." Unpublished Ph.D. dissertation, University of Minnesota, 1955.

20. Stryker, Sheldon. "Relationships of Married Offspring and Parent: A Test of Mead's Theory," *American Journal of Sociology*, Vol. 62 (1956), pp. 308–319.

21. Stryker, Sheldon. "Role-Taking Accuracy and Adjustment," *Sociometry*, Vol. 20 (1957), pp. 286–296.

22. Sullivan, Harry S. "Psychiatry: Introduction to the Study of Interpersonal Relations," in Patrick Mullahy (ed.), *A Study in Interpersonal Relations*. New York: Grove Press, Inc., 1949.

23. Taft, R. "Some Correlates of the Ability to Make Accurate Social Judgments." Unpublished Ph.D. dissertation, University of California, 1950.

24. Waller, Willard, and Reuben Hill. *The Family*. New York: The Dryden Press, 1951.

4

Transformations of Identity

ANSELM STRAUSS

UNIVERSITY OF CALIFORNIA MEDICAL CENTER,
SAN FRANCISCO

In interactionist social psychology, the individual is never considered to be an entity except insofar as it is an animal organism. Psychologically, the individual is emergent out of a social process and constantly develops or changes. This emergent and ever changing individual — called a "self" in interactionist terminology — has been well studied in its earliest or childhood stages. It has been rather ignored in its adult transformations, except in the study of deviant personalities. Although not the first to analyze the "normal" adult's transformations of self, Anselm Strauss here presents a highly significant statement of this phenomenon.

One of the most hotly contested areas in social psychology is the problem of personal change and development.* My aim is not to offer an assessment or a critique of extant writing, but to suggest a framework for studying changes that take place in adult years. Our best formulated theories of development —

* This article is reprinted, with the permission of the author and the publisher, from *Mirrors and Masks* (Glencoe, Illinois: The Free Press, 1959), pp. 89–109, 124–129, and 144–147. Copyright 1959 by The Free Press.

63

Freud's and Sullivan's — follow children until they are about to become men and women; and later changes, as in psychoanalytic accounts, are viewed mainly as variants of earlier development. Even that acute student of development, Erik Erikson, has restricted his focus to children and their immediate passage into adult life. The sociologist is, because of his concerns, struck by changes in persons, and in their sense of identity, as they move in and out of, and up and down within, social structures. Insofar as he is interested in personal identity, he quite literally has to be interested in the changes of adult life.*

DEVELOPMENT AS TRANSFORMATION

It will pay first to consider what is involved in the concept of "development." Presumably it refers to a progressive movement wherein the beginning, middle, and end bear some discernible relationships to each other. But the notion of development is a trap for the unwary and a battleground for some centuries of philosophic contention. Precisely what are the relationships that hold between beginning, middle, and end? This is the nub of the argument. A stand must be taken on this issue by anyone who wishes to account for and study changes in self-conception and behavior. There are two conceptions of development that are most commonly held by social psychologists. To these I wish to contrast a third, less usually assumed.

Visualize a path from its beginning to its end. Along this path runners are scattered, some just starting, others nearing the end. The end of the path represents the final goal; and the closer to it the runner, the more "advanced" he is. This is the metaphor underlying one conception of development; people are more or less developed along certain lines or in regard to certain tasks. The observer, who stands outside the race, possesses tools for measuring crudely or precisely the amount of progress. The metaphor assumes fixed goals or norms against which the aspirants' movements can be charted. The movement may be con-

---

* [Some recurrent problems of adult socialization are treated in Part Three, where Erving Goffman discusses aspects of adaptation to failure, Irwin Deutscher examines the transition to postparental life, and Ruth Cavan takes up the "transformations of identity" attendant upon old age. — Ed.]

ceived as a series of stages or as steps along a continuum. Any mother who has matched her child's progress against the Gesell age norms will find that this metaphor has a familiar ring. Like the idea of a ladder, or an ascent to heaven, arrival at the final goal is a resting place beyond which progress is not calculated. Too slow progress or too quick, as well as failure to reach the final norm, usually leads to "trouble."

Consider now another metaphor. We have before us an uncooked egg. We may choose to boil, scramble, or poach it, or make it into a dozen different kinds of omelet. Regardless of the treatment this egg receives, it remains an egg. Some people like their eggs hard, some soft, and some very finicky eaters draw finer specifications. To the extent that any claim is made that "this egg is now cooked," all this can mean is that in more or less degree the egg is finished. Up to the point where it becomes converted into charcoal and is really finished, the cooking of the egg represents a matter merely of degree: no matter how the egg changes in appearance, it is still "essentially" an egg.

Changes in people may be conceptualized in like fashion. Thus a person during his lifetime may seem to change considerably, but the essential person is assumed to be the same; he is after all the same person, albeit he may suffer severe damage in transit. This metaphor underlies much theorizing in social psychology. It is represented by the familiar conception that the essential core of personality is laid down early in life and that later changes are variants, although complicated ones, on the initial personality organization.

Development, then, is commonly viewed either as attainment, or as sets of variations on basic themes. In either case, you as the observer of the developmental pattern are omniscient; you know the end against which persons are matched, or you know the basic themes on which variations are composed. Neither metaphor captures the open-ended, tentative, exploratory, hypothetical, problematical, devious, changeable, and only partly unified character of human courses of action. Horace Kallen has put it well:

> Personal accounts of progress uncover no single pattern, no straight, inevitable line, developmental or other. They speak of regressions and other shifts of interest or direction; changes

of field, of method, and of tempo; of new lives, new careers supervening (10, p. 26).

Development (or the relations between "permanence and change," between "before and after") may be conceptualized as a series of related transformations. Etymologically the term "transformation" invites us to consider changes in form — changes in being, kind, or psychological status.

An example will illustrate this, and other related points as well. When children begin to learn a classificatory terminology — say, distinctions having to do with numbers or money — their initial conceptions are crude and inaccurate; but since classifications are always related to other classifications, never standing in isolation, even a very young child's classifications cohere, hang together. As he "advances," his earlier concepts are systematically superseded by increasingly complex ones. The earlier ones are necessary for the later; each advance depends upon the child's understanding a number of prerequisite notions. As the newer classifications are grasped, the old ones become revised or qualified, or even drop out entirely from memory. These changes in conceptual level involve, of course, changes in behavior, since behaving is not separate from classifying. Shifts in concept connote shifts in perceiving, remembering, and valuing — in short, radical changes of action and person. Hence a child going through different "stages of knowledge" is not merely acquiring more and more knowledge, but may be viewed as becoming transformed.

In speaking of children's development, a directional terminology of advancement or improvement is almost always used, although it need not be. Leaving aside questions of direction, it is perfectly clear that conceptual change — hence transformation — no less marks the course of adult careers. Utilizing the dual meaning of the word "terms," I am suggesting that in coming to new terms a person becomes something other than he once was. Terminological shifts necessitate, but also signalize, new evaluations: of self and others, of events, acts, and objects; and the transformation of perception is irreversible; once having changed, there is no going back. One can look back, but he can evaluate only from his new status.

Transformations of Identity

Some transformations of identity and perspective are planned, or at least fostered, by institutional representatives; others happen despite, rather than because of, such regulated anticipation; and yet other transformations take place outside the orbits of the more visible social structure, although not necessarily unrelated to membership within them. As a way of introducing these several dimensions of personal change, I shall discuss next certain critical incidents that occur to force a person to recognize that "I am not the same as I was, as I used to be." ("Turns occur in experience when the program is stopped in its tracks and the plan is gone with the wind." — 10, p. 72) These critical incidents constitute turning points in the onward movement of personal careers.

TURNING POINTS

For our purposes there is not much use in describing in detail what takes place at such turning points beyond noting the frequent occurrence of misalignment — surprise, shock, chagrin, anxiety, tension, bafflement, self-questioning — and also the need to try out the new self, to explore and validate the new and often exciting or fearful conceptions. Rather than discussing critical junctures in general, let us consider their typology. The list will not be a long one, but long enough to suggest the value both of extending it and of relating turning points to changes of identity.

A change in your relations with others is often so mundane, so gradual that it passes virtually unnoticed. Some incident is needed to bring home to you the extent of the shift. A marker of progression, or retrogression, is needed. When the incident occurs it is likely to strike with great impact, for it tells you: "Look! you have come way out to here! This is a milestone!" Recognition then necessitates new stances, new alignments. A striking example of the "milestone" is found in the autobiographies of many immigrants to America who later visited their native lands, only then realizing how little affinity they had retained, how identified they had become with America and Americans. Any return home, insofar as you have really left it, will signalize some sort of movement in identity. Some people literally go back home in an effort both to deny how far they have strayed and to prevent further defection.

Sometimes the path of development is foretold but is not believed, either because he who forecasts is distrusted or because his prophecy cannot be understood. Prophets not only point out new directions: they give you measuring rods for calculating movement if you happen to traverse the paths prophesied. This is certainly one of the critical experiences in the psychology of conversion. For instance, a recruit to a religious sect, only partly convinced, is told what will happen when he tries to explain his new position to his old minister, attempts to sell pamphlets to the heathen, and so on, and lo! events turn out as predicted. The prediction will be in terms of a new vocabulary, and consequently when the vocabulary is shown to be workable the recruit is well on the road toward adopting it in part or *in toto*. The point holds for any kind of conversion — occupational, political, or what not. A novice is told by the old-timer: "Your clients will be of such and such sorts and you'll have such and such experiences with them." When the graph of experience is thus plotted and confirmed, then the person can recognize his own transformation.

Forecasting is often institutionalized in such a fashion that public proclamation is made: "Said candidate has followed the predicted and prescribed path of experience and has gotten to the desired point." "Kneel, knight, and receive knighthood." "Come to the platform and receive your diploma." When paths are institutionalized, a candidate can easily mark his progress, note how far he has come, and how far he has yet to go. If there are the usual institutionalized acknowledgments of partial steps toward the goal, then these may constitute turning points in self-conception also. If the institutionalized steps are purely formalized, are no longer invested with meaning by the institution, or if the candidate believes them of no real significance, they will not, of course, be turning points for him.

Private proclamation to a public audience is quite another matter. Having announced or avowed your position, it is not easy to beat a retreat. Often you find yourself in interpersonal situations climbing out on a limb, announcing a position, and then having to live up to it. In a more subtle sense, one often marks a recognition of self-change by announcement, but this announcement itself forces a stance facing foward, since the way back, however tempting it may still look, is now blocked.

A related turning point — since ceremonial announcement often follows it — is the meeting of a challenge, either self-imposed or imposed by others. Any institution, for instance, possesses regularized means for testing and challenging its members. If you are closely identified with the institution, some tests will be crucial for your self-regard. If you pass them, everyone recognizes that you have met the challenge. However, some challenges, although they occur in institutional settings, are not themselves institutionalized. For instance, every student nurse early in her training must face the situation of having a patient die in her arms. For some nurses this appears to be a turning point for self-conception: the test is passed and she — in her own eyes at least — has new status; she can now think of herself as more of a professional. Crucial tests are imposed by individuals on themselves; if they pass they have been psychologically baptized, so to speak, but if they fail then a new path must be taken, a new set of plans drawn up. Naturally, failure does not always result in immediate self-transformation, but may lead to more complete preparation until the test is definitely failed or passed.

One potent form of self-test is the deliberate courting of temptation. Failure to resist it is usually followed by new tests or by yielding altogether. The fuller meaning of temptation is this: you are withdrawing from an old psychological status and coming into a new, and in doing so something akin to the "withdrawal symptoms" of drug addiction occurs. When you are able to resist temptation then an advance is signalized; but when no longer even tempted, you are well aware of having progressed still further. Institutions find it easier to check upon the overt resistance of their members than upon their covert desires. Genuine conversion means the death of old desires. "Backsliding" signifies a failure to resist temptation; frequent backsliding results in a return to previous status or change to yet another.

A rather subtle type of transforming incident occurs when you have played a strange but important role and unexpectedly handled it well. Whether you had considered this an admirable or a despicable role does not matter. The point is that you never thought you could play it, never thought this potential "me" was in yourself. Unless you can discount your acts as "not me" or as motivated by something not under your control, you bear the responsibility or the credit for the performance. Cowardly and heroic roles are both likely to bring unexpected realignment in self-regard. But more usual, and more subtle, are those instances where you find yourself miraculously able to enact roles that you believed — at least as yet — beyond you. Nearly every person new to a job finds himself, through no fault of his own, at some point taken by clients or fellow workers as of more advanced status than he is. This is akin to a light-colored Negro "passing" unwittingly as a white. Once having carried off the disguise, you realize something new about yourself. The net result is likely to be that you wish to experiment with this new aspect of yourself. Conversely, there are roles previously viewed with suspicion, even despised, that you now find yourself enacting with unexpected success and pleasure. You must either wash your hands óf it, actually or symbolically — as in *Macbeth* — or come to grips with this new aspect of yourself. . . .

Another kind of transforming experience, one with shattering or sapping impact, is betrayal — by your heroes, in fact by anybody with whom you are closely "identified." Betrayal implicates you as well as him, in exceedingly subtle ways. Consider three varieties. When you have closely patterned yourself after a model, you have in effect "internalized" what you suppose are his values and motives. If the model abandons these, he leaves you with a grievous dilemma. Has he gone over to the enemy? — then you may with wry smile redouble your efforts along the path he laid out when he was still pure. Or did he lead you up an illusory path of values? — then with cynicism and self-hate you had better abandon your former self too. A different species of betrayal, involving search for atonement, is illustrated by the stunned American mother whose son, a captured prisoner of the Chinese Communists, became converted to Communism and refused to return to America. The cry here is always: "Where did I go wrong that he, an extension of me, should go wrong?" A third variety of betrayal often goes by the name of "rejection" — that is, rejection of you after you had closely identified with him. Here the beloved has symbolically announced that you and your values are not right, or at least are not wholly satisfying. This is illustrated by second-generation rejection of immigrant parents and the drift away from them. Betrayal of this type consists, usually, of a series of incidents, rather than of a single traumatic event. During the course of day-to-day living, decisions are made whose full implications are not immediately apparent. People can go on deceiving themselves about paths that actually have been closed by those decisions. At the point when it becomes apparent that former possibilities are dead issues, the person stands at a crossroads. . . .

Enough has been said about various types of turning points to suggest that these points in development occur when an individual has to take stock, to re-evaluate, revise, resee, and rejudge. Although stock-taking goes on within the single individual, it is obviously both a socialized and a socializing process. Moreover, the same kinds of incidents that precipitate the revision of identity are extremely likely to befall and to be equally significant to other persons of the same generation, occupation, and social class. This is equivalent to saying that insofar as experiences and interpretations are socially patterned, so also will be the development of personal identities. Let us look next at some types of social patterning: those associated with regulated movements of persons into and from social positions in organized groups. This will enable us to place turning points into close conjunction with formal organizations, yet will not commit us to the position that changes of identity are invariably associated with social position in formal organizations.

REGULARIZED STATUS-PASSAGE [1]

Membership in any enduring group or social structure inevitably involves passage from status to status. In order that a group persist and flourish, each status must be filled, jobs must be done. The incumbents of positions die, retire, leave, fail, and sometimes betray the organization. New kinds of goals develop

[1] Becker and Strauss have given a similar but more elaborate treatment of this subject (3).

and so new positions are created. Other positions get sloughed off, and persons who previously filled them must shift or be shifted elsewhere. Lengthy retention in a given status may hide a genuine shift of social position, as old duties and prerogatives are dropped and new ones accrue. Unless a group were to be wholly undifferentiated, its members necessarily have to move up, down, and sideways.

Many passages of status are highly institutionalized, so that individuals move through them in orderly sequence. Professorial ranks in colleges and universities are an instance of such a step-by-step progression; but so is the normal movement from bride to wife to expectant mother to rearer of children. When movement is thus regularized, there must be predecessors and successors: people have been there before and will follow you. This gives continuity not only to the group or organization, but also to personal experience. In a host of ways, you are prepared for what is to come, are made aware of the immediacy of the next transition, are reminded that you have just now made a passage. The attainment of status may require that you have certain experience, and meet certain standards of conduct and performance; these, myth and story, example and direct instruction, are indispensable. The more subtle aspects of preparation include forewarning you that certain things will soon happen, that you will experience certain experiences, and feel certain feelings; and when you do, certain predecessors will stand ready with interpretations of such predicted events. Their interpretations embody the special language of the group. Ex post facto explanations are also at hand, so that when a person encounters situations for which he has no definitions, he will be offered ready-made ones. "We all went through this." "At your age, that happened to me too. It means that. . . ."

Providing that the definitions offered are not too many and too divergent, you are thereby moved along an orderly line of development. By organizing your action in terms of preferred rationale, you thereby confirm their usefulness and validity. I say validity because your action then can be easily named by other people, and familiarly, even comfortably, responded to. Merton in another connection has called this the "self-fulfilling prophecy" (12) — although I am emphasizing here primarily the continuity that an acceptance of rationale affords. Thus, advice given within an occupation to incoming personnel about clients serves to perpetuate certain relationships and experiences with the clients.

If conflicting rationales leave a person in definitional confusion, or if for other reasons he reaches novel interpretations of his experience, the regulated chain of status-progression is threatened. However, alternative explanations of given events may traditionally exist within a single institution, so that the acceptance by a novice of one or another explanation sets immediate conditions for the pursuit of alternative career routes. This, indeed, is true not merely at the inception of a career but at any point along it, providing that unexpected situations and experiences are traditionally rationalized. Thus a young professor who discovers that he has neither the ability nor the incentive for genuinely excellent research can find institutional sanction and rationale for devoting himself to building a reputation as an outstanding teacher of undergraduates.

When positional mobility follows known sequences, different motivations frequently become appropriate at each successive status. Passage from one to another involves not only changes of action and demeanor, but of the verbalized reasons that are associated with them. Indeed, the stability of a given social structure rests largely upon a proper preparation for these sequential steps. Motivations appropriate to earlier — and usually lower — status must be sloughed off or transmuted, and new ones added or substituted. This necessity is marvelously illustrated in a description by Arensberg and Kimball of family transition in Irish peasant families (1). At the time of the son's marriage, a series of cognate changes in status, act, and motivation are intended to occur simultaneously. The father must yield control of family policy and cease active work; the son must assume responsibility and ardently wish to do so; the mother must become a household guide and teacher to her son's wife; and the latter must remain temporarily subservient. But the younger woman must also be properly motivated to leave her own family, physically and psychologically, and to become a mother as quickly as possible. When her child is born, the young mother must enthusiastically assume full household responsibility.

Simultaneous with this momentous event, the old couple pass to a status of old age. This latter change carries with it an organization of perspective and activity that can be called "making ready for death," the next — and last — status. At any step of this complicated drama of progression, things will go awry if the actors lag behind or speed up unduly in their action or rationale. And, in fact, the strains in family and community life fall exactly at those points where the speed of transition gets out of alignment.

Even in relatively stable structures, where career paths are regular and well regulated, there always arise problems of pacing and timing. Ideally speaking, successors and predecessors should move in and out of offices at equal speeds, but they do not and cannot. Persons who are asked to move may be willing to do so, but must make actual and symbolic preparation to leave. Meanwhile, a successor may be waiting impatiently to take over. In status-passage, transition periods are a necessity, for people often invest heavily of themselves in a position, come to possess it as it possesses them, and it is no easy matter for them to sever themselves from it. If the full ritual of leave-taking is not allowed, a person may be for some time only partially in his new status. On the other hand, the institution stands ready with devices to make him forget, to plunge him into the new office, to point out and allow him to experience the gratifications accruing to it, as well as to force him to abandon the old. Where statuses pyramid so that each is conceived as the logical and temporal extension of the last, severance is not such a disturbing experience. But even here if a person must face his old associates in unaccustomed roles, problems of loyalty become knotty. For this reason, a period of tolerance immediately after formal admission to the new status is almost a necessity. This tolerance is rationalized with phrases like "It takes time," "He is not quite yet in it," "We all make mistakes when starting, until we learn that...."

But people not only drag their heels, they may be too zealous, too eager. Those who are new to a position often commit the indelicate error of taking formal promotion or certification much too literally, when actually there exist intervening informal stages that must be traversed before the full prerogatives of position are attained. This passage may involve tests of loyalty as well as the simple accumulation of information and skill. These informal status grades are referred to in the special language of rankings: "He's a *new* lieutenant" or "That board member is one of the old-timers." An overeager person may be kept in line by all kinds of controlling devices; for instance, a new sales manager discovers that it will take "just a little while" before things can be arranged so that he can institute the changes he envisages in his department. Even a newly appointed superior has to face the resentments or cautiousness of personnel who have preceded him in the organization; and he may, if sensitive, pace his "moving in on them" until he has passed unspoken tests.

When a man is raised to the rank of his former superiors, an especially delicate situation is created. Officially he is now equal to, or like, his former teachers and elders. But equality is neither created by that official act nor, even if it were, could it come about without a certain awkwardness. Imagery and patterns of responses must be rearranged on both sides, and strong self-control must be exerted in order that acts be kept appropriate — even to the self-conscious use of first names, often violating an outmoded but still strongly operative sense of propriety. Slips are inevitable, for although the new status may be fully granted, proper situational identities may be temporarily forgotten to everyone's embarrassment. The former subordinate may come eventually to command, or take precedence over, someone toward whom he previously looked for guidance. At the very least, the colleagues may have to oppose each other over some crucial issue which arises and divides people of the same rank. When former sponsors and sponsored now find it necessary to array themselves differently on such issues, recrimination becomes overt and betrayal explicit. It is understandable why men who have been promoted often prefer to take office, or are advised to do so, in another agency or organization or branch office, however great their desire for remaining at home.

The problems attending the speed of status-passage are merely part of the larger organizational problem of recruiting members for various posts. Recruitment is generally thought of only in connection with bringing newcomers into the structure; but insofar as replacements must be found for each position, on every level, personnel either must be brought in from the outside or trained in other internal positions. In both cases, persons must be induced to give up current endeavors and commitments in order to move onward and, usually, upward. Within the organization, certain persons must be deterred from aiming too high, but others must be induced to cease practicing prized skills and to give up clear satisfactions in exchange for the presumed rewards of the next position. If the latter rewards seem great enough, candidates for each position will be found; but if they are improperly motivated to move to the new position, they will experience considerable strain in transit. Until engineers become used to the idea that their careers frequently involve beginning as engineers and ending as administrators, they experience severe shocks to personal identity when as administrators they cease practicing their engineering skills. E. C. Hughes has recounted[2] the story of one engineer who dreamed a nightmare in which he had lost the capacity to operate a slide rule. In social science research nowadays, it has become necessary for some research professors to spend time and energy finding research money for their junior colleagues. "I spend my time on this. I'm always working on it, I spend my evenings writing letters, seeing people, telephoning. I have to make sacrifices in my own research, of course." (5, p. 293) The Harvard professor from whom this quote is taken must be ready and willing to append "of course" to his sacrifice of research and its satisfactions; otherwise his personal dissatisfactions will outweigh the benefits, accruing to his juniors and to the department, of his contribution toward the common organizational task of raising necessary funds.

Indeed, at every level of an organization, personal stress can arise if motivations are inappropriate for further passages. Self-conceptions may mesh with or grate against institutional arrangements for sequential movements. At Harvard University, few assistant professors can expect to attain the tenure ranks; most anticipate going to other colleges and universities after a maximum of five years. If an assistant professor regards his years at Harvard as stimulating and prestigeful preparation for a better post elsewhere, he is relieved of many strains of competition. But he must guard himself — and some do so insufficiently —

2 In personal conversation.

76

against putting down roots into the community and prevent himself from hoping, however vaguely, that he will be extended tenure. Harvard is able to recruit its assistant professors so effectively — from its own graduate schools as well as from other universities — only because this rank is an early step of a career that is completed elsewhere.

When occupancy of a status is accompanied by acute strain, there is an enhanced possibility that the regular or institutionalized sequence of steps will be abandoned. At these points, people break away in desperation or with defiance, leaving their occupations, families, social classes, and other such organizing frameworks of commitment and loyalty. If recruits are plentiful and not too much time, effort, and money have been expended upon them, their loss may be regarded as minimal. Otherwise steps must be taken to prevent such defection. The conditions that are causing personal stress must be examined, greater rewards offered, in order that stress can better be endured; and alternative career paths must be opened up, or at least seem to aspirants to have opened up. However, the occurrence of stressful situations may not force a man entirely out but merely lead him to aim at a different career within the organization or establishment, causing him to abandon the greater effort necessary to reach the top ranks or to shift his aspirations to other channels. Some choices of specialty and vocation involve this kind of shifting, as when one abandons a line of occupational endeavor but uses it or its skills to make the shift. Hence, in certain specialties, until the routes of entry become institutionalized, recruits are drawn from many fields, often from their failures or their rebellious members. This means that these men are embarked upon an uncertain though not necessarily hazardous future, since the sequences of status-passage have not yet been precisely laid down and sanctified by tradition.

When organizations and institutions are expanding, forming, disintegrating, or in any way changing radically, the personal lives of their members are rendered more tortuous and uncertain and at the same time more dangerous and more exciting. The opportunities for power and personal advance in expanding social structures are obvious, but even when the latter are disintegrating, some clever or fortunate people forge new career opportunities. The dangers of rapid organizational change — whether of expansion or contraction — can be illustrated by what happens to old-timers who reach high positions only to find these no longer carry distinctive prerogatives and honors. Danger also dogs the novice who blindly follows old career models, for a model always is in some significant regard out of date unless the times and the institutions are relatively stable. During periods of great institutional change, the complexities of career are further compounded by what is happening to the careers of those others with whom one is significantly involved. The ordinary ties of sponsorship weaken and break because those in positions to sponsor are focusing upon matters more immediately germane to their own careers. The lower ranks feel the consequences of unusual pressures generated among the ranks above. People become peculiarly vulnerable to unaccustomed demands for loyalty and alliance which spring from unforeseen organizational changes.

Insofar as careers can be visualized and implemented because of the relative stabilities of those social structures within which one has membership, the continuity and maintenance of identity is safeguarded and maximized, and methods of maintenance and restoration are more readily utilized and evolved. However, the movement from status to status, as well as the frustration of having to remain unwillingly in a status, sets conditions for the change and development of identities. Although my examples have been chosen mainly from work organizations, this way of looking at adult development is not at all restricted to occupational life. The lives of men and women can — theoretically, at least — be traced as a series of passages of status. Insofar as this is so, we most heartily agree with Erikson's striking statement that a sense of identity "is never gained nor maintained once and for all. Like a good conscience, it is constantly lost and regained. . . ." (6, p. 57)

PHASES: INSTITUTIONAL AND PERSONAL

I wish now to turn to temporary, if patterned, changes of persons and their behavior. "Temporary" is terminologically related to "temporal" and "time." The vocabularies of all societies cut and order the flow of time, and as Everett Hughes has called to our attention (9), when a society divides time into conventional units it thereby succeeds in introducing perio-dicities, repetitions, routines and high points into the lives of its members. During these periods, and associated with them — whether moments, hours, episodes, or seasons — certain acts are supposed to be performed, others are tabooed, and others are allowed providing anyone should avail himself of the oppor-tunity. Quite clearly this affects the course of interactions.

Turn this statement of institutional action into a statement of identity, and you would say that people are sanctioned to *be* different during different periods. The way to act during a celebration is as a celebrant; the way to act during a legal cross-examination is as accused, accuser, or witness. A status, as I remarked earlier, is likely to become a way of being as well as a way of acting.

A temporal dimension is implicit in all kinds of status. No one is assigned, nor may he assume, a position or status forever. Always there is a clause, whether hidden or openly acknowl-edged, whereby a man may be dispossessed or may dispossess himself of the status. Some statuses, as Nelson Foote has ap-propriately remarked, are socially "scheduled"; people enter and leave them at scheduled times, and generally from other posi-tions while moving toward still others. "Social scheduling is like a game of musical chairs, except that people know in advance when the next change is coming, and as a rule no one gets left out." (8) In less regulated mobility, people take up and drop positions in no particular order; but whether the status is as-sumed progressively, sporadically, or periodically, these very adverbs suggest the notion of a time period. A great many of these are named in the vocabularies of social chronology. During them people are licensed, obligated, sanctioned, and tabooed beings.

The matter of a temporal identity is made much more com-plicated because kinds of status themselves possess a scheduled inner structure. By this I mean merely that people are always entering and leaving them; also that people are always at one point or another in their occupancy. A convenient illustration is the Presidency of the United States, for it is clearly recognized that a President during his fourth year is in a different phase than during his first or sixth. Harold Laski has gone so far as to suggest that a President in his fourth year who is seeking re-election is, in fact, mainly engaged in seeking re-election (11). If such "phases" are sufficiently recurrent, they are likely to receive names. Although the steps of entrance, passage through, and exit from a status are not always perfectly clear, this phaselike character of status is worth analyzing. . . .

All groups recognize periods of time which, though they are much less institutionalized than those mentioned above, are yet conventionalized. In families, for instance, the parents may render the child incommunicado as a punishment: he must remove himself physically from interaction, must refrain from doing certain things, and must by command do another, such as meditate upon his transgression; and his re-entry into communication is preceded at least by some stated period of isolation or by a rite of apology. Punishment by isolation is generally less of a routine in family life than the one o'clock rest period, but it is nevertheless rather well governed by conventional understandings.

Such understandings are multitudinous, and can be drawn upon at will, as when one enters voluntarily upon some transitory phase. You signal that you have a headache, and will withdraw, or will listen but not actively participate in conversation. You may even go to sleep in public with the understanding, in some groups at least, that you are not to be disturbed. (I have heard jazz musicians use the suggestive phrase "to fall out.") Asked a question, you may declare yourself "in thought," not to be disturbed or asked further questions until you signal your return to the conversation. Such incidents suggest that all that you must do to elicit appropriate action from others is to announce your entrance into certain phases; you are given exemption, license, but also appropriate obligations; having slept, the sleeper is supposed to be refreshed; having thought, the thinker is supposed to have answers.

Viewed more longitudinally, interaction is punctuated by much longer phases than mere withdrawal from conversation for thought and sleep. A student may withdraw from a busy social life for several weeks to study for exams or to go on a prolonged reading kick. Conversely, he may plunge periodically into a social whirl. Erik Erikson has pointed to an eight-year period in the life of G. B. Shaw during which the great man declared a virtual moratorium on all ordinary commitments (6, pp. 51–55; 7). He resigned from a business post, at which he was by ordinary standards successful, left family and friends, left Ireland for England, and as Shaw says, "left a phase behind me, and associated no more with men my age until, after about eight years of solitude in this respect, I was drawn into the Socialist revival of the early eighties." He meanwhile employed himself in learning to write, which meant in the deeper sense, as both Shaw's account and Erikson's commentary make clear, utilizing his moratorium to work out a new sense of identity. Shaw is not alone; many people declare moratoria, albeit less radical ones. They also declare periods for the consolidation of psychological gains, periods for resting upon laurels after success, periods for personal trial or probation, periods for expiation of sins, periods for contemplation, periods for prolonged self-searching. All such periods, which themselves also consist of a series of phases, are much less institutionalized than are honeymoons, celebrations, and other such regulated episodes. Nevertheless, a person may often use conventional signs to indicate that he is entering, or is in the midst of such a period, and wishes to have his claims to it honored.

There is always the potential problem of legitimizing one's right to enter a phase that is not clearly institutionalized, for the signs adduced then for placement of self can be debated. School children thus sometimes encounter difficulties when trying to receive authorization to leave school grounds before dismissal time, unless they can produce unequivocal signs of illness; and some are compelled to remain when seriously, although not violently, sick. Legitimation is rendered easier when the claim to a phase conforms traditionally to what is expected at a given age. A young man is freer to wander aimlessly or to experiment with jobs than a middle-aged one. Legitimation is linked in this way with timing, as phases run athwart other phases. When phases are part of lengthier temporal periods, there is always the possibility that people may too quickly or too slowly pass through these periods. Any extraordinary pace must be justified. The patient who argues that he is sicker than the doctor thinks, and the patient who insists on getting out of bed before it seems that he should, are both bothersome to the doctor.

Actually, although I have been writing as if people were passing through a single phase at any given time, this is never so. Even in grief and deep mourning you only temporarily lay aside your other temporal identities, and during an extended period of mourning, you continually interrupt it to enter into quite different phases. Life consists not merely in adjudicating between the demands of stable kinds of status, but also in juggling differential temporal placement. On Monday morning, you may be entering the initial phase of one status, leaving another, and be midstream in several others. To which should you pay chief attention? The query suggests problems of self-legitimation and self-justification. These can never be fully or finally resolved, for you are forever moving on into new phases. . . .

THE SENSE OF PERSONAL CONTINUITY

The persistence of identity is quite another thing than its imagined persistence. In Erikson's terminology there is a difference between "a conscious sense of individual identity" and "an unconscious striving for a continuity of personal character," or between the former and "the silent doings of ego-synthesis." (7, p. 57)

Some of the conditions for the actual minimization of change, of course, have relevance for a person's lack of recognition of change in himself. A prefigured life-cycle, a standardized progression of social positions, not only actually minimizes crises but obscures those changes that occur and aids in explaining them away. The very names for a given status, as well as the presumed coherent complex of associated tasks, helps to dull any sense of personal change even when the actual behavior associated with the status becomes altered.

Through the years, much that a person recognizes as belonging characteristically to himself — as, for instance, an intense liking for foods characteristic of his ethnic group — obscures recognition of other, seemingly less important, shifts in taste and conduct. Awareness of significant change is a symbolic matter.

A change must be deemed important before it and kindred changes can be perceived as vitally important. Everyone's behavior changes in some regard but not in all; and which changes are worth taking into special account and which are trifling, peripheral, irrelevant, and even believed spurious does not depend merely upon the appearance or disappearance of actual behavior.

Each person's account of his life, as he writes or thinks about it, is a symbolic ordering of events. The sense that you make of your own life rests upon what concepts, what interpretations, you bring to bear upon the multitudinous and disorderly crowd of past acts. If your interpretations are convincing to yourself, if you trust your terminology, then there is some kind of continuous meaning assigned to your life as-a-whole. Different motives may be seen to have driven you at different periods, but the overriding purpose of your life may yet seem to retain a certain unity and coherence. Thus a late convert to a sect may view most of his life as actually spent in the service of the Lord and regard the early wastrel years as a necessary preparation to the later service; or certain events may stand out as deviant from the general stream of a career, thereby contributing, by their very rarity, a further unity to the main line. The deviant events may be discounted because they belong to earlier or more youthful phases.

> He thought of it as a youthful folly. He put his vote for Eugene Debs alongside his visit to a parlor house when he was twenty. Both were things he expected of growing boys (13, pp. 41–42).

Deviant events may be explained also as temptations, as illnesses, escapes, releases, last minute flings, and foolhardiness. Like other assignments of motive and meaning, those made about one's own self may — indeed must — change over the years. With new experiences, everyone discovers new meanings and orderings in his career.

Such terminological assessment is crucial to feelings of continuity or discontinuity. If past acts appear to fit together more or less within some scheme, adding up to and leading up to the current self, then "they were me, belong to me, even though I have somewhat changed." It is as if you were to tell the story of your life, epoch by epoch, making sense of each in terms of the end product. The subjective feeling of continuity turns not merely upon the number or degree of behavioral changes, but upon the framework of terms within which otherwise discordant events can be reconciled and related. Past purposes and dedications may be challenged and abandoned, but when viewed as part of a larger temporal design they do not plague one by feelings of self-betrayal. It is the very lack of design that is reflected subjectively in feelings of personal discontinuity, of wrecked or abandoned selves, or more mildly experienced in the lack of meaningful purposes, in conceptions of certain periods of one's life that were wasted, or senseless, or did not lead anywhere. Past identities can be reconciled, made to appear uniform despite their apparent diversity, only if they can be encompassed in a unified interpretation. A firm sense of oneness rests upon "coming to terms with self" — a suggestive pun. The terms of settlement are never over and done with; the point is magnificently illustrated by the ending of Balzac's *Père Goriot,* when an elderly man upon his deathbed almost questions his entire life, as he stands upon the brink of recognizing an abrupt transformation of self, but is released from confronting himself full-face by death (2).

The awareness of constancy in identity is, then, in the eye of the beholder rather than "in" the behavior itself. The point holds no less for biography than for autobiography. Camus has said:

> Looking at these existences from the outside, one lends them a coherence and unity which, in truth, they cannot have, but which appears evident to the observer. He sees only the outline of these lives, without taking account of the complicating detail (4, p. 275).

But the point is not merely that the observer misses complicating detail; it is that events must be ordered to be comprehended at all. Like other events, the details of any person's life may be conceptually organized and patterned by the observer and thus understood, explained, and managed. "We make art out of these (observed) existences." (4, p. 275) Different biographers organize more or less the same facts bearing upon someone's actions, and each arrives at a fairly unified but not necessarily congruent picture of the hero and the course of his life. Neither the biographer nor the autobiographer can afford to admit that more than a few of these puzzling, poorly understood actions are vitally important to the personal narrative. If they seem important, they will be woven somehow into the story — else disjuncture will be recognized and gaps sensed.

References

1. Arensberg, Conrad. *The Irish Countryman*. New York: The Macmillan Company, 1937.

2. Balzac, Honoré de. *Old Goriot*. New York: E. P. Dutton and Co., 1935.

3. Becker, Howard S., and Anselm Strauss. "Careers, Personality and Adult Socialization," *American Journal of Sociology*, Vol. 62 (November 1956).

4. Camus, Albert. "Art and Revolt," *Partisan Review*, Vol. 19 (May–June 1952), p. 275.

5. Committee of the Faculty Report. "The Behavioral Sciences at Harvard." Cambridge, Mass.: Harvard University, June 1954.

6. Erikson, Erik H. "Identity and Totality: Psychoanalytic Observations on the Problem of Youth," *Human Development Bulletin*, Fifth Annual Symposium (1954).

7. Erikson, Erik H. "The Problem of Identity," *American Journal of Psychoanalysis*, Vol. 4 (1956).

8. Foote, Nelson. "Concept and Method in the Study of Human Development." Paper delivered at an Oklahoma conference in Social Psychology.

9. Hughes, Everett. *Cycles and Turning Points: The Significance of Initiation in Human Culture*. New York: The National Council of the Protestant Episcopal Church, Faculty Paper, no date.

10. Kallen, Horace. *Patterns of Progress*. New York: Columbia University Press, 1950.

11. Laski, Harold. *The American Presidency*. New York: Harper & Brothers, 1940.

12. Merton, Robert K. *Social Theory and Social Structure*, rev. ed. Glencoe, Ill.: The Free Press, 1957.

13. Steinbeck, John. *The Wayward Bus*. New York: The Viking Press, 1947.

5

Appearance and the Self

GREGORY P. STONE

UNIVERSITY OF MINNESOTA

In most interactional processes there is an exchange not only of verbal symbols, but also of natural signs and of other non-verbal signs which set the conditions for the interaction. Among the latter are the "appearances" of the interacting persons as they perceive each other. The "appearance" covers many things, including body size and shape, "reputation" and "image," clothing, stance, and facial expression. In this chapter, Professor Stone takes Mead and other symbolic interactionists to task for neglecting this important dimension of interaction. Following the lead offered by Mead's perspective, Stone has sought empirical evidence of the meaning of appearance in the responses that appearances mobilize. In pursuit of his critique, he offers a thoughtful analysis of the role of "appearance" in interactions, and of its effect through the reflected image of others back on the self.

A primary tenet of all symbolic interaction theory holds that the self is established, maintained, and altered in and through communication. Seeking to probe this tenet, most investigations have emphasized discourse — or, somewhat inexactly, verbal communication — and have shown that language exerts a very great influence indeed upon the structure and process of the self. The present essay attempts to widen the perspective of symbolic interaction studies by isolating a dimension of communication that has received relatively little attention by sociologists and social psychologists — appearance. Except for psychoanalysts, some psychiatrists, and a few anthropologists, one finds almost no scholars willing to bend their efforts to the study of appearance.[1]

This paper seeks to demonstrate that the perspective of symbolic interaction, as it has been formulated by George H. Mead, requires (indeed, *demands*) a consideration of appearance for the adequate interpretation of social transactions as well as the careers of selves in such transactions. Mead's analysis of communication, it is suggested, suffers from what might be called a "discursive bias."[2] Consequently, there are crucial unanswered questions posed by his analysis of communication that can only be answered by extending and refining his perspective. This requires a demonstration that: (1) every social transaction must be broken down into at least two analytic components or processes — appearance and discourse; (2) appearance is at least as important for the establishment and maintenance of the self as is discourse; (3) the study of appearance provides a powerful lever for the formulation of a conception of self capable of embracing the contributions of Cooley and Sullivan as well as Mead;

[1] Erving Goffman (7) must be exempted from the indictment. Recently he has pushed sociological or social psychological analysis far beyond the conventional limits of a perspective that has restricted the study of social transactions to their linguistic characteristics, conditions, and consequences.
[2] Of course, the gesture is considered at length, and gestures may often be employed to establish appearances, as we shall see. However, Mead views the gesture as incipient discourse, more typical of communication in its rudimentary phases. The aptness of the vocal gesture for explaining the emergence of meaning in sub-social communication may be an important source of Mead's discursive bias. Even more than discourse, appearance presupposes an on-going social process for its meaning. Apparent symbols are often silent and are best intercepted by mirrors, while one's own ear always intercepts one's own vocal gesture about as it is intercepted by others. But mirrors are not always handy; so it happens that the silent appearance, even more than the vocal utterance, comes to require an audience which can serve as a mirror, reflecting one's appearance back upon himself.

and (4) appearance is of major importance at every stage of the early development of the self. These assertions are all empirically grounded in the author's long-term study of dress as an apparent symbol (16).

APPEARANCE, DISCOURSE, AND MEANING

According to Mead, meaning is established only when the response elicited by some symbol is the "same" for the one who produces the symbol as for the one who receives it.[3] "Same" appears here in quotation marks, because the responses are *really* never the "same." This is an integral feature of Mead's perspective and calls for some elaboration. The fundamental implication is that *meaning is always a variable.*

We can trace this variable nature of meaning to Mead's conception of the self as process and structure, subject and object, or "I" and "me." The "I" imbues the self with a certain tentativeness — a "certain uncertainty." As a consequence, any future line of action (for example, one's response to one's own symbolic productions) can never be fully anticipated. Mead put it this way:

> So the "I" really appears experientially as a part of the "me." But on the basis of this experience we distinguish that individual who is doing something from the "me" who puts the problem up to him. The response enters into his experience only when it takes place. If he says he knows what he is going to do, even there he may be mistaken. He starts out to do something and something happens to interfere. The resulting action is always a little different from anything which he could anticipate. . . . The action of the "I" is something the nature of which we cannot tell in advance (14, p. 177).

But the meaning of a symbol, as we have said, is premised upon the notion that the response called out in the other is the *same* as the response called out in the one who produces the symbol

---

[3] "Response" is usually the production of other symbols. The term is distinguished from "symbol" merely to permit the observer to shift his view as he analyzes what is going on in the social transaction. Actually, all that distinguishes a "response" from any symbol in question is its occurrence later in time. I am indebted to my colleague, Keith Miller, for this clarification.

— always a little different from anything which he could anticipate. Moreover, the other's response has the same characteristically unanticipatable quality.

Meaning, then, is always a variable, ranging between non-sense, on the one hand — the total absence of coincident responses — and what might be called boredom on the other — the total coincidence of such responses. Neither of these terminals can be approached very often in the duration of a transaction, for either can mean its end. It is seldom' that we continue to talk non-sense with others, and boredom encourages us to depart from their presence. Thus, meaning is present in communication when the responses that are symbolically mobilized only *more or less* coincide.

This raises the question of *guarantees* for the meaningfulness of social transactions. How can the transaction be prevented from spilling over into non-sense or atrophying into boredom? Because the self is in part an "I" — unpredictable — the risks of boredom are minimized; but, for Mead, the guarantee against non-sense in the transaction is "role-taking," or, more accurately, placing one's self in the attitude of the other. By placing one's self in the attitude or incipient action of the other and representing one's own symbolic production to oneself from that attitude, one guarantees that one's own response will be rather more than less coincident with the response of the other, since the other's incipient actions have become incorporated in the actions of the one producing the symbol. It is here, however, that a gap in Mead's analysis occurs, for a further question arises, and that question was not systematically considered by Mead: if role-taking is the guarantee of meaning, how then is role-taking possible? Obviously, one must apprehend the other's role, the other's attitude — indeed, the other's self — before one can take the other's role or incorporate the other's attitude.

At this point a shift in terminology is required to expedite the analysis of meaning and to provide initial answers to the questions that have been raised. Let us suggest that the guarantee against non-sense in the social transaction is heuristically better conceptualized as *identification*,[4] not role-taking or taking the other's attitude — at best a very partial explanation of how mean-

4 The precedent has been incisively established by Nelson N. Foote (4).

ing is established in social transactions. The term "identification" subsumes at least two processes: *identification of* and *identification with*. Role-taking is but one variant of the latter process, which must also include sympathy,[5] and there may well be other variants.[6] Nevertheless, the point to be made is this: identifications *with* one another, in whatever mode, cannot be made without identifications *of* one another. Above all, identifications of one another are ordinarily facilitated by appearance and are often accomplished silently or non-verbally. This can be made crystal clear by observing the necessity for and process of establishing gender in social transactions. Everywhere we find vocabularies sexually distinguished: there are languages for males only, languages for females only, and languages employed to communicate across the barriers of gender. Obviously, identifications of the other's gender must be established before the appropriate language can be selected for the upcoming discourse. Seldom, upon encountering another, do we inquire concerning the other's gender. Indeed, to do so would be to impugn the very gender that must be established. The knowing of the other's gender is known silently, established by appearances.

Appearance, then, is that phase of the social transaction which establishes identifications of the participants. As such, it may be distinguished from *discourse*, which we conceptualize as the text of the transaction — *what* the parties are discussing. Appearance and discourse are two distinct dimensions of the social transaction. The former seems the more basic. It sets the stage for, permits, sustains, and delimits the possibilities of discourse by underwriting the possibilities of meaningful discussion.

Ordinarily appearance is communicated by such non-verbal symbols as gestures, grooming, clothing, location, and the like; discourse, by verbal symbolism. Yet the relationship between the kinds of symbolism and the dimension of the transaction is not at all invariant. Gestures and other non-verbal symbols may be used to talk about things and events, and words may have purely apparent significance. In fact, appearances are often discussed,

---

[5] Mead himself distinguishes sympathy as a particular mode of "attitude-taking" in a seldom cited article (13); but for the empirical utility of the distinction, see Sheldon Stryker (17).
[6] An imposing taxonomy has been erected in Howard Becker (1).

while discussions often "appear" — that is, serve only to establish the identities of the discussants. In the latter case, the person may seem to be talking about matters other than identifications of self or other, but may actually be speaking only about himself. "Name-dropping" serves as an example. In the former case, which we will term *apparent discourse,* whole transactions may be given over to the discussion of appearances, and this occurs most often when some new turn has been taken by the transaction requiring re-identificatións of the parties. Indeed, apparent discourse is often *news* and vice versa.

Appearance and discourse are in fact dialectic processes going on whenever people converse or correspond. They work back and forth on one another, at times shifting, at other times maintaining the direction of the transaction. When the direction of the transaction shifts, appearance is likely to emerge into the discursive phases of the transaction; when the direction is maintained over a relatively long period of time and is uninterrupted, discourse is likely to be submerged in appearances. In all cases, however, discourse is impossible without appearance which permits the requisite identifications with one another by the discussants. One may, nevertheless, appear without entering the discourse. As Veblen suggested, we may escape our discursive obligations, but not our clothed appearances (19, p. 167).

APPEARANCE AND THE SELF

Appearance *means* identifications of one another,[7] but the question arises whether such identifications follow any ordered pattern. Mead's perspective insists that we look for the meaning of appearance in the responses that appearances mobilize, and we have examined more than 8,000 such responses supplied by interview materials to discern whether they are consistently patterned. Many responses are, of course, gestural in nature. One's appearance commands the gaze of the audience. An eyebrow is lifted. There is a smile or a frown, an approach or withdrawal. One

[7] The question of how the meaning of appearance is guaranteed is germane and recognized, but will not be treated here. Aside from the "teamwork" analyzed so carefully by Goffman in his *Presentation of Self in Everyday Life* (7), other guarantees are suggested in his "Symbols of Class Status." (6)

blushes with shame for the shamelessness of the other's appearance or with embarrassment at one's own. The nature of our data precluded the study of such gestural responses unless they were recorded by the interviewer. Consequently, apparent discourse was examined for the most part — talk about appearance aroused, in particular, by clothing. Over 200 married men and women living in a Midwestern community of 10,000 population supplied the talk. Of the many statements these people made about dress, only statements referring to those who wore the clothing in question were scrutinized. These were construed as identifications of the wearer. Here we shall be concerned for simplicity's sake with only two modes of such responses: (1) responses made about the wearer of clothes by others who, we shall say, *review* his clothing; and (2) responses made about the wearer by the wearer — we shall call these responses *programs*. A third mode of response is relevant, but will not be considered here — the wearer's imagination of others' responses to his dress.

When programs and reviews tend to coincide, the self of the one who appears (the one whose clothing has elicited such responses) is validated or established; when such responses tend toward disparity, the self of the one who appears is challenged, and conduct may be expected to move in the direction of some redefinition of the challenged self. Challenges and validations of the self, therefore, may be regarded as aroused by personal appearance. As a matter of fact, the dimensions of the self emphasized by Mead, Cooley, and Sullivan effectively embrace the content of the responses to clothing we examined in our quest for the meaning of appearance. In response to his clothes, the wearer was cast as a social object — a "me" — or, as we shall say, given some identity. A person's dress also imbued him with attitudes by arousing others' anticipations of his conduct as well as assisting the mobilization of his own activity. In Mead's terms, then, the self as object and attitude is established by appearance. However, the most frequent response to dress was the assignment of value-words to the wearer. One's clothes impart value to the wearer, both in the wearer's own eyes and in the eyes of others. Both Sullivan and Cooley underscore the relevance of value for any adequate conceptualization of the self; Sullivan, by referring to the self as comprised by the "reflected *appraisals* of others," Cooley, by emphasizing "imagined *judgments* of appearance." Finally, Cooley's emphasis upon self-*feeling* or the self as *sentiment* was provided with empirical support by this analysis. A person's clothing often served to establish a mood for himself capable of eliciting validation in the reviews aroused from others. The meaning of appearance, therefore, is the establishment of identity, value, mood, and attitude for the one who appears by the coincident programs and reviews awakened by his appearance. These terms require further discussion.

IDENTITY

It is almost enough to demonstrate the significance of the concept "identity" by referring to the rapidity with which it has caught on in social science. Recently re-introduced to the social sciences by Erik Erikson, the term has provided many new social-psychological insights. Specifically, fruitful inquiries into the sociological implications of the ego have been made possible by releasing the investigator from the commitment to argument and partisanship that alternative concepts such as "personality" demand. Identity, as a concept, is without any history of polemics. However, the impetus to discovery afforded by the term has been so great that its meaning threatens to spill over the bounds of analytic utility. Before its meaning becomes totally lost by awakening every conceivable response in every conceivable investigator (like the term "personality"), the concept must be salvaged.

Almost all writers using the term imply that identity establishes *what* and *where* the person is in social terms. It is not a substitute word for "self." Instead, when one has identity, he is *situated* — that is, cast in the shape of a social object by the acknowledgment of his participation or membership in social relations. One's identity is established when others *place* him as a social object by assigning him the same words of identity that he appropriates for himself or *announces*. It is in the coincidence of placements and announcements that identity becomes a meaning of the self, and often such placements and announcements are aroused by apparent symbols such as uniforms. The policeman's uniform, for example, is an announcement of his identity as policeman and validated by other's placements of him as police-man.

Such a conception of identity is, indeed, close to Mead's con-ception of the "me," the self as object related to and differentiated from others. To situate the person by establishing some identity for him is, in a sense, to give him position, and a pun permits further elucidation of the concept: identity is established as a consequence of two processes, apposition and opposition, a bring-ing together and setting apart. To situate the person as a social object is to bring him together with other objects so situated, and, at the same time to set him apart from still other objects. *Identity is intrinsically associated with all the joinings and de-partures of social life.* To have an identity is to join with some and depart from others, to enter and leave social relations at once.

In fact, the varieties of identity are isomorphic with the va-rieties of social relations. At least four different types of words were used to place and announce the identities communicated by clothing: (1) universal words designating one's humanity, such as age, gender, and community (we call these "universal" words because people everywhere make such distinctions); (2) names and nicknames; (3) titles, such as occupational and marital titles; (4) "relational categories," such as customer, movie-goer, jazz fan, and the like. Social relations, viewed as on-going trans-actions, can be classified according to the identities which must be placed and announced to permit entry into the transaction. Thus, *human relations* are those requiring the placement and an-nouncement of such universal identities as age, gender, or com-munity membership. *Interpersonal relations* are those that may only be entered by an exchange of names or nicknames,[8] while *structural relations* are those that may only be entered by ex-changing a name for a title. Finally, we may speak of *masses* as social relations that may be anonymously entered.

The distinction between interpersonal and structural relations seems, at this point, to have the greatest analytical utility. Since one's name ordinarily outlasts one's titles, interpersonal relations probably provide an important social basis for the continuity of

---

[8] This characterization of interpersonal relations is not reversible. The exchange of names does not guarantee that an interpersonal relationship will always be established.

identity. Structural relations, on the other hand, are more discontinuous and changing.

We can note how one's name is established by dress if we
imagine Teddy Roosevelt without the pince-nez, F. D. R. without the cigarette holder, or Thomas Dewey without the mous-
tache. One of our informants, a small-time real estate operator,
was well aware of the significance of clothing in his attempts to
personalize his occupational identity. Asked, "What do your
fellow workers say and think when you wear something new
for the first time on the job?" he replied:

> Well, I always have a new hat, and I suppose my clientele talks
> about it. But, you know, I always buy cheap ones and put my
> name in them. I leave them around in restaurants and places
> like that intentionally. It has advertising value.

The interviewer asked later, "Would you rather wear a greater
variety or a smaller variety of clothes on the job?" and the informant replied:

> A smaller variety so you will look the same everyday. So
> people will identify you. They look for the same old landmark.

In response to the same question, a working man who had recently opened a small business said:

> A smaller variety for both sales and shop. I think if a person
> dresses about the same continually, people will get to know
> you. Even if they don't know your name, you're easier to
> describe. I knew an insurance man once who used a wheel
> chair. Everyone knew him because of that chair. It's the same
> with clothes.

Distinctive, persistent dress may replace the name as well as
establish it!

On the other hand, one's career within the structural relation
is marked by changes of title, and the change of title demands
a change of dress. All of the men in this study were presented
with the following story:

> John had an excellent record as foreman in an automobile
> factory. Eventually, he and two other foremen were promoted
> to the position of division head. John was happy to get the job,

because of the increase in pay. However, he continued to wear his old foreman's vest and work clothes to the office. This went on for several months until the division heads he had been promoted with began to avoid him at lunch and various social gatherings. They had dressed from the beginning in business suits and had mingled more and more with older managerial employees. John found himself without friends in the office.

When asked, "What finally happened to John?" about 80 per cent of the men interviewed predicted termination, demotion, or no further promotion (5, pp. 47–51). One informant, interviewed by the writer, quite seriously suggested that John was a potential suicide.

Appearances, then, are interrupted in social structures as identities are set apart; appearances, so to speak, endure in interpersonal relations where identities are brought into closer proximity. Yet we find that, in the context of structural relations, identities are given a somewhat different cast than in interpersonal relations. In the former, identities are qualified along the axis of value; in the latter, more usually along the axis of mood.

QUALIFICATIONS OF IDENTITY:
VALUE AND MOOD

To engage meaningfully in some transactions it is enough to know merely "what" the parties are — to know their identities. This would seem often to be the case in the anonymous transactions of the masses. As Louis Wirth used to tell his students in his elaborations of the "massive" character of urban life, "You go to a bootblack to have your shoes shined; not to save your soul." The implication is, I think, that, when we become concerned with the bootblack's moods or his larger worth in terms of some scheme of value, our relations with him will lose their anonymous character. By so doing, we have, perhaps, disadvantaged ourselves of the freedom the city offers. Ordinarily, however, if transactions persistently engage the same persons or seem likely to continue into an ill-defined future, it is not enough merely to establish identities in the guarantee of meaningful discourse. Thus, when we are introduced to strangers who may become acquaintances or possibly friends, we *express* our pleasure with the introductions, and such expressions are ordinarily *appreciated* by those we have met. Or, meeting an acquaintance on the street, we inquire how he *feels* before the discourse is initiated. In a certain sense, interpersonal relations demand that the *moods* of the participants be established (as well as their names or nicknames) prior to the initiation of discursive phases in the transaction: that "Joe" or "Jane" is mad or sad will have definite consequences for the talk with "Jim" or "Joan."

Ordinarily, also, before a title is bestowed upon us or before we are invested with office, our identities must undergo qualifying scrutiny. In such cases, the qualification does not usually get accomplished in terms of our anger or sadness, but in terms of some assessment of our former careers and future prospects with reference to their *worth*. The tendency is to assess worth in terms of a relatively objective set of standards that can transcend the whim of the assessing one and the whimsy of the one assessed. Upon the initiation of what we have called structural relations, the *values* of the participating persons (as well as their titles) must be established.

Value and mood provide two fundamental axes along which the qualifications of identity are accomplished in *appraising* and *appreciative* responses to appearance. This seems obvious on the face of it: that a teacher is competent has different consequences for faculty–student transactions than that a teacher is a teacher; and that a teacher is temperamental or easy-going presents the possibility of a still different set of consequences for upcoming discussions. The differences between value and mood are suggested by the distinction that Park has made between interests and sentiments, that Helen Lynd has made between guilt and shame, or that Kenneth Burke has made between poetry and pathos (*poiema* and *pathema*). It is the difference between virtue and happiness, and, as we know full well, the virtuous man is not necessarily happy nor the happy man necessarily virtuous. The problem arises when we observe that happiness may be a virtue in some social circles or that one may be happy because he is virtuous (cynics might say "smug"). Value and mood, so patently distinguishable in discourse, merge together inextricably in experience. Can we conceive of feelings of pride without reference to a set of values? I think not, although it does seem possible to conceive of merit without feeling. Yet, in situations that are totally value-relevant, totally given over to matters of appraisal — the courtroom, the examination, the military review — the very constriction of feeling and mood, their suppression, may saturate the situation with a grim somberness that can transform dispassion into passion — as the austerity of the courtroom has provided a curiously fitting context for the impassioned plea; the silence of the examination room is interrupted by nervous laughter; the ordered rhythm of the march engenders song.

As Helen Lynd has written of guilt and shame, so we conceive value and mood:

> They are in no sense polar opposites. Both the guilt axis and the shame axis enter into the attitudes and behavior of most people, and often into the same situation. But there are for different persons different balances and stresses between the two, and it does matter whether one lives more in terms of one or the other (11, p. 208).

And we would add that one differentiating condition is the type of social relation that regularly mobilizes the time and attention of the person. Thus, we have found that value has a greater saliency for most men in their conceptions of self and others, while, for most women, mood has a greater saliency. This finding is ascribed in part to the American male's more frequent participation and absorption in the structure of work relations, in comparison with the American woman's more frequent preoccupation with the interpersonal relations she carries on with friends and acquaintances.

It is much more difficult to characterize value and mood than it has been to characterize identity. However, the responses to dress that were classified as words of value manifested the following references: (1) to *consensual goals*, such as wealth, prestige, or power; (2) to *achievement standards*, universalistic criteria applied to the assessment of one's proximity to or remoteness from such goals; (3) *norms* or rules regulating the pursuit of consensual goals; and (4) *moral precepts* stipulating valued behavior often employed in the assessment of character (e.g., cleanliness, politeness, thriftiness, and the like). Responses classified as mood-words were even more difficult to order, including references to ease and lack of ease in social transactions, liking, disliking, fearing, and dreading. Anxiety, monotony, rapture, and surprise also were included in the category, as were references to that ill-defined state which the informants called morale.

It may be helpful to borrow again from Helen Lynd, using her technique for contrasting guilt and shame to contrast value and mood. Table 1 attempts to state the social relations for which value and mood *ordinarily* have the greatest saliency, the nature of the criteria which are applied in the establishment of value and mood, the processes by which these qualifications of identity are established, and finally the consequences for the social relationship when identities are qualified along one or the other axis. I wish to emphasize that the summary presentation in Table 1 is in no way meant to be definitive, and that the axes which

TABLE 1

Value and Mood as Axes Along Which Qualifications of Identity Are Established

PHASES	VALUE AXIS	MOOD AXIS
Relational Basis	Structural relations	Interpersonal relations

Criteria	Universalistic
	  Abstract
	Objective
	  Detachment
	  Poetic (Pious)
	  Neutrality
	Scalar
		Particularistic
		  Concrete
		Subjective
		  Attachment
		  Pathetic
		  Affectivity
		Absolute

Establishment	Rationalized Investment Conformity–deviation with respect to universal rules or a social code Future reference Legitimated by appeals to the appraisals of others	Spontaneously communicated Preoccupation or rapture Ease–dis-ease with respect to engagement in social transactions Present reference Legitimated by appeals to the expressions of the self
Relational Consequences	Stratification	Rapport

are characterized as value and mood, although they are set down in a contrasting manner, are not meant to be established as polar opposites. In particular, *sentiments* represent a convergence of the two axes in the qualification of identity. Sentiments are valued feelings or felt values, as for example in Cooley's "looking-glass self" — the sentiments of pride or mortification are *expressive* responses to the judgments or *appraisals* of others.

ACTIVATIONS OF IDENTITY: ATTITUDE

In a brilliant discussion, Kenneth Burke has established the essential ambiguity of the term "attitude": an attitude can be looked upon as a substitute for an act — the "truncated act" of John Dewey — or as an incipient act — a "beginning" from the standpoint of George H. Mead (2, pp. 235–247). The establishment of identity, value, and mood by appearances represents the person as *there, stratified* or assigned a particular distance, and *rapt* or engrossed. There remains the matter of his activation, the assessment of the path along which he has traveled, the path he is traveling, and where he is about to go. These aspects of the person — that he has acted, is acting, and will act further — are also established by appearance. We refer to them as *attitudes*.[9] Attitudes are *anticipated* by the reviewers of an appearance, *proposed* by the one who appears.

Appearance *substitutes* for past and present action and, at the same time, conveys an *incipience* permitting others to anticipate what is about to occur. Specifically, clothing represents our action, past, present, and future, as it is established by the proposals and anticipations that occur in every social transaction. Without further elaboration, I think that this can be clearly seen in the doffing of dress, signaling that an act is done (and another

[9] Of course, the concept "attitude" is of central significance for the social psychology of George Herbert Mead, but, in some ways, it is the least satisfying of the terms we have characterized here. All the meanings of dress or appearance have an attitudinal or "activated" character. In particular, programs and reviews may be conceived as incipient, truncated, or on-going acts. It may be, in fact, that the concept "attitude" is of a different order from the concepts "identity," "value," and "mood," asking the observer to inquire not into the content or structure of the events under scrutiny, but rather to seize those events in their full-blown capacity as processes.

act about to begin), the donning of dress, signaling the initiation of a new act, and the wearing of dress, signaling that action is going on.

APPEARANCE AND THE SELF

The meaning of appearance, therefore, can be studied by examining the responses mobilized by clothes. Such responses take on at least four forms: identities are placed, values appraised, moods appreciated, and attitudes anticipated. Appearance provides the identities, values, moods, and attitudes of the person-in-communication, since it arouses in others the assignment of words embodying these dimensions to the one who appears. As we have noted earlier, this is only one part of the total picture.

Cooley, Mead, and Harry Stack Sullivan have reminded us often that such responses are reflexive in character, reverberating back upon the one who produces them and the one toward whom they are directed. In short, identifications of others are always complemented by identifications of the self, in this case, responses to one's own appearance. In a variety of ways, as a matter of fact, reviews of a person's appearances are intricately linked with the responses he makes to his own appearance. We have called the process of making identifications of the one who appears by that one a *program*. Programmatic responses parallel the responses that have been called reviews. One appears, reflects upon that appearance, and appropriates words of identity, value, mood, or attitude for himself in response to that appearance. By appearing, the person *announces* his identity, *shows* his value, *expresses* his mood, or *proposes* his attitude. If the meaning of appearance is "supplied" by the reviews others make of one's appearance, it is established or consensually validated, as Sullivan would have said, by the relative coincidence of such reviews with the program of the one who appears. In other words, when one's dress calls out in others the "same" identifications of the wearer as it calls out in the wearer, we may speak of the appearance as meaningful. It turns out, in fact, that this is the self, and this may be diagrammed as in Table 2.

In appearances, then, selves are established and mobilized. As the self is dressed, it is simultaneously addressed, for, whenever

TABLE 2

*Schematic Representation of the Meaning of Appearance,
Emphasizing the Validation of Personal Appearance*

PROGRAM OF APPEARANCE	REVIEW OF APPEARANCE			
	Placement	*Appraisal*	*Appreciation*	*Anticipation*
Announcement	Identity			
Show		Value		
Expression			Mood	
Proposal				Attitude

we clothe ourselves, we dress "toward" or address some audience
whose validating responses are essential to the establishment of
our self. Such responses may, of course, also be challenges, in
which case a new program is aroused. This intimate linkage of
the self and clothing was masterfully caricatured by a forty-
year-old carpenter's wife who was herself working in a local
factory. Our guess is that a few bottles of beer were conducive
to the spontaneous flow of words, but their import is none the
less striking. The woman had interpreted a modified TAT scene
as a religious depiction, and the interviewer asked her, after the
completion of the stories, which card she liked best:

> [Interviewer: Of those three, which did you like best? . . .]
> Oh, that is kinda hard for me to do. I like them all. This one
> here is good, and that one is good, and that one is good. I
> think, of course, religion should come first, but I still think
> this is first right here — of her trying to help this girl. [Note:
> the card depicts a well-dressed woman talking with another
> woman in rather drab masculine dress.] Looks to me like she
> is just telling her what she should do and how she should dress.
> Don't look very nice. I think that has a lot to do with a per-
> son's life afterwards. If they can get straightened out on their
> personal appearance, they can get straightened out in their
> religion a lot quicker. You take personal appearance; goes with
> their minds. Their mind has to work to go with that. They
> get that straightened out; I think they can go back to religion
> and get that straightened out. I don't go to church now, but I

used to be, and I am still, and always will be, regardless of what it is I ever do. I smoke a cigarette, drink a bottle of beer. I'm not Catholic. I'm Protestant. Church is my first thing. But this [informant hits the picture] comes first, before church. I don't care what anybody says. Clothes, our personal appearance, and getting our minds settled is how we should do. Some people don't believe that, but I do, 'cause you can go into a church and worship, but that ain't all that makes a go of this world. You have got to have something beside that. I don't care how much you worship. People can laugh at you. When you go into a church, they laugh at a girl dressed like this girl is or this woman is. They'll think she is not all there. But, if she gets herself fixed up, and looks nice, and goes to church like this picture here, they'll think she knows what she's talking about. I've seen too much of that. In other words, *clothes, personal appearance, can make one's life.* [Said slowly, deliberately, with much emphasis.] There is something about it that gives you courage. Some people would call it false courage, but I wouldn't. . . . I think anyone has to have a certain amount of clothes to give them courage. It ain't false courage either or false pride. It's just it. . . . Suppose it was just like it was when I went to that banquet tonight. Everybody told me how nice I looked, but I didn't think so. I had to feel right. . . . when I get the dress I feel right in, I feel like a million dollars. It makes an altogether different person out of me. That's an awful thing to say, but that's true for me.

Similar, but less dramatic, remarks abound in our interview materials. All point to the undeniable and intimate linkage of self and appearance. As a matter of fact, the analysis we have made permits a suggested modification of perhaps the best definition of the self in the social-psychological literature. Lindesmith and Strauss

> . . . think of the self as: (1) a set of more or less consistent and stable responses on a conceptual level, which (2) exercise a regulatory function over other responses of the same organism at lower levels (10, p. 416).

Dispensing with the notion of levels of behavior, which seems unnecessarily misleading (surely the self exercises a regulatory function over discourse — a set of conceptual responses!), we suggest the following definition: *the self is any validated program which exercises a regulatory function over other responses of the same organism, including the formulation of other programs.* What this definition does is spell out the regulatory responses — that is, one's announcements, shows, expressions, or proposals — while linking their consistency to the consensual validations of others. Such selves are established in significant appearances which provide the foundations of significant discourse and which, of course, may be played back upon and altered as the discourse transpires.

APPEARANCE AND THE EARLY EMERGENCE OF THE SELF

In explaining the emergence of the self, George H. Mead discusses at length the two stages of "play" and the "game." Prior to entering the stage of play, however, the child must have acquired a rudimentary language at least. We will call this early stage of rudimentary communication "pre-play." For Mead, the emergence of the self in society is inextricably linked to the expansion and consolidation of personal communication as the child participates in and successively generalizes an ever widening universe of discourse — that set of social relations that is mobilized by the symbols the child acquires. We may infer that the type of discourse changes in the different stages of the emergence of the self and shall suggest some possibilities. We shall demonstrate, however, the changing character of appearance in these stages. In particular, we will note how these changing appearances hinder or facilitate the establishment of sexual identity or gender for the child.

PRE-PLAY, INVESTITURE, AND THE
UBIQUITOUS MOTHER

It is very difficult to establish in any verifiable way how the child acquires its earliest significant symbols, whether they be gestures or words, because the investigator cannot enter into the rudimentary "prototaxic" communication of the infant. At best, he can observe, make inferences, and check those inferences out against the inferences of family members.

Appearance and the Self

It seems to be the case, however, that some "initiative" is required from the child in this early learning process. Cooley, for example, observed that parents imitate the noises and sounds of their very young children in greater degree than those children imitate the noises and sounds of parents (3, p. 25). These observations have since received further empirical support (12, p. 41). Apparently this phenomenon of "parental imitation" or, more accurately, parental re-presentation is usually linked with the infant's babbling. Through babbling, the child hits upon a word-like sound (often "ma-ma"). This sound is then re-presented to the child as a word, together with the appropriate behavior that is the meaning of the word. Through repetition, the child takes over the response pattern it calls out in the adult, and the sound consequently becomes a significant symbol within the domestic universe of discourse.[10]

Another hypothesis seeking to explain the infant's earliest entrance into communication has been proposed by I. Latif.[11] Initially, the presumed discomfort of the infant is "communicated" by a gross writhing and wriggling of the whole body, setting up a series of responses in the parental person — feeding, cuddling, diaper-changing, and so on. Over time these parental responses become differentiated out as the gross movement of the child is progressively curtailed. Ultimately, the mere beginning of movement can elicit the appropriate parental response. Significant gestures have been established.

The point in all of this is that the child enters discursive communication by, in a sense, "initiating" activity construed as symbolic by parental persons and established as meaningful by their persistent cooperative response. In contrast, the appearance of the infant is imposed. The diaper folded in front *invests* the child with masculinity; in back, with femininity. Or dressing the child in blue invests the child with masculinity; in pink, with

[10] There is further probative support for this hypothesis in the current research of Omar K. Moore at Yale University, where he is teaching two-and-a-half year old children to read and write. The child is first encouraged to "play" at an IBM typewriter — akin to babbling. An adult responds to the play by re-presenting the letter sound. Eventually the child takes over this response pattern of the adult and "learns" the letters of the keyboard.
[11] Discussed in Lindesmith and Strauss (10, p. 166).

femininity. In this way, the responses of the world toward the child are differentially mobilized. The world handles the pink-clad child and the blue-clad child differently. The pink-clad child is *identified* differently. It is "darling," "beautiful," "sweet," or "graceful"; the blue-clad child is "handsome," "strong," or "agile." At a very early age the investiture of the child provides the materials out of which the reflected sexual identity and its qualifications are formed. And in America the process of investiture is accomplished overwhelmingly by the mother.

One hundred and eighty-five of our informants were asked, "What is the earliest recollection you have of being made to wear particular clothes?" Then we asked, "Who made you wear them?" One hundred and twenty-six provided determinate answers to the question. Of these, 82 per cent named the mother as the "instrument of coercion"; 10 per cent named both parents. For more than 90 per cent of those recalling coercive investitures, the mother was recalled as the agent, usually the sole agent. There were no sex differences in these recollections. She was the sole agent for 83 per cent of the men and for 81 per cent of the women. She acted in conjunction with the father for 13 per cent of the men and for 8 per cent of the women.

It is sociologically significant, of course, that the prime agent of investiture for the men of this Midwestern community was a woman, and no matter how much we might be inclined to disparage Geoffrey Gorer's study of "the American people," these data do suggest that Gorer's "encapsulated mother hypothesis" has some basis in fact (8, pp. 55–68, 124–132).

Because of the ubiquity of the American mother as the prime agent of socialization for the child, it will be recalled, Gorer maintained that the "superego" of the American male was characterized by a significant feminine component manifested in extraordinary anxiety about and fear of homosexuality. We need not accept the entire line of analysis when we recognize, first, that the "significant other" for the male child in our sample has been almost unanimously recalled as the "significant mother," and, second, that the adequate early formulation of a sexual identity may have been impeded among men. Indeed, it may not be a "homosexual anxiety" that typifies American men as much as a generalized "sexual anxiety." If he is represented at all by the men of this Midwestern community, the American male may have found it difficult very early in life to establish who he was in sexual terms. Consequently, an adequate basis in which to "ground" subsequent announcements of maleness may not have been provided. As very young children, most of these men were invested with a program of appearance fashioned exclusively by women. This investiture process persisted beyond infancy, even, in some cases, into relatively late childhood. Their first reflected glimpse of themselves was provided by the eyes of a woman — a woman who, in fact, saw many of those men as girls. Some were dressed as little girls.

A fifty-three year old postal clerk provided a vivid recollection of the early stages in the life cycle as they were represented by dress:

> I can remember back in the South, forty-five years ago, the children — boys — always wore dresses up to the time they were three or four years old. When I was about five, six, seven, or eight, they wore those little Fauntleroy suits. God damn! I hated those. Then knickers came. I wore those until I was about fifteen year old. I was fifteen and a half when I had my first long pants suit.

A sixty-three year old carpenter, born on a Midwestern farm, suggests that the earliest dress of little boys was not restricted to Southern regions:

> Just one thing that always stood out in my mind. I wore dresses until I was six years old, and, as I remember, they were the Mother Hubbard type.

Knee pants, of course, were much more frequently recalled by the men in the sample as early garments in which they were forcibly dressed by the mother, and these were often interpreted as feminine representations. Asked to state his earliest memory of being forced to wear particular clothing, a twenty-seven year old oven-tender replied:

> Knee pants. [Interviewer: Who made you wear them?] Mother. [Interviewer: How did you feel about that?] I just felt like a girl in them. They reminded me so much of a dress.

The revulsion against being a "sissy," recalled by many of the male informants in the sample, was generally remembered in the context of investiture in short pants or "fussy" clothing. Again, the investiture was accomplished by the mother, whose decision they could not appeal.

Investiture takes on even greater significance for the interpretation of the meaning that clothing has for men in our society when we recall our earlier remarks about the establishment of identity. Identity, as it has been apprehended here, is only established in the collective or transactive process of announcement and placement. The knowing of gender is, as we have said, known silently. To appear in the dress of either sex is to announce one's gender, and the apparent announcement is seldom questioned. The gender is confirmed by ratifying placements. Dressed as someone he is not, by a ubiquitous mother, in clothing that is employed arbitrarily by his peers (and himself) to establish who he is, the American male may, indeed, have been disadvantaged very early with respect to the formulation of a sense of sexual identity. Advantages, rather, accrued to the female, who from the earliest age was dressed as she was by a mother from whose perspective she was provided with an adequate conception of herself in sexual terms.[12]

PLAY, COSTUME, AND DRESSING OUT

In his discussions of the development of the self (more exactly, the development of the "me"), George H. Mead does not concern himself so much with the establishment of the self *by* others — the phenomenon of investiture — as with the development of a self-conception *reflected* by the attitudes of others. Such attitudes or roles (Mead uses the terms interchangeably in his discussion of the self) are at first acted out. By acting out the role of the other, the child develops a conception of his own attitude or role as differentiated from and related to the adopted role. The acting out of the other's role is caricatured by the play of the child in which he amuses himself by acting out the role of

[12] There may be a generational problem involved, but we cannot consider that problem in this place. We are speaking here of those who were adults by 1950, and whose childhoods occurred in the 1930's or earlier.

the parents, the schoolteacher, the policeman, the cowboy, the Indian, the storekeeper, the customer, and various other roles that constitute the institutional fabric and legendary *personae* of the larger community or society. A mere consideration of these roles, incidentally, betrays the fact that at least two kinds of socialization go on in the stage of play. First, there is a genuine *anticipatory socialization* in which the child acts out roles that might quite realistically be expected to be adopted or encountered in later life, such as parental roles, common occupations, or customer. Second, there is a process of *fantastic socialization* in which the child acts out roles that can seldom, if ever, be expected to be adopted or encountered in later life — cowboy and Indian, for example. This is a point to which we will return.

Now this phase of play in the development of the self cannot be accomplished without costume. Acting out of role implies that one appear out of role. Play demands that the players leave themselves behind, so to speak. The players may do this symbolically by doffing their ordinary dress and donning extraordinary dress so that the play may proceed. Playing the role of the other requires that the player *dress out* of the role or roles that are acknowledged to be his own. Costume, therefore, is a kind of magical instrument. It includes all apparent misrepresentations of the wearer. As such its significance or meaning (the collective response that is mobilized — the coincidence of the wearer's program with the review of the other) is built upon the mutual trust of the one who appears and his audience. Collusion is required to carry off the misrepresentation: the parent, for example, cannot "really" insist that his child is, in fact, not a cowboy or a spaceman. Play is easily transformed into a vast conspiratorial secret, if it has not, in fact, begun secretly. As Huizinga has expressed it:

> The exceptional and special position of play is most tellingly illustrated by the fact that it loves to surround itself with an air of secrecy. Even in early childhood, the charm of play is enhanced by making a "secret" out of it. This is for *us,* not for the "others." . . . The "differentness" and secrecy of play are most vividly expressed in "dressing up." Here the "extraordinary" nature of play reaches perfection. The disguised or masked individual "plays" another part, another being. He *is*

another being. The terrors of childhood, open-hearted gaiety, mystic fantasy and sacred awe are all inextricably entangled in this strange business of masks and disguises (9, pp. 12–13).

This element of secrecy would seem to imbue the play of children with sentiment — a nexus of value and mood — establishing for the child *involvements* with the identities that are appropriated in play in addition to the sheer objective *commitments* to such identities, emphasized by Mead. Making the point in another way, it may be that the consequence of childhood play, at least for some children, is not merely the formulation of the self as an object — an identity — differentiated from and related to the objects of play, but the establishment of the self as a sentiment — a base of "show" and expression — as Cooley insisted.

All respondents were asked, "When you were a child, did you ever dress up in anyone else's clothes?" Of the 180 replying to the question, 35 per cent disavowed dressing up in other people's clothing when they were children. The disavowal was predominately male. Fifty-nine per cent of the men replying to the question maintained that they had not dressed up in other people's clothing when they were children, and that figure compares to 14 per cent for the women responding to the question. Again, in a sense, the male child seems to have been "disadvantaged" in the phase of play. The clothing of the others in his earliest social world is not made available to him.

Indeed, one of the still striking features of childhood costume is the fact that boys' costumes are sold in considerably greater quantities than are girls' costumes.[13] Commercial costumes are generally more fantastic than the costumes available from the cast-off clothing of family members. The disavowals of the men do not mean, of course, that the men did not dress out when they were children, but that they did not dress out in clothing ordinarily worn by other people. Assuming that the "dressing out" of men, at least in the higher ranges of the status order, was facilitated by commercial costume and that the "dressing out" of women was facilitated by the ordinary dress of others, it may well be that the early conception of self established by

[13] The assertion may be verified by telephoning the toy department in any large store. I have not yet found any exceptions to the rule.

men in the phase of play in this country and among the generations interviewed is, in fact, more fantastic than the early conception of self established by women, who can more often reflect
upon their own appearance in the dress of and from the standpoint of others who are the *real* population of their social world.
But this is a point for which we have no direct evidence.

Of course, the most striking difference between the sexes with
respect to the costume of play is, as we have said, found among
those who dressed up in other people's clothing at all when they
were children. More than half of the men did not, as Table 3
shows, and more than 85 per cent of the women did. Those who
did recall dressing up in other people's clothing when they were
children were asked whose clothing was worn, and the responses
were coded for the person standing in the most "objectively"

TABLE 3

*The Most Intimate Sources of Costume Mentioned by
Midwestern Men and Women in Their Recollections of
Childhood Play*

MOST INTIMATE SOURCES OF CHILDHOOD COSTUME	SEX OF RESPONDENTS				TOTALS	
	MALE		FEMALE			
	Num-ber	Per Cent	Num-ber	Per Cent	Num-ber	Per Cent
None	50	58.8	13	13.7	63	35.0
Parent, same sex	13	15.3	48	50.5	61	33.9
Parent, opposite sex	2	2.4	—	0.0	2	1.1
Sibling, same sex	6	7.1	10	10.5	16	8.9
Sibling, opposite sex	2	2.4	2	2.1	4	2.2
Extended kin	5	5.9	8	8.4	13	7.2
Unrelated adults and peers	7	8.2	14	14.7	21	11.7
TOTALS	85	100.1	95	99.9	180	100.0
$\chi^2 = 43.791*$				.05 > p < .001		

* The last five rows were combined in the computation of the chi-square,
which is for a sixfold table with two degrees of freedom. If the first row
is eliminated from the analysis, and the chi-square computed for the second row and the combined remaining rows by sex, then $\chi^2 = 4.432$, and
.05 > p > .02.

intimate relationship to the informant. Table 3 shows that the parent of the same sex as the informant was the most frequently mentioned source of childhood costume in play.

Yet the male is again "disadvantaged." Even if we exclude from the analysis those informants who could not recall dressing in other's clothing during childhood, men are still significantly underrepresented among those who dressed in the clothing of the father, and women are significantly overrepresented among those who dressed in the clothing of the mother. Childhood play was accomplished by donning the costume of the relevant adult female model — the mother — among the women of the sample, while many men were denied the costume of the relevant adult male model. Among the men who could recall dressing in other's clothing, brothers and extended kin acted as sources of costume in somewhat greater than expected proportions (as did sisters and mothers! — but the numbers there are very small), while, among the women making such recollections, the mother was the sole source of childhood costume noticeably overrepresented. Small wonder that we are tempted to generalize that the men of our sample had a difficult time developing an adequate conception of their sexual identity. The adult models were often not available to them.

It may well be that discourse takes on a characteristic form during the stage of play. For one thing, the speech of the child may be what Piaget has called "egocentric." (15) At least, the child enters the stage of play before his egocentric language dwindles to less than 25 per cent of his discursive communication as recorded by Piaget and his associates. At this point the child is capable of socialized speech. Piaget hypothesizes that this occurs around the age of 7 or 8. On the other hand, the discourse of play is highly suggestive of "parataxic" communication. Sullivan, incidentally, did not restrict the concept to the depiction of psychotic behavior:

> Now let us notice a feature of all interpersonal relations. . . .
> This is the parataxic, as I call it, concomitant in life. By this
> I mean that not only are there quite tangible people involved
> . . . , but also somewhat fantastic constructs of those people are
> involved. . . . These psychotic elaborations of imaginary people
> and imaginary performances are spectacular and seem very

strange. But the fact is that in a great many relationships of the most commonplace kind — with neighbors, enemies, acquaintances, and even such statistically determined people as the collector and the mailman — variants of such distortions often exist. The characteristics of a person that would be agreed to by a large number of competent observers may not appear to you to be the characteristics of the person toward whom you are making adjustive or maladjustive movements. The *real* characteristics of the other fellow at that time may be of negligible importance to the interpersonal situation. This we call *parataxic distortion* (18, pp. 25–26).

Consider a typical instance of play. The father returns home from work, is ambushed at the door, and "shot" by the young cowboy. The transaction has no "meaning" within the *real* father–son relationship — some psychoanalysts to the contrary notwithstanding! Instead, father and son are "of negligible importance to the interpersonal situation." The "fantastic constructs" of cowboy and Indian or "good guy" and "bad guy" are the relevant personifications or identifications with reference to which the discursive meaning is established. Of course, *as father*, the adult enables the young actor to carry off the performance, imbuing the play, as we have said, with a secrecy shared by *father and son*, charging the play with affect or mood.

THE GAME, THE UNIFORM, AND DRESSING IN

While the costume of play may be construed as any apparent misrepresentation of the self, permitting the wearer to become another, the uniform is precisely any apparent representation of the self, at once reminding the wearer and others of an *appropriate* identity, a *real* identity. The team-player is uniformed; the play-actor is costumed. When we asked our informants their earliest recollections of wanting to wear any particular item of clothing, they responded almost unanimously by recalling their earliest self-conscious appropriations of the dress of their peer groups. In a sense, the earliest items of clothing they wanted comprised the *uniforms* of the peer circle.

Among the men who experienced the wish for particular items

of clothing in late childhood, most were concerned with escaping the investitures of the mother. The tenor of their remarks conveyed the undesirability of the clothing they were forced to wear as mother's sons. Thereafter, beginning in early adolescence, their comments focused more and more on the desirability and necessity of conforming to the dress established by their peers or demanded by the dating situation. The women, on the other hand, were concerned from the earliest ages with the desirability of conforming to the dress of peers. Rather than rejecting their early identities as mother's daughters, they began generally to enter the "game of life" at an earlier age than men, and this was represented in part by their self-conscious wishes to don the uniform of their peer circles at earlier ages.

I do not regard these findings as surprising. Indeed, they have been discussed widely by sociologists and social psychologists. It is recognized that women "come of age" more rapidly than men in our society. My only intention here is to frame these data in the perspective of socialization as it concerns the early development of a self-concept in the stages proposed by Mead. Growing up is dressing in. It is signaled by the wish to dress like others who are, in turn, like one's self. The earlier representation of the self is formulated in play which is facilitated by costume. In play one does dress like others, but like others who are, in that case, unlike one's self.

In the stage of the "game," discourse undoubtedly takes on the character of developed speech — what Piaget called "socialized speech" or what Sullivan called "syntaxis." As the game is played, the person becomes an integral part of an on-going universe of discourse in every sense. The early socialization has been effected; a self has emerged. These stages and processes have been summarized in Table 4.

LATER SOCIALIZATIONS

It may well be the uneasiness attending the American's view of play and the game that inclines him to relegate such matters to the social world of children and disinclines him to acknowledge their central importance in adulthood. However, especially when we employ these processes to caricature socialization, we

TABLE 4

Tentative Model for the Investigation of Processes of Discourse and Appearance in the Early Establishment of the Self

STAGES OF EARLY SOCIALIZATION	DISCURSIVE PROCESSES	TYPES OF DISCOURSE	APPARENT PROCESSES	TYPES OF APPEARANCE
Pre-play	1. Parental representation of infant babbling as verbal symbols (Cooley, Markey) 2. Progressive curtailment of whole body movement by parental intervention (Latif)	Conversation of gestures (Mead) Prototaxis (Sullivan) Signal communication, or designation, as in "ma-ma"	Investiture	Representation as infant, young child, and gender
Play	Identification with discrete differentiated others as in role-playing (Mead) 1. Anticipatory socialization 2. Fantastic socialization	Egocentric speech (Piaget) Parataxis (Sullivan)	Dressing out	Misrepresentation of the self Costume
Game	Generalization and consolidation of other roles Taking the role of the "generalized other" or "team"	Socialized speech (Piaget) Syntaxis (Sullivan)	Dressing in	Representation of peer-group affiliation Uniform

should not ignore the fact that they occur throughout life. Life must be viewed as a continuous socialization, a series of careers, in which old identities are sacrificed as new identities are appropriated, in which old relations are left behind as new relations are joined. Each critical turning point of life is marked by a change of dress, and, ordinarily, the new upcoming "game" is rehearsed prior to the entry upon the appropriate field of play.

Such rehearsals may be looked upon as the play of the adult. Momentarily the self is misrepresented as the adult plays at the roles he expects to enact in a near future. Particularly for American men, these rehearsals differ from the play of children by virtue of their rather more "realistic" appropriateness. They are much more frequently genuine *anticipatory socializations*. The child plays many more roles than he will enact in later life, while the roles playfully rehearsed by the adult are generally those he firmly expects to enact later on. But his *fantastic socializations* are also different. More often than is the case for the child, they occur in private. In the bathroom, behind closed doors and before a secret mirror, the man may become for an instant a boxer, an Adonis, an operatic virtuoso. The fantastic play of the child occurs in public, usually in areas set aside by the adult community precisely for such fantastic performances. The fact that the play of the adult is more realistic or appropriate, or, if not, more private, does not gainsay its significance. The rehearsal is often a dress rehearsal, and the more critical the turning point, the more likely the rehearsal is designed as a full dress affair — leaving school and entering the adult world of work, marriage, baptism, and the institutionalized recognition of death.

More realistic than adult play is the adult game. Indeed, we can conceive of life as a series of games — contests and engagements — that mark the progress of careers, culminating in losses and victories for the participants. Participation in the many "games" of life is, again, always represented by appropriate dress which assists the players in their identifications of one another and helps those on the sidelines — the spectators — to know, in fact, what game they are watching. However, these — the play and games of adults — are matters we must leave for a subsequent analysis in another place.

Appearance and the Self

SUMMARY

In this article, we have attempted to show the importance of appearance for any general theory of communication that is developed in the perspective of symbolic interaction. We have attempted to show also that the self is established, maintained, and altered in social transactions as much by the communication of appearances as by discourse. In this regard, by analyzing many statements evoked by clothed appearances, we have suggested a definition of the self that may have greater empirical utility than existing definitions. Finally, we have staked out the significance of appearance in the early socialization processes. In doing these things, our "real" goal will have been realized if we have encouraged one or two of our colleagues or future colleagues to look at the cloth on which, as Carlyle noted long ago, society may, in fact, be founded.

References

1. Becker, Howard. "Empathy, Sympathy, and Scheler," *International Journal of Sociometry*, Vol. 1 (September 1956), pp. 15–22.
2. Burke, Kenneth. *A Grammar of Motives.* Englewood Cliffs, N.J.: Prentice-Hall, Inc., 1945.
3. Cooley, Charles H. *Human Nature and the Social Order.* New York: Charles Scribner's Sons, 1902.
4. Foote, Nelson N. "Identification as a Basis for a Theory of Motivation," *American Sociological Review*, Vol. 16 (February 1951), pp. 14–21.
5. Form, William H., and Gregory P. Stone. *The Social Significance of Clothing in Occupational Life.* East Lansing, Mich.: Michigan State University Agricultural Experiment Station Technical Bulletin 262 (November 1957).
6. Goffman, Erving. "Symbols of Class Status," *British Journal of Sociology*, Vol. 2 (December 1951), pp. 294–304.
7. Goffman, Erving. *The Presentation of Self in Everyday Life.* Edinburgh: University of Edinburgh Social Science Research Centre Monograph, No. 2, 1956.
8. Gorer, Geoffrey. *The American People.* New York: W. W. Norton & Company, Inc., 1948.

9. Huizinga, Jan. *Homo Ludens: A Study of the Play-Element in Culture*. London: Routledge & Kegan Paul, Ltd., 1949.

10. Lindesmith, Alfred R., and Anselm L. Strauss. *Social Psychology*. New York: The Dryden Press, 1956.

11. Lynd, Helen Merrell. *On Shame and the Search for Identity*. New York: Harcourt, Brace and Co., 1958.

12. Markey, John F. *The Symbolic Process and Its Integration in Children*. London: Kegan Paul, Trench, Trübner and Co., Ltd., 1928.

13. Mead, George H. "Philanthropy from the Point of View of Ethics," in Ellsworth Faris, Ferris Laune, and Arthur J. Todd (eds.), *Intelligent Philanthropy*. Chicago: The University of Chicago Press, 1930, pp. 133–148.

14. Mead, George H. *Mind, Self, and Society*, ed. by Charles W. Morris. Chicago: The University of Chicago Press, 1934.

15. Piaget, Jean. *The Language and Thought of the Child*. New York: Meridian Books, 1955.

16. Stone, Gregory P. "Clothing and Social Relations: A Study of Appearance in the Context of Community Life." Unpublished Ph.D. dissertation, Department of Sociology, University of Chicago, 1959.

17. Stryker, Sheldon. "Relationships of Married Offspring and Parent: A Test of Mead's Theory," *American Journal of Sociology*, Vol. 62 (November 1956), pp. 308–319.

18. Sullivan, Harry Stack. *The Psychiatric Interview*. New York: W. W. Norton & Company, Inc., 1954.

19. Veblen, Thorstein. *The Theory of the Leisure Class*. New York: Modern Library, Inc., 1934.

6

What Other?

EVERETT C. HUGHES

BRANDEIS UNIVERSITY

Interaction is the relationship between the self and certain others. The preceding essays have focused primarily upon the self; Professor Hughes now shifts the emphasis to a consideration of others. That the character of the other has a great deal of consequence for the interactive relationship and for the self should be evident at this point. In the course of his discussion, Hughes makes a plea for the revival and systematization of some of the concepts employed earlier in this century by Robert E. Park, Ellsworth Faris, and W. I. Thomas. For the first time in this volume, some of the implications of the symbolic interactionist approach for the practical problems confronting man — in his politics and his work, among other areas — are brought to light.

A playwright, novelist, or politician insensitive to the gestures and attitudes of others, and of some others more than other others, is hard to imagine. Indeed, what more common theme is there in literature — and in politics — than this? But systematic attention to the problem of degrees and directions of sensitivity to others turned up rather late among those who study human society in a would-be scientific way. Adam Smith was a John the Baptist in the field, when, in his *Theory of the Moral Sentiments*, he makes emulation account for so much of human behavior and suggests that the choice of models for emulation is fateful for any man. He is warning, however, not against choosing evil companions, but against taking models — of consumption at least — beyond one's effective reach.

This theme is almost the central one of that whole school of American sociologists and philosophers which included J. Mark Baldwin, Charles Cooley, George Mead, William Thomas, Robert Park, Ellsworth Faris, and their students. Perhaps one should mention Josiah Royce, William James, and John Dewey also, for these men and their variety of pragmatism were part of the same movement, each in his own time and fashion.

I need not remind anyone of the place of the theme of "others" in the work of Mead. Fewer people may be familiar with Thomas' classification of men into Philistine, Bohemian and Creative. One of the themes in that classification is the degree of one's sensitivity to others; another is selection of the others.

When I was a graduate student at the University of Chicago — Thomas' shadow was still there, Mead was still about, and my teachers were Park and Faris — practically all the courses were imbued with the problem of "others." In one of Park's classes a student disputed his statement that most social behavior stems from the fact that we keep an eye on others and their actual and probable reaction to what we do. Park retorted with a question, "Why did you wear pants to school on a pleasant May morning such as this? Think how nice it would feel to have the wind blowing around your legs." Park made a distinction between status and position, sometimes adding adjectives thus: *personal* status and *ecological* or *symbiotic* position. One of his students, Clarence Glick, wrote a dissertation on the Chinese of Hawaii showing that a man might achieve a considerable position in Hawaii while his personal status existed only in relation to the world he had physically left behind. Park spoke of symbiotic or survival relations without social interaction — that is, of relationships without any mutual sensitivity or interpenetration of attitudes and sentiments. This terminology, which was useful, has fallen by the way. Someone may do himself and social science a service by bringing together and systematizing what Park and his students did with the whole problem of sensitivity to others. Nor should Faris be overlooked. It was in a course of his that I first heard developed the notion that the whole fate of sectarian and other Utopian experiments turned upon keeping succeeding generations as impervious to the opinions of the godless as the founding fathers had been. It is an obvious notion, but one which — when enriched by comparative observation — leads to some of the most significant social studies. Indeed, it has lain behind much recent social research, such as that on the spread of influence in politics and consumption, and is the theme of all that is written about reference groups. In what follows, I simply add some thoughts on the subject, thoughts which I believe especially appropriate to our times and to the ever increasing breed of people who think of themselves as professional.

Pearl Buck's father, a *Fighting Angel*, knew no "other" but God; sometimes he seems to have thought that even God needed to be told his own mind. Certainly no human "other" could tell where God meant the Fighting Angel to preach the gospel. He violated all cartel arrangements of the denominational mission boards about what territories each could save souls in. He was so consumed by his calling that he could leave his wife alone to look after her sick children in a plague-ridden Chinese town while he went off to give some more souls their chance to hear the gospel and take it and be saved or leave it and be damned. God — and God as the Fighting Angel alone saw him — was his only colleague and his only kin.

Hitler confounding the smart Berlin lawyers when on trial for his Munich Beer Hall Putsch; Edmond Gosse's father (*Father and Son*) persisting in his belief in the creation of the world in one week in 4,004 B.C. in the face of the contrary evidence of geologists and their other scientific colleagues, including Darwin; many of the saints, the heretics and villains, have fanatically rejected the opinions of all "others" — wife, children, kin, friends, class, brothers in the faith, and professional colleagues.

They appear magnificently (if saints) or diabolically (if heretics or villains) indifferent to the opinions of any and all "others." Rather, they would appear indifferent were it not that their own testimony and the analyses of psychiatrists so often reveal that the certainty of their call covers and compensates for some ravaging uncertainty about who and what they are in the eyes of the very "others" they so fiercely defy. Or perhaps they suffer from some deep rejection by the "others" or from unwillingness to accept their humiliating verdict. The possibilities are many, but it is doubtful whether the apparent freedom of "true believers" from the influence of "others" is ever indifference; it is high-strung, not slack. It is not of the same order as that self-contained indifference to the opinions of "others" which one sometimes observes, perhaps more often in women and cats than in men and dogs; not callousness nor want of perceptiveness, but detachment, amused and even bemused.

If absence of direction toward and by "others" is of various kinds as well as degrees, the same is true of such direction itself. What is more pathetic and demoralizing than the fawning attempt to find favor with others not worthy of the suppliant — as one sees it sometimes in homosexuals of intellectual quality whose perversity consists in part of seeking the favor of lesser men than themselves. One thinks of the self-destruction depicted in André Gide's *La Porte étroite*, and *Si le grain ne meurt*. But in that kind of attention to "other," is it not some self-satisfaction that is sought? The "other" is, after all, but an instrument. How different is the thoughtful, sometimes tortured, attempt to understand and respond to the thoughts, feelings, and judgments of others in order that one may do them justice or that one may pursue more effectively some end to which one is devoted. This, too, requires a measure of detachment — as does all true understanding, even of those closest to us. The degrees and qualities of other-directedness — to use the happy phrase with which David Riesman has enlivened our discourse — are, however, but one aspect of the problem.

Another is that contained in the question "What other?" Indeed, degrees and qualities can scarcely be understood without reference to that question. One of the complications of civilized life is that one is confronted with a variety of "others," some of whose directions are not compatible with those of some others. None is completely compatible with all others. Once that oneness of the "others," attributed — correctly or not — to primitive societies, is gone, there is no finding it again except by conversion to a religious, political, artistic, or intellectual sect, disappearance into a monastery, or flight to some totalitarian state where thought and action are alike controlled by some central authority. In the latter case, some people seem always to seek underground some company of kindred souls, some "other" to give them courage in their struggle to remain spiritually independent of the massive *Big Brother* "other." One need not go to a totalitarian state to find this search for a supporting semi-secret "other"; it may be found wherever and whenever the pressure for conformity becomes oppressive — in a college town, in a closed profession, in a period of McCarthyism or even of Ike-ism — because weakness and blundering in high places are thought to require a more desperate and unquestioning support than strength combined with intelligence (for the weak and blundering man has little to fall back upon except the claim to loyal support that is, he believes, due him).

Certainly we are in a time when part of the very struggle to be a man is the search for one's "others." It takes intelligence to find the "others" that will bring out the best in one's self, and it takes courage to follow — no, not follow, but to walk abreast with that collective "other," ready made or created by mutual effort — when one has found it. Any one of us has certain ready-made "others" by virtue of his birth and the accidents of his schooling and career. Some of them are there from infancy, others gather about him later. Some creep upon him; others he chooses of his own will and seeks that admission to them which will reveal to him the direction in which he must travel if he is to be accepted as one of them.

Some people find, in this welter of "others," some complex balance or compromise among several. Others let one or another tyrannize them. The nature of the combinations and balances is part of the organization of society itself. Judging the relative influence of various "others" upon individuals is indeed one of the problems with which social surveys are most concerned.

Some people manage to remain responsive to only one "other" even in the midst of a complex society. This was the essence of the system of honor among Prussian army officers. Only another of his class could really offend, or give satisfaction for an offense. To be sensitive to the opinions of civilians or of the lower ranks was to be less than an officer and a gentleman. We are no longer a society of closed estates, some of them honorable in that strict sense. We disapprove alike of the dueling sword, used to keep one's face before his honorable peers, and of the horsewhip, used to keep lesser breeds respectful. But we have some very demanding "others" and a certain tendency to become so attached and sensitive to one of them that we lose other attachments and sensitivities.

One order of "others" in which this tendency is strong is the professions, those old and established as well as those new and on the make. Professionalism, in its valued sense, indicates a strong solidarity of those in an occupation combined with a high sense of duty to their clients and a well-developed code of conduct. In its pejorative sense, it refers to a sort of exclusiveness, a group-centrism that makes individual members impervious to the opinions, indeed, to the very terms of thought and feeling, of those outside their professional circle. The professions are not only "functional" in the peculiar sense in which that term has come to be used, they are hyper-functional to a pathological degree in some cases. For professionalism, however worthy the motives for pursuing it, has often led to a hasty crystallizing of the techniques, the apologia, and hence the substance of the training and qualifications required of those who would enter the occupation. This has been clearly true of social work, where the state of the art at a given period was hardened into a curriculum from which the schools of social work are recovering only now. It is also true of education, where certainly there was and is need for tremendous improvement of professional standards and the preparation for practice. The whole business has bogged down in a professionalism that is dogmatic, sometimes bigoted, and generally touchy and impatient of criticism from other "others" — parents, the public, or educated people not of the "educationist" ranks.

A new profession, one on the make, often takes as the common "other" toward which its members direct their conduct some other profession of longer history and firmer place. For social work, the outside looked-up-to "other" has been the psychiatric profession; for nurses, their troublesome superiors, the physicians; for psychologists, both physicians and biological scientists. For sociologists, the emulated outside groups are no doubt several. But the role of older brother is assumed by psychology and sociologists are inclined to allow it. Thus there is a sort of chain reaction: the psychologist must be either a therapist, following the model of the physician, or a scientist, following the model of physiologists or physicists. The sociologists must be scientists, following the psychologists both from wanting to emulate them and from fearing that they may steal their prerogatives. In our world of upwardly mobile occupations, as well as mobile individuals, there thus occurs a sort of collective other-directedness. When an occupational group is actively climbing, and has taken a model, it is likely to be especially severe in its demand for conformity to that model by those in its own ranks — just as a mobile individual puts pressure on his family not to disgrace him before sought-after company. It is to be suspected that some of the rather ritualistic following by sociologists of what are thought to be the only sound techniques of research is due to just such a desire to impress their elder scientific brethren, those who have won recognition as scientists. Somewhere in this complex of things one finds what one might call "bureaucratic other-directedness," an overweening following of the rituals which one believes will get him, by a sort of right, promotion to the next rank in the system in which he works and lives.

Every profession does its work in some social matrix in interaction with whatever kinds of people it defines as its clients, with colleagues in the profession itself and with people in related occupations, with people related to their clients in various ways and eventually with elements of the public. The very word "profession" implies a certain social and moral solidarity, a strong dependence of one colleague upon the opinions and judgments of others. In fact, one depends more upon the opinions of some colleagues than of others; and some professions are more guided by group opinion than are others. In our society it is inevitable that the professions should be among the more significant "others" toward which and by which conduct is directed, for we have more professions than ever and a larger proportion of the working force is in them. That makes it the more important that the relations between profession-directedness and sensitivity to the others involved in the drama of work should be kept flexible, complex, and in balance. A man who stakes all upon his reputation with his clients — patients, students, "cases" — is in great danger of being considered a quack. In fact, the essence of being a quack lies not in the quality of one's work, but in the "other" to which he directs his behavior. A professional who is completely client-directed, without regard to his professional colleagues' judgments, is likely to be declared a quack. He may, in fact, be either a charlatan or a brilliant innovator. The optimum balance between sensitivity to one's professional "other" and one's responsiveness to the people outside — fellow workers of other specialties or professions, one's own and other people's clients, the various parts of the public — will vary from one profession to another and from one situation to another. But in all cases there is some distribution of "directedness" among the various "others" who are involved in one's work. A man's great problem is to see to it that the balance is of his own making and that he finds it intelligently and with perception of the several "others."

One of the great glories of an urban civilization is the complex man, finely tuned to many of the "others" in his life-orbit, consciously selecting the impulses to which he will respond and not being deterred from responding because one of his "others" — and the offender is often the colleague "other" — claims his whole allegiance and demands that he accept and defend its current doctrines and techniques *in toto*. I take it that it is such a man whom William I. Thomas would have called "creative" and David Riesman would call "autonomous." He would be not an automaton, a guided missile, not a Fighting Angel, not a pachyderm impervious to pricks, not a reed blown about by the wind, but a man of many sensitivities who would attain and maintain, by his intelligent and courageous choice of the messages to which he would respond, by the choice of his "others," freedom of a high but tough and resilient quality.

In the academic and professional worlds, such a freedom will show itself in the choice of close colleagues, regardless of department or specialty. The more such freedom is stoutly and sensitively exercised, the more strength we will have to fight off attacks on academic and professional freedom. We will have more freedom to lose, but better weapons with which to defend it. We will also make much greater progress in our common enterprise of understanding man and society.

7

Reference Groups and Social Control

 TAMOTSU SHIBUTANI

UNIVERSITY OF CALIFORNIA, SANTA BARBARA

*The concept of "reference groups" has always been central in
interactionist theory, although it did not gain currency among
social psychologists until Herbert Hyman used the term in a
study published in 1942. It refers to the sources of values selected
by an individual for the guidance of his behavior, especially in
cases when a choice has to be made. Reference groups may be
groups of which the individual is a member, but sometimes they
may not. In all cases they provide direction for the behavior of
the individual concerned, and so constitute important sources of
social control. Dr. Shibutani pursues further the question
broached in the preceding chapter — "What Other?" While continuing to employ the more generally accepted term "reference
group," Shibutani's discussion indicates the many reasons why
the term is not entirely satisfactory (and why Rose, in his introductory chapter to this volume, prefers to substitute the term
"reference relationship"). In relating reference groups to social
control, the author implicitly suggests a seminal approach to the
study of social values. He points out the manner in which the
reference-group concept has been employed to refer to different*

Reference Groups and Social Control

kinds of social processes, and he defines it in such a way as to be consistent with the general orientation of this volume.

Martyrs of one sort or other are apparently found in all societies, and they usually become objects of curiosity, if not of vituperation.* Less unusual men also attract attention — the dedicated scientist who carelessly uses his pay check as a bookmark, the mountaineer who risks his life scaling dangerous peaks, or the boy in the tenement who practices his violin doggedly amid the taunts of his neighbors. Such conduct has been explained in several different ways, but an especially plausible hypothesis is suggested by Thoreau's famous lines: "If a man does not keep pace with his companions, perhaps it is because he hears a different drummer." Most individualists tend to be somewhat estranged from those immediately around them, but rarely do they live in complete isolation.

Such extreme cases of non-conformity provide a point of departure for the study of more frequently found forms of diversity. Deliberately, intuitively, or unconsciously each person performs for some kind of audience; in the drama of life, as in the theater, conduct is oriented toward certain people whose judgment is deemed important. In a complex society like ours, in which there are so many audiences, it often becomes necessary to identify the one for which an individual is performing in order to make his behavior comprehensible. The current popularity of the concept of "reference group" rests in part upon its utility in explaining behavior that is oriented toward audiences that are not obviously represented on the scene.

Sociologists have long been concerned with audiences, for they usually explain conduct in terms of social control. "Social control" refers not so much to deliberate influence or to coercion but to the fact that each person generally takes into account the expectations that he imputes to other people. The kinds of observations that have been accounted for in terms of what has been called the "normative function" of reference groups, one of the two "functions" they are alleged to have˙ (21, 28), can be

---

* This essay is a thoroughly revised version of "Reference Groups as Perspectives," *American Journal of Sociology*, Vol. 60 (1955), pp. 562–569. Copyright 1955 by The University of Chicago.

explained through the application of a long-familiar theory of social control to the conditions prevailing in modern mass societies. What is implied in the writings of Cooley, Dewey, Mead, Park, and Sapir must be stated more explicitly, however, since most of these men did not address themselves specifically to the study of mass societies. This task can be facilitated by making a distinction between (*a*) the *perspective* that is imputed to an audience and (*b*) the *people* who make up an audience.

PERSPECTIVES AND VOLUNTARY CONDUCT

Thomas (42, pp. 154–155) pointed out many years ago that what a person does rests largely upon his definition of the situation. It may be added that the manner in which he consistently defines a succession of situations depends upon his perspective. A perspective is an organized view of one's world, what is taken for granted about the attributes of objects, of events, and of human nature. The environment in which men live is an order of things remembered and expected as well as of things actually perceived. It includes assumptions of what is plausible and what is possible. Without such an order life would be chaotic; even doubts become possible only within an unquestioned frame of reference. Having such perspectives enables men to conceive of their ever changing world as being relatively stable, orderly, and predictable. As Riezler (33, pp. 62–72) puts it, one's perspective is an outline scheme which, running ahead of experience, defines and guides it. One of the most important things one can know about a person is what he takes for granted (30).

Mutual understanding and concerted action become possible only when presuppositions are held in common, but perspectives vary in the extent to which they are shared with other people. In many cases of schizophrenia the victim apparently defines situations from a standpoint that is incomprehensible to anyone else. He performs for some kind of audience, but it is one that he has presumably constructed in his imagination. Those suffering from paranoid disorders are not quite so isolated, but they live in pseudo-communities made up of personifications to whom convenient traits have been imputed (5, pp. 372–447). Less limited perspectives are found among those who are bound closely to one another. Cliques and families that remain aloof may develop distinctive orientations, and "provincialism" refers to an outlook that characterizes a small community.

The concept of "culture" designates the perspective that is shared by the people in a particular group. As it is used by Redfield (32, pp. 132–133), it refers to those "conventional understandings, manifest in act and artifact, that characterize societies." Since the understandings which make up such perspectives constitute the premises of action, those with the same cultural background engage in similar patterns of activity.

People with dissimilar perspectives define identical situations differently, responding selectively to diverse aspects of their environment. A prostitute and a social worker walking through a slum area notice different things. There is increasing experimental evidence that what is perceived depends largely upon what is anticipated. Especially revealing is the ingenious experiment by Bagby (1) comparing Mexican and American subjects. He set up ten pairs of slides to be viewed through a stereoscope. On one side he mounted pictures of objects familiar to most Mexicans — such as a matador, a dark haired girl, a peon. On the other he mounted a similar picture of objects familiar to most Americans — such as a baseball player, a blonde girl, a farmer. The corresponding photographs resembled one another in contour, texture, and the distribution of light and shadows. Although there were a few exceptions, in general the Americans saw only what was already familiar to them, and the Mexicans likewise saw only the scenes placed in their own culture. Thus, the selection and interpretation of sensory cues rests to a surprising extent upon expectations formed while participating in groups. Any change of perspectives — from becoming acquainted with a new culture or from some unusual experience, such as learning that one will die in a few months — leads one to notice things he had previously overlooked and to see the same familiar world in a different light.

Mead (27, pp. 152–164) contended that independently motivated men are able to engage in concerted action because each participant takes the role of the "generalized other." Each person perceives, forms judgments, and controls himself from the standpoint shared by the participants in a transaction. Since he forms a self-image from the same perspective as the others, he can anticipate their reactions to what he would like to do, inhibit inexpedient impulses, and thus guide his conduct along acceptable lines. Each socialized person, then, is a society in miniature. Once he has incorporated the culture of his group, it becomes his perspective, and he can bring this frame of reference to bear upon all new situations that he encounters. The fact that most people are able to control themselves in this manner is what makes society possible. In this connection it should be emphasized that when Mead spoke of the "generalized other," he was not referring to people but to a shared perspective.

Much of what a man does or refuses to do depends upon the kind of human being he regards himself to be. Studies of class consciousness are revealing. In his study of a labor union Goldstein (15) found that most of the engineers in the membership were opposed to strikes, the use of grievance procedures, and political action. These men formed their self-images from a middle-class perspective and defined union activities differently from the industrial workers. In his study of voting patterns in the 1952 presidential election, Eulau (12) found that the manner in which a man votes depends more upon the class with which he identifies himself than the class in which an observer might place him in terms of objective criteria.

The concept of "reference group" has been used in several ways, but its utility can be maximized when it signifies *that group whose presumed perspective is used by an actor as the frame of reference in the organization of his perceptual field.* Thus defined, it becomes apparent that all kinds of units may serve as reference groups. Attention should not be limited to organized groups that are readily identifiable. The audience for whom one performs may consist of a single person, a small handful of people with whom he is in sustained contact, a voluntary association, or some broad category of people — a social class, a profession, an ethnic group, or some community. A reference group is an audience, consisting of real or imaginary personifications, to whom certain values are imputed. It is an audience before whom a person tries to maintain or enhance his standing.

The contention that men think, feel, and see things from a collective standpoint is an old one which has been emphasized repeatedly by students of anthropology and of the sociology of knowledge. Why, then, the sudden concern with reference groups during the past few decades? Interest apparently arises from the peculiar characteristics of mass societies, societies that are held together through the media of mass communication (45, pp. 368–391). Although a number of scholars have contended that mass societies are lacking in organization, having many of the characteristics of crowds, closer examination reveals that they are actually held together by an infinite number of personal attachments and by moral obligations in specific contexts (37). Mass societies are pluralistic; even under totalitarian regimes, with their centralization of political power, social control is decentralized. Special problems arise from the fact that in such complex societies men sometimes utilize the norms of groups in which they are not ostensibly participating at the moment, sometimes of groups in which they are not recognized as members, and sometimes of groups that do not exist at all.

There is an extensive literature in which the term "reference group" designates a group with which a person compares his fate. This is another usage, and little can be gained from quarreling over the "correct" meaning of words. It is important to recognize, however, that a group which serves as a point of comparison is quite different from a group whose culture constitutes one's point of view. Any convenient group with which a person is familiar may be used in making comparisons; he can also compare himself with another individual or with an impersonal standard of measurement, such as a yardstick. As Stern and Keller (40) declare, however, the fact that people are aware of differences between groups does not lead them to adopt the standpoint of outsiders, even when the others are believed to be better off. Indeed, as Bott (2, pp. 159–216) shows in her study of English families, one need not even know very much about such groups, for any stereotyped conception suffices. Some writers (21; 28, pp. 283–284) have gone further and have contended that reference groups have a "comparison function" as well as a "normative function." To speak of two parallel "functions" of the same concept implies that the phenomenon is similar in all respects other than its "function." Although there are some superficial similarities, this is not the case. Are such groups formed under the same conditions? Do people acquire their norms in the same manner? Are they transformed under the same circumstances? The same label is unfortunately being used to refer to two different processes, and the attempt to combine them only adds to the already existing confusion. Turner (43) lists several ways in which groups may become involved in the formation of judgments, and it goes without saying that each should be labeled with a different symbol.

Cultural Pluralism in Mass Societies

Dewey (8, pp. 166–207), Park (30, pp. 36–52), and Sapir (35, pp. 104–109) emphasized that society exists in and through communication. Shared perspectives are the products of common communication channels. Despite the frequent recitation of this proposition, its full implications, especially for the analysis of mass societies, have not been fully appreciated. Variations in outlook arise through differential contact and association; the maintenance of social distance — through segregation, conflict, or simply reading different literature — leads to the formation of distinctive cultures. Thus, people in different social classes develop dissimilar modes of life not because of anything inherent in economic position but because similarity of occupations and the limitations set by income level dispose them to certain restricted communication channels. Some social scientists are out of touch with many segments of American life because they eschew many mass media programs, especially television, or expose themselves only condescendingly. Even the outlook that the *avant garde* thinks of as "cosmopolitan" is culture-bound, for it also is a product of participation in restricted communication channels — books, magazines, lectures, exhibits, and taverns which are off limits for most people in the middle classes.

In their study of relatively isolated societies, anthropologists are able to speak meaningfully of "culture areas" in geographical terms; in such communities each culture has a territorial base, for only those who live together can interact. But as Redfield (32) showed in his comparative study of four communities in Yucatan, culture areas are coterminous with communication channels. In modern industrial societies, because of the development of rapid transportation and the media of mass communication, people who are geographically dispersed can communicate quite effectively. Communication channels are now readily accessible, even to those who are illiterate. Since these networks no longer coincide with territorial boundaries, culture areas overlap and have lost their ecological foundations. Next-door neighbors may be complete strangers. Even in common parlance there is an intuitive recognition of this diversity of perspectives, and we speak meaningfully of people living in different social worlds — the world of high finance, the academic world, the world of children, or the world of the theater.

Each communication channel gives rise to a distinctive outlook. Since these channels differ in stability, range, and effectiveness, social worlds also vary along several dimensions. Worlds differ considerably in composition, size, and the territorial distribution of their participants. Some, like local cults, are small and concentrated; others, like the intellectual world, are vast and the participants are dispersed. Some, like many ethnic minorities, have a relatively homogeneous population; others, like most political parties, are utterly mixed. Worlds differ in the extent and clarity of their boundaries; each is confined by some kind of horizon, but this may be wide or narrow, clear or vague. Although some men regard their own perspective as absolute, the fact that social worlds are not coterminous with the universe of men is usually recognized. Those in the underworld know that outsiders do not share their values. Worlds also differ in exclusiveness and in the extent to which they demand the loyalty of their participants. Some are open only to those who dedicate themselves completely; one cannot be a part-time nun. But there are others in which most of the participants are only occasional spectators.

Social worlds differ considerably in their solidarity and in the sense of identification felt by their participants. Probably the strongest sense of solidarity is to be found in the various subcommunities — the underworld, ethnic minorities, the social elite, or isolated religious cults. Such communities are frequently segregated, and this segregation multiplies intimate contacts within and reinforces barriers against the outside. Another common type of world consists of the networks of interrelated voluntary associations — the world of medicine, the world of organized labor, the world of the steel industry, or the world of opera. These are held together not only by various organized groups within each locality but also by periodicals such as *Variety*, the *CIO News,* and specialized journals. Churches and fraternal organizations often have their own publications. Among the better organized of these worlds are the professions, which sometimes have a code of ethics more stringent than what is required of everyone by law. Finally, there are the loosely connected universes of special interest — the world of sports, the world of the stamp collector, or the world of women's fashions. Since the participants are drawn together only periodically by the limited interest they have in common, there are varying degrees of involvement, ranging from the fanatically dedicated to the casually interested. Since participation is usually quite extensive, the latest developments in sports, fashions, and various entertainment fields are carried in the media of mass communication, readily available for anyone who cares. Although these arenas are only loosely organized, the participants nonetheless develop similar standards of conduct, especially if their interests are strong and sustained. Fashion-conscious women can identify one another easily in their reciprocal appraisals, and enthusiastic fishermen encourage practices that give their prey a fighting chance to get away.

The various cultures found in mass societies are in many respects like those in stable, isolated communities. In each social world there develops a universe of discourse. Pertinent experiences are categorized in particular ways, and a special set of symbols is used to refer to them. The argot of soldiers, prostitutes, and drug addicts, as well as the dialects of ethnic minorities, differ from the standard tongue of the larger community, and these linguistic differences further accentuate social distance from outsiders. Each social world is a universe of regularized mutual response, an arena in which there is some kind of organization that facilitates anticipating the behavior of others. *Each social world, then, is a culture area, the boundaries of which are set neither by territory nor formal group membership, but by the limits of effective communication.*

A social world is an orderly arena which serves as a stage on which each participant can carve out a career. There are special norms of conduct, a set of values, a prestige ladder, and a common outlook toward life — a *Weltanschauung*. In the case of elite groups there may even develop a code of honor, holding only for those who belong; others are dismissed as somewhat less than human, those from whom bad manners may be expected. Career lines are organized, and there is usually an orderly sequence of steps through which one moves from apprenticeship to mastery. It is in terms of such ladders that aspirations are shaped, and a person who is on his way measures his progress by comparing himself with his predecessors, not with outsiders (17, pp. 56–67). Indeed, prestige ladders in the various worlds are so different that a man who reaches the pinnacle of success in one may be completely unknown elsewhere. In each world there evolves a different historical orientation, selectively emphasizing past events of special interest. Common memories are built up and reinforced within the limited communication network. In the lore of mountain climbers throughout the world, for example, there are tales of the extraordinary courage and skills of certain mountaineers, of daring rescues, and of great achievements against incredible odds. The grim determination of those assaulting the various peaks in the Himalayas can be understood only within such a context.

Many misunderstandings arise in our society from the fact that people who are living in the same community and even cooperating in a number of transactions are actually oriented toward different audiences. For example, intramural quarrels are common on college faculties. In his study of a liberal arts college Gouldner (16) was able to isolate several different types of career lines. There were some professors who had a strong sense of loyalty to the college community and took active part in various campus activities. There were others who pursued administrative careers, conducting themselves in ways most likely to bring promotions within the bureaucratic hierarchy. Still others were committed to their respective fields of specialization. Like technical experts in industrial firms they were sometimes suspected of not being "company men," for they complained continually about the excessive teaching load and the lack of opportunities for research. Although all professors are ostensibly committed to similar values, it is apparent that these men had different aspirations, sought status in different social worlds, and did not really understand one another. In pluralistic societies, then, it is not unusual for men to pursue goals that are incomprehensible to their neighbors.

Since perspectives are the products of communication, the groups to which they are imputed need not actually exist in real life. While most men are highly responsive to the views imputed to people with whom they are in direct association, reference groups may be imaginary — as in the case of artists who claim to be "ahead of their time," scientists who work for "humanity," or philanthropists who give for "posterity." Such individuals are unconcerned with immediate rewards and sometimes undergo incredible sacrifices in anticipation of being appreciated by some future audience that would presumably be more sensible than the people now living. They form self-images from a postulated standpoint imputed to people who may never come into existence. There are others who live in the distant past, idealizing some period in history and longing for the "good old days." They criticize current events from a standpoint imputed to people long since dead — like the Southerner pining for the days of the Confederacy. As in the case of the Medievalist, such people often acquire the outlook of their treasured era solely through books. The discontented differ from the psychotic in that their imaginary perspective is generally more limited in scope and is used only when engaging in a few specialized activities. There is also a more explicit awareness of the differences between a private world and the "reality" that enjoys consensus.

CONFORMITY AND SIGNIFICANT OTHERS

Even casual observation reveals the amazing variety of standards in terms of which Americans live. Because of the ease with which anyone can participate in several communication channels, each person may develop a number of perspectives. Each time he enters a new channel — subscribes to a new periodical, joins a new circle of friends, or purchases a television set for the first time — he is introduced into a somewhat different social world. For any individual there are as many reference groups as there are communication networks in which he becomes regularly involved. Of course, people differ in the range of their participation. Each person lives in an environment of which he is the center, and the dimensions of his effective surroundings are defined by the direction and distance from which news comes to him. Furthermore, the particular combination of social worlds differs from person to person. Simmel (39, pp. 127–195) noted that each individual stands at that point at which a unique combination of his social circles intersects. This geometric analogy is a happy one, for it enables us to conceive of the numerous possibilities of combinations and the various degrees of participation in each circle.

Where each person acquires a number of perspectives, incongruent and conflicting definitions are bound to arise. This need not lead to difficulties, however, and usually passes unnoticed. Most reference groups of a given person are mutually sustaining. A soldier who volunteers for hazardous duty may provoke anxiety in his family but is not acting contrary to its values; both his family and his comrades admire courage and disdain cowardice. Furthermore, even if one's behavior is inconsistent, as in the case of the proverbial terror of the office who is meek before his wife, it is not noticed if the transactions occur in dissociated contexts. Those who live in a pluralistic society tend to lead compartmentalized lives, shifting from one perspective to another as they participate in a succession of transactions that are not necessarily related. In each social world they play somewhat different roles, and they manifest a different facet of their personality. Furthermore, Bott (2, pp. 192–216) found that people confronted by conflicting norms tend to construct their own version of appropriate modes of conduct and then attribute this model to some group. This is consistent with the findings of Burchard (3) and of Edwards (10) that people tend to rationalize away observations that are inconsistent with their basic beliefs.

People become acutely aware of differences in outlook only when they are caught in situations in which conflicting demands are made upon them, all of which cannot possibly be satisfied. In his study of disasters Killian (22) reports that policemen, firemen, and public utilities workers were suddenly confronted with unexpected dilemmas. They were concerned with the safety of their own families, but their failure to stay on their jobs would result in costly delays in traffic control, fire-fighting, and rescue and relief work. Campbell and Pettigrew (6) describe the unenviable position of the Protestant clergymen in Little Rock, Arkansas, during the school integration crisis of 1957. Although most of them personally favored integration, they could not speak frankly without losing at least part of their congregation. Since each minister is judged in terms of how his church prospers, none could succeed within his profession without the support of his congregation. But for most people such conflicts are ephemeral. From time to time otherwise unnoticed contradictions are brought into the open, and painful choices are forced. But there are some people who find themselves chronically beset by such conflicts — people who occupy marginal status. The child of an immigrant (30, pp. 345–392), the foreman in a factory (47), the well-educated woman (23) — all live in the interstices of organized structures. In spite of the compartmentalization of their lives, personal maladjustments are not infrequent among marginal men, for they must violate the norms of one reference group no matter what they do (17, 102–115).

Dilemmas and contradictions of status force one to choose between reference groups. Such conflicts are essentially alternative ways of defining the same situation, alternatives arising from each of the two or more perspectives that might be brought to bear upon it. In the words of James (18, p. 295), "As a man I pity you, but as an official I must show you no mercy; as a politician I regard him as an ally, but as a moralist I loathe him." In playing roles in different social worlds, incongruent expectations are imputed to different audiences, and sometimes these differences cannot be compromised. The problem becomes that of selecting the perspective to be used in defining the situation.

On what basis is the choice made under such circumstances? One widely entertained hypothesis comes from the experimental study of small groups: a person tends to comply with the norms of the group that he finds more attractive. Festinger and his associates (13) report that subjects in more attractive groups tend to change their views upon discovering that other members disagree with them, even before anyone attempts to influence them. Along the same lines Merton (28, pp. 288–292) suggests that people who are eligible for membership in a group to which they aspire are more likely to respond to its demands. Dittes (9) also found that the extent to which an individual is influenced by a group depends upon its attractiveness; he discovered too, however, that those who have a low level of self-esteem are much more sensitive to group opinion. Some individuals apparently need the support of groups with prestige more desperately than others.

Another promising hypothesis, not necessarily inconsistent with the first, is derived from psychoanalysis (14) and from the work of Cooley (7, pp. 81–135) and Mead (27, pp. 144–164): *the choice of definitions depends upon one's sentiments toward the significant others who serve as representatives of reference groups.* "Significant others," for Sullivan (41, 18–22), are those individuals directly responsible for the socialization of an individual. Conventional meanings of all kinds are learned in social contexts; our orientations toward various objects are formed while interacting with specific people, and these intimate interchanges continue as the welding and assimilating matrix through which we are able to understand our universe. The extent to which any particular perspective is used rests upon the sentiments that develop toward such individuals. Those who feel that they had been treated with affection and consideration usually regard their personal obligations as binding under all circumstances and find it difficult not to comply. When the sentiments are negative, however, a person may go out of his way to spite his mentors by rejecting their expectations. A person who is somewhat isolated from real people may develop a sense of loyalty to an imaginary personification to whom all kinds of beliefs are imputed, or he may dedicate himself to a set of abstract principles learned from a book whose author he greatly admires.

Although the evidence is far from conclusive, it appears that many transformations of perspective are accompanied by a displacement of significant others. Marked changes of outlook occur in political and religious conversions. Autobiographies of converts as well as clinical studies reveal a typical natural history. There is usually a long period of frustration, marked by disturbances in interpersonal relations; the person often rejects his family and forsakes his friends as he becomes increasingly alienated from himself. Then the "lost soul" is introduced to a new communication channel, often by accident, and becomes aware of another way of looking at life. Experiences are reclassified, and the convert forms a new conception of himself (19, pp. 77–253). These new meanings are then reinforced by another set of significant others, and their sympathetic support is apparently a crucial part of all conversions. A similar pattern is found in the spectacular changes that take place in Alcoholics Anonymous. In this group the recruits are encouraged to assist more recent converts, thereby further enabling them to see themselves as being worthy of respect (34). More drastic changes in outlook are found in the development of psychosis and in the recovery from this condition. Again, early phases of the onset of psychosis are characterized by estrangement from significant others, and recovery involves the establishment of intimate ties, often with a psychiatrist (36). This led Burke (4, pp. 125–147) to refer to psychoanalytic therapy as a "secular conversion," contending that a patient learns a new vocabulary of motives and is thereby able to re-evaluate himself from another standpoint. Even less drastic transformations have been found by Newcomb (29) and by Pearlin (31) to be related to changes in associates.

Studies of social solidarity also reveal that conformity to group norms is related to favorable interpersonal relations. Since each person is capable of independent action, the persistence of any group depends upon the continued conformity of the participants to its norms. When enough people defect, the collective pattern collapses. Ethnic minorities break into factions and eventually disappear as increasing numbers become assimilated. Those who are among the first to become assimilated are generally the people who are alienated from others in the minority group (44, pp. 105–106). Studies of military morale also show that the men who are closely attached to their comrades risk death rather than disappoint them. But a demoralized unit is characterized by a high degree of individualism. The men distrust one another and refuse to take unnecessary chances. Each looks after his personal interests, and the group disintegrates with the first serious adversity (26, 38).

Cultures are not static entities. Norms are creatively reaffirmed from day to day in the social interaction of the participants (35, pp. 104–106). Those partaking in transactions approach one another with given expectations, and the actual occurrence of what is anticipated confirms and reinforces their orientations. In this way people who share a common culture are continually supporting one another's perspectives, each by responding to the others in expected ways. But in a mass society the responses of other people often vary, and the problem is that of ascertaining *whose* responses are ·needed in order to sustain a given point of view. Those in a social elite are not likely to become concerned if "peasants" do not understand what they are doing. People are selectively responsive only to the reactions of those who are included in their reference group, for it is primarily in their eyes that they attempt to maintain their standing. Each person seeks recognition primarily in *his* world.

SUMMARY AND CONCLUSION

To understand what a man does we must have some appreciation of his definition of the situation, and this requires knowing something of what he takes for granted. This is especially true in a pluralistic society, where different people approach the same situation from diverse standpoints and where the same individual utilizes dissimilar perspectives in different transactions. Being able to identify the audience for whom a man is performing, therefore, becomes a task of decisive importance. Usually the audience consists of the other people who are involved in the transaction, but this is not always the case. Audiences that are not immediately represented on the scene also exercise social control, and it is for this reason that the concept of "reference group" assumes such importance in the study of mass societies.

In what directions should further inquiries be made? Some sociologists have urged a more detailed study of the structure of organized groups, and no one can argue with the desirability of such knowledge. However, the theory under consideration directs our attention elsewhere. One task is the development of more effective techniques for the empirical study of perspectives, perhaps on the basis of such provocative discussions as those of

Burke (4), Landgrebe (24), and Mannheim (25). Second, we must learn more about the formation, maintenance, and dissolution of communication channels. Communication channels are not merely avenues of transmission; they consist of common understandings concerning who is to address whom on what topics with what degree of confidence. Studies such as those by Katz and Lazarsfeld (20) and Emery and Oeser (11) provide thoughtful beginnings, but much remains to be done. Third, one of the most difficult areas of inquiry is the study of the relationship between perception and interpersonal relations. Recent research reveals that what is perceived is related to sentiments. Wittreich (46) found in his study of the "Honi phenomenon" that people who are respected and are the object of affection do not appear distorted even when they are placed in a special experimental room in which everyone else appears grotesquely out of proportion. The relationship between people and perspectives is not yet clearly understood, but there is sufficient evidence to conclude that some kind of connection exists. Investigations along these lines will undoubtedly give us a better comprehension of social control in mass societies.

References

1. Bagby, James W. "A Cross-Cultural Study of Perceptual Predominance in Binocular Rivalry," *Journal of Abnormal and Social Psychology*, Vol. 54 (1957), pp. 331–334.

2. Bott, Elizabeth. *Family and Social Network*. London: Tavistock Publications, 1957.

3. Burchard, Waldo. "Role Conflicts of Military Chaplains," *American Sociological Review*, Vol. 19 (1954), pp. 528–535.

4. Burke, Kenneth. *Permanence and Change*. Los Altos, Calif.: Hermes Publications, 1955.

5. Cameron, Norman, and Ann Magaret. *Behavior Pathology*. Boston: Houghton Mifflin Co., 1951.

6. Campbell, Ernest Q., and Thomas F. Pettigrew. "Racial and Moral Crisis: The Role of Little Rock Ministers," *American Journal of Sociology*, Vol. 64 (1959), pp. 509–516.

7. Cooley, Charles H. *Human Nature and the Social Order*. New York: Charles Scribner's Sons, 1922.

8. Dewey, John. *Experience and Nature.* Chicago: Open Court Publishing Co., 1926.

9. Dittes, James E. "Attractiveness of Group as Function of Self-Esteem and Acceptance by Group," *Journal of Abnormal and Social Psychology,* Vol. 59 (1959), pp. 77–82.

10. Edwards, Allen L. "Rationalization in Recognition as a Result of a Political Frame of Reference," *Journal of Abnormal and Social Psychology,* Vol. 36 (1941), pp. 224–235.

11. Emery, Frederick E., and O. A. Oeser. *Information, Decision, and Action.* Melbourne, Austral.: Melbourne University Press, 1958.

12. Eulau, Heinz. "Identification with Class and Political Role Behavior," *Public Opinion Quarterly,* Vol. 20 (1956), pp. 515–529.

13. Festinger, Leon, *et al.* "The Influence Process in the Presence of Extreme Deviates," *Human Relations,* Vol. 5 (1952), pp. 327–346.

14. Freud, Sigmund. *Group Psychology and the Analysis of the Ego,* tr. by James Strachey. London: Hogarth Press, 1945.

15. Goldstein, Bernard. "The Perspective of Unionized Professionals," *Social Forces,* Vol. 37 (1959), pp. 323–327.

16. Gouldner, Alvin W. "Cosmopolitans and Locals: Toward an Analysis of Latent Social Roles," *Administrative Science Quarterly,* Vol. 2 (1957), pp. 281–306, Vol. 3 (1958), pp. 444–480.

17. Hughes, Everett C. *Men and Their Work.* Glencoe, Ill.: The Free Press, 1958.

18. James, William. *The Principles of Psychology.* New York: Henry Holt and Company, 1890, Vol. I.

19. James, William. *The Varieties of Religious Experience.* New York: Modern Library, Inc., 1936.

20. Katz, Elihu, and Paul F. Lazarsfeld. *Personal Influence.* Glencoe, Ill.: The Free Press, 1955.

21. Kelley, Harold H. "Two Functions of Reference Groups," in Guy E. Swanson, Theodore M. Newcomb, and Eugene L. Hartley (eds.), *Readings in Social Psychology,* New York: Henry Holt and Company, 1952, pp. 410–414.

22. Killian, Lewis M. "The Significance of Multiple-Group Membership in Disaster," *American Journal of Sociology,* Vol. 57 (1952), pp. 309–314.

23. Komarovsky, Mirra. "Cultural Contradictions and Sex Roles," *American Journal of Sociology,* Vol. 52 (1946), pp. 184–189.

24. Landgrebe, Ludwig. "The World as a Phenomenological Prob-

lem," *Philosophy and Phenomenological Research*, Vol. 1 (1940), pp. 38–58.

25. Mannheim, Karl. *Ideology and Utopia*, tr. by Louis Wirth and Edward Shils. New York: Harcourt, Brace and Co., 1936.

26. Marshall, Samuel L. *Men Against Fire*. New York: William Morrow & Company, 1947.

27. Mead, George H. *Mind, Self, and Society*, ed. by Charles W. Morris. Chicago: The University of Chicago Press, 1934.

28. Merton, Robert K. *Social Theory and Social Structure*. Glencoe, Ill.: The Free Press, 1957.

29. Newcomb, Theodore M. "Attitude Development as a Function of Reference Groups: The Bennington Study," in Muzafer Sherif, *Outline of Social Psychology*. New York: Harper & Brothers, 1948, pp. 139–154.

30. Park, Robert E. *Race and Culture*, ed. by E. C. Hughes, *et al.* Glencoe, Ill.: The Free Press, 1950.

31. Pearlin, Leonard I. "Shifting Group Attachments and Attitudes Toward Negroes," *Social Forces*, Vol. 33 (1954), pp. 47–50.

32. Redfield, Robert. *The Folk Culture of Yucatan*. Chicago: The University of Chicago Press, 1941.

33. Riezler, Kurt. *Man: Mutable and Immutable*. Chicago: Henry Regnery Co., 1951.

34. Ritchie, Oscar W. "A Sociohistorical Survey of Alcoholics Anonymous," *Quarterly Journal of Studies on Alcohol*, Vol. 9 (1948), pp. 119–156.

35. Sapir, Edward. *Selected Writings in Language, Culture, and Personality*, ed. by David Mandelbaum. Berkeley, Calif.: University of California Press, 1949.

36. Sechehaye, Marguerite (ed.). *Autobiography of a Schizophrenic Girl*, trans. by Grace Rubin-Rabson. New York: Grune & Stratton, 1951.

37. Shils, Edward A. "Primordial, Personal, Sacred, and Civil Ties," *British Journal of Sociology*, Vol. 8 (1957), pp. 130–145.

38. Shils, Edward A., and Morris Janowitz. "Cohesion and Disintegration in the *Wehrmacht* in World War II," *Public Opinion Quarterly*, Vol. 12 (1948), pp. 280–315.

39. Simmel, Georg. *Conflict and the Web of Group Affiliations*, tr. by Kurt H. Wolff and Reinhard Bendix. Glencoe, Ill.: The Free Press, 1955.

40. Stern, Eric, and Suzanne Keller. "Spontaneous Group References

in France," *Public Opinion Quarterly*, Vol. 17 (1953), pp. 208–217.

41. Sullivan, Harry S. *Conceptions of Modern Psychiatry*. Washington, D.C.: W. A. White Psychiatric Foundation, 1940.

42. Thomas, William I. *Social Behavior and Personality*, ed. by Edmund H. Volkart. New York: Social Science Research Council, 1951.

43. Turner, Ralph H. "Role-Taking, Role Standpoint, and Reference Group Behavior," *American Journal of Sociology*, Vol. 61 (1956), pp. 316–328.

44. Vogt, Evon Z. "Navaho Veterans: A Study of Changing Values," *Papers of the Peabody Museum*, Vol. 41 (1951).

45. Wirth, Louis. *Community Life and Social Policy*, ed. by E. W. Marvick and A. J. Reiss. Chicago: The University of Chicago Press, 1956.

46. Wittreich, Warren J. "The Honi Phenomenon: A Case of Selective Perceptual Distortion," *Journal of Abnormal and Social Psychology*, Vol. 47 (1952), pp. 705–712.

47. Wray, Donald E. "Marginal Men of Industry: The Foremen," *American Journal of Sociology*, Vol. 54 (1949), pp. 298–301

8

Breadth of Perspective

LEON H. WARSHAY

UNIVERSITY OF KANSAS CITY

In interactionist theory, as formulated particularly by John Dewey, rational thought is a function of the breadth of experience — direct or vicarious — available to the individual. Learning, too, is considered to be a function of the breadth of perspective. Critics of symbolic interaction theory frequently pose the question: How can one objectively study so subjective a phenomenon as "what goes on in people's heads"? Since role-taking and the selective perception, choice, and interpretation of symbols from the environment are precisely processes which do "go on in people's heads," this is a criticism which merits serious consideration. Professor Warshay provides methodological leads to the objective analysis of such subjective processes. He introduces the notion of "breadth of perspective" as a concept derived from Mead and Dewey and then proceeds to an empirical test of the validity of the concept and an empirical demonstration of its relation to other variables commonly employed in the social sciences.

"The individual organism," wrote George H. Mead, "determines in some sense its own environment by its sensitivity. The only environment to which the organism can react is one that its sensitivity reveals. The sort of environment that can exist for the organism, then, is one that the organism in some sense determines. If in the development of the form there is an increase in the diversity of sensitivity there will be an increase in the response of the organism to its environment, that is, the organism will have a correspondingly larger environment." (32, p. 245)

The present study, following what is undoubtedly a lesser emphasis in the work of Dewey and Mead, introduces a new concept for what may be a new variable — breadth of perspective — and seeks to "imbed" it within the general stream of knowledge of human interaction.*

The concept refers to the *range* of alternative solutions that one is able to bring to mind when presented with a problem. It thus focuses attention *not* upon the nature of the response *actually made*, but rather on the breadth of responses that one can call to mind *before* overtly responding. And it asks further: what accounts for the fact that, when presented with a problem, some people can "think of" more different *kinds* of alternative solutions — regardless of the one they may actually use, or the one that may succeed — than others?

Human problem-solving differs from that of the lower animals — according to symbolic interactionists, some Gestaltists, and several personality theorists — in that it involves the covert manipulation of abstract objects called symbols. A further cogent argument made by most of the above is that the simpler stimulus–response orientations do not fit much of man's behavior; this is the more true when emphasis is placed upon the more cognitive aspect, which is at least somewhat creative, less directly and simply related to situational variables, and therefore capable of more variation in problematic situations.

Nowhere, however, has attention been paid to the range of alternatives that one mulls over — or is able to mull over when stimulated — before responding; extensive examination of the literature has failed to unearth any previous similar emphasis (even the "number of responses" method for scoring the Rorschach, though similar, is hardly "number of *kinds* of *covert*

* This study was originally prepared as part of a Ph.D. thesis under the direction of Professors Arnold M. Rose and Roy G. Francis at the University of Minnesota.

responses"). True, John Dewey's definition of thinking is a behavioral version of perspective in that the individual begins to think — that is, to mull over alternatives — only when previously existing habit is insufficient to the task. This, however, does not conceptualize perspective in any way (for example, as a *cognitive structure*), but merely gives certain conditions (that is, blockage of habit) under which individuals mull over alternatives.

On the other hand, in the quote at the beginning of this article, George H. Mead hit the nail on the head when he referred to the "diversity of sensitivity" of the organism making for a "correspondingly larger environment." Earlier in the same source, Mead said the following:

> We can also recognize in such a general attitude toward an object an attitude that represents alternative responses. . . there is a readiness to act in . . . different ways with reference to the [object] . . . (32, pp. 11–12).

However, none of this has been followed up, either theoretically or empirically. Instead, the concern of students of human behavior has been with the kind, quality, intensity, rigidity, and other such aspects of *overt* responses. Whether the response be selective (as in voting or consumer behavior), directive or dominant (as in leader–follower or status relations), urban, empathic, hostile, neurotic, upper or lower class, correct (as in intelligence testing), or characteristic (as in some culture-and-personality studies), it has been the nature or character of the *single overt* response *actually made*, or likely to be made, that has been emphasized.

True, studies of covert processes have been made, involving, for example, memory, learning, reasoning, insight, and creative thinking of children, adults, neurotics, the aged, and the like. But nowhere, as far as this writer has been able to determine, has the range of kinds of alternative solutions to a problem — here called breadth of perspective — been studied, much less related to other things.

Because breadth of perspective as such is perhaps an important aspect of man, it has been selected as a focus of study. The discussion begins by treating the theoretical development of the concept and follows this up by analyzing the results of an empirical study of the correlates of the breadth of perspective of political precinct chairwomen. The theoretical discussion will delve more thoroughly into the nature of breadth of perspective and will imbed it within a theoretical orientation. The empirical study will relate the concept to as many other variables as appear relevant; for, if the breadth of one's perspective should turn out to be an important variable for sociologists and social psychologists to study, then it should be related in various ways to many of the more significant variables in the social sciences. The empirical study therefore will aim to examine a large number of correlates *extensively* rather than a few intensively.

THE NATURE OF BREADTH OF PERSPECTIVE

Perspective is a capacity or potential of the actor that he brings to a situation and which determines the kind of *meaningful* responses *possible* in that situation. *Breadth of perspective* refers to the broadness or scope of perspective, to the range of meanings and ideas that make it up.

The most general and relevant statement that one might make then is that the person with broad perspective is one who, when confronted with a problematic situation, is able to "see" more different alternate solutions to that situation than is the person of "narrow" perspective.

This study — and, therefore, breadth of perspective — does *not* deal with the following:

(1) the overt response actually made;
(2) the probability of a response being made;
(3) the effect of an overt (or even of a covert) response;
(4) the efficiency of covert or overt responses.

Instead, as indicated at several points above, the concern is with the number of different *kinds* of possible alternative solutions that the actor is able to think of, when stimulated, regardless of what may follow overtly.

THEORETICAL DEVELOPMENT

The work of recent decades in the social sciences appears unmistakably to lead to a number of assumptions relevant to the present interest. Five assumptions will now be listed and discussed.

1. *Perspective is a symbolic structure that the actor brings to situations, consisting of meanings (or concepts), ideas, and values in differing states of clarity and coherence.* The socialized human being thinks in terms of "categories [that are] developed in response to events," (9, p. 232) in terms of a "context of past experience . . . not haphazardly but organized into concepts, attitudes, and other determining tendencies." (48, p. 137) Included are new (at least to him) concepts or categories, not only arising out of interaction with others, but developing "by combinatorial activity as when one proposes the class of 'female presidents of the United States' . . or . . . centaurs," (9, p. 232) for "symbols are pregnant with possibilities of convergence and divergence, of combination and permutation. Meanings 'breed new meanings.' " (43, p. 25)

2. *Perspective serves as a frame of reference* (39), *running ahead of situations, making for definition of situations* (46). That behavior, perception, and memory are "affected" by previous verbal set (10; 29; 48, pp. 137, 313), cultural stereotypes (3, 4), and by one's values (8, 27, 36) has been fairly well established.[1] In any case, then, "to understand what a man does, we must get at . . . what he takes for granted and how he defines the situation." (41, p. 567)

3. *Perspective, therefore, determines the kind of definitions "possible" in a given situation, being broader for some and narrower for others.* A number of writers have pointed out this difference between people, beginning with the statement by Mead quoted above. Further examples are found in the following quotations:

> The number of ways in which an array of events can be differentiated into classes will vary with the ability of an organism to abstract features which some of the events share and others do not (9, p. 8).

[1] The findings of the last mentioned study — by Postman, Bruner, and McGinnies (36) — have been disputed and, in some cases, interpreted differently. See, for example, studies by Floyd Allport (1), Postman and Schneider (37), and Solomon and Howes (42).

... when an individual's vocabularies are limited in range, his knowledge of alternative paths of action is limited (43, p. 28).

The only motives which can be imputed are those which one himself understands. He cannot attribute to others, any more than to himself, motives not dreamed of; neither can he attribute motives in whose existence he does not believe (43, p. 11).

4. *Perspective is learned, largely through symbolic interaction.* This statement needs to be analyzed in two ways. The first is the psychological process through which thinking occurs which, to follow Dewey (17, 18), arises only when habitual response is blocked, with stress and/or discomfort ensuing. Only in this way is thought — the covert manipulation of concepts, ideas, and the like — possible. Some research into the response to prolonged deprivation, frustration, and persecution in Nazi Germany has shown it to consist often in the adoption of temporary frames of reference, increased planning, and increased problem-solving (2).

The second line of analysis is the linkage of the psychological process with social organization. That thinking is intricately linked, from the beginning, with the social process is the contribution of Dewey and Mead. The notion that "society not only continues to exist *by* transmission, communication, but . . . may fairly be said to exist *in* transmission, *in* communication" (16, p. 5) is central to Dewey's approach. Mead, building upon Dewey's beginning, identified the process or mechanism linking the "individual" to "society" as follows:

> Only in terms of gestures as significant symbols is the existence of mind or intelligence possible; for only . . . [thus] can thinking . . . take place. The internalization in our experience of the external conversations of gestures which we carry on with other individuals in the social process is the essence of thinking (32, p. 47).

Among the products of the above processes are what Mead called "attitudes," and what Rose refers to as "expectations":

> The expectations . . . specify or refer to a number of (1) *meanings* and (2) *folkways* or *values*, which together make up

the *culture* or subculture of the group. A meaning is simply a definition of an object . . . [it] usually indicates how an individual *may* act toward the object . . . [whereas the folkway or value] indicates how an individual *should* or *must* act toward an object (38, p. 8).

Perspective, as used here and as indicated in Assumption 1 above, refers to a person's meanings, values, concepts, and ideas — Mead's "attitudes" and Rose's "expectations." (Some prefer to think of meanings and values, incidentally, as different from, and as partial causes of, attitudes and expectations, but such distinctions are less important here.) That these are largely learned through interaction with others has been fairly well established. For example, evidence for the effects of social norms upon social, political, and racial attitudes (6, 15, 20, 26, 34), of social-class membership upon motives, attitudes, and values (7, 11, 14, 49), and of reference-group membership upon attitudes (12, 21, 23, 33, 40) is abundant.

Perhaps the more pertinent questions are just how and under what conditions the above social variables influence meanings, values, attitudes, ideas — that is, the parts of perspective.

5. *Symbolic interaction, involving as it often does role-taking and role-playing, leads to a good deal of one's perspective being closely organized around one's self or selves.* This assumption implies that while, on the one hand, an individual is a product of "social group(s) of which he is a member" (32, p. 6) or, as Cooley and Simmel have argued, he is the point of intersection of social groups or circles (13, p. 148; 41, p. 567), yet this is far from the whole story and need not imply that this is all there is to the relation of individual to society. Not all experiences are equally important (13, p. 144; 22, p. 179) or salient (12) to the individual and, because individuals differ in their degree of personal commitment, loyalty, and obligation to various groups, it is correct to argue that "endeavor is not always clearly linked with membership in well-organized groups," (43, p. 29) or necessarily with other social situations, for that matter.

Emphasis by Sullivan of the "significant other," (45) by Foote (19) and Strauss (43) of identification, and the work on reference groups after the ideas of Hyman (21) and Sherif (40) further stress the point made above[2] — that the relation between social experience, self — and, therefore, perspective — is not a very simple one.

Yet, it still must be argued that, with the above qualifications in mind, a good deal of one's concepts, values, meanings, and attitudes is intimately related to one's self organization, and that, in fact, one often acquires the former in the process of acquiring new selves, as examples of the socialization of children, the assimilation of immigrants, and of movement up or down an occupational hierarchy illustrate. One can posit the fact that interaction involves the sharing and exchange of identities (or self-concepts) — that for organized social behavior to proceed, each actor must know "who" *he* is and "who" the *other* is (19, p. 17) — without assuming at the same time that any given self is equally, or at all, involved in a given situation. Benjamins uses the distinction between "figure" and "ground" to make this point (5, p. 474) and Turner distinguishes between other attitudes that are "directed toward the self and those which are not," (47) calling the former interaction *reflexive.*

In any case, the above is the rationale for assuming that, since self-concept and perspective both arise via the same interactionist process, the positing of some kind(s) and degree of relationship between them is reasonable.

AN EMPIRICAL TEST: THE BREADTH OF PERSPECTIVE OF POLITICAL PRECINCT CHAIRWOMEN

THE PROPOSITIONS

With the above five assumptions behind them, six major propositions were set up for study, positing two broad kinds of variables as relevant to the prediction and accounting for variation in breadth of perspective from person to person. The first three propositions relate breadth of perspective to the actor's *past social experience,* and flow largely from Assumption 4; the second

[2] The above generalizations are restricted to the sociogenic aspect of personality — for example, role, self, value, meaning, concept, and the like. No discussion of biogenic or psychogenic aspects (for example, physiological tensions and reflexes — both conditioned and unconditioned — and simple habits and emotions) is necessary or relevant here.

three, but upon Assumption 5, posit relationships between breadth of perspective and *present self-concept(s)*. The propositions are that perspective is likely to be broader

1. the broader one's culture contact; [3]
2. if there has been sudden disruption of habit or change of role;
3. the more contact there has been with opposing ideas;
4. the broader one's self-concept(s);
5. the less ascribed one's self-concept(s);
6. the more situation-free one's modal self-concept.

A full discussion of the rationale for each proposition will be presented with the empirical findings below.

It is believed that the above propositions represent a reasonably broad, as well as a theoretically relevant, test of the potential value of breadth of perspective as a concept. However, to broaden the analysis and understanding still further, the following propositions — more peripheral to the central theory of the study — were also tested. The first five *peripheral* propositions (Propositions 7–11) state that perspective is likely to be *broader*

7. the higher one's income;
8. the higher one's social class;
9. the more years of formal education one has had;
10. the more urban one's background;
11. the more organizations in which one has held high office.

On the other hand, perspective is likely to be *narrower*

12. with increasing age;
13. with the tendency to read the popular mass media;
14. with the tendency to read material of one's membership groups.

These last eight propositions are admittedly narrower in scope, for the most part, than are the first six. However, since they include some of the more important variables in social life, they have been added, as indicated above, in order to explore more broadly the relevance of breadth of perspective to human behavior.

[3] Culture *contact*, rather than experience, was used. Although it is true that the work of George H. Mead, Kurt Lewin, William I. Thomas, and others has stressed not contact but "experience" (that is, "significant" contact or environment) as relevant to behavior, it proved necessary in this case to settle for a less desirable substitute.

Breadth of Perspective

As subjects for study, every Minneapolis precinct chairwoman available at the time of the study was interviewed; both major political parties were involved, 103 women in all being studied. Their selection kept constant gender and avocational role and enabled choice of problems relevant to that role.

Breadth of perspective was measured by presenting each subject with hypothetical problem situations, encouraging her to volunteer verbally, in a "permissive" setting, as many solutions as she could think of to each problem situation. Six problems in all were selected, three *familiar* (dealing with daily mundane problems taken from precinct politics) and three *unfamiliar* (as far removed as possible from their daily experience — for example, adventure, science fiction).

The basis for selecting and rating the problems was the judgment of a dozen political precinct chairwomen from St. Paul (the twin city of Minneapolis), six from each major party; it was assumed that the small St. Paul sample was similar to that in Minneapolis. Each chairwoman was presented with a list of 26 hypothetical problem situations, 15 "typical" political precinct problems adapted from political handbooks and eleven "unusual" non-political problems devised by the writer and several colleagues. The three most familiar, as judged by the St. Paul sample, and the three least familiar problems were then used in the study. The three *familiar* problems are the following:

> 1. Jane Marshall is appointed precinct chairwoman of her party in her precinct. She is advised that one of the most important jobs of a precinct chairman is to enlist the aid of people in her precinct for the various tasks to be performed in the campaign that is coming. She is faced with the problem of how to do this.

> 2. Precinct worker Dorothy Adams is faced with a problem which she has encountered in previous elections. Many voters just vote for candidates running for the higher offices, such as President, Governor, Senator, and Congressman, but leave out most of the smaller offices since they have never heard of most of these people. Therefore, the question is: How to get the

voters to vote for the party candidates running for these lesser offices.

3. Agnes Smith, chairman of her precinct, has been told by the precinct workers working under her that their main difficulty is that people won't register, and that people just don't see any use in voting since it is only one vote.

The three *unfamiliar* problems follow:

4. Mrs. Thomas, a widow, traveling one summer in South Africa, finds herself in the midst of a revolution. She hears that the U.S. consul has ordered evacuation of all American citizens within three days, after which transportation out of the country cannot be guaranteed. However, Mrs. Thomas is wounded during a skirmish and, by the time she is able to be moved, the three-day period has passed and all Americans have left the country. She is thus left in the interior of the country to solve her problem.

5. An American exploring in an African jungle one day has fallen and broken his leg. After lying there for an hour or so, unable to help himself, and faced with the prospect of lying there for days, he sees an African native, carrying a spear, walk by. The American is not sure whether the native, who is from a wild African tribe, has seen him or not.

6. A group of explorers from the Earth has landed on Mars and been taken prisoner by the Martians. The Martians think that the Earth people are animals, that the Earth people are not "rational" or "intelligent" beings the way they, the Martians, are; therefore, they put the Earth people in a large cage. The problem of the Earth people then becomes: How to demonstrate to the Martians that they (the Earth people) are not animals but rational beings *also*.

The six problems were printed on separate cards, each being handed, in turn, in the above order to the subject for her solutions.

Thus, a new *dimension* was added to the study in that one could now measure breadth of perspective in *familiar*, as against *unfamiliar*, problem situations and observe whether the other variables of the study (in Propositions 1 through 14) were related to them in the same manner. In fact, this distinction made necessary further theoretical analysis and increased the number of predictions eventually made.

The responses to each hypothetical problem situation were coded into broad categories and converted into standard scores. Therefore, each subject could be given two scores on breadth of perspective — one for familiar and the other for unfamiliar situations. Thus, data were collected to measure the *dependent* variable, breadth of perspective.

For the six major *independent* variables (Propositions 1–6), background data relevant to the first three propositions were gathered by going into each subject's past history; the Twenty Statements Test (the "Who Am I?)" was administered in order to obtain data relevant to the second three (25). One change was made, however, in the "Who Am I?" test in that twelve instead of twenty responses were asked for; the pretest experience suggested that twenty seemed too great a task and/or threat. This undoubtedly increased the probability of Type II statistical error.

For the more peripheral propositions (Propositions 7–14), additional background data from each subject's past and present were gathered, in keeping with the exploratory emphasis of the empirical study.

The "Who Am I?" test was presented first; second came the six hypothetical problem situations; and, to conclude the interview and data-gathering, questions on background and past experience were asked. The average interview lasted two and one-half hours, ranging from one to almost five hours.

THE FINDINGS: SOCIAL EXPERIENCE
VARIABLES (PROPOSITIONS 1–3)

Of the first three propositions, the second — that sudden disruption of habit or change of role makes for broader perspective — found no support whatever; in fact, the empirical results to some degree pointed in the opposite direction. Moreover, of the fourteen propositions tested, the second was the only one that failed to receive at least a modicum of support. It may be well to begin with this one.

Following the Dewey formulation that it is only when the actor's on-going habitual process is interrupted that it becomes possible for him to think of alternate responses to a situation, it was predicted that events such as disruption of family relationships by death, divorce, separation, and the like would broaden perspective, since these had presumably plunged the subject into new role expectations, frames of reference, etc. Instead, the following was the case:

(*a*) Habit disruption during the subject's *childhood* was *unrelated* to breadth of perspective. Measures of this variable were: death of one or both parents during subject's childhood, parents divorced or separated, subject had foster- or step-parents, subjects raised by people other than parents, and others. (*b*) Habit disruption during the subject's *adulthood* was *negatively* related to breadth of perspective. This was shown by the fact that subjects who were already adult when their parents died had narrower perspective in familiar situations; and this was particularly true of widows, in both familiar and unfamiliar situations (see Table 1); that this relationship may be attributed to age differences — between widows and non-widows, for example — was discounted since the above relationships held even when age was controlled.

Perhaps emotional factors are important here: the trauma of the habit disruption, of the sudden plunge into the new and uncomfortable role, may cause security-striving — a seizing of the near and familiar — and a consequent narrowing of perspective. This remains, of course, conjectural.

To turn now to the other propositions, Proposition 1, that broader culture contact broadens perspective, was widely supported by a number of different measures, to wit: number of culture areas lived in,[4] wide travel, broad reading of books and of the mass media, and membership in informal groups and circles (the last was related to perspective in familiar situations only). The only important *unrelated* measure of breadth of culture contact was membership in a variety of formal organizations (see Table 2).

Proposition 1 is perhaps the most crucial since it is assumed

[4] The Odum and Moore division of the United States into six culture areas was used (35).

Breadth of Perspective
TABLE 1
Sudden Disruption of Habit or Role
(Proposition 2)

Measures	Familiar Situations		Unfamiliar Situations	
	F or t Value	Level of Sig.	F or t Value	Level of Sig.
1. During subject's childhood				
a. death of one or both parents	F_3 *	......	F_3 *	......
b. parents divorced or separated	t *	......	t *	......
c. had foster or stepparents	t *	......	t 1.77	.10
d. raised by people other than parents	F_4 1.19	.20	F_4 *	......
e. looked after by others while living with parents	F_3 *	......	F_3 *	......
f. left alone part of day	t *	......	t *	......
2. During subject's adulthood				
a. both parents died (negative relationship)	t 2.56	.02	t 1.71	.10
b. widows and ex-widows (negative relationship)	t 2.62	.01	t 2.82	.01

* The asterisk stands for all values of F and t under 1.00. The subscript of F indicates the number of categories or "treatments" involved.

(Assumption 4, above) that perspective is learned via symbolic interaction and, therefore, broad contact with a variety of cultural ideas and meanings should broaden perspective.[5]

[5] That the direction of "cause" is not reversed — that is, that those with broader perspective are more likely to be *exposed*, or to *expose themselves*, to broader culture contact, rather than the other way around — was tested in the following manner. A measure of the number of culture areas lived in *before* age 18 was related to breadth of perspective and found to be statistically significant — although only in *unfamiliar* situations. (For familiar situations, $F_3 = 1.87$, and $p > .20$; for unfamiliar situations, $F_3 = 3.20$, and $p < .05$.) The reasoning behind this special test is that, before a given age (say, eighteen, as in this case), decisions about where to live are probably made by one's parents and not by oneself. This becomes, then, a "purer" causal situation, where causality, if "present," could have been exerted in but one direction. However, the possibility of perspective as

TABLE 2

Breadth of Culture Contact
(Proposition 1)

Measures	Familiar Situations		Unfamiliar Situations	
	F or t Value	Level of Sig.	F or t Value	Level of Sig.
1. Number of culture areas lived in	F_3 3.25	.05	F_3 5.08	.01
2. Total number of culture areas experienced	t 1.80	.10	F_4 2.79	.05
3. Number of *kinds* of newspapers and magazines read	F_3 3.64	.05	F_4 2.83	.05
4. Number of books finished	t 1.96	.05	F_6 3.49	.01
5. Number of *kinds* of books read	F_6 2.15	.10	F_6 2.59	.05
6. Number of *kinds* of formal organizations	F_3 *	......	F_3 2.26	.20
7. Number of *kinds* of informal groups	F_4 2.84	.05	F_4 1.47	> .20

The third proposition, that contact with opposing ideas broadens perspective, was selected as a more intensive test, and perhaps special example, of Proposition 1 — the broad culture-contact hypothesis. In any case, Proposition 3 was supported by the fact that the following were positively related to breadth of perspective: reading material which one dislikes, and number and per cent of opposite party friends (the latter to breadth of perspective in *unfamiliar* situations only). There was no relationship, however, to voting for opposite party candidates, or to tendency to read material favorable to the opposite party (see Table 3); in the case of the latter, however, it may be that there *is* a relationship in the "real world" — the probability of Type II statistical error is high — since only nine of the 103 subjects interviewed did any reading of material favorable to the opposite party so that, although the nine subjects had much broader perspective

---

cause still lingers, even before age eighteen, and may rest in the fact that it may have been the broad perspective of the parents or guardians that accounts for *both* the wide culture contact and the broad perspective of the offspring.

Breadth of Perspective

TABLE 3

Contact with Opposing Ideas
(Proposition 3)

MEASURES	FAMILIAR SITUATIONS		UNFAMILIAR SITUATIONS	
	F or t Value	Level of Sig.	F or t Value	Level of Sig.
1. Reads material which one dislikes	t 3.53	.001	t 3.09	.01
2. Number of opposite party friends	t *	....	t 2.03	.05
3. Per cent of opposite party friends	t 1.37	.20	t 2.03	.05
4. Reads material favorable to opposite party	t 1.17	.30	t 1.35	.20
5. Has voted for important opposite party candidates (curvilinear relationship) ..	F_3 *	....	F_3 1.31	> .20

than the others, this was too small a number for statistical significance.

The first and third propositions, as verified above, perhaps lend support to the speculative notion that it is *not* the individual who selects from his environment only what he "needs" to solve *fairly immediate* problems who has the broader perspective; but rather, it is the one who ranges far and wide to gain new and antagonistic points of view — regardless of clearly foreseeable usefulness — who has, or gains, perspective.

In any case, with the major exceptions above in mind, sufficient support for the relevance of certain kinds of *social experience* to breadth of perspective has been tentatively established.

THE FINDINGS: SELF-CONCEPT
VARIABLES (PROPOSITIONS 4–6)

The second three propositions rest on the assumption that interaction often involves self (Assumption 5). Hence, it seemed desirable to measure not only the actor's *past social experience* (for Propositions 1 through 3), but his *present self-conceptions* as well.

The instrument chosen to elicit the subject's self-concept(s) was, as said above, the Twenty Statements Test, an unstructured test.[6]

The first self-concept proposition (Proposition 4) — that the broader the self-concept, the broader the perspective — assumes that each self-concept or, more accurately, *category* of self-concepts, reflects a constellation of similar ideas and meanings; therefore, the more different *kinds* (categories) of self-concept, the broader the perspective. A code was devised under which each subject's self-concepts were classified into categories — for instance, one referring to family role, others to political, communal, occupational, and other roles, as well as to more "personal" identities that indicate trait, taste, value, and physical characteristics.

Partial support was given to the proposition in that subjects with the largest number of categories of self-concept had the broadest perspective in *familiar*, but not in unfamiliar, situations (see Table 4). A divergent self apparently is a help in broadening one's outlook in the more familiar situations only.

The *second* self-concept proposition (Proposition 5), following Ralph Linton's distinction (28, p. 115), uses a threefold

TABLE 4

Broadness of Self-Concept
(Proposition 4)

MEASURE	FAMILIAR SITUATIONS		UNFAMILIAR SITUATIONS	
	F or t Value	Level of Sig.	F or t Value	Level of Sig.
Number of *kinds* of self-concept or identity	t 2.52	.02	F_6 *	......

[6] The Twenty Statements Test asks the respondent to give twenty answers to the simple question "Who am I?" It was selected for the following reasons: (1) the question elicits the respondent's *subjectively* defined identities or self-concepts; (2) it does so in a "voluntary" manner rather than through elicitation from direct self-characterizations, group memberships, or indirect questions; (3) "Who am I?" is clearly a question relevant to the theoretical framework of the study; and (4) much empirical work with this instrument already exists, suggesting its usefulness for the purpose at hand (24).

classification of self-concept: "achieved (e.g., stamp collector, follower of Billy Graham)," "ascribed (e.g., woman, thirty-five, daughter)," and "impure ascribed," an intermediate category referring to apparently "ascribed" self-concepts where the possibility of achievement cannot be ruled out and to other self-concepts that, though achieved in a sense, cannot be seen as clearly achieved (e.g., middle-class, married, mother).

The results were meager (see Table 5) in that only "impure ascribed" self-concept was related — and in curvilinear form (with the extremes having the broader perspective) — to breadth of perspective, and then only in *familiar* situations.

TABLE 5

Degree of Ascription of Self-Concept or Identity
(Proposition 5)

MEASURES	FAMILIAR SITUATIONS		UNFAMILIAR SITUATIONS	
	F or t Value	Level of Sig.	F or t Value	Level of Sig.
1. "Achieved" self-concepts (actually, converse of "ascribed" plus "impure ascribed"), number of	F_4 *	......	F_4 *	......
2. "Ascribed" self-concepts, number of	F_3 1.34	> .20	F_3 *	......
3. "Impure ascribed" self-concepts, number of	F_3 3.38	.05	F_3 1.12	> .20

The third, and last, self-concept proposition (Proposition 6) refers to the actor's modal self-concept, to the manner in which he relates himself to the world about him — both in terms of *which context* and also with reference to how *specifically* and *clearly* he does so. A fourfold scheme, devised for other purposes (30, 31), was selected; it categorizes the subject's self-concepts, at a relatively low level of abstraction, into an A to D scheme. Type A refers to objective, concrete self-concepts (e.g., I have red hair; I live at 4117 S. Girard; I was born in 1896); Type B to objective self-concepts relating to social units or systems (e.g., I am a mother, interior decorator, Democrat,

Red Cross secretary); Type C to subjective self-concepts that cut across social units or systems (e.g., I am shy, like music, believe in radicalism); and Type D to subjective self-concepts that are too abstract, vague, general, and/or irrelevant to enable any reasonable degree of prediction within social contexts, as for Type B, or across them, as for Type C (e.g., Say hello to everyone; I am a pseudo-rational empiricist; I sometimes have the feeling, especially when tired, that things are disintegrating).

The above scheme was selected to test the proposition that, the more *situation-free* one's self-concepts, the broader one's perspective, particularly in the *less familiar* situations. In other words, people whose self-concepts are largely of Types C and D *organize* self in ways that happen to be relevant to a wider variety of situations than do those whose self-concepts are largely of Type B; the latter, if anything, would have broader perspective in the more familiar situations. Of the sample of precinct chairwomen, 73 had a majority or plurality of Type B, 23 Type C, and a handful of Type D and tied categories; there were no Types A.

The results supported the proposition as follows: in the *familiar* problem situations, there was no difference between subjects of Type B and a combined category of Type C, Type D, and Type C–D (tied); however, the latter did have the broader perspective in *unfamiliar* situations, supporting the idea that *situation-free* modal self-concepts are more likely to have broader perspective (see Table 6).

It therefore appears that some degree of *detachment* from social

TABLE 6

Modal Self-Concept: Relation to Social Contexts
(Proposition 6)

MEASURE	FAMILIAR SITUATIONS		UNFAMILIAR SITUATIONS	
	F or t Value	Level of Sig.	F or t Value	Level of Sig.
Degree of detachment from specific social contexts (Types C and D rather than Type B)	F_4 *	......	F_4 2.66	.10

contexts — in fact, even a great deal of this — does not harm breadth of perspective in situations relevant to those contexts (the familiar situations of this study, for example) and is of particular value in unusual social contexts (the unfamiliar situations of this study).

THE FINDINGS: BACKGROUND (PERIPHERAL) VARIABLES (PROPOSITIONS 7–14)

The background variables were related to breadth of perspective in the following ways: (*a*) In *both* familiar and unfamiliar situations, income, social class, and education were positively related to breadth of perspective; age was negatively related. (*b*) In *familiar* situations only, the tendency to read the popular mass media showed a curvilinear relationship, with the broadest perspective occurring at the two extremes; the tendency to read material of one's membership groups was negatively related to breadth of perspective. (*c*) In *unfamiliar* situations only, an exclusively urban background was positively related to breadth of perspective; leadership showed a curvilinear relationship, with the broadest perspective at the extremes. These results are summarized in Table 7.

The significance of the above relationships will be discussed in more organized fashion below. The writer wishes, however, to turn here to the question of leadership (Proposition 11) — which raises a theoretical issue. It actually is difficult to make a prediction about the breadth of perspective of leaders (leadership was defined as holding high office — president and vice-president — in organizations). On the one hand, because the leader has to act, to make fairly rapid and unambiguous decisions, *too broad* a perspective may be a luxury; on the other hand, one cannot conceive of the leader (in formal organization, at least, or in any other social context where "competition" for leadership obtains) as having *too narrow* a perspective. The best theoretically based prediction perhaps should be that, as an aggregate, the leaders' breadth of perspective should be more homogeneous (that is, the distribution of the breadth of perspective of leaders should have a smaller standard deviation) than that of followers as an aggregate.

TABLE 7

Background Variables
(Propositions 7–14)

VARIABLES	FAMILIAR SITUATIONS		UNFAMILIAR SITUATIONS	
	F or t Value	Level of Sig.	F or t Value	Level of Sig.
1. Income (7)	t 2.10	.05	t 2.88	.01
2. Social Class (8)	F_3 4.89	.01	t 1.93	.10
3. Education (9)	F_6 3.77	.01	F_6 3.02	.05
4. Age (12) (negative relationship)	F_4 3.99	.01	F_{10} 2.39	.05
5. Tendency to read the popular mass media (13) (curvilinear relationship) ..	F_7 2.68	.05	F_4 1.57	.20
6. Tendency to read material of one's membership groups (14) (negative relationship)	F_9 2.91	.01	F_9 *	......
7. Only urban background (10)	t 1.33	.20	t 2.23	.05
8. Leadership (the more organizations in which one has held high office) (11) (curvilinear relationship) ..	F_5 1.48	.20	F_5 2.71	.05

CONCLUSIONS

SUMMARY OF FINDINGS

The above empirical relationships have demonstrated that breadth of perspective is related, in great or small measure, to a number of important variables. Five of the six major propositions found at least a minimum of support — with even the one exception suggesting a new research direction — and a number of additional variables, important sociologically, also were seen to be related.

Out of the above, a number of conclusions might be formulated:

    1. Breadth of perspective in *familiar* situations:

        (*a*) is most narrow for those with a *passive* relation to their world — if widowhood, ascribed identity, tendency to read the popular mass media and material from one's membership groups imply a passive selection from or adjustment to one's social milieu; (*b*) profits most from broad contact with the *near* and *traditional;* for instance, membership in informal groups assumes wide contact within a narrow sphere, such as the local neighborhood or community; moreover, social class and education are, if anything, more closely related to breadth of perspective in familiar situations, though they are related in unfamiliar situations as well.[7]

2. Breadth of perspective in *unfamiliar* situations, on the other hand:

(*a*) suffers from too close attachment to social contexts (Type B was narrowest); (*b*) but is broadest with wide contacts with the *strange* and *distant* (for example, number of books finished, which implies contact with many ideas, some presumably strange and distant; and number and per cent of opposite party friends, which implies the same sort of contact, if not the type of person who "seeks" the strange and distant).

These two statements, expressed in rather abstract form, place many of the findings more neatly; coming after the examination of the empirical findings, they perhaps have a status similar to that of summary statements — at least, that is, without further theoretical and empirical work.

FINAL CONSIDERATIONS

In assessing the results, a number of theoretical and methodological questions may be raised.

1. *Relative value of the variables used.* The social experience variables (Propositions 1–3) and the background variables (Propositions 7–14) were, on the whole, more closely related to breadth of perspective than were the self-concept variables

[7] For example, in *familiar* situations, the F-ratio was significant when all three social classes (upper-lower, lower-middle, and upper-middle) were compared with one another; in the case of *unfamiliar* situations, however, it was only when the upper-lower and lower-middle were lumped and a t-test, running them against the upper-middle class, computed that statistical significance was obtained. Similarly, the relation of education to *familiar* perspective was clearer, in that it was perfectly linear (with six categories or "treatments"), whereas this was not quite the case for *unfamiliar* situations.

(Propositions 4–6). This may mean either that (*a*) the self-concept variables — at least as used here — are less relevant, or (*b*) there has been less research with the "Who Am I?" test, which may correspondingly be conceptually less well developed. The writer is inclined toward the second interpretation, since the one self-concept proposition that yielded clear results (Proposition 6 — modal self-concept) relied on a fourfold categorization used in several previous studies.

2. *Alternate explanations.* The nature of knowledge is such that alternate explanations of observed phenomena are always possible; in the present study, the alternate explanation of *verbal fluency* particularly suggests itself. If this is greatly involved in both breadth of perspective and the independent variables related to it, then one might have really been relating verbal fluency to itself in the case of many of the variables used, especially in the case of education, class, breadth of culture contact, travel, reading, and the like, but probably not in the case of variables such as widowhood, death of parents, modal identity, and so on.

3. *Causality.* The direction of causality is partly open (this problem was alluded to in Footnote 5); that is, it might be the case that people with broader perspective — or whose parents have broader perspective — are more likely to go to school, travel, move about, select friends who disagree with them, and so on. This argument, however, is undoubtedly weaker in the relation of breadth of perspective to factors such as widowhood, death of parents during subject's adulthood, and age.

4. *Interview bias.* Subjective factors in the interview situation may have distorted the results. To give one example, it could be that the interviewer got along better with the more literate women, eliciting more responses on all or most variables of the study; this alone could account for the relationships obtained between breadth of perspective and at least the following: education, social class, reading habits, wide travel, and number of culture areas lived in.

Further suggestions for improvement, modification, and extension of the study are the following:

1. To repeat the study, relating the independent variables to something with which this study was *not* concerned — namely, the *kind,* or *efficiency,* of the one overt solution actually (or

likely to be) selected. It is expected, in view of all of the above
theoretical considerations, that sufficiently different results would
follow.

2. To repeat the study with a population that differs in area
of interest, role, sex, education, and the like. One should expect
great similarity, for example, if the area of interest were to be
changed from politics to religion, since the theoretical distinction
is between *familiar* and *unfamiliar* situations, *not* political and
non-political. What the effect of altering some of the other
characteristics of the population would be is, at least in part, an
empirical question.

3. The data-collecting situation could be further altered, not
only in age, sex, and race of the interviewer, but in his approach
as well. One might vary the permissiveness of the situation, the
kind of problem (for example, make it non-hypothetical, present
non-social situations, require non-verbal overt responses), engage
in further probing (for example, further probing into the "Who
Am I?" self-concepts might raise the validity of, say, their classification into ascribed vs. achieved; furthermore, the presence
and/or strength of "trauma" might be investigated as a possible
explanation of the negative relationship between breadth of perspective and widowhood), ask for merely a general discussion or
analysis of the problem situations instead of specific alternate
solutions, and substitute mass filling out of questionnaires for
personal interviews.

Perhaps prematurely, four possible areas of application are
offered for the central variable of this study:

1. The area of *personnel selection*, when (*a*) the position calls
for broadness of understanding rather than quick decision and
where (*b*) an immediate but incorrect response can do more
damage than sober consideration of possibilities.

2. The area of *intelligence* theory and research, since breadth
of perspective offers perhaps a different dimension, or even conception, of intelligence — the "intelligent" person being the one
who can think of broad possibilities rather than selecting the one
"correct" choice out of several.

3. It suggests a typology of *leadership* positions or situations:
(*a*) one who must act instantaneously, (*b*) one who has the
choice of delaying action, and (*c*) one whose situation gives him

more time to mull over ideas. The three may differ in the breadth of perspective required and perhaps in its correlates as well.

4. Lastly, a broad perspective may be a necessary, or at least a contributory, condition to *neurosis*, for it may be that "weakness" of personality and/or certain kinds of situations *alone* are insufficient in themselves to make for neurosis where perspective is *narrow*.

SUMMARY THEORETICAL STATEMENT

The role that breadth of perspective plays in man's daily contact with his milieu differs from that of the usual problem-solving mechanisms that he calls into play.

The person with broad perspective is not necessarily, or often, the successful problem-solver in immediate situations; breadth of perspective is not analogous to social intelligence or even to intelligence in general. He is one who learns ideas, meanings, and values — but not for immediate use; they might be useful some time in the future, or perhaps never. He need not be practical in the usual sense and is not, therefore, rewarded by others in the usual way. The tests and criteria for selecting the successful do not usually fit him very well nor is he likely to have much value for them.

He has a variety of potential responses in his arsenal and these are often inconsistent. He is often, as Strauss says, a problem to himself (43, p. 28) and, therefore, a puzzle to others.

The question that has been asked in this study is, how to account for the difference between men such as the above and others. Positing a theory called symbolic interaction, and making extensive use of related theories and ideas, this study has tested for empirical relationships which, when integrated within one theoretical orientation, could serve as part of the answer.

In conclusion, breadth of perspective, as defined above, has not really been studied by students of human behavior. It may be encouraging that, despite the problems that had to be faced in the testing of a variable without hints from previous research, breadth of perspective has proved to be related not only to the central variables of the study, but also to several of the major variables in the social sciences. The consequence of this is that

Breadth of Perspective

(1) since many empirical relationships have been uncovered that were statistically significant and (2) this fact having made for much interplay back and forth between the findings and theory, the present study may now offer some direction for further theory and research.

There is now, perhaps, some basis for doing in the future what has not been very much attempted in the present study — more *intensive* research and analysis.

References

1. Allport, Floyd H. *Theories of Perception and the Concept of Structure.* New York: John Wiley & Sons, 1955.
2. Allport, Gordon W., Jerome S. Bruner, and E. M. Jandorf. "Personality Under Social Catastrophe," *Character and Personality,* Vol. 10 (1941), pp. 1–22.
3. Allport, Gordon W., and Leo J. Postman. *The Psychology of Rumor.* New York: Henry Holt and Company, 1947.
4. Bartlett, Frederic C. "Social Factors in Recall," in Theodore M. Newcomb and Eugene L. Hartley (eds.), *Readings in Social Psychology.* New York: Henry Holt and Company, 1947, pp. 69–76.
5. Benjamins, J. "Changes in Performance in Relation to Influences Upon Self-Conceptualization," *Journal of Abnormal and Social Psychology,* Vol. 45 (1950), pp. 473–480.
6. Bettelheim, Bruno, and Morris Janowitz. "Ethnic Tolerance," in Guy E. Swanson, Theodore M. Newcomb, and Eugene L. Hartley (eds.), *Readings in Social Psychology.* New York: Henry Holt and Company, 1952, pp. 593–602.
7. Bronfenbrenner, Urie. "Socialization and Social Class Through Time and Space," in Eleanor E. Maccoby, Theodore M. Newcomb, and Eugene L. Hartley (eds.), *Readings in Social Psychology.* New York: Henry Holt and Company, 1958, pp. 400–425.
8. Bruner, Jerome S., and Cecile C. Goodman. "Value and Need as Organizing Factors in Perception," in Theodore M. Newcomb Eugene L. Hartley (eds.), *Readings in Social Psychology.* New York: Henry Holt and Company, 1947, pp. 99–108.
9. Bruner, Jerome S., J. J. Goodnow, and George A. Austin. *A Study of Thinking.* New York: John Wiley & Sons, 1956.

10. Carmichael, Leonard, H. P. Hogan, and A. A. Walter. "An Experimental Study of the Effect of Language Upon the Reproduction of Visually Perceived Form," *Journal of Experimental Psychology*, Vol. 15 (1932), pp. 73–86.

11. Centers, Richard. *The Psychology of Social Classes.* Princeton, N.J.: Princeton University Press, 1949.

12. Charters, Werrett W., Jr., and Theodore M. Newcomb. "Some Attitudinal Effects of Experimentally Increased Salience of a Membership Group," in Guy E. Swanson, Theodore M. Newcomb, and Eugene L. Hartley (eds.), *Readings in Social Psychology.* New York: Henry Holt and Company, 1952, pp. 415–420.

13. Cooley, Charles H. *Human Nature and the Social Order.* New York: Charles Scribner's Sons, 1902.

14. Davis, Allison. "Socialization and Adolescent Personality," in Guy E. Swanson, Theodore M. Newcomb, and Eugene L. Hartley (eds.), *Readings in Social Psychology.* New York: Henry Holt and Company, 1952, pp. 520–531.

15. Deutsch, Morton, and Mary E. Collins. *Interracial Housing.* Minneapolis: University of Minnesota Press, 1951.

16. Dewey, John. *Democracy and Education.* New York: The Macmillan Company, 1916.

17. Dewey, John. *Human Nature and Conduct.* New York: Henry Holt and Company, 1922.

18. Dewey, John. *How We Think.* Boston: D. C. Heath and Company, 1933.

19. Foote, Nelson N. "Identification as the Basis for a Theory of Motivation," *American Sociological Review*, Vol. 16 (February 1951), pp. 14–21.

20. Horowitz, Eugene L. "Development of Attitude Toward Negroes," in Guy E. Swanson, Theodore M. Newcomb, and Eugene L. Hartley (eds.), *Readings in Social Psychology.* New York: Henry Holt and Company, 1952, pp. 491–501.

21. Hyman, Herbert H. "The Psychology of Status," *Archives of Psychology*, No. 269 (1942).

22. James, William. *Psychology.* New York: Henry Holt and Company, 1892.

23. Kelley, Harold H. "Two Functions of Reference Groups," in Guy E. Swanson, Theodore M. Newcomb, and Eugene L. Hart-

ley (eds.), *Readings in Social Psychology*. New York: Henry Holt and Company, 1952, pp. 410–414.

24. Kuhn, Manford H. "Preliminary Analysis of Self-Attitudes by Age, Sex, and Professional Training." Unpublished monograph, 1956.

25. Kuhn, Manford H., and Thomas S. McPartland. "An Empirical Investigation of Self-Attitudes," *American Sociological Review*, Vol. 19 (February 1954), pp. 68–76.

26. Lazarsfeld, Paul F., Bernard Berelson, and Hazel Gaudet. *The People's Choice*. New York: Duell, Sloan, and Pearce, 1944.

27. Levine, Jerome M., and Gardner Murphy. "The Learning and Forgetting of Controversial Material," in Guy E. Swanson, Theodore M. Newcomb, and Eugene L. Hartley (eds.), *Readings in Social Psychology*. New York: Henry Holt and Company, 1952, pp. 402–409.

28. Linton, Ralph. *The Study of Man*. New York: Appleton-Century Co., 1936.

29. Luchins, Abraham S. "Mechanization in Problem Solving: The Effect of *Einstellung*," *Psychological Monograph*, No. 248 (1942).

30. *Manual for the Twenty Statements Problem*. Kansas City, Mo.: Greater Kansas City Mental Health Foundation, Department of Research, January 1959 (rev.).

31. McPartland, Thomas S., and John H. Cumming. "Self Conception, Social Class, and Mental Health," *Human Organization*, Vol. 17 (1958), pp. 24–29.

32. Mead, George H. *Mind, Self, and Society*, ed. by Charles W. Morris. Chicago: The University of Chicago Press, 1934.

33. Merton, Robert K., and Alice Kitt. "Contributions to the Theory of Reference-Group Behavior," in Guy E. Swanson, Theodore M. Newcomb, and Eugene L. Hartley (eds.), *Readings in Social Psychology*. New York: Henry Holt and Company, 1952, pp. 430–444.

34. Newcomb, Theodore M. *Personality and Social Change*. New York: The Dryden Press, 1943.

35. Odum, Howard W., and Harry E. Moore. *American Regionalism*. New York: Henry Holt and Company, 1938.

36. Postman, Leo J., Jerome S. Bruner, and E. McGinnies. "Personal Values as Selective Factors in Perception," *Journal of Abnormal and Social Psychology*, Vol. 43 (1948), pp. 142–154.

37. Postman, Leo J., and B. H. Schneider. "Personal Values, Visual Recognition, and Recall," *Psychological Review*, Vol. 58 (1951), pp. 271–284.
38. Rose, Arnold M. *Theory and Method in the Social Sciences.* Minneapolis: University of Minnesota Press, 1954, Chapters 1, 5–13.
39. Sherif, Muzafer. *The Psychology of Social Norms.* New York: Harper & Brothers, 1936.
40. Sherif, Muzafer. *An Outline of Social Psychology.* New York: The Dryden Press, 1950.
41. Shibutani, Tamotsu. "Reference Groups as Perspectives," *American Journal of Sociology*, Vol. 60 (May 1955), pp. 562–569.
42. Solomon, R. L., and E. H. Howes. "Word Frequency, Personal Values, and Visual Duration Thresholds," *Psychological Review*, Vol. 58 (1951), pp. 256–270.
43. Strauss, Anselm L. *Identification.* Unpublished manuscript, 1956.
44. Strauss, Anselm L. (ed.). *The Social Psychology of George Herbert Mead.* Chicago: The University of Chicago Press, 1956.
45. Sullivan, Harry S. *The Interpersonal Theory of Psychiatry.* New York: W. W. Norton & Company, Inc., 1953.
46. Thomas, William I., and Florian Znaniecki. *The Polish Peasant in Europe and America.* Chicago: The University of Chicago Press, 1918.
47. Turner, Ralph H. "Role-Taking, Role Standpoint, and Reference-Group Behavior," *American Journal of Sociology*, Vol. 61 (November 1956), pp. 316–328.
48. Vinacke, W. Edgar. *The Psychology of Thinking.* New York: McGraw-Hill Book Company, Inc., 1952.
49. Warner, W. Lloyd, Robert J. Havighurst, and Martin B. Loeb. *Who Shall Be Educated?* New York: Harper & Brothers, 1944.

Part Two

THE INDIVIDUAL AND SOCIAL ORGANIZATION

9

Society as Symbolic Interaction

HERBERT BLUMER

UNIVERSITY OF CALIFORNIA, BERKELEY

Symbolic interaction provides a point of view toward society as well as toward the individual and interpersonal relations. In fact, it ties these things together in such a way that sociology cannot be divorced from social psychology. Professor Blumer, probably the leading living exponent of the symbolic interactionist approach, interprets the manner in which this approach views organized human behavior and social change differently from the currently fashionable approaches to social organization and social structure. In so doing, he makes a number of important distinctions, including that between an "object" (upon which meaning is conferred by an individual) and a "stimulus" (which has an intrinsic character identifiable apart from the individual). Professor Blumer also makes explicit some of the methodological implications of symbolic interaction theory.

A view of human society as symbolic interaction has been followed more than it has been formulated. Partial, usually fragmentary, statements of it are to be found in the writings of a number of eminent scholars, some inside the field of sociology and some outside. Among the former we may note such scholars as Charles Horton Cooley, W. I. Thomas, Robert E. Park, E. W. Burgess, Florian Znaniecki, Ellsworth Faris, and James Mickel Williams. Among those outside the discipline we may note William James, John Dewey, and George Herbert Mead. None of these scholars, in my judgment, has presented a systematic statement of the nature of human group life from the standpoint of symbolic interaction. Mead stands out among all of them in laying bare the fundamental premises of the approach, yet he did little to develop its methodological implications for sociological study. Students who seek to depict the position of symbolic interaction may easily give different pictures of it. What I have to present should be regarded as my personal version. My aim is to present the basic premises of the point of view and to develop their methodological consequences for the study of human group life.

The term "symbolic interaction" refers, of course, to the peculiar and distinctive character of interaction as it takes place between human beings. The peculiarity consists in the fact that human beings interpret or "define" each other's actions instead of merely reacting to each other's actions. Their "response" is not made directly to the actions of one another but instead is based on the meaning which they attach to such actions. Thus, human interaction is mediated by the use of symbols, by interpretation, or by ascertaining the meaning of one another's actions. This mediation is equivalent to inserting a process of interpretation between stimulus and response in the case of human behavior.

The simple recognition that human beings interpret each other's actions as the means of acting toward one another has permeated the thought and writings of many scholars of human conduct and of human group life. Yet few of them have endeavored to analyze what such interpretation implies about the nature of the human being or about the nature of human association. They are usually content with a mere recognition that "interpretation" should be caught by the student, or with a simple realization that symbols, such as cultural norms or values, must be introduced into their analyses. Only G. H. Mead, in my judgment, has sought to think through what the act of interpretation implies for an understanding of the human being, human action, and human association. The essentials of his analysis are so penetrating and profound and so important for an understanding of human group life that I wish to spell them out, even though briefly.

The key feature in Mead's analysis is that the human being has a self. This idea should not be cast aside as esoteric or glossed over as something that is obvious and hence not worthy of attention. In declaring that the human being has a self, Mead had in mind chiefly that the human being can be the object of his own actions. He can act toward himself as he might act toward others. Each of us is familiar with actions of this sort in which the human being gets angry with himself, rebuffs himself, takes pride in himself, argues with himself, tries to bolster his own courage, tells himself that he should "do this" or not "do that," sets goals for himself, makes compromises with himself, and plans what he is going to do. That the human being acts toward himself in these and countless other ways is a matter of easy empirical observation. To recognize that the human being can act toward himself is no mystical conjuration.

Mead regards this ability of the human being to act toward himself as the central mechanism with which the human being faces and deals with his world. This mechanism enables the human being to make indication to himself of things in his surroundings and thus to guide his actions by what he notes. Anything of which a human being is conscious is something which he is indicating to himself — the ticking of a clock, a knock at the door, the appearance of a friend, the remark made by a companion, a recognition that he has a task to perform, or the realization that he has a cold. Conversely, anything of which he is not conscious is, *ipso facto*, something which he is not indicating to himself. The conscious life of the human being, from the time that he awakens until he falls asleep, is a continual flow of self-indications — notations of the things with which he deals and takes into account. We are given, then, a picture of the human being as an organism which confronts its world with a mechanism for making indications to itself. This is the mechanism that is involved in interpreting the actions of others. To interpret the actions of another is to point out to oneself that the action has this or that meaning or character.

Now, according to Mead, the significance of making indications to oneself is of paramount importance. The importance lies along two lines. First, to indicate something is to extricate it from its setting, to hold it apart, to give it a meaning or, in Mead's language, to make it into an object. An object — that is to say, anything that an individual indicates to himself — is different from a stimulus; instead of having an intrinsic character which acts on the individual and which can be identified apart from the individual, its character or meaning is conferred on it by the individual. The object is a product of the individual's disposition to act instead of being an antecedent stimulus which evokes the act. Instead of the individual being surrounded by an environment of pre-existing objects which play upon him and call forth his behavior, the proper picture is that he constructs his objects on the basis of his on-going activity. In any of his countless acts — whether minor, like dressing himself, or major, like organizing himself for a professional career — the individual is designating different objects to himself, giving them meaning, judging their suitability to his action, and making decisions on the basis of the judgment. This is what is meant by interpretation or acting on the basis of symbols.

The second important implication of the fact that the human being makes indications to himself is that his action is constructed or built up instead of being a mere release. Whatever the action in which he is engaged, the human individual proceeds by pointing out to himself the divergent things which have to be taken into account in the course of his action. He has to note what he wants to do and how he is to do it; he has to point out to himself the various conditions which may be instrumental to his action and those which may obstruct his action; he has to take account of the demands, the expectations, the prohibitions, and the threats as they may arise in the situation in which he is acting. His action is built up step by step through a process of such self-indication. The human individual pieces together and guides his action by taking account of different things and interpreting their significance for his prospective action. There is no instance of conscious action of which this is not true.

The process of constructing action through making indications to oneself cannot be swallowed up in any of the conventional psychological categories. This process is distinct from and different from what is spoken of as the "ego" — just as it is different from any other conception which conceives of the self in terms of composition or organization. Self-indication is a moving communicative process in which the individual notes things, assesses them, gives them a meaning, and decides to act on the basis of the meaning. The human being stands over against the world, or against "alters," with such a process and not with a mere ego. Further, the process of self-indication cannot be subsumed under the forces, whether from the outside or inside, which are presumed to play upon the individual to produce his behavior. Environmental pressures, external stimuli, organic drives, wishes, attitudes, feelings, ideas, and their like do not cover or explain the process of self-indication. The process of self-indication stands over against them in that the individual points out to himself and interprets the appearance or expression of such things, noting a given social demand that is made on him, recognizing a command, observing that he is hungry, realizing that he wishes to buy something, aware that he has a given feeling, conscious that he dislikes eating with someone he despises, or aware that he is thinking of doing some given thing. By virtue of indicating such things to himself, he places himself over against them and is able to act back against them, accepting them, rejecting them, or transforming them in accordance with how he defines or interprets them. His behavior, accordingly, is not a result of such things as environmental pressures, stimuli, motives, attitudes, and ideas but arises instead from how he interprets and handles these things in the action which he is constructing. The process of self-indication by means of which human action is formed cannot be accounted for by factors which precede the act. The process of self-indication exists in its own right and must be accepted and studied as such. It is through this process that the human being constructs his conscious action.

Now Mead recognizes that the formation of action by the individual through a process of self-indication always takes place in a social context. Since this matter is so vital to an understanding of symbolic interaction it needs to be explained carefully.

Fundamentally, group action takes the form of a fitting together of individual lines of action. Each individual aligns his action to the action of others by ascertaining what they are doing or what they intend to do — that is, by getting the meaning of their acts. For Mead, this is done by the individual "taking the role" of others — either the role of a specific person or the role of a group (Mead's "generalized other"). In taking such roles the individual seeks to ascertain the intention or direction of the acts of others. He forms and aligns his own action on the basis of such interpretation of the acts of others. This is the fundamental way in which group action takes place in human society.

The foregoing are the essential features, as I see them, in Mead's analysis of the bases of symbolic interaction. They presuppose the following: that human society is made up of individuals who have selves (that is, make indications to themselves); that individual action is a construction and not a release, being built up by the individual through noting and interpreting features of the situations in which he acts; that group or collective action consists of the aligning of individual actions, brought about by the individuals' interpreting or taking into account each other's actions. Since my purpose is to present and not to defend the position of symbolic interaction I shall not endeavor in this essay to advance support for the three premises which I have just indicated. I wish merely to say that the three premises can be easily verified empirically. I know of no instance of human group action to which the three premises do not apply. The reader is challenged to find or think of a single instance which they do not fit.

I wish now to point out that sociological views of human society are, in general, markedly at variance with the premises which I have indicated as underlying symbolic interaction. Indeed, the predominant number of such views, especially those in vogue at the present time, do not see or treat human society as symbolic interaction. Wedded, as they tend to be, to some form of sociological determinism, they adopt images of human society, of individuals in it, and of group action which do not square with the premises of symbolic interaction. I wish to say a few words about the major lines of variance.

Sociological thought rarely recognizes or treats human societies as composed of individuals who have selves. Instead, they assume human beings to be merely organisms with some kind of organization, responding to forces which play upon them. Generally, although not exclusively, these forces are lodged in the make-up of the society, as in the case of "social system," "social structure," "culture," "status position," "social role," "custom," "institution," "collective representation," "social situation," "social norm," and "values." The assumption is that the behavior of people as members *of a society* is an expression of the play on them of these kinds of factors or forces. This, of course, is the logical position which is necessarily taken when the scholar explains their behavior or phases of their behavior in terms of one or other of such social factors. The individuals who compose a human society are treated as the media through which such factors operate, and the social action of such individuals is regarded as an expression of such factors. This approach or point of view denies, or at least ignores, that human beings have selves — that they act by making indications to themselves. Incidentally, the "self" is not brought into the picture by introducing such items as organic drives, motives, attitudes, feelings, internalized social factors, or psychological components. Such psychological factors have the same status as the social factors mentioned: they are regarded as factors which play on the individual to produce his action. They do not constitute the process of self-indication. The process of self-indication stands over against them, just as it stands over against the social factors which play on the human being. Practically all sociological conceptions of human society fail to recognize that the individuals who compose it have selves in the sense spoken of.

Correspondingly, such sociological conceptions do not regard the social actions of individuals in human society as being constructed by them through a process of interpretation. Instead, action is treated as a product of factors which play on and through individuals. The social behavior of people is not seen as built up by them through an interpretation of objects, situations, or the actions of others. If a place is given to "interpretation," the interpretation is regarded as merely an expression of other factors (such as motives) which precede the act, and accordingly disappears as a factor in its own right. Hence, the social action of people is treated as an outward flow or expression of forces playing on them rather than as acts which are built up by people through their interpretation of the situations in which they are placed.

These remarks suggest another significant line of difference between general sociological views and the position of symbolic interaction. These two sets of views differ in where they lodge social action. Under the perspective of symbolic interaction, social action is lodged in acting individuals who fit their respective lines of action to one another through a process of interpretation; group action is the collective action of such individuals. As opposed to this view, sociological conceptions generally lodge social action in the action of society or in some unit of society. Examples of this are legion. Let me cite a few. Some conceptions, in treating societies or human groups as "social systems," regard group action as an expression of a system, either in a state of balance or seeking to achieve balance. Or group action is conceived as an expression of the "functions" of a society or of a group. Or group action is regarded as the outward expression of elements lodged in society or the group, such as cultural demands, societal purposes, social values, or institutional stresses. These typical conceptions ignore or blot out a view of group life or of group action as consisting of the collective or concerted actions of individuals seeking to meet their life situations. If recognized at all, the efforts of people to develop collective acts to meet their situations are subsumed under the play of underlying or transcending forces which are lodged in society or its parts. The individuals composing the society or the group become "carriers," or media for the expression of such forces; and the interpretative behavior by means of which people form their actions is merely a coerced link in the play of such forces.

The indication of the foregoing lines of variance should help to put the position of symbolic interaction in better perspective. In the remaining discussion I wish to sketch somewhat more fully how human society appears in terms of symbolic interaction and to point out some methodological implications.

Human society is to be seen as consisting of acting people, and the life of the society is to be seen as consisting of their actions.

The acting units may be separate individuals, collectivities whose members are acting together on a common quest, or organizations acting on behalf of a constituency. Respective examples are individual purchasers in a market, a play group or missionary band, and a business corporation or a national professional association. There is no empirically observable activity in a human society that does not spring from some acting unit. This banal statement needs to be stressed in light of the common practice of sociologists of reducing human society to social units that do not act — for example, social classes in modern society. Obviously, there are ways of viewing human society other than in terms of the acting units that compose it. I merely wish to point out that in respect to concrete or empirical activity human society must necessarily be seen in terms of the acting units that form it. I would add that any scheme of human society claiming to be a realistic analysis has to respect and be congruent with the empirical recognition that a human society consists of acting units.

Corresponding respect must be shown to the conditions under which such units act. One primary condition is that action takes place in and with regard to a situation. Whatever be the acting unit — an individual, a family, a school, a church, a business firm, a labor union, a legislature, and so on — any particular action is formed in the light of the situation in which it takes place. This leads to the recognition of a second major condition, namely, that the action is formed or constructed by interpreting the situation. The acting unit necessarily has to identify the things which it has to take into account — tasks, opportunities, obstacles, means, demands, discomforts, dangers, and the like; it has to assess them in some fashion and it has to make decisions on the basis of the assessment. Such interpretative behavior may take place in the individual guiding his own action, in a collectivity of individuals acting in concert, or in "agents" acting on behalf of a group or organization. Group life consists of acting units developing acts to meet the situations in which they are placed.

Usually, most of the situations encountered by people in a given society are defined or "structured" by them in the same way. Through previous interaction they develop and acquire common understandings or definitions of how to act in this or that situation. These common definitions enable people to act alike. The common repetitive behavior of people in such situations should not mislead the student into believing that no process of interpretation is in play; on the contrary, even though fixed, the actions of the participating people are constructed by them through a process of interpretation. Since ready-made and commonly accepted definitions are at hand, little strain is placed on people in guiding and organizing their acts. However, many other situations may not be defined in a single way by the participating people. In this event, their lines of action do not fit together readily and collective action is blocked. Interpretations have to be developed and effective accommodation of the participants to one another has to be worked out. In the case of such "undefined" situations, it is necessary to trace and study the emerging process of definition which is brought into play.

Insofar as sociologists or students of human society are concerned with the behavior of acting units, the position of symbolic interaction requires the student to catch the process of interpretation through which they construct their actions. This process is not to be caught merely by turning to conditions which are antecedent to the process. Such antecedent conditions are helpful in understanding the process insofar as they enter into it, but as mentioned previously they do not constitute the process. Nor can one catch the process merely by inferring its nature from the overt action which is its product. To catch the process, the student must take the role of the acting unit whose behavior he is studying. Since the interpretation is being made by the acting unit in terms of objects designated and appraised, meanings acquired, and decisions made, the process has to be seen from the standpoint of the acting unit. It is the recognition of this fact that makes the research work of such scholars as R. E. Park and W. I. Thomas so notable. To try to catch the interpretative process by remaining aloof as a so-called "objective" observer and refusing to take the role of the acting unit is to risk the worst kind of subjectivism — the objective observer is likely to fill in the process of interpretation with his own surmises in place of catching the process as it occurs in the experience of the acting unit which uses it.

By and large, of course, sociologists do not study human society in terms of its acting units. Instead, they are disposed to view

Society as Symbolic Interaction

human society in terms of structure or organization and to treat social action as an expression of such structure or organization. Thus, reliance is placed on such structural categories as social system, culture, norms, values, social stratification, status positions, social roles and institutional organization. These are used both to analyze human society and to account for social action within it. Other major interests of sociological scholars center around this focal theme of organization. One line of interest is to view organization in terms of the functions it is supposed to perform. Another line of interest is to study societal organization as a system seeking equilibrium; here the scholar endeavors to detect mechanisms which are indigenous to the system. Another line of interest is to identify forces which play upon organization to bring about changes in it; here the scholar endeavors, especially through comparative study, to isolate a relation between causative factors and structural results. These various lines of sociological perspective and interest, which are so strongly entrenched today, leap over the acting units of a society and bypass the interpretative process by which such acting units build up their actions.

These respective concerns with organization on one hand and with acting units on the other hand set the essential difference between conventional views of human society and the view of it implied in symbolic interaction. The latter view recognizes the presence of organization in human society and respects its importance. However, it sees and treats organization differently. The difference is along two major lines. First, from the standpoint of symbolic interaction the organization of a human society is the framework inside of which social action takes place and is not the determinant of that action. Second, such organization and changes in it are the product of the activity of acting units and not of "forces" which leave such acting units out of account. Each of these two major lines of difference should be explained briefly in order to obtain a better understanding of how human society appears in terms of symbolic interaction.

From the standpoint of symbolic interaction, social organization is a framework inside of which acting units develop their actions. Structural features, such as "culture," "social systems," "social stratification," or "social roles," set conditions for their action but do not determine their action. People — that is, acting units — do not act toward culture, social structure or the like; they act toward situations. Social organization enters into action only to the extent to which it shapes situations in which people act, and to the extent to which it supplies fixed sets of symbols which people use in interpreting their situations. These two forms of influence of social organization are important. In the case of settled and stabilized societies, such as isolated primitive tribes and peasant communities, the influence is certain to be profound. In the case of human societies, particularly modern societies, in which streams of new situations arise and old situations become unstable, the influence of organization decreases. One should bear in mind that the most important element confronting an acting unit in situations is the actions of other acting units. In modern society, with its increasing criss-crossing of lines of action, it is common for situations to arise in which the actions of participants are not previously regularized and standardized. To this extent, existing social organization does not shape the situations. Correspondingly, the symbols or tools of interpretation used by acting units in such situations may vary and shift considerably. For these reasons, social action may go beyond, or depart from, existing organization in any of its structural dimensions. The organization of a human society is not to be identified with the process of interpretation used by its acting units; even though it affects that process, it does not embrace or cover the process.

Perhaps the most outstanding consequence of viewing human society as organization is to overlook the part played by acting units in social change. The conventional procedure of sociologists is (a) to identify human society (or some part of it) in terms of an established or organized form, (b) to identify some factor or condition of change playing upon the human society or the given part of it, and (c) to identify the new form assumed by the society following upon the play of the factor of change. Such observations permit the student to couch propositions to the effect that a given factor of change playing upon a given organized form results in a given new organized form. Examples ranging from crude to refined statements are legion, such as that an economic depression increases solidarity in the families of workingmen or that industrialization replaces extended families by nuclear families. My concern here is not with the validity of such propositions but with the methodological position which they presuppose. Essentially, such propositions either ignore the role of the interpretative behavior of acting units in the given instance of change, or else regard the interpretative behavior as coerced by the factor of change. I wish to point out that any line of social change, since it involves change in human action, is necessarily mediated by interpretation on the part of the people caught up in the change — the change appears in the form of new situations in which people have to construct new forms of action. Also, in line with what has been said previously, interpretations of new situations are not predetermined by conditions antecedent to the situations but depend on what is taken into account and assessed in the actual situations in which behavior is formed. Variations in interpretation may readily occur as different acting units cut out different objects in the situation, or give different weight to the objects which they note, or piece objects together in different patterns. In formulating propositions of social change, it would be wise to recognize that any given line of such change is mediated by acting units interpreting the situations with which they are confronted.

Students of human society will have to face the question of whether their preoccupation with categories of structure and organization can be squared with the interpretative process by means of which human beings, individually and collectively, act in human society. It is the discrepancy between the two which plagues such students in their efforts to attain scientific propositions of the sort achieved in the physical and biological sciences. It is this discrepancy, further, which is chiefly responsible for their difficulty in fitting hypothetical propositions to new arrays of empirical data. Efforts are made, of course, to overcome these shortcomings by devising new structural categories, by formulating new structural hypotheses, by developing more refined techniques of research, and even by formulating new methodological schemes of a structural character. These efforts continue to ignore or to explain away the interpretative process by which people act, individually and collectively, in society. The question remains whether human society or social action can be successfully analyzed by schemes which refuse to recognize human beings as they are, namely, as persons constructing individual and collective action through an interpretation of the situations which confront them.

10

The Interview
and the Professional Relationship

 MANFORD H. KUHN

STATE UNIVERSITY OF IOWA

Interviews may be classified in many different ways in terms of their purpose, but all of them are social acts. Some are consciously intended to convey messages and change behavior, but others are intended to be neutral. Considering the many value- and emotion-laden variables which must enter into every interview situation, it is doubtful whether any interview is truly neutral in the sense that it is merely a record of what is in the respondent's mind. Professor Kuhn's analysis suggests the potentialities of symbolic interaction theory for the practicing professions in which practitioner–client interaction is the major therapeutic instrument. He focuses on the problem of the middle-class social worker's ability (or inability) to take the role of lower-class clients and suggests that without such role-taking, effective casework is unlikely. Kuhn indicates that parallel situations have been observed in other practitioner–client relationships such as that between the middle-class schoolteacher and the lower-

193

class pupil. Finally, Professor Kuhn's essay reflects the manner in which symbolic interaction theory identifies needed areas of research.

The interview, far from being a kind of snapshot or tape-recording — a simple report either of fact or of emotional response — in which the interviewer is a neutral agent who simply trips the shutter or triggers the response, is instead inevitably an interactional situation. Within this context, the conceptualizations of symbolic interaction theory are more and more frequently being applied to the interview. The Maccobys write, for example, "The essential point regarding role relationship in an interview is that the interviewer must occupy *some* role, whether he wishes to or not...." (10, p. 463)

But if the interactional and role-playing nature of the interview has been pointed out, certainly the indicated corollary conceptualization has not been carried very far. For example, the unit for observation and analysis of interaction is the *social act* (4, p. 379; 16, pp. 123–126). If the interview is to be seen as interaction, then the interview should be examined in terms of the theoretical model of the social act. A considerable part of this paper is an attempt to apply certain salient aspects of this model to the interview.

THE SOCIAL ACT

The social act may be said to have three distinct parts: a beginning, a middle and an end (3). The beginning lies in self-indications, covert manipulation of symbols which in cross-section we call attitudes, or which longitudinally we call thinking; it is important to note that the beginning of a social act is not triggered, as the learning theorists say it is, by perceptions, but instead by giving one*self* cues to look for percepts. Nor is the beginning of the act seen as resulting from some state of drive; instead it is ordinarily *scheduled* (expected) from institutional agenda.

The middle part of the act is, of course, devoted to some kind of action but not necessarily gross physical or bodily movement. Instead, the universal kind of action involved in the social act is *talk* — conversation, communication, exchange, interchange. Conjoint activity which is so characteristic of the social act hinges on language. Some kind of lingual transaction is necessary if a team is to get itself organized, and most social acts involve a team. Even if a team has a continuous, running organization that antedates a particular act, it requires a set of signals, even if conventional and routine, to get organized for a particular act.

Conjoint activity is not uniform, identical action, but reciprocal action. Complementarity depends on organization, which in turn depends on self-conceived identities, communication for the ascription and mutual legitimation of roles, the rehearsal of role alternatives and the establishment of a plan of action. The middle part of the act involves all of these things plus the actual carrying out of the plan through the agreed-upon mutual role-playing.

The end of the act is commonly thought to come with the realization of the objective, and so indeed it may. But an act may end as it began — by virtue of institutional scheduling (the time for it gets all used up!) — and in any event it is by no means uncommon for an act to cease long before it is possible to assess whether it achieved its purpose or not. Perhaps it is most important to realize that the objective has played its part whether or not it has been achieved, for it is by virtue of a purpose that the act gets organized and hangs together at all.

It was in terms of its relation to the objective that Ellsworth Faris classified the act as being one of four varieties: immediate, delayed, frustrated, or retrospective (3). The immediate act has no middle and is essentially infrahuman, having no interruption during which the individual makes self-indications and thus intelligently redirects his activity. The delayed act is the common kind of act among human beings, being mediated by conversation and thought. The frustrated act is self-explanatory; it has its consequence in the fourth kind, the retrospective act, which, Faris said, has for its end the consideration of another act, usually this frustrated act. Faris believes that it is in the social act, especially in the retrospective act, that self and meaning arise, for it is here that continued and varied self-appraisal takes place.

Kenneth Burke has taken a dramatistic view of the social act, indicating four other concepts collateral with act which are requisite for its analysis: scene, agent, agency, purpose (2, p. x). Erving Goffman, who carries the dramatistic perspective even further, would substitute for *act* the term *performance* or even *encounter*, and he would substitute for *agent* the *team of performers* (6). The role-conventionalized characteristics of acts he calls *routines*, which take the place of *agency* in Burke's conceptualization. Much of Goffman's writing has to do with these routines — whether the players are taken in by their own routines, whether the audience is, and so on. He also makes much of the maintenance of front and of the appropriateness and supportiveness of the setting. While the dramatistic view may be too imprecise to form the basis for a rigorous social psychology, methodologically speaking, it may nonetheless provide very useful perspectives on the social act with which to analyze the participants in the social work interview, what they expect, what they are trying to do, and how they are trying to do it.

To sum up the relevant aspects of the model of the social act — in paraphrase of a definition I have presented elsewhere (7) — a social act is the basic unit for observation of human behavior. It consists of any activity defined as unitary by one or more participants who are objects to themselves. It may be said to have three distinguishable parts: (*a*) *anticipations* in the form of advance recipes for action, entries on the agenda, programming, scheduling, etc.; (*b*) *action*, organized and directed according to role, patterns for which have been established by social norms and invoked through expectations by significant others (reference groups), accompanied by continuing indication, self-appraisal, and redirection; (*c*) *consensual termination*, usually with symbolic goal achievement, but with no necessary relevance to the satisfaction of organic needs.

THE INTERVIEW AS A SOCIAL ACT

The analysis of the interview in terms of its nature as a social act has received very little if any attention either by behavioral scientists or social workers. Perhaps this is owing to the fact that the behavioral scientists have been much more interested in the interview as an information-getting tool than as a therapeutic instrument. As a technique for acquiring information the interview is, probably, less usefully differentiated into parts. As a therapeutic instrument, or as a constructed relationship to aid in the achievement of adjustment, the interview ought to be looked at carefully in terms of differential characteristics of the three parts of the social act.

In the beginning part, there is the problem of establishing the definition of the act itself. The social worker is apt to take the professional view which defines the act not as a single interview, as the client may very well do, but as a so-called process, involving a sequence of interviews, the establishment of a relationship, and then the controlled termination of that relationship. The social work viewpoint is that the client must come to share at least a minimal part of this view of the activity if the process is to be set up and be effective, but relatively little if any systematic attention has been paid to the ways in which clients vary in their definitions of the activity at the outset.

Who Is the Social Worker?

Logically prior even to this question of initial definition of "what is going to happen" is the question of definition of the participants by themselves and by each other. Who is the social worker? Who does she think she is? With whom does she compare herself? Who does the client think she is?

A study of social workers in Detroit by Norman Polansky and associates, published in 1953, found that the median salary of the social worker in Detroit was $411 a month or about $4,900 a year (15). The social worker in this study was modally a single woman. Next most frequently represented were married women, then came married men and then single men. The average income was approximately a third as much as that of the average physician in the United States and probably not more than a fifth as much as that of the average Detroit physician. Yet more than four-fifths of the social workers in this study held advanced degrees. About two-thirds lived in housing areas designated as "top third" areas in terms of income and rental rank of dwellers. Two-thirds of these social workers came from families with fathers who were either professional or semi-professional men or else were proprietors, managers, or officials. They rated their own class position in terms of Centers' four categories in almost the identical fashion Centers' professionals did: 83 per cent considered themselves middle class as against only 36 per cent of the national cross-section so defining themselves. They rated their prestige identically with the rating given social workers by Wayne University students, *but they rated their own ability to help people* (vis-à-vis other relevant professions) *significantly higher* than did these same Wayne University students. And social workers tended to take medicine as their most salient comparative reference category.

We have, in addition, the data from the North-Hatt NORC study of occupational prestige (11). *Welfare worker* ranked 46th among 90 occupations ranked by a national cross-section of the population (and the percentage rating given it by the cross-section further indicates that "welfare worker" as an occupation was very close to the median for these 90 occupations). This category ranked just below *trained machinist* and just above *undertaker;* perhaps more significantly it ranked in the percentage ratings five percentage points below *public school teacher* and five percentage points above *bookkeeper!*

In summary, we have in the social worker one who is modally a single woman from a near-upper-middle-class background, well-educated, whose occupational prestige is not very high and who is under no illusions about it, who has an income so low that it almost falls out of the range of even semi-professional incomes but who lives in quite good quarters, who compares herself occupationally with the physician, and who tends, in comparison with outsiders, to overrate her ability to help people (placing herself second only to doctors). She considers herself middle class, and — so the Detroit study reported — conceives her clients below her in class.

Our knowledge of the ways in which *clients* conceive themselves is contained only in non-comparable form in the case records and case histories. Their conceptions of the social workers' identities, their statuses, their roles are available to us only in anecdote and humor. Here clearly is a field for investigating.

The Interview and the Professional Relationship

How the Social Worker Would Redefine Her Role

The recent work of Hollingshead and Redlich indicates that psychotherapy of the sort that is at all comparable to the relationship involved in the interview-casework process occurs almost exclusively between the psychiatrist and patients whose class position most resembles his own: those from the top two classes (8). That the social worker would like to redefine her role is indicated by the frequent allusions in communications in the profession to a preferred or ideal function which would focus on marriage and family counseling and personality therapy, extricated from the public definition of the social worker's role as having to do with "welfare" and "poverty" and other matters associated with the lower class. This is a question having in only minor degree to do with money and income.

Possibilities for "Missing" the Client

The point is frequently made regarding psychotherapy that only people from class backgrounds similar to those of the psychiatrist can comprehend the aims and objectives of psychotherapy, its language, and the significance of its constituent parts. If this is true then one wonders about the middle part of the social act in the casework process, for the social worker is there modeling much of her activity, sharing much of the frame of reference, and using a good part of the vocabulary of the *psychiatrist*, and yet she deals in this social act with a participant who tends to come from the lowest of the socio-economic strata. Do we know with any certainty what the client thinks he is doing in the interview? Is this not frankly a form of quasi-captive psychotherapy done in the name of advancing the professionalization of social work but largely in ignorance of the attitudes and definitions of one of the two participants (perhaps in many instances an unconcern — since "we know best what is good for him"). The lower-class client is said to prefer pharmaceuticals to depth therapy; is he likely to understand permissive and non-directive interviewing?

Can we really be sure we know what is good for him? Much

attention has been drawn by Havighurst and Davis, and others, to the peculiarities of the relation between middle-class teachers and lower-class pupils. Middle-class members appear to have a certain compulsiveness and rigidity about almost all their rituals for living — courtesy, hygiene, language, and the like. These are apparently aggravated in the upwardly mobile role of teacher, and they are conducive to a sharp lack of rapport with any lower-class charges she may have.

Should not similar studies be directed to the probably equally interesting inter-class relationship involved in the social work interview? Is it possible that there is compulsiveness and rigidity about the permissiveness, the restrained and tacit role of the social worker? There would certainly seem to be some of this about her drive for "professionalization" on which this role hangs. In contrast to the school teacher, however, she would appear to be somewhat downwardly mobile. Does this have a distinctive effect in the interpersonal relation in the interview which is at the same time inter-class?

There appears to be some evidence that the psychiatrist tends to have patients who are somewhat like him in general attitudes, interests, tastes, preferences, and so on, in a way that goes beyond the class selectivity previously alluded to (8). The social worker is not ordinarily in a position to exercise any significant degree of control, at least directly, over the clients assigned to her, for they are assigned to, rather than accepted by, her. Yet this phenomenon, which is in the general realm of interpersonal attractions and avoidances, must play some kind of significant part in the social work interview. One does not have to be a devotee of extra-sensory perception to believe that affinity and avoidance can be and usually are subliminally communicated and that they have an effect on the nature, direction, and success of the social act. There is a considerable and growing literature on "interviewer effect" (9, pp. 177, 183–184, 193–195; 10), which in general deals with the effects of certain gross social categories to which the interviewer may belong on the responses of the subject or client, but I am unaware of any studies on the subject of "client effect." Certainly if we are to begin to comprehend the interactional nature of the interview we ought to probe this area.

The Interview and the Professional Relationship

RAPPORT

This leads us to — or, more accurately, it may be said to have already taken us into the middle of — a consideration of the subject of *rapport*. Rapport is probably by no means the intangible, mysterious thing it has been characterized as being. It involves, at bottom, simply the sharing of a common language, so that through shared frames of reference each person in what he has to say, or in each posture he takes, calls out in himself, incipiently, the response that these gestures, postures, and symbols call out in the other. Not only do differences in class spell differences in language, values and general perspective; so too, and often in greater degree, do differences in ethnic and national background, in age and in sex. The social worker frequently must deal with all these differences in a single client, for the lower socio-economic strata, obviously, contain disproportionate numbers of people from immigrant backgrounds, or from the Southern Appalachian highlands culture, Negroes, Puerto Ricans, and the like. Becker, Blanc, Leznoff, Vogt, von Hoffman, and Cassidy have recently called attention to special transcultural problems in interviewing (1) as has Paul (14). Benney, Riesman, and Star have shown the importance of age and sex differences in eliciting information in interviews (1, pp. 143–152). One would suppose that the therapeutic interview would present a setting in which these differences would be all the more likely to affect rapport and in greater degree, especially when these differences are compounded by other, cross-cultural and intra-class differences.

Rapport would appear to have much in common with transference. Is it not odd that we are accustomed to think of transference *bi*laterally, but to think of rapport only *uni*laterally. That is, we do not think about the rapport of the case worker with the client, except in a wholly negative way. The professional attitude, we have all heard a great many times, is one of *detachment*. To use Parsons' term, it is one of *affective neutrality*. This is only part of a somewhat paradoxical matter. The physician's attitude, after which the therapeutic social worker's role is fashioned, is not purely one of detachment, but instead, one of "concerned detachment." That is, he must of necessity be to a degree a party to the rapport. He must give support and encouragement. What, then, if his whole class and cultural orientation gives him a predisposition of revulsion, distaste, or even only mild unpleasantness in this intimate relationship of the interview? Would this not tend to preclude rapport on the part of the client — especially if he did not really know what this was all about?

The Interview as a "Performance"

Let us now consider the appropriateness and usefulness of the dramatistic model provided by Burke, Foote, and Goffman. In a situation marked, as we have seen this one to be, by certain distances in class and culture, the characterization of the relationship in the interview as one in which each puts on a "performance" for the benefit of the other seems especially appropriate. Each puts on his best "front," most calculated to impress the other; neither one will be quite "taken in by his own routine." The social worker, while trying to maintain the professional prescription of tacit self-constraint, will probe for the "dark secrets" she presumes the other to have (which tend in general to be of two kinds: derogated ways of behaving attributable to class, and detrimental emotional snarls attributable to the Freudian early-family romantic situation). If the client is at all sophisticated he will either conceal these secrets or use them to negotiate for whatever it is that he thinks he can get to his advantage out of the relationship. Each in his own way, but especially the social worker, will engage in what Goffman calls certain acts of *mystification* (6, pp. 44–46). These will involve on her part the use of certain esoteric words, the "management of the scene," and the allusion to powers outside the interview situation. The use of mystification she justifies to herself in terms of the "professional role," but actually its use is to create or maintain her authority to probe for dark secrets. She already holds two trump cards in this: her class superiority and her role of functionary in the agency. However, though her use of mystification tends to enhance her authority, it also tends to diminish rapport.

This is the predicament that the class and other cultural differences between social worker and client place the social worker in: control and rapport are both necessary, though paradoxical, requisites if the social act is to go as the social worker defines it. The interview will fall apart without control and will be meaningless without rapport. But the social distance between client and worker result in secrets on both sides, especially on the side of the client. The enhancement of control through mystification at this point on the part of the social worker will result only in the lessening of rapport, whereas rapport is the needed tool with which to disengage the secrets. The social worker's attempt to pry at this juncture into what Goffman calls the "back regions" (call it "backstage" if you like) where the client lives with those most intimate to him only increases the difficulties for rapport, even if it divulges a few secrets.

THE INTERVIEW AND IDENTITY

We may take a more positive, constructive view if we regard the social act, of which the interview is our special case, as the context in which any individual discovers himself and establishes his own identity. The interview, then, is not a situation — as it is commonly taken to be — in which a film (in the form of an interviewer) is exposed to an already established self which will then be developed (in the form of a case record) so that the image of the self can be studied and diagnosed. It is rather, at least ideally, a constructed situation in which an individual can act out, at least in conversation, the essentials of what Faris called the retrospective act, and which needs to be renamed the "conspective act" (for it has present and future reference as well as past reference; it does not stem alone from the past, frustrated acts, but also from anticipations and intentions). In this interview process the individual client is led to rehearse his past actions, the evaluations which others who matter to him put upon them, to consider alternatives, redirective actions, to imagine the responses of significant others to these, to define, assess, and reassess himself as an object with each rehearsal.

It would seem to be the prime requisite of the social worker that she present herself in this dialogue in such a way and in such a light that will most facilitate this rehearsal and this self-definition. To do this she must have achieved a certain degree of clarity in her own self-definition, and this requires much more than that she have successfully resolved her Electra complex! It involves a reasonable congruence between role ideal and role actuality. It involves her knowledge and understanding of the various cross-cultural and inter-class rhetorics involved in any client relationships she has. And it involves her understanding of the paradox of control and rapport and the aspects of the interview process for which each is distinctively requisite.

Nothing has been said thus far about the end of the social act. Relatively little is known about the nature and effects of the termination of a close relationship like the one under consideration. There have been continuing contributions to the literature from Freud's famous essay "Analysis Terminable and Interminable" (5) to the present, but there have been, to my knowledge, no empirical studies. The differences between the effects of termination of a social work interview sequence and those of termination of psychiatric psychotherapy may very well be great, for there are important respects in which the motives (which always refer to ends anticipated and thus have peculiar relevance to the end of the act) differ from each other.

An individual in trouble in either case welcomes a supportive relationship such as each is supposed to be, but there is a double demand for *anonymity* on the part of the person in trouble that is commonly less well met in the social work situation than in the psychiatric situation. One is the desire of the person in trouble to find a helper to whom he is anonymous. The other is that this helper be what I would call for want of a better term "socially impervious"; that is, that the helper be legally immune from the obligation to testify in court, and free from institutional pressures or controls which might induce or require him to reveal what has transpired. Since the social worker does not meet these requirements the client may confront the end of the relationship with ambivalences raised by the possibility of violation of confidence, or at least failure to achieve anonymity in some important respect or other.

The Interview and the Professional Relationship

SUMMARY

In this paper an attempt has been made to aid in the analysis of the therapeutic interview as conducted by social workers by applying to it some aspects of the model for the social act as constructed by social psychologists oriented to symbolic interaction theory. The simple differentiation of the act into a beginning, middle, and end, together with an analysis of the action which goes on in each part, points up the absence of certain crucial knowledge about the interview process. Self- and other-definitions by each participant, the goal definitions of each, especially in this case the client's, are important aspects of the initial part of the act, and none of these has been systematically studied. In the middle part of the act the effects of differences in class, culture, personality, and temperament were examined and again lack of needed information was pointed out. The dramatistic model was used in an attempt to widen perspective on the middle part of the act. It was pointed out that the end of the interview or interview process is perhaps the least studied aspect of all.

A model was presented for the action involved: the interview process is simply a special case of the conspective act in the course of which the individual rehearses his past and canvasses his present and future with the aim of self-indication, self-assessment, and self-definition. The professional relationship is one which maximally assists in this rehearsal and self-definition.

References

1. *American Journal of Sociology.* Special issue entitled "The Interview in Social Research," ed. by David Riesman and Mark Benney. Vol. 62 (September 1956).

2. Burke, Kenneth. *A Grammar of Motives.* Englewood Cliffs, N.J.: Prentice-Hall, Inc., 1945.

3. Faris, Ellsworth. "The Retrospective Act," *Journal of Educational Sociology,* Vol. 14 (October 1940), pp. 79–91.

4. Faris, Robert E. L. *Social Psychology.* New York: The Ronald Press Company, 1952.

5. Freud, Sigmund. "Analysis Terminable and Interminable," in Ernest Jones (ed.), *Collected Papers*, Vol. V. London: Hogarth Press, 1950, pp. 316–357.

6. Goffman, Erving. *The Presentation of Self in Everyday Life.* Edinburgh: University of Edinburgh Social Science Centre, 1956.

7. Gould, S. J., and William Kolb (eds.). *An English Language Dictionary of Social Science Concepts.* UNESCO, at press.

8. Hollingshead, August B., and F. C. Redlich. *Social Class and Mental Illness.* New York: John Wiley & Sons, 1958.

9. Kahn, R. L., and C. F. Cannell. *The Dynamics of Interviewing.* New York: John Wiley & Sons, 1957.

10. Maccoby, Eleanor E., and Nathan Maccoby. "The Interview: A Tool of Social Science," in Gardner Lindzey (ed.), *Handbook of Social Psychology*, Vol. 1. Reading, Mass.: Addison-Wesley Publishing Company, Inc., 1954, Chapter 12.

11. National Opinion Research Center. "Jobs and Occupations: A Popular Evaluation," in Reinhard Bendix and Seymour Lipset (eds.), *Class, Status and Power: A Reader in Social Stratification.* Glencoe, Ill.: The Free Press, 1953, pp. 411–426.

12. Newcomb, Theodore. *Social Psychology.* New York: The Dryden Press, 1950.

13. Newstetter, W. I. "Social Psychological Problems in Relation to Social Work Practice and Theory," in Muzafer Sherif and M. O. Wilson (eds.), *Emerging Problems in Social Psychology: The University of Oklahoma Lectures in Social Psychology Series III.* Norman, Okla.: The University Book Exchange, 1957, pp. 291–311.

14. Paul, B. D. "Interview Techniques and Field Relationships," in A. L. Kroeber (ed.), *Anthropology Today.* Chicago: The University of Chicago Press, 1953, pp. 430–451.

15. Polansky, N., W. Bowen, L. Gordon, and C. Nathan. "Social Workers in Society: Results of a Sampling Study," *Social Work Journal*, Vol. 34 (April 1953), pp. 74–80.

16. Young, Kimball. *Social Psychology*, 3d ed. New York: Appleton-Century-Crofts, Inc., 1956.

11

Dilemmas in the Doctor–Patient Relationship

ELIOT FREIDSON

NEW YORK UNIVERSITY

In the preceding chapter, Kuhn suggested that the physician–patient relationship is different, in some respects, from that of social worker and client. One such difference, according to Kuhn, was that the social worker is "assigned" a client while the physician "accepts" a patient. Physicians have long known that "the bedside manner" is an important adjunct to the physical treatment of a patient. But it is doubtful whether they have ever made a study of the various forms it may take and why it is necessary. Since the relation between doctor and patient is usually a voluntary one and positively motivated on both sides, one might assume that the relationship is also a cooperative one. But human interactions are complex. Professor Freidson examines the element of conflict in the doctor–patient relationship, thereby illuminating some of the complexities in human interactions generally.

Struggle between patient and doctor seems to have gone on

throughout recorded history.* Almost 2500 years ago, the Hippocratic corpus presented doctors' complaints about the nonprofessional criteria that people use to select their physicians (14, Vol. II, pp. 67, 281, 311), criticism of patients for insisting on "out of the way and doubtful remedies" (14, Vol. I, p. 317) or on over-conventional remedies like "barley water, wine and hydromel," (14, Vol. II, p. 67) and for disobeying the doctor's orders (14, Vol. II, pp. 201, 297). The physicians who have left us historical documents largely treat the patient as an obstacle, a problem of "management." From their point of view the patient is very troublesome, full of anxiety, doubt, and fear, insisting upon using his own scanty knowledge to evaluate the practitioner.

The patients who have left us documents often treat the physician as a potential danger to which one must respond cautiously and whom one must always be ready to evade. Patients have circulated stories about the occasions on which they successfully cured themselves, or continued to live for a long time in defiance of medical prognoses. This sort of literature may be represented by the Roman "epigram about a doctor Marcus who touched a statue of Zeus, and although Zeus was made of stone he nevertheless died" (22, p. 87), and by Benvenuto Cellini's mild little story:

> I put myself once more under doctor's orders, and attended to their directions, but grew always worse. When fever fell upon me, I resolved on having recourse again to the wood: but the doctors forbade it, saying that if I took it with the fever on me, I should not have a week to live. However, I made my mind up to disobey their orders, observed the same diet as I had formerly adopted, and after drinking the decoction four days, was wholly rid of fever. . . . After fifty days my health was reestablished (2, p. 128).

The struggle between physician and patient has continued into modern times. The cases recorded in Paul's volume (20), in the work of Saunders (24), Clark (3), and Koos (16), and in my own

* Reprinted, with some revision, from *Patients' Views of Medical Practice* (New York: Russell Sage Foundation, 1961), by permission of the author and publisher. Copyright 1961 by the Russell Sage Foundation.

study (8) have indicated that on important occasions patients do not necessarily do what they are told by physicians. They persist in diagnosing and dosing themselves and in assigning heavy weight to lay advice and their own personal dispositions. It is difficult to get them to cooperate wholly with health programs which, professionals believe, are for their own good (e.g., 4).

That the problem continues today is somewhat paradoxical, for it seems unquestionable that the medical practitioner has reached an all-time peak of prestige and authority in the eyes of the public as a whole. The physician of today is an essentially new kind of professional whose scientific body of knowledge and occupational freedom are quite recent acquisitions. His knowledge is far more precise and effective than it has ever been in the past, since for the first time in history it could be said that from " 'about the year 1910 or 1912 . . . [in the United States] a random patient with a random disease consulting a doctor chosen at random stood better than a 50–50 chance of benefitting from the encounter.' " (10, p. 13) The physician has obtained unrivaled power to control his own practice and the affairs that impinge upon it and the patient now has severely limited access to drugs for self-treatment and to non-medical practitioners for alternative treatment. But the ancient problem continues.

THE CLASH OF PERSPECTIVES

It is my thesis that the separate worlds of experience and reference of the layman and the professional worker are always in potential conflict with each other (cf. 1, 18). This seems to be inherent in the very situation of professional practice. The practitioner, looking from his professional vantage point, preserves his detachment by seeing the patient as a case to which he applies the general rules and categories learned during his protracted professional training. The client, being personally involved in what happens, feels obliged to try to judge and control what is happening to him. Since he does not have the same perspective as the practitioner, he must judge what is being done to him from other than a professional point of view. While both professional worker and client are theoretically in accord with the end of their relationship — solving the client's problems — the means by which this solution is to be accomplished and the definitions of the problem itself are sources of potential difference.

The very nature of professional practice seems to stimulate the patient on occasion to be especially wary and questioning. Professional knowledge is never complete, and so diagnosis, made with the greatest of care and the best of contemporary skill, may turn out to be inappropriate for any particular case. These mistakes may occur in two basic ways (cf. 13, pp. 88–101).

First of all, it is obvious that in every age, including our own, there are likely to be worthless diagnostic categories and associated treatments — sometimes merely harmless without contributing anything to cure, sometimes downright dangerous. As Shryock put it for an earlier time, "No one will ever know just what impact heroic practice [heavy bleeding and dosing with calomel] had on American vital statistics: therapy was never listed among the causes of death." (25, p. 111) In addition, in every age, including our own, there are likely to be diseases unrecognized by contemporary diagnostic categories — as typhoid and typhus were not distinguished before 1820, as gonorrhea and syphilis were once confused, and as mental diseases are no doubt being confused today. Thus, the best, most well-intentioned contemporary knowledge may on occasion be misdirected or false and some of the patient's complaints wrongly ignored.

Second, however, is a considerably more complex source of error that flows not from knowledge so much as from the enterprise of applying knowledge to everyday life. Insofar as knowledge consists in general and objective diagnostic categories by which the physician sorts the concrete signs and complaints confronting him, it follows that work assumes a routine character. This is the routine of classifying the flow of reality into a limited number of categories so that the individual items of that flow become reduced to mere instances of a class, each individual instance being considered the same as every other in its class.

The routine of practice not only makes varied elements of experience equivalent — it also makes them *ordinary*. This seems to be the case particularly in general medical practice. In general medical practice, while the range of complaints may indeed be unusually wide, the number of compaints falling within a rather narrow range seems to be overwhelming. In our day, for example, complaints that are categorized as upper respiratory infections are exceedingly common. Like malaria in the nineteenth century, they are so common that they are considered ordinary. And insofar as they are considered ordinary it is not legitimate for the patient to make a great fuss about the suffering they involve. His subjectively real pain is given little attention or sympathy because it is too ordinary to worry about. His likely response to this may be gauged by reading Dr. Raffel's account of the reception of his complaint of acute sinusitis (21, pp. 236–241).

What also happens is that more of reality than proves to be appropriate tends to be subsumed under the ordinary and commonly used categories. This agains seems to be in the very nature of professional practice — if *most* patients have upper respiratory infections when they complain of sneezing, sounds in the head, a running nose, and fatigue, then it is probable that it is an upper respiratory infection that is involved when *one* particular person makes the complaint. It may indeed be an allergy, or even approaching deafness (21, pp. 62–72) but it is not probable — that is to say, it has not commonly been the case in the past. The physician cannot do otherwise than make such assumptions, but by the statistical nature of the case he cannot do otherwise than to be sometimes wrong.

THE PATIENT'S PROBLEM

These problems of diagnosis are not only problems for the doctor but also problems for the patient. All the patient knows is what he feels and what he has heard. He feels terrible, his doctor tells him that there's nothing to worry about, and a friend tells him about someone who felt the same way and dropped dead as he was leaving the consulting room with a clean bill of health. The problem for the patient is: when are subjective sensations so reliable that one should insist on special attention, and when can one reasonably allow them to be waved away as tangential, ordinary, and unimportant; when is the doctor mistaken? The answer to these questions is never definite for any individual case, and indeed cannot be resolved decisively except by subsequent events. All of us know of events that have contradicted the judgment of the physician,[1] and of course many others that have contradicted the patient.

The situation of consultation thus proves to involve ambiguities which provide grounds for doubt by the patient. Furthermore, those ambiguities are objective. Most reasonable people will agree that the doctor is sometimes wrong, whether by virtue of overlooking the signs that convert an ordinary-appearing case into a special case or by virtue of the deficiencies of the knowledge of his time. He is less often wrong now than he was a hundred years ago, but frequency is not really the problem for the individual. Even if failure occurs once in ten thousand cases, the question for the patient is whether or not it is he who is to be that one case or not, a question that no one can answer in advance. If the evidence of his senses and the evidence of his knowledge and that of his intimate consultants are contradicted by the physician, the patient may feel it prudent to seek another physician or simply to evade the prescriptions he has already obtained.

The Role of Confidence

If it is true that the very practice of medicine, through the process of diagnosis, is permeated with objective uncertainty of which the patient may become aware, it is at least as important to understand why patients do cooperate with doctors as to un-

[1] In discussing one of the mammoth but well-intentioned and probably competent "professional" mistakes of the past, St. Theresa calls the practitioner's routine and easygoing attitude a temptation by the devil of the client: "[A spiritual director must not be] of the kind that teaches us to be like toads, content if our souls show themselves just capable of catching small lizards. . . . I believe the devil is very successful in preventing those who practice prayer from advancing further by giving them false notions of humility. He persuades us that it is pride that gives us such great aims, and that makes us wish to imitate the saints and desire martyrdom." (5, p. 89)

Most of the sensible priests who have devoted themselves to soothing underemployed women who fear for their souls have been lost to history. St. Theresa, however, has left them a monument in her ungrateful remarks about one of their harried colleagues, for they all ran the same risk of assuming that they were confronted by a hysterical lady rather than by a future saint. She, like the cancerophobic patient who actually turned out to have a sensational tumor, is the symbolic case that stiffens the backbones of those who wish to imitate the saints in spite of being told they are quite holy or healthy enough.

derstand why they do not. One reason seems to be the ignorance of the patient — he may not be aware of or be sensitive to the contingencies of practice. Another reason seems to be the kind of situation with which the patient is confronted — whether it is a crisis situation that motivates him to be sensitive to uncertainties, or a routine situation that blunts his sensitivity and attention. There is still another possible reason, however, which, if true, is more strategic than the patient's ignorance or the variable context of consultation. I refer to the special status of the professional in society that (unlike the businessman with his motto, *caveat emptor*) supposedly entitles him to a priori trust and confidence (11, p. 78).

The usual conception of confidence seems to be shallow and parochial. It is indeed true that under ordinary circumstances one goes to a doctor assuming that the doctor knows his business and that his judgment may be trusted, but it is no less true of the ordinary use of other services. It is a mistake to assume that the title "profession" confers a kind of expert authority on the practitioner which is greatly different from the authority of any fairly esoteric craftsman. Simmel pointed out some time ago that

> our modern life is based to a much larger extent than is usually realized upon the faith in the honesty of the other. . . . We base our gravest decisions on a complex system of conceptions, most of which presuppose the confidence that we will not be betrayed (29, p. 313).

Under normal circumstances we have confidence in a mechanic's ability to grease our car properly just as we have confidence in a physician's ability to prescribe the right drug for us and a pharmacist's ability to fill the prescription accurately. In the same fashion we have confidence in a variety of other service workers — appliance repairmen, bank clerks, carpenters, fitting-room tailors, and so on. Faith in the honest application of specialized ability by a consultant seems to be connected not only with the use of those who are called professionals, but also with the use of any kind of consultant whose work is fairly esoteric. Such confidence must exist if life is to function smoothly, routinely.

However, there seems to be a generic distinction in the way

the definition of the situation of consultation varies. On the one hand, there is an unthinking and fundamentally superficial sort of confidence that is automatically attached to any routine consultation. It is manifested in uncritical cooperation with the consultant. This sort of confidence sustains the doctor–patient relationship in about the same way it sustains any consultant–client relationship. It appears to waver when the client's expectations are not fulfilled by the consultant and when the problem of consultation comes to be seen as critical (that is, non-routine) to the patient. Questions arise when the consultant does not act as he is expected to, when the diagnosis seems implausible, when the prescription seems intolerable and unnecessary, and when "cure" is slow or imperceptible. They become pressing when the problem of consultation assumes what seem to be serious proportions. Under such circumstances what is needed to sustain the relationship is at least a different quantity if not a different quality of confidence.

It may be that it is this latter sort of confidence which is in the minds of those who make a special connection between professions and client confidence. Certainly it is true that three of the old, established professions deal with some of the most anxiety-laden topics of existence — the body, the soul, and human relations and property. Plumbing, internal combustion engines, and clothing are not likely to occasion as much anxiety. In this sense doctors, clergymen, and lawyers are more likely to require for their practice a special kind of confidence than are plumbers, mechanics, and fitting-room tailors. But, we may observe, it is precisely this special sort of confidence that is problematic for professions in general and medicine in particular; it is precisely this sort of confidence that does *not* flow automatically from professional status. Routine confidence is automatic, but grants no special advantage to the professions. Confidence in crises, however, is demanded but not necessarily obtained by consultants with professional standing.

THE ROLE OF CULTURE

One of the things that breaks routine and thereby suspends routine confidence is an occasion in which the patient's expectations are not met. Instead of prescribing what seems to the patient to be a good sensible remedy like barley water, wine and hydromel, or penicillin, the physician suggests that the patient go on a dietary regimen or simply take aspirin. Obviously, on such an occasion as this, we have in essence a clash of culture or education. The patient's culture leads him to expect what the doctor's culture does not suggest.

Cultural differences between patient and doctor have received a great deal of attention. The tenor of contemporary writings suggests that much patient–doctor conflict can be eliminated by reducing the differences between the two.

Some — particularly those writing about fairly exotic patients who cannot be expected to become "educated" quickly (17) — suggest that the physician should be able to get patients in to see him and to reduce conflict during consultation by adjusting himself to the patient's expectations. If, for example, his prospective patients interpret the professional attitude of detachment and impersonality to be hostile, the doctor should be prepared to behave in a less "professional" and more sociable way (3, p. 215). On the whole, the recent movement to bring social science into American medical schools seems to share this perspective: by teaching the prospective physician more about "the patient as a person," it is presumed that when he starts to practice he will be better equipped to understand, tolerate, and adjust himself to those expectations of the patient that contradict his own.

But how far can we expect the physician to adjust himself to the patient's lay (and sometimes bizarre) expectations without ceasing to practice modern medicine? There is of course a great practical difference between automatic and rigid compliance to a set of scholastic propositions and a more flexible kind of behavior, and certainly professionals would agree that the latter is likely to produce the "better" practitioner. But flexibility must remain within limits or it becomes "irresponsible." The physician can listen closely to the patient and adjust to him only so far. If his adjustment is too great, the physician must deny the heritage of special knowledge that marks him off as a professional — in effect, he ceases to be a professional. Thus, we may say that some conflict in the physician–patient relationship may indeed be forestalled by educating physicians to be somewhat more understanding and flexible with patients, but that there is a line beyond which the physician cannot go and remain a physician. Some patients' expectations cannot be met.

It might be suggested that at the point where the physician must stop adjusting, the patient must begin. After the physician has accommodated himself to the patient as far as he can, the patient should make all further accommodation if conflict is to be forestalled without destroying medical authority. With the proper "health education" it is believed that the patient will understand and believe in enough of modern medicine to be able to approach his illness from the same perspective as the physician. Thus, *patients* are to be changed so as to conform to the expectations of the doctor.[2]

The relation of health education to the reduction of conflict is, however, by no means clear. As one way of assessing it we might contrast the consequences of two extremes. First, we may ask, what sort of conflict exists when the patient has no "health education" at all — that is to say, no culturally determined expectations of the doctor. Situations like this are often found in veterinary and pediatric medicine — at least when the parent or owner of the patient does not take a surrogate sick role. Patients in both cases lack any health education. As such, they lack any of the knowledge that would lead them, when ill, to seek a physician. Unassisted, they are likely either to seek a familiar sympathetic person or, like the lion in the fable, lie helpless somewhere waiting for the chance and professionally unqualified kindness of an Androcles. If they should happen to strike upon a treatment situation, they prove incapable of indicating by any but the crudest and largely involuntary means — like a swollen paw and roars of distress — what it is that is wrong with them. Nor can they themselves be counted upon to follow or even to submit to the treatment prescribed; indeed, it often happens that they must be physically restrained to be treated.

It is patent that there are shortcomings in working with patients with no health education at all, but are there any virtues?

2 Talcott Parsons (19) in fact seems to define the role of the patient by reference to the expectations of the physician, for what he describes is not at all typical of what empirical studies show to be the expectations of patients and their lay consultants.

One is that while the patient may be incapable of illuminating his complaint by reason of his lack of education, he is also incapable of obscuring it by irrelevancies and misinformation, or compounding it by imaginative anticipation. Another is that he has no expectations about treatment, so that once the consultant establishes control there is no contradiction of his authority. Another is that simply by reason of the fact that the patient cannot cooperate it is permissible to use physical restraint, a very convenient device for practice that cannot be used on people who theoretically can but will not cooperate. And finally, apocryphal but worth citing nonetheless, the ignorant client, once won over, may, like Androcles' lion, show undying gratitude and devotion to his healer. If this is true, it is no mean virtue.

However, the virtues of the completely ignorant patient may seem small in the face of the shortcomings. After all, patients who are educated in health affairs will have the knowledge to allow them to recognize symptoms so as to come in to see the doctor in time, to give a useful history, and to cooperate intelligently with treatment. Surely people with the most health education will be more cooperative and will not struggle with the doctor.

It does not seem to be so simple. The physician is the one with the greatest possible health education, but there are good grounds for believing that he is not a very cooperative patient at all. The physician is reputed to be given to a great deal of self-diagnosis and treatment. This follows in part from his advanced health education, which makes him feel competent to diagnose himself "scientifically," and in part, like his susceptibility to drug addiction, from his privileged access to the medication that his self-diagnosis calls for. And when, after the long delay caused by self-diagnosis and treatment, the physician does seek the aid of another, he is reputed to be an argumentative and uncooperative patient incapable of repressing his own opinions in favor of those of his consultant.[3] This too seems to follow from his very health education, for it gives him a "scientific" position in which to

[3] The bad reputation of the doctor as patient is not limited to the United States. From the Soviet Union, Pondoev (22, pp. 104–105) observes, "If we ask any doctor he will agree with any other that the most difficult patient is a sick doctor. No other patient interferes so much with the doctor in his work as does the ailing doctor. . . . Nothing is more difficult than to convince the sick doctor that he is mistaken in his own diagnosis."

stand and counter that of his consultant, and it gives him a clear insight into the uncertainties of practice such that he may feel strongly justified in holding to his own opinion.

This view of physicians as patients is supported only by the plausibility of what is essentially gossip. It is made substantially more credible, however, when we look at the behavior of well-educated middle-class patients. Fairly well versed in modern medicine, they can on occasion cooperate beautifully with the physician, but on occasion they are also quite active in evaluating the physician on the basis of their own knowledge and shopping around for diagnoses or prescriptions consonant with their knowledge. They are more confident and cooperative on a routine basis, perhaps, but they are also more confident of their own ability to judge the physician and dispose themselves accordingly.

Whether health education resolves or encourages conflict in the doctor–patient relationship, then, seems to depend upon the situation. Where the well-educated, acculturated patient's expectations are being met (and they are more likely to be met by a physician than are those of worse-educated patients), his cooperation can be full and intelligent by virtue of the correspondence between his conceptions and those of the doctor. But by the nature of the case, so much of diagnosis and particularly treatment being a matter of opinion even within the profession itself, the patient's expectations will on occasion be violated: here his education is more likely to encourage conflict than to resolve it, for it allows the conflict to be justified by the same authoritative norms as those of the physician himself. A worse-educated patient may be far more manageable.

The Role of Latent Status

Thus far, the only clear way by which professional authority seems able to sustain itself consistently appears to lie in an at least partial compromise of the *content* of that authority — by taking patients' expectations into account and adjusting practice to them. At the point of adjustment to the patient beyond which professional authority must be sacrificed, however, an additional non-medical element may work to control the patient without compromise. In political affairs we would call it power; in professional affairs we lack an adequate term but might call it ability to intimidate.[4] This mode of resolving conflict flows not from the expert status of the physician but from the relation of his status in the community to that of his patient.

In the consulting room the physician may be said to have the manifest status of expert consultant and the latent status (cf. 9) of his prestige in the lay community. His latent status has no necessary relationship to his technical qualification to be an expert, but obviously impinges upon his relation to his patients. Indeed, latent status seems crucial for sustaining the force of manifest or professional status, for while many occupations possess expert knowledge, few have been able to control the terms of their work. The established professions, however, have obtained both the political power requisite for controlling the socio-legal framework of practice, and the social prestige for controlling the client in consultation. Both the power of the profession and the prestige of the practitioner are quite separate from the "authority" inherent in technical expertness. They seem to be critical conditions for reducing doctor–patient conflict *without* compromising expert knowledge. However, even when professional power and technical expertness are high, the relative prestige of the practitioner varies. It is not a constant. It has varied through history; within any particular society it varies from one practitioner to another; within any particular practice it can vary from one patient to another. What are the consequences of variation in relative latent status for the doctor–patient relationship?

When the physician has had a *lower* standing than his patient, "more on a footing with the servants" (6, p. 91), he is likely to have to be either complaisant or nimble or both to preserve the relationship. This necessity is clearest in instances in which social

---

[4] I find myself severely handicapped by this terminological problem. The physician has no administrative authority or power such as is attached to an office in an organization. The "authority" of his expert status is, as we have seen, problematic. But if he is, say, upper-middle-class, and his patient lower-class, he has leverage over his patient that does not rest on authority or expertness as such and that exists in spite of the fact that the patient is paying him for his service. To my knowledge there is no analytically appropriate term for this type of influence.

standing was accompanied by absolute power and in which the severest result could ensue from failure. For example:

> Astragasilde, Queen of France, on her death bed had begged her husband, Gontrano, to throw her doctor out the window immediately after her death, which was done with the greatest punctuality. . . . In the fifteenth century, John XXII burned an unsuccessful physician at Florence and, on this Pope's death, his friends flayed the surgeon who had failed to keep him alive (23, p. 365).

Under such circumstances the difficulties of practice according to strictly professional standards must be very great indeed — beyond fear of severe punishment for failure, considerable frustration could be caused by the way a patient of relatively high standing could effectively refuse to cooperate, as the difficulties of Dr. Henry Atkins, physician to Charles, Duke of Albany, indicated (15).

Even today it seems plausible to think that physicians of eminent and powerful men have a trying practice and that their behavior in the presence of superordinate patients will differ considerably from their behavior in the presence of "charity" patients in a hospital out-patient clinic (cf. 28, p. 211). Indeed, Hollingshead and Redlich observed that upper-class

> patients and their families make more demands of psychiatrists than other patients. . . . These patients and their families usually view the physician as middle class. In such relationships the psychiatrist is not in a position to exert social power; he is lucky if he is able to rely on professional techniques successfully. All too often he has to carry out complicated maneuvers vis-à-vis a critical, demanding, sometimes informed, and sometimes very uninformed "VIP." Some VIP's push the physician into the role of lackey or comforter, and some psychiatrists fall into such a role (12, p. 353).

Obviously, where the relative latent status of the physician is below that of the patient, he is not in a very good position to obtain cooperation. Overt or covert conflict seems likely to ensue.

On the other side we have a situation in which the physician has considerably higher standing than his patient. The most extreme example illustrating this is found in the case of James IV, King of Scotland, who practiced on his subjects. Here, while the physician's behavior might be qualified by his sense of paternalistic or professional responsibility, we should expect that his standing is sufficiently intimidating to the patient that, while the patient is in his hands, he will be in a position to impose the full weight of his professional knowledge. However, in response to his lack of control over his own fate, the patient seems to be inclined to adopt the defense of evasiveness. He may avoid coming in to see the physician in the first place — King James, as a matter of fact, paid his patients a fee to get them into his consulting room — or he may play dumb, listen politely while in the consulting room, and, once outside, ignore the physician's advice. Evasive techniques seem to be very common in instances where the physician is in a position to intimidate his patients. As Simmons has observed:

> The deference doctors receive as upper-status persons can easily be mistaken for voluntary respect and confidence. This error could prevent perception of substantial resentments and resistances of patients (26, p. 22).

CONCLUSION

This paper has argued that objective differences in perspective between physician and patient and uncertainties inherent in the routine application of knowledge to human affairs make for incipient conflict between patient and physician. Conflict occurs especially when the patient, on the basis of his own lay perspective, tries in some way to control what the physician does to him. It is more likely to occur when the patient defines his illness as potentially critical than when he sees it as minor and ordinary.

There seem to be three ways by which conflict may be forestalled, but each is problematic. The doctor may accommodate to the demands of the patient, but if he should do so extensively he ceases to be the doctor. The patient may be educated in health affairs so as to be more in agreement with the doctor, but education also equips him to be more self-confident and self-assertive in evaluating the doctor's work and seeking to control

it. Finally, the physician may attain such relatively high social standing as to gain an extra-professional source of leverage for controlling the patient, but the patient tends to answer by only superficial cooperation and covert evasiveness.

In the light of these dilemmas it might be asked how it is that medical practice can even persist, let alone grow as much as it has over the past fifty years. Pain and desire for its relief are the basic motives of the patient, and they are not diminished by any of the elements of contradiction in the doctor–patient relationship. The prospective patient will not stop seeking help, but the way these dilemmas are managed will figure in what he seeks help for, when he seeks help, the way in which he seeks help, whom he seeks help from, and how he will behave in consultation. How some of the dilemmas are managed, of course, also involves the physician — his willingness and ability to accommodate to the patient, and the presence of situations in which he must accommodate if he is to keep his practice. They are reflected in the way he tries to deal with the patient. Thus, the doctor–patient relationship is not a constant, as Parsons seems to imply (19), but obviously a variable. As I have tried to show elsewhere (7), systematic differences in the doctor–patient relationship such as Szasz and Hollander discuss (27) may be seen to flow from historical and situational variability in the strength and content of struggling lay and professional systems.

References

1. Becker, Howard S. "Some Contingencies of the Professional Dance Musician's Career," *Human Organization*, Vol. 12 (Spring 1953), pp. 22–26.

2. Cellini, Benvenuto. *The Autobiography of Benvenuto Cellini*, tr. by John A. Symonds. New York: Modern Library, Inc., n.d.

3. Clark, Margaret. *Health in the Mexican-American Community*. Berkeley, Calif.: University of California Press, 1959.

4. Cobb, Sidney, Stanley King, and Edith Chen. "Differences Between Respondents and Nonrespondents in a Morbidity Survey Involving Clinical Examination," *Journal of Chronic Diseases*, Vol. 6 (August 1957), pp. 95–108.

5. Cohen, J. M. (tr.). *The Life of Saint Theresa*. Baltimore, Md.: Penguin Books, Inc., 1957.

6. Eliot, George. *Middlemarch: A Study of Provincial Life*. New York: A. L. Burt Co., n.d.

7. Freidson, Eliot. "Client Control and Medical Practice," *American Journal of Sociology*, Vol. 65 (January 1960), pp. 374–382.

8. Freidson, Eliot. *Patients' Views of Medical Practice*. New York: Russell Sage Foundation, 1961.

9. Gouldner, Alvin W. "Cosmopolitans and Locals: Toward an Analysis of Latent Social Roles — I," *Administrative Science Quarterly*, Vol. 2 (December 1957), pp. 281–286.

10. Gregg, Alan. *Challenges to Contemporary Medicine*. New York: Columbia University Press, 1956.

11. Gross, Edward. *Work and Society*. New York: Thomas Y. Crowell Company, 1958.

12. Hollingshead, August B., and Frederick C. Redlich. *Social Class and Mental Illness*. New York: John Wiley & Sons, 1958.

13. Hughes, Everett C. *Men and Their Work*. Glencoe, Ill.: The Free Press, 1958.

14. Jones, W. H. S. (tr.). *Hippocrates*. London: William Heinemann, 1943.

15. Keevil, J. J. "The Illness of Charles, Duke of Albany (Charles I), from 1600 to 1612. An Historical Case of Rickets," *Journal of the History of Medicine and Allied Sciences*, Vol. 9 (October 1954), pp. 410–414.

16. Koos, Earl Lomon. *The Health of Regionville*. New York: Columbia University Press, 1954.

17. Mead, Margaret (ed.). *Cultural Patterns and Technical Change*. New York: International Documents Service (UNESCO), Columbia University Press, 1955.

18. Merton, Robert K. "The Role-Set: Problems in Sociological Theory," *British Journal of Sociology*, Vol. 8 (June 1957), pp. 106–120.

19. Parsons, Talcott. *The Social System*. Glencoe, Ill.: The Free Press, 1951.

20. Paul, Benjamin D., and Walter B. Miller (eds.). *Health, Culture and Community*. New York: Russell Sage Foundation, 1955.

21. Pinner, M., and B. F. Miller (eds.). *When Doctors Are Patients*. New York: W. W. Norton & Company, Inc., 1952.

22. Pondoev, G. S. *Notes of a Soviet Doctor.* New York: Consultants Bureau, Inc., 1959.

23. Riesman, David. *The Story of Medicine in the Middle Ages.* New York: Paul B. Hoeber, Inc., 1935.

24. Saunders, Lyle W. *Cultural Differences and Medical Care.* New York: Russell Sage Foundation, 1954.

25. Shryock, Richard H. *Medicine and Society in America.* New York: New York University Press, 1960.

26. Simmons, Ozzie G. "Social Status and Public Health," *Social Science Research Council Pamphlets,* No. 13, 1958.

27. Szasz, Thomas S., and Marc H. Hollander. "A Contribution to the Philosophy of Medicine," *A.M.A. Archives of Internal Medicine,* Vol. 97 (1956), pp. 585–592.

28. Turner, E. S. *Call the Doctor.* New York: St. Martin's Press, Inc., 1959.

29. Wolff, Kurt H. (ed. and tr.). *The Sociology of Georg Simmel.* Glencoe, Ill.: The Free Press, 1950.

12

Sociology of Occupations: The Case of the American Funeral Director

 ROBERT W. HABENSTEIN

UNIVERSITY OF MISSOURI

The sociology of occupations, in the core area of the study of social organization, has occasionally benefited from an interactionist approach, particularly under the leadership of Everett C. Hughes. In this essay, Robert W. Habenstein, a student of Professor Hughes, applies the point of view to the occupation of funeral director. A social process extends in both directions through time. Habenstein's article illustrates the manner in which a historical analysis of a process provides improved understanding of its current state. It is interesting to note the application in this essay of Max Weber's concept of the "ideal type" — or, as Howard (P.) Becker has called it, "constructive typology" — as a means of furnishing additional insight into the process of professionalization among funeral directors.

This chapter attempts to present in rather compressed form an occupational case analysis of a profession-oriented personal service occupation — funeral directing. The approach incorporates both historical and cross-sectional modes of analysis and leans rather heavily for conceptual apparatus upon E. C. Hughes's (3) work-and-self and Erving Goffman's (1) presentation-of-self formulations. Data have been gathered by the author in the course of a ten-year period of study of funeral directors and their work (2).

HISTORICAL BACKGROUND

EARLY MORTUARY BELIEFS

The basic beliefs which underpin modern deathways were set in the context of developing Christianity and represent only a partially integrated ideology defining the meaning of death and relating the dead to the living. From the early Hebrew mortuary pattern were drawn the more basic of Christian death beliefs, and these were overlaid with the teachings of Christ and the early Christian fathers. Greek and Egyptian contributions centered on the concept of unfettering the soul from the corporeal body, although to the Egyptians the soul later was reunited for eternity with the embalmed body. Generally early societies used the funeral as a mode of reaffirming social relationships, but rationalized procedures and the use of secular functionaries were brought into use predominantly by the Romans. Germanic and Scandinavian death beliefs supported Christian doctrines of a viable afterlife, but the role of flame and fire as a sacred, purifying agency, paralleling Classical Greek and Roman beliefs, conflicted with the Christian conception of the personal "calling up of the soul" by God, and the "safe escort by His angels." Until the present there has been an absence of integration in Christian beliefs concerning the precise nature of the body after death, and, for example, no consensus has ever been achieved on the practice of cremation.

Nevertheless *reverent* care of the dead as a sacred duty has been imperishably associated with Christian peoples everywhere and at all times, although the orientation to death has changed considerably in historical periods: ennobling in early Christian; grisly and materialistic in the Middle Ages; real and everyday after the Reformation and in the early colonial period in America particularly; elegiac and mournful in the nineteenth century; and, today, tragic but encapsulated by a popular aesthetic of beauty, undercut by alienation of the dead. Despite these varying orientations, the personal involvement of the bereaved in the disposal of the dead has been a firmly rooted aspect of the Christian tradition. From Christian Rome on, the crisis of death and the mobilization of emotion and action in the funeralization of the dead has more or less been subject to definition and control by established religion and its clergy. Although the Roman example of placing mortuary tasks partially within the domain of secular functionaries has a certain parallel to modern American funeral direction, the only fragment of Roman funeral tradition extending beyond the Dark Ages is found in fraternally organized burial-assurance societies of occupational groups.

TRADESMAN-UNDERTAKER

The beginnings of a commercial and industrial revolution, the breaking down of caste barriers and the rise of the bourgeoisie in the sixteenth and seventeenth centuries along with the emergence of a Protestant ethic opened the door to the secular furnisher for all classes of mourning paraphernalia previously associated with only the upper classes. This form of tradesman-undertaker appears in England in the late seventeenth century. Embalming, necessary in Egyptian religious beliefs pertaining to disposal of the dead, but incidental to Christian ideology, was in highly limited fashion reserved for the nobility and ranking clergy whose bodies, or portions thereof, were reserved for special burial or kept as religious relics. The embalming task through the eighteenth century was performed by anatomists, surgeons, and barber-surgeons, and in Europe it is still practiced in incidental fashion by physicians and surgeons.

During the eighteenth century the desire of all classes to keep the body "in state," reinforced during the great epidemics and plagues by the practice of keeping the bodies for several days to make sure that death had occurred, gave rise to an opportunity for undertakers to arrogate to themselves the embalming task, albeit in a rudimentary "sawdust and tar" fashion. These crude preservative measures were carried over to colonial America, but the secular tradesman-undertaker who combined numerous mortuary tasks into a recognized occupation did not, apparently, migrate to the New World in appreciable numbers, nor for that matter, do the records of seventeenth- and early eighteenth-century colonial history show such an occupation practiced natively by the colonists.

The Puritan emphasis in early colonial social organization had its expression in the treatment of the dead. Death was placed in the realistic context of everyday life, the dead were subject to virtually no alienation, and the funerals combined a simple, early Christian-like mode of burial with, paradoxically, rather vigorous festivities and more than a trace of grisly jollity — as evinced in the popular custom of epitaph construction. The abolition of English ecclesiastical law meant that the formal, legal controls of burial and funeral practices were haphazard and desultory, tending to be expressed in *ad hoc* sumptuary regulations. Although ecclesiastical definitions of mortuary behavior eventually sifted back into later colonial life, there has always been an indeterminacy in drawing the lines of action for the disposal of the dead. At the formal level, common law prevails, although in highly uncodified character.

As a consequence of the early indeterminacy in the who, how, and what of funeral actions, nurses, sextons, cabinetmakers, livery stable operators, and other factotums found opportunity to extend the scope of their functions to include mortuary tasks other than those which historically had been theirs (laying out the dead, coffin-making, grave-digging, hearse-providing, and the like). The spirit of enterprise, embodied in the new, evolving, expanding society gave encouragement to go beyond one's traditional work tasks and to arrogate others which might improve the status, income, and self-regard of the performer. This "open task" system has had general expression in the development of the American occupational system and is congruent with a fluid class structure. Thus the woodworker who in the earliest colonial times made a coffin upon demand found, as population and economic opportunity expanded about him, that it made economic sense to turn a part of his shop into a wareroom or coffin warehouse. The sexton, who tolled the bell and dug the grave, found that it required only a slight extension of office to increase the scope of "arrangements" and to furnish the goods and services that were increasingly involved in funerals. Again, the proprietor of hacks and coaches found that funerals, in a land where space was no object, often involved rather extended journeys and that the order of the funeral procession could be left neither to chance nor to individual discretion.

It was a short step from furnishing a hearse or coach for funeral use to furnishing other funeral paraphernalia and to assuming the function of procession *director*. On the other hand, the nurse, one of the earliest functionaries to whom one of the most sacred tasks — laying out the body — was first delegated, could find small justification for extending her function to include coffining, "funeralizing," "processionalizing," and "sacredizing" the body. The culture provided only small precedent for females in trade functions, although female undertakers were no novelty in England and her possessions. Moreover, the stretch in logic required to extend one's tasks from laying out the body to such functions as those listed above seems far greater for the nurse than for the sexton, cabinetmaker, and liveryman.

From the standpoint of theory of occupations and professions, this last point has some interesting implications. The role of the nurse has traditionally been one of mother surrogate. The affective component involved in carrying out this role is high, higher in the case where "nurse" refers to that kind of person who actually performs nursing services, broadly conceived, *inside* the context of familial relationships. This generally was the case in colonial times. It would appear that less strain would have attached to delegating the more personal or sacred aspects of care for the dead to the nurse than to any of the other categories of occupations "on the make," so to speak, for command of the undertaking functions. It may be noted in this connection that some adaptive measures were taken by the early morticians insofar as they attempted to include a woman "in attendance" with the operation of their funeral establishments.

By mid-nineteenth century we find, then, undertaking in America assuming many characteristics of a service occupation, with a set of tasks and functions organized into a pattern of behavior toward the dead that included laying out, coffining, and transporting the body to the grave. Around these central functions ancillary services, such as the furnishing of paraphernalia of mourning, clothing emblems, and remembrances were, to a greater or lesser degree, included. The role of the clergy as producer of sacred ritual and as comforter to the bereaved remained important, but only as one aspect of service rendered the living and the dead.

Thus, the first quarter of the nineteenth century became crucially important in the evolution of the modern American funeral director, for all basic undertaking functions were organized under a conventionally recognized name-category during this period. While there is some evidence to indicate that early undertaking was often defined within the context of town or municipal official functions, by 1850 this had given way in face of the emergent *undertaker as entrepreneur,* purveying a service or set of services for a charge. The practice of handing down one's trade to a son had already begun by this period, but more significant was the noticeable decline in the number of combinations of undertaking with trades and specialties, although in rural areas the combination of furniture sales and undertaking has had a functional vitality that has lasted into the present century.

From 1850 to 1960 the development of the funeral service occupation is characterized by the growth of a self-conscious, aggressive body of secular, quasi-professionally oriented, personal service performers of mortuary tasks, carrying out their activities within a context of business enterprise. Out of the total range of mortuary tasks that feature the mortuary complex in its entirety, the "undertakers" of the nineteenth century brought under their occupational aegis those of removal of the body; its preparation for burial, including embalming, restoration, dressing, and casketing; directing the drama of disposal; transporting the corpse to the grave; and with some important exceptions the general supervision of all ceremony and ritual involved in the funeral, including graveside services. Many other service items, such as notification of relatives, making cash advances, and counseling the bereaved on matters pertaining to the deceased's estate have been subsumed under the modern funeral director's role.

Although the basic rationale for mortuary tasks in America and Western society generally had been set in the matrix of early Christian and Hebrew belief, new tastes, values, and collective dispositions appeared in the nineteenth century to produce rather thoroughgoing changes in the patterns of disposal of the dead. In a period of rapid economic expansion and development, a correlative expansion of the burial culture is noticeable as Americans sought new ways to preserve, lay out, casket, and bury the dead. As the century progressed, traditional styles in coffins underwent substantial change; stone, terra cotta, glass, papier-mâché, iron, and other metals were given trial. Protection, durability, beauty, luxury, simplicity, and body preservation were among the major functions sought or claimed by these innovations in burial cases. While in the period 1800–1850 the coffin shop predominated, a new establishment, the coffin warehouse, was coming into being. In consequence, coffin-making separated out of the bundle of funeral tasks performed (usually) by the undertaker, and coffins, burial cases, and later caskets became progressively articles of manufacture. "Furnishing undertakers" appeared to supply necessary funeral paraphernalia to others in the trade and, as a result, there emerged, along with the part-time undertaking parlor-furniture store of rural areas, the small-time "crossroads" undertaker of towns and the "curbstone" undertaker of the cities. This type operated with a minimum of capital, merchandise, funeral equipment, and overhead costs. From the mid-nineteenth century until only recently, the field of funeral service has been crowded with such small, part-time undertakers, competing strenuously for a few funerals, renting most of their equipment, making use of manufacturers' display rooms, and providing the minimum of facilities for the funeral service they perform. As a social type among modern funeral directors they are still known deprecatingly as "curbstone" operators. By the turn of the century the manufacture of morticians' goods had become categorically separated from the functions of the funeral director and remains so today.

RISE OF EMBALMING

Embalming the dead for eternity has never been part of American deathways. Yet the impulse to preserve the dead long enough to permit appropriate obsequies has always been operative. The nineteenth century witnessed the attempt on the part of early coffin manufacturers to meet a variety of needs openly expressed, or latently present, in the desires of a rapidly expanding society whose members were more likely to seek the externalities of ceremony and ritual than to expend the time and attention necessarily demanded by social forms in a more static, traditionally-oriented society. Insofar as the funeralization process assumed more and more importance in the total mortuary complex, embalming and restorative practices became central to what was evolving as a distinctly American style of burial. Midway through this century, knowledge and techniques of arterial and cavity embalming diffused from medical and anatomical sources in Europe to physicians in America. After the Civil War the spread of body preservation, compared with usage in England and Europe, was startlingly rapid, especially in the Northern States and urban areas. Equally imposing was the rapidity with which undertakers armed themselves with the techniques of embalming, first in the name of sanitation, adding later the aesthetic rationale, and began to offer this additional service to their clientele. The commercial compounding of embalming fluids was lucrative, and the diffusion of technique and interest was enhanced with the appearance of "schools" and "institutes" of embalming. These were generally of one or two weeks' duration, sponsored by fluid-compounding companies, and consisted mostly of demonstrations and lectures by salesmen upon whom the trade had conferred the designation "professor" or "doctor," although few actually were trained in medicine. At the turn of the century the beginnings of formalized training in embalming were noticeable in the development of the proprietary embalming schools, which today, congruent with the professional aspirations of the field of funeral service, have been terminologically upgraded to "Schools of Mortuary Science."

AESTHETIC DRIFT

From 1900 to the present, the undertaker has changed both name and emphasis in the performance of his work functions. The cultural backdrop against which these changes can be seen reflects primarily an aesthetic drift which has placed increased stress on beauty-in-externality, a tendency to disassociate or repress the grimness and coarseness of most aspects of human affairs, and the encapsulation and isolation of human crises such as death.

Late nineteenth- and early twentieth-century America has increasingly sloughed off the moral, religious, and ethical freight of an earlier era. The popular "aesthetic of death" defined a new mode of response to death, transcending conventional and traditional definitions in the process. Nonetheless, if the modern stance toward death does not carry with it great moral and religious implications for behavior by the living, neither does it reflect a preoccupation with rationality and utilitarian values. Rather, the current aesthetic combines external beautification of things pertaining to death with a correlative rejection of the realities of a mundane world.

Moreover, there is little that may be called exemplary or cautionary in the modern definition of or response to death, or for that matter to the words said over the dead. In a nutshell, the new aesthetic of death as it has developed over the past century is expressive, non-rational, and projective in the sense that objects of and around death are suffused with a quality of beauty. To the funeral director, whether fully or dimly aware of it, this aesthetic is the imperative which shapes and gives content to his activities in the preparation of the dead and in organizing and directing the drama of human disposal.

Funeral behavior has come to be set in a context of drama whose staging calls for a variety of social forms including those embracing elementary collective phenomena. Comfort and the consideration of family feelings become something the funeral director must take into account; usually he does this by use of what Goffman has called "region management." This takes the form, among other things, of arranging special rooms and special attention for the bereaved family through the provision of a wing of the chapel where, removed from the gaze of the audience, family members may participate in the ritual of funeralization.

In addition to the special attention to the family, or the "hominess" factor, there is a social demand for exercising all ingenuity possible in creating the aesthetic atmosphere appropriate to the popular conception of a "nice" or, better, a "beautiful" funeral home. The cues afforded the funeral director in his search for appropriate artifacts are seldom abundant. He has the past record of experience, the experience of fellow funeral directors as he knows them or reads of them, and the vagaries of his own imagination.

One of the more interesting developments has been the building of a chapel in the funeral home. This phenomenon, which has picked up momentum in the past quarter century, indicates seemingly that the "hominess" requirement has become a necessity to be reckoned with, but does not constitute the dominant *raison d'être* of modern funeral establishments. The center of gravity, dramaturgically (as well as physically) speaking, has shifted from the parlor to the chapel. Moreover, the appearance of the chapel in the funeral establishment signalizes the inclusion of religious or quasi-religious functions within the funeral directors' scope of operations. The clergy come to the funeral chapel to take a necessary but not a commanding role in the funeral service. To say that the church has been removed to the funeral home by the funeral directors as a consequence of collective, rational deliberation would be a gross oversimplification. But the beauty and magnificence of the church chapel which has been added to the funeral home may be taken, on the other hand, to represent a "natural" development in the efforts of the modern funeral director to respond to — as well as capitalize upon — the developing aesthetics of death and burial in America.

The tendency for occupations to "language up" — that is, to replace old terms of the trade felt to be undesirable in connotation with new words whose images are arresting, "catchy," or of a different *métier*, so that lower-status occupations may share higher status through word-association — has been the subject of observation and comment by many students of the sociology of work. This process has been observed to be operative in funeral directing. The obvious and easily identifiable occupational terminological associations of funeral directors and embalmers include two major spheres: (1) medical practice and (2) human relations. In the area of embalming, especially, the nomenclature is highly associated with the language of medicine, medical science, and health.

Yet when one has taken from the language of funeral service

all allusions to human relations and medical science, there remains a substantial vocabulary of affect which rings the changes on the new aesthetics of death. Thus, the changing pattern of terms reveals a consistent movement toward avoidance of the harsh, the grim, and the objective. "Corpse" becomes "loved one"; "burial," "interment"; "embalming," "preparation"; "purchase," "selection"; "coffin," "casket"; "undertaker's parlor," "chapel" or "slumber room"; "selling," "counseling"; and "make-up," "restoration." Those words which fall least harshly upon the human ear have become the language of the mortician in his relations with the client.

ASSOCIATIONAL GROWTH

A final historical development is the growth and elaboration of associations. Within the decade following the Civil War, undertakers had increased greatly in number and, simultaneously, occupational self-consciousness began to appear in the form of gestures toward associational organization. Numerous problems presented themselves. Casket and coffin makers had reached that point of organized production where they constituted a manufacturing group with related interests. Embalming fluid manufacturing concerns were still in their infancy, and undertakers had not the slightest assurance that the compounds they used were effective or contained what the compounding companies claimed. New personnel with little or no experience were entering the field. Transportation of dead bodies involved railroads and especially the railway baggagemen, who handled the shipping cases while they were in transit. This latter group constantly pushed for higher standards of shipping, and undertakers found themselves in need of some organization to represent them not only to organized baggagemen but to other organizations and legal or quasi-legal bodies. Finally, there was the problem of establishing an unambiguous occupational identity.

In the late seventies local and state associational stirrings were noticeable; by 1880 Michigan had an Undertakers' Association, and within a year most of the states of the Midwest had followed. Some Eastern states came next, along with a regional (New England) association. In 1882 the first national association was organized and exists today as the major collectivity for the expression of the interests of funeral directors generally.

There were two basic motivations behind the associational activities of those in the field of funeral service: one was to protect the serious and established undertakers from excessive and harmful competition, and the other was to bring about a sense of professionalism within what had formerly been for many just a trade, or merely a sideline. The need for protection was evident to the funeral directors in Eastern and Midwestern states, where for some time it had been the case that nearly anyone who had a furniture store would have an ancillary line of caskets. It was not unusual, in fact, for coffins and cradles to be exhibited in the same area of the store! The ultimate consequence of such a proliferation of outlets was the rapid reduction of cases per undertaker.

It was standard practice of the casket manufacturers, who were multiplying rapidly, and of casket "jobbers" to encourage almost any interested person to lay in a stock of caskets and get into the undertaking business. Cloth caskets and cheap burial cases of all materials were either dumped on the funeral director or were left "on consignment" to newcomers to the occupation. Thus, the single most important trade problem of the funeral director who wanted to operate full time was protection from the kind of competition which would not only ruin his business but destroy all the good will that was in the process of being built up by full-time funeral directors generally.

The second motivation behind the organization of associations in the field of funeral service was the impulse to professionalize. The sanitation movement provided an additional area of organized attitudes to supplement the rationale of funeral directing as public service. Throughout most of the latter part of the nineteenth century one finds an expressed conviction on the part of most funeral directors who were association-oriented that theirs was the calling of the professional sanitarian.

Early leadership, in the main, was in the hands of fairly well-to-do and fairly well educated middle-class undertakers who leaned in the direction of creating a profession out of their trade. Nevertheless, business interests were not subordinated in the name of professionalism. Agreements with burial case manufacturers (later held in restraint of trade) were made at the associational level, and agreements with other collectivities such as baggagemen were negotiated. One of the more important collective gestures by the undertakers was their support of legislation establishing public health boards and creating boards of examination and licensure for their own occupation. Codes of ethics were propounded and accepted by the undertakers; unscrupulous operators were faced with collective disapproval if not control; committees on product and merchandise evaluation, education, techniques, and the like were formed in the interests of higher standards of competence and performance of task. Finally and importantly, conventional trade association procedures for the protection and enhancement of business interests were put into operation. The over-all goal embraced public respectability, upper-middle-class status, unfettered business operations featuring individualistic enterprise safe from cut-throat competition of mass-operators, and recognition of the professional character of the services performed.

STRUCTURE AND PROCESS

ECONOMIC SUBSTRUCTURE

In 1960 there were in operation about 24,000 funeral establishments, most of which have a small volume of business, nearly half with only one or two employees. Many funeral directors operate their own establishments with the help of family members or part-time workers. Approximately one-sixth are currently operated in combination with businesses such as furniture or hardware stores. There were approximately 58 deaths per funeral director in 1960 and about 70 deaths per funeral establishment. However the backbone of the funeral service operations consists of establishments handling 100–150 cases per year. About 10 per cent operate on a big-business or mass principle and stand roughly analogous in funeral service to the supermarket as over against the small, independent groceryman. The Pacific Coast region is not characterized by but certainly features the gigantic, big-business type of funeral establishment.

Analysis of the organization and distribution of funeral suppliers reveals what could scarcely be called an integrated set of expeditious actions calculated to give the ultimate in service and merchandise for the lowest cost. There is neither unification nor integration in the production and wholesaling of mortuary goods. Rather, small, medium, and large manufacturing concerns exist, often cheek-by-jowl in a paradoxical competitive relationship which serves often to increase the costs of service and merchandise. Proliferation of small productive units employing twenty-five or thirty persons has made for higher wholesale costs to the funeral director. It appears that a modicum of monopolistic practices, in this case, might redound to the public benefit.

Funeral directors cannot control appreciably the source of their supplies, nor can they affect the volume of their cases. Because entry into the field is not subject to such controls as would curtail the number of practitioners, and because funeral service has always been thought of as a fairly lucrative field, the number of persons competing for the relatively constant number of dead bodies fluctuates with the business cycle and other factors external to the field itself. The impulse to "merchandise up" becomes well-nigh irresistible in the face of the diminishing "average" number of cases that many funeral directors can expect in the normal course of competition. Thus, in light of an almost undefinable injunction or popular norm to bury the dead "decently," the funeral director has a somewhat fluid situation presented him in which his survival may well depend upon his taking a strong role in the defining of *what*, in the particular case, constitutes the "decent" funeral.

While special variables, some historical and some social, are shown to make the pattern of burial in America one of slight geographical differentiation, the overriding economic process at work is reflected in the tendency of the American funeral director to become increasingly aware of the impersonal requisites of business management, with special attention given to cost-accounting procedures. But as the process of rationalization of business procedures goes forward at the level of individual enterprise, there are few indications that a rationalization and integration of the field of funeral service as a whole are taking place. The organization of trade associations is indicative that collective measures are necessary, or felt to be necessary, but the programs of these collectivities are somewhat ambiguously oriented (1) toward keeping the field free from outside non-individual enterprise influences, (2) toward keeping the management of individual operators on a service basis, (3) toward representing the field to the public and other groups through public relations programs, and (4) in some cases, toward developing a sense of professionalism among funeral directors.

It is apparent, however, that some of the broader economic problems of funeral service operation as business enterprise have not been and may not be controlled by modes of collective organization of funeral directors: uneconomic competition, fluctuation in personnel and number of establishments, uncontrollable costs, including labor which no longer may be expected to be management-oriented, gross violations of business and professional ethics, such as untoward advertising, kickbacks, informal buying arrangements, cut-throat selling, and the failure to give value received — all in some degree represent problems to those funeral directors who seek to build and control a field of personal service in the image of the "higher professions."

NORMATIVE FRAMEWORK

No distinct and independent branch of law deals with the disposal of the dead; what mortuary law exists in America is based on common law and is relatively devoid of basic principles which might be harmonized with later precedents. Codification of existing statutes and decisions is consequently almost impossible. The underlying dimensions of burial norms are: (1) concern with the public interest; (2) concern with the rights of the departed; and (3) concern with the privileges, powers, and duties of the survivors. Public health considerations, based on sanitation necessities, are expressed in police powers of the state; under the principle of *pro bono mores* a decent burial becomes a social as well as an individual matter. Property rights in the body as a common law principle is in process of giving way, however, to an attenuated quasi property right which is surrendered or voided when its effect would have been "to deny the claims of reason and of human right and thereby permit violation of sound morals and human emotions."

Although the emphasis on health and sanitation has brought embalming and funeral direction under jurisdiction of state departments of health, and the occupation is licensed and supervised by state examining boards, the overriding normative demand for funeral directors at work is that they exercise utmost respect for the sacred object with which they deal, and that they likewise use appropriate skills of human relations in dealing with the bereaved. The discharge of such functions cannot take place within the confines of a contractual relation. Consequently a built-in insecurity exists in the occupation insofar as the funeral director can never be guaranteed security from damaging the feelings of his clients. Formal insurance may protect the pocketbook but not the reputation. At law, embalmers and funeral directors are not generally held to be professionals. The privileges given them are those which accrue to businessmen generally, although funeral expenses are given certain priorities in the settlement of estates. "Reasonable" funeral costs are expected and the courts customarily judge reasonableness on such criteria as social position, or status of the decedent, and the condition of the estate. A proper burial may legitimately consume one-third of the estate of the least well-off; in higher income brackets the amount generally allowed by courts will be proportionately less. The expression of social-class differences in burial, nevertheless, has greater legal sanction in America than, say, the provision of religious ceremony and the relating of the dead to the afterlife.

ESTABLISHMENT ORIENTATION

With respect to the social organization of funeral directing, two models of funeral "establishment orientation" have been constructed. These types are rational and analytic, but not abstracted to a highly formal level. Each consists of five elements or definitions of situation whose polar opposites make up the other type. The first type is called the "local funeral home" and as an establishment orientation is comprised of: (1) personal ("focalized") service of the funeral director to his client; (2) the reflection of community social structure in funeral service operations; (3) family-service orientation ("socially vested unit of operation"); (4) limited business goals; and (5) traditional orientation toward the personnel or "help."

The second type, denoted as the "mass-mortuary" reflects an opposite set of definitions vis-à-vis those of the local funeral home: the contact with the clientele is diffused through intermediaries and there is no one who is *the* funeral director in the establishment; community social structures are taken into account, but the operation of the mass principle demands a transcendence of community expectations and controls; the unit of operation is a socially divested "case," stripped of kinship and locality attachments; the goal of operations is unlimited business and an untrammeled growth of profit by conventional merchandising methods, including installment purchase and price advertising; and finally, to complete the configuration, a bureaucratic organization of personnel exists in which functionaries are related to the establishment by rational rather than traditional orientations.

Although these are ideal types, their appearance in concrete reality is not an impossibility. The "mass-mortuary" type is exemplified in the large-scale, corporate, big-business funeral establishment found in urban areas. The "local funeral home" inevitably has a community-neighborhood-family basis, and provides the cultural agar for the growth of professional–client relations. Such a type stands vulnerable, however, to the onslaught of massification, bureaucratization, unionization, and ecological metabolism.

WORK AND THE SELF

Outside the more formalized demands of education, training, character reference, and such economic imperatives as adequate financial resources and/or family connection with the business, there are contingencies and necessities of behavior that must be met by the funeral director by virtue of the particular nature of the work or service performed. Funeral homes run twenty-four hours a day and can never be left unattended. Clients, particularly of "local funeral homes," want the service of a funeral director whom they know personally, or who has served their families in the past. Consequently, such a funeral director feels the need to be constantly at hand; there is really no moment of his life safe from the demands of his clientele. Funeral directors are almost unanimous in stating that the work of the mortician is demanding of energy and spirit in a way which is seldom appreciated by the layman. Few people, they claim, realize the output of strength necessary for certain kinds of body handling. For example, new apartments tend toward narrower stairways and sharper turns; consequently "carrydowns" are always a problem, and many times the body will have to be brought down the back stairs. Ambulance cases require their own brand of special handling. In another area of the work there are the time-taking details, each needing special attention, yet most of which go unnoticed by the public. Funeral directors feel that the demands made on strength, energy, and spirit are never fully appreciated; this belief may be generic to the process of occupational mobility as a counterpart to the belief that the clientele is unable to assess the judgment of the practitioner.

In dealing with the bereaved, the funeral director operates in an atmosphere of tension, distress, and easily displaced hostility. Vulnerable as he is to the vicissitudes of the emotionally upset, he can never be sure that the funeral has been a success until the thank-you notes drift across his desk. Mistakes at any phase of the funeral cycle can be disastrous. Moreover, a cautionary tale pervasive in the occupational culture concerning a dropped and spilled casket during a funeral keeps the anxiety of funeral directors at a high level. Again, overpersonalizing of relations with the client may be as offensive as complete lack of sympathy. Small matters are often exaggerated in importance; nevertheless, the dramatic continuity of the funeral calls for a sustained expressive representation of appropriate gestures and symbols. For these and other reasons, funeral directors admit being "under a strain" from start to finish of any funeral. In the "local funeral home" mistakes reflect directly upon the funeral director, and their costliness must be measured in terms of self-regard as well as business repercussions. It follows that the "mass-mortuaries" seek to create a bureaucratic milieu in which the risk of mistakes can seldom be lodged in one person.

Occupational controls operate through formally constituted

state boards, through trade and quasi-professional associations, and through a rather nebulous colleagueship. Although professionally-oriented funeral directors would rather work out solutions to intra-occupational problems through joint action with their colleagues, the most effective agencies for prosecuting illegal operators, by bringing cases before state boards, are the state and local associations. Nevertheless, crucial controls requisite to professional performance of tasks are as yet lacking in the occupation.

The funeral director deals with objects which are simultaneously sacred and profane, loved and loathed. By concealment and backstage preparation he tries to remove the negative aspects of his work and present for display a non-loathesome, "restored" body. The artistry of such accomplishment is often unnoticed. This means that the first call, or removal call, important in numerous other ways, is not a part of the work of the funeral director that is represented publicly to the world with the same emphasis as the dramatic and directive functions. This fact is illustrated in the addiction to the term "funeral director" over "mortician." A funeral director today does not glorify his body-handling, and the pathological details of preparation are certainly not part of the stock of terms used in verbal intercourse with the clientele.

The embalming function seems destined, apparently, to remain "backstage," and embalmers who have hitched their occupational star to the pathological and clinical aspects of funeral service unhappily find themselves in rather low public esteem. With reference again to the "dirty work": by shifting attention from the mortuary to the dramatic, ritualizing, and directing functions, the funeral director is able to escape, partially at least, the onus of a functionary merely dealing with the dead.

One of the most effective instruments at the command of the funeral director in working in a constant atmosphere of sorrow and grief is what might be called his "language of death." Such language has both connotative and denotative dimensions. Connotatively, the language of the funeral director operates congruently with the aesthetic imperative of modern American mortuary behavior. Death and beauty are made virtually synonymous, and the cruel words are put into limbo. The corpse becomes the "loved one"; death is "eternal rest," and an aesthetically pleasing imagery envelops the realities of the situation. At such a level the funeral director can sustain himself personally; the representation of death in this manner permits him to interact with the bereaved over considerable lengths of time without the stress that comes with the exposure to the sharpness of raw grief and sorrow. The denotative part of the language of the funeral director is used propitiously when matters of action and rational decision are involved.

Finally, self-gratification among funeral directors is achieved from the aesthetic pleasure of directing a successful performance in the drama of disposal, in the expressions of gratitude received from the bereaved, by the feeling of having been of service to mankind, and through self-identification with an occupation felt to be in the process of achieving professional recognition.

CLIENT-AMBIVALENCE

An analysis of the public image of the funeral director based on case materials drawn from interviews and content investigation of popular literature reveals, in the writer's judgment, a profound ambivalence between funeral director and client — one which tinctures the interaction of the two at all points. The root of such ambivalence is social rather than psychological in the sense that the conditions for its emergence are socially discernible and the circumstances of its development and dissolution are explainable at the social level. Put simply, there is no inherent or instinctive reason why funeral directors must be regarded negatively. Yet the author's research shows an unmistakable ambivalence, less present in the relation of a specific client to *his* funeral director, but strongly in evidence in the public image of the mortician as an occupational category. The client-ambivalence explanation proposes that the current popular aesthetic of death makes for the alienation of the dead and demands at the same time the disposal of the dead within a setting of beauty. In face of the traditional Christian prescriptive for reverent, *personal* involvement in the care of the dead body, Americans delegate the task to a secular functionary — the funeral director. The clash of aesthetic impulse with traditional prescription provides the social basis of the client-ambivalence.

If the funeral director is subject to client-ambivalence because mortuary tasks which have long been normatively defined as part of the actions traditionally taken by the family, close friends, and neighbors are now delegated to him as a secular functionary, what then are the possible modes of directing the affective charge away from the negative pole of the ambivalent relationship? The aesthetic impulse to beautify the unpleasant by artifice and the alienation of the dead by the bereaved have made the funeral director an indispensable adjunct to American society. It is most highly unlikely that a radically different mode of disposal of the dead could make its appearance in the very near future. The delegation of mortuary tasks seems indubitably anchored in the American response to death. Yet the mortician interested in reducing client-ambivalence is faced with several large but poorly defined problems. Public fear of death, ignorance, and the activities of a few disreputable practitioners are blamed by funeral directors for the general antipathy toward the occupation. Consequently, they are unwilling to admit that there could be a significant, profound, culturally-based negative attitude toward them as a group, except as this feeling is defined as merely the response to a few "rotten apples in the barrel."

There is the realistic understanding by funeral directors that personal relationships with clientele, sustained in a neighborhood and community context, are important in achieving good "public relations." A "family" funeral director has a tremendously reduced amount of "delegation-distance." In caring for the dead his hands are not felt to be so impersonal, nor does the care seem merely perfunctory. A real, thoroughgoing, personal relation of funeral director to the clientele, then, suggests possibilities for the minimizing of client-ambivalence. This has been recognized to a minor degree by these funeral directors who are emphatic about the professional or personal-service aspect of their calling. Conflicting head on are the rather obvious and significant processes of elaboration, bureaucratization, and rationalization of establishment operation, and the consequent widening personal gulf between the modern funeral director and those whom he serves. Atop these problems and dilemmas is the reluctance of funeral directors and their representatives to go beyond mere verbal protestations of professionality to develop a set of standardized professional gestures: restriction of entry; setting of standards of competence and performance; inculcation of a sense of professional ideology into the new personnel; and the establishment of a sense of colleagueship among members throughout the field.

These, then, are some of the social realities that face the contemporary, mobility-conscious, American funeral directors. Realization of their goal of professional recognition is neither automatic nor inevitable. In the past seventy-five years funeral directors have emerged from a semi-pariah sub-caste of gloomy-demeanored "dealers in death" to a quasi-professional, socially respected (with some latent antipathy) occupation capable of conferring middle-class status on its members. Although no prediction will be hazarded as to the destiny of the occupation, it is the impression of the writer that funeral directors and their associations will retain the emphasis on expediency and occupational hedonism in meeting problems as they come up in the day-by-day course of events. Less likely is the possibility of their engaging in long-range programs aimed primarily toward achievement of professional status based upon an appreciation and understanding of the social organizational and social psychological factors that are involved in and characteristic of their work in caring for the dead.

References

1. Goffman, Erving. *The Presentation of Self in Everyday Life.* Garden City, N.Y.: Doubleday & Company, Inc., 1959.
2. Habenstein, Robert W. "The American Funeral Director and the Sociology of Work." Unpublished Ph.D. dissertation, University of Chicago, 1954.
3. Hughes, Everett C. *Men and Their Work.* Glencoe, Ill.: The Free Press, 1958.

13

Industrial Workers' Worlds: A Study of the "Central Life Interests" of Industrial Workers

 ROBERT DUBIN

UNIVERSITY OF OREGON

Part of the conception of the self includes what Robert Dubin calls "central life interests." In recent years, much of the research on the sociology of work has dealt with the professions or occupations "on the make" (that is, in the process of professionalization). It is not surprising, then, that considerable commitment of self to work has been discovered. However, on the basis of his study of industrial workers, Professor Dubin suggests that the kind of commitment found among professional, quasi-professional, or professionalizing groups is absent among industrial workers. To them, work is not a "central life interest" in the sense that the family and the community are. These findings should be read in the light of Tamotsu Shibutani's more theoretical discussion of reference groups.

The Individual and Social Organization

In an urban industrial society it seems more than pertinent to inquire into the world of industrial workers.* We are here concerned with defining this world in terms of the significant areas of social experience. For each area of experience our basic object is to determine whether it represents a life interest of importance to the worker. In particular, we will focus attention on work and the workplace to determine their standing as a central life interest to workers in industry.

The impact of industrialization and urbanization on human behavior is empirically noted and theoretically accounted for in the general sociological literature. Microscopic studies of industrial organizations and of "human relations" within them are producing their own observations and generalizations. The bodies of knowledge in general sociology and in industrial sociology are at variance on critical points. This study presents one part of a larger research linking general and industrial sociology. The linkage is made through an intensive study of the "central life interests" of industrial workers.

INTRODUCTION

It is a commonplace to note that work has long been considered a central life interest for adults in most societies, and certainly in the Western world. Indeed, the capitalist system itself is asserted to rest upon the moral and religious justification that the Reformation gave to work, as Weber and Tawney have pointed out (8, 9). Our research shows that for almost three out of every four industrial workers studied, work and the workplace *are not* central life interests.

This result is surely not startling to the general sociologist. He has already noted that the social world of urban man is continuously subdivided into areas of activity and interest, with each social segment lived out more or less independently of the rest. It seems highly plausible that the urban world, with its emphasis upon secondary and instrumental social relations, might indeed

* This essay is reprinted, by permission of the publisher, from *Social Problems*, Vol. 3 (January, 1956), pp. 131–142. Copyright 1956 by the Society for the Study of Social Problems. The research was conducted under a grant from the National Institute of Mental Health of the United States Public Health Service.

be one in which work has become secondary as a life interest.

The one large subject matter illuminated by industrial sociologists in the past decade has been the human relationships that surround job and task performance in the formal organizations of modern life (4, 5, 12). We are generally led to believe that informal human relationships at work are important to the individual industrial man — he finds that the informal work society presents opportunities for intimate and primary human interaction. Our research indicates that only about 10 per cent of the industrial workers perceived their important primary social relationships as taking place at work. The other 90 per cent preferred primary interactions with fellow men elsewhere than on the job!

This finding should jolt the industrial sociologist, if duplicated in subsequent studies. The result will be an important corrective to the naive assumption that complex and rational organizations of modern society, through which most of the society's business gets done, are effective or not as the human relations of their members are "good" or "bad."

In an era when loyalty is in the vocabulary of even the common man, the ways in which members become attached to and thereby loyal toward an organization are of central interest. Our research findings indicate that more than three out of five industrial workers have strong job-oriented preferences for those sectors of their experience that involve either a formal organization or technological aspects of their personal environment. This result (again perhaps surprising to the human relations expert) suggests that strong bonds of organization may be forged out of the impersonal aspects of work experience that attach the individual more or less firmly to his company or workplace.

These three problems taken together, then, are the subject of this report: (*a*) work as a central life interest; (*b*) the role and importance of primary social relations on the job; and (*c*) some sources of organizational attachment.

Theory

The theory underlying this study involves five basic points: (*a*) the axiom that social experience is inevitably segmented; (*b*) the assumption that an individual's social participation may be necessary in one or more sectors of his social experience but may not be important to him; (*c*) the logical conclusion that adequate social behavior will occur in sectors of social experience which are mandatory for social participation by the individual but not important to him; (*d*) the second conclusion that in situations of necessary but unimportant social participation the most direct and obvious features of the situation become bases for the individual's attachment to that situation; and (*e*) the third conclusion that primary social relations take place only in situations where the social experience is valued by the individual.

The axiom with which we start scarcely needs elaboration. The segmented character of experience is revealed in the round of daily activities where one kind of activity succeeds another; in the succession of days, and particularly the weekend days when leisure-time activity replaces remunerative work; in the physical separation of such significant locales as place of residence and place of work; and in the numerous autonomous organizations that serve special, and sometimes very esoteric, interests in our lives. This by no means exhausts the illustrations of ways in which social experience is divided into discrete parts, but it should serve adequately to demonstrate the reasonableness of our initial axiom.

It is equally obvious that participation in some segments or sectors of social experience may be necessary but not important to an individual. The significance of this assumption rests on the definition of important social experience. We are here concerned with a subjective state of mind. Some social experience is important because it is valued by its participants; some is important because it is necessary as a means towards an end, though slightly valued in itself. The ceremonial banquet for awarding football letters to the college team may be valued as public recognition of achievement. The meal eaten at the banquet is important, too, but only as the justification for naming the ceremony, not for its nutritive value or esthetic appeal. The kind of importance we are concerned with is illustrated by the ceremony, not the meal.

This assumption tells us that social experience is differentially valued. The form in which it is stated emphasizes the fact that participation takes place in some experiences because it is necessary and not because the activity is itself valued. We could equally well state the axiom as follows: only a portion of all social experience is important or valued by its participants. We have chosen the first formulation because it gives greater emphasis to the subject matter of this research — the fact that remunerative work may be required by the society but that this does not guarantee that it will be viewed as important or valued by workers.

Three propositions or generalized predictions follow from our two axioms. The first is that individuals will exhibit adequate social behavior in sectors of social experience in which participation is mandatory but not valued. This proposition, when converted to hypothesis form, becomes empirically testable. In its proposition form it makes a general prediction for any and all individuals. In the form of a hypothesis the prediction is limited to the particular data of the study and the actual empirical indicators used. For example, this proposition in our study becomes the following hypothesis: a significant proportion of industrial workers will rate non-job interests high in their value orientation on the Central Life Interests questionnaire. Our hypothesis as a prediction is completely consonant with the general proposition, but it is also directly related to the data of our study. The hypothesis is the bridge between the general proposition and the empirical data marshaled in testing the proposition. Any proposition can be converted to an indefinite number of hypotheses. Consequently, no confirmation of a single hypothesis can establish any proposition. The confirmed hypothesis does, however, lend support to the proposition.[1] Our research findings lend support to the three propositions set forth. We are not, of course, asserting that the propositions are thereby proven.

[1] This short methodological excursion is necessary for this paper but not adequate to do more than outline the steps through which the research proceeded. The writer is working on a monograph entitled *Theory Building in the Behavioral Sciences*, in which are set forth the details of one approach to theory building that, among other things, specifically relates axiom, law, proposition, hypothesis, and empirical indicator in a way to make theory both the beginning and the end result of empirical research.

The second proposition or general prediction is that an individual's attachment to a situation in which his social experience is not valued by him will be to the most physically and directly obvious characteristics of that situation. The pertinent hypotheses that flow from this proposition will be set forth below.

The third general prediction in proposition form is that primary human relations take place only in situations where the social experience is valued by the individual. By "primary human relations" we mean, of course, the relationships that occur in groups where the interaction is face-to-face, continuous, intimate, and shared over a wide range of subjects. The directly related hypotheses will be stated below.

RESEARCH PROCEDURE

This study was conducted in 1952–53 in three Middle-western plants employing a total of approximately 1,200 workers. The companies are located in different communities ranging in size from 35,000 to 125,000, all clearly urban units. The largest company makes industrial equipment, employing about 600 workers on two shifts in a wide and typical range of metal manufacturing and equipment assembly operations. The smallest company manufactures industrial, dress, and novelty gloves of cloth and leather with a work force of approximately 200 employees, who were represented by an A.F. of L. union. The third company produces printed and novelty advertising items and employs about 400 people.

Active cooperation was secured in each plant to carry on the total study, which included observations of work performance and work behavior, the anonymous completion of a series of separate questionnaires administered over a period of time and completed by 491 workers, and intensive recorded interviews with a sample of 120 selected employees.

We will report here the results of the Central Life Interests questionnaire only. This questionnaire was designed to determine whether the job and workplace were central life interests of workers or whether other areas of their social experience were important to them. We defined "central life interest" as the expressed preference for a given locale or situation in carrying out an activity. After a pretest, forty questions were selected for the Central Life Interests (CLI) schedule.

Each question represented an activity that had an approximately equal likelihood of occurring in connection with some aspect of the job or workplace, or at some definite point in the community outside of work. A third choice was added that represented an indifferent or neutral response to the question. An example of a typical question is the following:

I would most hate
................missing a day's work
................missing a meeting of an organization I belong to
................missing almost anything I usually do

The forty questions used dealt with the formal aspects of membership and behavior in organizations, the technological aspects of the environment, the informal group life experiences, and general everyday experiences. Each question was individually scored as a job-oriented response, as a non-job-oriented response, or as an indifferent response. The questions that applied to each of the four areas were then scored as separate groups by summing the responses to the individual questions in each group. Those workers who chose a work-related response on at least half the questions in each group and answered the remaining ones with a non-job or indifferent response, or who had at least 70 per cent of their answers made up of a combination of job-oriented and indifferent responses, were designated job-oriented workers. The remaining workers were designated non-job in their outlook because they responded with more emphasis upon non-job and indifferent choices. The indifferent response is not utilized as a separate category in this report.

By the same scoring procedure and using the same criteria a total classification was secured for each worker. This indicated whether he was job-oriented or non-job-oriented in his total pattern of responses on all forty questions.

Work as a Central Life Interest

Previous researchers have generally assumed that work must be a central life interest because so many are engaged in it. We make quite a different assumption about work. We assume that holding a job is simply evidence of adequate performance above some minimal level that justifies continued employment by the company. In short, we assume that social behavior is adequate in this sector of social experience. For us the research question becomes one of determining to what extent the job and its locale are central life interests to workers.

It will be recalled that our first proposition is that individuals will exhibit adequate social behavior in sectors of social experience in which participation is mandatory but not valued. Remunerative work is mandatory both in the general sense that most male adults (or female heads of households) are expected to work for a living and in the specific sense that each job is surrounded by many imperatives and requirements for its performance. We have thus assumed that continued employment is evidence of adequacy of social behavior and that holding a paying job is evidence of mandatory participation in the two senses mentioned.

Our hypothesis can now be stated as follows: a significant proportion of industrial workers will be classified as non-job-oriented when central life interest is measured with the CLI questionnaire.

Considering the pattern of responses to all the questions, we found that only 24 per cent of all the workers[2] studied could be labeled job-oriented in their life interests. Thus, three out of four of this group of industrial workers did not see their jobs and work places as central life interests for themselves. They found their preferred human associations and preferred areas of behavior outside of employment.

If this finding holds generally, the role and significance of work in American society has departed from its presumed historical position. Factory work may now very well be viewed by industrial workers as a means to an end — a way of acquiring income for life in the community. The factory as a

[2] $N = 491$, for this and all other percentages reported here.

locale for living out a lifetime seems clearly secondary to other areas of central life interest. The factory and factory work as sources of personal satisfaction, pride, satisfying human associations, perhaps even of pleasure in expressing what Veblen called the "instinct of workmanship," seem clearly subordinated in the American scene. The general and specific implications of this finding will be examined in the last section of this paper.

WORK AND INFORMAL SOCIAL RELATIONS

Our third general prediction of human behavior in proposition form was that primary human relations take place only in situations where social experience is valued by the individual. From the test of our first hypothesis we have strong evidence that the workplace does not provide social experience that is valued more highly than other experiences. It would follow, then, that we may expect a significant proportion of industrial workers to be non-job-oriented with respect specifically to informal group experiences when measured on the relevant portion of the CLI questionnaire. This is the hypothesis derived from the above proposition.

Informal group experiences are those relations between people that are not directly a product of an official relationship in an organization or related positions in a division of labor. Illustrative of informal social relations are those involving small talk, leisure-time behavior, friendship interactions, and affectional attachments. Questions such as the following were asked:

I would rather take my vacation with
...................my family
...................some friends from work
...................by myself
The people I would be most likely to borrow money from are
...................the people I know around town
...................anyone who would lend it to me
...................the people I know here in the plant
It hurts me more if I am disliked
...................by the people at work
...................by the people around town
...................by anyone I know

In all a total of fourteen questions were used to sample informal group experiences. A job-oriented or non-job-oriented score was secured for each worker for the informal group experience sector in accordance with the procedure set forth above.

Only 9 per cent of the industrial workers in the sample prefer the informal group life that is centered in the job. Nine out of ten of those studied clearly indicated that their preferred informal human associations and contacts were found in the community, among friends, and in the family.

The industrial sociologist has been impressive in demonstrating the informal group life of people associated together at work. But the relative significance of this kind of human experience in relation to the full round of life has never before been considered. If our findings are at all typical — and general sociological theory would predict the findings to be of this sort — then the workplace is not very congenial to the development of preferred informal human relationships.

Much action research and some company policy has implicitly or explicitly been grounded in the simple-minded assumption that improving, enriching, or facilitating the development of informal group life is both desirable as a goal (to develop "happy" workers) and necessary as a means (to improve production, decrease turnover, and so on). Now it can perhaps be suggested that, on balance, such well-intended efforts may be misdirected. The workplace is not the breeding ground of preferred informal human relationships; deliberate efforts to make it so may be relatively ineffectual. The possible exception, perhaps, is the one worker in ten who sees the job environment as his most likely source of desired informal group life.

The immediately preceding hypothesis tested its underlying proposition by asking questions directly about primary or informal social relations. We can make another test of the proposition by focusing upon the part of it that deals with valued social experience. One of the direct ways of getting at valued social experience is to ask questions that deal with activities giving pleasure, satisfaction, or general rewards which may be pursued in varying places and at varying times. For questions dealing with this area we have used the designation of "general experience." In terms of this approach to our third proposition, the hypothesis becomes: a significant proportion of industrial workers will not respond to work as a valued social experience when this is tested by the general experience section of the CLI questionnaire. Questions dealing with general experience include those concerning "the most important things I do," "the most pleasant things I do," "my ideas about getting ahead," "my worries," and "my interests." General experience was sampled in a total of nine questions on the basis of which each worker was classified as job-oriented or non-job-oriented in this area.

Only 15 per cent of the workers give job-oriented preferences. The rest — about eleven in thirteen — saw experiences of theirs that were sampled in the study as taking place somewhere away from the workplace.

It is immediately suggested that the emotional impact of work and the work environment seems to be remarkably low in terms of general life experiences. Not only is the workplace relatively unimportant as a place of preferred primary human relationships, but it cannot even evoke significant sentiments and emotions in its occupants. These two conclusions may, of course, be related. A large proportion of emotionally significant experience takes place in primary group relationships. If the informal work group is a matter of relative indifference to workers, then it is reasonable that general social experiences of emotional importance will not take place with high frequency in the workplace.

It seems fair to conclude that our hypotheses have been supported. When measured in terms of valued social experience, the workplace is preferred by only 15 per cent of the workers studied. When measured in terms of primary human relations, only 9 per cent of the workers report that the workplace provides their preferred associations. Thus, in terms of the workplace as a testing ground, we can conclude that the underlying proposition may well be valid: primary human relations take place only in situations where social experience is valued by the individual. Obviously, many more tests of this proposition must be made, but the present tests encourage its future exploration.

SOME BASES OF ORGANIZATIONAL ATTACHMENT

Max Weber has pointed out that, in formal organizations

based upon rational authority with staff units organized in bureaucracies, the staff members are loyal to the legally established, impersonal order of the organization (10). By implicit extension of this idea we can see immediately the possibilities of other sources of organizational attachment for members. In particular, we can examine the possibility that organizational attachment can be a product of the formal organization and its operations, and of the technology which surrounds work.

Our second general proposition was set forth in the following manner: an individual's attachment to a situation in which his social experience is not valued by him will be to the most physically and directly obvious characteristics of that situation. From our data we propose to test this in terms of experience in formal organizations and experience with technology.

The choice of these two kinds of experiences is based on clear grounds. Both kinds of experiences are direct and obvious. We have many daily evidences of our participation in an organization. We arrive at its building from home, enter into a specified location, do required jobs under the direction of organization supervisors, work with machines and equipment under operating conditions that are special to the work, and have our time spent and output measured and recorded as a basis for remuneration.

We know from the first portion of this study that a significantly large percentage of the industrial workers studied do not value the work situation in terms of its opportunities for informal group experiences and for general affective experiences. This suggests that the workplace provides an excellent opportunity to test our second proposition, because it generally meets the condition that it does not provide valued social experience for a large proportion of its participants. We can derive the following hypothesis from that proposition: a significant proportion of industrial workers will score job-oriented for their organizational experience when measured on the organizational section of the CLI schedule.

A sampling was made of typical relationships between members and organizations. Experience in the formal sector includes a number of different relationships between an organization, its officials, and its members. Hiring, joining, firing, disciplining, rewarding, directing, and ordering are illustrative of relationships of this sort. Some of these relationships were covered in the study and on the basis of his responses to seven questions, each worker was rated as job-oriented or non-job-oriented in the formal sector.

More than three out of five of the workers were scored as job-oriented with respect to their experiences in organizations: 61 per cent chose their companies as the most meaningful context to them when their life experiences in organizations were brought into their focus. Put another way, the most significant formal organization when judged in terms of standard and typical organizational ties and bonds is the employing one, the industrial company.

This conclusion should not be confused with the notion that these workers are saying they necessarily like their employer or the company for which they work. No such questions were included. The questions asked placed emphasis only upon choosing that situation or organizational context in which a particular behavior was best carried out, or in which the worker would most like to have it happen. Thus, he was asked to choose between getting a job promotion or "becoming a more important member in my club, church, or lodge"; between workplace or "an organization I belong to" as the locale where praise received produces greater happiness; between regretting most "missing a day's work" or "missing a meeting of an organization I belong to." These choices serve to illustrate the questions asked in order to seek information on attachment to the formal organizations in workers' lives. Like all the questions asked, those in the formal sector were designed to determine the central life interests of workers.

We may conclude, then, that the workers studied were not confusing a liking for their company or its officials with a preference for their workplace as the most important formal organization in their lives. It seems reasonably clear that a significant majority of these workers believed that the companies in which they worked provided the important or preferred opportunities for organizational experience. Further important implications of this finding will be examined below.

The second test of the general proposition underlying this section can be made through the following hypothesis: a significant proportion of industrial workers will be job-oriented for their experiences with technological aspects of their environments when measured on the technological section of the CLI questionnaire.

A sampling was made of experiences involving the relations between people and the technical aspects of their environment. The questions probing this aspect of experience gave the workers the opportunity to select the place or situation most preferred or desired for behavior directly involving relations with machines or technical operating conditions. The technical sector of experience was defined as that involving the relationships between an individual and his actual work operations. Tool, equipment, and machine maintenance; concern with job and operating techniques; overcoming operating problems; minimizing waste; accuracy of operations; quality of materials; and cleanliness and care of operations are illustrative of the kinds of relationships between an individual and technical aspects of his environment. These relations were sampled and another score on job vs. non-job orientation was secured for each worker for the technological sector of experience, based on a total of ten questions.

In the technological sector, 63 per cent of the respondents were scored as job-oriented. This is the highest proportion of job-oriented responses for any of the sectors of experience examined. It certainly seems notable that almost two out of every three of the workers studied identified their workplace as the locale of their preferred relationships with the purely technical aspects of their environment.

The meaning of this finding can, perhaps, be made clearer when we examine some of the kinds of questions asked. For the statement, "I don't mind getting dirty," the alternative responses were: "while working at home," "at anytime if I can wash up afterwards," "while working at the plant." The introductory phrase, "I most enjoy keeping," was followed by these choices of response: "my things around the house in good shape," "my hand tools and workspace on the job in good shape," "my mind off such things." Additional questions in this area included:

> Noise bothers me most
> ....when working at home
> ....when working at the plant
> ....hardly ever

Industrial Workers' Worlds

When I am doing some work
.................I am usually most accurate working at home
.................I seldom think about being accurate
.................I am usually most accurate working at the plant

It will be noted that an attempt was made to select those kinds of technical considerations that would have an equal likelihood of being relevant to the non-job and job environments. We feel certain that the high percentage of job-oriented responses is not the product of a bias in the questions asked that tended to favor the job environment.

The fact that the technological sector of experience is the most clearly job-oriented one suggests the desirability of a fresh appraisal of this dimension of social experience. In the past there has been considerable concern with the general meaninglessness of industrial work derived directly from a technology that makes work itself monotonous, repetitious, mechanical, and fragmentary. The human consequence of this has been generally assumed to be indifference, alienation, rebellion, or even personal disorganization and possibly mental disorder.

We can, however, return to one of Durkheim's important theoretical points and see another possible analytical approach to the problem of technology (2). It will be recalled that Durkheim stressed the organic solidarity that made whole the individual units, tasks, and jobs in a given division of labor. He was emphasizing, of course, the necessary unity and integration that must bind together the divided and separate tasks and functions constituting the given division of labor. Without such unity the parts cannot mesh properly with each other, with the result that the planned-for outcome (product or service) will not be forthcoming.

To Durkheim, this organic solidarity was a non-consensual one. People who were part of a given division of labor did not necessarily share with other members of it either a sense of common enterprise or a body of common values. To be sure, Durkheim clearly saw that consensus was essential to social unity, as his concept of mechanical solidarity illustrates. The connections between the two forms of social bond were a central research interest of his, but remain even to this day a set of mooted issues.

The Individual and Social Organization

It may now be possible to suggest that industrial employment is one of the important focal points in our society for experiences with technical environments. This kind of experience has meaning in a sociological sense because it signifies the interdependence of man with man even where there is no necessary common ground of values shared between them. The urban environment is heterogeneous — in values, in the backgrounds of its residents, and in their daily experiences. Diversity is one of the hallmarks of urban life. But underpinning this heterogeneity and diversity is a fundamental human interdependence that flows from the far-flung division of labor. The real experiencing of this interdependence and sensing of it comes from the daily job. On the job the urbanite learns more directly and acutely than anywhere else how dependent he is upon those about him. There may follow from this the unity of interdependent action that is such an impressive feature of industrial work. This can often be achieved even in spite of lack of consensus, as Goode and Fowler neatly demonstrated in their study of an industrial plant (3).

The characteristics of industrial work that are alleged to be disturbing to the individual (monotony, repetitiveness, mechanistic character, and overspecialization) are the very features that make obvious to its participants the nature of symbiotic or technological interdependence. In short, industrial work may be functional for the society because it sharply etches for the individual some awareness of the division of labor and its resultant interdependence.

Both of the hypotheses derived from our second proposition have been supported. This suggests that the proposition has merit. It certainly must be subjected to further test, but we now have some prospect that the tests will continue to sustain the general prediction about human behavior that it represents.

CONCLUSIONS

The industrial workers' world is one in which work and the workplace are not central life interests for a vast majority. In particular, work is not a central life interest for industrial workers when we study the informal group experiences and the general social experiences that have some affective value for them. Industrial man seems to perceive his life history as having its center outside of work for his intimate human relationships and for his feelings of enjoyment, happiness, and worth. On the other hand, for his experiences with the technological aspects of his life space and for his participation in formal organizations, he clearly recognizes the primacy of the workplace. In short, he has a well-developed sense of attachment to his work and workplace without a corresponding sense of total commitment to it.

In a more general sense this study has been designed to provide empirical tests for three propositions. We have evidence to believe that these propositions are worthy of further testing. It now seems reasonable to believe that individuals will exhibit adequate social behavior in sectors of social experience in which participation is mandatory but not valued. Where the social experience is not valued, the individual may still become attached to the situation of the experience in terms of the most physically and directly obvious features of that situation (as we examined it, the formal organization and its technology). Finally, we would predict that primary human relationships develop only in situations where the social experience is valued by the individual.

IMPLICATIONS AND SPECULATIONS

Several years ago the Corning Glass Company celebrated its centennial with a conference whose proceedings have been published under the title of *Creating an Industrial Civilization* (7). This suggests a theme for drawing implications from this study in a speculative vein. The emphasis is upon the future and the creative task that lies ahead.

Viewed from the standpoint of industrial management there are two broad and contradictory influences at work in the society. Work is no longer a central life interest for workers. These life interests have moved out into the community. Yet work was presumably once a central life interest. Much management activity in personnel and industrial relations is implicitly directed at restoring work to the status of a central life interest. Management's efforts and the main drift of social developments work at directly contrary purposes.

The second contradictory influence centers on the location of primary human relationships in the total social fabric. Some groups in management have accepted a philosophy and developed social engineering practices summed up in the phrase "human relations in industry." The major purpose of this movement is to center primary human relationships in work and make it functional for productivity. At the same time it seems evident that primary human relations are much more likely to be located at some place out in the community. The management efforts again seem to be at odds with social reality.

The first dilemma is perhaps best highlighted in the pronounced frustration that management practitioners experience with the relative failure of their efforts to engender a sense of participation in their work forces. Many have become convinced that it's all a matter of communication and semantics. If simple language is chosen, comic-book presentation is used, and "volume of impact" is raised, then employees will feel they are part of the "company team," a phrase commonly used. Other efforts have been directed at "participant management" and its latter-day descendant, "group dynamics." Here the chief goal seems to be to make a central life interest out of work by permitting some sharing by employees of decisions affecting their work routines.

None of these efforts have been crowned by remarkable success. Indeed, the group dynamics technique, which has much research background and a number of practical applications, seems singularly sterile. When the research findings indicate that the technique has not produced a material change in the output of an experimental group over an "old-fashioned" control group, the group dynamics approach is justified on the ground that it is easier on the emotional hide of those who are subjected to it.

Perhaps the issue is really not one of human manipulation after all. All the communication effort and group dynamics in the world will not alter the basic drift in our society away from a central life interest in work. Some of the older personnel techniques of supporting after-work activities, bowling leagues and bird-watching clubs, may really be more sensible. Company involvement in a constructive way in community affairs, in the non-work activities of its own employees as well as in a general sense, might be a more significant way to enhance attachment of employees to their company. Perhaps the basic problem is not one of central life interest in work after all, but one of enhancing the sense of attachment of participants to social organizations in which participation is necessary but not important to them. These are all questions that are suggestively derived from this study. They may be examined with profit.

The second dilemma has an interesting intellectual history in which theorizers and researchers, having established the concept of primary group and primary social relations (1, 6), proceeded to apply it indiscriminately to all kinds of social organizations. Whyte in his finest study (11) gave us a magnificent picture of primary relations in boys' gangs (community, not work, organizations). He has since attempted to discover the same primary group life in industry (12), with much less certainty of the results obtained. At least in this writer's opinion we have a good deal of evidence that there are non-official as well as official, or informal along with formal, relations in a business organization. But to call these "primary social relationships" may do grave injustice to a perfectly good concept.

It may very well be that those efforts of any managerial group in any kind of organization to center primary group life for a majority of employees in the workplace are misplaced. If our evidence is substantiated in other studies, the community is the locale of preferred primary social relations. To attempt to shift the locale to the workplace may be trying to reverse a social development that is not alterable in that direction.

This may not be an entirely undesirable prospect. Weber emphasized the impersonality and efficiency of modern bureaucratic organization. The efficiency can remain along with the impersonality, providing there are other points in the society where the primary social relations can be experienced.

The general conclusion of the Corning Glass Conference was that the problem of creating an industrial civilization is essentially a problem of social invention and creativity in the non-work aspects of life. Our great social inventions will probably not come in connection with work life; they will center in community life. This research certainly suggests the importance of this insight.

References

1. Cooley, Charles H. *Social Organization.* New York: Charles Scribner's Sons, 1924.

2. Durkheim, Emile. *Division of Labor in Society.* Glencoe, Ill.: The Free Press, 1947.

3. Goode, William J., and I. Fowler. "Incentive Factors in a Low Morale Plant," *American Sociological Review,* Vol. 14 (October 1949), pp. 619–624.

4. Homans, George C. *The Human Group.* New York: Harcourt, Brace and Co., 1950.

5. Roethlisberger, F. J., and W. J. Dickson. *Management and the Worker.* Cambridge, Mass.: Harvard University Press, 1934.

6. Simmel, Georg. *The Sociology of Georg Simmel,* ed. by Kurt H. Wolff. Glencoe, Ill.: The Free Press, 1950.

7. Staley, Eugene A. (ed.). *Creating an Industrial Civilization.* New York: Harper & Brothers, 1952.

8. Tawney, R. H. *Religion and the Rise of Capitalism.* New York: Harcourt, Brace and Co., 1926.

9. Weber, Max. *The Protestant Ethic and the Spirit of Capitalism.* London: George Allen and Unwin, Ltd., 1930.

10. Weber, Max. *Theory of Social and Economic Organization.* New York: Oxford University Press, 1947.

11. Whyte, William F. *Street Corner Society.* Chicago: The University of Chicago Press, 1943.

12. Whyte, William F. *Human Relations in the Restaurant Industry.* New York: McGraw-Hill Book Company, Inc., 1948.

14

Cooperative Evasions to Support Labor–Management Contracts

MELVILLE DALTON

UNIVERSITY OF CALIFORNIA, LOS ANGELES

*Although the symbolic interactionist rejects the equilibrium impli-
cations of functional theory (in effect he makes the diametrically
opposite assumption of inherent process or constant change), one
of the points of convergence between symbolic interactionism and
functionalism is illustrated in Professor Dalton's article. The interactionist seeks to discover the symbolic meaning or interpretation
which precedes the overt phase of the act, while the functionalist
focuses upon the unintended and/or unanticipated consequences
of the act. Since it is posited throughout this volume that actors
do respond symbolically — that is, in terms of definitions of the
situation — rather than to uniformly "objective" stimuli, their responses can frequently be expected to result in unintended consequences.*

*In the process of interaction, things are not always what they
seem. True goals may be camouflaged behind display goals, unconscious goals may lurk behind conscious ones; actions may be
intended — knowingly or unknowingly — to deceive. Evasions
have their place in behavior, and may even manifest themselves*

*in behavior seemingly in pursuit of the goals which are being
evaded.*

*Conflict groups, such as trade unions and management, may
thus actually be engaged in cooperation at times. This cooperation has a purpose, of course, in terms of the true goals of both
groups. Professor Dalton analyzes this phenomenon in the
present essay, which may be regarded as a complement of Professor Freidson's essay on the actual conflict manifesting itself
in the interaction between two persons presumably seeking to
cooperate.*

The great organizations of labor and management exist both to
lead and to compel their respective members toward generally
understood goals. As we all know, strikes, publicized sparring,
and reciprocal propaganda variously conceal, inhibit, and encourage progress toward these planned ends.

Many of us identify ourselves more with one group than the
other, and thus see one group as less moral, more violent, etc.
than the other. Various researchers, with a professional dis-
interest, have described the relations between union and management as struggles between power blocs, as an outgrowth of
occupational structure, a consequence of bigness and bureaucratic anatomy, type of leadership, and so on. Issues have been
approached philosophically and empirically, cosmically and mi-
croscopically, by teams and by individuals, by involved practitioners and by outside experts.

Our part in these compounds of inquiry and comment will be
limited to a sketch of (*a*) the contradictory pressures on leaders
inside each group, chiefly in the local (5, 12), (*b*) the interplay
between local activities and the guiding labor agreement drawn
up by top leaders, and (*c*) the consequences for the theoretical
organizations of union and of management. In doing this we
must bypass the inseparable and emotional issue of democracy
versus bureaucracy as opposed — or, as some say, "engaged" —
types of behavioral frameworks (3, 6, 10, 13).

Developing these three points forces us to think in terms of a
social interaction process through which the economic and
power pressures of the groups are expressed. A group may con-

sist of only two individuals. But neither an individual nor a group operates in a social vacuum. Neither is a mere set of fixed drives waiting for release in response to a stimulus. Rather each simultaneously influences and adjusts to the other through a shared awareness that allows each to assign the same meaning to their joint action. Alert to achieve goals and circumvent obstacles, the individual evades as he conforms, yields as he influences. By this means, A guides his own behavior and in effect controls the behavior of B, who orients himself and controls A by sharing the action. Leaders of groups behave similarly with their associates and with members of other groups. Each understands the other only as he is able to view himself from the other's position. Each reciprocally judges the other and *organizes* his own action in terms of what he perceives and intends. The whole process is informal. It is jointly open and covert and, as we shall see, may be quite out of keeping with the formal guides to which diverse groups are subject. Such interaction is an ongoing series of transactions and compromises.

Before looking at the play of groups on leaders, we must note functionaries as they are officially labeled at the local level. For the union, the bottom officer is normally the shop steward. In larger plants there is a committee of stewards, or a grievance committee, made up of "grievers," each of whom services one or more departments. This officer processes grievances to higher levels. At the plant level the top union officer is the president of the local. He of course coordinates the activities of the local and communicates with the national union, where authority lies and policy is made. Between the local president and the national union there are sometimes regional or conference officers who deal with certain problems.

Among the members of management, the lowest placed agent who discusses problems with the steward or griever is the first-line foreman. Above him may be a general supervisor, a department head, or the plant manager, who meets with the griever or president of the local to consider still unsettled grievances. Officers of the national union or its agencies meet with representatives of the company to discuss problems not settled in the plant.

The Individual and Social Organization

Some students consider that labor and management have the identical interest of mutual survival and welfare of the larger society. Others see this interpretation as a worthy ideal but an incomplete picture. They point to the volume of collective bargaining as obvious proof of opposed interests. There are probably both shared and conflicting interests. In general, each group is first concerned with preserving itself. However, at least in the larger and more influential firms, management also has a legal commitment to stockholders to achieve top production at least cost, and of course to control all personnel toward that end. On its side the union is committed to its personnel to win for them improved job comforts, a higher standard of living, a greater share of profits, protection of their jobs, provisions for retirement, and so on. A frequent assumption is that each group is unified, that all of its members will follow legal procedures and adhere to the written agreement. Reworded, our purpose is to show how leaders respect this picture by collaborating in complex ways to support it as they may simultaneously attack it. To do this we must follow the shifting and unlabeled alliances that form (a) to advance the interests of factions and individuals, (b) to adapt the logic of the labor agreement to personal agreement, and (c) to introduce changes without serious threat to the formal structure. Our analysis omits the atypical variables of "racketeering" in unions, collusion between union and management to exploit the public, and "white collar crime" in management.

Hiatuses between contractual assumptions and daily practice arise from several conditions. First, the agreement is unable to consider the many differences in tradition and practice among the locals. Top leaders may make every effort to incorporate the motley complaints from below. But the diversity in kind, weight, and support of issues is too great. So top levels deal chiefly with the more urgent issues that are backed by influential people. Concessions are made to certain local customs as long as they do not seriously challenge the contract.

A second factor is expediency at the bargaining table. Policy-makers are under pressure from constituents, the public, various community interests, and in many cases the Federal government. Hence top spokesmen of each group try to hammer out clauses favorable to their camp. Each group of course seeks to block or limit the too favorable phrases pushed by the other, and presses to incorporate its own. If the adversaries are both wily and verbally adroit, the finished document is nicely ordered and clearly ambiguous. The interpretive handbooks sent down by top leaders of each camp show this, as do actions in the shop. For example, the president of a local of 8,000 employees defended such manuals "because every statement's got a half-dozen meanings." Indicating the priority of local interest as well as the nominal respect for the contract is the consensus in both houses to use the contract only when they are unable to set up personal arrangements. Several factors provoke settlement outside the pact: irrelevant personal interests, rivalries too fluid for legal containment, variations in commitment to one's job, the play of the community on the firm, compulsions to win higher place in one's camp or, among union officers, to move over to management, and so forth.

Recital of departures from the contract must not obscure its importance. First, it does homage to the eye — it presents the negotiated ideal of order and shared responsibilities. As such it gives a statement of policy that becomes the focus of attention and the take-off for action — conforming or deviant — for the duration of the contract, which will be for a year or more, a long time in our changing world. Next, the document allows appraisal of current relations between signers. Planners who are "leaders" to the extent that they know the major aspects of developing unofficial trades are in a position to assess the balance of conforming and deviant behavior around the contract and thus test its merits and note weaknesses to correct in future negotiations. In this sense, the pact is a standard for organizing and dealing with the confusing reality. It limits snap judgments and forces logical justification for evasions or seemly concealment of them. If it were not compromised at times, it could not do these things or even survive between renegotiations. The pledge thus orders defined routes but adventitiously points new ways for the alert to detect and use in containing the struggle between order and freedom inherent in democracy.

The Individual and Social Organization

We can best follow the shifting interfusions of official and off-the-record bargaining at local levels by noting the relations between top union and rank and file, the pressure on local unionists and managers, and by looking at common events in the plant.

Top Union and Management

Moving from top to bottom of the hierarchies one can see the truce of legality and expediency between levels and across the verticals.

As top leaders of both union and management increasingly look and act alike, they may, under the pressures we noted, discover that they come nearer to seeing eye-to-eye with each other than they can with their respective constituents whom they may regard as obstacles to harmony. Both American (2) and English (16) union experts admit this.

Guided by their moral commitments and the upward pressure of a rank and file suspicious of collusion, the national leaders are also constrained to be like the managers in dress, manners, and poise if they are to negotiate effectively. Sharing these symbols may provoke hunger among unionists to share the managers' power and style of life. Certainly some unionists enter the ranks of management, thus weakening local union leadership (2).

The hushed disunities between the tops and bottoms of the hierarchies come out in the summer "institutes" and "workshops" on many university campuses. Here elected members of the union rank and file officially come for brief training in economics, collective bargaining, shop courses, and related subjects. Recreational, morale, and status functions are also served, especially in the games and picnicking shared by high officers and the rank and file. But in the lecture hall, officers of the national union (and invited managers) show a self-consciousness by sitting separately and in the rear. They want to observe what is being fed to the rank and file, but they do not want to be drawn into any open discussion with them.

As a lecturer at such events, the writer has been approached several times at the conclusion of a lecture (never of course twice by the same people at the same workshop) by both higher managers and national union officers (separately) and requested to conduct the lecture and discussion so that they would not be involved. I was reminded, separately, by both that their own camps contained persons competent to present the substance of my lectures, and that "the reason for getting an outsider" was for "purposes of impartiality." The separation in the lecture hall is often extended to sleeping quarters, with the rank and file staying on campus while the managers and national officials retire to hotels, apparently from choice, since facilities usually do not require the distinction.

The schisms between levels in unions have been discussed by Brooks (2), Herberg (6), Lipset (10), Wilensky (17), and others in terms of different outlooks and styles of living.

Pressures in the Local Union

We need to look at the adapted union roles from the shop level up to the president of the local. As administrators of the local, none of these officers have official *legislative* power. But their constructive facing of events too personal and fugitive for legal containment forces them, like judges, to make decisions and engage in actions which set precedents that must later be incorporated by policy-makers at higher levels. Hence, like judges, they legislate in effect.

The Shop Steward. As the man in direct contact with workers, this officer has a role vaguely comparable to management's publicized first-line foreman. He is always under pressure for favors. He must do a certain amount of research — or even internal espionage — for his higherups in the sense of getting at the source of conflicts within his camp and between it and management. He must learn who and what is involved, and interpret and police important new clauses. He must confer with his committee head to learn how to conceal necessary but illegal practices (for example, a more efficient work method — in terms of bonus pay — but one not yet legal); handle a trouble-maker among the workers, or check a hostile foreman; develop tactics for placating the few members of a job category which must be sacrificed for some majority in the shop who see the minority as temporarily expendable for winning a point with management that will be good for all in the long run, and so on. Or the steward may be pressed by an old friend — now in management — for help in concealing costly errors in production from higher managers, persuading a work crew not to force a "rotten grievance" at this time, etc. In any case the steward's official and actual functions are often far apart. To give them seeming concurrence he must work to develop an organization not contractually specified but one necessary for carrying out the contract.

Grievance Committeeman. Terminologies vary, but the griever is usually one of a larger committee. Since he typically serves in more than one area, he is subject to a greater range of pressures and consequently makes more serious compromises than the shop steward. His paper function of processing grievances — and collaborating with the committee — tells little of what he must do to get along.

More than the steward, he must justify to his rank and file the now revealed arbitrary and repercussive decisions that he or other grievers or the president have made. He must deal with the recurring attempts of ethnic majorities to discriminate against minorities. And in doing this he may have to make concessions to informal leaders among the rank and file in the form of private favors for their aid. Typical rewards would include (*a*) winning promotions that circumvent job tests required of others, (*b*) illegally punching their time cards in or out to reduce their work day, (*c*) working to secure transfers to more desirable jobs or into other departments without loss of seniority, (*d*) arranging for them to get a larger share of available overtime, (*e*) getting them more desirable days off, and so on. He cannot, of course, win such favors without aid from some member of management. This aid is given with the implicit understanding that he will "be a good fellow" when necessary. This means that he will (*a*) use his influence to win acceptance of "frozen" work schedules by rank and file, (*b*) refuse to present ominous grievances, (*c*) collaborate in evading staff people or inspectors, or rules that restrict "gentlemen's agreements," (*d*) enter into pacts that will not be revealed to other committee members, (*e*) not stand pat on the seniority principle, etc.

President of the Local. As the local's highest officer, the president coordinates its action, polices the contract, and communicates with the national union. These bald functions similarly give no picture of his crucial unwritten functions. As members of the grievance committee become involved in confidential schemes to temper their bargaining, the president's coordinative function becomes correspondingly elusive. He feels pressure from the national to conserve union funds by settling grievances preferably below the third step so as to escape the travel and maintenance costs of fourth- and fifth-step grievances. But bullying his juniors for details of their private bargaining with managers may throw matters into the open and tip issues into formal bargaining at high levels. Hence to get a working estimate of the favor-trading, he compares the partial reports of his grievers and sifts the real from the seeming by spot checks among rank and file and friendly supervisors. He remains officially ignorant but acts to contain the more dangerous issues. The process is more like that of managers on comparable levels than he would admit. The comparison can be extended. For as a militant cooperator with management, the president of the local knows of, and often honors, management's demand for compromise of the agreement when it makes problems for the enterprise. Accordingly he — as managers do with their superiors — withholds some information from national officers, who, as we saw, have their own disorientation toward troublesome locals. If the president's devotion to formalities prevents such elasticity, he may find both his local and the managers pressing him to resign (4, Chapter 5).

Frequently during summers he must engage in the supreme distortion of legal logic by becoming a *pro tem* manager to fill the roles of vacationing first-level foremen. A suspicious minority of the rank and file see this as a dangerous step toward becoming "management-minded," and demand reassurance.

Strauss (15) and the Rosens (11) have indicated somewhat comparable pressures on the "business agent," the analogue of the local president in the building trades.

The Individual and Social Organization

The list of pressures on union agents is not complete but is probably typical of middle-sized and large firms. Occurrence and resolution of tensions variously interlock with those of the managerial staff. And both are subject to demands from the rank and file for democratic settlements.

Before sketching the unauthorized organization to support the contract by experiment and surface conformity, we must note pressures on middle and lower managers. The first of course is to function and produce with minimum disturbance (7). Probably the best known pressure is the cumulative assault by union and higher management on the first-line foreman. One constraint on him is to maintain harmony among ethnic groups at the work level. This is obviously difficult when established majorities seek favoritism for themselves and harass minorities. The condition is aggravated for the foreman by the clash between public and internal policy in companies responsive to community pressures. For example, contrary to released statements, hiring officers may be ordered to hold the plant total of minority groups to the proportion they constitute in the community. The complex of actions by management, moves by minority leaders, statements in the press based on garbled leaks from the firm — all contribute to irritations and scapegoating that pass down by default for the uninformed foreman to deal with. Thus the compulsion is to use him as a buffer, and in effect to deny him a definitive status, without which he obviously must be everything demanded by everybody. Suspended in ambiguity, he seeks a tie with the worker, or with management, or, unfortunately, with both at once. Commonly he ends by forming a silent association with his own kind against the two. And this has considerable effect on union–management relations. For as a once-favored son now orphaned by rationality, he can neither be abandoned nor overlooked in decision-making by those who demand outward peace.

Top managers of corporations are of course legally committed to fight for efficient operation and favorable publicity. Where corporation units of different ages are widely dispersed, these coercive expectations invade all functions. In disparate situations they often become irrational and self-defeating prods. An instance is the logic that the less modern units should produce as much as the more modern. Another is the arranged competition among unlike departments to set records in production, safety, and low turnover and absenteeism. Guarded escapes from these burdens become hidden factors in labor relations. A case in point is the demand for "good relations" with the union but not good to the point of collusion. This pressure may lead department heads to alter work methods, conceal accidents, and distort reports with union cooperation and against the union.

A derivative pressure is reflected in the upward flow of reports on the state, or "solution," of all problems. These documents for the record require private understandings with clerical and staff experts who are similarly pushed, or ambitiously depart, from their planned functions.

Finally the department chief squirms under urgencies to reward skilled supporters among his subordinates. He cannot always do this as they expect — by promotion to less harried and richer posts in or out of the department. Instead he rewards them with material and social perquisites and exemption from some formal duties as he lives with the problem of not letting them escape.

This summary of role compromises among *individual* unionists and managers gives no picture of the coalitions to protect and guide the ostensible organization.

PRESERVATIVE ALLIANCES

As we saw, the direct unified pressures made by either union or management on the other are less defeating to the rational contract than (*a*) the situational pressures at different levels in the local as well as between it and the distant governing offices of each camp; (*b*) the unequal commitment of personnel; (*c*) the self-interested ingenuity of those moving up either of the heirarchies — or from union to management; (*d*) intrusion of community influences, and so on.

The events we presented as compromising individual roles may be more systematically grouped into the following types of informal regulation: (*a*) union control of official and potential members, (*b*) union and management control of rule-devotees, (*c*) union–management promotion of implicit policy, (*d*) union adaptation of national policy, and (*e*) management's punishment of its non-compromisers.

Union Control of Members. The union always has some need to regulate members who are entering management "permanently" or for a known period in the same firm. Usually members move up to the position of first-line foreman. If the aspirant is uncertain whether future reorganizations will drop him back to the work level, he may silently continue in the union as an illegal dues-paying member. This is likely if he has been aggressively influential in the union. For as he and the union agree, his promotion would give management an opportunity to fire him once he is legally out of the union. In cases of this kind, the union argues that the promotee was never a bona fide member of management, but was only "lent" to them.

Where the man is merely replacing a foreman on vacation but shows such zest for the role that he is considered by management as a candidate for their house, watchful unionists restrict information or production, or produce embarrassing information that reminds the aspirant of his uncertain role. Where the former unionist presumably enters management for the duration, but is realistic enough to know that reorganization and demotion are always possible, he may be sensitive to the knowledge imparted by some locals that former members now managers will, if demoted, retain or lose their seniority rights depending on the vote of the workers whom they supervised.

Union–Management Control of Rule-Devotees. In both union and management there are always some representatives of each of two extreme types. The first of these may be variously called formalists, absolutists, non-compromisers, or rule-devotees in terms of their attitudes toward law and formal controls in general. In our context persons of this type move forcefully only along authorized routes. They are usually lost in new or confused situations where guides are lacking.

The other type may be called informalists, relativists, compromisers, or rule-interpreters. Primarily they see rules as means and are prepared to be somewhat expedient in devising new means. Dominant figures in union and management are likely to be of this type. This is particularly true of union officers who are re-elected and rise in the hierarchy. Members of the first type who *do* climb to high place by some anomaly — as during a period when strong formalists are in demand and enter untested — are not likely to remain there. Under established and periodically renegotiated contracts they may be ousted by pressure from both camps. The ousters want deviation from the contract to deal with on-going contingencies, which means freedom to interpret it to preserve its dignity (as a restriction on the other camp!) while stretching it to justify a move. High officers of each house confidentially approve departures equivalent to a *carte blanche*, but warn members to "keep everything out of writing and don't involve me!" The attitude is reflected by one manager who argued, with respect both to the contract in his plant and directives on general policy from his central office, that "necessary exceptions can be made without changing policy — if it's done right." This sentiment is jointly extended to federal legislation, including the Taft-Hartley Act, which forbids union pressure on non-members to sign the check-off. In some cases local officers and management have cooperated for different reasons to coerce non-members to sign this approval for withholding union dues from their wages (4, Chapter 5). In such blurs of conflict and favor-trading there is little room for the formalist. After one explanation he is coerced in the name of the very thing he sees too narrowly for his superiors.

Joint Promotion of Implicit Policy. The inventive behavior we have discussed cannot of course operate by chance. Constructive cliques of unionists and managers see that it joins with official action and limits irrelevant or dangerous conduct. To channel the conflict they may help generate, these cross-cliques mold a body of emerging precedents into a tacit policy, some of which will in time be formalized.

A given clique's activities are usually confidential, for workable practices that leak to other departments may become widespread and lose their value by being copied or attacked by formalists as illegal. Need of secrecy obviously increases with such irregularities as: allowing a worker exemption from some rules in return for his doing operations he is not paid for; charging the time for reprocessing spoiled work to another department's account; or collaboration to promote a worker valuable for some functions but not the ones for which he is promoted. Secrecy naturally requires that members of, say, the grievance committee not reveal their private pacts to each other or to non-involved managers. The same holds for pact partners in management.

This seeming "collusion" is not conspiracy to exploit the public but to get the technical job done while controlling personal rivalries and expediently rewarding those able to make order out of confusion and camouflage their blend of the legal and illegal as they do it. Unbureaucratic cooperation of this kind covers the usual range of grievances, but also deals with control of foremen who see their role as more sharply defined than situations allow it to be, and with checking those staff experts who build their techniques first and then fail to find a problem to fit them.

The Local's Adaptation of National Policy. The local resists the national union in the sense that it acts autonomously in a way contrary to agreed policy. For example, it frequently rewards its strongest members by advancing them contrary to the seniority principle — when logic and ingenuity can be made to match — because effective supporters may lack seniority and those with seniority may lack what the leader needs. Ungranted autonomy is also exercised, as in management or any organization, by exempting favored members (those at least minimally competent *but* attitudinally akin) from formal tests for promotion required of the less favored; by penalizing the "troublemaker" or the "radical" member of minority ethnic groups through refusal to process grievances and debarment from choice jobs; by expending a minority of members in one occupational group to advance a majority in another group; by provoking a strike while telling the national that it could not be prevented; and so on. This behavior complements the national union's neglect as shown in its occasional misuse of union funds, favoring of some locals over others, and its empty formalizing to preserve itself and maintain dignity and moral correctness before the public (8, 9).

Cooperative Evasions by Labor and Management

Management's Punishment of Its Non-compromisers. Inability
to trade with the union is a bugaboo to upper managers. Usually
it is lower foremen and specialized experts who bridle at peaceful
concession. As we suggested above, the foreman's insecurity —
stemming from his lack of authority, narrow background, and
unprotected position on the fighting front between workers and
higher managers — is likely to make him more of a formalist
than a compromiser. His suffering disposes him to hit back with
absolutes against irritating workers and his "two-faced" superiors.
He either accepts a challenge to fight or passes it to higher-ups.
Rarely does he talk his way out or consider the problem for his
superiors. Hence the latter often reverse his decisions, withhold
symbols of membership in management, and dally in rewarding
him for his excellence in formalities. Second-level supervisors
are usually more flexible, but they too may favor the book so
much that they drop to first-level foremen without knowing
why.

As impatient young specialists, the experts often transfer their
textbook imagery without change into the shop. If they fail to
learn the language of concession and trade in favors, they are
punished on more counts than the foremen. First, their ideas are
rejected even when admittedly worth while. Or their proposals
are officially accepted but neglected in practice, so that unionists
and lower foremen, resenting rationality, may sabotage them.
When inflexible experts get in such trouble that they crave in-
formality, higher managers will stand on formality. Or management may not deny a griever's complaint that an expert's
threatening project is "crackpot" — and thus encourage union
resistance to it. Or executives may exploit the rigid expert's
plan by modifying it to ease pressure from the union. Finally,
in granting research funds to its various staffs of experts, management will favor compromising individuals over the uncom-
promising.

MUTED AUTONOMIES

Genuine "power struggles" are rare between union and management, as formal entities, at the local level (1). This is owing
in part to the bigness of the total camps, which places their
power at the top (1, 6), not in the local, and in part to the

presence of both formalists and informalists in each camp at the local level. This second condition encourages a variety of overlapping coalitions in the plant. On-going containment of frictions gives the local union (as it does the firm) an operative autonomy that enables it both to eat its cake and have it too. By *sub rosa* organization it escapes crippling legalities — or alters their intent. Local management in general cooperates in this and treats *its* distant higher-ups in much the same way. But when crises develop, the local calls on the national. The national similarly survives through the strength of multiple locals, yet departs from mere majority sentiments in order to please powerful minorities, or even to ignore some locals for a time.

Since the machinery behind this muted autonomy is not described by the official terminology, moral disturbances qualify action. Similar conditions have of course been common in the larger world from the time that ethics and action were separated. Ethical uncertainties may never be articulated in our context but they show up in the positions taken by the two action types, who become polar cynics. The formalists, for example, see the situation as "cold-blooded," and their informalist opponents as immoral. They doubt that life in their firm is typical and think that union–management relations are much better elsewhere. The informalists accept the concealed side of organization as a general truth, but think that "the way people are" the condition is inevitable and much the same everywhere.

Whether unionists or managers, the dominant informalists unwittingly reflect the advice of a late unionist: "Always remember, most people are wedded to formulas. They will fight for words when in terms of reality they would be willing to make concessions. There is no use in arguing about the formulas and words. That is meaningless and makes everybody stubborn. Let them have their formulas and take real concessions in exchange. They will be just as happy and you will get something genuine." (14)

References

1. Blumer, Herbert. "Social Structure and Power Conflict," in Arthur Kornhauser, Robert Dubin, and Arthur M. Ross (eds.),

Industrial Conflict. New York: McGraw-Hill Book Company, Inc., 1954, pp. 232–239.

2. Brooks, George W. "Reflections on the Changing Character of American Labor Unions," in L. Reed Tripp (ed.), *Industrial Relations Research Associations Proceedings, December 1956.* Madison, Wis.: Industrial Relations Research Association, University of Wisconsin, 1957, pp. 33–43.

3. Coleman, John R. "The Compulsive Pressures of Democracy in Unionism," *American Journal of Sociology,* Vol. 61 (May 1956), pp. 519–526.

4. Dalton, Melville. *Men Who Manage.* New York: John Wiley & Sons, 1959.

5. Derber, Milton, W. Ellison Chalmers, and Ross Stagner (with the cooperation of Milton Edelman). *The Local Union–Management Relationship.* Urbana, Ill.: University of Illinois, Institute of Labor and Industrial Relations, 1960.

6. Herberg, Will. "Bureaucracy and Democracy in Labor Unions," *Antioch Review,* Vol. 3 (Fall 1943), pp. 405–417.

7. Homans, George. "Industrial Harmony as a Goal," in Arthur Kornhauser, Robert Dubin, and Arthur M. Ross (eds.), *Industrial Conflict.* New York: McGraw-Hill Book Company, Inc., 1954, pp. 48–58.

8. Jacobs, Paul. "Comments on Bernstein's Paper on the Teamsters' Union," in Edwin Young (ed.), *Industrial Relations Research Association Proceedings, September 1957.* Madison, Wis.: Industrial Relations Research Association, University of Wisconsin, 1958, pp. 32–34.

9. Kleiler, Frank M. "William Morris Leiserson," in Edwin Young (ed.), *Industrial Relations Research Association Proceedings, September 1957.* Madison, Wis.: Industrial Relations Research Association, University of Wisconsin, 1958, pp. 95–101.

10. Lipset, Seymour Martin. "The Political Process in Trade Unions: A Theoretical Statement," in Walter Galenson and Seymour Martin Lipset (eds.), *Labor and Trade Unionism.* New York: John Wiley & Sons, 1960, pp. 216–242.

11. Rosen, Hjalmar, and R. A. Hudson Rosen. "Personality Variables and Role in a Union Business Agent Group," *Journal of Applied Psychology,* Vol. 41 (1957), pp. 131–136.

12. Sayles, Leonard R., and George Strauss. *The Local Union: Its Place in the Industrial Plant.* New York: Harper & Brothers, 1953.

13. Seidman, Joel. "Democracy and Trade Unionism: Some Requirements for Union Democracy," *American Economic Review*, Vol. 48 (May 1958), pp. 35–43.
14. Soule, George. *Sidney Hillman.* New York: The Macmillan Company, 1939.
15. Strauss, George. "Control by the Membership in Building Trades Unions," *American Journal of Sociology*, Vol. 61 (May 1956), pp. 527–535.
16. Wigham, Eric L. *Trade Unions.* New York: Oxford University Press, 1956.
17. Wilensky, Harold L. *Intellectuals in Labor Unions.* Glencoe, Ill.: The Free Press, 1956.

15

Types of Family Organization:
Child-Oriented, Home-Oriented,
and Parent-Oriented

 BERNARD FARBER

UNIVERSITY OF ILLINOIS

The interactionist approach to the study of the family, the most prominent exponent of which is Ernest W. Burgess, has long provided a major theoretical orientation for family research. In Chapter 12, Robert Habenstein illustrated the manner in which constructed types can be used to delineate forms of client–professional interaction; in the present chapter, Professor Farber applies such ideal types to identify forms of intra-family interaction. Like Habenstein, he provides types based upon empirically observed processes which never exist in their pure form; unlike Habenstein, Farber has been able to take an earlier typology (developed by Burgess) as a point of departure. Farber developed his classification in the course of a study of families that include a mentally retarded child. Although based on the pattern of interaction within the family, the classification appears to be useful in predicting various aspects of family organization.

E. W. Burgess' view of the family as a unity of interacting persons and his companionship-versus-institutional family typology have provided a basis for much research and thought in contemporary family sociology. This essay is concerned with a classification scheme stimulated by the Burgess typology and a description of various studies related to this scheme.

A major basis for the distinction between the institutional and companionship family according to Burgess is the source of social control for the family unit. The control of family behavior in the institutional family is derived from sources outside the immediate (or nuclear) family. The control of behavior in the companionship family is derived from mutual affection and aims at mutual compatibility of the family members. The typology implies that the institutional family has strong community ties, while the companionship family has a more or less symbiotic relationship with the rest of the community (1; 2, pp. 25–31).

In a study of families with a mentally retarded child, the Burgess typology was applied to determine whether the retarded child had a different effect on the marital integration of parents in families classified as oriented toward companionship or toward institutional continuity. In the course of this investigation, two problems were encountered which led to the abandonment of the attempt to classify families in the study as either companionship or institutional.

The first problem emerged when a third family type was found. On the basis of an intuitive analysis of case material, these families seemed "well-integrated." On various characteristics, however, this family type did not fit the companionship–institution classification. For example, as in the companionship family, parents found a primary source of emotional support in each other; at the same time, like parents in the institutional family, these parents placed much emphasis on children. Moreover, both in families classified as companionship and families classified as institutional, the husband and wife frequently strained toward upward mobility and were highly aware of their position in the community. (See 2, pp. 437–469) In the third type, however, the parents lowered their level of occupational aspiration and focused their lives on the home. Hence, although the institutional and companionship labels are supposed to describe alternative aims of family life, they fail to point out some essential distinguishing commitments of family members.

The second problem in classifying families emerged when families with no discernible pattern of aims in family life were encountered. Neither the companionship label, the institutional label, nor the third family type fitted these families. Several other classification schemes were attempted, but these also were inadequate.

Because of the problems encountered in attempting to use the companionship and institutional family scheme, a threefold classification scheme was developed (4). This scheme is presented below along with a description of supporting studies.

BASIS FOR TYPOLOGY OF FAMILY ORGANIZATION

The concept of predicament was used as a basis for developing the typology of family organization presented in this paper. The various kinds of family organization could then represent different solutions to these predicaments.

A predicament refers to a situation characterized by the presence of a perplexing problem. In the organization of the aspirations and expectations of family members, numerous perplexing problems exist.[1] In the typology developed in this paper, four persistent predicaments in family organization are used. These are problems of the primacy of (a) social-emotional versus instrumental values and norms, (b) short-run versus long-run considerations, (c) family commitments versus community commitments, and (d) gratification of parents' needs and desires versus gratification of children's needs and desires (6).

In the situation where the ordinary "cultural," ethnic, social-class, and occupational expectations are met by the family members without conflict or frustration, these predicaments in family organization may not be apparent to the members of an individual family. Family integrity is not threatened.[2] However, in the face of a severe crisis, the family members must decide

[1] Kirkpatrick has described 14 "dilemmas" of family organization (7, pp. 86–92).

[2] These statements regarding the family not in crisis are made dogmatically, but since they have not been tested, they should be considered as speculative.

which aspects of family life are to be given highest priority if family integrity is to remain intact. The problems of organization, which are latent in their disruptive effects under ordinary circumstances, then become vital issues with regard to the integrity of the family in crisis. Hence, it is suggested that the typology of family organization be based upon kinds of solutions given to particular predicaments which become apparent in a crisis situation. Since the family in crisis must solve these problems to maintain its integrity, study of the family in crisis becomes a useful tool for understanding the process of family organization.

The four predicaments in family organization used as a basis for the typology are described more fully as follows.

1. *Social-Emotional (Personal Relations) Versus Instrumental (Family as an Institution) Values and Norms.* Social-emotional values and norms generally pertain to the development of a system of personal relations between family members. Social-emotional valuation would be reflected in a high preference given to values and expectations related to companionship, personality development, emotional security, and affectional satisfaction. In contrast, from the viewpoint of the family as an institution, instrumental values and norms pertain to the continuity of the family unit through generations, administration of family affairs, and the place of the family among other institutions. Instrumental valuation would be reflected in a high preference given to values and expectations related to economic security, physical health of the family members, a respected place in the community, and adherence to moral and religious principles in developing role expectations.

2. *Role-Orientation Versus Career-Orientation.* A *role* can be described as the organization of an individual's activities in an institution such as the family at any particular time. A *career* is regarded as progression by an individual through a series of roles.

Problems faced by family members necessarily change during crisis and in the normal course of the family life-cycle. The succession of problems stimulates changes in roles of the family members. Insofar as the family exists as a system of careers, a marked shift in one career in the system affects the other careers. With respect to each career in the system, the sequence of role changes can be orderly as opposed to haphazard from an observer's viewpoint and anticipated as opposed to unanticipated from the family members' perspective. In part, the orderliness of the development of the career system depends upon the anticipations of the family members with respect to future role changes within each career. Hence, the extent to which the family members are oriented toward potential role changes may affect family organization.

Anticipation of potential role changes affects family organization when new roles are developed to meet a change in circumstances at a point in time. One manner of developing roles is for family members to consider only short-run consequences and immediate personal gain. This kind of development can be considered as "role-oriented" — that is, the members focus upon problems in the current family situation and minimize possible long-term consequences. A second way of developing roles is for family members to give minimal consideration to short-run consequences in the family. This kind of development can be described as "career-oriented."

The distinction between role- and career-orientation does not necessarily imply that in career-oriented families the members consider alternatives more carefully than members in role-oriented families do. Rather, the emphasis here is on the kind of perspective given priority in redefining expectations of the individual members.

Potentially, in every family, the following situation may exist for the husband and wife: (*a*) both are consistently career-oriented; (*b*) one spouse is consistently career-oriented and the other role-oriented; (*c*) both are consistently role-oriented; (*d*) there is personal inconsistency in role- versus career-orientation.

3. *Commitment to Internal (Family) Versus External (Community) Organization.* In a society based primarily upon kinship considerations, the predicament of choosing between family commitments and community extra-family commitments may not occur. However, in contemporary urban society, parents can develop strategies for maintaining or increasing their commitment and consequent participation in other institutions and thus give priority to the development of a successful career in these insti-

tutions. Or the parents can develop a different set of strategies for withdrawing from a good many activities in the community and thereby give priority to their domestic careers.

Commitment to "successful" institutional participation in the community other than the family is regarded in this essay primarily in terms of the middle-class social system. The middle-class social system is regarded as oriented toward achievement in socio-economic status. When conflicts arise between the middle-class career and domestic career and when the solution of these conflicts involves much time and/or effort, the parents must give priority to one career consistently if they are to minimize tension in the system of family roles. In a crisis the parents are regarded as having to choose between achievement in (*a*) the middle-class status system and (*b*) their home life by giving priority to *one* sequence of roles.

4. *Life-Career Gratification Priorities: Parents Versus Children.* Many parents sacrifice their own needs and desires for the sake of their children. These parents organize not merely their daily routine and recreation in accordance with the child's needs, but also long-range financial and educational planning. Other parents believe that their own life-career needs should assume priority over those of their children when there is a conflict. In any particular family, the parents may agree or disagree on whose life-career is to be given priority in long-range planning — parents or children.

Types of Family Organization

The types of family organization resulting from the combinations of alternatives chosen as solutions to the four predicaments are presented below. Each combination of alternatives determines a particular type of family organization. However, not all combinations are regarded as effective in maintaining high family integration.

For the purpose of the present investigation, the content of family careers is defined in terms of the structuring of family life in middle-class American society. It is assumed that the wife's role revolves around the home while the husband's role is primarily aimed at relating the home to the community. That is, the wife is generally responsible for the internal relations of the family, whereas the husband is responsible for keeping the family a going concern in relation to the rest of the community. Insofar as this division of roles occurs, the wife is in the position of balancing the demands of the husband with those of the children. Successful mediation by the wife of the husband's and children's demands and needs would be necessary for the smooth coordination of activities within the family.

Effective solutions to the family predicaments depend upon the coalitions formed by the husbands and wives to formulate decisions to resolve or minimize the crisis. Generally, the task of the husband in achieving high marital integration is to adapt his family role in such a way as to minimize contradictory demands made on his wife. Theoretically, this can be accomplished in one of three ways: (*a*) by instituting a sharp division of labor, (*b*) by a coalition between husband and wife giving priority to social-emotional activities in structuring family life, and (*c*) by a coalition between wife and husband giving priority to achieving goals in the community social structure. These three strategies are described below as child-oriented, home-oriented, and parent-oriented.

Since all three of these strategies are concerned with consistency in the allocation of priorities over time, they all tend to be career-oriented rather than role-oriented. However, failure to resolve any of the predicaments in a consistent manner would affect the extent of integration.

With respect to solutions of the predicaments, the *child-oriented family* is regarded as giving priority to instrumental (family as an institution) over social-emotional (personal relations) norms and values, community-status commitments over home-life commitments, and children's gratifications over parents' gratifications. These solutions to the predicaments can be accomplished through a sharp division of labor between husband and wife. Through this division of labor, community-status commitments would not conflict with the priority of children's over parents' gratifications. The activities related to community status could be delegated to the husband and those related to children's gratification to the wife. The rationale for this kind of organization would be provided by the priority of the family as an institution over the norms and values of personal relations: the parents agree that the most important task in family life is the maintenance of the family unit as an on-going concern vis-à-vis all other social groupings.

The *home-oriented* family is viewed as giving priority to social-emotional (personal relations) norms and values over instrumental (family as an institution) norms and values, home-life commitments over community-status commitments, and children's gratifications over parental gratifications. Inasmuch as ordinarily little conflict can occur between home-life commitments and children's gratification, there is little need for specialization in carrying through the home-oriented solution: both parents concentrate on structuring congenial interpersonal relations in the home. The middle-class model of the family described earlier places the wife in the position of mediating between demands of the husband and children. With both parents concentrating on social-emotional relations, the wife would lose her status as the social-emotional leader and the husband would become *the* central figure in the family.

In the *parent-oriented* family the priority system is as follows: social-emotional (personal relations) norms and values over instrumental (family as an institution) norms and values, community-status commitments over home-life commitments, and parents' gratification over children's gratification. Ordinarily, there would be little conflict between community status and parents' gratification as priorities. However, in order to carry through these solutions in the face of the priority of personal over familial norms, the parents would have to develop an equalitarian organization to make their set of solutions internally consistent. This equalitarian organization would place stress upon personal development and social skill of all members of the family. In this organization, the primary activities of the wife become those of (*a*) reinforcing such goals as the acquisition of artifacts and social contacts symbolic of success in middle-class society, and (*b*) developing skills to collaborate with her husband in his work or social contacts in the community. To compensate for the wife's assumption of achievement functions, the husband would have to perform some of the social-emotional activities ordinarily performed by the wife.

Types of Family Organization

In each of the above three types, a clear-cut focus of the parents upon a single aspect of family life is implied. Families falling into a fourth or residual category, however, are regarded as either (a) lacking in focus or common orientation in career priorities, or (b) being organized in their systems of roles in such a way as to impede gratification pertaining to a common orientation. Hence, the residual category is considered as the grouping of kinds of family organization not conducive to high marital integration in critical situations.

In the studies reported in this paper, in which the primary aim was to explore consequences of applying the three family types, little analysis was made of the cases falling in the residual category. Possibly, a systematic analysis of these residual families would reveal other strategies of family organization facilitating high integration in a crisis situation. Analysis of the residual category of families is also discussed later in this paper in the section on unresolved problems of the typology.

Empirical Investigation of the Family Types[3]

In order to be a useful research tool, types of family organization should make possible predictions regarding various aspects of family behavior not directly associated with the typology. In addition, however, there should be some indication that results are not merely an artifact of the research procedures. The investigations, hence, focused upon the following problems: (a) correspondence of classification procedures to ranking of values by the parents, (b) the relationship between the family types and marital integration, and (c) variation among the family types in children's perceptions of their parents' dissatisfaction with their behavior.

Families with a mentally retarded child provided the material for most of the studies described below. Experts on mental retardation generally recognize that the presence of a severely retarded child places a heavy strain on family relations. The

[3] The studies described in this paper were supported by grants from the Psychiatric Training and Research Fund of the Illinois Department of Public Welfare and (M 3207) National Institute of Mental Health, U.S. Public Health Service.

typology was regarded as especially appropriate to the study of families in crisis. Hence, families with a retarded child were considered as a fitting population for an initial exploration of the adequacy of the typology for understanding family life.

In several of the studies, because of the small number of cases falling into any one of the three major categories, results for the three categories were combined for comparison with the residual-category results. Findings for the three categories were combined only when a preliminary analysis showed that the results for all three family types bore that same relationship to the residual-category results.

RANKING OF DOMESTIC VALUES

In a study of 233 families with a retarded child, the families had been classified as child-oriented, home-oriented, parent-oriented or residual category on the basis of criteria derived from the generalized description of the family types.[4] The question arose whether parents classified according to these criteria would tend to assign a high rank to domestic values supposed to be important in the particular family orientation.

Each parent had been asked to rank a list of ten domestic values in the order of their importance to successful family life. The list included: (*a*) a place in the community, (*b*) healthy and happy children, (*c*) companionship, (*d*) personality development, (*e*) satisfaction in affection shown, (*f*) economic security, (*g*) emotional security, (*h*) moral and religious unity, (*i*) everyday interest, and (*j*) a home.

The findings are presented below in terms of the mean rank assigned.

[4] The study is reported in Farber (4). The sample consisted of families living in the Chicago area in which both husband and wife were interviewed. The parents (*a*) were Caucasian, (*b*) generally had a high school education, (*c*) earned a median of about $6,000 per year, (*d*) were more often in white collar than blue collar occupations, and (*e*) had been in contact with a parents' association for promoting the welfare of the mentally retarded. With respect to religion, 46 per cent of the parents were Protestant, 34 per cent Catholic, 13 per cent Jewish, and 7 per cent none, atheist, agnostic, or did not respond to the question on religion. The mentally retarded children were (*a*) aged 16 or under, (*b*) born in the present marriage and (*c*) generally had an IQ under 50. A study of problems in sampling families with a retarded child is also reported in Bernard Farber (3).

Types of Family Organization

1. Wives in traditional or child-oriented families tended to stress (in order) healthy and happy children, a home, and moral and religious unity.

2. Wives in home-oriented families placed highest value on healthy and happy children, companionship, and emotional security.

3. The wives in parent-oriented families stressed the same values as those in home-oriented families, but the parent-oriented wives had a different order of preference — companionship, healthy and happy children, and emotional security.

Hence, the wives in the child-oriented families seemed to stress the traditional aims of family life, whereas the wives in both home-oriented and parent-oriented families stressed social-emotional aspects of interaction, with the parent-oriented wife placing a greater emphasis on companionship.

Consistent with the above interpretations of wives' rankings as stemming from three kinds of value-orientations were the findings on their rankings of personality development and economic security among the ten items. These two values seemed to epitomize the distinction between the institutional and personal-relations value systems.

1. The mean rank for the wives in child-oriented, home-oriented, and parent-oriented families on personality development was respectively 7.2, 6.1, and 5.3 (with 5.3 as the highest mean rank).

2. Similarly, the mean rank for the wives in the three family types on economic security was (in the order above) 5.8, 7.2, and 8.2, with the child-oriented wives assigning the highest mean rank to economic security.

These results add support for the contention that the family types represent consistent value systems of the wives in these families.

The results of the husbands' ranking were generally similar to those of their wives.

1. The traditional or child-oriented husbands ranked moral and religious unity highest and followed it with healthy and happy children and companionship, with economic security fourth.

2. The home-oriented husbands ranked a home and companionship as tied for the highest rank, closely followed by emotional security and then healthy and happy children.

3. The parent-oriented husbands, however, stressed companionship, emotional security, and healthy and happy children.

The husband in child-oriented families stressed familial, traditional values — moral and religious unity, children, and economic security. The home-oriented husbands and parent-oriented husbands both emphasized emotional security and healthy and happy children; the home-oriented husband, however, placed a home and companionship highest in their list of values, whereas the parent-oriented husband ranked only companionship highest. These results were, therefore, consistent with the characterization of the integrative family types in the general descriptions.

In addition, just as wives in all family types tended to rank healthy and happy children high, regardless of family type, husbands tended to assign a high rank to companionship as well as children. The significance of healthy and happy children in this sample may be that the parents believe the retarded child has created many problems for their marriage. The presence of problems may then mean that the husbands do not find the companionship they seek in the family. However, similar high rankings on healthy and happy children and companionship in two small samples with normal children only in Champaign and Danville, Illinois, suggest that a general cultural norm related to the sexual division of labor is operating.[5]

MARITAL INTEGRATION AND FAMILY ORIENTATION

The types of family orientation had been developed initially to determine which strategies of family organization were associated with the maintenance of high marital integration in a crisis situation. In the analysis, then, marital integration was considered as a function of two factors: (*a*) type of family orientation and (*b*) severity of the crisis. (In a more general study, problems in

[5] An unpublished study. The Champaign sample consisted of both parents in 63 Catholic families with a child in a parochial junior high school. The majority of the fathers were in white collar occupations, the parents were Caucasian and generally in their forties, and there was an average of 3.7 children per family. The Danville sample consisted of 54 husbands and wives who were reached through the PTA council. The Danville sample was predominantly Protestant, somewhat younger than the Champaign sample, and families were smaller.

broad cultural values such as the possible contradiction between "children" and "companionship" could be introduced as a third factor.)

The severity of the crisis was operationally defined in terms of a series of propositions concerning the relationship between marital integration and circumstances surrounding the retarded child and his family. The procedure by which the circumstances were classified as unfavorable, unpredictable (middle category), or favorable to marital integration is summarized elsewhere (4, pp. 29–35). The classification scheme rests upon the effects on marital integration of the sex of the child, socio-economic status, parents' marital integration prior to the birth of the retarded child, religion, and birth order of the retarded child. Most of these effects had been tested in a previous analysis (3). The remainder were drawn from case material. The specific sets of circumstances classified in terms of their severity with respect to marital integration are presented in Table 1.

In the study of the relationship between extent of marital integration and type of family organization, the relative effects on marital integration of parent-, child-, or home-oriented organization, and the strategy of placing the retarded child in an institution were examined, with the following results.

1. For each level of favorableness of circumstances, regardless of whether the child was at home or in an institution, child-, home-, and parent-oriented families showed a higher mean marital integration than residual-category families. However, the difference in mean marital integration score between the child-, home-, or parent-oriented families and those in the residual category was greatest for families faced with unfavorable circumstances. The results suggest that the more severe the family crisis, the greater is the need to develop a parent-, child-, or home-oriented type of organization to maintain family integrity.

2. However, when only the child-, home-, and parent-oriented families were studied (and the residual-category families were omitted), the difference in mean marital integration between parents with a child in an institution and a retarded child at home *increased* with each level of *decrease* in favorableness of circumstances. As a result, in circumstances classified as unfavorable, child-, home-, or parent-oriented families with a child in an

TABLE 1

Classification of Combinations of Circumstances on Basis of Their Favorableness to the Marital Integration of Parents of Severely Mentally Retarded Children

Set No.	Sex of Child	Favorableness of the Set of Circumstances	Circumstances				No. of Cases	Mean Marital Integration Score
			Marital Prediction Score	Social Status	Religion	Birth Order of Retarded Child		
1a	Boy	Favorable	High	Middle	Catholic	First	8	4.50[a]
		Favorable		Lower	Catholic	Not first	7	4.14
		Unpredictable	High	Lower	Catholic	Not first	11	3.27
		Unfavorable	Low	Lower	Catholic	Not first	11	2.91
1b	Boy	Unpredictable		Middle	Non-Catholic	Not first	33	3.58
		Unfavorable		Lower	Non-Catholic	First	17	2.41
1c	Boy	Unpredictable	High	Lower	Non-Catholic	Not first	9	3.33
		Unfavorable	Low	Lower	Non-Catholic	Not first	6	2.83
2	Boy	Favorable	High	Middle		First	15	4.15[a]
		Unfavorable	Low	Middle		First	28	2.86
3	Girl	Favorable	High	Middle	Non-Catholic		27	4.07
		Unpredictable	High	Middle	Catholic		7	3.29
4	Girl	Favorable	High	Lower		Not first	18	4.06
		Unpredictable	High	Lower		First	10	3.20
5	Girl	Unpredictable	Low				33	3.55

Note. In blank spaces in the table, the circumstances of the family are regarded as unimportant for the classification of favorableness and, therefore, no category is specified in classifying the case.

[a] Categories are not mutually exclusive. Cases applying to both categories are placed in the latter one listed.

298

institution had a substantially higher marital integration than parents in the same orientation categories with a child at home. In contrast, residual-category families showed no consistent difference in degree of marital integration between families with a child in an institution and those with a child at home. The results relating to institutionalization suggest that although a consistent child-, home-, or parent-oriented organization influences degree of marital integration, kind of family organization is only one of a combination of strategies for maintaining high family integration in the face of crisis.

3. An attempt was made to determine whether additional patterns of attributes in the residual-category cases were related to high marital integration. One pattern was uncovered, but it was itself related to the severity of the crisis. When families faced with favorable circumstances had only one child (the retarded child) and kept this child at home, they generally had very high marital integration. If parents faced with unfavorable circumstances kept their only child (who was retarded) at home, however, they generally had very low marital integration.

The study described above indicated the role of type of family orientation in the relationship between degree of marital integration and severity of family crisis. Consistency in family orientation as a solution to a number of predicaments also suggests that marital integration of the child-, home-, and parent-oriented families is stable over time. To test the stability of integration, two samples were used. In one sample, in which all children were normal, 57 couples in Champaign, Illinois, were retested after a one-year lapse. In the second sample, 55 Chicago families with a retarded child were retested after a three-year lapse of time.[6] In each sample, the results were:

1. The absolute shift in number of units in marital integration score from the first to the second interview was greater for residual-category families than for child-oriented, home-oriented, or parent-oriented families.

2. The mean downward shift in marital integration scores at the upper levels of marital integration (that is, 5 and 6 in a range of 0–6) for residual-category families was about three times the

[6] An unpublished study. The initial Champaign sample is described above in Footnote 5 and the larger Chicago sample in Footnote 4.

shift for child-oriented, home-oriented, or parent-oriented families.

Hence, the results on marital integration indicated that type of family orientation was a factor not only in the degree of marital integration but also in the stability of integration.

PARENT–CHILD RELATIONS AND FAMILY ORIENTATION

If the type of family orientation is an important factor in family life, it is reasonable to expect that the quality of parent–child relations will be affected by the kind of orientation. In the following studies, the relationship between family orientation and the child's perception of his parents' dissatisfaction was examined. There were two sets of analyses. In the first analysis, different kinds of stress situations related to the family types were described; in the second, differences in children's perceptions were studied in terms of type of family orientation.

In the studies of parent–child relations, families were classified by type of orientation on the basis of the *parents'* interviews; the focus of the analysis was on 109 *children's* perceptions of their parents' dissatisfaction with their behavior. The children were normal siblings (aged 11–16) of a retarded child.[7]

The study of stress situations related level of performance described by the child and degree of parental dissatisfaction which he perceived (8). Three categories of activities were used: (*a*) individual instrumental activities (such as household chores), (*b*) group family activities (such as helping care for siblings), and (*c*) extra-family activities (such as working, dating, or staying out late).

---

[7] This sample is part of a study of 374 Chicago families with a retarded child. The first phase of that study which dealt with family factors in institutionalization was reported in Farber, Jenne, and Toigo (6). The second phase is concerned with normal siblings of the retarded child. In the second phase, only responses pertaining to one normal child in the family, aged 11–16, were used. The mean age of the 51 boys in the study was 13.0 years and that of the 58 girls was 12.6. In this sample, about three-fifths of the parents had completed high school, over half of the fathers were in white collar occupations, median annual income was $6,450 in 1958, and there was a mean of 2.5 children per family. The sample was restricted to families with a severely retarded child, aged 15 or under, born in the present marriage.

Types of Family Organization

Children in child-oriented families tended to show the highest performance level in individual instrumental activities; the consequence of failure to perform particular individual instrumental activities, however, was related to the sex of the child in the child-oriented family. In this family type, although both boys and girls frequently reported high performance levels on individual instrumental activities, when a boy reported low performance, he generally did not perceive much parental dissatisfaction. However, girls in child-oriented families perceived much dissatisfaction when their performance of individual instrumental activities was low.

In home-oriented families, the performance level of individual instrumental and extra-family activities was low; performance of group family activities was high. Even when performance of individual instrumental activities was low, there was little parental dissatisfaction perceived by the child. Other results were in the middle range.

In parent-oriented families, the performance level of individual instrumental activities was especially low and that of extra-family activities especially high. Furthermore, when the child's performance level of extra-family activities was low, he generally perceived much parental dissatisfaction with his performance.

Among families in the residual category, regardless of the level of performance, the children generally perceived a higher degree of parental dissatisfaction than did the other children.

The results suggest that pressures or difficulties in a particular area of activity could have quite different meaning to families of different orientations. Inability or unwillingness on the part of a family member to fulfill instrumental family expectations would be viewed as a major problem in child-oriented families but not in home-oriented or parent-oriented families. Events which hamper congenial intra-family relations would be regarded as a great difficulty in home-oriented families but not in child-oriented or parent-oriented families. Parent-oriented families would regard as highly stressful inability on the part of a family member to engage in skillful social interaction outside the family. However, inability to participate skillfully in extra-family activities would be relatively unimportant in child-oriented and home-oriented families. Thus, a child's difficulty in school work might be regarded as a major problem in child-oriented families, a minor difficulty — if noted at all — in home-oriented families, and a problem primarily insofar as it affects the child's social activities in parent-oriented families.

The second analysis pertaining to parent–child relations was concerned with the association between family type and the manner in which the child perceives parental dissatisfaction (5). The above results suggest that the children in child-, home-, and parent-oriented families are sensitive to particular kinds of parental expectations. The parental dissatisfaction perceived by children in the residual-category families, however, was generally independent of their level of performance; hence, they may not receive sufficient feedback from the parents to regulate their performance of specific activities. Thus, we would expect that the residual-category children would perceive parental dissatisfaction in a more global fashion than would the children in child-, home-, or parent-oriented families.

To test this expectation, two scales were correlated. The extent to which the child regarded the parent as dissatisfied with his instrumental activities (such as school work, help at home, seriousness, advice-taking) was correlated with the extent to which the child perceived the parent as dissatisfied with his social-emotional activities (such as being friendly and trusting people, showing affection to friends and to parents, and feeling sorry for those in trouble). The interpretation was that the higher the correlation, the more global is the child's perception of parental dissatisfaction.

In the child's perception of the mother, both boys and girls showed a lower correlation between the instrumental and social-emotional scores in the child-, home-, and parent-oriented families than in residual-category families. In the families classified as residual, generally, when the score on one index was high, so was the other score. The results, thus, were those expected: children in consistently oriented families perceived a greater distinction between instrumental and social-emotional behavior in their impressions of their mother's expectations than did other children.

In the child's perception of the father, for boys, the results were also in the anticipated direction. For girls, however, the daughters of child-, home-, or parent-oriented parents actually showed the least distinction between instrumental and social-emotional perceived dissatisfaction. The finding for the girls suggests that the father–daughter relationship in these family types deserves special study.

Generally, the study of effects of family type on parent–child relations indicates that kind of family orientation is associated with kinds of activities regarded as stressful and with the manner in which the child perceives parental dissastisfaction.

UNRESOLVED PROBLEMS RELATING TO THE FAMILY TYPOLOGY

Although the studies cited above indicate that the classification of families as child-oriented, parent-oriented, or home-oriented may be a useful research tool in gaining insights into family organization, the findings were not wholly unequivocal. Several problems were raised:

1. Many families fell into the residual category. Among families with a retarded child, one-half to two-thirds of the cases in each sample were classified as residual; in the sample of families with all normal children, about one-third of the cases fell into the residual category. One reason for the large number of cases in the residual category is technical. With only crude indices for classifying families, rigorous standards were set in the exploratory studies so that only the "purer" cases would be classified as child-oriented, home-oriented, or parent-oriented. A second explanation is that, as suggested in the description of the predicaments, there are numerous "solutions" which are not conducive to high integration. Furthermore, each parent may prefer a different solution. A third reason is that the conceptual scheme upon which the typology is based has not been fully exploited. Logically, eight rather than three family types can be depicted by the scheme. These are shown in Table 2. A refinement of indices relating to the combinations of priorities established as solutions to the predicaments discussed earlier in the paper would make possible the study of the associations between solutions X_1 to X_5 in Table 2 and marital integration and parent–child relations.

2. Are the family types related to particular stages in the family life cycle? In an analysis involving the 57 Champaign, Illinois, families with normal children and 55 Chicago families with a retarded child, the relationship between type of family orientation

TABLE 2

Types of Family Organization as the Establishment of Priorities in Alternative Commitments Constituting Predicaments in Family Life

TYPES OF FAMILY ORGANIZATION	ALTERNATIVE GIVEN PRIORITY IN PARTICULAR TYPE OF FAMILY ORGANIZATION[1]		
	Social-Emotional (Personal) Versus Instrumental (Family as an Institution) Norms and Values	*Family Group Commitment Versus Community Commitment*	*Life-Career Gratification: Parents Versus Children*
Child-oriented	Family as an Institution	Community	Children
Home-oriented	Personal Relations	Family Group	Children
Parent-oriented	Personal Relations	Community	Parents
X_1	Personal Relations	Community	Children
X_2	Family as an Institution	Family Group	Children
X_3	Family as an Institution	Family Group	Parents
X_4	Family as an Institution	Community	Parents
X_5	Personal Relations	Family Group	Parents

[1] In all of these assignments of priorities as solutions to predicaments, the priority of career-orientation over role-orientation is assumed. Career-orientation is considered as necessary to permit the maintenance of high family integration in a crisis. This assumption too should be tested.

and (*a*) age of the youngest child and (*b*) age of the husband was examined. The youngest child in the parent-oriented family was much younger than that in the home-oriented or child-oriented family. The mean ages were 7.8 years for the child-oriented families, 9.4 for the home-oriented families, and 3.9 for the parent-oriented families. The youngest child in the parent-oriented family was generally of pre-school age. Similarly, the age of the

Types of Family Organization

husband in the parent-oriented families was generally lower than that in the child-oriented or home-oriented families. The mean age for husbands in child-oriented families was 45.2, the mean in the home-oriented families was 44.9, and the mean in parent-oriented families 38.1. The chances of the parent-oriented husband's being under forty were much greater than those of the child-oriented or home-oriented husband. The theoretical formulation, however, does not indicate a relationship between age and type of family orientation. Further investigation would determine more adequately the extent to which age and type of orientation are related in the general population.

3. The typology was developed in terms of families in which the primary worker is the husband. The wife, in the conception of the family considered, either stays at home or works at a part-time job. To what extent can the typology explain variation in family organization when both husband and wife are primary workers? Can the typology, with modifications for missing personnel, be used in the study in which a parent is missing through divorce, death, or hospitalization?

CONCLUSIONS

This paper has described the development of a series of studies based on Burgess' suggestion that the family be viewed as a unity of interacting persons. Unity was regarded as coalition formation on the basis of the structure of interaction. Personality was here thought of in terms of the value orientations connected with particular roles. Categories of families, resembling in some ways the Burgess institution-versus-companionship typology, were described as child-oriented, home-oriented, parent-oriented, and residual. The categories of family orientation were considered as forms of organization to handle life-career predicaments of the family members. Evidence was presented concerning these categories of organization as providing insight into family life.

Perhaps the revision of the Burgess typology presented in this essay will facilitate the testing of specific characteristics of the family related to the institution–companionship types.

Because most of the evidence related to the family orientations has come from studies of families with a retarded child, the extent of generalization may be open to question. However, comparable research on families with normal children only is anticipated.

References

1. Burgess, Ernest W., and Harvey J. Locke. *The Family*. New York: American Book Co., 1953.

2. Burgess, Ernest W., and Paul Wallin. *Engagement and Marriage*. Philadelphia: J. B. Lippincott Co., 1953.

3. Farber, Bernard. "Effects of a Severely Mentally Retarded Child on Family Integration," *Monographs of the Society for Research in Child Development*, Vol. 24 (1959), Appendix C.

4. Farber, Bernard. "Family Organization and Crisis: Maintenance of Integration in Families with a Severely Mentally Retarded Child," *Monographs of the Society for Research in Child Development*, Vol. 25 (1960).

5. Farber, Bernard, and William C. Jenne. "Family Organization and Children's Perception of Parental Satisfaction with Their Behavior." Paper presented at the International Conference on the Family, New York, 1960.

6. Farber, Bernard, William C. Jenne, and Romolo Toigo. "Family Crisis and the Decision to Institutionalize the Retarded Child," *Council of Exceptional Children Research Monograph Series*, Series A (1960).

7. Kirkpatrick, Clifford. *The Family as Process and Institution*. New York: The Ronald Press Company, 1955.

8. Liebman, Carol S. "Family Type and Child's Perception of His Mother's Satisfaction with His Behavior." Master's thesis, Department of Sociology, University of Illinois, 1960.

16

Social Stratification
and the Political Order

HOWARD BROTZ

SMITH COLLEGE

*Social status and stratification are related at once to the political
order and to the respect which individuals grant each other in
private life. They become especially meaningful conceptions in
a society when there is a divergence between privately held
standards and those which prevail politically. It is within this
context that Professor Brotz examines social status and stratification, and thus brings interactionist concepts into the analysis of
social organization.*

Although the study of social stratification has made tremendous
progress in the last decades, there still remains, as specialists in
this field have noted, a theoretical difficulty.* There are certain
types of individuals or groups whom it is extremely difficult to fit
into the main status hierarchy of a community in a convincing
and unambiguous way (7, p. 27). Minorities as a whole and in-

* Reprinted, with the publisher's permission, from *The American Journal
of Sociology*, Vol. 64 (May 1959), pp. 571–578. Copyright 1959 by the
University of Chicago.

dividual members of them, whose status in outside social circles is marginal by virtue of their origins, are prominent examples. Of even greater theoretical significance, however, are those familiar cases of individuals who have great political authority but lower social status. How is one to rank, for example, a governor who is openly a member of a minority which is excluded from elite social clubs? He might not even be able to afford, politically, to join one of these clubs were an invitation to do so proffered.

The usual way of resolving this difficulty is, in practice, to describe the society in terms of discrete hierarchies — a status hierarchy, status hierarchies of subgroups, hierarchies of authority and power. Within limits this will work very well. If individuals who are marginal members of minorities, such as assimilated members of the minority upper classes, cannot be clearly placed within the main status hierarchy, at least their marginality in their relations with the minority can be clearly described, as numerous studies have shown.

Nonetheless, as a general theoretical orientation this is far from satisfactory; it abandons what is most valuable in the theoretical rationale of the central importance of social stratification, that is, the understanding that a society must have some over-all principle that establishes what is respected and that even the presence of conflicting standards in itself exhibits a principle.

As is readily understandable, theoretical difficulties will have empirical repercussions. In the absence of a comprehensive principle that adequately explains the precise relationship of the crucial hierarchies of social status and political authority to each other, one is without adequate guidance in determining how decisive each is in shaping the structure and character of the society. Without such a principle there is no brake against the mutual reduction of these hierarchies to each other, although this has predominantly been in the direction of reducing authority to status, that is, treating the former as a criterion of the latter.

This reductionism, if pressed to the logical extreme, could lead to such conclusions as that it is more important to be the president of a private university than to be president of the country. And, in general, the whole sphere of status may be invested with an importance which it may not possess. If people "count" socially and have little or no influence in setting the tone of that society, one cannot simply regard their status as an unequivocal index of their importance without begging the whole question of what it means to "count." Furthermore, from within the perspective of a status hierarchy, conceived of as the main hierarchy to which all others are reduced, one is compelled to be silent about or to minimize the importance of such things as class conflicts which press for a solution in political terms. There has always been an uneasy lack of articulation in American sociology between the approaches of Warner and Lynd.

Is there a way of untying the Gordian knot without cutting it? Is there a way of interrelating the various hierarchies in the society without fundamentally reducing them one to the other? I suggest the following approach as an alternative, which, though provisional, has already proved useful in actual research.

Social stratification may be best understood by relating it to the political context in which it arises and is maintained. This political context is the sphere in which various interests — the poor, the rich, the middle class, religious factions, minority ethnic groups — compete for a share of political authority, for the power, that is, to establish what is publicly respected in that society. The outcome is a hierarchy of all the interests which effectively claim some right to be heard in determining this hierarchy, which becomes thus a measure of their political strength. The recent changes in the segregation laws following upon the northward migration of the Negro are a convenient case in point. The claims of the Negro can no longer be ignored because he is now a political force to be reckoned with. Yet the fact that he cannot be elected to governorships, let alone the presidency, must equally be taken into account in estimating his political strength at a given time.

This hierarchy, which is characterized in its essential respects by the kind of political interest which dominates it, is the political order. Such, for example, would be plutocracy, aristocracy, or democracy in its older political meaning. In this sense it is not primarily defined by a set of legal-institutional arrangements or by an equality in the direct management of political affairs from public offices. (These, in any but the smallest societies, must always remain in the hands of a minority of the people.) It is defined rather by a distribution of political power within a broad civic body — rather than a narrow one based, for example, upon a high property qualification — which distribution will be reflected in the interests advanced in the public arena, the kind of men selected for public life, and the moral and cultural standards these men uphold.

Within a range, democracies can vary in the composition of the politically predominant class. As Lubell has shown, the middle class in the United States holds the balance of political power. Its strength, as measured by its ability to establish the standard for participation in public life, is shown in an interesting way by his analysis of minorities. None of the American minorities, as he makes clear, was aroused into political protest when it was at the very bottom of society and its grievances were heaviest; nor have sheer numbers been sufficient for political power. The Mexican-Americans in the Southwest are a sizable group. Yet, economically depressed in the lowest stratum of society, they are politically inert. For a minority to become conscious of itself as a political entity and of its right to enter the public realm, make political claims in its interest, and elect public officials from within its own ranks, it must have some foothold in the middle class, with all that this implies in terms of educational, economic, and social qualifications (10, pp. 79–85). In this sense the political order establishes the attributes of the "first-class" citizens and is, in fact, constituted by the kinds of men who are the first-class citizens (12, pp. 1–85). As understood in this way, the political order is more comprehensive than and prior to any other hierarchy and for two reasons which are really the reciprocal of each other.

The first is that the attributes of the first-class citizens, of those who can hold their heads up in public with all the self-confidence of a ruling class, of those whose attributes are not handicaps to them in public life, will be the standards that are really respected in that society. This is the import of not having to conceal one's attributes and qualities. A self-made man in a society dominated by self-made men has an altogether different bearing from what he would have in a hereditary aristocracy. By the same token, an aristocracy which rules can affect tastes in a way which it can hardly do when after a democratization the very remnants of its position are suspect. If power, in short, is ashamed to become visible, it cannot exert moral authority. To the extent, then, that a group is publicly authoritative and its standards and outlook are the ruling principles, it sets the tone for the whole society. Just as a single institution will be influenced by the example of the men who direct it, so will the entire institutional fabric of a society be affected by the kind of men who are held in public respect and whose standards can never be simply ignored. Even those who privately despise the standards of the ruling class do so all the more because they have to acknowledge in some way its authoritative position.[1]

The second reason is simply the political implication of the above: this is, that from within the perspective of human societies as political societies, the composition of the body of first-class citizens cannot help but be the crucial internal political question. It is, in fact, *the* political basis of civil wars and revolutions. When one considers the central role of moral evaluation in social and political life, it must follow that human beings cannot be neutral about the kinds of men in their society who have genuine, public authority and about the things for which they stand. Even a man who seeks martyrdom above all other things, though this is hardly the model for political activity, would have to admit that he requires a political framework in which authority cares about his opinions.

If the political order, then, is the public or authoritative distribution of respect, social stratification is based on the rank or esteem which individuals grant each other in an essentially private sphere. It is thus to be contrasted with every form of authoritative determination of rank, prestige, legal status, privilege, honor, or dishonor — by political, legal, or ritual sanctions — where the respect with which an individual will be treated is

[1] A complete analysis of this problem cannot be attempted here. It may suffice, simply to indicate the direction which the analysis would have to take, to note the implication of the difference between purely private power and public authority — of the differences, for example, between a leader of a political party or faction with armed men at his disposal and a general of an army or between a presidential candidate and the man as president. In each of the latter cases the man can raise a moral claim to rule, by virtue of the fact that he can speak as a representative of the whole, which the former cannot. By empirical observation one would then have to show how clearly this moral claim is the basis of respect in the constitution of human societies.

commensurable with and based upon his political strength. Such, for example, would be the deference granted to an absolute monarch who holds the power of life and death over his subjects or, at the other extreme, the public humiliation of powerless groups regarded as pariahs, where they are not allowed to use the ordinary wells or drinking fountains or are required to wear a distinctive garb. Similarly, we may regard the stratification of a caste system or an estate system as the political order, noting that political action which is or nearly is revolutionary in character is usually required to bring them to an end.

In sharp contrast to this, social status in its modern and, perhaps, essential meaning and the correlative conceptions of social stratification, social equality, and social inequality constitute an independence of the political order. They arise as meaningful elements in the life of a society and, significantly, as conceptions of it[2] when there is an important divergence between what some sizable group regards as ideal and the kind of men who have either political authority or the wealth which it is possible to accumulate within that political framework.[3] Wealth, because of the universal admiration it commands and the power it makes possible, is something about which political beings can never be neutral. The implications of this are seen whenever aristocracies are displaced from power or come into competition with a rising bourgeoisie. Class distinctions, based on their qualifications in the past, are generated and invested with seriousness as a way of ridiculing the ascendant class to which they would have been oblivious in the period when they firmly ruled. By the same token, in every capitalist democracy there is a chronic divergence between the political dominance of the average man and the self-

---

[2] The earliest date in the English language for the term "status," meaning social standing, is 1820 (*Oxford English Dictionary*). Tocqueville, to my knowledge, does not use the term "social equality" at all. For Bryce, however, it becomes a problem to clarify the meaning of the term "equality" and to distinguish between its political and social forms (4, Vol. II, pp. 615–626).

[3] They thus presuppose, as an ultimate cultural precondition, a society in which the idea has taken shape that there are ideals of this character or, more specifically, moral-political standards with which to judge the distribution and use of wealth and power. Cf. Edmund Burke's analysis of the way in which the manners of chivalry formed the character of modern Europe (5, pp. 73–74).

Social Stratification and the Political Order

esteem of the successful man, let alone those who have pretensions to a hereditary, aristocratic status.

Now no society can so control a man's mind that it can prevent him from making a private judgment about the worth of himself and others, and very few men, if any, do not think that they are better than they are actually treated. Insofar as these facts are at the root of social stratification, it is thus rooted in the private character of thought and in the workings of vanity and pride, hence in human nature itself. But, for social stratification to emerge, it must be more than completely private or subjective. It must be "social." It must, that is, rest upon shared opinion which thus presupposes some institutions or more or less informal groups to fix them and be their carriers. This, in turn, presupposes a political order which permits freedom of association for informal groups and voluntary associations — freedom not merely in a formal legal sense but in the additional sense of freedom from those social pressures which would make it impossible for the groups to hold together. The fact that the freedom is constituted by the political order, however, means that the very independence of that order is derivative. Social stratification is derivative not merely because its very reason for coming into existence is that it is a reaction against a specific type of political order. More fundamentally, it is because it requires political freedom to exist at all and thus presupposes a specific political framework. This particular framework is the liberal state.[4]

Now the most clear-cut manifestation of social stratification is, of course, the formation of social classes which takes place when people have the freedom to choose those with whom they will associate and those whom they will marry — choices which are not dictated by any political necessity. This organization of private life reaches its apogee in "Society," which in its pure

---

[4] Some of the difficulties of contemporary stratification theory arise from the fact that it has universalized in concepts what are only the particular properties of this type of society. L. A. Fallers (9) explicitly deals with the problem of analyzing the stratification of a society which lacks the very idea of social strata as understood in the West. This use of the comparative method to become aware of possible ethnocentricity in the conceptions of a theoretical framework itself and, hence, of the possibility of a more comprehensive understanding of these conceptions is a novel and important contribution.

form looks as though it is completely separated from the "state." This thus echoes the distinction between state and society which is the main tenet of liberal theory of the nineteenth century. In its pure form, as it exists for all practical purposes in the United States, outside the diplomatic circles in Washington, and in France (11, p. 38), it is completely autonomous, completely independent of any political pressure in determining its members. Otherwise it would lose its private character. As such, it determines its own rules of admission to its private circle — one form or another of a convivial set — and in so doing confers social status or standing. All social qualifications — wealth, birth, personality, education, even political authority itself — are translated by it, which in practice means its private ruler, in independence of the political order and as freely as it wishes, into its own qualifications for admission. To conform completely to the pure type, it would have to have the right to exclude any one whom it wishes.[5] It would thus be impossible in a perfect despotism where the despot would fear the existence of any autonomous groups as a threat to his power.

What does social stratification "do" in modern societies? As may already be evident, the point of view underlying this analysis is that the basic integrative structure of a society is the political order. This is the locus of all serious claims in the society, which by virtue of the nature of social and political life cannot be concerned with the right to the friendship or the convivial association of another. Friendship, in other words, when it becomes politically compulsory, is no longer friendship. When social distinctions, however, become matters of public treatment, such as the right to enter public schools, the right to public employment, and even rights in quasi-public situations such as the right to enter restaurants, then these distinctions are capable of becoming serious and, hence, political issues. Thus the way in which all the serious and conflicting claims are resolved, whether they are in some degree harmonized or whether they have

[5] Unlike the registers of titled nobility in Europe, one's name can be dropped from the *Social Register* on the grounds of conduct. The only "politicized" *Social Register* is that of Washington, D.C., which automatically lists the President, all United States Senators (but not Representatives), etc.

traveled such a course that they can be settled only by an appeal to force, gives to a society whatever integration it possesses. As suggested by Hobbes and others, a disintegrated society is one which is on the brink of or actually engaged in civil war. To the extent, then, that the political order is the integrative structure, we may say that statesmanship, tact, and diplomacy are the integrative or political arts.

In the light of this we may say that the functions of social stratification, conceived now as the formation of private groups and voluntary associations, are twofold. The first is to provide a depoliticized "escape" from the political order in the creation of a sphere which is on the surface of things independent of that order. Tocqueville has stated this in a way which goes to the heart of the matter:

> No state of society or laws can render men so much alike but that education, fortune, and tastes will interpose some differences between them; and though different men may sometimes find it their interest to combine for the same purposes, they will never make it their pleasure. They will therefore always tend to evade the provisions of law, whatever they may be; and escaping in some respect from the circle in which the legislator sought to confine them, they will set up, close by the great political community, small private societies united together by similitude of conditions, habits, and customs.
>
> The Americans, who mingle so readily in their political assemblies and courts of justice, are wont carefully to separate into small distinct circles in order to indulge by themselves in the enjoyments of private life. Each of them willingly acknowledges all his fellow citizens as his equals, but will only receive a very limited number of them as his friends or his guests. This appears to me to be very natural. In proportion as the circle of public society is extended, it may be anticipated that the sphere of private intercourse will be contracted; far from supposing that the members of modern society will ultimately live in common, I am afraid they will end by forming small coteries (15, Vol. II, pp. 215–216).

This is confirmed by the ambiguity of social stratification. Everyone knows who the President is. By the same token every enlisted man knows who is an officer. Where he will be punished for not knowing, it is no longer a "social" distinction. By contrast, practically no one knows who the leaders of "Society" are except those who are actually in it. There is, thus, no need for mutual agreement about the precise standards of social status except within a class and those classes adjacent to it. The bases of precise social distinctions within a circle, the things that are really esteemed and regarded as worthy of prestige, may not only be unknown but for all practical purposes be inconceivable to people in distant circles. What, for example, does a policeman in London know or even care about the relative social standing of the colleges in Oxford? What does an enlisted man think about the standing of an officer, as such, in the officers' club? Even servants can have, what are from their employer's point of view, very strange notions, indeed, about the social status of the family to which they are attached. Along these lines almost all the difficulties which have legitimately perplexed specialists in this area have arisen from the initial assumption of a unitary status hierarchy. As the theory of reference groups and research on them, among other things, has so abundantly confirmed, this cannot possibly exist in a large, complex society. What exists is a multiplicity of circles which are linked together by personal contacts and the mass media. The result of this is that from within the various circles there are different perspectives of the stratification system and, hence, different hierarchies (16, p. 19).

This is not to suggest that there are not broad areas of agreement upon standards within the society as a whole. Where agreement is genuinely clear cut and widespread, however, such as there is in the United States upon respect for the attributes of middle-class status, it will invariably be an aspect of the political order or of something which competes with government for its political functions.[6] Respect for these attributes, in other words, would not be so clear cut or widespread were they not publicly

---

[6] Cf. Churchill's remarks: "The East India Company's Army of Bengal had long been of ill-repute. Recruited mainly in the North, it was largely composed of high-caste Hindus. Brahmin privates would question the orders of officers and N.C.O.s of less exalted caste. Power and influence in the regiments frequently depended on a man's position in the religious rather than the military hierarchy. . . . This was bad for discipline." (6, p. 67)

authoritative, if the middle class, that is, were not really the first-class citizens.

The methodological implication of the above is that the analysis of social stratification must be "repoliticized" in order to bring out its essential features.[7] Only by making the composition of that class which publicly and, hence, effectively sets the ruling standards in the society the focal point of analysis can one avoid one of the chief conceptual difficulties of much of stratification theory, namely, reified fragmentation of subgroups from the society as a whole. For example, to return to the question of minorities again, granted that they may to a great degree live in their own social worlds, have their own internal criteria of prestige, and altogether do not "fit" into the non-minority status hierarchy of the community as a whole, the fundamental fact still remains that middle-class members of such a minority, and, of course, the group as a whole when it becomes middle class, can make a political claim to be treated as first-class citizens, which completely breaks through the boundary of the community. The minority, in other words, becomes integrated or politically linked in the decisive respect to the main axis of the society which is obscured by regarding its social life as the basis of the exhaustive conceptual framework. All in all, one may say that only in the light of the authoritative character of the political order can the essentially private, ambiguous, and non-authoritative character of much of what takes place in the sphere of social class stratification be seen as such. Unless the latter is fitted into the more comprehensive conceptual framework, it becomes almost impossible to account, first, for the political weakness of upper social classes as classes and, second, for the fact that their very emphasis on status is a reaction to their loss of genuine authority.

The second aspect of social stratification concerns its political functions. These are to provide a sphere in which a group or class can arise and maintain itself as some type of intermediate

---

[7] Cf. Dahrendorf (8, pp. 144–145), whose analysis points to similar conclusions. Cf. also in this respect the important words of caution of Bendix and Lipset (3, pp. 82–85) against the danger of any approach which, by denying that political claims and interests may have a rational or reasonable ground, explains away the facts of political life.

authority in the society as a whole. This would be a class which, in spite of its lack of a ruling position, still has sufficient self-confidence, respect, and coherence openly to oppose the ruling standards set by the political order. Briefly, we examine three possible varieties of such authority.

The first type is that which exists in a capitalist democracy without a hereditary aristocracy, such as in the United States. There the members of the upper social classes as well as the clergy, educators, and those members of the professional classes in general who still have the bearing, the style of life, and the outlook of the older professional man, even though they must bow politically to the middle class, still can make a moral claim to be heard. On the one hand, there is considerable respect for these groups among the middle class as a whole by virtue of its religious heritage as well as the heritage of Western civilization in general. On the other hand, these groups, by virtue of the freedom they possess, accept the democracy in a way which they were not prepared to do in 1800 when the election of Jefferson appeared to them like the beginning of mob rule (1, pp. 59–60). In fact, it would be fair to say that they have forgotten that there ever was once such an issue. For both these reasons, even though they are not publicly authoritative on a national level in the same way in which they set the tone of eighteenth-century New England (1, p. 54), they cannot be simply dismissed. With the exception on the federal level of certain enclaves within the civil service, which in any event, as the attack by McCarthy showed, hardly have the coherence of the British civil service (14), their sphere of influence has been the local community (2). Much of this influence is the purely private power that wealth makes possible that can be exerted not only locally but nationally as well. With this we are not concerned in this analysis. What is of interest here is merely the extent to which they do wield influence and power that is not purely private but does have a moral foundation, that is to say, the extent to which they enjoy consent.[8] In general, one may offer the provisional hypothesis that, the larger the city, the less authoritative will these groups be in any issue that involves a conflict about a democratization, such as, for example, on the

[8] See above, Footnote 1.

lowering of school standards. In these respects such groups have their greatest influence in the smaller suburban communities, where the dominant tone is set by the upper middle class.

A second type of such power is that which existed in prewar France and Germany, where the upper classes which had been displaced from power by a democratization, and inflamed furthermore by ideological cleavages, never fully accepted the parliamentary regimes. From their positions in the civil service and more particularly in the army, they exerted what power they possessed to destroy these regimes (11, p. 36).

A third type is that which exists in a totalitarian society. In view of the absence of freedom, it is more a potential than a normal feature of the society. What is of interest in the present context is the way in which groups, such as the economic managers in Soviet Russia, can develop an *esprit de corps* and certain non-ideological standards of political behavior oriented toward administrative, technical expertise. As such, these conflict with the methods of the autocratic dictatorship, which, relying for its support upon the ideological party, prefers such demagogic techniques as the "crash drive" to raise production levels in industry. Though these groups can become influential when the autocracy is weakened, their political strength relative to that of the party politicians is indicated by the triumph of Khrushchev, the party leader, over Malenkov, who sought a base of support in the more educated, professional bureaucracy. Nonetheless, the general problem of whether such groups can exert influence within the regime promises to be one of the most interesting lines of research about stratification in totalitarian societies.[9]

References

1. Adams, Henry. *The United States in 1800*. Ithaca, N.Y.: Great Seal Books, 1955.
2. Baltzell, E. Digby. *Philadelphia Gentlemen*. Glencoe, Ill.: The Free Press, 1958.

[9] Cf. Myron Rush's (13) penetrating analysis of the tension between the party and the state bureaucracy in Russia.

The Individual and Social Organization

3. Bendix, Reinhard, and Seymour M. Lipset. "Political Sociology," *Current Sociology*, Vol. 6 (1957), pp. 82–85.

4. Bryce, James. *The American Commonwealth*, 2d rev. ed. London: Macmillan and Co., Ltd., 1889.

5. Burke, Edmund. *Reflections on the Revolution in France*. New York: E. P. Dutton and Co., "Everyman's Library," 1910.

6. Churchill, Winston. *A History of the English-Speaking Peoples*. London: Cassell, 1958.

7. Cuber, John F., and William F. Kenkel. *Social Stratification in the United States*. New York: Appleton-Century-Crofts, Inc., 1954.

8. Dahrendorf, Ralf. *Soziale Klassen und Klassenkonflikt in der industriellen Gesellschaft*. Stuttgart: Ferdinand Enke Verlag, 1957.

9. Fallers, L. A. "Despotism, Status Culture, and Social Mobility in an African Kingdom," *Comparative Studies in Society and History*, Vol. 2 (October 1959), pp. 11–32.

10. Lubell, Samuel. *The Future of American Politics*. Garden City, N.Y.: Doubleday & Company, Inc., Anchor Books, 1956.

11. Luethy, Herbert. *France Against Herself*. New York: Meridian Books, 1957.

12. Marshall, T. H. *Citizenship and Social Class*. Cambridge, Eng.: Cambridge University Press, 1950.

13. Rush, Myron. "The Economic Managers," *New Leader*, May 12, 1958.

14. Spann, R. N. "Civil Servants in Washington," *Political Studies*, Vol. 1 (1953), pp. 143–161; 228–245.

15. Tocqueville, Alexis de. *Democracy in America*, tr. by Francis Bowen. New York: Alfred A. Knopf, 1945.

16. Warner, W. Lloyd, Marchia Meeker, and Kenneth Eells. *Social Class in America*. Chicago: Science Research Associates, 1949.

17

Social Bases of Political Commitment: A Study of Liberals and Radicals

 WILLIAM KORNHAUSER

UNIVERSITY OF CALIFORNIA, BERKELEY

The social act as seen by symbolic interactionists is a continuous process of defining the situation, with each definition evolving, in large part, out of antecedent definitions. In effect, the act becomes a continuous series of contingencies. Once a choice has been made, there may be a commitment to it which will determine most of the steps in a future course of action. Professor Kornhauser here analyzes the process of forming a commitment and adhering to it among political liberals and radicals. Although real differences are pointed out between the radical and liberal self-commitments, attention should be drawn to the even greater contrast with the industrial workers' lack of commitment to work, as portrayed by Dubin in Chapter 13. For the radical, "work" is politics, and it is clearly his "central life interest."

To incur a commitment is to become more or less unavailable for alternative lines of action. Commitment entails more than merely voicing a choice, although a pledge or promise certainly is a simple way of becoming committed. The additional element in commitment is the "force of circumstances" to which one becomes exposed by virtue of pursuing a course of action. A commitment consists in the various relations which are formed in the process of acting in a certain direction, so that to shift the line of action requires changing these relations.

The relations formed in the course of striving for a goal possess certain general characteristics. They include much more than was bargained for in the initial decision to seek the goal. The unanticipated relations result from the nature of the effort (or means) required by the goal. They are binding on the individual who would continue to seek the goal. Hence, commitments are *requirements* for seeking a goal (cf. 3, pp. 225–259).

One kind of circumstance surrounding any sustained effort to achieve a goal consists in other relations and goals. Thus a certain course of political action may enforce a wide range of nonpolitical relations. The *interdependence of spheres of action* is responsible for many of the attributes of commitment. This circumstance creates tension and resistance, as commitments generated in the course of seeking one goal clash with requirements of other goals. The individual faces the problem of integrating the various relations which command his allegiance. To say that an individual seeks conflicting goals usually means that he cannot fulfill both sets of commitments engendered by them. Therefore, *the strength of a commitment can be measured by the number of social spheres for which it enforces lines of action.*

The idea of commitment, then, implies more than choice, and also more than what we initially believe to be our obligations as a result of the choice. We may *feel* committed and yet not *be* committed; and we may be committed without full cognizance of that fact. Appreciation of what is comprised in a commitment may come only when we try to break it; then the consequences of our involvement are revealed to us, often for the first time.

In order to explore the social bases of commitment, we studied a group of people whose goals engendered high commitment, and compared them with people whose goals summoned only limited commitment. We also studied people who broke off each kind of commitment. We selected radical political goals as ones which produce strong commitment, and liberal political goals as ones which invite only moderate commitment. Our sample was composed of leaders of radical political groups in Chicago, namely, Communist and Trotskyist organizations, and of the major liberal political organization in Chicago, the Independent Voters of Illinois (affiliated with Americans for Democratic Action). We found people who had terminated their commitments by asking these leaders for the names of persons they knew who had quit the organization after having held similar positions. Since we sought intensive interviews covering a wide range of topics, we had to impose severe limits on the number of people studied. We secured case histories of 20 presently active local leaders of radical organizations, and of 10 who quit these organizations and revolutionary politics altogether. We also secured the same number of cases of present and former leaders of the liberal organization. Our analysis of these 60 cases first treats the political commitment of the radical, and then the political commitment of the liberal.

Social Bases of a Radical Commitment

Radicals stand apart from society, living their lives primarily as "outsiders." Politics must be of unsurpassable importance for them to give of themselves thus. By the same token, the political future must hold great promise of success. High expectations on both counts are necessary for the radical's commitment. This confidence in the future clashes with the poverty of radical achievements in present-day America. Faced with innumerable disconfirming events on all sides, the radical party in America continuously must contend with what it is wont to call "defeatist tendencies."

A radical leader noted that, among new recruits, political expectations often are excessive, even by radical standards:

> One of the toughest problems we [leaders] face is the great hopes new comrades bring into the party. They are expecting the revolution to be right around the corner. When it doesn't come, they get discouraged and may leave the revolutionary movement. We have to teach them that immediate victory is not in sight. That's tough to do. Revolutions are only made when the objective conditions are ripe. A professional revolutionary knows this and is braced for defeats.

The Individual and Social Organization

A radical in the process of breaking from his party was able to reveal the strain between high expectations and low achievements as he first began to experience it:

> The more optimistic among us expected revolutionary conditions to follow the war. The party would never admit this, but when you're in the revolutionary movement, you have to think the revolution is coming in five or ten years. Or, at least, you have to believe that the revolution is coming in your lifetime! You have to think that! You can't keep up the pace unless you have that hope.

Radicals, then, face the continuous problem of maintaining high expectations in the face of disconfirming events. Resolution of the problem cannot be made simply by lowering expectations, since revolutionary demands for change are of such scope and weight as to require sustained effort at the expense of other aspects of life, and this in turn requires overriding belief in the promise of political success. Instead, adaptation to the wide gap between expectations and achievements tends to be made by *enforced isolation* from people who do not hold revolutionary goals.

Our case histories show that persons currently holding revolutionary goals are isolated from the community, whereas persons who have terminated their ties to radical groups are not isolated. Specifically, radicals generally do not have close ties with persons who are not radicals, nor do they seek a professional career outside the political movement.

Revolutionary groups seek to place their members in jobs where they can make a political contribution. For example, members frequently are instructed by party leaders to take a job in a plant to help organize or penetrate a trade union. The hard core of the party consists of members on the party staff or members who are working in jobs through which they can be politically effective. One radical followed this party expectation in the selection of work for several years, but then he took a job with no political potential:

> I can't do any union work where I am now. It's too small a shop. I could go into a bigger shop, but I don't want to. I'm glad to have a breather for awhile. There is nothing stirring

nowadays. I figure it's better for the party [*sic*] as well as for me to do some other things during this quiet period. I want to do some writing and reading, work on my inventions, see new friends. . . . My job gives me a chance to get some more money.

Although it is of course possible to disengage oneself from politically relevant work for short periods of time without divorcing oneself from radical politics, once the individual begins to satisfy non-political gratifications in his work it will be more difficult for him to give them up for political action. In this case, the respondent's *private* interests in writing, reading, working on inventions, seeing friends, and making money portend a movement away from radical politics. As a matter of fact, this person quit radical politics a year or so after we first interviewed him.

The radical who is effectively insulated from influences outside the radical movement does not attach an important value to his work over and above its political significance. He does not change jobs simply to gain more money, nor does he expend major energies to gain promotions and to advance a career. Where the radical's job has political potential, the party demands that he use it to advance its interests. This means that a union official, for example, must be prepared to sacrifice his career in the labor movement if party leaders decide that this is the course required by the political needs of the party. The harshness of this commitment is indicated by the frequency with which union leaders have broken with radical groups.

Where a job does not have political potential, the committed radical will seek a job which consumes the minimum amount of time, leaving him with the most freedom to engage in political work. The radical commitment involves the full use of "spare time" for political purposes.[1]

A radical discussed the problem in these terms:

I would take a university job if the circumstances seemed right; at least, I would do it for a short time. I can't see myself working in business much longer. The crucial thing is that I get a job with the most freedom to do what I want —

[1] Almond's study based on interviews with former Communists reports findings similar to ours on this point (1, pp. 147-151).

working for the party. For a well-educated Marxist, party work is fulfillment enough. You can get your prestige and you can use your skills there [in the party]. It has tremendous status to be a party staff member. That's my ultimate aim.

By virtue of his political goal, the radical activist is required to reject the pursuit of a career. His political relations enforce this commitment, for example, by not leaving him time to develop new interests. Party members are so busy with party activities that they are effectively insulated from outside influence.

A second major indication of the enforced isolation of the radical is his lack of personal ties to people who are not also radicals. None of the radicals we interviewed had close friends and members of his immediate family who did not also belong to the same political group. The radical's lack of personal ties outside his political group is not a matter of his choice alone. His political associates enforce it. The tendency for the community to ostracize the radical for his politics also plays a role in isolating the individual, as the following account of one individual's experiences shows:

> Former friends and associates thought I was dead wrong in my politics, that I was a threat to the community, and did everything they could think of to cut me off and ruin me. Now they think I'm just eccentric — it's gone that far! I have faced the whole range of intimidations. But I haven't curtailed my actions. Once you are in, there is no going back, even if you wanted to.

The radical will seek to terminate personal ties outside the party, not merely because he is constrained to do so, but also because he feels uneasy with people who do not share his central mission in life. When asked to describe his closest friends, a radical replied:

> When you are in the party for many years, as I have been, you develop warm bonds with your comrades. I have had a few friends outside the party, but they can never be as close friends. They can't be friends at all if they are hostile to the party. You never feel as comfortable with an outsider as you do with your comrades. But each of us has to work out these personal problems as best he can, always keeping in mind that personal considerations must be changed to fit the needs of the party.

In order to continue actively seeking radical goals, the individual needs to give up personal ties outside the radical group; he also must develop new personal relations within the radical group. Unless he terminates outside relations, the individual will be exposed to conflicting demands. Unless he forges new ties within the group, the individual will be exposed to disillusionment and discouragement. When the radical must maintain his political allegiance in order to maintain his personal relations and social status, then he will be less ready to entertain doubts about that allegiance. Too many non-political relations are at stake to judge the political relationship in purely political terms. If the political relationship does not find support in non-political attachments, then it can readily be disrupted by disconfirming events in the political world.

Festinger and his colleagues have shown how a small sect in Chicago was able to sustain itself in spite of the fact that its key expectation — that the world would come to an end on a certain date — was not fulfilled (2). One of the reasons why the sect did not disintegrate when its prophecy failed was that the participants were bound together in close personal relations and provided strong support for one another in the face of failure. So, too, with our radical groups: their prophecies have by and large also failed; yet they frequently have maintained their cohesion because they have not formed merely a special-purpose association of like-minded people but a closed *society* in which a variety of needs are fulfilled. To leave such a group is not merely to terminate a political relationship: it also entails the rupture of all kinds of non-political relations.

One of our respondents who is a leading radical illustrates to what extent a political relationship may come to involve a total commitment. He joined a radical party when he was a young man. A short time later he was appointed to the staff of the party. At this point, he changed his name at the direction of the party. Shortly thereafter, he married a girl who also worked on the party staff. Now his name, his job, and his wife were all acting to support his political goals. During this period he terminated all personal relations with people who were not also in the party, and built up a completely new circle of friends. He also gave up any aspirations for a career outside the party.

At the same time, the radical's politicalization of his personal relations tends to attenuate them. Non-political relations become *restricted* by incorporation into the political relation. This is especially true of personal relations, for this kind of social bond involves mutual trust and spontaneity, something which cannot be given fully and easily where political tests are always being applied (cf. 1, pp. 118-125). Thus radicals insist that the movement comes before personal relations, which means that those who leave the movement cut themselves off from all personal as well as political consideration.

The social bases of the radical commitment are further revealed by the kinds of orientations and relations that characterize persons who defect from radical groups. The process of defection involves the loss of political hope, rather than an initial change in political values or in the assessment of the group's adherence to these values, and the growth in concern for personal interests, which are felt to be threatened by the radical commitment. Corresponding to this change in orientation, defection is associated with certain changes in personal relations: the loss of personal relations with political associates, which signifies the failure to fulfill the radical commitment, and the development of close ties to persons who are not political associates, which also violates the radical commitment. We shall first consider changes in orientation by persons who have quit radical politics, and then changes in personal relations.

One of our respondents expressed his changing political orientation in these terms:

> The party's isolation made me feel that there was no point in being a Communist and sacrificing my whole life. The party was through, and I didn't feel like sticking around as a caretaker, even though I still believe the party is right.

We may view the sense of increasing hopelessness of the radical party as a rationalization for the desire to jump back into the mainstream of society; or it may be that the desire to return to the community results from the judgment that political life appears increasingly pointless. In all probability, the two grow together, indistinguishable from one another. Loss of political expectations is closely associated with a shift in orientation away from the group and toward the self. When this happens, as it did in the following case of a person who left the Communist party, the individual sees himself caught between a political commitment and the satisfaction of personal interests.

> I still hold to the same position of Marxism. I just decided that I came first. It wasn't worth the sacrifices to stay in. Nothing can be done now, anyway. Yes, I've changed a lot in recent years. I've always been an egotist. I finally decided I didn't want to be a martyr. I want to get a good job, not too good, but sufficient so that I don't worry about money. And lead a normal life for a change.

As doubts about the possibilities of political effectiveness grow, concern over the impact of political relations on personal interests grows apace.

> When I went to work at [a business firm], I didn't want to be known as a radical. I didn't want to be an outsider. I got to know a lot of people there who would have thrown me over if they knew. Not to mention the boss. I've seen too many lives wasted by those who have cut themselves off from everything to be a radical. They have made tremendous sacrifices to do it. They have never made a decent living, they have turned down good jobs, they have made their families suffer. Brilliant people who could have made a real success of their lives. Thrown away for a cause that can't ever be successful. Socialism will never come in this world!

Our interviews show a consistent pattern of inner conflict over leaving radical politics. One of our respondents made this conflict very clear.

> I'm not doing anything political these days. I've lost contact for the most part. It's hard to be active along with a job and family. . . . I'm getting older. I have two kids. You start thinking about putting something away for them. Against all these things, when you've been in the movement for years, you feel a duty to go on, you feel like hell when you don't. So what do you do? When things become quiet, you let your wife pull you out. Maybe if things were really happening, then you would choose the movement and let the family go.

People leave radical politics when they come to define the

situation as a choice between a hopeless political cause and a hopeful personal life. In order for the lines to be so drawn, the individual must have more or less fully divorced himself from significant personal relations *within* the political group, or failed to have developed such relations in the first place. Termination of a radical commitment tends to occur when several of the individual's closest personal associates have decided to break their radical commitment. They may not make such a decision consciously as a group; they may not leave together. But the fact is that most of the ex-radicals we interviewed reported that they talked over the question of leaving with intimates in the party, and that they left the party at about the same time.

It would be an oversimplification to conclude that the individual quits a radical group when he decides to sacrifice his political relations in favor of his personal relations. In the first place, there must be a process of political disillusionment, usually born of pessimism over the party's future. In the second place, it is too neat to suppose that the individual's personal relations all function to keep him in the political group or to pull him away from the political group. Generally, the individual's personal relations pull him in both directions simultaneously. The evidence we have collected points to a net balance on the side of personal relations which pull the individual who quits radical politics away from his political commitment (cf. 1, pp. 300–324). But consider the case of one of our respondents who quit radical politics in spite of the influence of close friends:

> I had friends in the party I wanted to keep. They were my closest friends, and I knew that it meant losing them [if I quit]. The party won't have anything to do with the fellow who breaks. He's a renegade, finished, dead. Once you have been in, you can't leave without this stigma.

This respondent reports that when he quit, he made a strenuous effort to keep in touch with a few of his closest friends. Belying his own prediction, this effort met with some success, but only because he remained ideologically sympathetic to the party.

Once outside the radical movement, former members frequently associate with one another, at least during the early period of their alienation from radical politics. The tendency for ex-radicals to seek one another out helps bridge the great distance between the world of radical politics and the community. In effect, they are leaning on one another for support in their often painful return to the society from which they had withdrawn.

As people who have terminated their membership in a radical group reintegrate themselves into society, they slowly give up their radical ideas. Among our respondents there is no case of a dramatic shift to the opposite extreme, as in the much-celebrated cases of ex-Communists returning to the Catholic Church or joining the political right. It might be expected that a certain proportion of ex-radicals will overconform to the dominant political temper of the community in their anxiety to be accepted. But among our respondents this type of response does not appear.

A final word about the consequences of defection for radicalism itself. Defection from a radical group has much more serious consequences for radicalism as an organized movement and as an ideology than does defection from a liberal group. For when a radical drops out of a political organization, he cuts himself off from radical influences and becomes more open to influences which operate to change his ideas and values. But the liberal, adhering to ideas and values closer to widely held views, may sustain them without active membership in an organization. The liberal rarely becomes isolated from the community in the first place on account of his politics. On the contrary, the liberal's political action generally heightens his ties to the community.

Social Bases of a Liberal Commitment

Liberals lead only part of their lives as political men. Politics may be judged to be very important, but liberals can be politically active without great expectations. Politics may be hopeful, but liberals can commit a part of their lives to the pursuit of political goals without the conviction that success is imminent or certain. They have not invested that much of themselves in politics to feel basically threatened if political demands are not realized.

If the limited nature of liberal expectations and demands reduces the danger of political disillusionment, by the same token it poses the problem of maintaining political interest. The gap between the liberal's expectations and achievements tends to be so small as to provide little *incentive* for political action. This is the opposite of the problem facing the radical, who must suffer a very great disparity between expectations and achievements. The liberal's weak political motivation is illustrated by one of our respondents who quit liberal politics:

> I resigned from IVI last year. I had too many other things to do. It was a question of where to put my time. And, frankly, I was bored! The meetings became awfully boring, just terribly dull. Instead of discussing issues, all the time was spent talking about how to raise funds. I tried to stir up discussions on issues, but didn't get anywhere.

An IVI leader observed that "with no major election for some time if there is no transfer of interest somewhere, interest will die." The modest goals of liberal groups fail to summon the intense energies available to radical groups. Nor is a liberal organization prepared to use the full energies of many of its members even if they were forthcoming. There is relatively little *work* to be done in a liberal organization, precisely because its goals are so limited. Many a liberal group seeks to make work for its members, but this merely serves to underscore the problem rather than to solve it. In short, liberal goals invite only moderate commitment to political activity.

At the same time, the liberal's commitments to non-political goals tend to be strong and demanding. This applies especially to his professional goals, and also to his family obligations. Running throughout our interviews with liberals are statements to the effect that "I can't put in so much time"; "IVI is taking up too much of my time"; "I'm neglecting my work"; "My family objects to my politics because I'm never home"; "Now that the children are out of the way [going to school], maybe I can give some more time to IVI"; "When my partner comes back from his vacation, then I can go to IVI meetings again"; "When you get older, you can't maintain the same pace in political action because you have so many more responsibilities."

Respondents were asked what kinds of political action they enjoyed and what kinds they disliked. In every interview with liberals, a ready and definite reply was forthcoming, specifying what was pleasurable and what was distasteful. Representative liberal responses referred to personal gratifications derived from backstage maneuverings in deciding whom to endorse for public office, the promotion of candidates, and the excitement of election night, and to the tedium of such routine work as door-bell ringing. Only two radicals expressed such preferences or dislikes. The others replied with such answers as: "I never really thought about that." "I don't like campaigning, but it is all necessary." "It is serious business." One radical said:

> This [political action] is not a pleasurable matter. It is a difficult and serious matter. I don't enjoy any of the work. It's just something that has to be done.

Here is additional evidence that the characteristic motivational problem facing radicals is maintaining political expectations, and that of liberals is sustaining political interest.

The liberal group cannot seek to generate or sustain political interest among its participants in ways analogous to those employed by the radical group. Given its basic acceptance of the political order, and its limited demands for change, the liberal group can neither claim from its members nor use "the whole of their lives." Furthermore, the wholly political man is an anti-liberal conception in and of itself. Liberalism implies pluralism in interests and relations. Liberal groups are thus debarred from seeking to absorb the whole of their members' lives, nor can they seek to insulate their members from the larger society. Quite the contrary. *A liberal group finds strength in the multiple ties its members establish to the community.*

Radicals are constrained to avoid deep involvement in a career outside of politics; liberals are valued for their successful business or professional careers. Membership in a radical group is an *exclusive* relationship; members of liberal groups characteristically have multiple group affiliations. Radicals are required to confine close personal relations to other members of the political group; liberals are expected to value a diversity of beliefs among their close associates. These three major differences between liberals and radicals in the social bases of the political commitment will be considered in order.

Two-thirds of the liberals we interviewed occupy high professional and business positions. Two-thirds of the radicals hold considerably lower occupational positions. This difference in occupational status is reinforced by the political commitment. We have already shown that radicals are discouraged from placing career interests ahead of political interests. In contrast, liberal leaders are sought among the members of certain major law firms, universities, and businesses in order to gain access to their skills, contacts, money, and prestige. Much of the power of the liberal group consists in the influence of individual members, rather than in the power of organization. The strength of the liberal group depends more on its *selective recruitment* of leaders, whereas the strength of the radical group depends more on its *intensive socialization* of leaders.

All of the liberals we studied who have remained active in IVI were also members of at least three civic or reform groups in addition to their political affiliation. In contrast, only two radicals maintained any organizational affiliations in addition to their membership in the political group. The groups to which liberals belong have memberships which overlap one another and that of the political group. A cross-tabulation of names appearing on the letterheads of six major liberal organizations in Chicago shows that a large number of persons appear on more than one letterhead. In fact, about one-half of the total list of names on six letterheads are accounted for by about one-fourth of the people. Half or more of the names on each letterhead also appear on one or more of the other five letterheads. Furthermore, the most active leaders of each group are more likely to appear on more than one letterhead than are the less active persons. One of our respondents analyzed this "community of liberal leaders" from his own experience:

> My work in housing led me into conferences of the Mayor's Commission on Human Relations, because housing always leads to race relations. From this, I was invited on the board of the American Civil Liberties Union and the Chicago Council Against Racial and Religious Discrimination. Then, I was

working with an IVI leader, who asked me to serve on that board. And I've been on the board of the Chicago Council on Foreign Relations, Committee for the Nation's Health, Housing Conference of Chicago, and probably a dozen more I don't even remember. *Once you get involved in one of these groups, you meet people who are in other groups and they invite you to join the boards of these other groups.* They're all interlocking directorates. . . . What happens is you get to be something of a name in these circles, so you get invited to all these committees and boards, because each group figures your name will appeal to certain other people.

Thus, where the radical commitment enforces isolation from the community, the liberal commitment enforces participation in it.

The liberal's personal relations also testify to a broad community involvement. Whereas all the radicals we studied had most of their friends in the party, only one liberal did so. The other liberals report that their friends were often very different from them politically, that they "go across the board politically," that they run the "whole gamut of political views." These respondents refer to the diversity of political views among their friends with no regret. They would not have it any other way, because "one does not want to appear to be choosing his friends on a political basis," and "differences of opinion make for a more interesting life," and "everyone has a right to his own political views." Frequently, these liberals try to proselytize friends who are not IVI members. But politics rarely is a condition of friendship. By and large, *the liberal commitment does not involve a shift in the locus of the personal world.*

At the same time, those who have persisted in their liberal loyalties have *some* strong personal ties with other members of IVI. These ties typically were formed outside the political group and carried over into politics. Or, if they were formed in political contexts, they subsequently were integrated with associations outside of politics. Thus members of a liberal group are absorbed into the organization only to a limited extent. Even in a liberal group, however, some personal ties are needed to lend stability to the pursuit of liberal political goals through organized efforts. This is indicated by an examination of those who left the liberal group.

Those who quit IVI did not have close personal relations within the group; nor did they belong to other civic or reform associations. Thus, there were few social supports for the political relation, and few social obligations contingent upon it. Consequently, when pressures from professional or family roles increased, the fragile political ties readily collapsed.

Representative of our respondents who quit liberal politics was a man who had been very active in IVI for several years. At the same time he was just breaking into a large law firm. Then he received a sudden promotion in the firm, and shortly thereafter began to cut down on his political action. When he mentioned how much time he used to put into politics, he quickly added:

> Please don't write that down! I would hate to have my firm know about this!

This person seized upon a minor disagreement with IVI as an occasion to break off his commitment. The incident would have been quickly forgotten by this man unless he were looking for an excuse to quit. After that incident, he stated:

> Now I'm through with politics. When I withdrew my political career came to an end. It's more comfortable looking in from the outside. I enjoyed it while it lasted, but I'm sure I'll never get involved again. I have a busy and growing law practice which I couldn't risk by being politically active.

In short, those who quit IVI had two major characteristics in common prior to their withdrawal: (1) few personal ties within IVI, and (2) few ties to the larger community of which IVI is a part. They left IVI under the following conditions: certain personal interests either conflicted with the political affiliation, or simply were not being satisfied by the political affiliation. In several cases, disturbances in their political relations within IVI facilitated the withdrawal, but in all cases the decisive factor appears to be the pull of outside family and professional commitments. In no case did a person arrive at a new ideological position, and leave the group on that basis. In several cases, there is evidence that IVI may be rejoined sometime in the future.

Involvement in a liberal political group generally is an *extension* of involvement in a wider community of professional, civic, and personal relations. Rather than weakening ties to the community, liberal politics tends to strengthen multiple attachments to the community. As a result of the integration of the liberal political group in the larger society, the individual who joins a liberal group does not become dependent primarily on political associates to satisfy primary-group needs. This difference from the radical is only a matter of degree, however. Liberals who do not find *any* gratifying personal relations in their political life are also likely to withdraw from politics.

When the individual does drop out of a liberal group, his political beliefs generally remain more stable than does the individual who quits a radical group. The liberal is closer to widely held views and therefore can sustain liberal values even after he gives up membership and participation in a liberal organization. This is to say that radical beliefs require much more *organizational support* than do liberal beliefs. Radical groups tend to become closed societies, set apart from the community, whereas liberal groups are open associations.

CONCLUSION

The radical suffers from a very wide disparity between what he has learned to expect about ultimate political victory and day-to-day political achievements. As a consequence, he is prey to doubts about the worth of sacrificing a life in the community. The radical group seeks to counter these tendencies among its members by separating them from the community and absorbing them into the movement. The community cooperates by ostracizing those in its midst who are believed to be radicals. Insofar as this isolation is enforced by the political group and the community, the individual avoids cross-pressures between his political and non-political relations. The radical incurs commitments far transcending his political obligations, especially pressures on him to terminate involvement with work associates, family, friends, neighbors, etc., who are not also radicals. In addition, he incurs commitments to fellow radicals which are not specific to the political enterprise, often including obligations of a highly personal nature. All of his relations support the political allegiance by being *fused* with the political role, which *dominates* the non-political roles. This is the only way the radical can integrate his political and non-political roles, precisely because the radical movement is isolated from and at war with the larger society. For under these conditions, a web of non-political involvements, by requiring the individual to maintain his political allegiance in order to sustain his personal relations, is a major source of support for radical goals. Movement away from radical politics is at the same time movement back into the community. Persons in the process of breaking their ties to a radical group, as well as those who have already defected, form multiple relations in the community. Persons securely attached to radical groups, on the other hand, have no such relations and therefore are not readily vulnerable to threatened deprivations at the hands of the community.

The liberal suffers from *too small* a disparity between his political expectations and achievements. The gap is so small that it provides little *incentive* to engage in political action. The liberal is vulnerable to loss of political interest. Unlike the radical group, the liberal group cannot seek to isolate its members from competing interests and loyalties, because it is part of the community. It also cannot seek to absorb its members into the group, since its goals and activities permit only the limited use of its members' energies. Instead, the liberal group constrains the individual to form and sustain multiple involvements in the community. The sustenance of political interest is facilitated when the liberal shares multiple ties with other members of his political group — as colleagues, as friends, in voluntary associations. In this case, political ties are supported by non-political relations centering in the community rather than in the political group. These independent *mediating* relations help to support the political goal by stimulating political interest in it. Furthermore, this is the only way the liberal can integrate his political and non-political relations just because the liberal group is part of the community. If he does not *differentiate* his political and non-political relations, he is more likely to face cross-pressures between them. If he *shares* non-political concerns with some of the people with whom he also shares political concerns, but does not confound them (as does the radical), he is less likely to face cross-pressures between them. Conflict may arise from increasing involvement in one role which requires decreasing involvement in other roles. An element of stability in the allocation of involvement among several roles is introduced by sharing different involvements with some of the *same* people. For then the expectations of each role include expectations that the other roles will be performed.

But this is not to say that the liberal's non-political relations are contingent on his fulfilling political obligations to the extent that this is true for the radical. Liberal goals enforce much less commitment than do radical goals. But then liberal goals entail much less sacrifice of personal interests outside of politics, and therefore do not need such strong support. Furthermore, liberal values are much more consistent with the culture of the larger society, whereas radicalism is a deviant subculture. In general, the more distinctive the subculture, the more precarious it is, and therefore the greater the commitment it requires.

References

1. Almond, Gabriel A. *The Appeals of Communism.* Princeton, N.J.: Princeton University Press, 1954.
2. Festinger, Leon, *et al. When Prophecy Fails.* Minneapolis: University of Minnesota Press, 1954.
3. Selznick, Philip. *TVA and the Grass Roots.* Berkeley, Calif.: University of California Press, 1949.

18

Collective Dynamics: Process and Form

KURT LANG

GLADYS ENGEL LANG

QUEENS COLLEGE, NEW YORK

Ever since the formal study of social psychology began, it has included a special sub-field, generally misnamed "collective behavior," to which the Langs here address themselves. Insofar as the subject is distinct from the rest of social psychology, it is that it is based on communication through natural signs rather than significant symbols. However, except in the extreme stages of crowd excitement, the distinction is not absolute, because few concrete human behaviors are grounded on any abstraction formulated out of the social scientist's heuristic interest. But crowds, panics, rumors, fads, and similar collective phenomena are characterized by a relatively large number of expressions and effects of natural signs. Since other animals than man also communicate by means of natural signs, a large part of this sub-field might logically be considered as part of general psychology. Nevertheless, practically all general psychologists eschew the field — indeed, many deny its existence. For this reason, and because students of "collective behavior" have actually studied it only in man's behavior, it belongs historically with sociological social psychology.

As a field of sociological interest, collective behavior has its roots in the late nineteenth century, in the concern of Tarde, Sighele, LeBon, and others with the psychology of the crowd. In the thinking of continental psychologists, the "crowd" stood for an array of collective phenomena, ranging from the shifts of public sentiment exhibited in fashion or on the stock market to the far-reaching social changeover, sparked by revolutionary movements, from some occasional fracas on a city street to the mob despoiling a city, from the emotional outbursts of a revival meeting to the far-flung orgiastic activities of predatory groups, from emotional responses of entire nations to specific crises in parliament. The epidemic-like way in which behavior catches, and the irrational or socially deviant nature of behavior when people, on given occasions, are subjected to the psychological intoxication of large numbers, seemed to be the common element in all these "crowd" phenomena. LeBon claimed that almost any multitude was capable of being transformed into a psychological crowd. The crowd potential, he said, slumbers within every individual.

These crowd-like phenomena were also the subject matter of the field to which Park and Burgess first gave concise definition. But in differentiating the crowd proper and other crowd-like phenomena, they offered a more refined framework for including a variety of similar phenomena within a single area of inquiry. Thus Park and Burgess (21) — and subsequently Blumer (1) — pointed out how the crowd proper, the public, and the mass differed from each other both in their over-all pattern of action and the nature of the interaction within each.[1] Between the crowd and these other forms of collective behavior there were certain formal differences. Still, common to all these phenomena were patterns of interaction marked by relatively greater *spontaneity, transitoriness,* and *volatility.* It is these properties rather than the irrational behavior of individuals under the sway of collective psychological forces or the pressures of "group in-

[1] A similar clarification of the catchall term *Masse* took place among German sociologists in the 1920's. (See 3 and 8.)

fluence" as such that set the phenomena of collective behavior apart, as a distinct category, from other patterns of interaction where the participants are equally aware of and responsive to each other's presence.

By *spontaneity*, we mean nothing more than that the participants react so as to be governed primarily by the mood of the moment, not that the interaction is completely random. Emotions ordinarily contained are let loose in the collective dread of the panic, the collective hostility of the ugly mob or gang, in the uninhibited weeping at a revival meeting. The member of the public feels free to speak his own mind, while the social movement is the vehicle by which accumulated grievances get an airing.

Transitoriness means that the interaction results in relatively impermanent forms. The phase of enthusiasm passes quickly. The group of demonstrators dispersed by the police disintegrates into nothingness, unless it contains an organized nucleus to call them together later in further action. Audiences mobilized in response to a particular program can be held only if the appeal stimuli are repeated.

Finally, it is the lack of orientation on the part of participants to a body of norms and traditions that accounts for the *volatility* of interaction, for the unexpected emergence of new forms of activity and organization. "Collective behavior," wrote Blumer, "is concerned in studying the ways by which a new social order comes into existence." (1, p. 169) Turner and Killian add that in collective behavior there are developed "norms which are not envisaged in the larger society and may even modify or oppose these broader norms." (29, p. 12) When a plurality acts contrary to expectations, definitions, and rules which are considered valid in a situation, their usefulness as normative standards declines. The individual becomes to some degree confused, and the structure — that is, the shared assumptions by which relationships are regulated — becomes fluid. In seeking a way out of their bewilderment, people interact and communicate with others. But since the responses of others to one's own behavior can no longer be predicted on the basis of abstract norms, no one individual or group of individuals is capable of directive influence.

"The most elementary form of integration by which mere

Collective Dynamics: Process and Form

aggregates of individuals assume the character of social groups is the simple dominance of a mood." (20, p. 631) In such a situation, there occurs a collective reorientation, if not of actions, then at least of thought and sentiment. Whatever the pattern that emerges, it lacks as yet the rules of procedure, the division of labor, the collective representations, and so forth that we usually consider the mark of a group, with all that the term "group" implies. We speak of these interactionist phenomena as collective *dynamics* in order to differentiate them clearly from those other organized patterns of interaction that are reducible to status and role. The interaction, in deviating from the structured pattern, entails at least a temporary transformation of that structure.

It is our thesis that sociologists have invested much less effort in characterizing the processes that account for the emergence of new collective forms than to the description and classification of the forms themselves. In this discussion, we focus on the dynamics: the forms are to be understood as processes of transformation within some kind of social order.

COLLECTIVE FORMS AND COLLECTIVE PROCESSES

When the norms of a group temporarily lose their efficacy as a guide to conduct, characteristic forms of collective behavior are likely to appear. The form such interaction takes is affected by whether the group is physically dispersed or in close contact but the nature of the transformation by which the form emerges is not. For instance, the demoralization of a single platoon in panic flight represents a process of transformation analogous to the demoralization accompanying the defeat of an entire nation. A group of school children turns into a mob attacking the class scapegoat through a process similar to that by which an entire people, gripped by war fever, embarks on a nationwide witch hunt. Again, the process by which the vague anxieties and hopes of the disinherited everywhere crystallize into a widespread movement to overthrow the social order is, in terms of the crystallization that takes place, essentially the same as that by which a particular radical sect (religious or political) comes into being.

The partial transformations that any social system undergoes in the face of unsettling influences can be subsumed under five basic processes. Each process represents a collective response growing out of unstructured interaction. The product cannot be predicted from such prior understandings, norms, values, etc. as could be designated as its social structure. If one focuses on the conditions prerequisite for the continuation and persistence of organized collective life, each process appears both as a negation of structure and as a temporary reorientation by some group or segment of the population towards new events or feelings that have remained unrecognized:

> *Demoralization:* the loss of meaningful relationship to the values and activities of some collectivity because changes in the balance of rewards make adherence no longer attractive.

> *Collective defense:* the spontaneous psychological integration of a collectivity on the basis of emotions that are normally contained and conventionalized.

> *Collective redefinition:* the dissemination of information from anonymous sources via fugitive channels in response to a puzzling event that is of general concern.

> *Mass conversion:* the wholesale change of basic allegiances within a group or among a plurality of persons, as during a revival or a period of political change.

> *Crystallization:* the congealing through conflict of forms developed in spontaneous interaction into a cohesive nucleus that provides the active cell for wider social movements.

Only with regard to the process of demoralization is our conceptualization set forth in any detail. Demoralization represents the essence of the many forms sociologists have designated as unrest. Other processes are only sketched.[2]

DEMORALIZATION

Morale measures the capacity of members of a collectivity to pursue, despite disruptive influences, an objective recognized as legitimate. High group morale expresses itself in *esprit de corps*

[2] A more complete treatment of these collective processes will be found in our *Collective Dynamics* (New York: Thomas Y. Crowell Company, 1961).

and optimism. But the ultimate test lies in the continued performance and coordination of roles in situations of stress. The
demoralized individual is one for whom social values and group
goals have lost their meaning. Collective demoralization designates a progressive retreat from these values and goals by many
participants into a state where they no longer care. The process
must always be defined in relation to a recognized norm within
some group structure.

An extreme state of demoralization, whether individual or collective, cannot last long. If the individual or the collectivity
somehow fails to adapt and reintegrate, they will in each instance
literally go to pieces. Extreme panic in the individual precipi-
tates mental illness, while in group panic private and particularistic goals gain ascendancy over values and goals necessary to group
persistence. The individual aspects of this phenomenon differ of
course from the collective ones. Individuals within a group may
remain clear-headed and act rationally though the group itself
gradually disintegrates.

Forms of individual behavior designated as panic range from
inactivity in the form of political, moral, or general apathy to
such precipitous actions as the ill-advised dumping of securities
as stock market values momentarily slump, from frantic escape
activity to the confused and uncoordinated behavior of many
persons hit by disaster, from the individual stunned by terror to
hyperactivity. On the individual level, each response may constitute an adaptation to a situation that is beyond one's own control. The rifleman, ordered to advance, "freezes" to avoid dangerous exposure to the fire of a well-entrenched enemy; the
small-time speculator, having overextended himself financially,
sells at a loss just to remain solvent; motivated by an overwhelming concern to save their families, people use roads that others
are trying to keep clear for rescue work. Yet in such instances,
the adaptive behavior of the individual interferes with an adaptive
collective response.

To define collective panic as an escape mob in which the competitive scramble for safety interferes with the maximization of
collective effort obscures the underlying similarities between the
particular form which collective demoralization may take and a
variety of syndromes, more frequent in occurrence (7). Even

more important, because of certain superficial similarities with other forms of disorder in physical-contact groups, the escape mob is often classified — in our opinion, falsely — as belonging to a category of crowd phenomena where the participants act in what is essentially a solitary fashion. As pointed out, the persistent pursuit of collective purposes has long been the distinguishing feature of the sociological idea of morale (16). The escape mob is only one of many forms, generically similar, which result in the progressive undermining of group purposes. This generic similarity can be described in terms of an underlying process of collective demoralization, whether disorganization becomes manifest in competitive flight or in other ways, such as apathy.

As a collective process, demoralization entails the disruption of two elements essential to the functioning of a group: *cognitive definitions* and *affective ties*. By cognitive definitions we mean the patterns of expectations and intellectual schemes by which nature and society are transformed into a meaningful world. Persons become disoriented when the unexpected or unfamiliar partially eclipses or shatters their basic understandings. But aberrant events, though they often precipitate demoralization, are hardly a sufficient condition, since individuals are tied to each other not only by shared definitions but also by "moral" bonds. When external danger that cannot be mastered or internal dissension that cannot be resolved weakens the affective ties that normally weld a group into a cohesive unit, it becomes panic-prone because of demoralization. The balance between the controls exerted by the relevant group interest and the tendency to follow more exclusive interests has shifted to the side of the latter. The less the attachment to the group, the less salience its norms have for individual conduct. Any activity in pursuit of specific and private ends contributes to demoralization, because it interferes with the attainment of collective goals and impedes the rational and ordered adaptation to a changed situation by the group as a whole.

To disrupt and demoralize a solidary group firmly bound by mutual bonds requires considerably greater pressure on individuals than in the case of a group bound only by the coincidence of its members' self-interest. The relationship between the two variable quantities — amount of stress and strength of affective ties — is diagrammed below. Each plus sign designates a factor that tends to produce demoralization. One is most likely to find panic and disintegration when groups with weak affective ties face extreme stress. Studies of the military, for example, indicate the ineffectiveness of the individual combat replacement and the

Conditions Inducing Demoralization

AFFECTIVE TIES	STRESS	
	Moderate	*Extreme*
Strong		+
Weak	+	+ +

disruptive impact of enemy fire which keeps soldiers on the battle field from communicating with each other (17, 19, 26). The feeling of being alone, more than anything else, contributes to the rifleman's headlong flight at the sight of the unexpected.

Of the two elements, magnitude of stress, which is situationally determined, seems the more variable, while the strength of affective ties helps to explain primarily why objectively similar stress situations have different effects on different groups. The two are rather intimately related in the subjective assessment of danger. It would seem, however, that the objective threat is largely mediated in its effects through the comfort and concern a person expects from others in the situation.

The altogether unexpected, when it occurs, produces the most extreme states of terror. The greatest fear is the vague and indefinite fear of the unknown (22). In his study of post-operative patients in a surgical ward, Janis found those most realistically informed about the discomforts likely to be experienced were able to rehearse the situation mentally by "worrying." The confirmation of predictions, as well as the increased faith in the surgeon which resulted, reassured them. By contrast, those who could face the operation only by unrealistically denying its danger and discomforts reacted with hostility and uncooperativeness as convalescents (12). For those caught in any sudden disaster, the world seems to disintegrate. It is common for persons, at first, to consider themselves directly in the center of the impact area, abandoned by everybody. Faith in the protective capacity of the community is restored only gradually.

But under certain conditions, cumulative exposure to danger also undermines the belief in the protective capacity of the group, on which so much of one's emotional allegiance and confidence in personal survival is based. For example, a progressive deterioration of morale invariably follows a period of uninterrupted service in the line without rest and recuperation. Both the loss of friends and feelings of guilt for their loss promote fatalistic expectations, while the emotional ties are not easily transferred to men replacing those lost (9, 24).

That demoralization should follow whether the "worst" is anticipated or comes wholly unexpectedly seems a paradox. Mac-Curdy (18) has tried to account for it. The morale among a population subject to bombardment, he holds, is a function of the ratio of those who have suffered remote-misses to those having suffered near-misses. A near-miss is a close call. It may be physically close or psychologically close, as when injury is suffered by someone dear to him. While near-misses are unnerving, remote-misses reaffirm confidence in one's invulnerability. The person remains physically and psychologically unscathed; his faith in the collective enterprise, as part of which he withstood the danger, remains unimpaired. He can trust fate. Confidence begins to wane only after serious losses have destroyed the feeling of invulnerability, and the group has, so to speak, psychologically failed the individual.

As a statement of the basic factors affecting morale, the near-miss hypothesis is just a bit too mechanical. It attributes progressive demoralization to an increase in the number who suffer near-misses but does not explain why in some groups demoralization occurs after rather slight losses, an effect that must be attributed to pre-existing group factors. More significant, a society is not a mere quantitative aggregate. The multiple group memberships and the way each is integrated to form the structure of a society must also be considered. The fabric of any army or of a community may be disrupted even while the individual units continue to function intact.

Collective Dynamics: Process and Form

The maintenance of in-group solidarity in the small unit contributes to demoralization when it interferes with the performance of roles necessary for the survival of the larger unit. Many a military commander has failed because he has over-identified himself with his men. McClellan, Lincoln's first commanding general, is said to have been incapable of assuming responsibility for orders that meant sure casualties. In never following through on his advances, he probably prolonged the war and the suffering of his soldiers (31). A World War II general, eminently successful in combat, could never transcend the perspective of unit commander. He always reached his divisional objective but at the expense of the theater effort and consequently was dismissed. In the last analysis, the capacity of a collectivity to function under stress depends not only on the performance of individual members vis-à-vis other members, but on the way in which the efforts of primary groups are integrated into a larger structure.

The bearing of multiple group memberships within a complex social fabric on the forms of demoralization has been pointed out by Killian (15). The fact that the individual is bound to the community in many different ways increases the potential for role conflicts, which in the disaster situation are all too often resolved in favor of the primary group. Apprehensiveness about the safety of loved ones, known to be near the impact area, interferes with effective rescue work and leads some to desert their disaster stations. In the closing months of World War II, mass desertions effectively dissolved the German *Wehrmacht*, as units suffered heavy casualties and hope of victory faded. The primary ties through which the soldier was bound to the army were shattered, and primary-group ties to families again became of paramount concern, especially where the latter had suffered bomb damage and needed their male head (25). The same underlying process is exhibited in a nation torn by tribal, regional, or party loyalties which interfere with an adaptive response. In fact, this concentration of loyalties on some alienated primary group is a main form of demoralization within an abstract secondary group. Thus, strikes may be broken as wives plead with their husbands to go back to work to keep their children fed.

The process of progressive demoralization, whatever its concrete form, can be defined and described only in relation to some kind of social framework. Mass apathy, collective flight, a wave of predatory activity are among its many manifestations. It is not the behavior per se but its failure to sustain or its tendency to undermine social values or collective efforts that mark it as demoralization. Mass panic — as in the run on the banks during a depression — and the escape mob are merely different forms that emerge once social bonds have been weakened. To equate demoralization with any particular manifestation is to confuse form with process.

COLLECTIVE DEFENSE

The phenomenon of social unrest, resulting from the communication of personal restlessness to others, is generally used to explain the apparent spontaneity and impulsiveness with which a multitude of persons act when they enjoy momentarily, as in a crowd, support from others. Social unrest means the activation of emotions and motives, normally held in check, that are destructive of groups and thus illustrative of demoralization. Under certain circumstances, however, the individual motives coalesce into a collective response, usually of a highly emotional nature, that seems inappropriate or, at least, out of proportion to the provocation. Their coalescence under the sway of group emotion into conventionalized or explosive activity can be interpreted as a collective defense against anxiety associated with those emotions and impulses whose open expression brings the individual in conflict with the society.

Any defensive operation, so far as the individual is concerned, effects a reconciliation between social demands and impulsivity. Every individual learns techniques for managing the tensions generated by the irreconcilable nature of the two sets of demands. Symbolic processes are basic to the exercise of self-control. Still, an unsocialized neurotic potential, not under the control of symbolic activities, exists in every individual. This potential manifests itself in behavior and attitudes that are compulsively repeated irrespective of their appropriateness or practical utility. The concept of defense mechanisms by which inner anxiety is managed has become indispensable to the study of personality.

What has often been noted is that the specific forms individual defenses take are culturally typed. They depend on the availability of roles compatible with the patterns that serve specific individuals. They depend furthermore on the existence of occasions during which the open or conventionalized expression of emotions is tolerated. Beyond that, when people of similar background thrown together are subjected to stress, they often respond by developing the same neurotic symptom or bodily disturbance.

The psychiatric literature contains some dramatic examples of collective symptoms formed suddenly under the influence of others (4, 10, 13, 27). In each of these situations, the common symptom, spontaneously developed in interaction and communication, resulted in a collective redefinition that permitted the individual to give in to his submerged motives without thereby violating the group codes. Thus the participants continued to behave in an essentially solidary fashion. To illustrate: Strecker reports that a unit, which had performed in an exemplary fashion under fire, suffered within a short span of time about five hundred "gas casualties," every one of which proved, upon examination, to have a purely psychosomatic origin. No evidence was found of contact with gas. The various symptoms attributed by the soldiers to the effects of gas opened a route of escape from group obligations, one that was socially sanctioned and elicited sympathy. The collective utilization of the symptom (they were not malingerers), though demoralization in terms of institutional performance, effected a compromise between individual demands and group codes, in which the latter were upheld. This accounts for its contagious spread. That scapegoating, revivalist cults, xenophobia, and similar phenomena that are crowd-like in character redirect emotions so as to preserve the collectivity has often been pointed out. Again the process involved in scapegoating, cultish orgies, and so on appears similar, regardless of whether the particular forms occur in specific groups or on a much wider scale.

Collective defenses, it is hypothesized, develop with explosive suddenness when tension has accumulated but "built-in" safety valves,[3] permitting conventionalized relief, are lacking and/or are forcibly suppressed. The crowds that form spontaneously always reflect social cleavages, insofar as the behavior attracts only those whose psychological needs are not officially recognized in the structured arrangements of society. Many forms of collective defense are officially sanctioned by those who see their own purposes being advanced in this way. For instance, the collective paranoia of a nation in wartime is considered irrational only after the nation has had a chance to sober up.

COLLECTIVE REDEFINITION

The emergence of new social definitions is part and parcel of just about every phenomenon of collective dynamics. There are many ways in which collective redefinitions come about, but among these, the rumor process seems to be the most elementary. In our terms, rumor is not defined by its content, i.e., as untruth or distortion or scientifically unreliable information, nor by its forms, i.e., as information transmitted serially by word-of-mouth. A rumor is what emerges via the rumor process, and the rumor process refers exclusively to those unorganized and fugitive efforts to arrive at definitions when social orientation is necessary but (1) formal (structured) channels of information, on which people expect to rely, break down or are discredited; (2) no single individual is in possession of the information necessary for defining the situation; and (3) some kind of validation from "authorized" sources is missing. Rumor thus serves to define a situation whenever more authentic information is lacking but some action is required. The information needed for social orientation diffuses by way of the rumor process, from sources which remain anonymous by way of fugitive channels. In this way rumor often provides the definitions members in some collective enterprise need to act in concert. Lacking other means of testing the validity of the definition, people accept it because others accept it.

[3] The notion of customs that act as safety valves was first developed in 1902 by Heinrich Schurtz in *Altersklassen und Männerbunde*. (See also 5, 6.)

Usually an item of information is labeled a rumor in order to discredit it. Yet rumors persist with such tenacity because they sustain definitions congruent with the aims of some collectivity. A person's reputation, for example, may be considered the sum total of what people choose to believe about him. In the case of a controversial figure, the rumor material will be of a highly partisan nature, and objective validation except in the case of blatant untruths is practically precluded. What is a fact for one side is dismissed as rumor by the other. On the other hand, stories of Belgian franc-tireurs, dressed as priests and harassing German soldiers, when circulated with official approval in World War I, ceased to be rumors and became official information. The activities of a German Fifth Column whose sabotaging activities accounted for unexplained defeats and on that basis commanded constant vigilance served the Allied cause well in World War II. Both stories were considered patent falsehoods by later research (16, 29), but because they had been officially validated, printed in newspapers, used in cartoons, celebrated in books and on the screen, referred to in speeches, and publicized in still other ways, they were at that time widely accepted as fact.

What marks information as rumor is its *sub rosa* existence among persons who develop assessments at variance with what is officially condoned. The segment of the population among whom a rumor circulates is always, to that extent, alienated from those who disapprove. The important part that rumor and myth (in the sense that Sorel employed the term) play in crowd behavior, in social movements, and during revolutions, or in financial panics and military life is readily documented. The significance of rumor lies in the sanction it gives to matters, irrespective of their truth or falsehood, that remain unacknowledged by those whose function it is to provide information and interpretation (23).

Mass Conversion

By the term mass conversion we designate a wholesale shift in self-attitudes, not necessarily religious ones, in a direction that is discontinuous with earlier commitments. The changes observed among those who participate in therapeutic groups, or who undergo the type of training which is required of the Chinese Communist cadres, or who are forced to submit to intensive indoctrination as were American prisoners in the Far East, as well as the successful proselyting by a religious sect or by a radical movement, the turnover in values in a period of revolutionary fervor, and so on can all be considered conversions *if* they involve a relatively permanent commitment to antithetical values. Conversion in the individual should not be confused with the temporary hysteria or mystical experiences that sometimes accompany and sometimes are required for acceptance into a specific cult. On the contrary, these outbursts, especially when deliberately aroused by invoking fears of some devil and hell for wayward believers, appear more representative of the process of collective defense than of a collective change in values.

The most frequently studied forms of conversion relate to the religious realm, and the more fundamental the importance of religious values the more likely it is that change in that area will require a conversion. Careful observation reveals, however, that the majority of religious conversions occur only gradually and as the fruition of a protracted search for religious experience (2, 34). In view of this, the religious "awakening" so highly prized by some Protestant sects as a test of religiosity is rarely discontinuous with the person's prior commitment. The change it effects is actually an initiation into the full religious responsibility of an adult member.

From a psychological point of view, whether there can be a *complete* about-face in fundamental values is debatable. Some psychological antecedents to the "new" beliefs seem to be present in every convert. In the view of William James, a conversion meant that the submerged side of a divided self was brought to the fore. To this extent, he held, any role change has some of the earmarks of conversion; for example, the President on a holiday is a changed man, but he can re-enter the role appropriate to his office at will. The role change generally looked on as conversion appears as discontinuous because of social definitions: the transition is not accepted as a normal part of a person's life career. Furthermore, the convert is not only reborn; he is "renamed," that is, he is given a new identity and a sense of selfhood anchored in new group affiliations from which he can return only with the greatest difficulty. His defection is complete; the convert burns his bridges or, as the Chinese put it in their thought-reform program, cuts his tails.

Mass conversion, then, can be viewed as a collective movement in status or as a shift in the norms of some group which fundamentally reorients the relationship of participants to the rest of society, even while the participants strive to maintain consistency. The mass of potential converts is found among those partly excluded from what they consider effective participation in society. Hence, psychologically or socially, their relation to the social universe in which they live is tenuous. When a break with others tends to isolate one of these individuals, it often results in mental illness; when it offers new fellowship and confirmation of the new beliefs, it constitutes a conversion.

CRYSTALLIZATION

The congealment, through repetition, of fluid and transient patterns into a body of norms constitutes crystallization. Of course, roles continually change in some manner and new conventions are born out of the cumulative changes. But the coalescence of alienative tendencies is of special significance in collective dynamics for two reasons: the alienated nucleus which is formed offers a reliable source of support for pathological tendencies (for example, the adolescent gang leader's paranoid projections are confirmed by gang codes); the alienated nucleus forms the active cell through which agitation and proselyting activities of larger social movements are conducted. In terms of the process by which it originates, the sectarian association, whatever its specific form, represents the product of crystallization (11, 28, 33).

The adjective "sectarian" carries no religious connotation but signifies that such an association is a secondary or schismatic phenomenon that arises in cleavage from the existing social order. Its members have turned away from the world, either in active protest or in seeking moral perfection only for themselves. This gives rise to two subtypes: the gang and the sect. Both are products of opposition; both develop their internal structure and solidarity in conflict with a world experienced as hostile

The Individual and Social Organization

IMPLICATIONS FOR RESEARCH

In substituting the term "collective dynamics" for the more conventional "collective behavior," we wish to emphasize that the interactions under study are in process and that the relationships between the participants have not yet congealed into some kind of recurrent pattern of interaction, namely a structure. What happens should be understood as a temporary disruption of or deviation from some established pattern. We would stress also that in collective dynamics the particularistic aspects of the phenomenon are less important than the general processes which account for its emergence. To look only at what happens to a particular rumor and how it spreads, for example, is to lose sight of the dynamics by which a collectivity becomes rumor-prone and the way in which the new definition, in reflecting some underlying cleavage, also constitutes a collective realignment. Of course, patterns like rumor can be studied only in the concrete instances in which they occur. Consequently, the materials on specific cases are a major source of data, which can be supplemented by surveys (to test specific hypotheses about their distribution) and by experimental observation of corresponding small-scale phenomena (to test specific hypotheses about antecedent conditions or the processes themselves).

Since the occurrence of the collective patterns we have been discussing cannot very easily be predicted in advance, it requires mobile research teams to study them in real life. The investigators must be something of detective-reporters, forever keeping their eyes open and their ears to the ground. Rigid commitment to only one method of data collection will mean loss of many of the most interesting aspects of the phenomenon. Their chameleon-like character demands flexibility in observation.

Their lack of structure notwithstanding, the processes of collective dynamics do not occur in an altogether chaotic and random manner. In fact, the assumption that they follow some general pattern is indispensable. It is a pattern, however, that has to be reconstructed from many minutiae. Because of their ephemeral existence, the phenomena of collective behavior are observable only when one is close to the event, whereas in the case of organized structures, the persistent perspectives of participants occupying relatively fixed positions can, because certain typical interactions constantly recur, be studied over time. To get data on these same perspectives when behavior is not governed by status constitutes a real problem.

In the unorganized collectivity, momentary and partial perspectives become spontaneously integrated, through communication, into transitory and volatile patterns. It is imperative that one begin by sampling the various perspectives from which the disintegrative tendencies are experienced. For this, the commonly used indices of status often do not suffice. The collective behavior phenomenon arises as the perceptions growing out of individual perspectives become modified and adapted to each other.

Because the participation in collective behavior phenomena always suggests the existence of some cleavage, though perhaps not acknowledged, the phenomenon needs to be studied in its totality, which includes the opposition to it. For example, the crowd consists not only of an active core of instigators; timid followers, passive bystanders, the behavior of potential victims, even the impression gained by a mass media audience, all contribute to what the crowd is all about. To be able to command data of such complexity, the investigator needs, above all, something that might be called sensitivity to the social atmosphere. Such sensitivity involves at least two entirely different components: (1) theoretical sophistication, which sensitizes him to significant clues he might easily ignore, and (2) trained imagination, which enables him to display insight and imaginatively reconstruct from these clues the total situation as part of which the various direct and indirect participants interact.

References

1. Blumer, Herbert. "Collective Behavior," in A. M. Lee (ed.), *Principles of Sociology*. New York: Barnes & Noble, Inc., 1946.
2. Clark, Elmer T. *The Psychology of Religious Awakening*. New York: The Macmillan Company, 1929.
3. Coln, Gerhard. "Die Masse," in Alfred Vierkandt (ed.), *Handwörterbuch der Soziologie*. Stuttgart: Ferdinand Enke Verlag, 1931.

4. Eissler, Ruth. "Riots," in *Psychoanalytic Study of the Child*, Vols. 3–4. New York: International Universities Press, 1949.

5. Erikson, Erik H. *Childhood and Society*. New York: W. W. Norton & Company, Inc., 1950.

6. Freud, Sigmund. *Totem and Taboo*, tr. by A. A. Brill. New York: Moffat, Yard and Co., 1918.

7. Fritz, Charles, and Eli S. Marks. "The NORC Studies of Human Behavior in Disaster," *Journal of Social Issues*, Vol. 10 (1954), pp. 26–41.

8. Geiger, Theodor. *Die Masse und ihre Aktion*. Stuttgart: Ferdinand Enke Verlag, 1926.

9. Grinker, Roy R., and John H. Spiegel. *Men Under Stress*. Philadelphia: The Blakiston Company, 1945.

10. Gruenberg, Ernest M. "Socially Shared Psychopathology," in Alexander H. Leighton *et al.* (eds.), *Explorations in Social Psychiatry*. New York: Basic Books, Inc., 1957, pp. 201–229.

11. Hobsbawm, E. J. *Social Bandits and Primitive Rebels*. Glencoe, Ill.: The Free Press, 1959.

12. Janis, Irving L. *Psychological Stress*. New York: John Wiley & Sons, 1958.

13. Johnson, Donald. "The Phantom Anesthetist of Mattoon," *Journal of Abnormal and Social Psychology*, Vol. 40 (1945), pp. 175–186.

14. Jong, Louis de. *The German Fifth Column in the Second World War*. Chicago: The University of Chicago Press, 1956.

15. Killian, Lewis M. "The Significance of Multiple Group Membership in Disaster," *American Journal of Sociology*, Vol. 57 (January 1952), pp. 3–14.

16. Lasswell, Harold D. "Morale," in *Encyclopædia of the Social Sciences*. New York: The Macmillan Company, 1937.

17. Mandelbaum, David. *Soldier Groups and Negro Soldiers*. Berkeley, Calif.: University of California Press, 1952.

18. MacCurdy, John T. *The Structure of Morale*. Cambridge, England: The University Press, 1943.

19. Marshall, S. L. A. *Men Against Fire*. New York: William Morrow & Company, 1947.

20. Park, Robert E. "Collective Behavior," in *Encyclopædia of the Social Sciences*. New York: The Macmillan Company, 1937.

21. Park, Robert E., and Ernest W. Burgess. *Introduction to the*

Science of Sociology. Chicago: The University of Chicago Press, 1921.

22. Riezler, Kurt. "The Social Psychology of Fear," *American Journal of Sociology,* Vol. 49 (May 1944), pp. 489–498.

23. Rose, Arnold M. "Rumor in the Stock Market," *Public Opinion Quarterly,* Vol. 15 (Fall 1951), pp. 461–486.

24. Shils, Edward A. "Primary Groups in the American Army," in Robert K. Merton and Paul F. Lazarsfeld (eds.), *Continuities in Social Research: Studies in the Scope and Method of "The American Soldier".* Glencoe, Ill.: The Free Press, 1950, pp. 16–39.

25. Shils, Edward A., and Morris Janowitz. "Cohesion and Disintegration in the *Wehrmacht," Public Opinion Quarterly,* Vol. 12 (Summer 1948), pp. 280–315.

26. Stouffer, Samuel A., *et al. The American Soldier,* Vols. I and II of *Studies in Social Psychology in World War II.* Princeton, N.J.: Princeton University Press, 1949.

27. Strecker, Edward A. *Beyond the Clinical Frontier.* New York: W. W. Norton & Company, Inc., 1940.

28. Thrasher, Frederick M. *The Gang.* Chicago: The University of Chicago Press, 1927.

29. Turner, Ralph H., and Lewis Killian. *Collective Behavior.* Englewood Cliffs, N.J.: Prentice-Hall, Inc., 1957.

30. Van Langenhove, Fernand. *Growth of a Legend.* New York: G. P. Putnam's Sons, 1916.

31. Williams, T. Harry. *Lincoln and His Generals.* New York: Alfred A. Knopf, 1952.

32. Wolfenstein, Martha. *Disaster.* Glencoe, Ill.: The Free Press, 1957.

33. Yablonski, Lewis. "The Delinquent Gang as a Near-Group," *Social Problems,* Vol. 7 (Fall 1959), pp. 108–117.

34. Zetterberg, Hans L. "Religious Conversion as a Change of Social Roles," *Sociology and Social Research,* Vol. 36 (January 1952), pp. 159–166.

19

Beyond Utopia: The "Beat Generation" as a Challenge for the Sociology of Knowledge

 ELWIN H. POWELL

UNIVERSITY OF BUFFALO

The "sociology of knowledge" is a branch of sociology which studies the relations between social conditions and intellectual productions, such as science, literature, and the products of the mass media of communication. While tracing its origins to certain German social philosophers of the nineteenth century, including Karl Marx, it took on an interactionist orientation in the twentieth century, particularly in the writings of Max Weber and Karl Mannheim. The "social conditions" that constitute the independent variable in the sociology of knowledge are found to be broader and more complex than those usually discussed in theoretical writings. Although the promise of the sociology of knowledge is great, there have been few researches systematic enough to merit the appellation of scientific study. Professor Powell here delineates the first steps in a study in the sociology of knowledge dealing with a highly specialized contemporary form of semi-popular literature — that produced by the so-called "beat generation." In this analysis, as in several previous chapters, the notion of degree of involvement in or commitment to a role becomes salient.

The sociology of knowledge explores the relationship between social existence and conceptual systems (56, pp. 103–130).* Critics have charged that the traditional sociology of knowledge of Karl Mannheim and Ernest Grunwald is a theoretical impossibility, that it is defeated by its own logic, that it fails to satisfy the requirements of scientific method (12; cf. 46). But for Mannheim science was something more than the formulation of limited hypotheses to be tested by available facts; it was "a struggle to obtain insight" and that, as Willard Waller says, "forces us to the admission that all science is half art. It depends upon perception reconstructed and fitted together in imagination, upon an artistic re-creation of events." (59; cf. 50) Working in this way Mannheim was able to grasp the essential spirit of our time as few other sociologists have done (61). The sociology of knowledge is not so much a discipline as a perspective, an approach, or, in Waller's words, "a process of looking at events until they become luminous." (59, p. 288)

Under the influence of Marx, Mannheim was initially preoccupied with class position as an existential determinant of knowledge or thought (6; 7, pp. 1–50). Briefly, the "insiders" — in Western capitalist society, the bourgeoisie — driven to defend their position of relative advantage, develop an ideological mode of thought which serves to rationalize and justify the established social order. The "outsiders" — the proletariat, the dispossessed — develop a utopian mentality which envisages and seeks the transformation of existing institutions. Ideology is conservative; utopia revolutionary.

But today, as Daniel Bell has pointed out, both ideologies and utopias have vanished, leaving in their wake the void of *anomie* (5, pp. 21–37, 369–377). Mannheim clearly foresaw the consequences of such a condition — a dehumanization of the arts, an

---

* Revision of a paper presented at the Annual Meeting of the American Sociological Association, New York, 1960. For the basic conception of this paper, I am indebted to Mr. Kenneth Bowden of the London School of Economics.

emergence of a "matter of factness" in all spheres of cultural life, an ethics of "genuineness" and "frankness" replacing the more heroic ideals (41, p. 230). Deprived of meaningful participation in the social system, the mind or self loses its structure and direction, sinking into a kind of torpor which requires ever more violent stimulation to arouse it. Reason itself is held in abeyance and the pursuit of long-range goals is abandoned for the pleasures — and the anguish — of the moment. "A thirst arises for novelties, unfamiliar pleasures, nameless sensations," writes Durkheim, describing the symptoms of *anomie*, "all of which lose their savor once known. [Finally] the whole fever subsides and the sterility of all the tumult is apparent." (19, p. 256)

Anomie has become the *Weltanschauung* of a generation. Long before the "beat generation" was named, its contours had been delineated. In 1951 *Time* called it a "silent generation" and commented on its diminished ambitions (57). David Riesman emphasized the apathy and conformity of the new generation (54). But it was not until the mid-fifties that the generation had its own spokesmen — and a fitting name. Writers like Jack Kerouac and Allen Ginsberg not only articulated but embodied the mood of the generation. Alternating between lassitude and frenetic excitement, the "beat" life is both a "drag" and a "kick." The beatnik lives the paradox of an acquiescent rebellion.

THE SOCIO-HISTORICAL SOURCES OF THE BEAT GENERATION

Discussing the problem of generations, Mannheim remarks that generational position "bears a certain structural resemblance to class position; it does not imply membership in a concrete group but rather a location . . . within a social whole." (42, pp. 289–290) In mass societies where ties to community and class are weak there may develop a kind of pseudo-identification with an age group, a generation. As a result of rapid change and upheaval or extensive vertical mobility, generations tend to split off from each other. The son no longer follows inexorably in the path of the father and must of necessity seek orientation outside the kinship circle (20, pp. 115–185). Awareness of "generations" is heightened; a youth culture and a youth problem may emerge (4, 16, 27). Parental beliefs seem all but irrelevant to the new world of the young, a condition evident in America since the turn of the century. "By 1912," writes Allen Churchill, "almost for the first time in history a young generation had come of age bringing with it a deep sensation of restlessness." (13, p. 23) Santayana observed the same phenomenon in 1913: "Men were giving up the search for lasting values and firm intellectual conclusions . . . and placing a premium on sheer vitality, on movement, change and emotion." (43, p. 115)

The decisive break with the old order came after World War I with the "lost generation." (14, pp. 3–12) The 1920's witnessed a revolution in manners and morals coincident with a growing indifference to political and economic realities. The subjective and interpersonal took precedence over the institutional, a mood reflected not only in the arts but in the great growth of psychology and psychoanalysis. An earlier "utopian" generation had expressed itself in the populist, progressive, and socialist movements, aimed at some kind of modification of the social system. But since 1920 rebellion has been a private matter; in the words of Richard Hofstadter, "Bohemianism triumphed over radicalism." (29, p. 284)

The lost generation represents more than the crisis of the intellectual. Uncertainties created by the uprooting effects of urbanization, industrialism, and the unpredictable machinations of corporate capitalism ended in the general bewilderment of the Depression. In 1930 there was a generation literally lost — jobless and adrift in a world where effort bore no relation to reward and *anomie* had become a way of life (17).[1]

Not until the late 1940's were there signs of a new generation and then there was no drama of lost illusions. "The generation of the forties," writes John Aldridge, "could never be lost because the safe and ordered world had never been theirs . . ." In fact, "it seemed at times as if the movement toward revolt, having been carried to its logical end in the twenties, had reversed itself and become a movement back to respectability." (2, pp. 118–119)[2] Out of this soil grew the curious blend of sheer nihilism

[1] For the political climate, see Daniel Bell (5, pp. 286–295).
[2] This study could be regarded as a literary documentation of *anomie*. The beat generation had come into being before Kerouac named it in 1955. Vance Bourjaily, Norman Mailer, Gore Vidal, and Truman Capote

and trite conventionality which characterizes the beat generation.[3]

Though fancier connotations have since been discovered, the word *beat* originally meant what it said: exhausted, or, as John Clellon Holmes expresses it, "emptied out . . . a state of mind from which all unessentials have been stripped, leaving it receptive to everything around it." (31, pp. 13–27) Consequently the beatnik is obsessed by a craving for experience, for people who are "mad to live, mad to talk, mad to be saved, desirous of everything at the same time . . ." as Jack Kerouac put it in *On the Road* (34, p. 8). Experience for the beatnik is a series of discrete sensations — that is, kicks. Seeking an immediacy of response, he wants to *dig* the universe — and his literature is at its best when it seeks only to convey that feeling. *On the Road* is a wonderfully uncomplex book. It is honest, fresh, exuberant — and pointless.[4]

In his frantic race the beat is not so much in action as he is in flight. After reaching San Francisco the narrator of *On the Road* says, "Here I was at the end of America — no more land — and now there was nowhere to go but back." (34, p. 78) Essentially bored, he needs constant excitement; implicitly passive, the beatnik structures his world to make himself the victim of forces beyond his own control. It is not accidental that the drug addict — the man helplessly hooked — is the persistent hero of beat literature, something of a martyr without a cause. Allen Ginsberg's *Howl* opens with the line

> I saw the best minds of my generation destroyed by madness, starving hysterical naked. . . . (24, p. 164)

---

are far more talented writers than Kerouac and Ginsberg, but they only describe the beat ethos where the latter embody it.

[3] In Robert Fitch's words: "The residue of Bohemian faith survives in an older generation; it is the young . . . who believe in respectability." (22, p. 133) But a superficial acquiescence to middle-class values should not be mistaken for commitment; often the bourgeois is more thoroughly anomic than the Bohemian.

[4] Kerouac's genius lies precisely in his uncontrived, almost unconscious portrayal of the essential aimlessness of the generation. Eugene Burdick likens him to a sensitive eyeball that sweeps and perceives but is not connected with a brain (10).

Beyond Utopia

Don Jacobson says that Mr. Ginsberg could not write his poem about one suffering soul; it had to be nothing less inflated (and companionable) than a generation.[5] Yet Ginsberg has voiced the mood of an age which is unable to experience the individual as a person — an Other, a Thou. Ginsberg's poetry for all its obvious flaws has an authenticity about it which is missing in academic poetry, still pondering the daisies and daffodils. For the beat generation, "life is no longer a jungle . . . but a junkyard — a collection of battered and rusted forms." (24, p. 119) The beats have tried to conceptualize, or rather depict, the urban scene; Ginsberg asks:

> What sphinx of cement and aluminum bashed open their skulls
> and ate up their brains and imagination?
> Moloch! Solitude! Filth! Ugliness! Ashcans and unobtainable
> dollars! Children screaming under stairways! Boys sobbing
> in armies! Old men weeping in parks! (24, p. 17)*

But despite a veneer of social determinism, the connection between prevailing conditions and the institutional order is never clarified. If the beatnik objects to the world as it is, the most he would ever propose as a program of reform, says Holmes, "would be the removal of every social and intellectual restraint to the expression and enjoyment of his unique individuality." (31, p. 23) To each his own kicks. Social protest rarely gets beyond the stage of hating cops, which may explain the strange popularity of the beat rebellion among the conservative press: *The New York Times, Mademoiselle,* and *Esquire* were the first to discover the beats and bring them to national attention, not without concealed admiration. Kerouac's first novel, *Town and City,* which is tame enough for any woman's magazine, describes the proletarianization of a New England family during the Depression of the 1930's without saying an unkind word about capitalism. The moral of the story is simply "that's the way the ball bounces."

[5] Don Jacobson, "America's Angry Young Men: How Rebellious Are the San Francisco Rebels?" (32) Not very, he says.
* Copyright 1956 & 1959 by Allen Ginsberg. Reprinted by permission of City Lights Books.

The beats are notably apolitical. The "administered life" of the modern state leaves no room for the radical, and the sources of power are too remote to inspire either interest or antagonism. Only the deluded utopian believes he can decisively modify the system and only the "squares" are content to work within the network of civic or voluntary organizations which help only to perpetuate a system already perceived as false. For the beats, liberals are as square as conservatives. To Mary McCarthy's charge that the new generation has given up the battle of standards and ideas, Anatole Broyard replies, "Ah, the luxury of ideas and standards. The rhetorical questions they [the generation of the thirties] flattered themselves with! Who shall own the machinery of production? What is art? A decade of charades! The students here are from the new school where they have just been asked, 'What is the meaning of meaning?'" (8, p. 398) The beatnik is neither reactionary nor revolutionary; he is simply the anarchist in waiting. Existing society is a sham, a "shuck"; his reaction to it is a kind of passive resistance. He "opts out"; he plays it cool; he disaffiliates.

Kenneth Rexroth, an older man of impressive talents, is the leading philosopher of the beat generation. As a philosophic anarchist he would, like Kropotkin, replace Society by Community. For Rexroth, "the organic community of men is a community of love (eros) but to attain it, it is necessary to disaffiliate from the 'social lie — the social order, the state and capitalist system.'"[6] But who is affiliated in the first place? Is it possible to disaffiliate from a mass society? (1, p. 4) In order to renounce status, one must have status. Therefore, the beat affiliates with a new community in order to validate his disaffiliation from a larger society.

THE BEAT COMMUNITY: CULT WITHOUT CREED

In Bohemia the beatnik finds the status denied him in the larger world. The sociology of Bohemia is a fertile field for investigation. Bohemia has been called the underworld of art — and also the free republic of the mind (44, pp. 136–154; 55).

[6] As quoted in Lawrence Lipton (38, pp. 294–296). See also Kenneth Rexroth (51).

Beyond Utopia

Harvey Zorbaugh saw in the Bohemia of the 1920's a release from rural provincialism, destined to disappear as urbanization "Bohemianized" the whole society (62, p. 104). But Bohemia has not wholly disappeared and is in fact reviving — with a difference. Where the older Bohemian sought "refuge from community opinion," the new Bohemian — the beatnik — seems determined to call forth the response, if not the censure, of the wider society. He is not content to live in freedom and solitude, in the Bohemia that produced a Eugene O'Neill and an Edna St. Vincent Millay. Instead he advertises his deviation, with a beard and special dress which amounts to a virtual uniform. In Bohemia, the beatnik finds an audience and a role to play; his is the "party" Bohemia which derives from Maxwell Bodenheim and Professor Seagull (13).

"The Bohemianism of the 1920's," writes Norman Podhoretz, "represented a repudiation of the provinciality, philistinism and moral hypocrisy of American life. It was a movement created in the name of civilization. . . . But that of the 1950's is a different kettle of fish. It is hostile to civilization; it worships primitivism, instinct, energy, 'blood.' To the extent it has any intellectual interests at all they run to mystical doctrines, irrationalist philosophies. . . . Its only art . . . is cool jazz. . . . Its bop language is a way of demonstrating solidarity . . . and expressing contempt for coherent rational discourse which being a product of the mind is in their view a form of death." (48, pp. 308–309; 49) Yet contempt for rational discourse is not confined to the beatnik in an age which uses rationality only in the choice of means not in the evaluation of ends.

The prototype of the beatnik is the psychopath — the man dissociated from his own feelings and therefore requiring even more violent jolts to jar him out of his own lethargy (40).[7] The beat movement has been called a revolt of the right, not the left; a form of neo-facism, with the motorcyclist in black leather jacket in the role of the SS. In an uncanny work Max Picard has analyzed the profound cultural discontinuity which gave rise to Hitlerism, and here can be seen a disturbing analogy

[7] The beatniks have sought a model to emulate in the Negro. However, the Negro is not beat in the sense of being devoid of inner vitality as is the disaffiliated white.

to the beats. It is a mood which says, "I am totally alone; nowhere is there a pulse, a life around me, and beyond me there is nothing but nothingness. . . . In this world of discontinuity the ego is not even the center of a destroyed world; it merely is like some projection on the empty screen of a cinema. . . ." (47, p. 184) Actually, the beat movement has two dimensions, what Herbert Gold calls the "authentic beast . . . the frozen thug — and the literary fleas who are mainly Ivy League desperadoes." (25, p. 349)[8] The latter are mouthpieces for the former and at times come close to rationalizing or justifying crimes which most of us find abhorrent. Clellon Holmes, for instance, reports a case in which one youth stabbed another and then said to his victim: "Thanks a lot. I just wanted to know what it felt like." Such a crime, says Holmes, was "neither insane nor perverted. . . . It was the sort of crime envisaged by the Marquis de Sade a hundred and fifty years ago — a crime which the cruel absence of God made obligatory if a man were to prove that he was a man and not a mere blot of matter." In the crime Holmes sees a "longing for values . . . the longing to do or feel something meaningful . . . a sobering glimpse of how completely the cataclysms of this century have obliterated the rational, humanistic view of Man on which modern society was erected." But the reaction to this, on the whole, Holmes continues, "is not calculated immorality . . . but a return to an older, more personal code of ethics which includes the inviolability of comradeship, the respect for confidences, and an almost mystical regard for courage — all of which are the ethics of the tribe, rather than the community; the code of a small compact group living in an indifferent or a hostile environment, which it *seeks not to conquer or change, but only to elude.*" (31, pp. 21–22)

But looking deeper, or longer, at the beat generation the tribal

---

[8] As Gold remarks: "The thugs say 'man' to everyone — they can't remember anybody's name. But Ginsberg and Kerouac are *frantic*. They care too much and they care aloud . . . mostly for themselves but it's a beginning. The hipster is past caring." (25, p. 350) Gold continues: "The experience [the hipster] craves is simple, dark and in any case inevitable to all of us sooner or later — immolation. He is not content to wait. Mortality terrifies him; better death at once than the long test of life. He expresses his fantasy with convulsive violence, trying to disguise the truth from himself . . . using breathlessness as a surrogate for energy. But . . . the jitters are not an active state of being." (25, p. 354)

character vanishes and becomes the transient solidarity of the herd. The confidences become a mere ventilation of the ego — strangers "spilling" to each other — and the comradeship is without duration. The hero of *On the Road* is very casually betrayed, or rather deserted, by his best friend at the end of the book. Theirs is the comradeship of crisis or circumstance, as in any army where people find themselves together, share common experiences, then disperse. New situations bring new friends, who fall in the slots vacated by the last occupant. Thus there is no real interpenetration of minds; people do not "take the role of the other" in George Mead's sense; they play roles, theatrically. Life is not so much a dialogue as a collective monologue.

Since it needs only signals, not symbols, the herd can operate on monosyllables — the stylized argot of the hipster is adequate for purposes of identification but not communication. "When the hipster began to talk," writes Anatole Broyard, "he re-edited the world with new definitions . . . jive definitions, from jibe meaning to agree or harmonize. . . . Since articulateness is a condition for, if not actually a cause of anxiety, the hipster relieved his anxiety by disarticulating himself. He cut the world down to size — reduced it to a small stage with few props and a curtain of jive. In a vocabulary of a dozen verbs, adjectives and nouns he could describe everything that happened in it. . . . Everything was dichotomously solid, gone, out of this world, or nowhere, sad, beat, a drag. . . ." (9, p. 115)

The beat cult grew out of the jazz community (45). The cult has its special heroes — Dylan Thomas and Bird Parker among the more notable — and its rites of marijuana, jazz, and, lately, coffee-house poetry. Marijuana offers the possibilities of group intoxication, an eminently social experience.[9] Heroin is another matter; the addict is the ultimate beat, totally disaffiliated not only from society but reality, where time is abolished and space transcended.[10] The play at mysticism and Zen Buddhism has a similar

[9] As Lawrence Lipton puts it: "The joint is passed around the pad and shared, not for reasons of economy but as a social ritual. Once the group is high the magic circle is complete . . . a symbol of and a preparation for the metaphysical orgasm . . . a sense of *presence*, a here-and-nowness . . . a heightened sense of awareness and immediacy." (38, p. 171)
[10] Alexander Trocchi (58) is the best available account of the philosophy of heroin-use. For a sociological account, see Harold Finestone (21).

object, a return to a mindless mode of being.[11] The jazz and poetry sessions, often sophomoric, still have the saving grace of play and occasionally they have produced a bitter distillate of the pathos of the age, as in Kenneth Rexroth's "Thou Shalt Not Kill: A Memorial for Dylan Thomas." The effort to restore poetry to a spoken context has removed the ambiguity and neologism from modern verse, but for the most part has left only a residue of inanity. Ginsberg, in a recorded reading of *Howl*, holds his own poetry up to ridicule, as if he could not afford to take himself seriously. But in the beat literature there are flashes of unsustained brilliance which contain a critique of a civilization, such as Diane DiPrima's one sentence nightmare: "Get your cut throat off my knife." (18)

Much of the beat movement is a publicity stunt of the squares who control the mass media; nevertheless, the spread of the beat fad probably indicates a generalized search for heresy. The beat has grown up as a counter image for the "square"; in many ways he is a parody on the organization man. Real beatniks are now, allegedly, rented out to enliven parties given by suburban matrons and advertising executives.[12] For contrast to the animated, well-groomed respectability of the organization man, the beat can provide a sullen, unshaven counterpoint. The beat pursues failure in order to assure his disaffiliation from the success values of the square; the new prosperity has produced its new poverty. The drive for failure may explain the beatniks' preoccupation with the outcast. But the outcast is only a symbol of disaffiliation, not an object of compassion; in fact, there is surprisingly little sympathy for the drug addict and there is almost no understanding of the American Negro, whom they so ludicrously try to imitate.[13] Seeking to dissociate themselves from an other-directed society, the beats have succeeded only in playing another variation on the same theme.

[11] Zen can be a serious and rigorous discipline as in Allan Watts (60); usually it is simply silly as in Jack Kerouac's *The Dharma Bums* (33).
[12] *New York Times,* November 30, 1959.
[13] Kerouac has no real comprehension of drug addiction and his conception of the Negro is naive in the extreme (34). John Clellon Holmes (30) shows a far more penetrating insight, but none of the beat literature on addiction has come up to the standard of Nelson Algren's *Man with the Golden Arm* (3). William Burroughs' *Naked Lunch* (11) is so terrifying that it loses the quality of terror.

THE BEAT ETHOS: THE OTHER SIDE OF OTHER-DIRECTION

David Riesman's *The Lonely Crowd* has been called the most influential book of the 1950's (39). Like Mannheim, Riesman combines the imagination of the artist with the objectivity of the scientist. Riesman pictures the other-directed man as of a "found generation." (52)[14] Polite, content except for a bit of status anxiety, suburban-bound, a good consumer — the seeming antithesis of the beatnik.

Actually the other-directed and the beatnik are polarities of the same process. The one is in quest of belonging, the other disaffiliation, but the belongingness of the other-directed is an illusion and the beat philosophy of disaffiliation is only a rationalization of an already accomplished fact. Both are profoundly isolated and anomic (28).

"The beat generation," says Clellon Holmes, "finds the valueless abyss of modern life unbearable. . . . Even the young slum hoodlum is almost exclusively concerned with the problem of belief, albeit unconsciously." (31, p. 31) But the beatnik has failed to discover a belief system — a hierarchy of values — which would enable him to differentiate the trivial from the significant and thus enable him to transcend the immediate context of his life.[15] The beat scene is the American scene — a disjointed world where all things are equally sacred, equally profane. For Kerouac the filling station is holy, the mountain is holy. "We love everything," he told a national television audience, "Billy Graham, the Big Ten, rock and roll, Zen, apple pie, Eisenhower — we dig it all. We're in the vanguard of the new religion."[16] At other times Bach, Plotinus, and Proust are thrown in for good measure, though Marx and Freud are square. But happily the beatnik is still a long way from the true believer, for to believe in everything is to believe in nothing.

Beat art is more a reflex than a reconstruction. Kerouac is celebrated because he wrote six novels in six months and seriously compares himself to Goethe, who could work forty years on a

[14] One interviewee is quoted as typical ". . . In 15 years I expect a constant level of happiness." (52, p. 432)
[15] On values, see William L. Kolb (31).
[16] As quoted in Herbert Gold (26, pp. 155–156).

single poem, who of all men struggled for light and clarity, not only in art but in science.[17] For science the beat generation has not even shown a casual curiosity. The patient, often painful, process of inquiry is a *drag*. To question is to risk frustration; it is much easier just to dig everything and be done with it.

The beat scene is one where only the *moment, not* the *process,* of interaction comes into focus, where people have encounters rather than involvements. Just as men and women are stripped out of the context of past and future, leaving only a raw present, so too their art and their religion and their lives disintegrate into kicks. After the kick subsides, the person is left precisely where he was before — in the bored morass of self. Again, we see a state of *anomie*, where the person, in Durkheim's words, "has nothing in the past as a comfort against the present's affliction, for the past was nothing to him but a series of hastily experienced stages. . . . Weariness alone . . . is enough to bring disillusionment, for he cannot in the end escape the futility of an endless pursuit." (19, p. 256)

For the beat generation, distracted motion takes the place of purposive action. Significantly, David Riesman now seems to feel that it is not so much conformity as aimlessness which characterizes the new suburban life (53). The beat and the square, more than either realizes or admits, are cut from the same cloth. The dilemma is that of Kerouac's character who has "nowhere to go but everywhere." (34, p. 28) Since there is no basis for choosing one direction over another, the final alternative is to lapse into that dark inertia which is just beneath the neon surface of American life.

CONCLUSION

Mannheim speaks about the disappearance of social tension which accompanies the decline of ideology and utopia. In the effort to "reach out beyond the tensionless situation," several

[17] One would suppose that in comparing himself to Goethe Kerouac was only "capping the squares," yet he seems to believe himself (36); for a devastating analysis see Caroline Freud (23). "The beatnik is simply a bourgeois fantasy . . . a rebel without repercussion . . . who scandalizes and interests only the middle class public from which he springs." (23, p. 42)

adaptations are possible: (1) affiliation with the radical left; (2) scepticism and disenchantment; (3) a refuge in the past which "through a romantic reconstruction seeks to spiritualize the present." Yet as modes of reality-transcendence none of these are quite suited to the contemporary scene. The left has been closed since the 1930's and the possibilities of disenchantment were exhausted by the lost generation of the 1920's. Refuge in the past, except for Southerners, has never been a real alternative for the historyless America. However, Mannheim delineates a fourth type which seems strikingly descriptive of the beat generation: "Shut off from the world, this group consciously renounces direct participation in the historical process. [That is, it disaffiliates.] . . . An ahistorical ecstasy . . . is now placed in all its nakedness in the very centre of experience. [Recall the beat play at mysticism and the search for 'kicks.'] We find one symptom of this [Mannheim continues] in modern expressionistic art, in which objects have lost their original meaning and seem simply to serve as a medium for the communication of the ecstatic. [Beat art is wholly subjective, largely meaningless to the uninitiated.] Similarly . . . in philosophy, Kierkegaard . . . ultimately driven to a bare ecstatic 'existence as such.' But when the ecstatic element . . . turns inward and gives up its conflict with the immediate concrete world [of culture and politics], it tends to become gentle and innocuous or else to lose itself in pure self-edification." (41, pp. 233–234)

References

1. Aldridge, John. *In Search of Heresy: American Literature in an Age of Conformity*. New York: McGraw-Hill Book Company, Inc., 1956.

2. Aldridge, John. *After the Lost Generation: A Critical Study of the Writers of Two Wars*. New York: The Noonday Press, 1958.

3. Algren, Nelson. *Man with the Golden Arm*. Garden City, N.Y.: Doubleday & Company, Inc., 1949.

4. Becker, Howard. *German Youth: Bond or Free*. London: Routledge & Kegan Paul, Ltd., 1949.

5. Bell, Daniel. *The End of Ideology: On the Exhaustion of Political Ideas in the Fifties.* Glencoe, Ill.: The Free Press, 1960.

6. Bottomore, T. B. "Some Reflections on the Sociology of Knowledge," *British Journal of Sociology,* Vol. 7 (March 1956), pp. 53–57.

7. Bottomore, T. B., and M. Rubel (eds.). *Karl Marx: Selected Writings in Sociology and Social Philosophy.* London: Watts & Co., 1956.

8. Broyard, Anatole. "Village Cafe," *New Directions,* Vol. 13 (1950), pp. 398–401.

9. Broyard, Anatole. "A Portrait of the Hipster," in Chandler Brossard (ed.), *The Scene Before You.* New York: Rinehart & Co., Inc., 1955, pp. 113–120.

10. Burdick, Eugene. "The Innocent Nihilist Adrift in Squaresville," *The Reporter* (April 3, 1958), pp. 30–33.

11. Burroughs, William. *Naked Lunch.* New York: Avon Books, 1958.

12. Child, Arthur. "The Theoretical Possibility of the Sociology of Knowledge," *American Journal of Sociology,* Vol. 51 (July 1941), pp. 392–418.

13. Churchill, Allen. *The Improper Bohemians: A Recreation of Greenwich Village in Its Heyday.* New York: E. P. Dutton and Co., 1959.

14. Cowley, Malcolm. *Exile's Return: A Literary Odyssey of the 1920's.* New York: The Viking Press, 1934.

15. Davidson, Richard. "Moon Over MacDougal Street," in Elias Wilentz (ed.), *The Beat Scene.* New York: Corinth Books, 1960, pp. 37–38.

16. Davis, Kingsley. "The Sociology of Parent–Youth Conflict," *American Sociological Review,* Vol. 5 (August 1940), pp. 523–535.

17. Davis, Maxine. *The Lost Generation: A Portrait of American Youth Today.* New York: The Macmillan Company, 1936.

18. DiPrima, Diane. "13 Nightmares," in Seymour Krim (ed.), *The Beats.* Greenwich, Conn.: Fawcett Publications, 1960, pp. 78–84.

19. Durkheim, Emile. *Suicide,* tr. by George Simpson. Glencoe, Ill.: The Free Press, 1951.

20. Eisenstadt, Samuel N. *From Generation to Generation: Age Groups and Social Structure.* Glencoe, Ill.: The Free Press, 1956.

21. Finestone, Harold. "Cats, Kicks and Color," in M. Stein, *et al.* (eds.), *Identity and Anxiety*. Glencoe, Ill.: The Free Press, 1960. pp. 435–449.

22. Fitch, Robert E. "The Bourgeois and the Bohemian," *Antioch Review*, Vol. 16 (Summer 1956), pp. 131–145.

23. Freud, Caroline. "Portrait of the Beatnik," *Encounter*, Vol. 12 (June 1959), pp. 42–46.

24. Ginsberg, Allen. *Howl and Other Poems*. San Francisco: The City Lights Pocket Bookshop, 1956.

25. Gold, Herbert. "Hip, Cool, Beat — and Frantic," *The Nation* (November 16, 1957), pp. 349–355.

26. Gold, Herbert. "The Beat Mystique," in Seymour Krim (ed.), *The Beats*. Greenwich, Conn.: Fawcett Publications, 1960, pp. 155–156.

27. Gould, Julius. "The Komsomol and the Hitler Jugend," *British Journal of Sociology*, Vol. 2 (December 1951), pp. 305–314.

28. Gutman, Robert. "Review of the Unsilent Generation," *Commentary* (April 1959), pp. 362–366.

29. Hofstadter, Richard. *The Age of Reform*. New York: Alfred A. Knopf, 1955.

30. Holmes, John Clellon. *The Horn*. New York: Random House, 1953.

31. Holmes, John Clellon. "The Philosophy of the Beat Generation," in Seymour Krim (ed.), *The Beats*. Greenwich, Conn.: Fawcett Publications, 1960.

32. Jacobson, Don. "America's Angry Young Men: How Rebellious Are the San Francisco Rebels?" *Commentary* (December 1957), pp. 475–480.

33. Kerouac, Jack. *The Dharma Bums*. New York: The Viking Press, 1958.

34. Kerouac, Jack. *On the Road*. London: Andre Deutsch, 1958.

35. Kerouac, Jack. *The Subterraneans*. New York: Grove Press, Inc., 1958.

36. Kerouac, Jack. "Beatific: On the Origins of a Generation," *Encounter*, Vol. 13 (August 1959), pp. 57–61.

37. Kolb, William L. "The Changing Prominence of Value in Sociological Theory," in Howard Becker and Alvin Boskoff (eds.), *Modern Sociological Theory*. New York: The Dryden Press, 1957, pp. 93–132.

38. Lipton, Lawrence. *Holy Barbarians.* New York: Julian Messner, Inc., 1959.

39. Lynes, Russell. "What Are Best Sellers Made Of?" *New York Times Book Review* (December 27, 1959), pp. 1, 15.

40. Mailer, Norman. "The White Negro," in *Voices of Dissent.* New York: Grove Press, Inc., 1954, pp. 197–214.

41. Mannheim, Karl. *Ideology and Utopia,* tr. by Louis Wirth and Edward Shils. New York: Harcourt, Brace and Co., 1951.

42. Mannheim, Karl. *Essays on the Sociology of Knowledge.* London: Routledge & Kegan Paul, Ltd., 1952.

43. May, Henry F. "The Rebellion of the Intellectuals, 1912–1917," *American Quarterly,* Vol. 8 (Summer 1956), pp. 114–126.

44. Mehring, Walter. *The Lost Library: The Autobiography of a Culture,* tr. by Richard and Clara Winston. Indianapolis, Ind.: The Bobbs-Merrill Company, Inc., 1951.

45. Merriam, Alan P., and Raymond Mack. "The Jazz Community," *Social Forces,* Vol. 38 (March 1960), pp. 211–222.

46. Merton, Robert K. "Karl Mannheim and the Sociology of Knowledge," in *Social Theory and Social Structure.* Glencoe, Ill.: The Free Press, 1957, pp. 489–508.

47. Picard, Max. *Hitler in Ourselves,* tr. by Heinrich Hauser. Chicago: Henry Regnery Co., 1947.

48. Podhoretz, Norman. "The Know Nothing Bohemians," *Partisan Review* (Spring 1958), pp. 305–318.

49. Podhoretz, Norman. "The New Nihilism and the Novel," *Partisan Review* (Fall 1958), pp. 576–590.

50. Redfield, Robert. "The Art of Social Science," *American Journal of Sociology,* Vol. 54 (November 1948), pp. 181–190.

51. Rexroth, Kenneth. "Disengagement: The Art of the Beat Generation," in Eugene Feldman and Max Gartenberg (eds.), *The Beat Generation and the Angry Young Men.* New York: Citadel Press, 1959, pp. 323–338.

52. Riesman, David. "The Found Generation," *American Scholar,* Vol. 25 (Autumn 1956), pp. 421–436.

53. Riesman, David. "The Suburban Sadness," in William M. Dobriner (ed.), *The Suburban Community.* New York: G. P. Putnam's Sons, 1958.

54. Riesman, David, *et al. The Lonely Crowd.* New Haven: Yale University Press, 1951.

55. Snyderman, George, and William Josephus. "Bohemia: The Underworld of Art," *Social Forces*, Vol. 18 (December 1939), pp. 187–199.

56. Taylor, Stanley. *Conceptions of Institutions and the Theory of Knowledge*. New York: Bookman Associates, 1956.

57. *Time*, "The Younger Generation" (November 5, 1951), pp. 46–51.

58. Trocchi, Alexander. *Cains Book*. New York: Grove Press, Inc., 1960.

59. Waller, Willard. "Insight and the Scientific Method," *American Journal of Sociology*, Vol. 40 (November 1934), pp. 285–297.

60. Watts, Allan. *The Way of Zen*. New York: Mentor Books, 1959.

61. Wolff, Kurt H. "The Sociology of Knowledge and Sociological Theory," in Llewellyn Gross (ed.), *Symposium on Sociological Theory*. Evanston, Ill.: Row, Peterson and Company, 1959, pp. 567–602.

62. Zorbaugh, Harvey. *The Gold Coast and the Slum*. Chicago: The University of Chicago Press, 1932.

Part Three

STUDIES IN
SOCIAL PROCESS

20

Social Problems and
Social Processes

ERNEST W. BURGESS

UNIVERSITY OF CHICAGO

*The structure and culture of human society are constantly in
flux. Usually the changes have some kind of internal order, even
though they are so complex that valid prediction, based on scientific knowledge, of the course of any given change is only partially possible. The internal order, in the sense that one stage
flows out the preceding stage and leads more or less inevitably
to the succeeding stage, justifies the name of "process." To open
this section on social processes, Professor Ernest W. Burgess delineates the nature of the basic social processes.*

*Some social conditions and processes are out of harmony with
certain social values, and when these affect a sizable number in
the population in substantially the same way, they may be called
"social problems." The development of a social problem and the
course of its solution, if any, is itself a social process. Professor
Burgess' article thus sets the stage for the consideration of human behavior as social process and social problem.*

Studies in Social Process

THE NATURE OF SOCIAL PROBLEMS

Conceptions of the nature of social problems have had an interesting history. Five main implicit or explicit theories of the nature of social problems will be briefly presented as indicating the development of insight into the nature of social problems and objectivity in their definition and analysis.

(1) *Social problems as an aggregate of individual organic pathology.* This point of view has been developed by biologists and psychologists who have been mainly concerned in the study of what they regarded as pathology in individual cases and then generalized to an aggregate of like individuals. Early explanations of delinquency and crime fall under this classification.

Lombroso (10) and his followers described criminals as constitutional inferiors to be identified by stigmata of degeneracy. Goddard (8, Chapter 1) and other psychologists ascribed juvenile delinquency and other social problems largely to feeble-mindedness to an extent not confirmed by later investigations. Alexander and Healy (1) after intensive psychoanalytic study of a few cases of adult criminality attributed the cause of crime to neuroticism. They admitted, however, that they were unable to explain why certain neurotics became criminal while others remained law abiding except to assume that there was a biological difference between them. It was evident that the explanation of social problems as an aggregate of individual pathology was entirely inadequate and that the explanation was not to be found in biological and psychological processes.

(2) *Social problems as social pathology.* The term social pathology implied that social problems were abnormal in comparison with the accepted norms of conventional society. They were behavior in violation of what was defined as right by the mores and by the prevailing ethical standards. The early books on social pathology and social problems by sociologists reflected this point of view (4, 7, 14).

(3) *Social problems as social and personal disorganization.* The consideration of social problems as a breakdown in the social structure represented an advance in sociological thinking. Society was viewed as a system of social controls in which its members were incorporated and in which they participated. Social and

personal disorganization occurred with a weakening of these controls over all or a part of the members of society (3, 12, 13).

Two criticisms have been leveled against the theory of disorganization as an explanation of social problems. One is that it implies that disorganization is always pathological, which is false to the facts. The other is that there is frequently smuggled into the analysis an adverse value judgment.

(4) *Social problems as conflicts of value.* Conflicts of value typically arise and create the following types of social problems: (*a*) conflict between representatives of two societies or of two groups in the same society; (*b*) conflict between the values of conventional society and those of unconventional groups or of persons within the society; (*c*) conflict of values in proposing alternative solutions to a problem; and (*d*) conflict of values in administering a program for the solution of a social problem.

These conflicts of values are often the surface expressions of deeper cultural conflicts of nationality, economic, religious, and political groups within a society (2, 5, 6).

(5) *Social problems as process.* The conception of social problems as social process recognizes their essential constructive function in the adaptation of a society and its culture to social change. The emergence of social problems is natural and inevitable. The resolution of social problems is necessary for personal growth in the individual and for progress in a society. The appearance and solution of social problems constitute the dynamics of the social process.

The concept of social process transcends while it includes the concepts of social disorganization and conflict of values. By placing social disorganization within the social process its constructive function of mediating social reorganization becomes evident. The conflict of values is also placed in the larger context of its function in the adaptation of the culture of a society to social change.

Ecological and Economic Processes

Two processes both of which are essentially non-social interact with the social process. These are the ecological and the economic processes. They are considered here because in their effects rather than in their nature they condition the operation of strictly social processes. Their influence needs to be understood to present a complete analysis of social processes and social problems.

Human ecology is the discipline which studies the effects of the physical environment upon human populations by the processes of economic competition, symbiosis, mobility, and distribution of populations and their activities over an area.

The ecological processes distribute population, groups, and individuals in their location and residence. Accordingly the technique of plotting the distribution of social phenomena by their territorial distribution is a useful tool in the study of social problems. The phenomena thus plotted include such social problems as juvenile delinquents, criminals, drug addicts, broken homes, divorces, desertions, gangs, and mental disorders.

By plotting the data of these and other social problems by natural or artificial areas, rates of incidence have been computed. By means of repeating this procedure over points in time, trends have been established. Signal examples of generalizations made possible in this way. are the theory of concentric urban zones, the concentration of cases of juvenile delinquency in the inner zones of industrialization, residential deterioration, and social and personal disorganization and the gradual thinning out of cases of delinquency in zones outward to the periphery of the city.

Analysis by the ecological method does not provide of course a complete explanation of any given social problem. But it is a good starting point. It excludes certain explanations and raises questions that are to be answered by other methods of research.

An excellent demonstration of the use of the ecological method in the study of a social problem is the book by Shaw, McKay and collaborators on *Juvenile Delinquency in Urban Areas* (16). Data are presented for representative cities of the United States showing rate of delinquency by concentric zones. Correlations are also presented on the association of juvenile delinquency with other social problems.

The economic process defined in its relation to social processes is the evolution of technological changes in the economy, that is, in the system of the production of goods and distribution of income. An example is the effect upon the system of land tenure as a result of a technological change in agricultural methods of production as related to the preceding and the following familial and societal organization. In Yugoslavia the wooden plow requiring several oxen was associated with the extended family system. The introduction of the more efficient iron plow led to the breakdown of the large family group into its component independent nuclear units of husband, wife, and children (9).

In conjunction with the other social processes (cultural, societal, and political), the economic process determines the occupational stratification, the income levels, and the standard of living of a society. Many social problems have been correlated with the lowest income levels of a society. Among these are inadequate housing, broken homes, divorce, desertion, juvenile delinquency, criminality, alcoholism, most forms of mental disorder, venereal diseases, and prostitution (16).

An examination of these social problems indicates that while the economic factor is undoubtedly present, no one problem is exclusively determined by it. Every one of these may occur with individuals and families of average and high income. It is also evident that where low income is present other processes — cultural, societal, and political — are also involved.

The economic like the ecological process can seldom if ever be regarded as the direct cause of a social problem. Social problems take shape in the operation of cultural, societal, and political processes. But the economic process exerts a powerful indirect influence.

THE SOCIETAL PROCESS

The term "societal process" is used here to denote the organization, disorganization, and reorganization of a society, community, or social group. The societal process is maintained by the interaction of persons of social groups within a social system and by the interaction of each social system with other social systems which result in change in the social structure.

Theoretically, the first phase of a societal process is the organization of previously unorganized persons into a social organization to work together for a desired goal. Every such organization makes certain demands and even hardships upon the individual members which are willingly borne because of faith in the goal. According to Malinowski a myth develops which touches the deepest emotions of man — his fears, his hopes, his passions, his sentiments — as it validates the social order and justifies the existing social scheme. Analogues to the myth may be found among historical peoples in the doctrine of the divine right of kings to rule in the European nations of the past, the rule of the proletariat and the withering away of the state under communism, and the democratic belief that any American boy can become president of his country. By formal and informal methods of education, values are inculcated upholding the existing social order.

The second phase of a societal process begins with evidence of disorganization. This is manifest in the unrest of those who either are under the greatest pressure and burden of the demands of the existing organization, who have been exposed to alternative forms of social organization, or who are temperamentally or emotionally unstable. The developing social unrest may lead to personal disorganization by alcoholism, gambling, delinquency, criminality, dissipation, *anomie,* and so on. Or it may take various forms of protest and agitation against the status quo, or be channeled into movements aimed at social reorganization. All these manifestations of personal and social unrest are stigmatized as equally pathological by the upholders of the social order. They condemn particularly those who question the established order and are planning to change or challenge its existence. Powerful forces are marshaled by the supporters of the status quo. These measures include the program of rewards and punishments and the compulsion to uniformity and conformity to the ritual of conventional behavior.

The third phase of the societal process is that of reorganization. This eventuates in the success of one of the movements to reorganize the social structure, which now becomes the established social order. This new social order in its turn is subject to disorganization and reorganization as the social situation again changes as a result of technological discovery or other economic conditions.

Social disorganization is always accompanied by problems of concern to the given society, to one of its constituent groups, or to the individuals immediately affected. But beyond this, social disorganization is a necessary prelude to social reorganization, which usually makes for the greater general welfare. The problem for the social scientist, then, is the question of bringing about social reorganization with a minimum of social unrest and of its accompanying problems of personal disorganization.

At any given point in historical time a society has a certain extent of social and personal disorganization. Problems arising in each situation should be studied not only in the context of these three phases of the social process but also in the perspective of the historical type of social structure. The nature of many a social problem can be determined only by an analysis of the factors involved in its development within a social structure. Another way of saying this is that every society has social problems which are characteristic of its social structure. For example, the land-tenure system of inheritance of rural Ireland, France, and other Western European countries provided for the authority and support of the aging patriarch. But it delayed the taking over of the management of the farm by the son and the introduction of more scientific methods of agriculture. In large-scale business organizations of the present a conflict typically develops between the formal bureaucratic organization and the informal organization of the employees of the company. In the United States a small percentage of unemployment is deemed by economists to be desirable for the efficient operation of the economy and therefore unemployment insurance is necessary. In the Soviet Union unemployment is practically nonexistent in the government-operated economy.

The societal process in conjunction with the economic, cultural, and political processes creates social stratification in all modern societies. The different social classes have a solidarity of interest in conflicts of their society with other societies. But within a given society the problem of the conflict of classes develops and may be intensified during election campaigns and in the period of collective bargaining, which may culminate in a strike. The relatively new field of industrial relations is devoted to research in management–labor policies and practices. One objective is the introduction of democratic procedures in decision-making.

In the United States and other societies social stratification takes place not only by economic classes but on the basis of such factors as age, sex, race, ethnic origin and religion. This country has an open-class structure which permits greater social mobility than in other countries. Yet discrimination exists to a greater or less degree wherever the lines of social stratification are drawn.

This system of social classes accentuates the problem of communication. Each group of a society has its own language. There arises, therefore, the need of expediting inter-communication to promote mutual understanding of points of view and the values that otherwise remain divisive.

The Cultural Process

The cultural process needs to be analyzed as it affects the rise and continuance of social problems in the context of social change and of the societal process or organization, disorganization, and reorganization. The values of a static societal order such as that of a primitive society or of an isolated cultural island tend to be stationary, while those of a modern society are in a process of evolution. The changes in values may be either slow or rapid as in a time of crisis, re-examination, and revision.

The culture of a society as an organized system of values tends to be non-adaptive to economic and social change. This produces what William F. Ogburn has defined as cultural lag (15). A technological invention is favorable to innovation in the economic and social systems, but its introduction may be hampered and delayed by the prevailing cultural values.

This is one of the situations that leads to a conflict of values between the standpatters and the innovators who are endeavoring to establish the new values which will facilitate and sanction the adoption of the innovation. Almost always there is an interplay of the cultural and the economic process in this situation. There are vested economic interests on the part of those resisting change and the prospect of economic gain or other advantages on the part of those advocating the introduction of the innovation.

Anthropologists and sociologists have stressed cultural relativity in relation to the rise and persistence of social problems.

William Graham Sumner has expressed this point of view in its most extreme form in his dictum, "the mores can make anything right." Conversely, they can make anything wrong. As an illustration of the validity of this principle there seems to be no behavior that has been stigmatized as wrong in certain societies and subcultural groups that is not sanctioned as right in others. Examples are therefore legion. Among these are polygamy, polyandry, promiscuity, divorce, lying, stealing, infanticide, murder.

"The definition of the situation" is a concept introduced by William I. Thomas to explain the rise and persistence of culturally sanctioned or disapproved behavior by social groups. He points out that in some cases the definition may seemingly be fortuitous. For example, among some African tribes the birth of twins is regarded as a sign of good luck. In neighboring tribes it may just as unaccountably be considered as certain to bring bad luck. The point is that in every group there is a range of behavior which bears the social definition of being either good or bad.

In every society or group there are those who are in control of the process of defining the situation. The institutions of a society — economic, educational, religious, political — act, in general, to maintain the existing values. The introduction and propagation of new values are generally promoted by voluntary associations, established for this purpose. The situation becomes one of cultural conflict, with both sides competing for the approval of the public. Often, as in the case of Protestant churches and the explosive issue of birth control, an institution gradually modifies its position and finally accepts and sanctions the innovation. The mores are the dominant values of a society. They are accepted as the conduct making for the welfare of a society. They have the acceptance either of the great majority of the members of the society or of its dominant classes. Deviations from them are condemned and entail social if not legal penalty. Deviations from the mores are regarded as the problems of a society. Certain of the mores of American society may be examined from this point of view.

Individualism is a dominant value in American society that arose under the conditions of a pioneering and frontier situation. The ideology of individualism still holds sway, although the frontier is no more and we have evolved from a rural free enterprise situation to an urban large-scale industrial civilization. Despite high percentages of failures, hundreds of thousands of Americans embark every year upon the individualistic venture of setting up their own business.

The old economic definition of individualism is being replaced by a cultural form of individualism. The stress now is upon ways of maintaining and enhancing personal development under conditions of modern life. The movements of adult education, art appreciation, music appreciation, the Great Books courses all emphasize the autonomy of the individual.

Organization is an American value of growing significance in modern society — in interpersonal relations, in intimate groups, in voluntary associations. The rapid rise of large-scale organizations has seemingly dwarfed the role of the individual and led to the emergence of the organization man. Consequently the values of team play are being emphasized. A loud dissenting voice is sounded by William Harrison Whyte in *The Organization Man*, which calls upon individuals to throw off the yoke of subservience and assert their autonomy and creativity. This situation creates a problem with economic, social, and personal ramifications. The rugged individualism of the past is out of step with the times. The socialized individualism is just beginning to take shape in the reorientation of values of democratic collective action.

Democracy has been and continues to be a dynamic value of American society. The ideology of democracy received its first full expression in the social relations of people in a pioneer society and has had application to political behavior in the abolition of slavery, in the political, economic, and social emancipation of women, in industrial relations, and in the current movement to abolish educational, residential, and other forms of segregation of the Negro. It is perhaps a paradox to point out that the dynamic idea of democracy creates both the perception of the problem and supplies the motivation of effort that leads to its solution. That the expression of the democratic way of life is not complete in the United States is evident in the forms of existing discrimination by race, by social class, and by religion. But the barriers to equality of opportunity are not insurmountable and indeed in individual cases may act as a spur rather than as a handicap to achievement. The potentialities of the value of democracy are far from spent as an indicator of social problems and as an instrument for their treatment.

Humanitarianism is a deep-seated value in the American mores. The disposition to act for the welfare of unfortunate members of the community was strong and personal in pioneer America. With the growth of industry and the urban way of life it has evolved into a huge complex of services under private and public auspices, such as community chest campaigns with their millions of beneficiaries. Perhaps with the great majority of people humanitarianism is largely emotional and not subject to analysis in its relation to the other concepts of our dominant values of individualism, democracy, and organization. An outstanding exception was the enactment of old age and survivors' insurance which was an expression of all four of these values in a form that gave full recognition to the meaning of each under modern conditions of life in this country. Thus a great step forward was taken in the elimination of poverty in old age. The controversy now raging over the form of medical care for older persons may be viewed as a struggle between the pioneer conception of welfare and its new expression, which takes into account the values of autonomy, individualism, and democracy.

So far we have considered the dominant values in American society. In the study of social problems it is necessary to point out the many subcultural groups within American culture. Every group has its own culture and set of values. These values control the behavior of its members even when they conflict with those of the larger society. So heterogeneous is American society as compared with nearly all other countries that aside from a few dominant values we should perhaps speak of cultural pluralism rather than of a unified homogeneous culture. This fact makes for the conflict of values and for a solution in terms of toleration of differences.

THE POLITICAL PROCESS

The political process, as the term is used in this chapter, is not confined to governmental action. It includes the process of collective action of leadership, public opinion, and propaganda, as well as procedures of legislation, judicial action, and administration of laws. The governmental aspects of the political process function not only through elected or appointed representatives but also through the pressure of interest groups, industrial and commercial associations, labor unions, medical associations, and many others too numerous to mention. These seek the enactment of legislation they support and the defeat of bills they oppose.

The instrumentality of government is increasingly being used for the enactment of legislation at the national and state level by social reformers to obtain the solution of social problems. Notable successes have been obtained by federal and state legislation prohibiting child labor, workingmen's compensation for industrial accidents, old age and survivors' insurance, permanent disability insurance, aid to dependent children, old age assistance, general relief, pensions for the blind.

A reform may have consequences quite different from those anticipated by its proponents. A notable case in point was the adoption of the Nineteenth Amendment to the Constitution, which prohibited the manufacture and sale of intoxicating liquors. The movement of national prohibition had been energetically pushed by the Anti-Saloon League and supported by ministers and leading laymen of Protestant churches. The years of prohibition witnessed the growth of bootlegging, the corruption of public officials, the rise of organized crime and widespread violation of the law. One basic explanation for the failure of prohibition was the cultural conflict between rural and small town people with strong convictions on the evils of alcohol and the tradition of urban ethnic groups of drinking as an accepted element of their social life. Another basic explanation was the erroneous belief of the advocates of prohibition that legislation could affect the personal habits of people. This restriction went against the mores of individualism and democracy, with their emphasis upon the autonomy of the person.

One cause of the failure of reform in the United States is the public reliance upon legislation in forbidding condemned behavior and providing punishment for violations. A striking illustration is provided by current measures in this country to prohibit the sale, possession, and use of narcotics. Actually this punitive method defeats its objective of reducing the sale of narcotics and the number of addicts. Under these conditions the price of the drug becomes abnormally high and the addict resorts to crime to secure funds for its purchase. Also under these conditions of repression and harassment, addicts tend to form a closed social group and to attract newcomers into membership. It is clear that drug addiction should no longer be treated as a crime but as a socio-medical problem, with treatment by clinics and by private physicians.

An even more striking illustration of the failure of measures as practiced by courts and other law-enforcing agencies to effect reformation is the case of the juvenile delinquent. Gabriel Tarde, with his rare insight as a judge, observed that the criminal is created by his act and by the way society treats his act (18). Delinquent acts are committed by nearly every adolescent. But the great majority never become delinquents because they do not go through the delinquency-making process. Only a minority are arrested by the police and appear in court, and still fewer are sent to reformatories. The great majority are treated by their parents and by their informal re-incorporation into neighborhood activities. The true delinquent gets his self-conception as a delinquent through the experience of his formal treatment by police, the detention home, the court, and the correctional institution. The juvenile court, with its ancillary services, has failed in its objective, namely, the reformation of the juvenile delinquent.

The social process has now been analyzed in terms of its component processes — societal, cultural, and political. A social problem needs to be examined from the standpoint of each of these processes. It then becomes necessary for complete understanding and control to combine the findings from each of the processes into a larger whole. This means that the study of social problems is interdisciplinary and does not belong to any one field.

SOCIAL SCIENCE RESEARCH AND SOCIAL ACTION

Social problems arise, become defined, remain unresolved, or are solved in the social processes of adaptation to, or control of, economic and social change.

Society now, in ever increasing degree, is directing its own destiny. Through scientific discoveries and technological inventions, society is now engaged in making the economic and social changes to which it must adapt or which it must subject to social control. It has, however, far less effective means for working out solutions to the social problems resulting from economic and social changes. It can be argued that, in the present stage of the development of social science, complete control of social problems is impossible and probably undesirable. Nevertheless, a few comments on the reasons for the lag in the solution of social problems may be offered.

1. *The single-discipline approach.* One of the reasons for the failure, or only partial success, of efforts in the solution and control of social problems is the prevalence of a single-discipline approach. Illustrations of this tendency to assign a problem to one field of social science are numerous. The treatment of juvenile delinquency is still largely on an individual basis because of the dominance of treatment by psychologists and psychiatrists. Yet sociologists have demonstrated by their research the significant factors of the gang and of the absence of neighborhood organization to provide activities for children and youth. A paradoxical situation has until recently existed in teaching and research where the family has been assigned to sociology and child study to psychology. Population problems by historical accident are now largely in the field of sociology. It is evident that their solution also requires biological, economic, anthropological, and political science research. Labor problems have been studied mainly by economists. At present sociologists and political scientists are also concerned with them. Problems of international relations were for a long time monopolized by political scientists and historians. Today representatives of the other social sciences are engaged in research in this field.

2. *The slow development of interdisciplinary research.* As is evident from the analysis of the interaction of economic, societal, cultural, and political processes, a social problem and its solution seldom if ever are confined to one or two of these processes but generally result from the interaction of all of them. This fact hampers the efforts of those who attempt the application of social science findings to the understanding and control of social problems. Too often at present the diagnosis of a social problem and

its treatment proceed from the viewpoint, findings, and methods of control of one of these disciplines. Instead, a total approach is necessary using the data and methods of all the disciplines relevant to the understanding and control of any given problem.

A recent study of the "Criteria of Aging and Determinants of Retirement" was conducted by a physiologist, a medical psychologist, an experimental psychologist, an economist, and a sociologist. Each investigator, independently of the others, studied the same cases of one group of employees 40 to 44 years of age and those of a second group of employees 60 to 64 years old. The findings showed the older group with somewhat less physical fitness for employment, somewhat greater incidence of brain damage, more abnormality of the retinal arteries of the eye, less psychomotor capacity, and more frequent self-perception of being old. Nevertheless, the productivity of the older workers as a group was as high as that of the younger workers. There were, however, equally great individual differences in productivity within each age group. All the workers were on individual incentive pay (17).

It is now feasible on the basis of this interdisciplinary study to construct a battery of tests that will give a preliminary method of assessing aging that is functional rather than chronological. The explanation of why the production of older workers is as high as younger workers remains a subject for further research.

There is imperative need for the study of social problems by the interdisciplinary approach. This type of study may of course be made by a person who is a competent investigator in two or more fields. The ideal project would, however, be carried through by a research team of scholars from the different relevant disciplines.

3. *There is a distinct place for exploratory research on social problems.* The intensive study of individual cases has its distinctive contribution. The social scientist needs to become familiar with the human beings who are the subjects of his investigations. He should come to know them in all their individuality. In this way he is enabled to perceive a particular social problem in its human significance. It is in this sense that Thomas and Znaniecki refer to the life history as the perfect sociological document (19).

Too often the exploratory phase of a research project is cut short, or no time at all is allowed for it. The investigator begins with a set of assumptions and proceeds to construct his questionnaire upon them. In this way he may omit consideration of an important variable and not be able to ask the right questions.

The nature of the phenomena of social problems calls especially for an exploratory period of inquiry. The essential nature of a social problem is generally quite different from its external appearance. Accordingly, a project with no adequate exploratory preparation may lead to quite superficial and even meaningless conclusions.

4. *The value of experimental projects.* There is real need at present in the field of social problems for projects that are not remedial but are preventive. They should be considered as experimental projects. They should be based on, or at least related to, the findings of social science research.

Such an undertaking is the Chicago Area Project, a neighborhood program for the prevention and control of juvenile delinquency. It was instituted in 1934 by Clifford R. Shaw of the Illinois Institute of Juvenile Research and of the Behavior Research Fund in cooperation with committees of local citizens in three Chicago neighborhoods with high delinquency rates.

The project was democracy in action at "the grass roots." The local committees in these immigrant neighborhoods undertook the same degree of sponsorship and responsibility as do similar local committees in residential neighborhoods. The decision-making on policies and programs was in their hands. They raised funds locally and obtained grants from the Community Fund. They took the responsibility for the prevention of juvenile delinquency and the constructive treatment of youthful offenders. This assumption of responsibility by a local group of a welfare program for the children of the neighborhood may be judged to be the best evidence of its success.

The continued existence of the committees and the taking of additional responsibilities is another criterion of success. Other criteria of success are the development of similar projects in other communities with high rates of delinquency, the formation of a Federation of Community Committees, the cooperation of the local committees with the juvenile court, the juvenile police, and the probation officers. The evidence is convincing that self-governing groups of local citizens will take responsibility for the problem of juvenile delinquency, will raise funds for its support, and will develop an effective program of activities for non-delinquent as well as delinquent children.

It can be confidently predicted that the present small number of experimental projects will multiply in the future. It is also to be expected that they will rely more and more on research findings on social problems.

5. *The need for thoroughgoing evaluation of projects.* Evaluation of the existing programs of welfare services is almost non-existent. The public assumes that a program is worth while because of the social and public prominence of its board of directors. The board of directors has confidence in the competence of the staff director of the project. The workers on the project have faith in their methods of work because of their professional training in them. Consequently no thoroughgoing evaluation is made. Of course, so-called evaluations may be made, but they tend to be made in terms of whether or not the services of the welfare agency meet standards in the field; unfortunately, the existing standards of service have not been evaluated.

Projects for the control of social problems should, wherever possible, have a built-in evaluation. A project of this type was the study of Highfields, an experimental treatment center. The purpose of the project was to find out the feasibility of operating a new type of treatment center which would exemplify the new knowledge of the nature and causes of juvenile delinquency secured by psychological and sociological research.

The Highfields project demonstrated these important facts: (*a*) that an informal residential center with a small staff of four to six persons and housing twenty boys with serious delinquency records could be set up and operated successfully; (*b*) that an atmosphere of rehabilitation could be established among the boys that would counteract the development of delinquent acts and behavior; (*c*) that the youth would participate freely and frankly in sessions of guided group interaction; (*d*) that they would be able to gain increasing insight into the factors which had led them to become delinquent; (*e*) that at the end of three or four months' residence in Highfields the large majority would acquire a determination to be law-abiding in the future; and (*f*) that in comparison with a similar group of boys with reformatory experience they showed a much better record of remaining nondelinquent after returning to the community.

Two evaluations were made of the effect of the experience of youth at Highfields in comparison with those at Annandale, the state reformatory to which the Highfields groups would probably have been committed had Highfields not been established. H. Ashley Weeks found that, after one year of freedom in the community, only 16.5 per cent of the boys from Highfields as compared with 48.9 per cent of those from Annandale engaged in new delinquencies (11). The second comparison reported in *The Highfields Story* was of the Highfields youth with an Annandale Reformatory sample selected before the establishment of Highfields. This comparison was made in order to remove any bias which might have been introduced by the judges' sending better risks for reformation to Highfields than to Annandale. The difference was still much in favor of Highfields, but with a smaller margin — 18 per cent of the Highfields boys as against 33 per cent of the Annandale boys returned to delinquency after one year in the community.

An evaluation such as that at Highfields gives assurance that a new method of dealing with a social problem is successful and can be adopted elsewhere under favorable administrative conditions.

The concept of social problems as a social process discloses the essential nature of their study. A social problem in modern society changes as it is being studied. It also changes because it has been studied. A problem that at first yields to a remedy may later become resistant to it.

The basic reason is that a social process with its component problems is a continuous flow of interaction and intercommunication of persons, groups, and societies. Research upon social problems introduces a rational and objective element into the social process, which, in the long run, should reduce the conflict aspect in attempts to solve social problems and conserve their positive contributions to human welfare. Social problems

Social Problems and Social Processes

in their total impact upon society may, therefore, be regarded by sociologists as natural, inevitable, modifiable, and normal.

References

1. Alexander, Franz, and William Healy. *Roots of Crime*. New York: Alfred A. Knopf, 1935.
2. Cuber, John F., and Robert A. Harper. *Problems of American Society: Values in Conflict*. New York: Henry Holt and Company, 1948.
3. Elliott, Mabel A., and Francis E. Merrill. *Social Disorganization*. New York: Harper & Brothers, 1934.
4. Ellwood, Charles A. *Sociology and Modern Social Problems*. New York: American Book Co., 1912.
5. Frank, Lawrence K. "Social Problems," *American Journal of Sociology*, Vol. 30 (January 1925), pp. 462–473.
6. Fuller, Richard C. "The Problem of Teaching Social Problems," *American Journal of Sociology*, Vol. 44 (1939), pp. 419–425.
7. Gillin, John L. *Social Pathology*. New York: Appleton-Century Co., 1946.
8. Goddard, Henry H. *Feeble-Mindedness, Its Causes and Consequences*. New York: The Macmillan Company, 1914.
9. König, René. "Changes in the Western Family," *Transactions of the Third World Congress of Sociology*, Vol. 4. Amsterdam: International Sociological Association, 1956, pp. 67–74.
10. Lombroso, Cesare. *Crime, Its Causes and Remedies*. Boston: Little, Brown and Co., 1911.
11. McCorkle, Lloyd W., Albert Elias, and F. Lovell Bixby. *The Highfields Story*. New York: Henry Holt and Company, 1958.
12. Mills, C. Wright. "The Professional Ideology of Social Pathologists," *American Journal of Sociology*, Vol. 49 (September 1943), pp. 165–180.
13. Mowrer, Ernest R. "A Study of Personal Disorganization," *American Sociological Review*, Vol. 4 (1939), pp. 475–487.
14. North, Cecil C. *Social Problems and Social Planning*. New York: McGraw-Hill Book Company, Inc., 1932.
15. Ogburn, William F. *Social Change*. New York: The Viking Press, 1922.

16. Shaw, Clifford R., and Henry D. McKay. *Juvenile Delinquency in Urban Areas.* Chicago: The University of Chicago Press, 1942.

17. Summary of papers presented at the seminar on "Criteria of Aging and Determinants of Retirement." Chicago: Industrial Relations Center, University of Chicago.

18. Tarde, Gabriel. *Penal Philosophy.* Boston: Little, Brown and Co., 1912.

19. Thomas, William I., and Florian Znaniecki. *The Polish Peasant in Europe and America.* New York: Alfred A. Knopf, 1927.

21

Social-Action Systems
and Social Problems

S. KIRSON WEINBERG

ROOSEVELT UNIVERSITY

The study of social problems has always been a major area of sociological research, but usually this research has been of a purely empirical nature rather than guided by sociological theory. In recent years, several attempts have been made to remedy this deficiency, and several papers following in this volume constitute such attempts, using interactionist theory. Professor Weinberg introduces the series by offering a general plan for approaching the study of social problems with an interactionist theory.

Static and Dynamic Approaches to Social Disorganization

Social disorganization, viewed as a function of a society's inability to solve its problems, implies an image of society as a symbolic-action unit with varying capabilities for coping with crises and problems. Social organization becomes a function of society's capabilities for constructively forming and changing its institutions to solve problems; and as a societal equilibrium, it becomes a dynamic process with continual changes to meet its

o

altering needs. Since problems of the static folk society differ from those of the dynamic urban society, diverse models of social organization are required for each. The model folk society has few problems, but has few action systems. The model urban society has effective action systems to solve its many problems. In this paper we will describe the effectiveness of the action systems as a function of social organization in three types of societies: (1) the simple folk society; (2) the *laissez-faire* urban society; and (3) the emerging planned urban society.

An action system consists of the ideologies, institutionalized services, programs, and personnel which are required to meet or to solve given social problems. This action approach to social organization is consistent with a scientific perspective of problem-solving; it is consistent with ideologies pertaining to controlled social change and social planning but upholding personal freedoms; and it is consistent with accrued knowledge and programs which aspire to reduce social problems such as juvenile delinquency, insanity, alcoholism, or marital conflict (21). This dynamic approach contrasts with the passive or static approach to social organization, which regards the inert social structure with minimal stress as the model societal equilibrium and which discounts or ignores existing or potential action systems capable of achieving social reorganization. The static model of social organization emphasizes societal order, inter-generational continuity, role symmetry, and a consensus geared to a tradition-bound past. Its ideal societal representation becomes the culturally homogeneous, informally controlled, kinship-centered, and isolated village society. This model of society might be a gauge to a *laissez-faire*, urban community, which also lacks effective action systems to handle its social problems. Hence it would view the model society as one with few social problems. From this static view a dynamic society germinates its own disorganization; the same elements that make a society dynamic, also make it disorganized (42; 43, pp. 17–37).

In the growing city of the nineteenth and early twentieth centuries, the festering slums, physical deterioration, squalor, crime, and prostitution, contrasted with the orderly rural community and the small village, which were relatively free of these symptoms (13, 30). The village or rural community is represented to some urban dwellers as a model organization (8, 28). But at the present this model remains a nostalgic hope rather than a realistic urban ideal. In fact, the urban model consists of a stable, but flexible and changing, technologically complex, well-administered, industrialized community that can recognize and, with the required techniques and public support, develop effective programs to solve its problems (7, 9, 17). Even a contemporary urban community lacking services and programs to meet many social problems, nonetheless has an intricate coordination of services in feeding, transporting, equipping, housing, medically treating, entertaining, and regulating millions of inhabitants, which far surpasses the coordination of the hamlet or village (1, 36, 42). But the services and personnel of a *laissez-faire* society in a city which attempts to deal with the personality problems of its inhabitants, are very inadequate (14, pp. 112–135; 28). This social inadequacy results in part from an image of the person and of society.

THEORETICAL BASES OF SOCIAL ACTION

The conception of the society and the person as symbolic-action units is derived largely from the philosophic systems of pragmatism, a forerunner of symbolic interactionism in social psychology (3, 20). Pragmatism regarded action as the means for testing the accuracy of an hypothesis, and hence as the locus of reality. William James's formulation of a pragmatic test of truth, Dewey's theory of instrumentalism, and George H. Mead's philosophy of action developed and represented this position (10, 18, 23, 24). This view was applied to the person as an actor, but was not as readily applied to society, which was analyzed as a unit emerging from interpersonal relations. But from this philosophy, society, too, can be viewed as a symbolic-action system. Its consensus about the means and ends of action in society gives interaction a dynamic twist (5). Societal responses result from deliberation and discussion among the members, who select a course of action to meet the given problem. On a parallel basis, the individual who selects a course of action after reflection, also debates within himself in a process called an "inner forum." (23)

This tendency to liken society to the individual as a symbolic-action system has been recently discouraged by past misleading analogies. Society had been likened to an organism, or had been characterized as having a "group mind," like that of the thinking individual. Both analogies have been refuted and discarded. Still, society and the individual have common features which are comparable. Both are communicative units capable of concerted and planned action. Both units can mobilize, anticipate, and execute ideas as a prerequisite to symbolic action and interaction (31). When societal consensus is perceived as being oriented toward action, customs become meaningful as traditionally standardized ways of solving problems, while enacted institutions become "organized forms designed to satisfy group needs." (7; 23; 43, pp. 17–37).

SOCIAL-ACTION SYSTEMS IN DIVERSE TYPES OF SOCIETIES

The components of social action include: (1) societal orientation towards social problems; (2) active and latent institutionalized forms to deal with social problems; and (3) the kinds of equilibrium which are achieved as a consequence.

These components of social-action systems become clear when the tradition-bound folk society and the *laissez-faire* society are compared with the contemporary partly planned urban community.

THE FOLK SOCIETY

The folk society is sometimes considered a model of social organization. Its degree of organization can be determined by these criteria:

First, it does not experience the crises and the intense strains which characterize the rapidly changing urban society. Second, its modes of disorganization vary from those of urban society, and hence these forms of disorganization are not readily discerned. In many folk societies, juvenile delinquency and adult crime are minimal, almost nonexistent, as contrasted with urban society; but other problems, such as infectious diseases, malnutrition, lack of personal fulfillment, and infant mortality, are quite prevalent. Third, its depiction as being ideally organized has resulted from the way folk societies, especially the exotic and nonliterate societies, have been studied. These cultures have been reconstructed on the basis of ideal norms, and from behavior patterns which were assumed to be homogeneous and consistent. Hence one, two, or several informants were considered adequate for an anthropologist in reconstructing a culture. But in this reconstructive process, relatively slight attention was devoted to the social deviants or to the changing and informal norms as distinct from the ideal and formal norms of the culture (12, 42). Consequently the reconstructed norms of many folk or exotic societies emphasized their harmony and symmetry and their lack of deviation and disorganization. Frequently the knowledge which the social anthropologist would gain from his informants would not necessarily penetrate to the more meaningful facets of the culture, nor would his informants necessarily have insight into or reveal all the discordant facets of the society. In brief, the anthropologists were concerned with the ways that societies were organized, not with the ways they were disorganized.

Although the folk society is depicted as a model of social organization by which to gauge urban societies, the two types of societies are not really comparable because their problems differ. Some problems of the folk society reflect their inability to cope with serious social problems, especially biological problems. Other social problems, such as deviant behavior, are few in folk societies because of informal, face-to-face social controls, because of the homogeneous value systems, and because of inter-generational continuity which effectively restrained the individual members. But these social characteristics are not always sufficient restraints because of separation between age groups, such as between adolescents and adults. Consequently delinquent practices existed among Alorese and the Chagga, and rape existed among the Samoans (12, 26).

The interpersonal stresses also were manifestly great in some folk societies because of witchcraft practices, hovering threats of supernatural punishments and general interpersonal hostilities, such as existed among the Mundugumor, the Alorese, and the Manus (12, 25, 26). In many nonliterate societies the personalities were relatively shallow emotionally because of early parent–child relationships. These persons were unable to express intense and bindingly intimate relationships; such shallow relations existed among the Trukese, Alorese, Samoans, and Marquesans (12, 19, 26). The forms of deviant behavior which would emerge from deviant subcultures within the society were rare among nonliterate and small folk societies because these societies were culturally homogeneous. Prejudice and discrimination were not marked in tribal societies which were in-groups, but definitely characterized their relations with captured out-group tribes. The problems of old age were not prevalent in folk societies because relatively few people survived beyond the age of fifty. In some simple societies such as the nomadic Siriono, persons about age 35 and older were left to forage for themselves as the tribe moved on (41, pp. 382–396). Disorganized behavior on the individual idiosyncratic level was prevalent in folk societies. Certainly many nonliterate personalities were the equivalent of our neurotics, and some also were psychotic and acting-out types. For example, institutionalized deviation occurred among the Comanches, who tolerated the hostile and destructive pranks of braves called "contrary ones" because they excelled as warriors (19). Linton has maintained that psychotics were few in many nonliterate societies because they did not survive. Certainly the nonliterate person was not more stable than the urban person. Although tradition-bound societies manifested indulgence toward infants, partly to avoid infant mortality, the period after weaning could have been traumatic for the child in many nonliterate societies because of the lack of adequate foods and the abrupt changes in social relationships. Furthermore, childhood in many of these societies was considered an unimportant stage in the life-cycle, and its value was of consequence only insofar as it led to adulthood. The child of these nonliterate and folk societies had considerably less value than the child of the child-centered, future-oriented societies, such as the United States. In terms of self-fulfillment, inter-generational continuity and control had adverse as well as beneficial consequences for the member of the folk society. On the one hand, they enabled the individual to have a clear image of his adult role as distinct from the hazy image which the urban person has of his. On the other hand, they reduced or delayed his tendency toward emancipation from his parents in his personality development. For example, in some pastoral societies which practised the bride-price, the father would marry off his daughter to collect cattle as the bride-price, but would delay his son's marriage until his acquired cattle reproduced enough calves to pay for his son's bride as well as leave some cattle for himself. The son's prolonged passivity which could result from this type of marital arrangement contrasts with the urban individual's attitude of assertive emancipation.

Since the static folk society aimed to conserve the past, it did not encourage new action systems for dealing with deviant behavior. Many folk societies had rudimentary or no action systems to protect society or to treat their deviants. For example, Fortune found that Dobuans had "no machinery for dealing with insane and delinquent persons." (15, pp. 53, 54) Men who ran amuck were dangerous at all times, but were not restrained. Instead people scampered away into the bush, claiming that the afflicted persons would be all right the next day. But this tolerance reflects the lack of social-action systems which were able to deal effectively with this disorder.

In some folk societies built-in informal controls, however limited, perhaps prevented deviant behavior, while suggestive psychotherapeutic techniques did counteract disordered behavior. Many folk action systems operated within the traditional framework of magic, were indirect, did not improve by testing, were geared to an inert society, and were oriented toward present problems from a perspective of the past. Many folk societies were not compelled to cope with new and challenging experiences. Perhaps some of these societies would not have survived severely critical experiences.

The survival of the Alorese, a South Sea people, hung "on a very thin thread," according to Kardiner. Their low level of cooperation and their tenuous grip on the external environment rendered them completely immobilized in a crisis. They survived apparently because of the absence of external enemies. They had low norms of achievement, no investigative drive, no admiration of strength, and no interest in order. They lacked effective techniques either to manipulate or to change their environment (12, 19).

The Ifaluk people, in the central South Seas, as a contrary instance to the Alorese, had a highly organized society. They experienced minimal anxiety and few conflicts. They valued cooperation, non-aggressiveness, kindliness, and generosity (37). They did not experience a discrepancy between their sanctioned goals and their means to attain them. Their economic system did not permit extreme discrepancies of wealth, and their distribution system provided economic care for the aged, the ill, and the bereaved. Politically, they respected and identified themselves with their chieftains. Although they felt hostility, they usually inhibited it or, at most, expressed their hostility and anxiety in fantasy. But the striking fact about the Ifaluk society is that "not one individual" recalled a single incident of murder, rape, robbery, or fighting, although there were a few cases of psychoses.

In this tradition-bound tribe, social problems were scarce, but corrective systems also were few. Although they had sanctioned outlets for socially shared strains, they had no institutionalized outlets for idiosyncratic strains, so that those few persons afflicted became psychotic or severely neurotic. Specifically, to avert shared strains, the Ifaluk displaced their aggressions to malevolent ghosts. "Although Ifaluk socialization provoked a potentially explosive problem by stimulating hostility in a people whose ethos prohibits the expression of hostility, the Ifaluk religion served to resolve the problem by providing the people with malevolent ghosts against whom their hostility could be released with impunity." (37)

When the deviants were openly aggressive, however, the society had no techniques to deal with them except by the ineffectual means of condemnation. In brief, in this highly organized folk society, few forms of deviant behavior existed, and the built-in preventive action systems within the culture offset these culturally induced hostilities. However, when new problems arose outside the scope of their customs, the Ifaluk had few techniques to deal with them, and did not devise any (37).

The level of social equilibrium in a folk society depended upon the inherent stresses within the culture, because most folk societies lacked the orientation, flexibility of adaptation, and the tribal support to meet new and critical changes. Their acceptance of pathology as an integral part of sacred societal conditions implied an institutional equilibrium that itself was static and frequently sacred. Their action systems were tradition-bound, geared to the past, and not amenable to improvement by experimentation. Their social organization sustained an equilibrium by encountering few new problems, in marked contrast to the urban community, which is continually meeting new problems.

THE LAISSEZ-FAIRE URBAN COMMUNITY

During the early twentieth century, the static model of social organization was regarded by sociologists as a contrasting ideal to the disorganization prevalent in many areas of American cities (8). This static model was an understandable ideal for the characteristic *laissez-faire* city.

The *laissez-faire* doctrine, as applied to urban affairs, advocated the least possible governmental interference in improving society, minimized governmental responsibility for social problems, maintained the least taxes for administering government, and favored the fewest programs and services to cope with social problems. People were appraised by their economic roles, whether as utilities or commodities, and were analyzed from a biogenetic perspective. The successful people were considered the fit people; the poor, as failures, were the unfit. From this Sumnerian view, the middle and upper classes had no obligation to promote the welfare of the lower classes, whose members comprised the predominant number of deviants (38).

This individualistic *laissez-faire* doctrine rationalized the minimal social-action systems and depreciated the lower classes:

> If, as the Spencerians and the Social Darwinists asserted, competition was the law of life, there was no remedy for poverty except individual self-help. The poor who remained poor must pay the price exacted by nature from all the unfit. Any interference in their behalf, whether undertaken by the state or by unwise philanthropies, was not only pointless, but absolutely dangerous. Protecting the weak in the struggle for existence would only permit them to multiply and would lead to no other result than a disastrous weakening of the species; it would thwart nature's plan of automatic, evolutionary programs toward higher forms of social life (2, p. 19).

This ideology emphasized that personality change and social change were basically biological and genetic problems which would be resolved in competitive struggle and with governmental noninterference. In nominalistic fashion, social institutions were considered products of the bio-psychological make-up of people. People who represented problems had to be eliminated in the biological way by not reproducing themselves and by not being helped, rather than by being rehabilitated. This ideology meant that society would be improved eventually by selectively sifting the biologically fit from the unfit, who were the deviants (2).

Although the state protected the law-abiding and successful individuals, it had no responsibility for improving unfit individuals. The action systems which were consistent with this philosophy were designed to protect society, and to punish or to segregate forcibly those deviants who threatened existing institutions and the safety of society (2; 14, pp. 112–135).

The social problems concentrated about the derivatives of poverty. The lower classes were considered the dangerous classes, and dependency frequently was categorized like criminality, while alcoholism was considered one very significant cause of poverty (2). The social problems which clamored for amelioration arose from poverty, including unemployment and dependency, prolonged working hours, the sweatshop, industrial accidents, child labor, women in industry, and bad housing. The basic corrective measures were oriented around effective legislation, which at least would remove the most offensive conditions.

In defining and dealing with deviants, the conception of rehabilitation and correction was minimized, and the essential equilibrium was that based upon suppression and forcible sequestration. The institutions for these purposes consisted of the prison, the insane asylum, the workhouse, and the almshouse. These action systems, then, created a specific equilibrium within the society, which by its techniques accepted a high rate of deviation and was ineffective in reducing or even in defining the problems adequately. On the other hand, the upper and middle classes were somehow portrayed as not having problems or even as not being deviants. White collar offenders, for example, were not recognized in legal systems nor even in sociological literature until about 1940, when this mode of crime was defined and analyzed by Sutherland (39).

But a humanitarian ideology also emerged as a rationale for dealing with squalor and human suffering. It emphasized that institutional and legal changes, rather than individual changes, were necessary to solve or to reduce the existing problems (14, pp. 112–135). Small private charities, social agencies, and neighborhood settlements strove to care for and to alleviate the condition of the poor, the homeless, and the orphaned. Because institutions and services were not established easily, imaginative individuals dreamed about or started utopian retreats where social problems would be few or eliminated. Their model of social organization was the small society.

American cities of the late nineteenth and the first quarter of the twentieth century, had few adequate services to deal constructively with social problems. Political administrators were frequently corrupt, inadequately trained, and incompetent. Social and psychological sciences were underdeveloped and were not applied, while the public was indifferent to and generally unable to change corruption and intolerable conditions.

In the early twentieth century, the "muckrakers" described the shocking conditions in the slums and factories. Their literary works sometimes influenced legislation and inspired new programs. Reformers led intermittent crusades against outrageous conditions. When they lacked an educated and aroused citizenry to support them, their efforts for social change sometimes became futile. At other times their clamor for needed change was effective, as in the case of Dorothy Dix and the insane asylum. In general, because of intense opposition, the word "reform" itself aroused controversy.

The prevalent suspicion of and opposition to corrective social change and social planning frustrated effective social action. Social improvements were gained only after intense social agitation. This method of effecting social change still exists in some measure for certain social problems in many present American cities. For example, widespread scandal can arouse the citizens to force changes in official personnel, laws, and procedures, or to create new programs which are designed to deal with social problems. At that time the social movements, whether brief or prolonged, frequently did not achieve the desired results because the action was counteracted by hostile groups and because knowledge was inadequate and money insufficient to cope with these problems.

In cities in other countries, such as in Brazil, Peru, and Venezuela, people may endure considerable abuse until they discharge their pent-up tensions by mob behavior or revolution. Their emotional reactions to social problems result in discharging tensions instead of in seeking rational solutions. This collective reaction is irrational, impulsive, ineffective, and frequently merely a search for a scapegoat. When elites turn over, as in a revolution, the changed power structure also may not create an effective action system for solving existing problems. On the other hand, in societies where knowledge is accessible, social pressure may inaugurate necessary changes. After World War II the exposés of the conditions of many state mental hospitals became so effective that many needed changes followed. The riots in the prisons also have affected certain modifications in prison custody and organization. The police scandals in Chicago have been the bases for needed and constructive changes. Sometimes, before effective changes take place, several intense reactions to scandal occur. In Chicago, police scandals occurred early in the twentieth century, again in 1930, were repeated in 1952 and once more in 1959–60, when a reorganization of the police department was initiated.

Perhaps the core of urban disorganization resides in uncontrolled urban migration, mobility, and growth. The urban migrant presumably escapes the intense informal control from his village, but many urban migrants have encountered social disorganization within the village and small town (29, pp. 243–266). Slotkin found that varying degrees of disorganization characterize the village groups from which urban migrants come (35, pp. 33–37). Possibly, their very migration may facilitate or intensify this village disorganization. But their early settlement in the city is one of intense disorganization. Since the urban migrants were regarded as economic utilities and their other needs overlooked, they had few social agencies to facilitate their total adjustment to the urban community. When the *laissez-faire* ideology prevailed, these disorganizing processes were considered natural and inevitable, and few if any steps were taken to direct or control them. In brief, the basic social problems in the *laissez-faire* city consisted in poverty and its effects. People were appraised by their economic roles, and the behavior of poor people was viewed as emerging either directly or indirectly from their poverty. In the nineteenth and early twentieth centuries their poverty was regarded as the result of their individual depravity or personal deficiency. From an institutional perspective the basis of social problems and deviant behavior resided in uncontrolled urban growth and urban mobility. These social problems included, among others, poverty, dependency, child labor, women in industry, housing, along with delinquency, crime, and alcoholism. These social problems were basically aspects of an economic constellation of problems in which poverty was considered the effect of personal difficulties and, in turn, the result of individual depravity and deficiency. The action systems of the city or state were designed to suppress deviant behavior by punishing or forcibly segregating the serious deviants. Small private agencies performed token duties to alleviate the effects of destitution and to treat social deviants. Hence the level of equilibrium was such that the rates for varied social problems remained high.

EMERGING ACTION SYSTEMS IN CONTEMPORARY
URBAN COMMUNITIES

The contemporary urban community in the United States has overcome the *laissez-faire* doctrine in several basic ways. It has recognized governmental responsibility for the welfare of its citizens and for controlled social change (6). It has accepted social planning and corrective social changes which do not throttle individual liberties (4). It has accepted higher taxes to defray the cost of government services and the application of the immensely accruing knowledge of the social and psychological sciences for dealing with social problems, especially those resulting from deviant behavior (7, 33, 43). It has trained personnel for these purposes (11). The attitude toward planning was clearly expressed by Truman after the enactment of the Employment Act of 1946. He rejected the view that people are the victims of immutable economic laws "about which we can only predict." Instead, he emphasized that "our economy, within reasonable limits, will be what we make it, and intelligent human action will shape our future." These attitudes toward planning by federal, state, or municipal intervention have become incorporated into the accepted thinking and practice of American society. They are consistent with the establishment of social-action systems to counteract social problems. This view maintains that the deviant individual can become rehabilitated and re-incorporated into society instead of being punished by or ostracized from society. The deviant is viewed not as a biogenetic inferior, but as an interpersonal emergent, albeit sometimes with ambivalence: as a threat to society and at the same time as a potentially rehabilitated law-abiding citizen.

The problems of urban society have become more pertinent and pressing because of the rapid spread of urbanization in the United States. About 70 per cent of the population in the United States reside in cities, especially in metropolitan areas. The emphasis on social organization must realistically be based upon devising action systems to meet the emerging social problems and not upon futile wailings concerning the inevitability of these urban problems. The level of equilibrium in the urban society becomes a significant criterion of the efficacy of these action systems.

Ideally, society's capacity to eliminate a given social problem would be the optimum societal equilibrium. But this ideal organization of society is a hope imported from the biological sciences. It is inspired by prevention programs against infectious diseases such as yellow fever, diphtheria, or cholera, the incidence of which has been minimized. But the societal equilibrium for social problems would be more realistic and hence more modest. This level of equilibrium for dealing with social problems would be measured by reduced annual rates for specific social problems. The reduction of annual rates over a time span would indicate the effectiveness of the action systems.

The third level of societal equilibrium would result from similar annual rates over a time span for specific social problems. This means that the action systems would be sustaining instead of reducing the existing prevalence of social problems (42).

Social-Action Systems and Social Problems

The fourth level of equilibrium — or more appropriately, disequilibrium — would intensify social disorganization as indicated by the increased annual rates for diverse social problems. This disequilibrium occurs among transition areas which new ethnic and/or economic groups invade and from which the resident groups are in process of leaving. In the interim, social controls decline, an anomic condition prevails, and the formal law-enforcing agencies are inadequate to cope with the increased deviant and disorganized behavior (27). Thus the established and new residents with declining morale become passively resigned to crime, gambling, alcoholism, prostitution, and other forms of manifest deviant behavior.

To counteract urban problems we may characterize urban action systems which pertain to two broad types of problems. These action systems include (1) the rehabilitation of the urban physical setting and its functions, and (2) the reduction of deviant behavior. But the latter actions systems are subdivided into (a) those which suppress deviant behavior, and (b) those which strive to re-orient and to rehabilitate the social deviants.

The rehabilitation of the physical city has become accepted as standard American practice (11). The improvement of housing, the renewal and the conservation of deteriorated urban areas, the planning of traffic, and the remaking of the central city are needs that require long-range planning to anticipate the cumulative changes that arise in a rapidly evolving urban society. But these plans frequently meet resistance from many quarters. Hence the blueprints of planning frequently are not carried out. For example, slum clearance in large cities such as Chicago, St. Louis, or New York is considered urgent. One accepted way of reducing physical blight is by the common enterprise of the city and the federal government because costs for such projects are higher than many local communities can afford. This kind of cooperative effort was initiated by Chicago and New York. In 1957 the Mayor of St. Louis characterized this cooperative need to a Senate Subcommittee as follows:

> The city of St. Louis is in the midst of a great effort to destroy the decay and blight in its very center. Our citizens have voted to spend over a hundred million dollars for capital improve-

ments during the next few years. But the total cost of rebuilding our city is simply beyond our present financial resources. . . . the Federal government . . . has the major tax resources in our country today to cooperate most effectively with our large cities in the renewal of their residential, commercial, and industrial areas (17).

But physical blight and housing shortages have created competition for homes, have intensified discrimination against individuals for housing, have intensified urban squalor, and furthermore are related to many social problems.

Because the federal government has lagged in coping with many of these problems, a federal Department of Urban Affairs and Housing has been suggested. But also effective legislation for urban affairs on a national and state level has lagged because of the underrepresentation of urban people in the various legislatures. Senator Douglas has pointed out that "cities are the Cinderellas of American life" — underrepresented in the State legislatures, in the national House of Representatives, in the Senate, and in the administration (17). One estimate is that slum clearance would take more than one hundred years if it proceeded at its present relatively inactive pace. Despite this slow activity, every large city has from one to several planning commissions and agencies to rehabilitate its deteriorated areas as well as to improve other facets of the urban community.

The action systems to counteract the varied forms of social deviation, such as crime, are more complex and more difficult to implement successfully. On the level of suppression, these action systems include the criminal laws, the institutionalized modes of detection, and the adjudication of the offenders. Perhaps the criminal laws would be more effective in reducing crimes if detection and conviction were more certain and if severe penalties were meted out for certain offenses. For example, in Ohio the long sentences imposed upon convicted drug peddlers were instrumental in markedly reducing drug addiction in that state. It does not follow, however, that capital punishment should be sustained or extended, because severe penalties would not necessarily be deterrents, and the death penalty might impede conviction.

The direct suppression of crime by detection involves the police

Social-Action Systems and Social Problems

and allied law-enforcing personnel. The organization, training, and professionalization of police work have improved considerably. The political barriers to effective police work, however, remain formidable, particularly because of the corruption and patronage wrought by political influence and because of the jurisdictional lags in overlapping authority between county and city and the fragmented authority vested in the inefficient police forces of every hamlet and township. The need for a metropolitan police force as a unit becomes definitely urgent.

As an action system to maintain the safety of the citizens, the police can be compared precisely for degrees of effectiveness in different cities and political jurisdictions. Thus, federal law-enforcement agencies would rate as being more effective than many municipal law-enforcement agencies.

Furthermore, action systems vary in their effectiveness in suppressing different types of crime. For example, direct offenders are far more likely to be detected and convicted than are syndicate offenders. According to the Chicago Crime Commission, for 926 murders committed by syndicate offenders from 1919 to 1960 in Chicago, there were only 17 arrests, or 1.8 per cent, and the percentage of convictions was less than 1 per cent. Witnesses did not testify for fear of reprisal, and the police did not seek the killers (32, p. 28). This weakness of the suppressive branches of the action systems for dealing with syndicated crime means that the resulting level of equilibrium for this type of crime is low. In several large cities it is reflected in a resigned acceptance of syndicated crime by the citizens, who feel that the syndicated offenders usually will resort to reprisal against witnesses and will not be caught or penalized for their crimes. By contrast, different offenders such as burglars and robbers, despite some corrupt practices in their adjudication, are sought, frequently apprehended, and frequently convicted and sentenced. Of a total of 260 homicides committed in Chicago during 1952, 223 arrests were made, or 85.7 per cent of the total homicides; and of 320 persons charged with murder, 90 were found guilty of homicide and 31 persons for lesser offenses — a combined percentage of 37.8 per cent. The action system for suppressing direct offenders is thus more effective than the system for suppressing syndicated offenders.

TABLE 1

Action Systems for Four Selected Social Problems in the Chicago Area*

ASPECT OF SOCIAL ACTION	TYPE OF SOCIAL PROBLEM			
	Schizophrenia	*Juvenile Delinquency*	*Alcoholism*	*Prostitution*
1. Approach to Deviant: Suppression versus Treatment	Minimal suppression and considerable treatment	Suppression and some treatment	Suppression and some treatment	Considerable suppression and little or no treatment
2. Treatment Agencies	9 clinics and counseling centers; 5 private hospitals; 3 state hospitals; 350+ psychiatrists**	1 state juvenile institute; 3 private agencies	2 clinics; c.10 private sanitariums	2 veneral disease centers

3. Forced segregation or custodial institutions	3 state hospitals; 3 federal hospitals; 1 county agency for temporary observation	2 detention homes and 1 reformatory	Lock-ups	Lock-ups
4. Prevention Programs	c.6 programs (mental health programs)	c.5 programs	None known	None known
5. Training institutes for professional and allied personnel	c.8 training institutes	c.4 training institutes	None known	None known
6. Public Education	Widespread	Widespread	Limited	None (for rehabilita- or control)
7. Research: Programs and Inquiries	c.10 projects	c.5 projects	1 project	None

*Data taken in part from 38, pp. 157, 165, 166, 170, 172–178; and *Chicago Classified Telephone Directory* (Chicago: R. R. Donnelly Corp., 1959), pp. 1504–32, 1781–82.

** *Biographical Directory of the American Psychiatric Association* (New York: R. R. Bowker Company, 1958, pp. 455, 456) lists 297 members and fellows for Chicago and about 50 for the suburbs immediately surrounding Chicago, but there are psychiatric practitioners who are not members of the APA.

On the rehabilitation-prevention level for deviants, the ideal objectives assume that with the application of optimum treatment techniques the deviants would be rehabilitated, and the improved social conditions and personality stability would remove or minimize the very bases for the rise and existence of deviant behavior (7). Rehabilitation at best is difficult and is achieved only for some deviants. Progressively more effective techniques for rehabilitating alcoholics and drug addicts have been developing; but almost no progress has been made for rehabilitating psychopaths or prostitutes. The techniques for treating and hence reducing emotionally disordered behavior and delinquency have definitely progressed. In consequence the public has revised its image of these deviants, regards many of them as amenable to rehabilitation, and is willing to subsidize treatment as well as research programs, although the money allotted still is inadequate for effective wide-scale programs. The treatment techniques for psychoses generally and for neuroses are more effective than those for delinquency and alcoholism, and far more effective than those for prostitution. In fact, the prostitute is viewed as a source of immorality or of venereal disease, or as a sex offender. Consequently she has no agencies to which to turn for rehabilitation, because there are no agencies which specifically treat the prostitute (43). Furthermore, few techniques to facilitate the rehabilitation of the prostitute exist.

To demonstrate the discrepant degrees of effectiveness of the action systems dealing with the diverse social problems, we have compared the action systems which deal with schizophrenia, juvenile delinquency, alcoholism, and prostitution. We have considered the following components of these action systems for comparative purposes: (1) the approach to the particular type of deviation, (2) the treatment agencies, (3) the voluntary and forced custodial agencies, (4) the prevention programs, (5) the institutions for training personnel, (6) the research programs, and (7) the programs for educating the public.

When the action systems which are designed to cope with these forms of social deviance are appraised for the Chicago area, we find that these systems, when ranked from most to least effective, pertain respectively to (1) schizophrenia, (2) juvenile delinquency, (3) alcoholism and (4) prostitution (36).

Social-Action Systems and Social Problems

When the most and least effective action systems are compared, we find many clinics, hospitals, and private psychiatrists for schizophrenia but almost no treatment agencies that are specifically designed to rehabilitate prostitutes. There is considerable research for the former, virtually none for the latter. There are training programs for personnel and programs educating the public about schizophrenia, while there are no training programs for personnel and no programs for educating the public about rehabilitating the prostitute. Consequently, the action systems for schizophrenia, despite the limitations of treatment techniques, are far more effective than those for prostitution. This extreme divergence in the effectiveness of the action systems of these two problems illustrates the diverse ways in which society responds to different social problems. We have shown in Table 1 a more detailed comparison for the four social problems.

In conclusion we have emphasized that within contemporary urban communities the mode of attaining a societal equilibrium resides in the types of action systems which are designed to reduce the extent of the social problems. This approach points to a different societal model of social organization than the static small society which has been used as a contrasting ideal for the *laissez-faire* city. Contemporary urban trends indicate that action systems are being devised and improved to cope more effectively with the prevalent urban social problems. These trends include a reduction of the modes of disorganization which contribute to deviant behavior, and the continued development of effective rehabilitative services, institutionalized programs, and trained personnel to deal successfully with social deviants. But these trends show an uneven development for different social problems.

References

1. Angell, Robert C. *The Integration of American Society.* New York: McGraw-Hill Book Company, Inc., 1941.
2. Bremner, Robert H. *From the Depths: The Discovery of Poverty in the United States.* New York: New York University Press, 1956.
3. Buckley, Walter. "Structural-Functional Analysis in Modern

Sociology," in Howard Becker and Alvin Boskoff (eds.), *Modern Sociological Theory*. New York: The Dryden Press, 1957, pp. 236–259.

4. Buell, Bradley, and Associates. *Community Planning for Human Services*. New York: Columbia University Press, 1952.

5. Cassirer, Ernst. *Philosophy of Symbolic Forms*, Vol. I. New Haven: Yale University Press, 1953.

6. Chase, Stuart. *Democracy Under Pressure: Special Interests vs. the Public Welfare*. New York: Twentieth Century Fund, 1945.

7. Clinard, Marshall B. *The Sociology of Deviant Behavior*. New York: Rinehart & Co., Inc., 1957.

8. Cooley, Charles H. *Social Organization*. New York: Charles Scribner's Sons, 1912.

9. Cuber, John F., Robert A. Harper, and William F. Kenkel. *Problems of American Society: Values in Conflict*. New York: Henry Holt and Company, 1956.

10. Dewey, John. *Human Nature and Conduct*. New York: Henry Holt and Company, 1922.

11. Dewhurst, J. Frederic. *America's Needs and Resources: A New Survey*. New York: Twentieth Century Fund, 1955.

12. Du Bois, Cora. *The People of Alor*. Minneapolis: University of Minnesota Press, 1944.

13. Faris, Robert E. L. *Disorganization: Personal and Social*. New York: The Ronald Press Company, 1955.

14. Fine, Sidney. *Laissez Faire and the General Welfare State: A Study of Conflict in American Thought: 1865–1901*. Ann Arbor, Mich.: The University of Michigan Press, 1960.

15. Fortune, Reo. *Sorcerers of Dobu*. Boston: Little, Brown and Co., 1932.

16. Fuller, Robert C. "The Problem of Teaching Social Problems," *American Journal of Sociology*, Vol. 44 (1949), pp. 415–435.

17. Hartley, Eugene L., and Gerhart D. Wiebe (eds.). "Urban Renewal in Selected Cities," in *Casebook in Social Processes*. New York: Thomas Y. Crowell Company, 1960, pp. 158–217.

18. James, William. *Pragmatism*. New York: Longmans, Green and Co., 1907.

19. Kardiner, Abram. *Psychological Frontiers of Society*. New York: Columbia University Press, 1945.

Social-Action Systems and Social Problems

20. Levy, Marion J. *The Structure of Society*. Princeton, N.J.: Princeton University Press, 1952.

21. Lynd, Robert S. *Knowledge for What?* Princeton, N.J.: Princeton University Press, 1949.

22. Mannheim, Karl. *Freedom, Power, and Social Planning*. New York: Oxford University Press, 1950.

23. Mead, George H. *Mind, Self, and Society*, ed. by Charles W. Morris. Chicago: The University of Chicago Press, 1934.

24. Mead, George H. *The Philosophy of the Act*, ed. by Charles W. Morris. Chicago: The University of Chicago Press, 1938.

25. Mead, Margaret. *Sex and Temperament in Three Primitive Societies*. New York: William Morrow & Company, 1935.

26. Mead, Margaret. *From the South Seas*. New York: William Morrow & Company, 1949.

27. Merton, Robert K. *Social Theory and Social Structure*. Glencoe, Ill.: The Free Press, 1949.

28. Mills, C. Wright. "The Professional Ideology of Social Pathologists," *American Journal of Sociology*, Vol. 49 (1944), pp. 169–180.

29. Miner, Horace. *Timbuctoo*. Princeton, N.J.: Princeton University Press, 1953.

30. Mowrer, Ernest R. *Disorganization: Personal and Social*. Philadelphia: J. B. Lippincott Co., 1942.

31. Parsons, Talcott, and Edward A. Shils (eds.). *Toward a General Theory of Action*. Cambridge, Mass.: Harvard University Press, 1951.

32. Peterson, Virgil. *Reports on Chicago Crime, 1957*. Chicago: Chicago Crime Commission, 1957.

33. Powers, Edwin, and Helen Witmer. *An Experiment in the Prevention of Delinquency: The Cambridge-Somerville Youth Study*. New York: Columbia University Press, 1951.

34. Rose, Arnold M. "Theory for the Study of Social Problems," *Social Problems*, Vol. 4 (January 1957), pp. 189–199.

35. Slotkin, James Sydney. *From Field to Factory*. Glencoe, Ill.: The Free Press, 1960.

36. *Social Service Directory of Metropolitan Chicago: 1958*. Chicago: Welfare Council of Metropolitan Chicago, 1958.

37. Spiro, Melford E. "Cultural Heritage, Personal Tensions and Mental Illness in a South Sea Culture," in Marvin K. Opler (ed.),

Culture and Mental Health. New York: The Macmillan Company, 1959, pp. 141–170.

38. Sumner, William Graham. *The Forgotten Man and Other Essays.* New Haven: Yale University Press, 1918.

39. Sutherland, Edwin H. "White Collar Criminality," *American Sociological Review,* Vol. 6 (February 1941), pp. 1–12.

40. Symes, Lillian. "The Great American Fact-Finding Farce," *Harper's Magazine* (February 1932), p. 354.

41. Weinberg, S. Kirson. *Society and Personality Disorders.* Englewood Cliffs, N.J.: Prentice-Hall, Inc., 1952.

42. Weinberg, S. Kirson. "Static and Dynamic Models of Social Disorganization Theory," *Social Problems,* Vol. 23 (1958), pp. 339–346.

43. Weinberg, S. Kirson. *Social Problems in Our Time.* Englewood Cliffs, N.J.: Prentice-Hall, Inc., 1960.

22

The Differential-Association
Theory of Crime

DANIEL GLASER

UNIVERSITY OF ILLINOIS

The late Professor Edwin H. Sutherland was closely identified with the interactionist theory in social psychology but specialized in studies of criminal behavior. His specific theory — called differential association — is an explanation of the major forms of crime in interactionist terms. It regards crime as a type of human behavior which society labels deviant or criminal. Professor Daniel Glaser not only summarizes Sutherland's theory but extends and refines it.

Evolution of the Theory

The term "criminology" is reported to have been coined by the popular press in the late nineteenth century as an abbreviation for "criminal anthropology." (9) Its use in much of Europe still connotes primarily the physical anthropological study of criminals. A latent function of academic sociology in America appears to have been to serve as a repository for left-over areas of societal or cultural study not clearly claimed by social science departments established before sociology. Accordingly, criminology, along with demography and the study of inventions, acquired an academic resting place in sociology which is rather unique to the United States. In Europe, criminology still is most commonly a specialty of law or medicine faculties; in the United States it has turned up in departments other than sociology at only a few institutions.

With the proliferation and expansion of sociology departments in American universities in the early twentieth century, and with the public increasingly demanding attention to "the crime problem" after World War I, the 1920's and 1930's saw a rapid increase in the number of American sociologists who became specialists in criminology. Their problem was to "explain" crime, and in this connection, they first had to cope with the older European literature in criminology, of strong biological orientation, which was extensively republished in the United States during the second decade of the twentieth century. Criminology textbooks and courses by American sociologists during the period between the two World Wars, and some even today, devote more time to summarizing and attacking the non-sociological literature on crime than to presenting substantive sociological propositions.

During the early twentieth century, many non-sociologists modified earlier biological explanations of crime. In Italy, Marxist influence led Ferri and others to try to blend economic and biological explanations (7). In France, drawing from experience as a magistrate and from his postulated "laws of imitation," Gabriel Tarde interpreted crime as a product of human association, reaching conclusions strikingly similar to much sociological writing several decades later (25). The psychiatrist Healy in the United States (15) and the psychologist Burt (1) in Britain each examined hundreds of delinquents, listing as "causes of delinquency" any presumed deviation from normalcy which they encountered, including deviations in health, intelligence, family conditions, education, and numerous other variables.

The first major contribution by American sociologists to empirical knowledge on crime was made at the University of Chicago by a series of studies providing systematic evidence that young criminals are highly associated with each other. Thrasher reported the actual or alleged names and locations of 1,313 gangs among juvenile delinquents in Chicago, and showed the functions these gangs served in delinquency (26). Shaw and McKay presented statistics, maps, and case studies which showed, among other things, that delinquency was concentrated in a limited portion of the city, that about 90 per cent of delinquents committed their offenses in company with other delinquents, and that their ties with other offenders and other sources of social support for criminal attitudes became more extensive the more they participated in crime (21).

In the first textbooks on criminology written by sociologists, which appeared in the 1920's, and in most such works still today, the basic formulation of theory is essentially the same as that of most non-sociologist writers, including early writers like Ferri, Healy, and Burt, whom we have cited. This is the so-called "multicausal" or "multiple factor" theory of crime. Its essence is that crime is a consequence of many causes, of which the most often cited include mental deficiency, economic distress, broken homes, association with criminals, and personality defects. The principal polemics of these theorists are against anyone whom, they charge, overemphasizes a single factor.

Differences between sociologists and other multiple-factor theorists have not been great with respect to the variety of causes recognized. Rather, differences have arisen from the relatively high weight which sociologists give to association with criminals and enculturation in criminal subcultures, and their lesser emphasis on alternative "causes." However, most presumed correlates of crime cited by others are included in the sociological multifactor catalogues.

In this setting, when as a young sociologist at the University of Illinois Edwin H. Sutherland was asked to teach criminology and to prepare a text in that field, he readily assimilated multicausal theory. As he put it: "I took pride in my broadmindedness in including all kinds of factors and in not being an extremist like the geographic determinists, the economic determinists, the biological determinists, or the mental-tester determinists." (2, p. 14) This was apparent in 1924 when his *Criminology* appeared. Fifteen years later, however, after a series of intellectual stimulations at the University of Minnesota (1926–1929), the University of Chicago (1930–1935), and at Indiana University thereafter, he says:

> It was my conception that a general theory should take account of all the factual information regarding crime causation. It does this either by organizing the multiple factors in relation to each other or by abstracting from them certain common elements (2, p. 18).

He also felt association alone to be inadequate as an explanation for crime since:

> . . . some people who reside in delinquency areas commit crimes, some do not. Any concrete condition is sometimes associated with criminal behavior and sometimes not. Perhaps there is nothing that is so frequently associated with criminal behavior as being a male. But it is obvious that maleness does not explain criminal behavior. I reached the general conclusion that a concrete condition cannot be a cause of crime, and that the only way to get a causal explanation of criminal behavior is by abstracting from the varying concrete conditions things which are universally associated with crime (2, p. 19).

The Third Edition of Sutherland's text, issued in 1939 as *Principles of Criminology*, contained the first publication of his "differential association" theory. In essence, it asserts: (*a*) the techniques and the "specific direction of motives, drives, rationalizations and attitudes" of criminal behavior are learned in interaction with other persons within intimate personal groups; (*b*) almost always in American society a person encounters a mixture of behavior which defines the legal codes as rules to be observed and behavior favorable to violation of the legal codes, and hence he experiences "culture conflict in relation to the legal codes"; (*c*) the principle of differential association "refers to both criminal and anti-criminal associations and has to do with counteracting forces" affecting one's definition of appropriate behavior; the principle is that "a person becomes delinquent because of an excess of definitions favorable to violation of law over definitions unfavorable to violation of law"; (*d*) the learning of criminal and anti-criminal behavior "involves all of the mechanisms that are involved in any other learning," is an expression "of the same needs and values," and is a function of the "frequency, duration, priority, and intensity" of differential associations with criminal and with anti-criminal behavior (2, pp. 8–10; 24, pp. 77–79).

As Sutherland interpreted his theory, all of the conditions predominantly — yet incompletely — correlated with crime, such as poverty, parental neglect, or personal traits, "have a causal relation to criminal behavior only as they affect the person's associations." (2, p. 25) Strongly influenced by Lindesmith at Indiana to strive to employ Znaniecki's "analytic induction" method of theory formation, Sutherland endeavored to phrase and to rephrase his theory so that it would account for the genesis of every case of crime which he encountered (2, pp. 17–18; 28). He particularly urged sociological study of those offenses commonly interpreted as having a genesis not readily accounted for by differential association, such as kleptomania, pyromania, incest, embezzlement, white collar crimes, and offenses allegedly committed under the influence of alcohol by persons who do not commit crimes when not under alcohol. If his theory would not account for these offenses, then his method would oblige him to revise his theory, or to divide crimes into categories each of which has a distinct genesis, then limit his theory to the class of crimes the genesis of which it explained. His posthumous papers suggest that he expected the theory to be revised from such research, but that he had not yet encountered what he considered to be adequate evidence for its systematic revision or delimitation.

THE THEORY'S STRUGGLE FOR EXISTENCE

Sutherland's theory was presented in nine propositions on two pages of his text. Illustration, elaboration, and interpretation of these nine propositions was not systematic in the rest of that volume. In the two-page formulation, the nine propositions and the commentary which is provided for each are rather dissimilar in scope. Indeed, it is not clear whether "differential-association theory" refers only to the sixth proposition, on "excess of definitions favorable to criminal behavior" (which he identifies as the "principle" of differential association), to all nine propositions taken collectively, or to the entire chapter in which they appear. His students and followers, notably Cressey, refer to the two-page, nine-proposition formulation as the theory, and we have taken this view (but have attempted a tighter integration of the theory, mostly in Sutherland's own words, in the four-segment synopsis presented in the preceding section).

Given this deficiency of formulation, and the polemical orientation especially characteristic of the literature of would-be sciences such as criminology, it is understandable that Sutherland's theory came under attack.

Cressey lists several errors of those critics whom, he says, "do not always understand what Sutherland was talking about." Most serious, perhaps, is the error of assuming that the theory is concerned only with criminal behavior patterns, neglecting Sutherland's simultaneous reference to *anti*-criminal patterns at almost every point of his theory. This error is understandable, however, since Sutherland applies his theory almost entirely to data on criminals, rather than to data on anti-criminals, ex-criminals, or other non-criminals. Secondly, Sutherland referred to association with patterns of *behavior*, but many of his supporters (including this writer) and most of his opponents frequently express his theory in terms of association with *types of persons*, criminal or anti-criminal. As Cressey points out: "One can learn criminal behavior patterns from persons who are not criminals, and one can learn anti-criminal behavior patterns from . . . professional crooks . . . and gangsters." Another type of error cited by Cressey is the practice of treating differential association as referring only to the learning of techniques for crime, rather than acquiring motivations and rationalizations. Still another type of misrepresentation sets forth the theory as concerned only with the "raw ratio of associations" — their frequency alone — neglecting Sutherland's stress on priority, intensity, and duration of differential association (6).

It was primarily in order to achieve more effective communication of what I conceived as Sutherland's theory that I proposed some years ago a reformulation of the theory as "differential identification," with the basic principle: "A person pursues criminal behavior to the extent that he identifies himself with real or imaginary persons from whose perspective his criminal behavior seems acceptable." (10) Later, it was also suggested that "differential reference" or even "differential learning" might be more adequate than "differential association" to convey in modern social-psychological language Sutherland's ascription of crime to the net effect of social learning, including socially derived motivation (11). Korn and McCorkle seem to be reformulating Sutherland's theory as differential "commitment" to various groups, adding an interesting and testable principle of "intensiveness" and "extensiveness" of commitments, but not basically altering Sutherland's image of the social genesis of crime (16, Chapter 14).

A second group of criticisms of Sutherland's theory can be distinguished as those which expect the theory to apply to the explanation of phenomena other than criminal behavior. For example, some writers seem to want the theory to account for the origin of criminal and anti-criminal association. While this is an area of inquiry to which one might reasonably progress in the course of applying differential-association theory, it clearly takes one to types of theory designed for other purposes, such as accounting for concentration of certain conditions in the slums, or for aspects of social stratification. A somewhat different form of unreasonable expectation by critics of differential association is the claim that the theory does not account for personality conditions associated with crime. This is unreasonable in that they have not demonstrated that any specific personality attributes other than criminal orientations and rationalizations, which are accounted for by differential-association theory, are regular antecedents of crime. Thus far investigations have shown that persons involved in crime are quite diverse with respect to non-criminal attributes of personality commonly investigated by personality tests.

A third variety of criticism of Sutherland's theory consists of claims that the theory does not fit certain categories of crime. Some of these claims pose issues as to whether the behavior considered can properly be called "crime," such as "unpremeditated" or "adventitious" offenses, and some juvenile delinquency (like delinquent but non-criminal disobedience to parents). Most other such claims involve unusual offenses, like pyromania, and have never been tested by research. Only two of these claims which the writer has thus far encountered seem to come from extensive research which clearly indicates that differential-association theory does not account for the genesis of the offense. These involve the crimes of trust violation and simple check forgery (4, 17).

A fourth major type of criticism of differential association is the observation that criminal behavior obviously occurs in part as a function of differential opportunities to commit criminal or non-criminal acts as alternative means to a given end. While there are arguments for and against the proposition that over any appreciable period of time almost everyone has opportunities to commit crime, it certainly is not true that everyone always has access to non-criminal means to attain his ends. There is increasing evidence that large segments of the population shift to economically oriented crime primarily when opportunities for legitimate employment diminish (13). Sutherland observed that differential association accounts for differences in recourse to crime in a given state of economic distress, but it might be usefully complemented by a theory taking into account the inverse relationship between some crime and opportunities for non-criminal achievement of the goals of crime.

TESTABILITY

The final type of criticism to be considered is that which contends that differential-association theory cannot be tested. This charge, if valid, would render the theory unacceptable, since it is a canon of science that any theory must be capable of being subjected to empirical tests which conceivably could prove it false (20). In this connection, Glueck inquires: "Has anybody actually counted the number of definitions favorable to violation of law and definitions unfavorable to violation of law, and demonstrated that in the pre-delinquency experience of the vast majority of delinquents and criminals, the former exceeds the latter?" (14) While the answer to this would at first appear to be negative, it should be noted that an abstract theory is not tested directly by empirical observation; it is validated or invalidated by tests of operational hypotheses deduced from the abstract theory. Our problem is to consider whether differential-association theory generates testable hypotheses.

Glueck's reference to definitions favorable or unfavorable to violation of the law comes from Sutherland's sixth proposition, called by Sutherland "the principle of differential association." However, seen as a whole, the nine propositions of his theory specify that several aspects of orientation to criminal and anti-criminal behavior (technique, rationalizations, etc.) are learned as a function of several aspects of association (priority, intensity, intimacy, etc.), and only in this context does the "principle of differential association" become meaningful. In this context the "definitions" phraseology seems to be a means of making a summary reference to the net effect of social learning processes, that is, all that is learned which is relevant to one's consideration of violation or non-violation of the legal codes.

It follows from the foregoing interpretation that one way to test Sutherland's theory without actually counting what Glueck calls the "number" of definitions would be to measure indices of the aspects of association specified in the theory, and to measure their correlation with observable criminal behavior, assuming the definitions to be an intervening variable. Sutherland's "definitions" term seems to come from W. I. Thomas' "definition of the situation," and in today's behavioral science idiom he might have used the term "orientations." At any rate, in the light of the foregoing analysis, the theory may be considered testable if operational indices of association and of criminal behavior can be deduced. The "definitions" concept then becomes an intervening variable, conceptualized but not directly indicated, in this respect resembling the concept "genes" in genetic theory and the concept "atom" in chemical theory, despite the vast differences between these theories.

The phrase "epistemic correlation" has been employed to designate the extent to which a particular type of observation is indicative of an abstractly conceived condition (19, Chapter 7). Since Sutherland asserts that most people, at least in America, experience both criminal and anti-criminal associations, and several aspects of each are relevant (priority, intensity, etc.), many indices of association are available. Indeed, indices of opposite types of association may be observed in any subject. It would follow that there will be only an imperfect epistemic correlation between any single type of relevant observation and the net association of subjects with criminal and anti-criminal behavior. Some tests of differential association are diagrammed in Table 1. These happen to be tests in which the hypotheses were validated. However, three major sources of limitation in testability,

TABLE 1

Four Empirical Tests of Differential Association Theory

Association with criminal behavior → *Criminal behavior*		*Association with anti-criminal behavior* +→ *Criminal behavior*	
Residence in high delinquency area → Arrest rates		Unseparated non-criminal family +→ Delinquency commitment	
Association with criminal behavior → *Criminal behavior*		*Association with anti-criminal behavior* +→ *Criminal behavior*	
Pre-prison regularity of employment →+ Discharge from five-year parole		Truancy → Arrest rates	

Key:
  Concepts: italicized phrases
  Observations (operationally defined indices): roman phrases
  Positive Epistemic Correlations: plain vertical lines
  Negative Epistemic Correlations: vertical lines with short cross-line
  Positive Theoretical Relationships: plain arrows connecting concepts
  Negative Theoretical Relationships: cross-lined arrows connecting concepts
  Hypothesis of Positive Correlation: plain arrows connecting observations
  Hypothesis of Negative Correlation: cross-lined arrows connecting observations
Note that there must be an even number of negative correlations or negative theoretical relationships. (This system of diagramming was learned by the author at the American Sociological Society meetings in Detroit in 1956 from Professor Robert Hamblin, now of Washington University in St. Louis.)

rather than invalidity of differential-association theory, could account for findings of no significant correlation between the observations (set in roman type) connected by arrows:

1. Epistemic correlations between the total associations with which differential-association theory is concerned and any available index of these associations necessarily are limited because each index reflects only a segment of an individual's total associations (school, family, neighborhool, and so on).

2. Each index for those segments can only be assumed to signify the relative extent of criminal or anti-criminal association there; residence in high delinquency areas, for example, can be assumed to signify more exposure to pro-criminal behavior than residence in low delinquency areas in most cases, but not necessarily a predominant influence of criminal over anti-criminal influences.

3. Since known criminal behavior is relatively infrequent in the general population, its relationship to antecedents is not likely to be manifested with statistical significance unless samples are extremely large, or are especially selected so that the group in which criminal behavior is manifest approaches 50 per cent of the sample. The lower the epistemic correlation, the more this sampling requirement of high "antecedent probability" of the criterion event (criminal behavior) becomes necessary for evidence of any relationship (18). That is why criminological causation research is most fruitful in analysis of recidivism for known delinquent or criminal populations (where it occurs in about half of the cases), or in comparison of a matched delinquent or criminal group with a non-delinquent or non-criminal control group.

Sutherland's theory deals with the net influence of criminal and anti-criminal association, while the tests illustrated in Table 1 involve only one of these types of association. However, there is much evidence that many indices of association with criminal behavior are highly correlated with one another (criminal record, truancy, residence in high delinquency area, and the like), that many indices of association with anti-criminal behavior are also highly intercorrelated (regularity of work record, cohesiveness of family, and so on), and that there is an inverse relationship between these two groups of indices. That is why, in Table 1, the same indices can be designated as having a positive epistemic correlation with association with criminal behavior or a negative correlation with association with anti-criminal behavior.

A numerical score which might be assumed to be correlated with the net ratio of definitions favorable and unfavorable to crime acquired through association conceivably could be procured by multiple correlation analysis. This is the method employed in criminological prediction research, using more or less sophisticated systems of deriving weights. (The discriminant function method, of course, involves a much more rational analysis than the so-called Burgess or Glueck weighting systems.)

Unfortunately, integrated tests are not available in criminological prediction literature because studies thus far have always mixed predictors which can be deduced to be indices of association with criminal or anti-criminal behavior and predictors which cannot readily be deduced as such indices. In a recent survey of this literature, however, I have shown that the group of predictors having the highest association with an index of criminal behavior (parole violation or delinquency) in each study include a markedly higher proportion of predictors deducible from differential-association theory than the group of predictors having the lowest association with the index of criminal behavior (12). The most effective predictors deducible from the theory and positively related to later parole violation or delinquency are indices of the extent of prior criminal record, truancy, and alienation from parents; those with highest negative relationships are regularity of prior work record, age at first arrest, and age at first leaving home. Among the poorest predictors have been measures of physical strength, number of siblings, dominant parent, and psychological test scores.

Two major exceptions to support of differential-association theory in criminological prediction research are that the most effective predictors also include type of prior offense and immediate job expectation. At least one of the types of prior offense highly associated with recidivism, forgery, cannot reasonably be inferred to be more of an index of prior association with criminal behavior than the less recidivistic type of offense (17). Job expectation may be an index of prior regularity of work record, but insofar as it is a function of involuntary unemployment due to fluctuations in the business cycle, it also reflects differential opportunity somewhat independent of prior associations.

Much more direct indices of differential association have been employed by Short, who procured from delinquents and non-delinquents responses to a series of questions on the delinquency of their first friends, most often seen friends, longest known friends, and best friends. These were presumed indicative, respectively, of priority, frequency, duration, and intensity of delinquent association. The results generally supported Sutherland's theory, particularly for boys rather than girls, for older rather than younger boys, for institutionalized rather than non-institutionalized delinquents, and especially with respect to the most intense — "best friend" — associations (22). Later, Short asked delinquents and non-delinquents questions on both the delinquency and the anti-criminality of their best friends. This yielded even more marked and consistent support for differential-association theory (23).

Wheeler has validated differential-association theory with a rather unique index of what might be called definitions favorable to conformity to conventional moral codes. He procured reformatory staff and inmate opinions on the most proper conduct of several alternatives in a series of hypothetical prison situations in which an actor was faced with a complex moral choice. Inmates most deviant from staff in their choices were judged lowest in conformity. These were the inmates with earliest and most frequent arrests, which was taken as an index of priority and frequency of contact with criminal patterns. An unanticipated finding was a low negative relationship between number of correctional institution commitments (taken as an index of intensity of contact with criminal patterns) and conformity to staff moral norms. Wheeler interprets this as due to the high number of alcoholic forgers in his sample who were both highly conforming in moral choices and frequently committed to institutions (27).

A misperception of the function of theory may develop if we accept without qualification Short's conclusion that operationalization of Sutherland's variables, at which Short has brilliantly led the way, enhances knowledge if it leads to "transformation of the theory by specification." (23) As Philipp Frank points out with repeated illustrations from the history of science, a major function of abstract theory is to serve as a code for summarizing myriad detailed observations; these are the observations which validate operational hypotheses deduced from the theory. The generalizations of theory which are validated become accepted as the principles of a science. These principles lose their utility for the analysis of new types of data if they lose their generality.

The foregoing does not mean that theory should not be revised to fit unanticipated findings, but the canon of parsimony in science creates pressure for drastic reconceptualization wherever a theory must become too highly qualified and cumbersome in order to account for observations. As Frank says: "Every acceptance of a debatable theory is due to a compromise between . . . agreement with facts and efficiency as a code." (8, p. 341) A theory is most useful if a diversity of useful hypotheses can readily be deduced from it (that is, if it can be operationalized in many ways for analysis of many problem situations). A theory's validity is never known conclusively or finally, although increased confidence may be inspired if there is a diversity as well as a high volume of validating test results.

Survival of the Fittest Theory

Commenting on the utility of the phlogiston theory of oxidation for 150 years after evidence contradicting it was known, but before the significance of oxygen was recognized, James B. Conant writes:

> Does it argue for the stupidity of the experimental philosophers of that day? Not at all; it merely demonstrates that in complex affairs of science one is concerned with trying to account for a variety of facts and with welding them into a conceptual scheme; one fact is by itself not sufficient to wreck the scheme. A conceptual scheme is never discarded because of a few stubborn facts with which it cannot be reconciled; a conceptual scheme is either modified or replaced by a better one, never abandoned with nothing left to take its place (3, p. 173).

In the light of the criticisms discussed in the preceding section, let us consider whether differential-association theory should be replaced by an alternative theory already available, or whether a modification of differential-association theory can be suggested to make it more adequately meet the effective criticisms which it has encountered.

The most prevalent theory in American criminology textbooks is multiple causation, which asserts that crime is a function of numerous variables, but does not indicate their interrelationship. Unless a testable proposition is set forth to rank, weight, or otherwise interrelate multiple variables, the proposition that crime is a function of many variables does not provide a basis for deducing hypotheses which observation could prove false. One can always subdivide or find a correlate of any variable which might be proposed as a basis for an alternative theory. This makes multi-causal theory untestable, and for this reason, it cannot be considered a scientific conclusion.

The other leading competitor of differential-association theory in criminological literature is the psychoanalytic view of crime as a breakdown of controls over innate impulses, or other breakdown or absence-of-control theories analogous to the psychoanalytic model. While this may be useful for encompassing certain behavior called "delinquency" in some literature, such as temper tantrums, it fails to account for the social sources of learning in what the courts more commonly call delinquency and crime (see 12 for fuller discussion).

By comparison with its principal competitors then, differential association stands fairly secure.

Earlier, this paper indicated some deficiencies of Sutherland's formulation in communicating what his supporters have interpreted as his meaning. Several modes of reformulating Sutherland's theory were noted. It also was reported that two types of criticism of differential-association theory have been supported by research. The first is that the theory does not account for most cases of at least two types of offense, trust violation and forgery. The second is that the theory does not take adequately into account the extent to which the genesis of crime is a function of fluctuations in opportunity for non-criminal achievement of the goals of crime.

The peculiar association between much persistent lone forgery and chronic alcoholism makes more adequate theory for that type of forgery highly dependent on development of a more satisfactory theory of the etiology of chronic alcoholism. While there may be other felonies in addition to forgery and trust violation which are peculiarly independent of a social learning process, Cressey has pointed out the questionable basis for assuming this independence in most so-called compulsive crimes (5). Our analysis leaves the conclusion that differential association still is the most satisfactory theory for interpreting the great bulk of major crimes, particularly larceny, burglary, and robbery, which comprise 90 per cent of felonies tabulated in the F.B.I.'s *Uniform Crime Report.*

For guidance in predicting the criminality of the majority of currently convicted offenders, who show appreciable evidence of both criminal and anti-criminal orientations, I have suggested that a "differential anticipation" theory of criminality might be developed to conceptualize simultaneously both the principles of differential-association theory and the influence of fluctuations in non-criminal opportunities (12). Since this type of prediction problem continually confronts judicial and correctional officials, such a frame of reference may be eminently practical. It is hoped that the elaboration and testing of such a formulation can be achieved in the currently burgeoning research in federal, state, and local judicial and correctional systems. Every theory such as differential association, which evolved from efforts to encompass conceptually an accumulation of empirical data, risks being but a step in the further evolution of theory, as long as procurement of new data continues.

References

1. Burt, Cyril. *The Young Delinquent.* London: University of London, 1925.
2. Cohen, Albert, Alfred Lindesmith, and Karl Schuessler (eds.). *The Sutherland Papers.* Bloomington, Ind.: Indiana University Press, 1956.
3. Conant, James B. *Science and Common Sense.* New Haven: Yale University Press, 1951.
4. Cressey, Donald R. "Application and Verification of the Differ-

ential Association Theory," *Journal of Criminal Law and Criminology*, Vol. 43 (May–June 1952), pp. 43–52.

5. Cressey, Donald R. "Differential Association and Compulsive Crimes," *Journal of Criminal Law, Criminology and Police Science*, Vol. 45 (May–June 1954), pp. 29–40.

6. Cressey, Donald R. "Epidemiology and Individual Conduct: A Case from Criminology," *Pacific Sociological Review*, Vol. 3 (Fall 1960), pp. 47–58.

7. Ferri, Enrico. *Criminal Sociology*. Boston: Little, Brown and Co., 1917.

8. Frank, Philipp. *Philosophy of Science*. Englewood Cliffs, N.J.: Prentice-Hall, Inc., 1957.

9. Geis, Gilbert. "Sociology, Criminology, and Criminal Law," *Social Problems*, Vol. 7 (Summer 1959), pp. 40–47.

10. Glaser, Daniel. "Criminality Theories and Behavioral Images," *American Journal of Sociology*, Vol. 61 (March 1956), pp. 433–444.

11. Glaser, Daniel. "The Sociological Approach to Crime and Correction," *Law and Contemporary Problems*, Vol. 23 (Autumn 1958), pp. 683–702.

12. Glaser, Daniel. "Differential Association and Criminological Prediction," *Social Problems*, Vol. 7 (Summer 1960), pp. 2–6.

13. Glaser, Daniel, and Kent Rice. "Crime, Age and Employment," *American Sociological Review*, Vol. 24 (October 1959), pp. 679–686.

14. Glueck, Sheldon. "Theory and Fact in Criminology," *British Journal of Delinquency*, Vol. 7 (October 1956), pp. 92–109.

15. Healy, William. *The Individual Delinquent*. Boston: Little, Brown and Co., 1924.

16. Korn, Richard R., and Lloyd W. McCorkle. *Criminology and Penology*. New York: Holt-Dryden, 1959.

17. Lemert, Edwin M. "The Behavior of the Systematic Check Forger," *Social Problems*, Vol. 6 (Fall 1958), pp. 141–149.

18. Meehl, Paul E., and Albert Rosen. "Antecedent Probability and the Efficiency of Psychometric Signs, Patterns, or Cutting Scores," *Psychological Bulletin*, Vol. 52 (May 1955), pp. 194–216.

19. Northrop, F. S. C. *Logic of the Sciences and the Humanities*. New York: The Macmillan Company, 1947.

20. Popper, Karl. *The Logic of Scientific Discovery*. New York: Basic Books, Inc., 1959.

21. Shaw, Clifford R., and Henry D. McKay. *Delinquency Areas.* Chicago: The University of Chicago Press, 1929.

22. Short, James F., Jr. "Differential Association with Delinquent Friends and Delinquent Behavior," *Pacific Sociological Review,* Vol. 1 (Spring 1958), pp. 20–25.

23. Short, James F., Jr. "Differential Association as a Hypothesis: Problems of Empirical Testing," *Social Problems,* Vol. 7 (Summer 1960), pp. 14–25.

24. Sutherland, Edwin H., and Donald R. Cressey. *Principles of Criminology,* 5th ed. Philadelphia: J. B. Lippincott Co., 1955.

25. Tarde, Gabriel. *Penal Philosophy.* Boston: Little, Brown and Co., 1912.

26. Thrasher, Frederick H. *The Gang.* Chicago: The University of Chicago Press, 1927.

27. Wheeler, Stanton H. "Social Organization in a Correctional Community." Unpublished Ph.D. dissertation, University of Washington, Seattle, 1958.

28. Znaniecki, Florian. *The Method of Sociology.* New York: Farrar & Rinehart, Inc., 1934.

23

Role Theory, Differential
Association, and Compulsive Crimes

 DONALD R. CRESSEY

UNIVERSITY OF CALIFORNIA, LOS ANGELES

*In the last chapter, Daniel Glaser pointed to some of the reasons
why truly useful scientific theories admit of exceptions. One of
the reasons is that popular concepts — like "crime" — encompass
a variety of disparate and sometimes even unrelated behaviors
(except in the sense in which the public brings them together and
lumps them under one rubric). Students of crime who have found
the differential-association theory most useful have always been
aware that this theory does not explain several categories of
crime. Glaser cited some of Donald Cressey's work to illustrate
this point. In analyzing compulsive crime as an apparent exception to differential-association theory, Professor Cressey makes a
distinctive contribution to general interactionist social psychology.*

Edwin H. Sutherland's theory of differential association, introduced in 1939, purports, among other things, to identify the
general process by which persons become criminals.* This

---

* The material in the second and subsequent sections of this chapter is
reprinted, with some revision, from (16); the permission of the *Journal of*

theory, like Sutherland's subsequent work and the work of those who have used his theory, is social psychological in emphasis, and it relies heavily on the theories of George Herbert Mead (45). Nevertheless, the implications of Mead's ideas for explanation of criminal conduct have never been fully explored. This chapter represents only a preliminary exploration of the way Meadian theories can be used in analysis of a small segment of all criminal behavior, "compulsive crime." The relationship between the theory of differential association and role theory will be explored by examining the degree to which so-called "compulsive crimes" are an exception to the former.

The essential idea in Sutherland's theory is that all criminal conduct is learned in a process of social interaction. He stated that "criminal behavior is learned in interaction with persons in a pattern of communication," and then went on to say that the specific direction of motives, drives, rationalizations, and attitudes — whether in the direction of criminality or anti-criminality — is learned from persons who define the legal codes as rules to be observed and from persons whose attitudes are favorable to violation of legal codes. "A person becomes delinquent because of an excess of definitions favorable to violation of law over definitions unfavorable to violation of law."[1] In modern society, the two kinds of definitions exist side by side, and one person might present contradictory definitions to another at different times and in different situations. Sutherland called the process of receiving these two kinds of definitions "differential association," because what is learned in association with criminal behavior patterns is in competition with what is learned in association with anti-criminal behavior patterns. "When persons become criminals, they do so because of contacts with criminal behavior patterns and also because of isolation from anti-criminal patterns." These contacts, however, "may vary in frequency, duration, priority, and intensity."

Criminal Law, Criminology, and Police Science to reprint these pages is gratefully acknowledged. Parts of the introductory section appeared first in (17).
[1] For a complete statement of Sutherland's theory, see Sutherland and Cressey (56, pp. 74–81). Unless otherwise identified, all quotations of Sutherland are from this source.

Numerous interpretative errors have arisen because readers have not understood what Sutherland apparently was trying to say; also, Sutherland's theory has been criticized on many grounds. These errors and criticisms have been reviewed elsewhere (17). It is important to observe here, however, that the two principal types of criticism are related both to each other and to the question of whether behavior such as kleptomania and pyromania can be handled by the theory of differential association.

One general kind of criticism holds that the theory over-simplifies the process by which criminal behavior is learned (2; 5, p. 183; 6; 11; 13; 15; 22; 23; 24; 25; 27; 36, p. 299; 37; 52; 57; 63). Such criticism ranges from simple assertions that the learning process is more complex than the theory states or implies to the idea that the theory does not adequately take into account some learning mechanism, such as differential identification. But it is one thing to criticize the theory for failure to specify the learning process accurately and another to specify in detail which aspects of the learning process should be included and in what way. Sutherland himself said only that "the process of learning criminal and anti-criminal patterns involves all the mechanisms that are involved in any other learning." This statement reveals a faith that broader social psychological research will yield specific descriptions of learning mechanisms. Yet, as Schrag has recently pointed out, statements such as "the individual internalizes the norms of his group," and "stimulus patterns that are active at the time of the response eventually acquire the capacity to elicit the response," are illustrations of assertions that cannot be confirmed or denied but which stand, at present, as substitutes for general social psychological descriptions of the process by which persons learn social behavior (51). Criminological theory can be no more precise than the general social psychological theory of which it is a part. Nevertheless, criminologists have not taken full advantage of such general theory as exists (50). It is for this reason, as we shall see below, that compulsive crime is often viewed as exceptional to Sutherland's principle.

A second popular form of "criticism" of differential association is not, strictly speaking, criticism at all, for it merely indicates that some kinds of criminal behavior seem to be exceptions to the theory. Thus, it has been said that the theory does not apply to rural offenders (6, 7), to landlords who violated OPA regulations (8), to criminal violators of financial trust (15), to "naive check forgers" (38), to white collar criminals (12, p. 240; 36, p. 299), to perpetrators of "individual" and "personal" crimes (9; 10; 12, p. 229; 13), to "irrational" and "impulsive" criminals (19, p. 402; 61, pp. 197–198), to "adventitious" and/or "accidental" criminals (13; 19, p. 402; 22; 32), to "occasional," " incidental" and "situational" offenders (13; 19, p. 402), to murderers, non-professional shoplifters, and non-career type criminals (13), to persons who commit crimes of passion (32), and to men whose crimes are perpetrated under emotional stress (18, pp. 347–348). Of these comments, only the first five — those referring to rural offenders, landlords, trust violators, check forgers, and some white collar criminals — are based on research. Even more significantly, at least two authors have simply stated that there are exceptions to the theory; the kind of behavior thought to be exceptional is not specified (3, p. 159; 58, p. 340).

The fact that most of the comments about exceptions are not based on research means that most of the "criticisms" actually are proposals for research. Should a person conduct research on a particular type of offender and find that the theory does not hold, a revision is called for, providing the research has actually tested the theory, or part of it. As indicated, this procedure has been used in five instances, and these instances should be given careful attention. But in most cases, there is no real evidence that the behavior said to be exceptional is in fact exceptional.

Some so-called "exceptions" seem to be listed in order to emphasize the importance of an alternative, and contradictory, general theory of individual conduct. For example, statements to the effect that "personal," "individual," "emotional," "impulsive," and "irrational" crimes are exceptions to the differential-association process are likely to be only indications of adherence to a theory holding that emotional disorders and defects of various kinds, once established "in" the person, determine conduct, regardless of social relationships. Similarly, promotion of concepts such as "impulsive crime," "crimes of passion," and "irrational crime" is, like use of the concept "compulsive crime," likely to indicate a belief that some types of criminal conduct are "obviously exceptional" to the kind of associational process discussed by Sutherland and, more generally, by followers of Mead.

Sutherland's generalization is stated in universal form, as a description of the etiology of all criminal behavior. Hence, the discovery of cases of behavior which is *crime* and whose genesis and development has not followed the process Sutherland described will call for either a modification of the generalization or a redefinition of the concept "crime."[2] As indicated, the important point in Sutherland's theory is the principle that all criminal behavior is learned in a process of social interaction, and to prove or disprove the theory we must carefully examine behavior to which the label "crime" is applied but which does not appear to have been learned in such interaction.[3] "Compulsive crime" is the best example of such behavior.

THE LEGAL-PSYCHIATRIC CONTROVERSY

Before such re-examination of compulsive crime can be made, however, it is necessary to review briefly the three fundamental points in the legal-psychiatric controversy about whether behavior said to be "compulsive" also is "crime." The issues are fairly clear. First, in the criminal law, under the M'Naghten rules, the stigma "insanity," not "crime," is applied to legally harmful behavior perpetrated under circumstances such that the defendant was unable to distinguish between right and wrong. This is to say, in more sociological terms, that he was unable to contemplate the normative consequences of his acts. If it is observed that a

[2] Many criminologists now argue that crime is not a homogeneous phenomenon and that it is therefore unwise to attempt universal scientific generalizations about it. While there is merit in this argument, it is not pertinent to the present discussion. (See 14.)

[3] Some apparent exceptions were pointed out by Sutherland himself (55). Similarly, crimes which in the criminal law are based on strict liability rather than on proof of criminal intent almost immediately appear as possible exceptions. One distinguished student of the criminal law holds, however, that strict liability offenses have so little in common with other crimes that they should not be included in the ambit of the criminal law (29, pp. 280, 296). Thus, the apparent exception seemingly calls for a revision of the concept "crime," rather than a revision of the theory. Such a redefinition of the crime concept, incidentally, would have serious effects on current generalizations about "white collar crimes," many of which are of a strict liability type.

so-called "compulsive criminal" *did* contemplate the normative consequences of his behavior, the behavior is classed as crime, rather than insanity.

Second, psychiatrists insist that some of the behavior which results in legal harm ("compulsive crime") has essentially the same characteristics as does compulsive behavior generally. As a general category of neuroses ("psychasthenia," "anankastic reactions," etc.), compulsive acts are described as irresistible behavior which the person in question often recognizes as irrational but is subjectively compelled to carry out (18, p. 364). Such acts are considered as irrational because they are thought to be prompted by a subjective morbid impulse which the person's "will" or "judgment" or "ego" cannot control. Malumud, for example, states that psychasthenias or anankastic reactions "have in common the fact that the patients feel themselves compelled by some inner force and against their own will or reason to think, act or feel in an abnormal manner," and that compulsive acts are "forms of behavior which the person carries out consciously without knowing the reason for such activity or for reasons which he knows have no logical foundation." (44; cf. 1, pp. 149–150) In other words, behavior described as compulsive is thought to be completely determined by the inner impulse or compulsion, and while the genesis of the compulsion might lie in a social context, once it has been formed it apparently operates as an entity, agent, or element in itself. Thus, the overt act is considered as prompted entirely "from within," and present contact with values concerning morality, decency, or correctness of the overt behavior in no way affects the actor, in the last analysis, either in deterring him from acting or in encouraging him to act (cf. 66).

It is argued by psychiatrists, then, that in cases of "compulsive crime" the actor *does* know right from wrong and does contemplate the normative consequences of his acts (that is, he recognizes the behavior as irrational, foolish, wrong, illegal, etc.), but *nevertheless* exhibits the behavior because it is prompted from within by a force which he is powerless to resist. Lorand, for example, cites three case histories as evidence that "compulsive stealing" is a subconscious act of aggression against the parents or parent surrogates. He points out that there were faults in the critical appreciation of the factors of reality, and that "all showed an overwhelmingly strong instinctual drive which clouded the function of the critical faculty. They were unable, consciously, to resist, and they could not prevent the breaking through of strong drives from within that lead to stealing." (42, cf. 44) If the legal harm resulting from such behavior actually is crime, then it obviously is exceptional to the differential-association theory. The "criminality" in "compulsive crime" would depend not upon former contacts with differential values concerning law-abidingness, but upon a non-social agent or process.

Third, some jurists have adopted a position similar to that of the psychiatrist. This is apparent from the fact that the courts of about fourteen states hold that the consequences to the actor of the perpetration of a legal harm can be avoided by showing that while the defendant knew right from wrong his behavior was prompted by an "irresistible impulse." (35) The "irresistible impulse" and "compulsive crime" concepts seem to have at their base the same assumptions inherent in the old faculty psychology concepts "moral perversion," "moral imbecility," "inhibitory insanity," "affective mania," "monomania," and so on, each of which implied a psychological disorder which has no connection with the "intellect" or "knowing" or "reasoning" faculties (43). Most modern psychiatrists claim that theirs is not a faculty psychology since what was formerly considered as emotional and intellectual faculties is now considered as one — the total personality. But while this "integration" theory is affirmed by psychiatrists as they oppose the M'Naghten rules, it is denied when they support notions of "compulsive crime" or "irresistible impulse." (See 29, pp. 523–524.) While there is disagreement among psychiatrists, it appears that most of them agree with the legal theory of those jurisdictions allowing the irresistible impulse defense, and many of them contend that those judges not allowing it are backward, ignorant, or stubborn. Wertham is a noteworthy exception. He writes that "the criminal law which makes use of the conception of irresistible impulse is not an advance belonging to the present 'scientific social' era. It is a throwback to, or rather a survival of, the previous 'philosophical psychological' era. The concept of irresistible impulse derives from a philosophical, speculative, synthetic psychology. It forms no part of and finds no support in the modern dynamic psycho-analytic study of mental process." (47, p. 164) Elsewhere, the same author has stated that there is nothing in the whole field of psychopathology which corresponds to the irresistible impulse, and that compulsions play no role in criminal acts (64, pp. 13–14). Bromberg and Cleckley recently took a similar position: "The concept of sudden 'irresistible impulse' in an otherwise perfectly normal organism is unsupported by modern psychiatric knowledge." (4)

MENTALISTIC ASSUMPTIONS OF LAW AND PSYCHIATRY

This divergence in opinion and viewpoint is enhanced by the fact that an assumption of "mind" is implicit in the psychological orientations of both psychiatry and criminal law, so that each discipline has a "mentalistic" approach to human behavior. In criminal law, the "right and wrong test" assumes the existence of a mind which, when normal and mature, operates in such a way that the human has conscious freedom to choose rationally whether or not a crime shall be committed. The mind impels the person only in the direction "he" wishes to be impelled. But a mind which is immature or "diseased" cannot make intelligent choices, and a defendant possessing such a mind is considered incapable of entertaining criminal intent. Such an assumption tends to equate rationality and sanity, and it is necessary to fix "responsibility" for acts (cf. 4, 28). Although psychiatrists often denounce this jurisprudential assumption on the ground that it ignores the facts of science (see, e.g., 26) their denunciation is possible only because of emphasis on a different mentalistic construct. In writing of "compulsive crime," at least, most psychiatrists assume a mind with only one significant difference from the one assumed by most jurists. Here, the mind is said to be subject to casual emotional experiences, especially early sexual experiences, which give it characteristics such that at the present moment of action it completely determines the person's choice — and, consequently, his overt behavior — in a manner which usually is completely unconscious and unknowable without the help of a psychiatrist. The deeply hidden emotional forces of the mind are thought to compel the actor even if "he" knows

Differential Association and Compulsive Crimes

the action is illegal, and "he" has no choice in whether the action shall be undertaken. The chief difference between such psychological forces or "mainsprings of action," and instinctive "mainsprings of action" is that the former are "unconscious." (See 33.) Foote has pointed out that in spite of the seductive appeal which is exerted by the hope of reducing human behavior to some simple and permanent order through finding certain "basic" imperatives underlying it, criticism has negated every naming of the "mainsprings of action." (20)

Mentalistic assumptions of both kinds must be clarified and supplemented in order to determine whether "compulsive criminality" is an exception to the differential-association theory. As long as criminality is said to have its etiology in a rather mysterious "mind," "soul," "will," or "unconscious," there will be no possible way for generalizations about criminality to be subjected to empirical tests or observations which would settle the issue. Also, so long as "compulsiveness," as traditionally described, must be determined by specialists rather than judges or juries, jurists will resist discussion of it in their courts and the legal-psychiatric controversy will continue.

A Sociological Theory of Motivation

Behavior traditionally considered as "compulsive crime" can be handled and clarified without the assumption of "mind" or a basic biological or psychic imperative by application of the sociological hypothesis that there are differences in the degree to which acts are controlled by the linguistic constructs (words or combinations of words) which the actor has learned from his social groups. Since the use of linguistic constructs depends upon contacts with social groups, this amounts to differences in the degree to which the actor participates in group experiences. In sociological role theory, differences of this kind are considered differences in the *motivation* of the actor, although this concept is used in a sense quite different from the use in psychiatry. Motivation here refers to the process by which a person, as a participant in a group, symbolically (by means of language) defines a problematic situation as calling for the performance of a particular act, with symbolically anticipated consummation and consequences (20). Motives are not inner, biological mainsprings of action but linguistic constructs which organize acts in particular situations (cf. 46), the use of which can be examined empirically. The key linguistic constructs which a person applies to his own conduct in a certain set of circumstances are motives; the complete process by which such verbalizations are used is motivation.

The great difference between this conception of motivation and the notion that motives are biological or are deeply hidden in the "unconscious" may be observed in the use of the concept "rationalization" in the two systems. In psychiatry it usually is said that one "merely rationalizes" (*ex post facto* justification) behavior which "has really been prompted by deeply hidden motives and unconscious tendencies." (48, p. 49; see also 33; 65, p. 9) In the other system, which uses a non-mentalistic conception of motivation, it is held that one does not necessarily "merely rationalize" behavior already enacted but acts because he has rationalized. The rationalization is his motive. When such rationalizations or verbalizations are extensively developed and systematized the person using them has a sense of conforming because they give him a sense of support and sanction (40, pp. 307–310). An individual in our society, for example, may feel fairly comfortable when he commits an illegal act in connection with his business for, after all, "business is business." But not all verbalizations are equally developed or systematized, and in some instances the use of the verbalizations does not, therefore, receive such extensive support and sanction. The individual in these instances does not have a comfortable sense of conforming. The person in the above example probably would not feel as comfortable if his illegal act were perpetrated according to the verbalization "all businessmen are dishonest." Motives can be treated, then, as "typical vocabularies (linguistic constructs) having ascertainable functions in delimited societal situations" (46) and, as such, they may be examined empirically.

Using this conception of motivation, it is immediately apparent that not all behavior is equally motivated; there are differences in the degree to which behavior is linguistically controlled. Certainly some behavior is performed with almost no social referent, that is, with the use of no shared verbalization.

For instance, behavior which is physiologically autonomous is clearly non-motivated since the release of energy appropriate to performing the behavior does not depend upon the application of a linguistic construct. Similarly, if one's behavior has been so conditioned by his past experiences that he behaves automatically, in the way that Pavlov's dogs behaved automatically at the sound of the bell, he is not motivated. Genuinely fetishistic behavior probably is of this kind. However, it is equally certain that other behavior cannot be enacted unless the actor has had rather elaborate and intimate contact with linguistic constructs which are, by definition, group products. Such behavior is motivated, and it may be distinguished from automatic behavior by the fact that it has reference to means and ends. If a person defines a situation as one in which there are alternatives, if there is evidence of planning, evidence of delaying small immediate gains for larger future gains, or evidence of anticipation of social consequences of acts, he is motivated.

APPLICATION OF THE MOTIVATION THEORY TO "COMPULSIVE CRIME"

When this theory of motivation is applied to the problem at hand, it may be seen that if behavior traditionally considered as "compulsive crime" were clearly non-motivated or autonomous then the legal-psychiatric controversy would have been resolved long ago since, if such were the case, the behavior easily could be subsumed under the legal concept "insanity." If "compulsions" "in" a person "came out" in the same way that his whiskers "come out," then even in the most "anti-psychiatric" court there would be no question of his legal responsibility, and his behavior would not, in fact, be designated as crime. In this case, there would be no problem about whether the behavior were an exception to the differential-association theory but, instead, the behavior would lie outside the definition of the phenomenon (crime) with which the differential-association theory is concerned. Non-motivated behavior of this kind which resulted in legal harm would not be unlike the behavior of a sleeping or drugged person whose hand was guided by another to the trigger of a gun aimed at a victim's head. Such behavior is not planned by the actor, and precautions against detection are not taken because the ability to use the language symbols normally pertinent to the situation is absent or deficient.[4] If behavior is nonmotivated the actor cannot possibly entertain "criminal intent."

In most cases now labeled "kleptomania," "pyromania," and the like, however, the actors appear to be motivated in the same way that other criminals are motivated. Consequently they are, in the terminology of the criminal law, "responsible." They select secluded places in which to perpetrate their acts, plan their activities in advance, realize that they will be arrested if detected, and do many other things indicating that there is a conscious normative referent in their behavior. Certainly most acts traditionally described as "compulsive crime" are clearly quite different from autonomous behavior having no normative components, in spite of the fact that the two are usually assumed to be identical or at least very similar. Possibly it was observation of the significant difference between the two that led Alexander and Staub to argue that while the impulse in kleptomania, pyromania, and compulsive lying is an unconscious one, an impulse foreign to the ego, yet the act is not completely unconscious, as is the case, they hold, in compulsive neuroses generally (1, pp. 95–97). Gault (21, pp. 163–166) uses kleptomania and pyromania as illustrations of the psychopathic personality. That is, they are considered as

> a form of outlet for a nature that is unbalanced by reason of the dominance of the egocentric disposition. . . . They take what does not belong to them not so much as a result of blind impulsion; not *quite* "blind impulsion" because the kleptomaniac is at pains to conceal not only his act but the products of his stealing. . . . We are forced to conclude that in the general run of instances of this nature we are dealing with unreasoned

[4] Although it is not recommended, because it probably would lead to even more confusion than now exists, the criminal law theory which exempts some persons from liability because they lack "responsibility" might easily be restated in these terms. Those persons — generally psychotics and very young children — who are now excused on the grounds that they cannot distinguish between right and wrong either have not acquired or have lost the ability to control language symbols. In fact, on a level that now seems very unsophisticated, this principle was recognized as early as the thirteenth century, when Bracton formulated what erroneously has been called the "wild beast test."

impulsion to get goods to amplify one's store, to gratify one's desire for possession, and therefore magnify one's self. In other words, here is the egocentric disposition. This language suggests a purposive character of the behavior — and it is so that it results in obtaining goods.

However, many other authorities claim that the evidence of deliberation and intent in acts of pyromaniacs and kleptomaniacs does not in and of itself signify sanity (39, p. 182; 54, p. 258). Thus, while it is not easy to classify precisely certain acts as motivated or non-motivated, since men do not always explicitly articulate motives, the sociological framework at least affords an opportunity to classify correctly the great proportion of the acts ordinarily labeled "compulsive crime." Using that framework, illegal conduct which is motivated would be classed as "crime" and illegal acts which are non-motivated would be classed as "compulsion" and would fall within the legal category "insanity."

Non-scientific Criteria of Compulsive Criminals

Accurate classification of this kind would be valuable, since in the current system it appears that compulsive-crime concepts are no less "wastebasket categories" than is the "psychopathic personality" concept. Casual observation indicates, at least, that the application of the "compulsive crime" label often accompanies the inability of either the subject or the examiner to account for the behavior in question *in terms of motives which are current, popular, and sanctioned in a particular culture or among the members of a particular group within a culture.* For example, one criterion, usually overlooked, for designating behavior "kleptomania" rather than "theft" is apparent lack of economic need for the item on the part of the person exhibiting the behavior. This may be observed in at least two different ways. First, the probability that the term "kleptomania" will be applied to a destitute shoplifter is much lower than the probability that it will be applied to a wealthy person performing the same kind of acts. "Kleptomania," then, often is simply a short-hand way of saying, as the layman does, "That woman is rich and can buy almost anything she desires. She does not need (economic) to steal.

She must be crazy."[5] An interesting but erroneous assumption in such logic is that the behavior of normal persons committing property crimes is explainable in terms of economic need. This assumption, coupled with the empirical observation that wealthy persons sometimes do commit major property crimes, led to the erroneous conclusion by two sociologists that such crimes must be prompted by "greed" rather than "need." (3, 1st ed., p. 43) Among psychiatrists, contradiction of the same assumption, through observation of the fact that wealthy persons do sometimes commit minor property crimes, results in the notion that larcenous behavior of wealthy persons must be "compulsive." The economic status of the observer probably is of great importance in determining whether he thinks a person is not in economic need and is consequently compulsive. Whether or not the misconduct is considered "disproportionate to any discernible end in view" (30, p. 771) conceivably will depend a great deal upon the attitudes of the examiner rather than upon those of the offender. That is, a poor person might consider that a middle-class person had no need to steal and that his stealing must be the result of "greed" or a "compulsion," while a middle-class person probably will entertain this notion only as it refers to upper-class persons whose incomes far exceed his. If all psychiatrists were poverty-stricken, the proportion of shoplifters called "kleptomaniacs" probably would be much higher than it is. And if it is assumed that the larcenous behavior of wealthy persons is, because they are wealthy, "compulsive" then there is little opportunity for determination of possible contacts with behavior patterns conducive to crime.

Second, the absence, from the observer's standpoint, of eco-

---

[5] Compare: "In kleptomania we have individuals who steal, but their stealing has a number of important differences from ordinary theft. For one thing, the purely predatory element present in common theft is lacking here. The subject steals not because of the value and the money he gets from the stolen articles — that is, not for their mercenary value — but entirely for what they mean to him emotionally and symbolically. One often observes this in rich women who have no need for the article they steal and, in point of actual fact, dispose of it almost immediately after the article has been stolen. While the symbolic nature of such stealing is often evident on the surface, we not infrequently come across cases of stealing the nature of which is not so obvious, so that one is puzzled to figure out whether we are dealing with kleptomania or ordinary theft. Many such cases are found in our prisons." (34)

nomic need is used as a criterion for designating persons as "kleptomaniacs" in cases in which the particular articles taken appear to be of no immediate use to the subject. For example, Alexander and Staub do not consider as kleptomanic the behavior of a physician (a "neurotic criminal") who had been taking medical books and supplies, but his "theft of porcelain figures which were new and actually of no value is more in the nature of a kleptomanic act," and Wallerstein has stated that a case "was hardly kleptomania in the usual sense because the articles were pawned or sold for money." (1, p. 168; 62) Although they have not been explored in this connection, Veblen's arguments about the great desirability in our culture of acquiring money merely as a means of accumulating economically "useless" goods might have a bearing here (49, 60). If his thesis were followed it would seem, at least, that there is little logical justification for designating as "criminal" the behavior of one who stole money with which to buy "useless" goods while at the same time designating as "compulsive" the stealing of the goods themselves.

This criterion also is used for designating even poor persons as "kleptomaniacs" in instances of repetitive taking of what appear to be economically useless goods. However, the fact that mere repetitive taking need not indicate a compulsion may be illustrated by the case of a gang of boys who went from store to store in a large city stealing caps. They would enter a store and each boy would steal a cap, leaving his own on the counter. The group would then move to another store where the stolen caps would be left on the counter, and new ones would be stolen. This practice would continue until the gang members became bored with the game. It is not difficult to distinguish such behavior from what is called kleptomania because it was perpetrated by a number of boys acting together, because it appears to have been done as play[6] and, most important, because it was perpetrated by boys closely approaching the cultural stereotype of the delinquent or criminal. Even a psychoanalyst probably would not assume that the caps were sex symbols or fetishes, although it is not inconceivable that he would do so.[7] However,

---

[6] In discussing legal problems of kleptomania, Hall says, "But mere repetition tends to prove habit, not abnormality." (29, p. 517; cf. 59)

[7] Karpman (34) reports the case of a man who burglarized women's

if one of the boys at a later date repeated alone the same kind of thefts, the probability that he would be labeled a kleptomaniac would be high. And if the boy were a member of a wealthy family the probability of his being labeled a kleptomaniac would be even higher.

In fire-setting cases the absence of obvious economic need also is used, in the traditional system of thought, as a criterion for applying the term "pyromania," but here the absence of other popular motives is used as well. If it can be determined easily that one burned property in order to collect insurance, in order to get revenge, or in an attempt to conceal a criminal act, or if there is ground for believing that he had some other conventional motive, then the probability that he will be designated a "pyromaniac" is low. However, if none of these is immediately apparent, and especially in instances where the thing burned has no great economic value, the probability that the term will be applied is much higher. Traditionally, pyromania has been, then, like kleptomania, a residual category. One investigator states that of all the varieties of incendiarists, the pyromaniac is the most difficult to detect "because of the lack of motive." (31)[8]

---

apartments, taking both money and female intimate garments. By using the case as an illustration of "fetishistic kleptomania," he puts great emphasis upon the taking of the garments and almost ignores the taking of money. Gault (21, pp. 163–166) has made the following significant statement about such psychiatric practices: *"The attempt that some have made to lay the foundation for cases of this nature in repressed sex motives and to interpret the objects stolen as so many symbols that they have in relation to the sex aspect of experience is a very unconvincing procedure. . . .* The case is doubtless not so simple. The sex urge is only one of many that actuate the human organism. For instance, let us assume that a clothespin or a rubber hose found among the stolen goods of a kleptomaniac is a symbol. Symbol of what? The answer, according to the present writer's opinion, is that *its symbolic character depends upon what the investigator is interested in finding."* (Italics added.)

[8] Psychoanalysts make much of the assumed sex symbolism in cases of non-economically motivated incendiarism. Thus, in one case of repeated burning of grass on vacant lots it was asserted that the lots symbolized the subject's father, that by driving onto the lot with his father's automobile the subject identified himself with his father and his sex organ and performed the act of incest on his mother, that the subject's effort to help in extinguishing the fires was symbolic of an unconscious wish to atone for his sin, and that the splashing of water on the fire was a symbolic repetition of a regression to the urethral phase of his libidinal

Differential Association and Compulsive Crimes

In contrast to what appears to be current practice, when a sociological theory of motivation is used, the apparent inability of a person to explain his actions to the police, to a psychiatrist, or even to himself is not considered sufficient for classifying those actions "compulsive." Using that theory, it may be observed that most criminals, in fact, when asked to explain their acts either recite the popular motives involved or respond that they do not know. For example, one might say, as did a criminal who had stolen a whole truckload of groceries, "I didn't want to take them but I had to because I was hungry." This response may be compared with that of a person arrested for taking small objects from a store: "I didn't want to take them but I just had to take them," and with that of a person who had burned an automobile, "I just wanted to stir up some excitement." As indicated above, such rationalizations are not necessarily *ex post facto* justifications for acts — and if they are not, then there is no logical justification for classifying one person as a "thief" and the others as "compulsive." Motives are circumscribed by the actor's learned vocabulary.

Sociological Role Theory Applied to "Compulsive Crime"

But sociological theory can do more than correctly classify the large proportion of defendants said to be compulsive. The literature on role theory* provides a framework not only for understanding the behavior of such defendants, but for understanding their inability to account for their behavior as well. Closely related to the theory of motivation which has been outlined is that aspect of role theory which deals with the relationship between the person's identification of himself as a "social object" and his subsequent behavior. In order to play a social role, one must anticipate the reactions of others by taking the role implicitly before it is taken overtly. He must look at himself from another's point of view. By hypothesizing the reactions of others, the person looks upon himself as an object and, consequently,

---

development, in which phase the subject was said to have had erections which he relieved by urinating (53).
* [In the terminology of this book, "role theory" is equivalent to "symbolic interactionist theory." — *Ed.*]

identifies himself as a particular kind of object. He then performs the role which is appropriate to the kind of social object with which he has identified himself. The vocabulary of motives employed in the performance of the role also is a corollary of this self-identification. But at various times and in different situations the person may identify himself differently, so that he is able to play many, often even conflicting, social roles. Again, his identification of who he is and what he is determines the roles he plays (20).

For example, one might in the course of a day identify himself as a father in one situation, as a husband in another situation, and as a property owner in another situation. The motives employed in the performance of each role will reflect his particular identification. A similar phenomenon may exist in respect to so-called "compulsive crime." For example, a person might in some situations identify himself as a kleptomaniac, since that construct is now popular in our culture, and a full commitment to such an identification includes the use of motives which, in turn, release the energy to perform a so-called compulsive act. The more positive the conviction that one is a kleptomaniac the more automatic his behavior will appear. The subject's behavior in particular situations, then, is organized by his identification of himself according to the linguistic construct "kleptomania" or its equivalent. In the framework of role theory, it is this kind of organization which makes the behavior recognizably recurrent in the life history of the person. The fact that the acts are recurrent does not mean that they are prompted from within but only that certain linguistic symbols have become usual for the person in question.

If this theory were applied, we would not expect apprehended shoplifters, some of whom conceive of themselves as kleptomaniacs, to provide a logically consistent or even "correct" explanation for their behavior. For example, one who has behaved according to a set of linguistic constructs acceptable to himself in one role (kleptomaniac) might later discover that both the behavior and the constructs are unacceptable to himself in another role he is playing or desires to play (father, property owner). In that case there will be a high probability of denial to himself in the second role that "he" behaved at all. His conception of himself from one point of view results in denial of the action: "I wasn't myself when (or if) I did that," "I wasn't feeling well that day," "I couldn't be the criminal you seek — I couldn't do a thing like that," etc. On the other hand, his continued conception of himself according to the symbolic constructs which were used in behaving in the first place probably will result in open confession that "he" behaved: "Stop me before I do it again," "I have no control of myself," "That which is 'in' me comes out in situations like that," "I did it and I'm glad," etc.

In interviewing persons who, according to role theory, have identified themselves with "compulsive criminals" of some sort, we should not expect them to realize that "who they are" depends upon language symbols and, hence, upon arbitrary ascriptions by others. One who identifies himself as a "kleptomaniac," for example, will be prone to accept such a conception of himself as ultimate reality. Even those observers or examiners who use the traditional notion that compulsive behavior is an expression of an "inner spring of action" have considered the subject's conception of himself as absolute rather than as a group product. As one sociologist has pointed out, "Because our learning has more often than not been perfected to the point where cognitive judgments in standardized situations are made instantaneously, and the energy for performing the appropriate behavior is released immediately, it has been an easy mistake for many observers to suppose that the organic correlates came first and even account for the definition of the situation, rather than the reverse." (20)

In our present state of knowledge we cannot be entirely sure how one gets committed to particular identities and motives in the first place, but, as indicated, the process certainly is one of social learning. Differential association is a theory of social learning specifically applied to criminal behavior, and it contends that, in the terminology used above, the identifications and motives of criminals are acquired through direct personal contacts with persons sharing those identifications and motives. This theory may have many defects, in that it does not precisely or adequately describe or integrate all the aspects of the processes by which criminality is learned, but it describes the processes by which one becomes a "compulsive" criminal as well as it describes the processes by which one becomes a "non-compulsive" criminal. "Compulsive criminality," as traditionally described, is not of such a nature that it necessarily is an exception to the differential-association theory.

SUMMARY AND CONCLUSIONS

1. The assertion that "latent forces of such phenomena as compulsive stealing and fire-setting are understood" (41, p. 323) is not warranted.

2. If the traditional assumption that all "compulsive crime" is motivated entirely "from within" is correct, then the use of the words "compulsive" and "crime" together is erroneous. If the behavior actually were prompted "from within" it would be subsumed under the legal concept "insanity," not "crime."

3. Re-examination of "compulsive crime" concepts in the framework of sociological theories of motivation, identification, and role-playing indicates that most of the legally harmful behavior traditionally labeled "compulsive" actually is "motivated" and has a developmental history which is very similar to that of other "motivated" behavior. That legally harmful behavior which is automatic ("non-motivated") cannot be considered as crime.

4. Since the developmental processes in so-called "compulsive criminality" are the same as the processes in other criminality, "compulsive crimes" are not, because of something in their nature, exceptional to the differential-association theory. Upon closer empirical examination it probably will be demonstrated that criminality which has traditionally been assumed to be "personal" is actually a group product, and this criminality will become of more concern to the sociologist than has been the case in the past.

References

1. Alexander, Franz, and Hugo Staub. *The Criminal, the Judge, and the Public.* New York: The Macmillan Company, 1931.
2. Ball, John C. "Delinquent and Non-delinquent Attitudes Toward

the Prevalence of Stealing," *Journal of Criminal Law and Criminology*, Vol. 48 (October 1957), pp. 259–274.

3. Barnes, Harry E., and Negley K. Teeters. *New Horizons in Criminology*, 3d ed. Englewood Cliffs, N.J.: Prentice-Hall, Inc., 1959.

4. Bromberg, Walter, and Hervey M. Cleckley. "The Medico-legal Dilemma — A Suggested Solution," *Journal of Criminal Law and Criminology*, Vol. 42 (March–April 1952), pp. 729–745.

5. Caldwell, Robert G. *Criminology*. New York: The Ronald Press Company, 1956.

6. Clinard, Marshall B. "The Process of Urbanization and Criminal Behavior," *American Journal of Sociology*, Vol. 48 (September 1942), pp. 202–213.

7. Clinard, Marshall B. "Rural Criminal Offenders," *American Journal of Sociology*, Vol. 50 (July 1944), pp. 38–45.

8. Clinard, Marshall B. "Criminological Theories of Violations of Wartime Regulations," *American Sociological Review*, Vol. 11 (June 1946), pp. 258–270.

9. Clinard, Marshall B. "Criminal Behavior Is Human Behavior," *Federal Probation*, Vol. 13 (March 1949), pp. 21–27.

10. Clinard, Marshall B. "Research Frontiers in Criminology," *British Journal of Delinquency*, Vol. 7 (October 1956), pp. 110–122.

11. Clinard, Marshall B. "The Sociology of Delinquency and Crime," in Joseph Gittler (ed.), *Review of Sociology*. New York: John Wiley & Sons, 1957, pp. 465–499.

12. Clinard, Marshall B. *Sociology of Deviant Behavior*. New York: Rinehart & Co., Inc., 1957.

13. Clinard, Marshall B. "Criminological Research," in Robert K. Merton, Leonard Broom, and Leonard Cottrell (eds.), *Sociology Today*. New York: Basic Books, Inc., 1959, pp. 509–536.

14. Cressey, Donald R. "Criminological Research and the Definition of Crimes," *American Journal of Sociology*, Vol. 56 (May 1951), pp. 546–551.

15. Cressey, Donald R. "Application and Verification of the Differential Association Theory," *Journal of Criminal Law and Criminology*, Vol. 43 (June 1952), pp. 43–52.

16. Cressey, Donald R. "The Differential Association Theory and Compulsive Crimes," *Journal of Criminal Law, Criminology, and Police Science*, Vol. 45 (June 1954), pp. 29–40.

17. Cressey, Donald R. "Epidemiology and Individual Conduct: A

Case from Criminology," *Pacific Sociological Review*. Vol. 3 (November 1960), pp. 47–58.

18. Dorcus, Roy M., and G. Wilson Shaffer. *Textbook of Abnormal Psychology*. Baltimore, Md.: The Williams and Wilkins Company, 1941.

19. Elliott, Mabel A. *Crime in Modern Society*. New York: Harper & Brothers, 1952.

20. Foote, Nelson N. "Identification as the Basis for a Theory of Motivation," *American Sociological Review*, Vol. 16 (February 1951), pp. 14–22.

21. Gault, Robert H. *Criminology*. Boston: D. C. Heath and Company, 1932.

22. Glaser, Daniel. "Criminality Theories and Behavioral Images," *American Journal of Sociology*, Vol. 61 (March 1956), pp. 433–444.

23. Glaser, Daniel. "Review of *Principles of Criminology*," *Federal Probation*, Vol. 20 (December 1956), pp. 66–67.

24. Glaser, Daniel. "The Sociological Approach to Crime and Correction," *Law and Contemporary Problems*, Vol. 23 (Autumn 1958), pp. 683–702.

25. Glaser, Daniel. "Differential Association and Criminological Prediction," *Social Problems*, Vol. 8 (Summer 1960), pp. 6–14.

26. Glover, Edward. "The Diagnosis and Treatment of Delinquency," in L. Radzinowicz and J. W. C. Turner (eds.), *Mental Abnormality and Crime*, Vol. 2 of *English Studies in Criminal Science*. London: Macmillan and Co., Ltd., 1949, pp. 279–280.

27. Glueck, Sheldon. "Theory and Fact in Criminology," *British Journal of Delinquency*, Vol. 7 (October 1956), pp. 92–109.

28. Green, Arnold W. "The Concept of Responsibility," *Journal of Criminal Law and Criminology*, Vol. 33 (February 1943), pp. 392–394.

29. Hall, Jerome. *Principles of Criminal Law*. Indianapolis, Ind.: The Bobbs-Merrill Company, Inc., 1947.

30. Healy, William. *The Individual Delinquent*. Boston: Little, Brown and Co., 1918.

31. Hoyek, Camille F. "Criminal Incendiarism," *Journal of Criminal Law and Criminology*, Vol. 41 (March–April 1951), pp. 836–845.

32. Jeffery, Clarence R. "An Integrated Theory of Crime and Criminal Behavior," *Journal of Criminal Law and Criminology*, Vol. 49 (April 1959), pp. 533–552.

33. Karpman, Benjamin. "An Attempt at a Re-evaluation of Some Concepts of Law and Psychiatry," *Journal of Criminal Law and Criminology*, Vol. 38 (September–October 1947), pp. 206–217.

34. Karpman, Benjamin. "Criminality, Insanity and the Law," *Journal of Criminal Law and Criminology*, Vol. 39 (January–February 1949), pp. 584–605.

35. Keedy, E. R. "Irresistible Impulse as a Defense in Criminal Law," *University of Pennsylvania Law Review*, Vol. 100 (May 1952), pp. 956–993.

36. Korn, Richard R., and Lloyd W. McCorkle. *Criminology and Penology*. New York: Henry Holt and Company, 1949.

37. Leader, Arthur L. "A Differential Theory of Criminality," *Sociology and Social Research*, Vol. 26 (September 1941), pp. 45–53.

38. Lemert, Edwin M. "Isolation and Closure Theory of Naive Check Forgery," *Journal of Criminal Law and Criminology*, Vol. 44 (October 1953), pp. 296–307.

39. Lichtenstein, Perry M. *A Doctor Studies Crime*. Princeton, N.J.: D. Van Nostrand Co., Inc., 1934.

40. Lindesmith, Alfred R., and Anselm Strauss. *Social Psychology*. New York: The Dryden Press, 1949.

41. Lindner, Robert M. *Stone Walls and Men*. New York: The Odyssey Press, 1946.

42. Lorand, Sandor. "Compulsive Stealing," *Journal of Criminal Psychopathy*, Vol. 1 (January 1940), pp. 247–253.

43. Lowrey, Lawson G. "Delinquent and Criminal Personalities," in Joseph McV. Hunt (ed.), *Personality and the Behavior Disorders*. New York: The Ronald Press Company, 1944, pp. 799–801.

44. Malamud, William. "The Psychoneuroses," in Joseph McV. Hunt (ed.), *Personality and the Behavior Disorders*. New York: The Ronald Press Company, 1944, pp. 851–852.

45. Mead, George H. *Mind, Self, and Society*, ed. by Charles W. Morris. Chicago: The University of Chicago Press, 1934.

46. Mills, C. Wright. "Situated Actions and Vocabularies of Motive," *American Sociological Review*, Vol. 5 (December 1940), pp. 904–913.

47. New York University School of Law. *Social Meaning of Legal Concepts — Criminal Guilt*. New York: New York University School of Law, 1950.

48. Noyes, Arthur P. *Text-Book of Modern Psychiatry.* Philadelphia: W. B. Saunders Company, 1940.

49. Schneider, Louis. *The Freudian Psychology and Veblen's Social Theory.* New York: King's Crown Press, 1948.

50. Schrag, Clarence. "Review of *Principles of Criminology,*" *American Sociological Review,* Vol. 20 (August 1955), pp. 500–501.

51. Schrag, Clarence. "Some Foundations for a Theory of Correction," in Donald R. Cressey (ed.), *The Prison: Studies in Institutional Organization and Change.* New York: Henry Holt and Company, 1961, Chapter 8.

52. Short, James F., Jr. "Differential Association as a Hypothesis: Problems of Empirical Testing," *Social Problems,* Vol. 8 (Summer 1960), pp. 14–25.

53. Simmel, Ernst. "Incendiarism," in Kurt R. Eissler (ed.), *Searchlights on Delinquency.* New York: International Universities Press, 1941, pp. 90–101.

54. Stekel, Wilhelm. *Peculiarities of Behavior.* New York: Liveright Publishing Corp., 1924, Vol. 1.

55. Sutherland, Edwin H. "The Relation Between Personal Traits and Associational Patterns," in Walter C. Reckless, *The Etiology of Delinquent and Criminal Behavior.* New York: Social Science Research Council, 1943, pp. 131–137.

56. Sutherland, Edwin H., and Donald R. Cressey. *Principles of Criminology,* 6th ed. Philadelphia: J. B. Lippincott Co., 1960.

57. Sykes, Gresham, and David Matza. "Techniques of Neutralization: A Theory of Delinquency," *American Sociological Review,* Vol. 22 (December 1957), pp. 664–670.

58. Taft, Donald R. *Criminology.* New York: The Macmillan Company, 1956.

59. Tiebout, H. M., and M. E. Kirkpatrick. "Psychiatric Factors in Stealing," *American Journal of Orthopsychiatry,* Vol. 2 (April 1932), pp. 114–123.

60. Veblen, Thorstein. *The Theory of the Leisure Class.* New York: Modern Library, Inc., 1934.

61. Vold, George B. *Theoretical Criminology.* New York: Oxford University Press, 1958.

62. Wallerstein, James S. "Roots of Delinquency," *Nervous Child,* Vol. 2 (October 1947), pp. 399–412.

63. Weinberg, S. Kirson. "Theories of Criminality and Problems of

Prediction," *Journal of Criminal Law and Criminology*, Vol. 45 (December 1954), pp. 412–429.

64. Wertham, Frederic. *The Show of Violence*. Garden City, N.Y.: Doubleday & Company, Inc., 1949.

65. White, William A. *Insanity and the Criminal Law*. New York: The Macmillan Company, 1923.

66. Zilboorg, Gregory. "Misconceptions of Legal Insanity," *American Journal of Orthopsychiatry*, Vol. 9 (July 1939), pp. 540–553.

24

Some Relevant Directions for Research in Juvenile Delinquency

IRWIN DEUTSCHER

SYRACUSE UNIVERSITY

The symbolic interactionist approach leads the analyst to consider definitions of the situation. After examining a sample of statistics on juvenile delinquency, Irwin Deutscher finds no consistent evidence of an increase in the phenomenon. On this basis he suggests that, in order to arrive at a "solution" to the problem, efforts must be made to understand the public definitions, which may be partly responsible for its existence. Professor Deutscher asks that we look more closely at the interactionist question: what is the relationship between the way others define a person and the person's definition of himself? Finally, this article contains a plea for studying the process of becoming a delinquent in place of studies of static traits and characteristics of delinquents.

Unlike more static and less complex societies, ours is characterized by an ever varying progression of fads and fashions — in clothing, housing, food, religion, education, child-rearing patterns, and *social problems.**[1] Professional publics, as well as so-called lay publics, are susceptible to seduction by such popular movements. It is hardly coincidence that sociologists and psychologists manifest a heightened intensity in their research on such phenomena as the adjustment of European immigrants to American urban life, conflict between labor and management, race relations, problems of the family, the organization and purpose of our prisons, mental health, and the like at times when there is great popular interest in these matters. Perhaps the most fashionable bandwagon rolling today is the one which flies the banner bearing that amorphous legend "Juvenile Delinquency."[2]

The only reasonable conclusions that can be drawn from the sometimes invalid and frequently unreliable data on delinquency trends, is that *there is no consistent evidence of any general increase in the rates of misbehavior among children and adolescents.*

In an excellent discussion of the pros and cons in interpreting delinquency trends, Teeters and Matza present delinquency rates from 1918 to 1957 for the Cleveland area. By and large those rates were considerably higher during the years 1918–1934 than they were in 1957. In the late thirties they dropped somewhat only to rise again during World War II (23).[3] In Philadelphia, Monahan has contrasted 1923 data with the years 1949–1954 and his curves show practically no difference in delinquency rates between these two periods of time (18). In Buffalo, New York, the delinquency rate (age 7–15) in 1957 is almost identical with the rate in 1950, with only minor variations during the inter-

---

* Reprinted, with considerable revision, from the author's contribution to *Casework Papers* (New York: Family Service Association of America, 1960) with the publisher's permission.

1 For analyses of the role of fad and fashion, see Herbert Blumer (3), Richard T. La Piere (13, pp. 185–195), and Ralph H. Turner and Lewis M. Killian (24, pp. 207–217).

2 A recent Roper survey indicates that Americans rate juvenile delinquency as the most serious moral problem out of eleven issues submitted to them. "The leading problems by per cent of those who consider them serious: juvenile delinquency, 89 per cent; dishonest labor leaders, 88 per cent; government officials accepting bribes, 81 per cent; policemen taking graft, 74 per cent; school segregation, 71 per cent; advertisers making false claims, 67 per cent; international disarmament, 66 per cent. Last two items: rigged quiz shows on TV, 41 per cent; disc jockeys taking money from record companies, 34 per cent." Reported in *Phi Delta Kappan* (19).

3 It is interesting to note that the wartime rise and fall revealed in most statistics is not as pronounced in the Cleveland area.

vening years. In that city the trend in youth arrests (age 16–20) shows a steady decline during the decade 1947–1957 (8, pp. 4, 6). Statistics from the District of Columbia show a constant decline in that city's delinquency index between the years 1954 and 1958 (10, p. 2). In the county containing Syracuse, New York, the delinquency rates in 1957 are almost identical with those in 1940. The City Youth Bureau rates when taken alone show a decline in the rate per thousand (age 7–15) from 51 in 1950 to 43 in 1957 (20, p. 2). The New York State Youth Commission reports that in 1959 delinquency rates in the upstate area were the lowest in twenty-two years and in New York City they were lower in 1959 than they had been in the preceding year (9).

The data cited above derive mainly from studies focused on limited geographic areas. When large quantities of data, presumably describing delinquency in the United States as a whole, are thrown together, the conclusions drawn are usually the reverse: such data tend to show an alarming upsurge in delinquency. For example, the Federal Bureau of Investigation's *Uniform Crime Reports* indicate a continuing rise in delinquency since the immediate postwar decline. On the basis of these data, the Children's Bureau tells us that "juvenile delinquency in the United States . . . has increased each year for the past decade." (15, pp. 2–3; 21, pp. 3–4) Although it is reasonable to assume that data derived from a more limited area are more reliable than those which purportedly describe behavior on a national level,[4] the direction of delinquency rates remains inconclusive. Such sophisticated observers as Bloch and Flynn have concluded, largely on the basis of the F.B.I. data, that "juvenile delinquency cases are rising." (2, p. 33) Although there is an obvious difference between numbers of cases and rates standardized to compensate for shifts in the age composition of the population, Teeters and Matza have shown that the difference between rates and numbers is usually not enough to account for the variations observed through time (23, p. 207). There are exceptions, however. Contrary to the declining rates indicated by the New York State Youth Commission, the State Charities Aid Association reported sharp and

---

[4] "Reasonable," in that the populations, definitions, reporting, and recording systems all tend to be more homogeneous and more consistent in limited geographic areas than in wider areas.

consistent increases both in New York City and upstate New York (26, p. 1). A re-analysis of these data, employing age standardized rates rather than the percentage increases originally reported, reveals no changes through time.[5]

The purpose of this paper is not to document the well-known fact that delinquency statistics are often inconsistent,[6] nor is it to underscore the fact that we do not actually know that there has been any increase in misbehavior among children and adolescents in recent years. Rather, the basic point to be made on the following pages is simply that it doesn't make any difference what the figures tell us because the actual behavior of the youngsters involved is not the only factor in the creation of a social problem. Surely a social problem exists: there is a delinquency problem regardless of what the statistics say and regardless of how many young people are behaving or misbehaving.

DIRECTION #1: RESEARCH ON PUBLIC IMAGES OF CHILDREN AND ADOLESCENTS

If, as suggested above, the definition of a social problem such as delinquency is to some degree independent of the rates of behavior, it would appear appropriate to examine variables other than the behavior per se. Specifically, it is proposed that there is need for a better understanding of the dynamics of public reactions to and definitions of delinquency, including the manner in which such reactions and definitions impinge on adolescent and child behavior. The fact that adolescents do not always behave in conformity with the ways adults would prefer them to behave creates a problem. The popular term which has become fashionable in describing this problem is "juvenile delinquency." Note that there are two independent factors which make this a problem (in addition to giving it a name): (*a*) the behavior of the adolescents and (*b*) the reaction of the adult community. It is true of any social problem that it can be defined as a relation-

---

[5] Unpublished communication from Kenneth W. Kindelsperger, Syracuse University Youth Development Center, to David Hunter, The Ford Foundation, July 14, 1959.

[6] For a description of some of the basic difficulties in obtaining and analyzing statistics on crime and delinquency, see Edwin H. Sutherland and Donald R. Cressey (22, pp. 25-50).

ship between these two factors: behavior on the one hand, and reactions to that behavior on the other. Van Vechten has expressed this phenomenon in terms of what he calls a "tolerance quotient." (25)[7] Taking some liberties with his formulation, we can put it this way:

$$\text{Extent of a Social Problem} = \frac{\text{Amount of Deviant Behavior}}{\text{Amount of Community Tolerance}}$$

It is apparent that this ratio can become large either through an increase in the numerator (for example, delinquent behavior), or a decrease in the denominator (community tolerance toward adolescent misbehavior). It goes without saying that a sudden surge in one — real or apparent — can create a reaction in the other and a spiraling effect can be produced, similar, for example, to the relationship between steel prices and steelworkers' wages.

This leaves us, then, with a double-barreled approach to the problem. We can examine the behavior of adolescents and we can examine the public reaction to that behavior. There has been little if any research on public images of adolescent misbehavior and, in terms of the above definition of a social problem, this is equally as important a phenomenon for research as the behavior itself. There are, of course, many publics and they have varying potential influences on the self-concepts (and therefore the behavior) of adolescent boys. For example, what are the differential images held by peers, by girls, by teachers, by parents, by policemen, by businessmen? According to one body of theory in social psychology, people react toward others in terms of the images they hold of those others and this reaction is a determining factor in creating the image those others hold of themselves (6, 16).[8]

This social-psychological problem of the relationship between definitions of the self and definitions by others is of crucial importance to those concerned with the problem of early identification and with that creature known as the "pre-delinquent."

[7] For an attempt to apply this concept to a number of diverse social problems, see Edwin M. Lemert (14).
[8] See also the writings of William James and John Dewey.

Exactly what is the effect on a child's definition of himself and his expected role in society to label him a delinquent or pre-delinquent? What is the effect on others (teachers, parents, peers, neighbors, and so on) to know that such a label has been applied? How is the interaction process and eventually the socialization process affected by such naming or identification? There are emotional answers to these questions and there are theoretical answers, but there is little research evidence. One of the few empirical tests of Mead's social psychology appears to support the hypotheses that the way in which others respond to a person is related to that person's self-conception, that the person's perception of other people's responses to him is related to his own self-conception, and that his self-conception is related to his estimate of the generalized attitude of others toward him (17). Translated into the specific context of the present problem, this would indicate that it is tenable to suggest that public images of adolescents have an effect on the manner in which they think of themselves. If we can assume that the way in which people think of themselves affects their behavior, we are confronted with some compelling evidence of the need for further research along these lines in our quest for understanding delinquent behavior.

DIRECTION #2: THE DEVELOPMENT OF OPERATIONAL TYPOLOGIES OF ADOLESCENT BEHAVIOR AND MISBEHAVIOR

It is apparent that the term "juvenile delinquency" is inadequate as a concept to guide research or, for that matter, any other purpose, except perhaps a study of popular stereotypes. One of the best recognized and most poorly coped with problems in research on social problems in general and delinquency in particular, concerns the unit of study. To lump under one rubric a nine-year-old girl who runs away from home, the zip-gun-toting members of a Manhattan bopping gang, the calculating groups of adolescents who methodically and efficiently strip cars and dispose of their produce through a fence, and the teen-age Kansas boy who deliberately blasts his father's head off with the family shotgun — to lump these all under one behavioral concept is patently absurd. Any research which employs such a concept in endeavoring to understand the behavior of children or adolescents can hardly hope to transcend the quality of the concept.

There is a need to identify homogeneous kinds of behavior which make sense scientifically, in place of the legal, clinical, or correctional categories which have been derived for other purposes. Such typologies need to have solid roots in current social science theory and need to distinguish clear and meaningful categories of behavior (or misbehavior) which "makes sense" empirically. For example, Donald Cressey (7), following Sutherland, has taken some steps toward thinking through a theory of "behavior systems" which might facilitate the development of a set of typologies of so-called delinquent behavior. More recently Cloward and Ohlin (4), drawing on Merton's classic formulation of "Social Structure and Anomie," have developed a theory of opportunity systems which differentiates types of youthful gangs in a manner which is theoretically sound and empirically reasonable. No such conceptual system can hope to encompass the totality of the hodge-podge that is labeled "delinquency." Much of such behavior is not sufficiently systematic to fall under the umbrella of Cressey's "behavior systems," and certainly the organized gang behavior with which Cloward and Ohlin are primarily concerned represents only a fragment of the variety of deviant behavior engaged in by children and adolescents. There have been, of course, other efforts in the direction of classification[9] but much more intensive and systematic work is needed in this area. When homogeneous types which are different from other homogeneous types have been identified, much of the confusion which results from attempting to study and to understand adolescent misbehavior as if it were a single phenomenon will have been eliminated.

DIRECTION #3: THE SHIFT FROM "FACTORS" TO "PROCESS"

In discussing the need for theoretical typologies, it should be clear that the reference was to types or categories of behavior or

[9] In an unpublished paper entitled "Criminal Motivation: An Attempt at Codification," Jackson Toby has begun to lay the foundations for a typology of deviant behavior based on the motivating forces acting on the deviant. See also William C. Kvaraceus and Walter B. Miller (12, pp. 50–55) and Lester E. Hewitt and Richard L. Jenkins (11).

motivation, *not to types of people or personalities.* Perhaps the foremost reason why there is so little understanding of the processes which lead to deviant behavior is that investigators have seldom bothered to look for them. Instead, they have dissipated their research energies in a fruitless search for factors, bewildering themselves with the fallacious behavioristic assumption of stimulus–response, in the fruitless quest for "causes." Such a conception of the etiology of deviant behavior has been no more productive than the earlier assumption that people who misbehave are inherently depraved, either as a result of the influence of the devil or the defectiveness of their genetic composition. The older assumption at least had the advantage of not being as wasteful of research funds, intellectual energies, or clinical time.

Although these "factor" schools vary in content, the principle is constant: there are certain traits or characteristics which distinguish deviant types from the rest of us. They may be mentally deficient, pear-shaped, slack-jawed, epileptic, psychotic, poor, orphaned, or have any one or a combination of personality, family, or social traits. The factors suggested may be sociological, psychological, psychiatric, biological, physical, or economic. All of them entertain the same fallacious notion that there is a simple cause which brings about misbehavior. Currently popular "causes" of delinquency range from toilet training to television to the existence of working mothers and the absence of reading skills. Obviously none of these, or any other which might be fashionable at a given moment, is a necessary and sufficient cause of adolescent misbehavior. There were, for example, delinquents before the advent of television and there are today delinquents who do not watch television and certainly many young people who do watch it without behaving abominably as a result. Any purported "cause" must fail this test of validity.

In place of the quest for causes in the factorial sense, research needs to seek to achieve an understanding of the varieties of socialization — the on-going life careers of young people with their frequent crises and turning points, their alternatives and choices, and the patterns of the paths which develop. Studies in this area will lead to an understanding of both conforming and deviant behavior and the routes which lead to both. What kinds of deviant behavior are harmless short expeditions without permanent consequences and with a rapid return to the conforming routes? What kinds of misbehavior lead to other kinds which eventuate in a sequence of behavior that may be identified as a delinquent career? Is it possible to identify potentially dangerous configurations of decisions or choices among adolescents? What sorts of day-to-day crises do adolescents see themselves confronted with? To what extent do they resolve these themselves and to what extent are they resolved for them by others? What is the differential influence of "others" (peers, girls, adults, parents, teachers, etc.) on the adolescent decision-making process? Can empirical typologies representing varieties of adolescent careers be identified?

It is suggested that these are the kinds of questions which can serve as productive guides to research in this area. The basic assumption involved in this approach is that misbehavior is of the same nature as any other kind of behavior and arises through the same general processes of socialization. Regardless of personal traits or characteristics, any individual given the proper configuration of circumstances and associations can become a criminal, a drug addict, a drunk, or a delinquent. As E. H. Sutherland phrases it: ". . . the development of criminal behavior is considered as involving the same learning processes as does the development of the behavior of a banker, waitress, or a doctor. The content of learning, not the process itself, is considered as the significant element determining whether one becomes a criminal or a non-criminal." (22, p. 58)

Direction #4: Knowledge of Norms Is Essential to Understanding Deviations

Sutherland's statement provides a natural bridge to the final direction for research proposed in this paper. If the difference between the deviant and the conformist lies in the differential contents of learning during the socialization process, then a crucial area of understanding must be those points at which the deviant finds himself gravitating out of conforming orbits and those influences which exert gravitational pressures both away from and back toward the conforming orbits. Is it unreasonable to suggest that before any kind of deviation can be understood, there must be some grasp of the norm from which that deviation occurs? It would seem apparent, for example, that without a basic understanding of normal skin tissue development, there is little possibility for corrective measures in cases of skin cancer. Moving closer to home, sociologists have fumbled for decades with the concept of social disorganization, largely because of a failure to recognize the prerequisite need to understand social organization. There is no hope of understanding the processes leading to delinquent behavior without understanding the conforming or non-delinquent paths from which they diverge.

There are conceptual clues to the approach to this kind of research already in the theoretical literature. Ruth Benedict, in a classic paper, has spelled out one of the crucial trouble spots in the socialization process (1). Her concept of "Continuities and Discontinuities in Cultural Conditioning" is particularly apropos of the growth and development problems of the contemporary American (and perhaps urban European) adolescent. A great deal could be learned by looking into the ways in which we do and do not provide continuous evolutionary processes by which a child can make the transition to adulthood without trauma — or, at least, accepting the system for what it is, by seeking to identify the ways in which some children manage to attain some success in achieving adulthood without getting into trouble.

DISCUSSION

Having suggested what, in the opinion of the writer, might be some of the more relevant directions for future research in delinquency to take, it remains necessary to clarify a few residual matters. Such directions will lead to better comprehension of the "how" and "why" of young people's behavior. Studying the "how" involves focusing upon the dynamics underlying behavior. Studying the "why" means focusing upon the earlier sequence of experience which has resulted in the current pattern of behavior. Such knowledge will ultimately help reduce occurrences of undesirable behavior among children and adolescents, or stated positively, will help them develop more adaptive behavior.[10] Reference to the reduction of occurrences implies *prevention rather than cure*. An understanding of the processes leading to various forms of delinquent and non-delinquent behavior will facilitate intervention in those processes under conditions which indicate the development of maladaptive careers. If it is known how and where the socialization process goes "wrong," it is possible to deflect it before it does so.

The most effective means of relieving the pressures now bearing down on the plethora of clinicians attempting to cope with delinquent children is to find ways of cutting down on their supply. Therapy, counseling, and casework are slow processes largely oriented to individual patients or clients. For every child who benefits by such treatment, there are at least two others to take his place. This hardly appears to be an efficient means of coping with a large-scale social problem. It provides little more than a stopgap — a valiant effort to do what is possible to hold the line until effective preventive measures can be evolved.

There is an inherent danger in the kinds of research which have been suggested here. It lies in the facile assumption of one or another type of group determinism. It is fallacious to see adolescent careers as if they were a railroad track with occasional switching points at which the person can be shoved onto another line. As important as the influence of others is on our lives, we are not simply pushed around by them. The acting individual partakes in the process and influences it; he is not a helpless pawn in the grasp of the conformity-demanding group. The problem of the ways in which innovation and change develop within the group is an important one and one about which little is known.

George H. Mead offers some highly suggestive insights in his concept of the "conversation of gestures." (16, pp. 253 ff.) It is possible that innovation begins in a group with certain tentative, sometimes non-verbal, types of feelers. These feelers are subtly put forth by a member who determines the extent to which they can be pursued in terms of the kind of response they receive from other members of the group (5, pp. 59–65). Hu-

[10] This paragraph is paraphrased from "A General Research Orientation for the Syracuse University Youth Development Center," a staff paper edited by the present writer and published by the Center. I particularly wish to acknowledge the assistance of David Hunt in the formulation of the ideas expressed in this paragraph, as well as elsewhere.

mor, for example, may be one of the key types of exploratory gesture utilized in efforts to determine the group's willingness to accept radical or exotic ideas, primarily because a "half-joking" suggestion always leaves open a clear avenue of retreat: "I was only kidding." If the response should tend to be serious and accepting, the "joker's" interpretation of the gesture can be revised accordingly: "I really mean it." It is also conceivable that innovation can occur without the intent of the joker. This can develop when a pure and simple attempt at humor is taken as possibly serious and the taker's response becomes an exploratory gesture in an effort to test that possibility. It is conceivable that if more were known about the nature and functions of adolescent humor, a better understanding of how change takes place in adolescent values would result.

In this paper it has been suggested that more research energy be expended on the effect which others — particularly adults — have on the creation of juvenile delinquency and on the concepts of themselves which young people develop as a result of adult definitions. It is important, too, that efforts be made to clarify conceptually the kinds of behavior with which we are concerned — that just what is meant by "juvenile delinquency" be specified in a theoretically and empirically meaningful way. An attempt has been made to point out that, in the opinion of this writer, one of the reasons research progress in this area has been so slow is that we have been traveling up a dead-end road in our fruitless search for simple cause-and-effect relationships in our quest for factors, traits, and characteristics. It was suggested that this quest be abandoned and replaced with efforts to understand the nature of the processes which lead to delinquent careers and how they depart from and differ from the careers of non-delinquents. Finally, a plea was made for recognition of the need to understand these "normal" patterns and processes before there can be hope for comprehension of deviations from the norm.

References

1. Benedict, Ruth. "Continuities and Discontinuities in Cultural Conditioning," *Psychiatry*, Vol. 1 (May 1939), pp. 161–167.
2. Bloch, Herbert A., and Frank T. Flynn. *Delinquency: The*

Juvenile Offender in America Today. New York: Random House, 1956.

3. Blumer, Herbert. "Collective Behavior," in Alfred McClung Lee (ed.), *New Outline of the Principles of Sociology.* New York: Barnes & Noble, Inc., 1946, pp. 217–218.

4. Cloward, Richard, and Lloyd E. Ohlin. *Delinquency and Opportunity.* Glencoe, Ill.: The Free Press, 1960.

5. Cohen, Albert K. *Delinquent Boys.* Glencoe, Ill.: The Free Press, 1955.

6. Cooley, Charles H. "Looking Glass Self," in his *Human Nature and the Social Order.* New York: Charles Scribner's Sons, 1902, pp. 152 ff.

7. Cressey, Donald R. "Criminological Research and the Definition of Crimes," *American Journal of Sociology,* Vol. 56 (May 1951), pp. 546–551.

8. *Delinquency and Youth Crime.* Buffalo, N.Y.: Research Report of the Buffalo Youth Board, 1958.

9. "Delinquency Drops in City and State," *The New York Times,* April 25, 1960.

10. *A Delinquency Index for the District of Columbia.* Washington, D.C.: Interdepartmental Committee of the District Government, March 9, 1959 (mimeographed).

11. Hewitt, Lester E., and Richard L. Jenkins. *Fundamental Patterns of Maladjustment.* Springfield, Ill.: State of Illinois, 1946.

12. Kvaraceus, William C., and Walter B. Miller. *Delinquent Behavior.* Washington, D.C.: National Education Association, 1959.

13. La Piere, Richard T. *Collective Behavior.* New York: McGraw-Hill Book Company, Inc., 1938.

14. Lemert, Edwin M. *Social Pathology.* New York: McGraw-Hill Book Company, Inc., 1951.

15. *A Look at Juvenile Delinquency.* Washington, D.C.: Children's Bureau Publication No. 380, 1960.

16. Mead, George H. *Mind, Self, and Society,* ed. by Charles W. Morris. Chicago: The University of Chicago Press, 1934.

17. Miyamoto, S. Frank, and Sanford M. Dornbusch. "A Test of Interactionist Hypotheses of Self-Conception," *American Journal of Sociology,* Vol. 61 (March 1956), pp. 399–403.

18. Monahan, Thomas P. "On the Incidence of Delinquency." Paper read at the annual meetings of the Eastern Sociological Society, Boston, April 1960.

19. *Phi Delta Kappan.* Vol. 41 (June 1960), p. 410.

20. "Progress Report on Inventory Research." Syracuse, N.Y.: Youth Development Center, November 20, 1958 (ditto).

21. *Report to Congress on Juvenile Delinquency.* Washington, D.C.: Chilren's Bureau Publication.

22. Sutherland, Edwin H., and Donald R. Cressey. *Principles of Criminology.* Philadelphia: J. B. Lippincott Co., 1955.

23. Teeters, Negley K., and David Matza. "The Extent of Delinquency in the United States," *Journal of Negro Education,* Vol. 28 (Summer 1959), pp. 200–213.

24. Turner, Ralph H., and Lewis M. Killian. *Collective Behavior.* Englewood Cliffs, N.J.: Prentice-Hall, Inc., 1957.

25. Van Vechten, C. "The Tolerance Quotient as a Device for Defining Certain Social Concepts," *American Journal of Sociology,* Vol. 46 (July 1940), pp. 35–42.

26. *Youth in Custody* (Part II). New York: New York State Committee on Children and Public Welfare of the State Charities Aid Association, January 1959.

25

On Cooling the Mark Out:
Some Aspects of Adaptation
to Failure

ERVING GOFFMAN

UNIVERSITY OF CALIFORNIA, BERKELEY

Employing as a point of departure the interaction process between the confidence man and his "mark," Erving Goffman considers the social processes by which transformations in self-concept and social role are consciously and deliberately facilitated by others. Although the author is principally concerned with devices by which individuals are persuaded to accept failure, his suggestion that some processes require "cooling in" rather than "cooling out" is illustrated by one of the processes observed in the next chapter, where children are seen to "cool in" their parents for a life without them. Socialization is a continuous process of learning to abandon old roles and self-conceptions and to acquire new ones. Professor Goffman skillfully explores some of the means by which this process can occur and some of the consequences when it does not occur.

On Cooling the Mark Out

In cases of criminal fraud, victims find they must suddenly adapt themselves to the loss of sources of security and status which they had taken for granted.* A consideration of this adaptation to loss can lead us to an understanding of some relations in our society between involvements and the selves that are involved.

In the argot of the criminal world, the term "mark" refers to any individual who is a victim or prospective victim of certain forms of planned illegal exploitation.[1] The mark is the sucker — the person who is taken in. An instance of the operation of any particular racket, taken through the full cycle of its steps or phases, is sometimes called a "play." The persons who operate the racket and "take" the mark are occasionally called "operators."

The confidence game — the "con," as its practitioners call it — is a way of obtaining money under false pretenses by the exercise of fraud and deceit. The con differs from politer forms of financial deceit in important ways. The con is practiced on private persons by talented actors who methodically and regularly build up informal social relationships just for the purpose of abusing them; white collar crime is practiced on organizations by persons who learn to abuse positions of trust which they once filled faithfully. The one exploits poise; the other, position. Further, a con man is someone who accepts a social role in the underworld community; he is part of a brotherhood whose members make no pretense to one another of being "legit." A white collar criminal, on the other hand, has no colleagues, although he may have an associate with whom he plans his crime and a wife to whom he confesses it.

The con is said to be a good racket in the United States only

* Reprinted, with the publisher's permission, from *Psychiatry: Journal for the Study of Interpersonal Relations*, Vol. 15, No. 4 (November 1952), pp. 451–463. Copyright 1952 by The William Alanson White Psychiatric Foundation, Inc.
[1] Terminology regarding criminal activity is taken primarily from Maurer (1) and also from Sutherland (4). The approach that this paper attempts to utilize is taken from Everett C. Hughes of the University of Chicago, who is not responsible for any misapplications of it which may occur here. The sociological problem of failure was first suggested to me by James Littlejohn of the University of Edinburgh. I am grateful to Professor E. A. Shils for criticism and to my wife, Angelica S. Goffman, for assistance.

because most Americans are willing, nay eager, to make easy money, and will engage in action that is less than legal in order to do so. The typical play has typical phases. The potential sucker is first spotted, and one member of the working team (called the "outside man," "steerer," or "roper") arranges to make social contact with him. The confidence of the mark is won, and he is given an opportunity to invest his money in a gambling venture which he understands to have been fixed in his favor. The venture, of course, *is* fixed, but not in his favor. The mark is permitted to win some money and then persuaded to invest more. There is an "accident" or "mistake," and the mark loses his total investment. The operators then depart in a ceremony that is called the "blowoff" or "sting." They leave the mark but take his money. The mark is expected to go on his way, a little wiser and a lot poorer.

Sometimes, however, a mark is not quite prepared to accept his loss as a gain in experience and to say and do nothing about his venture. He may feel moved to complain to the police or to chase after the operators. In the terminology of the trade, the mark may "squawk," "beef," or "come through." From the operators' point of view, this kind of behavior is bad for business. It gives the members of the mob a bad reputation with such police as have not yet been fixed and with marks who have not yet been taken. In order to avoid this adverse publicity, an additional phase is sometimes added at the end of the play. It is called "cooling the mark out." After the blowoff has occurred, one of the operators stays with the mark and makes an effort to keep the anger of the mark within manageable and sensible proportions. The operator stays behind his team-mates in the capacity of what might be called a cooler and exercises upon the mark the art of consolation. An attempt is made to define the situation for the mark in a way that makes it easy for him to accept the inevitable and quietly go home. The mark is given instruction in the philosophy of taking a loss.

When we call to mind the image of a mark who has just been separated from his money, we sometimes attempt to account for the greatness of his anger by the greatness of his financial loss. This is a narrow view. In many cases, especially in America, the mark's image of himself is built up on the belief that he is a pretty shrewd person when it comes to making deals and that he is not the sort of person who is taken in by anything. The mark's readiness to participate in a sure thing is based on more than avarice; it is based on a feeling that he will now be able to prove to himself that he is the sort of person who can "turn a fast buck." For many, this capacity for high finance comes near to being a sign of masculinity and a test of fulfilling the male role.

It is well known that persons protect themselves with all kinds of rationalizations when they have a buried image of themselves which the facts of their status do not support. A person may tell himself many things: that he has not been given a fair chance; that he is not really interested in becoming something else; that the time for showing his mettle has not yet come; that the usual means of realizing his desires are personally or morally distasteful, or require too much dull effort. By means of such defenses, a person saves himself from committing a cardinal social sin — the sin of defining oneself in terms of a status while lacking the qualifications which an incumbent of that status is supposed to possess.

A mark's participation in a play, and his investment in it, clearly commit him in his own eyes to the proposition that he is a smart man. The process by which he comes to believe that he cannot lose is also the process by which he drops the defenses and compensations that previously protected him from defeats. When the blowoff comes, the mark finds that he has no defense for not being a shrewd man. He has defined himself as a shrewd man and must face the fact that he is only another easy mark. He has defined himself as possessing a certain set of qualities and then proven to himself that he is miserably lacking in them. This is a process of self-destruction of the self. It is no wonder that the mark needs to be cooled out and that it is good business policy for one of the operators to stay with the mark in order to talk him into a point of view from which it is possible to accept a loss.

In essence, then, the cooler has the job of handling persons who have been caught out on a limb — persons whose expectations and self-conceptions have been built up and then shattered. The mark is a person who has compromised himself, in his own eyes if not in the eyes of others.

Although the term "mark" is commonly applied to a person who is given short-lived expectations by operators who have intentionally misrepresented the facts, a less restricted definition is desirable in analyzing the larger social scene. An expectation may finally prove false, even though it has been possible to sustain it for a long time and even though the operators acted in good faith. So, too, the disappointment of reasonable expectations, as well as misguided ones, creates a need for consolation. Persons who participate in what is recognized as a confidence game are found in only a few social settings, but persons who have to be cooled out are found in many. Cooling the mark out is one theme in a very basic social story.

For purposes of analysis, one may think of an individual in reference to the values or attributes of a socially recognized character which he possesses. Psychologists speak of a value as a personal involvement. Sociologists speak of a value as a status, role, or relationship. In either case, the character of the value that is possessed is taken in a certain way as the character of the person who possesses it. An alteration in the kinds of attributes possessed brings an alteration to the self-conception of the person who possesses them.

The process by which someone acquires a value is the process by which he surrenders the claim he had to what he was and commits himself to the conception of self which the new value requires or allows him to have. It is the process that persons who fall in love or take dope call "getting hooked." After a person is hooked, he must go through another process by which his new involvement finds its proper place, in space and time, relative to the other calls, demands, and commitments that he has upon himself. At this point certain other persons suddenly begin to play an important part in the individual's story; they impinge upon him by virtue of the relationship they happen to have to the value in which he has become involved. This is not the place to consider the general kinds of impingement that are institutionalized in our society and the general social relationships that arise: the personal relationship, the professional relationship, and the business relationship. Here we are concerned only with the end of the story, the way in which a person becomes disengaged from one of his involvements.

In our society, the story of a person's involvement can end in one of three general ways. According to one type of ending, he may withdraw from one of his involvements or roles in order to acquire a sequentially related one that is considered better. This is the case when a youth becomes a man, when a student becomes a practitioner, or when a man from the ranks is given a commission.

Of course, the person who must change his self at any one of these points of promotion may have profound misgivings. He may feel disloyal to the way of life that must be left behind and to the persons who do not leave it with him. His new role may require action that seems insincere, dishonest, or unfriendly. This he may experience as a loss in moral cleanliness. His new role may require him to forgo the kinds of risk-taking and exertion that he previously enjoyed, and yet his new role may not provide the kind of heroic and exalted action that he expected to find in it.[2] This he may experience as a loss in moral strength.

There is no doubt that certain kinds of role success require certain kinds of moral failure. It may therefore be necessary, in a sense, to cool the dubious neophyte in rather than out. He may have to be convinced that his doubts are a matter of sentimentality. The adult social view will be impressed upon him. He will be required to understand that a promotional change in status is voluntary, desirable, and natural, and that loss of one's role in these circumstances is the ultimate test of having fulfilled it properly.

It has been suggested that a person may leave a role under circumstances that reflect favorably upon the way in which he performed it. In theory, at least, a related possibility must be considered. A person may leave a role and at the same time leave behind him the standards by which such roles are judged. The new thing that he becomes may be so different from the

[2] Mr. Hughes has lectured on this kind of disappointment, and one of his students, Miriam Wagenschein, has undertaken a special study of it (5).

thing he was that criteria such as success or failure cannot be easily applied to the change which has occurred. He becomes lost to others that he may find himself; he is of the twice-born. In our society, perhaps the most obvious example of this kind of termination occurs when a woman voluntarily gives up a prestigeful profession in order to become a wife and a mother. It is to be noted that this illustrates an institutionalized movement; those who make it do not make news. In America most other examples of this kind of termination are more a matter of talk than of occurrence. For example, one of the culture heroes of our dinner-table mythology is the man who walks out on an established calling in order to write or paint or live in the country. In other societies, the kind of abdication being considered here seems to have played a more important role. In medieval China, for instance, anchoretic withdrawal apparently gave to persons of quite different station a way of retreating from the occupational struggle while managing the retreat in an orderly, face-saving fashion (see 6, p. 178).

Two basic ways in which a person can lose a role have been considered; he can be promoted out of it or abdicate from it. There is, of course, a third basic ending to the status story. A person may be involuntarily deprived of his position or involvement and made in return something that is considered a lesser thing to be. It is mainly in this third ending to a person's role that occasions arise for cooling him out. It is here that one deals in the full sense with the problem of persons losing their roles.

Involuntary loss seems itself to be of two kinds. First, a person may lose a status in such a way that the loss is not taken as a reflection upon the loser. The loss of a loved one, either because of an accident that could not have been prevented or because of a disease that could not have been halted, is a case in point. Occupational retirement because of old age is another. Of course, the loss will inevitably alter the conception the loser has of himself and the conception others have of him, but the alteration itself will not be treated as a symbol of the fate he deserves to receive. No insult is added to injury. It may be necessary, none the less, to pacify the loser and resign him to his loss. The loser who is not held responsible for his loss may even find himself taking the mystical view that all involvements are part of a wider con game, for the more one takes pleasure in a particular role the more one must suffer when it is time to leave it. He may find little comfort in the fact that the play has provided him with an illusion that has lasted a lifetime. He may find little comfort in the fact that the operators had not meant to deceive him.

Secondly, a person may be involuntarily deprived of a role under circumstances which reflect unfavorably on his capacity for it. The lost role may be one that he had already acquired or one that he had openly committed himself to preparing for. In either case the loss is more than a matter of ceasing to act in a given capacity; it is ultimate proof of an incapacity. And in many cases it is even more than this. The moment of failure often catches a person acting as one who feels that he is an appropriate sort of person for the role in question. Assumption becomes presumption, and failure becomes fraud. To loss of substance is thereby added loss of face. Of the many themes that can occur in the natural history of an involvement, this seems to be the most melancholy. Here it will be quite essential and quite difficult to cool the mark out. I shall be particularly concerned with this second kind of loss — the kind that involves humiliation.

It should be noted, parenthetically, that one circle of persons may define a particular loss as the kind that casts no reflection on the loser, and that a different circle of persons may treat the same loss as a symbol of what the loser deserves. One must also note that there is a tendency today to shift certain losses of status from the category of those that reflect upon the loser to the category of those that do not. When persons lose their jobs, their courage, or their minds, we tend more and more to take a clinical or naturalistic view of the loss and a non-moral view of their failure. We want to define a person as something that is not destroyed by the destruction of one of his selves. This benevolent attitude is in line with the effort today to publicize the view that occupational retirement is not the end of all active capacities but the beginning of new and different ones.

A consideration of consolation as a social process leads to four general problems having to do with the self in society. First, where in modern life does one find persons conducting themselves as though they were entitled to the rights of a particular status and then having to face up to the fact that they do not possess the qualifications for the status? In other words, at what points in the structures of our social life are persons likely to compromise themselves or find themselves compromised? When is it likely that a person will have to disengage himself or become disengaged from one of his involvements? Secondly, what are the typical ways in which persons who find themselves in this difficult position can be cooled out; how can they be made to accept the great injury that has been done to their image of themselves, regroup their defenses, and carry on without raising a squawk? Thirdly, what, in general, can happen when a person refuses to be cooled out, that is, when he refuses to be pacified by the cooler? Fourthly, what arrangements are made by operators and marks to avoid entirely the process of consolation?

In all personal-service organizations customers or clients sometimes make complaints. A customer may feel that he has been given service in a way that is unacceptable to him — a way that he interprets as an offense to the conception he has of who and what he is. The management therefore has the problem of cooling the mark out. Frequently this function is allotted to specialists within the organization. In restaurants of some size, for example, one of the crucial functions of the hostess is to pacify customers whose self-conceptions have been injured by waitresses or by the food. In large stores the complaint department and the floorwalker perform a similar function.

One may note that a service organization does not operate in an anonymous world, as does a con mob, and is therefore strongly obliged to make some effort to cool the mark out. An institution, after all, cannot take it on the lam; it must pacify its marks.

One may also note that coolers in service organizations tend to view their own activity in a light that softens the harsher details of the situation. The cooler protects himself from feelings of guilt by arguing that the customer is not really in need of the service he expected to receive, that bad service is not really deprivational, and that beefs and complaints are a sign of bile, not a sign of injury. In a similar way, the con man protects himself from remorseful images of bankrupt marks by arguing that the mark is a fool and not a full-fledged person, possessing an inclination towards illegal gain but not the decency to admit it or the capacity to succeed at it.

In organizations patterned after a bureaucratic model, it is customary for personnel to expect rewards of a specified kind upon fulfilling requirements of a specified nature. Personnel come to define their career line in terms of a sequence of legitimate expectations and to base their self-conceptions on the assumption that in due course they will be what the institution allows persons to become. Sometimes, however, a member of an organization may fulfill some of the requirements for a particular status, especially the requirements concerning technical proficiency and seniority, but not other requirements, especially the less codified ones having to do with the proper handling of social relationships at work. It must fall to someone to break the bad news to the victim; someone must tell him that he has been fired, or that he has failed his examinations, or that he has been by-passed in promotion. And after the blowoff, someone has to cool the mark out. The necessity of disappointing the expectations that a person has taken for granted may be infrequent in some organizations, but in others, such as training institutions, it occurs all the time. The process of personnel selection requires that many trainees be called but that few be chosen.

When one turns from places of work to other scenes in our social life, one finds that each has its own occasions for cooling the mark out. During informal social intercourse it is well understood that an effort on the part of one person (ego) to decrease his social distance from another person (alter) must be graciously accepted by alter or, if rejected, rejected tactfully so that the initiator of the move can save his social face. This rule is codified in books on etiquette and is followed in actual behavior. A friendly movement in the direction of alter is a movement outward on a limb; ego communicates his belief that he has defined himself as worthy of alter's society, while at the same time he places alter in the strategic position of being able to discredit this conception.

The problem of cooling persons out in informal social intercourse is seen most clearly, perhaps, in courting situations and in what might be called de-courting situations. A proposal of marriage in our society tends to be a way in which a man sums up his social attributes and suggests to a woman that hers are not so much better as to preclude a merger or partnership in these matters. Refusal on the part of the woman, or refusal on the part of the man to propose when he is clearly in a position to do so, is a serious reflection on the rejected suitor. Courtship is a way not only of presenting oneself to alter for approval but also of saying that the opinion of alter in this matter is the opinion one is most concerned with. Refusing a proposal, or refusing to propose, is therefore a difficult operation. The mark must be carefully cooled out. The act of breaking a date or of refusing one, and the task of discouraging a "steady," can also be seen in this light, although in these cases great delicacy and tact may not be required, since the mark may not be deeply involved or openly committed. Just as it is harder to refuse a proposal than to refuse a date, so it is more difficult to reject a spouse than to reject a suitor. The process of de-courting by which one person in a marriage maneuvers the other into accepting a divorce without fuss or undue rancor requires extreme finesse in the art of cooling the mark out.

In all of these cases where a person constructs a conception of himself which cannot be sustained, there is a possibility that he has not invested that which is most important to him in the soon-to-be-denied status. In the current idiom, there is a possibility that when he is hit, he will not be hit where he really lives. There is a set of cases, however, where the blowoff cannot help but strike a vital spot; these cases arise, of course, when a person must be dissuaded from life itself. The man with a fatal sickness or fatal injury, the criminal with a death sentence, the soldier with a hopeless objective — these persons must be persuaded to accept quietly the loss of life itself, the loss of all one's earthly involvements. Here, certainly, it will be difficult to cool the mark out. It is a reflection on the conceptions men have — as cooler and mark — that it is possible to do so.

I have mentioned a few of the areas of social life where it becomes necessary, upon occasion, to cool a mark out. Attention may now be directed to some of the common ways in which individuals are cooled out in all of these areas of life.

On Cooling the Mark Out

For the mark, cooling represents a process of adjustment to an impossible situation — a situation arising from having defined himself in a way which the social facts come to contradict. The mark must therefore be supplied with a new set of apologies for himself, a new framework in which to see himself and judge himself. A process of redefining the self along defensible lines must be instigated and carried along; since the mark himself is frequently in too weakened a condition to do this, the cooler must initially do it for him.

One general way of handling the problem of cooling the mark out is to give the task to someone whose status relative to the mark will serve to ease the situation in some way. In formal organizations, frequently, someone who is two or three levels above the mark in line of command will do the hatchet work, on the assumption that words of consolation and redirection will have a greater power to convince if they come from high places. There also seems to be a feeling that persons of high status are better able to withstand the moral danger of having hate directed at them. Incidentally, persons protected by high office do not like to face this issue, and frequently attempt to define themselves as merely the agents of the deed and not the source of it. In some cases, on the other hand, the task of cooling the mark out is given to a friend and peer of the mark, on the assumption that such a person will know best how to hit upon a suitable rationalization for the mark and will know best how to control the mark should the need for this arise. In some cases, as in those pertaining to death, the role of cooler is given to doctors or priests. Doctors must frequently help a family, and the member who is leaving it, to manage the leave-taking with tact and a minimum of emotional fuss.[3] A priest must not so much save a soul as create one that is consistent with what is about to become of it.

A second general solution to the problem of cooling the mark out consists of offering him a status which differs from the one he has lost or failed to gain but which provides at least a something or a somebody for him to become. Usually the alternative presented to the mark is a compromise of some kind, providing

[3] This role of the doctor has been stressed by W. L. Warner in his lectures at the University of Chicago on symbolic roles in "Yankee City."

him with some of the trappings of his lost status as well as with some of its spirit. A lover may be asked to become a friend; a student of medicine may be asked to switch to the study of dentistry;[4] a boxer may become a trainer; a dying person may be asked to broaden and empty his worldly loves so as to embrace the All-Father that is about to receive him. Sometimes the mark is allowed to retain his status but is required to fulfill it in a different environment: the honest policeman is transferred to a lonely beat; the too zealous priest is encouraged to enter a monastery; an unsatisfactory plant manager is shipped off to another branch. Sometimes the mark is "kicked upstairs" and given a courtesy status such as "Vice President." In the game for social roles, transfer up, down, or away may all be consolation prizes.

A related way of handling the mark is to offer him another chance to qualify for the role at which he has failed. After his fall from grace, he is allowed to retrace his steps and try again. Officer selection programs in the army, for example, often provide for possibilities of this kind. In general, it seems that third and fourth chances are seldom given to marks, and that second chances, while often given, are seldom taken. Failure at a role removes a person from the company of those who have succeeded, but it does not bring him back — in spirit, anyway — to the society of those who have not tried or are in the process of trying. The person who has failed in a role is a constant source of embarrassment, for none of the standard patterns of treatment is quite applicable to him. Instead of taking a second chance, he usually goes away to another place where his past does not bring confusion to his present.

Another standard method of cooling the mark out — one which is frequently employed in conjunction with other methods — is to allow the mark to explode, to break down, to cause a scene, to give full vent to his reactions and feelings, to "blow his top." If this release of emotions does not find a target, then it at least serves a cathartic function. If it does find a target, as in "telling off the boss," it gives the mark a last-minute chance to re-erect his defenses and prove to himself and others that he

[4] In his seminars, Mr. Hughes has used the term "second-choice" professions to refer to cases of this kind.

had not really cared about the status all along. When a blow-up of this kind occurs, friends of the mark or psychotherapists are frequently brought in. Friends are willing to take responsibility for the mark because their relationship to him is not limited to the role he has failed in. This, incidentally, provides one of the less obvious reasons why the cooler in a con mob must cultivate the friendship of the mark; friendship provides the cooler with an acceptable reason for staying around while the mark is cooled out. Psychotherapists, on the other hand, are willing to take responsibility for the mark because it is their business to offer a relationship to those who have failed in a relationship to others.

It has been suggested that a mark may be cooled out by allowing him, under suitable guidance, to give full vent to his initial shock. Thus the manager of a commercial organization may listen with patience and understanding to the complaints of a customer, knowing that the full expression of a complaint is likely to weaken it. This possibility lies behind the role of a whole series of buffers in our society — janitors, restaurant hostesses, grievance committees, floorwalkers, and so on — who listen in silence, with apparent sympathy, until the mark has simmered down. Similarly, in the case of criminal trials, the defending lawyer may find it profitable to allow the public to simmer down before he brings his client to court.

A related procedure for cooling the mark out is found in what is called stalling. The feelings of the mark are not brought to a head because he is given no target at which to direct them. The operator may manage to avoid the presence of the mark or may convince the mark that there is still a slight chance that the loss has not really occurred. When the mark is stalled, he is given a chance to become familiar with the new conception of self he will have to accept before he is absolutely sure that he will have to accept it.

As another cooling procedure, there is the possibility that the operator and the mark may enter into a tacit understanding according to which the mark agrees to act as if he were leaving of his own accord, and the operator agrees to preserve the illusion that this was the case. It is a form of bribery. In this way the mark may fail in his own eyes but prevent others from discovering the failure. The mark gives up his role but saves his face. This, after all, is one of the reasons why persons who are fleeced by con men are often willing to remain silent about their adventure. The same strategy is at work in the romantic custom of allowing a guilty officer to take his own life in a private way before it is taken from him publicly, and in the less romantic custom of allowing a person to resign for delicate reasons instead of firing him for indelicate ones.

Bribery is, of course, a form of exchange. In this case, the mark guarantees to leave quickly and quietly, and in exchange is allowed to leave under a cloud of his own choosing. A more important variation on the same theme is found in the practice of financial compensation. A man can say to himself and others that he is happy to retire from his job and say this with more conviction if he is able to point to a comfortable pension. In this sense, pensions are automatic devices for providing consolation. So, too, a person who has been injured because of another's criminal or marital neglect can compensate for the loss by means of a court settlement.

I have suggested some general ways in which the mark is cooled out. The question now arises: what happens if the mark refuses to be cooled out? What are the possible lines of action he can take if he refuses to be cooled? Attempts to answer these questions will show more clearly why, in general, the operator is so anxious to pacify the mark.

It has been suggested that a mark may be cooled by allowing him to blow his top. If the blow-up is too drastic or prolonged, however, difficulties may arise. We say that the mark becomes "disturbed mentally" or "personally disorganized." Instead of merely telling his boss off, the mark may go so far as to commit criminal violence against him. Instead of merely blaming himself for failure, the mark may inflict great punishment upon himself by attempting suicide, or by acting so as to make it necessary for him to be cooled out in other areas of his social life.

Sustained personal disorganization is one way in which a mark can refuse to cool out. Another standard way is for the individual to raise a squawk, that is, to make a formal complaint to higher authorities obliged to take notice of such matters. The con mob worries lest the mark appeal to the police. The plant manager must make sure that the disgruntled department head does not carry a formal complaint to the general manager or, worse still, to the Board of Directors. The teacher worries lest the child's parent complain to the principal. Similarly, a woman who communicates her evaluation of self by accepting a proposal of marriage can sometimes protect her exposed position — should the necessity of doing so arise — by threatening her disaffected fiancé with a breach-of-promise suit. So, also, a woman who is de-courting her husband must fear lest he contest the divorce or sue her lover for alienation of affection. In much the same way, a customer who is angered by a salesperson can refuse to be mollified by the floorwalker and demand to see the manager. It is interesting to note that associations dedicated to the rights and the honor of minority groups may sometimes encourage a mark to register a formal squawk; politically it may be more advantageous to provide a test case than to allow the mark to be cooled out.

Another line of action which a mark who refuses to be cooled can pursue is that of turning "sour." The term derives from the argot of industry but the behavior it refers to occurs everywhere. The mark outwardly accepts his loss but withdraws all enthusiasm, good will, and vitality from whatever role he is allowed to maintain. He complies with the formal requirements of the role that is left him, but he withdraws his spirit and identification from it. When an employee turns sour, the interests of the organization suffer; every executive, therefore, has the problem of "sweetening" his workers. They must not come to feel that they are slowly being cooled out. This is one of the functions of granting periodic advancements in salary and status, of schemes such as profit-sharing, or of giving the "employee" at home an anniversary present. A similar view can be taken of the problem that a government faces in times of crisis when it must maintain the enthusiastic support of the nation's disadvantaged minorities, for whole groupings of the population can feel they are being cooled out and react by turning sour.

Finally, there is the possibility that the mark may, in a manner of speaking, go into business for himself. He can try to gather about him the persons and facilities required to establish a status similar to the one he has lost, albeit in relation to a different set of persons. This way of refusing to be cooled is often rehearsed in phantasies of the "I'll show them" kind, but sometimes it is actually realized in practice. The rejected marriage partner may make a better remarriage. A social stratum that has lost its status may decide to create its own social system. A leader who fails in a political party may establish his own splinter group.

All these ways in which a mark can refuse to be cooled out have consequences for other persons. There is, of course, a kind of refusal that has little consequence for others. Marks of all kinds may develop explanations and excuses to account in a creditable way for their loss. It is, perhaps, in this region of phantasy that the defeated self makes its last stand.

The process of cooling is a difficult one, both for the operator who cools the mark out and for the person who receives this treatment. Safeguards and strategies are therefore employed to ensure that the process itself need not and does not occur. One deals here with strategies of prevention, not strategies of cure.

From the point of view of the operator, there are two chief ways of avoiding the difficulties of cooling the mark out. First, devices are commonly employed to weed out those applicants for a role, office, or relationship who might later prove to be unsuitable and require removal. The applicant is not given a chance to invest his self unwisely. A variation of this technique, which provides, in a way, a built-in mechanism for cooling the mark out, is found in the institution of probationary period and "temporary" staff. These definitions of the situation make it clear to the person that he must maintain his ego in readiness for the loss of his job, or, better still, that he ought not to think of himself as really having the job. If these safety measures fail, however, a second strategy is often employed. Operators of all kinds seem to be ready, to a surprising degree, to put up with or "carry" persons who have failed but who have not yet been treated as failures. This is especially true where the involvement of the mark is deep and where his conception of self had been publicly committed. Business offices, government agencies, spouses, and other kinds of operators are often careful to make a place for the mark, so that dissolution of the bond will not be necessary. Here, perhaps, is the most important source of private charity in our society.

A consideration of these preventive strategies brings to attention an interesting functional relationship among age-grading, recruitment, and the structure of the self. In our society, as in most others, the young in years are defined as not-yet-persons. To a certain degree, they are not subject to success and failure. A child can throw himself completely into a task, and fail at it, and by and large he will not be destroyed by his failure; it is only necessary to play at cooling him out. An adolescent can be bitterly disappointed in love, and yet he will not thereby become, at least for others, a broken person. A youth can spend a certain amount of time shopping around for a congenial job or a congenial training course, because he is still thought to be able to change his mind without changing his self. And, should he fail at something to which he has tried to commit himself, no permanent damage may be done to his self. If many are to be called and few chosen, then it is more convenient for everyone concerned to call individuals who are not fully persons and cannot be destroyed by failing to be chosen. As the individual grows older, he becomes defined as someone who must not be engaged in a role for which he is unsuited. He becomes defined as something that must not fail, while at the same time arrangements are made to decrease the chances of his failing. Of course, when the mark reaches old age, he must remove himself or be removed from each of his roles, one by one, and participate in the problem of later maturity.

The strategies that are employed by operators to avoid the necessity of cooling the mark out have a counterpart in the strategies that are employed by the mark himself for the same purpose.

There is the strategy of hedging, by which a person makes sure that he is not completely committed. There is the strategy of secrecy, by which a person conceals from others and even from himself the facts of his commitment; there is also the practice of keeping two irons in the fire and the more delicate practice of maintaining a joking or unserious relationship to one's involvement. All of these strategies give the mark an out; in case of failure he can act as if the self that has failed is not one that is important to him. Here we must also consider the function of being quick to take offense and of taking hints quickly, for in these ways the mark can actively cooperate in the task of saving his face. There is also the strategy of playing it safe, as in cases where a calling is chosen because tenure is assured in it, or where a plain woman is married for much the same reason.

It has been suggested that preventive strategies are employed by operator and mark in order to reduce the chance of failing or to minimize the consequences of failure. The less importance one finds it necessary to give to the problem of cooling, the more importance one may have given to the application of preventive strategies.

I have considered some of the situations in our society in which the necessity for cooling the mark out is likely to arise. I have also considered the standard ways in which a mark can be cooled out, the lines of action he can pursue if he refuses to be cooled, and the ways in which the whole problem can be avoided. Attention can now be turned to some very general questions concerning the self in society.

First, an attempt must be made to draw together what has been implied about the structure of persons. From the point of view of this paper, a person is an individual who becomes involved in a value of some kind — a role, a status, a relationship, an ideology — and then makes a public claim that he is to be defined and treated as someone who possesses the value or property in question. The limits to his claims, and hence the limits to his self, are primarily determined by the objective facts of his social life and secondarily determined by the degree to which a sympathetic interpretation of these facts can bend them in his favor. Any event which demonstrates that someone has made a false claim, defining himself as something which he is not, tends to destroy him. If others realize that the person's conception of self has been contradicted and discredited, then the person tends to be destroyed in the eyes of others. If the person can keep the contradiction a secret, he may succeed in keeping everyone but himself from treating him as a failure.

Secondly, one must take note of what is implied by the fact that it is possible for a person to be cooled out. Difficult as this may be, persons regularly define themselves in terms of a set of attributes and then have to accept the fact that they do not possess them — and do this about-face with relatively little fuss or trouble for the operators. This implies that there is a norm in our society persuading persons to keep their chins up and make the best of it — a sort of social sanitation enjoining torn and tattered persons to keep themselves packaged up. More important still, the capacity of a person to sustain these profound embarrassments implies a certain looseness and lack of interpenetration in the organization of his several life-activities. A man may fail in his job, yet go on succeeding with his wife. His wife may ask him for a divorce, or refuse to grant him one, and yet he may push his way onto the same streetcar at the usual time on the way to the same job. He may know that he is shortly going to have to leave the status of the living, but still march with the other prisoners, or eat breakfast with his family at their usual time and from behind his usual paper. He may be conned of his life's savings on an eastbound train but return to his home town and succeed in acting as if nothing of interest had happened.

Lack of rigid integration of a person's social roles allows for compensation; he can seek comfort in one role for injuries incurred in others. There are always cases, of course, in which the mark cannot sustain the injury to his ego and cannot act like a "good scout." On these occasions the shattering experience in one area of social life may spread out to all the sectors of his activity. He may define away the barriers between his several social roles and become a source of difficulty in all of them. In such cases the play is the mark's entire social life, and the operators, really, are the society. In an increasing number of these cases, the mark is given psychological guidance by professionals of some kind. The psychotherapist is, in this sense, the society's cooler. His job is to pacify and re-orient the disorganized person; his job is to send the patient back to an old world or a new one, and to send him back in a condition in which he can no longer cause trouble to others or can no longer make a fuss. In short, if one takes the society, and not the person, as the unit, the psychotherapist has the basic task of cooling the mark out.

A third point of interest arises if one views all of social life from the perspective of this paper. It has been argued that a person must not openly or even privately commit himself to a conception of himself which the flow of events is likely to discredit. He must not put himself in a position of having to be cooled out. Conversely, however, he must make sure that none of the persons with whom he has dealings are of the sort who may prove unsuitable and need to be cooled out. He must make doubly sure that should it become necessary to cool his associates out, they will be the sort who allow themselves to be gotten rid of. The con man who wants the mark to go home quietly and absorb a loss, the restaurant hostess who wants a customer to eat quietly and go away without causing trouble, and, if this is not possible, quietly to take his patronage elsewhere — these are the persons and these are the relationships which set the tone of some of our social life. Underlying this tone there is the assumption that persons are institutionally related to each other in such a way that if a mark allows himself to be cooled out, then the cooler need have no further concern with him; but if the mark refuses to be cooled out, he can put institutional machinery into action against the cooler. Underlying this tone there is also the assumption that persons are sentimentally related to each other in such a way that if a person allows himself to be cooled out, however great the loss he has sustained, then the cooler withdraws all emotional identification from him; but if the mark cannot absorb the injury to his self and if he becomes personally disorganized in some way, then the cooler cannot help but feel guilt and concern over the predicament. It is this feeling of guilt — this small measure of involvement in the feelings of others — which helps to make the job of cooling the mark out distasteful, wherever it appears. It is this incapacity to be insensitive to the suffering of another person when he brings his suffering right to your door which tends to make the job of cooling a species of dirty work.

One must not, of course, make too much of the margin of sympathy connecting operator and mark. For one thing, the operator may rid himself of the mark by application or threat of pure force or open insult.[5] In Chicago in the 1920's small businessmen who suffered a loss in profits and in independence because of the "protection" services that racketeers gave to them were cooled out in this way. No doubt it is frivolous to suggest

[5] Suggested by Saul Mendlovitz in conversation.

that Freud's notion of castration threat has something to do with the efforts of fathers to cool their sons out of oedipal involvements. Furthermore, there are many occasions when operators of different kinds must act as middlemen, with two marks on their hands; the calculated use of one mark as a sacrifice or fall guy may be the only way of cooling the other mark out. Finally, there are barbarous ceremonies in our society, such as criminal trials and the drumming-out ritual employed in court-martial procedures, that are expressly designed to prevent the mark from saving his face. And even in those cases where the cooler makes an effort to make things easier for the person he is getting rid of, we often find that there are bystanders who have no such scruples.[6] Onlookers who are close enough to observe the blow-off but who are not obliged to assist in the dirty work often enjoy the scene, taking pleasure in the discomfiture of the cooler and in the destruction of the mark. What is trouble for some is *Schadenfreude* for others.

This paper has dealt chiefly with adaptations to loss: with defenses, strategies, consolations, mitigations, compensations, and the like. The kinds of sugar-coating have been examined, and not the pill. I would like to close this paper by referring briefly to the sort of thing that would be studied if one were interested in loss as such, and not in adaptations to it.

A mark who requires cooling out is a person who can no longer sustain one of his social roles and is about to be removed from it; he is a person who is losing one of his social lives and is about to die one of the deaths that are possible for him. This leads one to consider the ways in which we can go or be sent to our death in each of our social capacities, the ways, in other words, of handling the passage from the role that we had to a state of having it no longer. One might consider the social processes of firing and laying-off; of resigning and being asked to resign; of farewell and departure, of deportation, excommunication, and going to jail; of defeat at games, contests, and wars; of being dropped from a circle of friends or an intimate social relationship; of corporate dissolution; of retirement in old age; and, lastly, of the deaths that heirs are interested in.

[6] Suggested by Howard S. Becker in conversation.

And, finally, attention must be directed to the things we become after we have died in one of the many social senses and capacities in which death can come to us. As one might expect, a process of sifting and sorting occurs by which the socially dead come to be effectively hidden from us. This movement of ex-persons throughout the social structure proceeds in more than one direction.

There is, first of all, the dramatic process by which persons who have died in important ways come gradually to be brought together into a common graveyard that is separated ecologically from the living community.[7] For the dead, this is at once a punishment and a defense. Jails and mental institutions are, perhaps, the most familiar examples, but other important ones exist. In America today, there is the interesting tendency to set aside certain regions and towns in California as asylums for those who have died in their capacity as workers and as parents but who are still alive financially.[8] For the old in America who have also died financially, there are old-folks homes and rooming-house areas. And, of course, large cities have their Skid Rows which are, as Park put it, ". . . . full of junk, much of it human, i.e., men and women who, for some reason or other, have fallen out of line in the march of industrial progress and have been scrapped by the industrial organization of which they were once a part." (3, p. 60) Hobo jungles, located near freight yards on the outskirts of towns, provide another case in point.

Just as a residential area may become a graveyard, so also certain institutions and occupational roles may take on a similar function. The ministry in Britain, for example, has sometimes served as a limbo for the occupational stillborn of better families, as have British universities. Mayhew, writing of London in the mid-nineteenth century, provides another example: artisans of different kinds, who had failed to maintain a position in the prac-

[7] Suggested by lectures of and a personal conversation with Mr. Hughes.
[8] Some early writers on caste report a like situation in India at the turn of the nineteenth century. Hindus who were taken to the Ganges to die, and who then recovered, were apparently denied all legal rights and all social relations with the living. Apparently these excluded persons found it necessary to congregate in a few villages of their own. In California, of course, settlements of the old have a voluntary character, and members maintain ceremonial contact with younger kin by the exchange of periodic visits and letters.

tice of their trade, could be found working as dustmen (2, pp. 177–178). In the United States, the jobs of waitress, cab driver, and night watchman, and the profession of prostitution, tend to be ending places where persons of certain kinds, starting from different places, can come to rest.

But perhaps the most important movement of those who fail is one we never see. Where roles are ranked and somewhat related, persons who have been rejected from the one above may be difficult to distinguish from persons who have risen from the one below. For example, in America, upper-class women who fail to make a marriage in their own circle may follow the recognized route of marrying an upper-middle-class professional. Successful lower-middle-class women may arrive at the same station in life, coming from the other direction. Similarly, among those who mingle with one another as colleagues in the profession of dentistry, it is possible to find some who have failed to become physicians and others who have succeeded at not becoming pharmacists or optometrists. No doubt there are few positions in life that do not throw together some persons who are there by virtue of failure and other persons who are there by virtue of success. In this sense, the dead are sorted but not segregated, and continue to walk among the living.

References

1. Maurer, David W. *The Big Con.* Indianapolis, Ind.: The Bobbs-Merrill Company, Inc., 1940.

2. Mayhew, Henry. *London Labour and the London Poor.* London: Griffin, Bohn, 1861, Vol. II.

3. Park, Robert E. *Human Communities.* Glencoe, Ill.: The Free Press, 1952.

4. Sutherland, Edwin H. *The Professional Thief.* Chicago: The University of Chicago Press, 1937.

5. Wagenschein, Miriam. " 'Reality Shock': A Study of Beginning School Teachers." Master's thesis, Department of Sociology, University of Chicago, 1950.

6. Weber, Max. *The Religion of China*, tr. by Hans H. Gerth. Glencoe, Ill.: The Free Press, 1951.

26

Socialization for Postparental Life

IRWIN DEUTSCHER

SYRACUSE UNIVERSITY

Anselm Strauss's essay in this volume examined the changes in adult personality in a general way. Irwin Deutscher now takes up a specific transformation — one that results from the growing-up and leave-taking of children. Significantly, and properly in interactionist tradition, he calls this a process of socialization, a term usually reserved for the process of induction of small children into society. Thus he considers this particular transformation a continuation of the lifelong process of social learning, and a number of alternative means of learning to play a new role are suggested.

The notion of life careers — of a developmental process — as a perspective for viewing the etiology of individual or institutional behavior is not new (see 15). The word "career" itself carries the connotation of a progressively developing sequence of *work* experiences. It need not, however, be restricted to the experiences of individuals. The "natural history" approach to institutional development employs an identical perspective (14). In attempting to understand and describe the family career, or stages in the development of the American family, the concept

Socialization for Postparental Life

of the "family cycle" has been frequently, although not intensively, employed (see 4, Chapter 2; 13; 22, Chapter 20). Perhaps more than any other analyst, Paul C. Glick has consistently exploited this concept in an effort to direct his analysis of demographic shifts in family structure (11, 12). In this paper some of the social-psychological problems of transition from one phase of the family cycle to another will be examined.[1]

The Postparental Phase of the Family Cycle

The span of time from the beginning of a family with the marriage of a young couple, the bearing, rearing, and marrying of their children, through the time when they are again alone together, until the ultimate death of one or both of them, is referred to as the family cycle. Cavan has described as thoroughly as anyone variations in family organization through the family cycle. She sees the cycle as "significant in that with each stage, changes occur in the family membership and consequently in family organization, roles, and interpersonal relationships." (3, pp. 262–263; 4, pp. 28–38) This paper focuses on the transition from the phase during which children are being launched into the adult world to the phase Cavan calls postparental: "The postparental couple are the husband and wife usually . . . in their forties and fifties. . . . The most obvious change is the withdrawal of adolescent and young children from the family, leaving husband and wife as the family unit." (3, p. 573)

In the family career pattern of a large segment of our adult urban population, this appears to be emerging as a new phase of the family cycle, largely as a result of two demographic shifts: the fact that these people can expect to live considerably longer than their parents or grandparents and the fact that they averaged fewer children over a shorter span of years than their parents or grandparents.[2] The typical couple of two generations

[1] This paper is based on a part of the author's doctoral dissertation (6). The research was facilitated by a pre-doctoral research training fellowship from the Social Science Research Council and a grant from Community Studies, Inc., of Kansas City, Missouri.

[2] Although it may appear that, in terms of average number of children, the offspring of the current crop of postparental couples are reverting to the patterns of older generations, this reversion is more apparent than

ago had a life expectancy which enabled them to survive together for thirty-one years after marriage, two years short of the time when their *fifth* child was expected to marry. But, "the decline in size of family and the improved survival prospects of the population since 1890 not only have assured the average parents of our day that they will live to see their children married but also have made it probable that they will have one-fourth of their married life still to come when their last child leaves the parental home." (11)

The Problem of Transition

In her classic formulation of "Continuities and Discontinuities in Cultural Conditioning," Ruth Benedict highlighted the problem of socially structured impediments to continuous socialization through the life cycle. She begins with the observation that there are certain discontinuities in the life cycle which are facts of nature and inescapable; thus, "Every man who rounds out his human potentialities must have been a son first and a father later and the two roles are physiologically in great contrast." (1) The important point, however, is that there is a great deal of variability in the way in which the transition is effected in different societies. Moving from Benedict's focus on the transition between childhood and adulthood to a focus on the transition from the launching to the postparental stage of the family cycle, and shifting from the concepts of "culture" and "conditioning" to the concepts of "role" and "socialization," we have a perspective within which to view the problems of transition and the modes of adaptation to postparental life.

Theoretically, it might be expected that the transition to postparental life would be a difficult one for the middle-aged spouses to make. Since this is an emerging phase of the family cycle, few of those entering it can find role models: in most cases one

real: "The fact that the crude birth rate has been higher in the postwar period than in the 1930's is due primarily to the operation of two factors: a larger proportion of women have been marrying at younger ages, and more of those marrying have started their families relatively soon after marriage. These factors may have only a minor effect on the final average number of children that women will have borne by the end of the childbearing period . . ." (10, p. 215) of their own parents was dead before the last of their **own** siblings was launched. This lack of anticipatory socialization — the absence of an opportunity to take the role of a postparental spouse, to rehearse the part before having to play the role themselves — ought theoretically to make for an extremely difficult situation after the children leave home. Much of the descriptive literature indicates that this, indeed, is a dangerous time of life (2, p. 626; 5, p. 404; 9, p. 3; 16, pp. 353–354; 17; 18, p. 79; 21, p. 7; 22, p. 43). *Nevertheless, despite expectations based on both theory and clinical experience, when urban middle-class postparental couples describe their life, the hurdle does not appear to have been insurmountable and the adaptations are seldom pathological.*[3]

In discussing postparental life, middle-aged spouses clearly reveal that it is not sound to assume that anticipatory socialization is absent because this is a new stage of the family cycle — that is, because middle-aged couples of today have not had the experience of observing their parents make such a transition. In spite of the fact that the identical situation could not be observed and rehearsed — that there was no opportunity to learn to take the role of the other by observing others — *analogous* situations exist in one's own life. Sussman recognizes this when he suggests that "most parents are gradually prepared to some degree for the day when their children marry and leave home by their periodic absences away at school or elsewhere." (20)[4] Such periodic absences do not, however, represent the full extent to which such socialization by analogy can occur.

Situations such as these provide an opportunity for the parent to rehearse in his own mind what life will be like when his children are gone. Anomalously, he himself becomes the "other" whose role he has an opportunity to take. Even though these practice situations may not be considered as permanent, impor-

[3] Observations made and materials cited below are derived from intensive interviews with 49 urban middle-class postparental spouses. The investigator gathered sufficient data on family characteristics from approximately 540 middle-class households to determine whether or not they met his criteria of postparental. Those selected were between 40 and 65 years of age, had from one to four children all of whom had been launched, and both parents were alive and living together. Self-selection occurred in only two cases where the family refused to be interviewed.

[4] A similar perspective can be found in John Sirjamaki (19, p. 135).

tant, or serious (they are more nearly instances of "playing-at-roles" than "role-playing") it will be seen that they provide the continuity in role conditioning — the socializing opportunity — that is needed. The word "opportunity" is used advisedly. Individuals react to the socialization process in different ways; on some it "takes" and on others it doesn't. The simple fact that an individual is provided with a potentially socializing experience does not necessarily result in his defining it as such or in his being socialized as a result of the experience. The remainder of this paper will be devoted to an examination of what these socializing opportunities are and the manner in which they appear to facilitate the transition to postparental life.

Opportunities for Anticipatory Socialization

Change as a Culture Value. One of the underlying cultural values of our contemporary society is the focus on change for its own sake. In a sense all Americans are socialized from early childhood to believe that change is both inevitable and good. The notion that things will not remain the same — politically, economically, or socially — is an integral part of our national ethos. Otherwise there could be no Horatio Alger myth. Otherwise the political slogan "It's time for a change" could not have been so effective as it obviously was in 1952. Otherwise Southern segregationists would not concede that the best they can do is fight a *delaying* action against integration. Change apparently is accepted as something both natural and inevitable by the vast majority of the members of our society. Such a value provides a general conditioning for the acceptance of new and different situations regardless of their specific nature.

In our interviews, we find evidence that middle-class urban Americans have internalized this value and are able logically to relate it to the family cycle. One mother observes philosophically that "it seems like life spaces itself. You look forward to finishing up one space but then another space always pops up. When this is accomplished something else comes along." The clearest statements, however, come from two of the fathers. One of them, when asked how it felt to become a grandfather responded that "like most things in my life, it's just a matter of course. Things can be expected, like you expect changes in jobs and expect children to be married. Natural events come afterward and you take those things as a matter of course." This process, felt to be "natural" in our society, is described in full detail by the other father:

> Of course you hate to give up your daughter, but I think we all understand that is the way of life; you can't stand still; you can't be the same forever. Life moves on and that is the most natural thing. You see them grow. You see them graduate from high school. Then you see them graduate from college — you follow along. It is changing all the time. First it is childhood. You hold them on your lap then you go walking with them. Then you see them through high school. I was her chauffeur, all the time taking her to social functions. She went through music school, then she got a bachelor of arts, then we sent her for four years to Juilliard and she got her bachelor's and master's there. Then she comes out and teaches in college for one year and then she gets married and settles down.

It is clear that at least some people are aware of a life cycle and a family cycle and are resigned (if not committed) to a philosophy of change. Whether or not one is willing to accept the conditioning effect of a basic cultural emphasis on change *per se*, there remain several more specific types of experiences which provide parents with an opportunity for anticipatory socialization.

The Temporary Departure of Children. Opportunities for middle-class parents at least to play-at a postparental role frequently occur when the children leave home for college. However, such opportunities are exploited to varying degrees, or, to put it another way, the experience is defined differently by different couples. Some parents make no mention of the possibility of college as a socializing experience for themselves. Presumably many of these do not see that possibility. On the other hand, there are others who see clearly what is happening. A mother claims that "The breaking point is when your children go away to college. After that you grow used to it. By the time they get married you're used to the idea of their being away and adjust to it."

The question "Do you think your child was ready to marry when he did?" brought out the functionality of the college experience. One father responded, "Yes, I thought she was. She had already gone through college — those five years of college and two years working. She was ready to get married." More important is that the college experience meant that he was now ready for her to get married. This kind of projection — the notion that college is training for the child to get away rather than training for the parent to release him — is expressed most clearly by a mother:

> It's only natural, when you have a family of three without any relatives near by, to notice a gap when she gets married. Of course, the first adjustment is when they go away to school; that's the first break. It's healthy for an only child to go far away to school. It makes them more self-sufficient. She had been in school away from home since she was sixteen and I think she was very well adjusted. Being away like that she learned to be independent, and make her own decisions and take responsibilities on her own. It was a sort of training period which prepared her [*sic;* "us"?] for leaving us [*sic;* "her"?].

Another mother says of her recently married son, "We had gotten used to just being by ourselves while he was in the Navy and away at college." This brings us to another frequently occurring opportunity for parents to play at the postparental role: the departure of children for military service. Life experiences tend to be evaluated in comparison with other experiences. They are not just good or bad; they are better or worse. Apparently it is better to lose a child through marriage than through war: "My most unhappy time was around the war years when my boy was in service. I worried over him coming back; he was missing several times." This is the kind of socialization that gives a parent a sense of relief to have a child home and married. We learn from another mother that, "When he was sent overseas, I was so worried about him over there that it was a relief when he got married and settled down." The importance of this as a learning experience is illustrated by the mother whose three children are now married, but who says of the time when her son went into service and she still had two others at home, "I think that the lonesomest part of my life I ever had was when my son was in service. We missed our boy." Her husband, interestingly enough, explicitly states that the Army experience serves as preparation for marriage. When asked if he thought his children were mature enough to get married, he responded: "Well, I thought more so about the boy because he was in the Army, but I did think that she (the daughter) should have waited."

Being in the armed forces serves both to wean the parents away from the children and the children away from the parents. Still another mother reports that:

> After he came out of the service he had aged a lot. He used to confide in us about life and to tell us about everything that was happening in school. But after he went into service he changed. We always spent our afternoons together — both the children. We'd go out for drives or picnics or something like that. But after he came home from service he didn't do that anymore. He wasn't contented to be at home.

But then, after the anguish of wartime separation, another woman implies that it is good just to know that the child is safe and is in this country:

> He was in the Second World War and he was overseas. And after having been so far away from home he feels like he's practically right here, because we can telephone and it's just 50 miles. After having been in Europe a couple of years, you know 50 miles away is "at home."

There are other experiences which, like college or service in the armed forces, give parents an opportunity to practice living without their children. Nearly a quarter of the families interviewed had parted with their children for extended periods of time while they were still in their teens. For example, there is the son who couldn't get along with his father: "My son used to say that as much as he would like to stay here, he couldn't take things off of his dad any longer. So I never insisted on him staying. He left a couple of times and would come back." Then there is the child with the wanderlust: "That boy wasn't interested in anything except to hitchhike — just to get as far as he could and to see what he could see. He was walking when he was eight months old and has been walking ever since." More common than either of these two experiences is the departure of children prior to marriage in search of work. Although this sometimes occurs with daughters, it is more frequently the sons who leave for this reason:

> (Do you remember how you felt when you first found out he was going to get married?) Yes, he was the first one. Both of them are married now. It was all right. He was able to take care of himself. He was away from home a lot. He and the oldest boy were up in Detroit on defense work. They have really been away from home a long time — ever since 1940.

> (How did you find it when the children left? Did you have a lot of time on your hands?) Well, that came gradually. The war had something to do with that. They were both in the war before they got married and we were alone then. And the youngest one went to aviation school. He was just barely 18 when he got his first job in Texas. Then he went to Phoenix and then he came home and then he went into service. And the other boy was at home for a while and then he had to go. So with their coming and going it kinda eased off gradually.

Finally, in connection with these temporary departures of children prior to marriage, a word should be said about the modern middle-class urban high school complex. In some cases it results in the home being little more than a place to sleep and certainly in infrequent contacts with the parents. This reaction was obtained only from fathers. Possibly mothers maintain closer contacts with their children — especially with daughters — during the high school years. Be this as it may, one father reports that:

> There is a difference when they grow older — particularly when they went to high school. Naturally they got their own friends and you saw less of them than you did before. They'd come home from school late and then they'd have a game or maybe the girl would have a date and you might see them at dinner time, but you probably wouldn't see them until breakfast — or maybe after the game or date.

Another father stated that the "best years" were when his boys were around nine or ten: "(When they started to grow up did you feel that they were growing away from you?) No, but when they go to high school they have different ideas and interests than the people at home have." There is, however, another side to this coin. The proud father of a high school athlete was asked when was the happiest time of his life: "Oh — that kid of mine — the things he did when he was in high school. It was like living your life over again. I guess I really enjoyed that period."

On the basis of such observations, there is reason to believe that there are bridges — transitional learning experiences which aid parents in adapting themselves to postparental life. These appear to provide continuity in role conditioning. Such "rehearsals" are not as difficult as "opening night," the real and permanent departure of the children which will come later. They are defined as temporary and are broken by regular visits home or the expectation that the children will at some time again return to live at home. But the "temporary" can gradually shift into the permanent without any traumatic transition: "My daughter went to California, to Berkeley, to go to school. Then she decided to work there a while and then she got married out there and she has lived there ever since." The fact that these socializing experiences occur at a time when the parents are still extremely active with their own affairs should not be ignored. It is probably easier to prepare for and accept such a transition in early middle age than in later years when it will actually occur. When one mother was asked how she made out at home with the children all off to college, she shrugged off the question with "Oh, I don't know. I was just too busy to be bothered about anything."

Life Without Father. If there are temporary departures of the children which provide parents with an opportunity to practice the postparental role, there is also a combination of recent historical events and cultural expectations which have provided middle-class fathers with an additional opportunity to practice this role. The historical events are the Great Depression and the Second World War; the cultural expectations are those related to the middle-class notion of "work." Unlike some of the temporary departures of children mentioned in the preceding section, a temporary shattering of the family constellation due to the exigencies of war, work, or economic depression can be rationalized as beyond the control of those involved — attributed to immitigable external forces. Such rationalization is not always possible when the family break-up results from a unilateral decision on the part of a child to leave home for reasons related to education or work. When opportunities to engage in these pursuits are locally available, the parents may view the child's decision as a rejection of themselves. Such a definition of the situation (whether accurate or inaccurate) is hardly conducive to promoting a smooth transition into postparental life.

Some fathers, owing to the press of circumstances, have lived for extended periods of time away from their wives and children.

> I was having a rough time. I was six months or a year on WPA and when I got off that I couldn't find anything. But I had a brother in Portland, Oregon, so I went out there and it seems I was away from mother (wife) and the kids for close to a year and a half.

> During the war my husband was on a swingshift and worked nights and then he was in the Hawaiian Islands for a year working for the Navy.

> Let me tell you how it was. On a certain day I had $50,000 in the bank and a $25,000 home paid for and all the trimmings to go with it. Three months later I borrowed $25 to send my wife and children up to Kansas City (from Oklahoma). It was months before I got things straightened out enough to join them.

> My husband was 38 and the company sent us to Ottawa (Kansas). The draft board there just had a high quota and they scraped the bottom of the barrel. That's how they got him.

Nearly one in every five of the families interviewed was broken for extended periods of time under circumstances similar to those described above. It is relevant that these experiences most often were narrated in response to questions about how close the father was to the children when they were growing up.

Socialization for Postparental Life

A somewhat more common experience (also usually discussed in relation to that same line of questioning) is the detachment of the father from his growing children and his lack of involvement in their activities as a result of his being "on the road." One third of these middle-class fathers found it necessary to travel regularly during some phase of their work career, and in all but one case this was defined as alienating the father from the children. When asked if she felt that she was closer to her children than her husband, one wife answered, "I think I was, definitely, because my husband is a traveling man. I really reared the children; most of the time he was only home Saturdays and Sundays." Other wives of traveling men tend to respond in like manner:

> He travels from Monday to Thursday and he's in Thursday evening until Monday morning. (Do you think this had anything to do with his relationship with the children when they were growing up?) Yes, quite a bit! They didn't have the companionship with their dad that I thought they should have had.

This is not a one-sided "mama's" point of view. As the following couplets excerpted from husband and wife interviews reveal, the husbands are in essential agreement on this matter:

> (1) *Wife:* (Do you think your husband's occupation kept him away from the boys?) Very definitely! It was unfortunate too. He felt he was just not able to devote the time to them and it was not up to me to say what he should and should not do. (He was out of town a good part of the time?) Yes, when they were young he was gone a great deal. Then later on he had so much responsibility in the office. He was the kind that went early and stayed late. You see he had had considerable trouble when he was younger, seeing his mother working and slaving while his father was ill and he didn't want me to have to do the same thing. *That* result has been fine. But as for the boys, he never did have much time for them.

> *Husband:* (Did you feel that your job kept you away from your children — that you didn't have enough time to spend with them?) I didn't have enough time to spend with them. When I was traveling I was away a great deal, and then when

I went into the office my job there kept me on the job from early in the morning until dinner time and then I worked a good many nights at home. So I didn't have too much time with them.

* * * * *

(2) *Wife:* (Which one of you was closer to the children when they were younger?) I would say I was. For one thing, he was gone so much. He would only see them on weekends. So I would definitely say they were closer to me. They respect their father and think a lot of him, but they wouldn't bring their problems to him as much as they would to me.

Husband: (Tell me how your work affects your family life?) Well, like the average man gets up and goes to work every morning. *I* am out for a week! Now that we have better highways and faster cars you can make most all your territory in a week's time. I used to make a lot of two and three weeks' trips because we had slower cars and not very good highways and it took just that much longer.

Although improvements in transportation may have reduced the periods of absence, they still exist. However, simply because a man travels does not mean that he has become detached from his children and family. A railroader and his wife demonstrate how a family can be tightly knit because his absence for short periods results in his being home for five or six day "weekends." This traveling man had the opportunity to be closer to his family than most who do not travel:

(Do you think it took you away from your family too much to be on the road?) Well, I was away from the family. Like a trip from here to Omaha and Colorado it was two nights and one day away and come in and sleep a day and then go right back out again when I had to make two round trips. So I was four nights off on the road, but then I'd come in and I'd have five days off one time and six the next.

And from his wife:

Yes, he was on the road a lot. He was on the Super Chief on the Santa Fe Main Line. He was on that train for eleven years. (Would you rather he worked at something that kept him home?) Oh my no! He liked his work. He was on the railroad for 44 years. (Do you think his being away from home affected his relationship with the children?) No, no; they were always regular companions — all of them. He knew the children as well as I did.

As has been indicated in some of the passages cited, even when father is at home, he may be so in body only, being engrossed in his work day and night whether on the road or in town. When this kind of commitment to work evolves, men whose work never takes them out of town may see less of their families than some who, like the railroader, travel a great deal. One mother generalizes: "I think most men are so occupied with their work that they sort of leave that (rearing of children) to the mother." A father whose work has never taken him out of town concurs: "I'm afraid I left most of bringing him up to his mother. Lots of times when he was growing up I had to work late. I wouldn't get home till 9:30 or 10:00 at night and I'd be out to the office at 5:00 in the morning."

It is important, however, that this parental detachment not be overemphasized. Not all middle-class fathers orient themselves to the work role so strongly. There are certainly some who leave their work at the office: "I have no night work. My work is at the office and when I leave the office I'm through until the next day, regardless of what I've got. I've never made a practice of bringing work home." There are others who emphasize that, in spite of many temptations, they have steadfastly refused to take their work out of the office.

It would seem that there are a good many cases among urban middle-class families where life goes on without father during the years when the child is growing up. As dysfunctional as this may be to the family at that stage, it does provide the fathers with continuity in role conditioning which can stand them in good stead at the later postparental stage when the time comes for the children to depart permanently.

The Mother-in-Law Myth as a Conditioning Device. If the work role helps to condition fathers for the departure of their children, at least some mothers appear to be provided with a conditioning device which is the distinctive property of their sex. That device is the cultural myth of the mother-in-law: "As soon as my youngsters were born I made up my mind that I was not going to be a mother-in-law like you read about." Such a resolution, if intended seriously, could go far in preparing a mother to accept the departure of her children. In addition to the folklore on the mother-in-law, there is the reality of experience:

> My son got married before he even finished his education. He was only seventeen years old, but I did not say a word! I don't think it's good policy. That can be a very tender spot. I know because I went through it. I had a mother-in-law — well, she was just butting into everything all the time. I just resolved never to act like that myself. The Bible says something about to hold your peace. And that's not prose. That's just the way it should be. People when they get married should get away from relatives. Far enough away so that it takes three days for a postcard to get to them and three more for it to get back.

The following mother expresses the same opinion even more vehemently:

> I'll go to the county home before I'll live with any of my children. I have very definite ideas on that. Because I had his mother with us every winter for 20 years whether I had room for her or not and it *doesn't* work and I very *definitely* will *not* do a thing like that! If I have to take a dose of strychnine first, I won't!

Humor is, of course, an effective form of social control — especially in an increasingly other-directed society. Mothers, like everyone else, are sensitive to the pleas of the mass media for conformity. They want to be "good" mothers-in-law and Evelyn Duvall's study indicates that they are — that the mother-in-law is not nearly the center of conflict in America that she is often thought to be (7). It is very possible that a more accurate statement would be that the mother-in-law is not nearly the center of conflict that she *used* to be. The pressures of experience and folklore as indicated in the passages cited above may have brought about a shift in the self-conception of mothers-in-law and in the role which they play. In any event, at least in some cases, these myths and experiences provide an opportunity for mothers to anticipate and prepare themselves for postparental life — a socializing opportunity.

Survivals of an Older Family Pattern. The postparental phase of the family cycle was described earlier as a newly emerging phenomenon resulting from increasing longevity and decreasing fertility. No longer is it true, as it was at the turn of the century, that both parents will have died before the last of their children was launched. However, as with any emerging phenomenon, fragmentary survivals of the earlier pattern remain. In such cases, there is, in effect, no transition to make — these people have no postparental period. Take, for example, the couple with six children ranging in age from 31 to 44, with three of them married and residing in the metropolitan area and a fourth divorced and living at home. Their daily life remains essentially the same as it has always been, although the work is somewhat lighter and the economic situation somewhat more secure:

> (Tell me just how you spend a typical day nowadays?)
> Well, I do my housework in the morning and then I get meals again, and the children will come in once in a while and sometimes I go down to one of my daughters'. That is all I do. I have a fine family. They are all good Christian children and I am just as proud of them as I can be.

Life has changed so little for this couple that they even argue about the same kinds of trivialities they did thirty years ago:

> . . . take that rug there in the dining room. I didn't like the color but he bought it anyway because it was a good buy. It was a remnant. But it seemed to me that a rug is something that you have to live with for a long time and it ought to satisfy you. But he said that I had had my way with the wallpaper so he went ahead and bought it.

An extended family need not be one of procreation; even with few children, postparental couples may refer themselves to a large family of orientation. This older pattern manifests itself in the case of a couple one of whose two married children is now living in Minneapolis. In spite of this, there is a plethora of parental siblings, in-laws, nephews, nieces, and grandchildren —

all part of a second- and third-generation Irish clan residing in the Kansas City area:

> (Tell me what you do with your time these days?) Well, we are quite home people, that is, with the grandchildren, the daughter, and his (husband's) people. He has seven brothers and they are all living in Kansas City, and we are very close to one another — the husbands and wives. We have picnics, and we go from home to home for little parties and then I have my sisters too and they live here. You know, we just enjoy family. I have brothers and sisters and he has all brothers. So that gives me a lot of sister-in-laws too. So we are very family people — very home people.

This kind of extended family support appears to lessen the trauma of the disintegration of the family of procreation. Most families, however, find themselves far more isolated from "kinfolk" in the modern American city.

SUMMARY AND CONCLUSIONS

We have seen that several conditioning situations present themselves as potential aids in the socialization of parents for postparental life. These situations provide an opportunity to anticipate postparental roles, not by taking the role of the other in the usual sense, but by experiencing analogous situations which are quasi-postparental and which enable the parents to play-at anticipated roles. There is the underlying value in our society on change for its own sake — a value which can be applied to the particular case of change in the family structure; there are the temporary departures of children during the adolescent years for college, service in the armed forces, and a variety of other reasons; there is the modern complex of urban high school life, which can move the children into a world which is foreign to their parents; there are the exigencies of the work situation which often remove the middle-class father from the family during the years when the children are growing up; there is the myth and the reality of the mother-in-law which some mothers internalize as lessons for themselves. In addition, remnants of the older extended family pattern which tend to reduce the impact of the transition cannot be ignored.

Socialization for Postparental Life

It was stated earlier that *theoretically* this could be assumed to be a difficult transition to make, largely because of the absence of role models — the absence of socialization to play postparental roles. However, middle-aged couples whose children have left home indicate that there are opportunities for them to learn these new roles before they are thrust upon them.

It was also stated earlier that much of the descriptive literature indicates that this is a difficult period of life. By and large such observations are based on clinical experiences with persons who have so much difficulty in making the transition that they must seek outside help. The small group of postparental spouses interviewed by the present writer represent a random sample of such people who discussed their lives in their own living room. Although definite conclusions cannot be drawn from the responses of this small fragment of the population, they have managed to provide us with some notion of the variety of alternative modes of anticipatory socialization available to their ilk. It would appear from their comments that it is reasonable to assume that people do have opportunities to prepare for postparental life and, in addition, that most of them take advantage of these opportunities.

This phase of the family cycle is seen by the majority of middle-aged spouses as a time of new freedoms: freedom from the economic responsibilities of children; freedom to be mobile (geographically); freedom from housework and other chores. And, finally, freedom to be one's self for the first time since the children came along. No longer do the parents need to live the self-consciously restricted existence of models for their own children: "We just take life easy now that the children are grown. We even serve dinner right from the stove when we're alone. It's hotter that way, but you just couldn't let down like that when your children are still at home."

References

1. Benedict, Ruth. "Continuities and Discontinuities in Cultural Conditioning," *Psychiatry*, Vol. 1 (1938), pp. 161–167.
2. Burgess, Ernest W., and Harvey Locke. *The Family: From In-*

stitution to Companionship. New York: American Book Co., 1945.

3. Cavan, Ruth S. *The American Family.* New York: Thomas Y. Crowell Company, 1953.

4. Cavan, Ruth S. *Marriage and Family in the Modern World.* New York: Thomas Y. Crowell Company, 1960.

5. Christensen, Harold. *Marriage Analysis.* New York: The Ronald Press Company, 1950.

6. Deutscher, Irwin. "Married Life in the Middle Years: A Study of the Middle Class Urban Postparental Couple." Ph.D. dissertation, Department of Sociology, University of Missouri, 1958.

7. Duvall, Evelyn M. *In-Laws: Pro and Con.* New York: Association Press, 1954.

8. Duvall, Evelyn M. "Implications for Education Through the Family Life Cycle," *Marriage and Family Living*, Vol. 20 (November 1958), pp. 334–342.

9. Duvall, Evelyn M., and Reuben Hill. *The Dynamics of Family Interaction.* National Conference on Family Life, Inc., 1948 (mimeographed).

10. Freedman, Ronald, Pascal K. Whelpton, and Arthur A. Campbell. *Family Planning, Sterility and Population Growth.* New York: McGraw-Hill Book Company, Inc., 1959.

11. Glick, Paul C. "The Family Cycle," *American Sociological Review*, Vol. 12 (April 1947), pp. 164–169.

12. Glick, Paul C. "The Life Cycle of the Family," *Marriage and Family Living*, Vol. 17 (February 1955).

13. Hiltner, Helen J. "Changing Family Tasks of Adults," *Marriage and Family Living*, Vol. 15 (May 1953), pp. 110–113.

14. House, Floyd N. "The Natural History of Institutions," in *The Development of Sociology.* New York: McGraw-Hill Book Company, Inc., 1936, pp. 141–157.

15. Hughes, Everett C. *Men and Their Work.* Glencoe, Ill.: The Free Press, 1959.

16. Kinsey, Alfred, Wardell B. Pomeroy, Clyde E. Martin, and Paul H. Gebhard. *Sexual Behavior in the Human Female.* Philadelphia: W. B. Saunders Company, 1953.

17. Lowrey, Lawson G. "Adjustment Over the Life Span," in George Lawton (ed.), *New Goals for Old Age.* New York: Columbia University Press, 1943, pp. 8–9.

18. Pollak, Otto. *Social Adjustment in Old Age*. New York: Social Science Research Council, Bulletin 59, 1948.
19. Sirjamaki, John. *The American Family in the Twentieth Century*. Cambridge, Mass.: Harvard University Press, 1953.
20. Sussman, Marvin B. "Parental Participation in Mate Selection and Its Effect Upon Family Continuity," *Social Forces*, Vol. 32 (October 1953), pp. 76–77.
21. Tibbitts, Clark. "National Aspects of an Aging Population," in Clark Tibbitts and Wilma Donahue (eds.), *Growing in the Older Years*. Ann Arbor, Mich.: The University of Michigan Press, 1951.
22. Waller, Willard, and Reuben Hill. *The Family: A Dynamic Interpretation*. New York: The Dryden Press, 1951.

27

Self and Role in Adjustment During Old Age

RUTH SHONLE CAVAN

ROCKFORD COLLEGE

The increasing national attention to the problems of older persons has concentrated on such material questions as income, health, housing, and recreation. While this emphasis is appropriate in that public opinion tends to focus on public solutions to problems, and these material problems are most directly susceptible to public or political solutions, the approach neglects the social-psychological problems characteristic of aging in American society. The latter problems are illuminated by interactionist concepts, as Ruth Cavan shows, and her analysis offers a basis for a realistic attack on these problems. This chapter picks up the life cycle where the last one left off. Although there are substantive similarities and differences in the transitions into the postparental and the elderly role, it is clear that the abstract process of socialization is the same regardless of the particular phase of the family cycle.

The concepts of self-conception, role-taking, and role-playing — as developed by George H. Mead (7), Charles Horton Cooley

(3), and others (1, 4, 8, 10) — have possibilities for a significant analysis of adjustment to old age.* They are here applied, first, to retirement from occupation, which is commonly accepted as the most acute adjustment that the older man has to make. The concepts are further tested in brief analyses of the adjustment of the retired man to his family, the adjustment of the widow, and adjustment to grandparenthood. These situations should be regarded as illustrative of the way in which the three concepts may illuminate adjustment in old age.

Retirement

Both self-conceptions and the social roles through which they find expression are culturally determined. Moreover, some conceptions and roles have higher public esteem than others. For example, the "ideal" male self-conception is the mature adult who is at the height of his powers in a position that he has reached competitively through his own efforts. The self-made man in general is more highly respected than the one who steps in at the top because of family contacts; the employed man outclasses the unemployed or the retired; the self-supporting man has a higher status than the one who depends upon some form of assistance or pension, unless he has earlier contributed to the pension. These different valuations are extremely important at the time of retirement.

At the point of retirement, we may make a generalized picture of the male. He has a well-ingrained self-image as competent, successful at some level of work, usefully productive, self-supporting, and able to provide for his family. This image has been built up over years of time by the favorable reactions of his family, friends, co-workers, and those segments of society whose opinion he values. He has, moreover, found a kind of work — a social role — that permits him to express his self-image satisfactorily, and he is firmly incorporated into a physical environment and a group of co-workers which make it possible for him to carry out his role.

Using the concepts employed above, let us consider what hap-

* The present paper was read at the Twentieth Groves Conference on Marriage and the Family, May 1, 1957, East Lansing, Michigan.

pens at the point of compulsory retirement.[1] First, the means of carrying out the social role disappears: the man is a lawyer without a case, a bookkeeper without books, a machinist without tools. Second, he is excluded from his group of former co-workers; as an isolated person he may be completely unable to function in his former role. Third, as a retired person, he begins to find a different evaluation of himself in the minds of others from the evaluation he had as an employed person. He no longer sees respect in the eyes of former subordinates, praise in the faces of former superiors, and approval in the manner of former co-workers. The looking glass composed of his former important groups throws back a changed image: he is done for, an old-timer, old fashioned, on the shelf. Fourth, he cannot accept this new evaluation for several reasons. He has had the old self-image for so many years that it has become part and parcel of him and is no longer dependent upon the current reflection of himself that he sees in the words and gestures of others. Long ago he internalized satisfying group reflections which now form a kind of independent self-conception. His self-image therefore is in conflict with the reflection he now finds in the attitudes and actions of others. Any movement toward solving the conflict is made difficult because the new self-image offered by those around him is of lower valuation than his internalized self-image.

Therefore at retirement we have a man still motivated by his old self-conception, but separated from his previous roles and many of his previous evaluative groups. He is a true social isolate. Moreover, the faint traces of a new self-image that he sees reflected in old and perhaps new groups is distasteful and unrewarding. His emotional reactions are likely to be distressing.

We will not go into the changes in this general sequence made by such factors as ill health, voluntary retirement, or retirement of the person who dislikes his work.

Let us look rather at what would be necessary to give a retired person a satisfying adjustment experience.[2] The same concepts are involved as in the original building up of a self-image.

[1] For additional light on retirement, see Dubin (5), Havighurst and Albrecht (6, Chapter 7), and Streib (9).
[2] The article by Becker and Carper (1) on the process of identification of young men with an occupation has implications for retirement adjustment, since some of the same processes are involved.

Self and Role in Adjustment During Old Age

First, there would need to be a culturally approved set of values for old age as the basis for a new self-conception. At present, old age is more or less of a vacuum; culturally, it has few real values. Second, these values would have to be accepted and respected by society itself and by the specific groups to which the retired person belonged. Without these two steps the retired person is almost helpless to change his self-image in a constructive manner. His new self-image will develop as his original self-image developed — through finding in others an evaluation of himself as a retired person which he can internalize. Third, new roles are needed through which the retired person may find expression for his new self-image.

Two difficulties exist at present. (*a*) To be satisfying, the new self-image offered by society should be the equivalent in respect of the one he has lost through retirement. A solution is found in partial retirement or in the transition from active worker to consultant. The old self-image may then be retained. Other solutions are less happy. One new self-conception offered to the retired man is the man of leisure who makes a career of leisure-time activities. While recreation has a definite value, to make a career of recreation, hobbies, and the like goes against deeply instilled values. The playboy has never held the respect given to the industrious producer. Another new conception offered by society is the image of oneself as old — that is, identification with old age itself. The names of clubs often suggest simply an old age self-conception: Golden Age Club, Borrowed Time Club, Three-Quarter Century Club, Senior Citizens, and so on. Thus the lawyer, doctor, philanthropist, shop superintendent, and foreman are all invited to stop being their former selves and to become generalized old age selves.

(*b*) The second difficulty is that many retired men have no real social group to replace their former co-workers. Many recreational and other programs are offered to the retired by social welfare or recreational workers, who make up a group in which the retired man does not have membership. Recall that the self-image is created by the evaluation of a group in which the person has membership. In time, the recreational club may form its own social group exclusive of social workers and may create some new self-conceptions. Such self-conceptions are often limited, however, in that they may not be capable of expression in any group except the club itself.

The present rush to find activities to fill leisure time for old people will not solve the problem of retirement adjustment satisfactorily. The two basic ingredients for adjustment are a culturally approved concept of an old age self held in respect by groups that are meaningful to the old person, and provision to express overtly the implications of the self-image. These elements usually are not present in the present programs devised for the old.

Adjustment of the Retired Man to His Family

An important adjustment that the retired man has to make is to his family. At the time a man retires his immediate family usually consists only of his wife. The wife, like the husband, has a long established self-image. For a woman now in her sixties, the basic self-image is usually that of wife, mother, homemaker, with a peripheral self of church or community worker, which is in reality but an extension of the homemaker self. Her image has been reflected with approval by family, friends, and community. Her overt role has consisted in establishing the tone of the home, doing or managing the housework, planning and purchasing, giving her husband sympathy and support in his work, and in earlier years rearing children. She has already made one change in her self-image when her children married and left home. Although this change is difficult for some women, it actually is less difficult than the retirement adjustment of the husband. The wife still receives a favorable reflection of herself from those around her, for her married and self-supporting children are a credit to her; and she retains much of the old self-conception and attendant role in continuing as homemaker and companion for her husband. Moreover, society has provided a new self-image for the woman who finds her life too constricted after children leave. The middle-aged employed woman now is socially accepted, and many types of work are open to her. She may devise some mixture of the old and new selves or she may discard the old homemaker self-image and develop a new employed-woman self-image. However, with the present group of retired husbands, the percentage of working wives is low, and the self-image usually is that of wife, homemaker, and retired mother.

Before the retirement of the husband, the self-images and the social roles of husband and wife were neatly dovetailed. It was conceded that the husband's role had slightly higher social status and that he was the head of the family. In her own home, however, the wife reigned supreme. Her self-conception included her queenship in the dominion of the home.

When the retired husband finds himself without his usual means of expression of his self-conception through his work role, he may try to work out a new role at home, without materially changing his self-image. Like a bull in a china shop, we have a man whose self-conception tells him to be competent, decisive, and productive, electing to express this self in a situation in which the available roles are already well filled by his wife, who, within her home, visualizes herself as competent, decisive, and productive. The husband's entrance into the situation tends to create tension in the former coordination between himself and his wife with respect both to their self-images and their roles. The husband sometimes attempts to express his superior status by assuming the decision-making roles in the home; or he may become a self-appointed expert, either criticizing or making suggestions regarding the way in which his wife manages the home. In thus attempting to give expression to his self-conception, he threatens his wife's image of herself. The wife is not opposed to having help in her housekeeping, but her self-conception calls for subordinates who take directions from her. Here, then, is a serious conflict between husband and wife in terms of their self-conceptions and roles. The problem is not one of what housework the husband will do, but of how the self-conceptions of husband and wife will be readjusted. If she retains her superior status and its self-image, his self-conception is damaged; if the husband takes control, the wife's self-conception is damaged.

Often husband and wife go through a period of incipient or actual conflict while self-images and roles are adjusted to a new orientation. Often these adjustments work out very well, especially if increasing age diminishes the desire of both husband and wife for full-time work. In other families, however, little change occurs in the self-images. Accommodation may be made only in roles, as some functions are assigned to the husband and the two overtly carry out coordinated roles. But each may feel dissatisfied and frustrated, with the result that there is bickering between the two.

WIDOWHOOD

Eventually each family dwindles to one person, and this person is more likely to be the wife than the husband. Only the widow will be discussed.

Instead of looking at widowhood only in terms of loneliness and lack of support, it is helpful to consider it also in terms of self and role. As we have just seen, the self-conceptions as well as the roles of husband and wife become well coordinated during the period when the husband is working; after the husband's retirement, and a transitional period of tensions, the coordination may become even closer with a new orientation. The death of the husband therefore severely disturbs the self-image of the wife. In a sense the two self-images have come to form one unit, a kind of family self-conception carried out jointly by husband and wife. Must the widow expand her self-image to include that of her husband, or must the family concept shrink to match her self-image? One may surmise that sometimes one thing happens and sometimes the other. Some widows seem to acquire the attributes of their former husbands; other widows never seem to recover from the bisecting blow of death. The widow may assume the overt roles or tasks of her husband, but this move may be because of necessity. It is in the intangible adjustment of self-image that the heart of the problem of adjustment lies.

If the widow is to modify her self-image, we must go back again to the conditions under which new self-images arise — the culturally acceptable pattern for self-conceptions, and groups of which the widow is a member which will help her achieve a new self-image through their approving evaluation of her change. Fortunately in the case of widowhood, the culture has devised several appropriate self-conceptions. It is important also to recall that the widow usually retains at least some of her old group memberships. She will receive a favorable reflection from her groups if she is courageous, if she attacks practical problems realistically, if she increases her civic or church work, and so forth.

It is at the point of widowhood that adult children often enter the picture, sympathetically offering the mother a home with the family of one of them. If the shock of death has been severe or if there are not sufficient financial resources for continued independence, such a move may be wise. It involves, however, some serious changes in self-conceptions for all concerned. We will consider primarily the situation of the widow. She is now very much in the position of the man who has experienced compulsory retirement. She retains her former self-image as competent housekeeper, companion to her husband, and so forth. But she has no way in which to enact the appropriate roles to give expression to this self-image. As in any well-coordinated household, the members of the younger family have developed self-images and roles that fit together to produce a unified family. It often seems impossible for such a unified family to open to admit an old relative in any except a subordinate — and, to the old person, almost disgraceful — status. Moreover, if the move has carried the widow into another city, she loses her supporting group of friends. Her children's friends are kind to her but do not accept her as an important person with a self of her own. She is Charlie's aunt or Ida's mother. Hence the widow who moves into a younger functioning family in a new community has none of the elements for the construction of a satisfying new self-image. Unless the family is wise enough to help her find a new and respected self-image and accompanying role, she is likely to deteriorate rapidly in personality or to become chronically complaining and disgruntled. It should be emphasized here that the step needed is not to provide love and activities alone, but also to provide a new and valued self-conception which will receive approval and which may be appropriately expressed.

GRANDPARENTHOOD

Finally, a word about the grandparent self-conception. Often this self-conception has been absorbed into the personality during the fifties or early sixties, especially on the part of women. In fact, some women visualize themselves as grandparents before a child is born and eagerly await the birth of a grandchild so that they may express the grandmother self-image in an appropriate role.

During middle age, men may be proud of their grandchildren, but perhaps do not savor the role completely until after retirement. At first, the man may have some difficulty in accepting the grandfather self as the culture defines it. In the patriarchal and to some extent in the patri-centered family, the grandfather self-image was one of authority and responsibility. Now, however, change has swept away this often satisfying self-image. As the culture defines the grandfather self-image and social role they are maternal in nature. The approved grandparent self is really a grandmother self-conception, whether the holder is the grandfather or the grandmother. Unless the child's own father is dead or not functioning in his role, the grandfather has little opportunity to function in the father role, which is one of financial supporter and source of authority as well as teacher and friend. The child's father guards his self-image and role jealously because they contribute to his conception as head of his family. The maternal role is less precisely defined and may be filled concurrently or successively by a number of different people, each of whom may develop some degree of maternal self-image. In this array of people who fill a maternal role toward the child the retired grandfather takes his place. He must see himself in relation to his grandchild not as a secondary father but as a minor form of mother. His role is to baby-sit, spoon in food, and trundle the baby around in its carriage. If he resents the role, he may arouse some resentment in turn from the baby's mother, who is often pressed for a responsible subordinate. If he accepts the role and develops a slightly masculine grandmother self-image, he may receive an emotional experience that he missed when his own children were young and his time was absorbed in earning a living for them. But to enjoy it he must genuinely be able to acquire a grandparent conception of himself and discover the values in the conception, for the self-image and the role differ widely from the man-of-affairs self and role which dominated his earlier years. Fortunately, the elements for developing a grandparent self are present in the culture. Since children are highly valued in the United States, the mere possession of a grandchild brings respect (or even envy) from friends and from society in general. Since the maternal type of grandparent image is virtually the only one in existence in the United States, the retired man trundling the baby carriage does not feel out of place. The baby comes to love the kindly man who helps to care for it, and the hurried mother adds her thanks. Thus the members of the man's social group approve of the self-image and he sees himself reflected on all sides as a good grandfather filling a valued position.

CONCLUSION

This essay has attempted to point out the way in which the concepts of self-conception based upon role-taking (Mead) and social role-playing can be helpful in analyzing certain kinds of adjustment in old age and in suggesting how better adjustment could be manipulated. The necessary elements for forming, maintaining, or modifying self-conceptions are socially approved self-images and social roles for their expression, and a group that supports these self-images and roles. To achieve or modify a self-image, the person must be a member of one of these groups and must value the group's evaluation of himself. He will then incorporate within himself the self-image approved by the group. He will need continued membership and the opportunity to enact an appropriate role. These elements are all present at the point of original formulation of self-images in youth, but are partially or completely lacking at the point of reformulations in old age.

References

1. Becker, Howard S., and James W. Carper. "The Development of Identification with an Occupation," *American Journal of Sociology*, Vol. 61 (January 1956), pp. 289–298.
2. Cavan, Ruth S., Ernest W. Burgess, Robert J. Havighurst, and Herbert Goldhamer. *Personal Adjustment in Old Age*. Chicago: Science Research Associates, 1949.
3. Cooley, Charles Horton. *Human Nature and the Social Order*. New York: Charles Scribner's Sons, 1922 (rev. ed.).

4. Coutu, Walter. "Role-Playing vs. Role-Taking: An Appeal for Clarification," *American Sociological Review*, Vol. 16 (April 1951), pp. 180–187.

5. Dubin, Robert. "Industrial Workers' Worlds: A Study of the 'Central Life Interests' of Industrial Workers," *Social Problems*, Vol. 3 (January 1956), pp. 131–142. [Reprinted as Chapter 13 of the present volume.]

6. Havighurst, Robert J., and Ruth Albrecht. *Older People*. New York: Longmans, Green and Co., 1953.

7. Mead, George Herbert. *Mind, Self, and Society*, ed. by Charles W. Morris. Chicago: The University of Chicago Press, 1934.

8. Merrill, Francis E. "The Self and the Other: An Emerging Field of Social Problems," *Social Problems*, Vol. 4 (January 1957), pp. 189–207.

9. Streib, Gordon F. "Morale of the Retired," *Social Problems*, Vol. 3 (April 1956), pp. 270–276.

10. Turner, Ralph H. "Role-Taking, Role Standpoint, and Reference-Group Behavior," *American Journal of Sociology*, Vol. 61 (January 1956), pp. 316–328.

28

A Social-Psychological
Theory of Neurosis

ARNOLD M. ROSE

UNIVERSITY OF MINNESOTA

By some historical accident, the study of the unhappy or disturbed personality has been assigned to physicians, perhaps the least equipped of all investigators of man to deal with the problem. Unlike others in the biological sciences, physicians have next to no training in scientific methodology, and — more important — they are trained to look for causation in the organism rather than the organization. By reacting against their training and social heritage, and led by one of the outstanding geniuses in human history (Sigmund Freud), physicians in the psychoanalytic tradition have been able to develop a significant theory of personality disturbances. But the biologistic heritage of even these brave innovators has prevented them from examining social-psychological factors fully. The present essay offers one possible social-psychological contribution to the understanding of personality disturbance, an interactionist one.

The analysis of the causes of human behavior of certain types

537

has often been beset by two types of logical difficulties.* One is the monistic explanation in which the search for causation is directed to only one set of determining forces. In the case of pathological behavior (psychosis and neurosis), the monism has most frequently been that of biological determinism or of explanation in terms of disturbances in the transfer of libido (as analyzed by Freud and his followers). The most diverse forms of mental disturbances, in individuals with the most diverse life histories, have been analyzed in terms of the same set of causes. The effort to correct this error by means of a theory involving pluralistic causation has sometimes resulted in the second logical difficulty to be mentioned here. This is the procedure of discovering a list of causes without indicating their relative importance or their manner of interaction. It is not particularly helpful to know that biological, psychological, economic, cultural, and social interactional forces underlie the diverse manifestations of mental disturbances, even though this may be a true statement. Logicians have found that useful causal theories distinguish between the one "sufficient" cause and the several "necessary" causes for a given type of phenomenon — thus gaining some of the advantages of a monistic explanation — and that causation generally involves a complex interplay of forces in which each is effective only when in certain relationship to others.

When now offering a social-psychological theory of neurosis, I wish to avoid both of these errors even though the theory does not yet have sufficient empirical grounding to allow me to be sufficiently detailed concerning the exact relationship of this factor to other causal factors. We must be able to conceive that a given behavioral disturbance has its roots in a given social-personal situation, but that this situation operates to cause the mental disturbance through the creation of physiological unbalances and that it is necessary to restore the physiological balance as well as the social-personal situation to remedy the mental disturbance. To use a perhaps overly simple example: A "worry" induced by relatively insuperable objective social conditions may

* A condensed form of this paper was presented at the Fourth World Congress of Sociology (Stresa, Italy; August 1959), and appears in the *Proceedings* of that Congress (published by the International Sociological Association; Louvain, Belgium, 1960).

result in such a deprivation of sleep that the physiological changes ensuing produce mental disturbances. A necessary step in the treatment of this problem might very well be the administration of drugs to induce sleep, even though the "cause" of the problem is a social one. It is difficult to get out of the theological habit of separating the mind from the body and to recognize that all mental processes are also body processes, so that nothing social or psychological ever happens without biological concomitants. And yet it is proper and necessary to make a social or psychological analysis. In other words, our theory does not claim to exhaust the causal statements that might legitimately be made concerning neurosis; it merely suggests one significant variable which is relatively amenable to control. We must also learn to conceive that a given theory may be highly appropriate for the understanding of one kind of mental disturbance, but quite inappropriate for another kind of mental disturbance. It is not necessary to claim that our hypothesis explains each and every manifestation of neurosis; we merely expect that it helps to explain most forms of neurosis, and we leave the explanation of marginal forms of neurosis to other theorists.

With these cautions before us, a specific social-psychological theory of neurosis will be set forth. Any claim that this theory covers all the varied forms of mental disturbance is specifically denied, although — because the dividing line between neurosis and psychosis is often thin or arbitrary — it might be that such borderline phenomena as "involutional melancholia," at least in its mild form, are capable of being understood in terms of the theory. Our definition of neurosis will simply be "inability to act reasonably effectively[1] — within the material means and limitations present — for the achievement of socially acceptable and personally accepted[2] goals, because of anxiety or because of com-

[1] What is reasonably effective action is, of course, not precise and somewhat arbitrary. The criterion is what the individual and his associates consider to be reasonably effective action.

[2] By "socially acceptable" is meant acceptance by the valued associates of the individual — that is, his reference membership groups. By using the term "acceptance" rather than "desired" we imply that the groups are at least willing to tolerate the individual's goals, even if they do not always evaluate them highly. By juxtaposing "socially acceptable" and "personally accepted" we imply a modicum of harmony in goals between the individual and his society, not a perfect harmony or conformity.

pulsions which camouflage anxiety." The theory does not rule out the possibility of other factors being important in the etiology of neurosis — as, for example, a traumatic experience which conditions an individual to certain hysterical behavior. The theory further refers to only one social-psychological element in what must necessarily be a complicated matrix of causation. The theory applies only to the behavior covered in our definition of neurosis; if another definition is used the theory may be rendered inappropriate.

Our theory is based on the social psychology of Charles H. Cooley and George H. Mead, who held that a "self," reflecting the reactions of others toward it, is an important intervening variable in human conduct. Observations of human behavior in a variety of settings have supported this conception and recently Manford Kuhn has undertaken laboratory experiments which demonstrate that one's opinion of oneself is significantly influenced by a sharply negative reaction from others concerning oneself.

The hypothesis offered here takes up where Kuhn leaves off. A factor in the chain of events leading to neurotic behavior is the induction of a person's negative attitude toward himself, and this may develop in a variety of ways — not only by sharply negative reactions from others. A significant and consistent pattern of self-deprecation, whether conscious or not, is the independent variable. The repression of this attitude may result in hysterical forms of neurosis, rather than the more direct anxiety symptoms. The individual's negative attitude toward himself is related in different degrees and ways to other people's reaction toward him. It is an essential element of Cooley's concept of the "looking-glass self" and of Mead's concept of the "me" that part of the self is a reflection — albeit sometimes distorted — of other people's reactions to the person in question. If the reaction of others is generally negative, and the individual gets a correct perception of this negative reaction, and if he accepts this negative evaluation, our proposition is that the individual becomes neurotic. In other words, an element in the chain of causes leading to neurosis is held to be the social-psychological factor of psychological self-mutilation. The psychoanalyst Carl Jung recognized this in speaking of a sense of "loss of significance" as a major factor in adult neurosis (4). A depreciated or "mutilated" self is a major factor in the development of a neurosis, we hypothesize, because an individual's ability to accept strongly held values of any kind and to act effectively to achieve those values is a function of his conception of himself — a conception that he is an adequate, worth-while, effective, and appreciated person. The mental state is similar to that of the person who commits what Durkheim calls "egoistic" suicide. The difference lies solely in that the individual either retains a compunction against suicide or else is not sufficiently organized to engage in the act of suicide. The psychoanalyst Alfred Adler had a comparable self-image theory of neurosis, although he tended to limit the concept of a negative self-image to those who had an "organ inferiority."

Certain temporary phenomena should not be confused with the more permanent self-devaluation here considered. Some negative reactions from others, some erroneous interpretations of others' reactions as unfavorable to ourselves, occasional moods of mild depression, are a part of everyday experience and hardly incapacitate an individual except for a very short time. The acceptance of a negative attitude toward oneself has to occur over a period of time to produce a neurosis. There is one significant exception to this: a psychological trauma, a crippling single incident of sharp self-devaluation, may create a neurosis for a significant period of time, although the individual generally recovers if a chain of negative events does not follow.

It is clear that the interactional process is central in this theory of neurosis. Rejection and devaluation by others are probably the most important cause of devaluation of self, provided the individual is not so psychotic or psychopathic that he cannot perceive the opinions of others.[3] Of course, an accurately perceived negative evaluation from others may be rejected by the individual concerned, but in such a case the individual generally has accepted what is for him the higher, more valued opinion of a small select group — perhaps even a group not in immediate social contact with him. The "looking-glass self" is not a mere reflection.

---

[3] There are other sources of incorrect perceptions of the opinions of others — including institutionalized sources. We are referring here to grossly incorrect perceptions, which we believe to be associated with psychosis or psychopathy.

it involves selection and evaluation, and hence the resulting self-image is far from being the image of the individual as seen by others with whom the individual interacts.

This selective and evaluative process can also give rise to a second type of self-disparagement — that in which the individual selects the negative reactions of others and gives them prime importance among the wide range of others' reactions to build his conception of himself. Persons who do this have a perfectionist attitude, and even slight blows to their egos are accorded a subjective importance out of all proportion to their objective importance (in the eyes of a neutral observer). Such a perfectionist or "over-sensitive" attitude probably grows out of certain childhood experiences of a harsh nature, and hence may be thought of as psychogenic. At any rate, the tendency to overrate the negative reactions of others serves to inflict regular blows on one's conception of self. Over the course of time, our hypothesis holds, this is a link in the chain of causes that produce neurosis.

It is to be noted that at first these two types of neurotics are able to communicate with, and receive communications from, others as well as non-neurotic people can. There is no immediate interruption of communication such as is generally associated with psychosis. In fact, it is in the process of communication that the neuroses develop. However, if the self-deprecation persists and becomes greatly exaggerated, communication becomes interrupted and/or distorted. The disturbed individual concentrates his attention on himself to the partial exclusion of all other external stimuli. His very preoccupation with the unworthiness, uselessness, and hopelessness of his self tends to restrict communication with others. Others no longer have to carry on their deprecation from the outside — although they may tend to do so as the individual fails to conform to their social pressures — for the self-deprecatory process comes to be reinforced by itself. The individual's obvious unhappiness, which makes him unattractive to others, and his own concentration of attention on himself, tend to isolate him. Thus there are certain tendencies toward an interruption of communication and a withdrawal from reality which are productive of a psychosis on the border of neurosis — usually called "involutional melancholia," at least in its milder form. On the other hand, unless the individual withdraws himself physically from social relations, the usual stimuli of everyday life intrude on his attention and keep him in some touch with reality. Thus the neurotic is only partly out of touch with reality, insofar as he over-selects the negative responses of others to the relative exclusion of the positive ones and insofar as his attention is concentrated on himself to the partial exclusion of some external stimuli; but if the neurotic further withdraws himself from society and broods almost exclusively on his unhappy self and its psychic pains, an involutional process with melancholia as its external manifestation will result. Karl Menninger describes the similarity of involutional melancholia to the neuroses:

> In this condition (melancholia) sufficient contact with reality may be maintained so that the individual, for all his self-destructiveness, does not endanger the lives of others, and may even co-operate in efforts to redirect or reshape his own life. For this reason, melancholia is sometimes described as a neurosis rather than a psychosis. But some victims of melancholia abandon all loyalty to reality and may be extremely deluded and even homicidal. The mechanisms are the same as in the so-called neurotic form, but the surrender of object attachment and of reality testing here is much greater (7, p. 213).

Davidoff expresses the ambiguous distinction between neurosis and involutional melancholia by holding that there is a difference between "the nonpsychotic involutional syndrome" and "the involutional psychosis." (2, p. 189)

The symptoms characteristic of involutional melancholia are those of extreme anxiety and depression. The melancholic individual is able to communicate with others, but in this communication he immediately makes it clear that he has a highly negative attitude toward himself. His inability, failure, and unworthiness are drawn to exaggerated proportions. A melancholic man will typically emphasize his belief that his life has been a failure. A melancholic woman will typically emphasize that she is not capable of doing anything right. The bodily symptoms are appropriate to these attitudes: there is much weeping and whining, wringing of the hands, negative shaking of the head, "long" expression on the face, high body tension. The melancholic's stated belief that nothing is worth while for him (except perhaps for something obviously unobtainable) is reflected in his activity: sometimes futile gestures are made in the direction of doing something constructive, but most of the time the melancholic seems "content" to sit back and contemplate his miserable state in his usual agitated manner. Any slight incident of a mildly unpleasant sort is awarded great importance in the melancholic's thought and conversation; any incident of a pleasant sort is glossed over and quickly forgotten. Attempts at suicide are not uncommon.

Our examination of the statistical incidence of involutional melancholia, even recognizing the great inadequacy of most statistics on mental disorder, reveals two persistent facts: women are more likely to have involutional melancholia in our society than are men, and the women typically have their first onset between the ages of 45 and 55, while men have their onset typically between the ages of 55 and 70 (8). These facts have led many psychiatrists to associate melancholia with glandular changes going on in the body in connection with the loss of sexual powers, particularly with the menopause in women and other physiological changes associated with aging (2, pp. 187–204, esp. 188). But the facts are equally compatible with a social-psychological theory about the changes of life roles. Women in our society typically lose their child-rearing function and much of their household-caring function during the fifth decade of their lives, and men — whose sexual potency has been declining gradually since the age of 20 — typically lose their occupational functions at about the age of 65 and begin to foresee this loss about ten years earlier. The "normal" procedure at such a critical juncture is to assume a new life role, which is of course facilitated by some earlier preparation for taking on such a new life role. The process is easier for men, since the socially expected life role for men past the age of 65 is one of leisure (including hobbies, travel, puttering around the house). But it is more difficult for a woman at the age of 45 to assume a new life role, because she is too young to retire (both in terms of her physical strength and in terms of social expectations). Our culture does not specify a "typical" role for the middle-aged woman whose child-rearing days are over, and the choices before her involve new efforts and skills on her part: she can find a job commensurate with her social status and abilities, she can become regularly active in civic or social affairs, she can play a larger part in the lives of her husband or her now-grown children (who often do not want her "interference"). Because of lack of previously acquired skill, because of the difficulty in engaging in these activities when one begins them at the age of 45, because of the outside world's frequent resistance, a woman may often fail to make a satisfactory transition to a new role. A man between the ages of 55 and 60 may also fail, if he thinks of himself as a failure in his occupation and finds that he cannot compete with younger men, and if he has never developed any skills or interests in the uses of leisure, or if he is especially unhappy about retiring from his occupational role. Our culture values highly the occupational role for men and the child-rearing role for women, and when these are lost, the individual's value goes down sharply unless he can find a new role for himself. In certain other societies a middle-aged person automatically takes on a new role of influence and prestige, and there is no decline in the individual's sense of his own worth.

The relationship of these facts and interpretations to our theory of neurosis should now be apparent. People who, for one reason or another, fail to make a satisfactory role transition (which our culture requires at about the age of 45–50 for women and 60–65 for men), especially if they find that their achievements have not been up to their expectations and hence cannot retire content with their laurels, are likely to develop persistent negative attitudes toward themselves. The central element in this negative attitude is that life is meaningless. This entails a sense of worthlessness, a loss of motivation, a belief in one's inability to achieve anything worth while. Such a complex tends to be persistent, as our culture does not offer any ready solution of the problem, and no happy accident is likely to change the situation (as might occur in other difficult problems of life). The individual feels himself aged or aging, and this feeling adds to the sense of hopelessness. The result is a persistent psychological beating of the self with a circular intensification of the process. Soon the individual is no longer able to control his feelings of anxiety and depression. It is as though the individual commits suicide mentally, but forgets to do it, or loses the capacity to do it, physically. After deciding he is not going to have anything more to do with life, he finds himself still alive, with the usual sorts of body needs. The latter naturally become very annoying; hence they tend to become the major object of attention and chief source of worry. Many such persons do attempt suicide, but others have certain compunctions against it or fears of it.

This extreme form of neurosis is generally known to psychiatrists as involutional melancholia. Failure to make a subjectively satisfactory transition in life role is not the sole cause of persistent self-deprecation, of course, but it may very well be the most frequent cause. Also there seem to be certain types of personalities who are especially susceptible to melancholia, personalities who are especially rigid and hence least able to find new life roles when the culture does not automatically offer them (1, p. 412; 5; 6, p. 567; 9, p. 19).

The theory applies, of course, to milder forms of neurosis than involutional melancholia. In the case of compulsive-obsessive neuroses, the individual is hypothesized to seek reassurance — to combat his negative attitude toward himself — by some form of repetitive behavior. Repetition of thought or behavior provides a way of "hanging on," of assuring oneself that something is stable even when one does not have confidence in one's perceptions, actions, or thought processes because he conceives of himself as generally inadequate. The specific compulsion or obsession is thus a mere symptom, although the choice of it is undoubtedly related to some significant experience in the life of the neurotic individual.

If reality is persistently bleak, it might be wiser for the individual not to face it completely, at least not for a certain period until a sense of self-confidence can be restored. People have to be taught to avoid persistent self-deprecation, as much as they have to be taught to face reality. Modern Western culture is weak in the social crutches which tend to compensate individuals for personal dissatisfaction with life: the belief in a just hereafter, the belief that God sets trials for people to test them, a strong family and church system which forces people into activity despite their personal disinclination. In the modern Western setting where these things are weak or non-existent, the wise psychiatrist should function partly as a priest, not only in the sense that he can serve as a confessor to relieve guilt feelings and other repressions, but also in that he can help people to turn their minds temporarily from the misery of their personal lot. Such avoidance of reality is necessary if only to let the body restore its physiological balance, which is inevitably unbalanced by the persistent anxiety and depression.

Having a neurotic individual avoid reality is, of course, a temporary device, a first step, since — if our theory is correct — the cure of neurosis must involve changing his situation and/or getting him to redefine his situation. Both of these require contact with reality at least most of the time. If the basis of a neurosis is persistent self-deprecation because the individual is in an objectively unpleasant situation, such as having to face uniformly negative judgments on the part of others or finding oneself without a meaningful life role, a major part of treatment should not be psychotherapeutic but consist of helping the individual move into a more favorable situation. That is, the unfavored individual should be brought into a new social environment, and the roleless individual should be taught a new role. An effective psychotherapy must be allied with these procedures, and should consist in helping the individual to redefine his relationship to his environment. If, on the other hand, the difficulty is not "objective" but results from the neurotic person's tendency to interpret his social situation in personally unflattering terms, there is not any point to changing the situation, and psychotherapy is all-important. Part of the psychotherapy still consists, however, in helping the individual to redefine his situation — in this case, bringing the definition closer to reality. The problem of getting at the sources of the neurotic's tendency to interpret his social situation as more unfavorable to him than it objectively is, cannot be helped by our theory. Freudian or other familiar theories of neurosis would be more successful at this point in guiding psychotherapy. Shock or drug treatment has also been found to be successful in some cases in bringing the melancholic to recognize the social world around him and to realize his relationship to it, and this sometimes aids redefinition and hence at least is a partial "cure."
(3) Our own contribution here limits itself to a psychotherapy of redefining the situation, redefining the self through a redefinition of the situation, and to a broader treatment process which involves changing the objective social situation. The goal is the development of a positive attitude toward the self, and a realistic

recognition of the attainable ways in which the changing self can continue to function in a changing social environment.

This is not Couéism nor "positive thinking." The individual must *do* those things which are in accord with his own values and which reflect the values of some social group that he rates highly. He must be able to congratulate himself occasionally and receive congratulations from esteemed others. This involves his social actions and not merely his personal thoughts. The therapy, therefore, must include putting him into a situation where he can engage in self-satisfying action with some fair degree of success and where he can receive some degree of recognition by others for this success. If neither changing the situation nor redefining the situation is possible for a given neurotic individual — perhaps because of his advanced age — it may be that "adjustment" can be achieved only by psychologically separating the individual from the stark reality of his life. For such an individual, self-delusion may be the only alternative to complete apathy and depression or suicide. The important thing is to maintain the integrity and the value of the self, even if — in the extreme instance — this means loss of contact with reality.

References

1. Brew, M. F., and Eugene Davidoff. "The Involutional Psychoses, Prepsychotic Personality and Prognosis," *Psychiatric Quarterly,* Vol. 14 (1940).

2. Davidoff, Eugene. "The Involutional Psychoses," in Oscar J. Kaplan (ed.), *Mental Disorders in Later Life.* Stanford University, Calif.: Stanford University Press, 1945.

3. Fishbein, Isadore Leo. "Involutional Melancholia and Convulsive Therapy," *American Journal of Psychiatry,* Vol. 106 (August 1949), pp. 128–135.

4. Jung, Carl G. *Modern Man in Search of a Soul.* New York: Harcourt, Brace and Co., 1933.

5. Malamud, William, S. L. Sands, and Irene T. Malamud. "The Involutional Psychoses: A Socio-psychiatric Study," *Psychosomatic Medicine,* Vol. 3 (October 1941), pp. 410–426.

6. Malamud, William, S. L. Sands, Irene T. Malamud, and P. J. P. Powers. "The Involutional Psychoses: A Socio-psychiatric Fol-

low-Up Study," *American Journal of Psychiatry*, Vol. 105 (February 1949).

7. Menninger, Karl A. *Man Against Himself.* New York: Harcourt, Brace and Co., 1938.

8. Palatin, Phillip, and James F. MacDonald. "Involutional Psychoses," *Geriatrics*, Vol. 6 (1951).

9. Titley, W. "Prepsychotic Personality of Patients with Involutional Melancholia," *Archives of Neurology and Psychiatry*, Vol. 36 (1936).

29

Self-Conception and Physical Rehabilitation

THEODOR J. LITMAN

UNIVERSITY OF MINNESOTA

A sudden and drastic deterioration of the body is likely to result in a changed conception of the self. If Rose's hypothesis, stated in the preceding chapter, is correct — if the change results in a negative conception of the self — the individual becomes neurotic in the sense that he is unable to engage in effective action leading to his rehabilitation. If his conception of self remains positive, and yet realistically takes into account ("accepts") the physical deterioration, the individual is able to undertake the rigorous and often painful rehabilitation program, even when he knows he will never be physically whole again. In verifying these hypotheses, Theodor Litman demonstrates that interactionist theory has value for the practice of medicine. His study, in the methodological tradition of Alfred R. Lindesmith's study of drug addiction and Donald Cressey's study of embezzlement, makes a contribution to Mead's hypotheses concerning self-conception, as well as giving support to Rose's hypotheses about neurosis and self-acceptance. The parallel should also be noted between the present chapter and Irwin Deutscher's earlier chapter on delinquency, where the point was made that in order to solve a social problem one has to be concerned with popular definitions of the problem as well as with the behavior of the people who have or present the problem.

THE PROBLEM

Human behavior, in general, may be considered as a manifestation of three primary sets of influences: biogenic, sociogenic, and psychogenic.* Few human actions are the exclusive result of any one of these. Rather, most involve a complicated combination of all three. This is clearly illustrated in the case of the physically disabled. Consider, for example, the following account of the incontinence of the paraplegic by Dr. Morris Grayson of New York University's Bellevue Medical Center:

> Such a system definitely has a physical, psychological, and social component. The [paraplegic] patient cannot control his urine and feces because of the severance of the nervous control (physical); the patient may use this symptom as a means of expressing his hostility toward the environment or as a means of accentuating his dependent needs (psychological); the patient may refuse to leave his wheel chair because of the fear of voiding and being seen or smelled by the people around him (social). Thus to think of incontinence as a purely physical symptom is to ignore reality. Psychological and social pressures persist in the urogenital area whether the cord is severed or not. Finding the physical reason for a symptom does not exclude the psychological and social components. The same approach to other physical symptoms must be used if one is really to understand what is going on in the patient (21, p. 56).

The fact that social and psychological factors may play an important part in the care and treatment of the patient has been

* This paper is based on information derived from research undertaken as part of a larger project supported in part by a fellowship, MF10,468, from the Division of Research Grants, National Institutes of Health. I am greatly indebted to Professor Arnold Rose for his helpful suggestions in the formulation of the hypotheses and guidance of the study throughout its stages. A fuller report is available in my Ph.D. thesis at the University of Minnesota.

increasingly recognized by the medical profession itself. This has been particularly true in the field of physical rehabilitation. As Dr. Francis J. Braceland observed:

> Any physical anomaly, however benign, and whether constitutional or acquired, can be the source of serious disturbances in the life of an individual. A nose, the contour of which offends only the owner may be as formidable an obstacle to adjustment as a major amputation. The problems of rehabilitation are, therefore, extensive and extremely complex. They arise in the wake of accidents and crippling diseases and also with acute and chronic illnesses, and very importantly with the attrition of years. . . . Medicine is finding that to fulfill its obligations in a changing epidemiology and a changing culture, it is not enough to apply the insights and techniques of pure science. It is equally important to treat the patient against the background of his environment and in light of the personal, interpersonal and social meaning of the illness. Illness represents a serious threat to the patient as a self-sufficient, intact individual, and hidden forces operating within him may have much to do with its course and outcome. These influences cannot be ignored in any treatment program for any illness or any handicap, they spell the difference between success and failure in our efforts and they are indeed basic materials with which to work (9, p. 211).

A similar point of view has been expressed by the Director of the Office of Vocational Rehabilitation, Mary E. Switzer:

> This drive to accomplish his own rehabilitation must come from within himself and we must be sensitive too in the factors that can help or hinder establishing this indispensable primary base for rehabilitation. Increasingly we are learning that human motivation is influenced by many things. Especially important are the psychological and social factors of an individual's life. These factors are important to consider early in our planning for the whole program of rehabilitation for the individual and in the evaluation of each step of its development (44, p. iii).

It is not surprising, then, that a recent report of the Committee on Rehabilitation of the American Medical Association cited as one of its objectives the need to study the problems and interrelationships of medical, social, educational, and vocational aspects of rehabilitation (10).

Physical rehabilitation, broadly defined, envisages the maximal physical, mental, social, vocational, and economic recovery possible for any given condition (24, p. 43). While the goals attained may vary according to the individual case, Kessler and Abrahamson suggest that a thorough survey of both the patient and his environment is a prerequisite for the establishment of a program which will serve his ultimate purpose. With the disability itself considered as a limiting condition, increasing emphasis must be placed on the patient's innate and residual abilities (24).

Through the combined efforts of personnel from all services in the hospital, departments of physical medicine and rehabilitation attempt to accomplish their task by an appeal to the team approach (22, 37). Cognizant that the physician alone has neither the time nor technical skill necessary to provide all the services required by the severely involved physically handicapped patient during his course of treatment, the assistance of many professionally trained, paramedical personnel is mobilized. Staff members may include physical therapists, occupational therapists, rehabilitation nurses, clinical psychologists, social workers, vocational counselors and speech pathologists.[1] Together, as the "rehabilitation team," they provide the necessary services to permit each patient to achieve maximal independence within his own capabilities (22).

Despite this socio-psychological orientation, there has been relatively little social-psychological research on the problems of physical illness and rehabilitation. A few of the studies that have been made include those by Barker, Wright, Dembo and associates (3, 4, 6, 14, 15, 16, 46, 47) on acceptance and adjustment to physical disability; Seidenfeld (40, 41) and Davis (12, 13) on poliomyelitis; Mueller (30, 31), Thom (45), and Berger (7, 8) on the personality patterns of persons with spinal cord injuries; Schwartz (39) on the use of social workers in the treatment of left hemiplegia; and MacGregor (27) on disfigurement.

---

[1] Although professionally qualified within their own specialties, it is clearly understood that the paramedical staff is not trained to substitute for the physician in medical evaluation, diagnosis, or prescription (22).

Perhaps one of the most vexing problems encountered in the practice of physical medicine and rehabilitation is the differential response of the orthopedically disabled to their total treatment program. This is especially true with respect to the individual's application to the difficult work of physical therapy. There, ". . . acts formerly performed in an unthinking and automatic fashion now represent challenges to functionless nerve patterns and unresponsive joints and muscles. The most elementary forms of self-care must all be relearned arduously and often the physical equipment is inadequate for the task." (45, p. 473) Discussing the response of the spinal cord injured, Mueller observed:

> A certain amount of initial resistance was found in many patients to rehabilitation activities requiring physical and mental effort on their part. Characteristic reactions were: indifferent, ambivalent and depressive attitudes toward the future and the possibilities it could hold for them socially and vocationally, indecisiveness and feelings of insecurity; and assuming a submissive and dependent role in life, with accompanying immature emotional behavior (30, p. 191).

In an address given before the Thirty-third Annual Session of the American Congress of Physical Medicine and Rehabilitation, Schmidt described two types of patients commonly found in practice:

> Most patients accept their handicaps and appreciate what is being done for them and will cooperate fully in the treatment. These patients usually gain the maximum improvement in the shortest time. They are encouraged by every little improvement and strive to assist the therapists in their work.
> The other type is the individual who gives up. Such patients realize their disability but feel that they can never expect to regain any great measure of improvement. They go along in a half-hearted way, never display any enthusiasm and as soon as they leave the department, forget everything and instead of doing things to help them, they relax and allow the nurses to wait on them (38).

The effect of a rather sudden, often unexpected disablement upon an individual may necessitate a great deal of personal adjustment. For example, a robust mechanic and excellent woodsman may find that he is unable to use his legs or grasp even the simplest eating utensil with his hands. Such common activities as dressing, washing, and going to the bathroom become arduous chores. In addition to coming face to face with the realistic limitations and adaptations imposed by his condition, he must also modify his conception of self (6, 46). On the basis of the available evidence, Barker reports that one's attitude toward his disability may vary widely and have little relation to the degree of disability itself. It may, however, be related to the individual's pre- and post-morbid personality and experience (5, p. 85).

In our society, the "body whole" and "body beautiful" have attained high social value. The disabled, Barker and Wright note, "often is regarded by himself and others as inferior, not only with respect to his specific limitations but as a total person. He may feel shame, inferiority, even worthlessness. . . . [They] are confronted with a serious situation because two basic psychological needs of man are the need for self-esteem . . . and the need for social status. For optimal adjustment these needs must be satisfied in some degree." (6, p. 18) A similar view has been expressed by Kessler:

> Imperfection in nature is always more or less abhorrent to the human mind. Man has tended to make a fetish of beauty, and the human figure is regarded as acceptable only when it is normal. When it is abnormal, or deviates in any way from the ideal, the repulsion is equally strong. . . . because of the widely different public attitude, the cripple often comes to regard himself in the same manner and as a result of brooding, loneliness and ill-treatment actually becomes mentally as well as physically unstable (23, p. 19).

Unfortunately, although theoretically relevant and practically significant, few empirical studies have been directed to an examination of the relation between self-conception and physical disability. However, the research that has been done suggests that the relation is a significant one.

For example, Fishman, using projective techniques, found that the self-concept constituted one of the factors which determined adjustment to leg prosthesis among forty-eight above-the-knee

amputees (18). In another study of one hundred hospitalized
service amputees and plastic surgery cases, White, Wright, and
Dembo noted the following self-feelings associated with disability: (*a*) fear that it is not "me as a person but my injury" that
is of primary importance to the other; (*b*) fear that the injury
devaluates him as a person; (*c*) guilt connected with the feeling
of being a burden; (*d*) conflict between the desire for dependence
and independence; and (*e*) feelings of self-pity (46). Still another investigation of the differential effect of dissimilar disabilities upon self-perception led Shelsky to conclude that (*a*) an overt
or visible injury does not necessarily have more of an effect upon
self-concept than a non-visible injury or illness; (*b*) amputees can
more readily evaluate their abilities and disabilities than the tuber-
culous; (*c*) a physical loss seems to be incorporated into the
self-concept more adequately and with less general damage than
an all-pervasive illness such as tuberculosis (42).

While limited in number, these studies have served to demonstrate the integral relationship between self-conception and physical incapacity. Nevertheless, there are at least two questions
which as yet remain unanswered. First, to what extent does the
self-conception influence the patient's response to the rigorous
program of rehabilitation as instituted within the hospital setting? Second, is there a relationship between one's acceptance
of his disabled condition and his self-conception? It is to a consideration of these problems that the remarks to follow have
been addressed.

The emergence of "self" as a theoretical construction achieved
its most complete formulation within the rich tradition of symbolic interaction. To the symbolic interactionist, the self as "me"
may be perceived as the reflection of the attitude of one's fellows
toward himself. Mead and Cooley referred to the full development of self as an organization of the individual attitudes of
others into social or group attitudes which become an individual
reflection of the over-all systematic pattern of social behavior in
which both the individual and the others participate (11, 29).
The self, then, is comprised not only of individual attitudes but
an organization of the attitudes of the social groups to which
one belongs. The "I," or self-conception, on the other hand, is
the individual's reaction to the imagined response of others to

Self-Conception and Physical Rehabilitation

oneself. It is related to the response of others and the individual's perception of those responses. Outside this tradition, Alfred Adler, a psychoanalyst, has suggested that physical defects, congenital or acquired, may raise feelings of inferiority or inadequacy within the individual which in turn create various compensatory mechanisms in behavior (1, 2). It is upon this general, theoretical framework that the analysis to follow has been based.

Although analytically brilliant and rich in insight, the Mead-Cooley approach has often been charged with operational weakness. However, the investigations of Kuhn and McPartland (25, 26) and Reeder, Donohue, and Biblarz (34) among others in the past few years have demonstrated its empirical applicability. In this study, we have attempted through the use of social-psychological research procedures to determine the influence of self-conception upon patient response in physical rehabilitation. In general, our attention has been directed to an examination of two basic hypotheses:

1. There is a direct relationship between a person's conception of self and his response to a program of physical rehabilitation.

> (a) Patients with poor self-conceptions — that is, characterized by feelings of individual worthlessness, inadequacy, perceived social unacceptability — will tend to lack initiative, drive, effort, and cooperation in their rehabilitation program.
>
> (b) Patients who are able to evaluate the reactions of others toward the disability favorably and who possess feelings of personal adequacy and worth will actively engage in their care and treatment as instituted within a rehabilitation facility.

2. If an individual has been able to accept his disability and its limitations realistically, he will more likely maintain a favorable conception of self, even though his body is no longer able to function in the usual ways and others show various signs of concern, interest, and curiosity. In contrast, if he either is unable to accept his condition or does so poorly, his self-conception will be negative. On the basis of her examination of the autobiographical accounts of the physically handicapped, Wright suggests: ". . . when the person has a well-balanced, accepting attitude toward his disability, he is more likely to feel that others question him and stare at him because they simply wonder about

him — how he gets along, or how his prosthesis works . . . than when he himself is ashamed of his disability. If, however, the person basically rejects his disability and himself, he will tend strongly to resist the curiosity of others, feeling that he is being regarded negatively, with aversion and pity. His self-concept defines for him the kind of person he is as an 'object' of stimulation to others." (47, p. 209)

Research Procedures

One hundred orthopedically disabled patients, fifteen years of age and older, undergoing rehabilitative treatment at the Department of Physical Medicine and Rehabilitation, University of Minnesota Hospitals, and at the Elizabeth Kenny Institute, Minneapolis, Minnesota, were interviewed over a period of fifteen months.[2] As in any empirical study, the selection of the sample, to a large extent, determines the limitations and restrictions imposed upon any subsequent generalizations from the data found. Included in this study were only those disabilities which had a fairly sudden onset of accidental or disease origin, resulting in loss or impaired use of the extremities of a rather serious nature requiring extensive rehabilitation. The types of orthopedic conditions studied may be seen in Table 1.

In each case, the physical presence of the paralyzed member(s) was retained while use and function were inhibited. Since the body remains physically intact and the effects of disfigurement and distortion upon others are minimized, there is maximum opportunity for the individual's own evaluation of what has happened to him in relation to others to affect his self-conception. The possible effects of speech and memory problems led to the exclusion from consideration of patients with moderate to severe brain damage. Within the range of these criteria, the sample comprised all patients who underwent rehabilitation at the two

[2] Initially, 105 patients were interviewed. Five of these, however, were eliminated from the study for the following reasons: one patient had a past history of psychiatric disorder, one patient was under the age of 15, one patient's condition was psychiatric in origin rather than physiological or neurological, one patient was senile, and the results of one interview were invalidated by the respondent's failure to cooperate fully.

Self-Conception and Physical Rehabilitation
TABLE 1

Distribution of Sample by
Type of Disability

Disability	No. & %
Poliomyelitis	25
Paraplegia[a]	25
Quadriplegia	33
Guillian-Barré Syndrome	8
Hemiplegia (Right, Left)	6
Demyelinating Disease[b]	3
Total (N = 100)	100

[a] Also includes paraparesis and transverse-myelitis.
[b] Etiology unknown.

medical facilities during the period, July 1959 to October 1960. Whether the composition of this sample may be considered representative of the physically handicapped in general or those at the two rehabilitation centers in particular may be open to question. The reader, therefore, is cautioned in advance about the generality of these findings because of the sample limitations (35, pp. 256–272).

Respondents were asked to indicate their degree of agreement with a series of forty items designed to measure their self-conception. The statements were derived from the analysis of approximately seventy medical records, from personal observation, and from a systematic examination of the rehabilitation literature. As formulated by Mead, Cooley, and Adler, self-conception was considered as a function of the individual's sense of personal worth and adequacy and his evaluation of the attitudes of others toward him. Each respondent was asked the following general question:

> Many people behave differently and have various attitudes toward their illness. The following is a series of statements made by patients with a condition similar to your own. Concerning which of these would you: Strongly Agree, Agree, Be Undecided, Disagree, Strongly Disagree? Wherever possible, let your own experience determine your answer.

Here are some of the statements on the list:

1. People can't stand to look at me. [*Appearance before others*]
2. There is little future for a person who has been paralyzed. [*Personal adequacy*]
3. When with a group of people, everyone stares at me. [*Reaction of others*]
4. No one in a condition such as mine should ever be put in a responsible position. [*Adequacy for employment*]
5. I worry about the way people will react to my disability. [*Concern about the reaction of others*]
6. A person who is physically disabled can not have a normal married life. [*Marital and sexual adequacy*]
7. The way people act, you'd think they were doing you a favor just being with you. [*Reaction of others*]

Although apparently reliable,[3] the scale has only face validity. Nevertheless, the individual items were judged to be valid on the basis of personal observation, examination of the hospital records, and discussions with the members of the staff. A self-conception score was computed for each patient.[4] Individuals who scored below the mean of this distribution were considered to have a good or favorable conception of self. Those whose scores were above the mean were regarded as having an unfavorable or poor self-conception.

Response to rehabilitation was measured in several ways. The patient's performance in physical therapy was evaluated by his or her therapist on the basis of a series of items, derived from Myatt (32), indicative of effort expended, cooperation, drive, interest, initiative, desire for self-help, and so on.[5] Each patient's

[3] The scale has an even–odd reliability coefficient of .771, uncorrected. Upon application of the Spearman-Brown Prophecy formula, $r = .871$.

[4] The scores on the self-conception scale ranged from 54 to 119. The mean score was 87.95.

[5] In her rejection of the use of purely objective self-care and ambulation ratings, Myatt argues: ". . . the points of improvement cannot be accepted as absolute values. For instance a patient who received a self care score of 96 upon arrival had only 4 points to move in order to achieve the highest score. Thus his range of improvement is curtailed. . . . There is a difference in the amount of effort required for improvement in the upper limits of the scale than in the lower limits. In the latter case . . . time and proper nursing care alone could be responsible for the patient's gain in strength . . ." (32, p. 36) "Although the validity of subjective

numerical evaluation, divided by ten for ease of computation, formed the PT Rating. In addition, the attending physician noted the patient's over-all motivation and performance along a weighted five-point continuum of Superior, High, Average, Low and Minimal (32), his rehabilitation potential,[6] proposed level of independence, estimated progress, and acceptance of his condition. A rehabilitation score for each case was then calculated as PT rating plus physician's evaluation.[7] Patients who scored above the combined mean (therapist rating plus physician "average" rating) were considered "poor" respondents, those below as "good." While the patients were also evaluated in occupational therapy and pre-vocational testing, not all cases received this type of treatment and therefore analysis of any relationships would only be speculative and would require further investigation.

FINDINGS

An examination of Table 2 reveals that response to rehabilitation, as measured by the total rehabilitation scores, is significantly related to self-conception. Whereas 77 per cent of the patients who had favorable self-conception scores exhibited a good response to rehabilitation, 64 per cent of those with negative conceptions of self were considered as "poor" patients. Looking at

---

judgments is always questionable, it was decided that in the present situation such judgments would be more likely to reflect the patient's intent than would the more objective scores. It was believed that the reliability of ratings would be relatively high because of the strong group feeling among staff members, the frequent conferences, and the cooperative manner of dealing with the patients." (32, p. 41)

[6] The rehabilitation potential refers to the patient's estimated ability or capacity to benefit from a rehabilitation program as determined by various diagnostic procedures and the physician's professional judgment. It should be noted, however, that before admission to candidacy for rehabilitation, all patients are carefully evaluated to determine their suitability for treatment. In general, only patients who are believed capable of rehabilitation are accepted. The estimation, here, was made at least one month after admission. To what extent this evaluation includes both attitudinal and motivational components as well as recognition of the patient's actual performance has not been determined.

[7] As head of the "rehabilitation team," the attending physician has the opportunity to observe the patient's response in all phases of his treatment; the evaluation of the therapist, on the other hand, is limited to the patient's response to the arduous program of physical therapy per se.

TABLE 2

*Response to Rehabilitation as Measured by
Rehabilitation Scores, by Self-Conception*

SELF-CONCEPTION	RESPONSE TO REHABILITATION:	
	Good	*Poor*
Positive	41	12
Negative	17	30
$\chi^2 = 17.34$; $df = 1$; $p < .001$; $N = 100$		

the data from a different direction, 71 per cent of the "good" patients had favorable self-conceptions. Similarly, a negative self-conception was found in 71 per cent of the cases whose response was poor. This relationship is illustrated by the following case histories drawn from our files:

U104 is a single, middle-aged woman, with moderate involvement of the lower extremities. During her period of treatment, she was a passive, unmotivated patient who required a great deal of encouragement and prompting. As described by the staff: "She feels that her age is her biggest handicap and that it is pretty hopeless to find factory work at her age and anyway she would 'hate it.' 'I'm so old maybe you people don't want to bother with me.' . . . The general picture is that of a highly intelligent small-town woman trapped by circumstances and accepting of the trap. She is good looking, intelligent, and not greatly handicapped physically. . . . Client needs occasional interviews to manage her self doubts until she is actively in school or at work. She has made great progress in overcoming personal devaluation and a feeling of hopelessness, but I feel she is not yet completely out of danger of sliding back into her old self-concept."

U103 is seventeen years old, male, polio-quadriplegic. He is intelligent, energetic, and extremely well motivated, despite severe involvement. Throughout his treatment, he attempted to devise various "gimmicks" and procedures to aid and assist self-care. His conception of self was extremely favorable. Both family and friends had accepted him as a useful member of the community and showed great interest in his treatment and plans for the future.

Self-Conception and Physical Rehabilitation

When the evaluation of the physical therapist alone was used as an index of patient response, a similar relationship was found (Table 3). Once again, patients with favorable self-conceptions received relatively good ratings and those with negative self-conceptions were rated poorly. Although the two variables seem rather strongly associated, this of course does not prove a cause-and-effect relationship.

TABLE 3

Physical Therapist Rating
by Self-Conception

SELF-CONCEPTION	PT RATING:	
	Good	Poor
Positive	38	15
Negative	18	29
$\chi^2 = 11.27$; $df = 1$; $p < .001$; $N = 100$		

As one might suspect, there was a direct relationship between patient response and rehabilitation potential (Table 4). In other words, patients whose potential for rehabilitation was considered favorable exhibited initiative, drive, and determination in their treatment, while those with an unfavorable potential were passive, lacked drive, and were generally unmotivated. As Table 5 demonstrates, however, self-conception and rehabilitation po-

TABLE 4

Response to Rehabilitation as Measured
by Rehabilitation Scores,
by Rehabilitation Potential

REHABILITATION POTENTIAL	RESPONSE TO REHABILITATION:	
	Good	Poor
Favorable	44	17
Unfavorable	14	24
$\chi^2 = 12.02$; $df = 1$; $p < .001$; $N = 99$[a]		

[a] Rehabilitation potential undetermined in one case.

TABLE 5

Self-Conception by Rehabilitation Potential

REHABILITATION POTENTIAL	SELF-CONCEPTION:	
	Positive	*Negative*
Favorable	36	25
Unfavorable	16	22
$\chi^2 = 2.69;\ df = 1;\ N = 99$[a]		

[a] Rehabilitation potential undetermined in one case.

tential were not significantly related. When the influence of the patient's rehabilitation potential was held constant, the relationship between self-conception and rehabilitation response remained statistically significant (Table 6). In those cases in which rehabili-

TABLE 6

Response to Rehabilitation as Measured by Rehabilitation Scores, by Self-Conception, with Rehabilitation Potential Held Constant

Rehabilitation Potential Favorable:		
SELF-CONCEPTION	RESPONSE TO REHABILITATION:	
	Good	*Poor*
Positive	31	5
Negative	13	12
$\chi^2 = 8.54;\ df = 1;\ p < .01;\ N = 61$		
Rehabilitation Potential Unfavorable:		
SELF-CONCEPTION	RESPONSE TO REHABILITATION:	
	Good	*Poor*
Positive	10	6
Negative	4	18
$\chi^2 = 7.82;\ df = 1;\ p < .01;\ N = 38$		

tation was considered "doubtful," 71 per cent of the patients with "good" ratings had positive self-conceptions. Moreover, 63 per cent of those with positive self-conceptions responded well in treatment despite an unfavorable potential. It is interesting to note, however, that among those whose potential was considered favorable, slightly over half (52 per cent) of the patients with a negative conception of self were regarded as "good" performers. This would seem to indicate that if prognosis is relatively good, a negative self-conception may not act as a deterrent to treatment.

In addition, there is also evidence that the nature of the self-conception — for example, whether bitterness or resignation is present — may play an important part in determining the patient's response. In several of the cases interviewed, patients with negative self-conceptions and bitter feelings regarding their physical condition were found to be highly motivated and evaluated as excellent candidates in rehabilitation. Here, it would seem that the individual has such a distasteful conception of self that every effort may be directed toward alteration of the physical state believed to be the cause of it. Thus, a thirty-five-year-old paraplegic, completely dissatisfied with his condition and its limitations, bitter about his role in society and negative toward himself, exhibited diligence and enthusiasm in treatment. Through possible physical restoration, he sought to alter his own condition and the perception of others of him. Unfortunately, once maximal physical capacity is reached and the patient is forced to face up to its limitations — that is, that he will never again be physically "normal" — productive effort might decline and a desperate search for miracle cures and new and different treatment procedures and facilities might ensue. For example, a thirty-seven-year-old male, paralyzed from the waist down due to spinal surgery, expressed anger toward the circumstances surrounding his hospitalization, disgust with his condition, and doubt and bewilderment concerning his future. During the early days of his treatment, he was depicted as a marvelous, if not inspiring patient. Later, however, his interest and enthusiasm fell off. He became openly hostile toward staff members and his productivity declined markedly. Discharged at the completion of his program, still depressed and unadjusted to his disability, Mr. E144 returned home only to seek the services of a chiropractor and the relief of "zone therapy."

On the basis of these and other cases, we would suggest that a negative self-conception when accompanied by a sense of bitterness or rejection may lead to a favorable response to treatment. If the individual is unwilling to give in to his conception of self, he may seek to modify it through alteration of his physical state, believed to be the source of his problems. The possibility of improvement through treatment offers the "I" an opportunity to reject the unfavorable "me." However, once the limitations of treatment have been reached, the individual may continue to look for some "miracle cure" or give in to his conception of self with a resulting loss in motivation.

As mentioned earlier in this paper, the attending physician was asked to determine, on the basis of his professional judgment, how well he felt the patient had progressed in his rehabilitation program.[8] Data from Table 7 indicate that there was a significant relationship between the patient's estimated progress and his conception of self. Among those who progressed beyond expectation, 68 per cent had positive self-conceptions. In contrast, 81 per cent of the patients who failed to achieve normal progress, conceived of themselves unfavorably. While 94 per cent of the individuals with favorable self-conceptions attained normal or

TABLE 7

*Patient's Estimated Progress
by Self-Conception*

| SELF-CONCEPTION | ESTIMATED PROGRESS: | | |
	Beyond	*Normal*	*Below*
Positive	13	36	3
Negative	6	27	13
$\chi^2 = 10.23$; $df = 2$; $p < .01$; $N = 98$[a]			

[a] Physician was unable to estimate the patient's progress in two cases.

[8] The patient's progress was described as: Far Beyond Expectation, Beyond Expectation, Normal Progress, Below Expectation, Far Below Expectation. For purposes of analysis the two extremes were combined to indicate beyond and below normal progress.

higher than normal progress, only 72 per cent of those who had poor self-conceptions did as well. Moreover, approximately four times as many patients with unfavorable self-conceptions progressed below expectation as those with positive conceptions of self.

The medical literature suggests that there is a direct relationship between acceptance of one's condition and response to rehabilitation (20, 45). Data in Table 8 tend to lend support to this argument. In addition, it has been hypothesized here that one's ability to "accept" his disability may be directly associated with his conception of self. The evidence from this study demonstrates that the two variables are indeed significantly related (Table 9). Among patients who had not accepted their condition or did so unfavorably, 76 per cent had negative self-conceptions. On the other hand, of those who had accepted their condition, 69.8 per cent had maintained a positive conception of self.

TABLE 8

Response to Rehabilitation as Measured by Rehabilitation Scores, by Acceptance of Condition

ACCEPTANCE OF CONDITION	RESPONSE TO REHABILITATION:	
	Good	Poor
Accept	49	14
Not Accept	3	22
$\chi^2 = 32.03$; $df = 1$; $p < .001$; $N = 88$[a]		

[a] Of the twelve patients whose acceptance could not be determined, six received poor rehabilitation scores and six good rehabilitation scores.

The reciprocal relation — that is, the influence of self-conception upon acceptance — appears somewhat less tenable. For while 88 per cent of those with positive self-conceptions did accept their condition, 50 per cent of the patients with negative self-conceptions were also characterized as accepting their condition. Therefore, it appears that a negative conception of self

TABLE 9

Self-Conception by Acceptance
of Condition

ACCEPTANCE	SELF-CONCEPTION:	
	Positive	*Negative*
Accept	44	19
Not Accept	6	19
$\chi^2 = 15.36$; $df = 1$; $p < .001$; $N = 88$[a]		

[a] Physicians were unable to determine acceptance or non-acceptance in twelve cases. Of these, three had positive self-conceptions and nine negative self-conceptions.

alone does not account for failure to accept one's disabled condition.

SUMMARY AND CONCLUSIONS

This study attempted to ascertain the relationship between self-conception and response to a medical regimen of physical rehabilitation. Upon analysis of the data, the following significant relationships were noted:

1. Response to rehabilitation as determined by a combined physician and therapist evaluation is associated with self-conception.

2. A similar relationship was found to exist when response to rehabilitation was measured by the therapist rating alone.

3. Although significantly related to patient response, rehabilitation potential was not related to self-conception. Moreover, when the patient's potential was controlled, the relationship between self-conception and rehabilitation response remained significant. Yet it was noted that, when potential is favorable, patients may or may not respond well to treatment if their self-conception is negative.

4. As estimated by the attending physician, progress in treatment was also found associated with conception of self.

5. As suggested by the medical literature, the ability of the patient to accept his condition is associated with his response

to treatment. Although self-conception and acceptance are also directly associated, patients whose self-conceptions are poor may or may not accept their condition.

The evidence would seem to demonstrate that self-conception does play an important part in determining the patient's response in physical rehabilitation. Nevertheless, before drawing any general conclusions from this study, the reader is again reminded of the particular limitations imposed upon the research by the population sampled. To what extent these findings may be generally applicable to the physically disabled in the United States as a whole, or those undergoing treatment at the two facilities surveyed, remains open to question.

Yet the findings provide presumptive evidence for several practical suggestions. As discussed earlier, the conception of self may be considered an evaluation of and reaction to one's perception of the attitudes of others toward him. Two implications flow from this: (*a*) the public needs to be educated in the possibilities for rehabilitation and in the importance of helping the patient sustain a positive conception of himself, and (*b*) orienting and counseling the patient in the importance of maintaining a positive self-conception as a means of meeting the demands of the difficult rehabilitation program would be of value.

The investigations of Barker, Wright, and associates upon the attitudes of the non-injured toward physical disability revealed two basic responses: (*a*) unwarranted pity and (*b*) treatment as an object of curiosity (6). It is not surprising then that they report that the injured individual feels himself to be a person set apart from people at large (6). Similarly, we found that a majority of the patients interviewed felt that people outside the hospital did not understand the problems of the physically handicapped. Moreover, many patients themselves admitted that they were unaware of what was involved in a physical disability, its limitations, implications, and possibilities. Consequently, not only were they unable to take the role of the disabled when well, but they were also unprepared to play the role of the disabled when afflicted.[9] A program of public education directed toward alter-

9 Barker, Wright, *et al.*, suggest that this may be a function of the patient entering the state of the injured with the attitudes of the non-injured (3, 4, 6).

ing the stereotyped picture of the "cripple" as an unproductive, hopeless drag upon society appears indicated. Moreover, movies, lectures, demonstrations, and tours of rehabilitation facilities have been suggested by the patients as a means of implementing the program.

It is also suggested that the patient must be made aware of his role in society and the ability of the disabled to handle their problems socially and vocationally as well as physically. On the basis of our interviews, the accomplishments of other patients with similar disabilities may serve to exemplify what can be accomplished. In addition, intensive psychological counseling may be useful.

While this exploratory study has confirmed an association between self-conception and response to rehabilitation, a number of other interesting facets to the problem warrant further examination. A few suggestions for future research may be mentioned in passing.

First, a longitudinal study designed to measure changes in self-conception over time. In several cases, patients reported changes in both their attitude toward self as well as toward treatment after either prolonged hospitalization or extended periods at home.

Second, it would be useful to determine who makes up the patient's reference group. To whom does he refer, from whom does he draw his social perceptions — is it the staff, other patients, family, friends, the "generalized other"?

Third, development of a standardized, refined scale of self-conception to include determination of the nature of self-feeling — that is, whether bitterness, rejection, resignation, and so on.

Fourth, extension of the present study, both intensively and extensively, to include a larger number of disabilities, increased sample size, tested at various stages in the rehabilitation program and after discharge.

In conclusion, this study has served to demonstrate the feasibility of introducing the symbolic interactionist formulation of self-conception as a research variable in the determination of factors influencing the differential response of the orthopedically disabled to a program of physical rehabilitation.

Self-Conception and Physical Rehabilitation

References

1. Adler, Alfred. "Study of Organ Inferiority and Its Physical Compensation: A Contribution to Clinical Medicine," *Nervous and Mental Disease Monograph*, No. 24 (1917).

2. Adler, Alfred. *The Practice and Theory of Individual Psychology*. New York: Harcourt, Brace and Co., 1924.

3. Adler, D., G. Ladieu, and T. Dembo. "Studies in the Adjustment to Visible Injuries: Social Acceptance of the Injured," *Journal of Social Issues*, Vol. 4 (1948), pp. 55–61.

4. Barker, Roger G. "The Social Psychology of Physical Disability," *Journal of Social Issues*, Vol. 4 (1948), pp. 28–35.

5. Barker, Roger G., and others. *Adjustment to Physical Handicap and Illness*, 2d ed. New York: Social Science Research Council, 1953.

6. Barker, Roger G., and B. A. Wright. "The Social Psychology of Adjustment to Physical Disability," in J. F. Garrett (ed.), *Psychological Aspects of Physical Disability*. Office of Vocational Rehabilitation, Rehabilitation Service Series No. 210, 1953, pp. 18–32.

7. Berger, S. "Paraplegia," in J. F. Garrett (ed.), *Psychological Aspects of Physical Disability*. Office of Vocational Rehabilitation, Rehabilitation Service Series No. 210, 1953, pp. 46–59.

8. Berger, S., and J. F. Garrett. "Psychological Problems of the Paraplegic Patient," *Journal of Rehabilitation*, Vol. 18 (September–October 1952), pp. 15–17.

9. Braceland, Francis J. "The Role of the Psychiatrist in Rehabilitation," *Journal of the American Medical Association*, Vol. 165 (September 21, 1957), pp. 211–215.

10. Committee on Rehabilitation, American Medical Association. "Report of the Committee on Rehabilitation," *Journal of the American Medical Association*, Vol. 164 (August 31, 1957), reprint.

11. Cooley, Charles H. *Human Nature and the Social Order*, rev. ed. New York: Charles Scribner's Sons, 1922.

12. Davis, Fred. "Definition of Time and Recovery in Paralytic Polio Convalescence," *American Journal of Sociology*, Vol. 61 (May 1956), pp. 582–588.

13. Davis, Fred. "Polio in the Family." Unpublished Ph.D. dissertation, University of Chicago, June 1958.

14. Dembo, T., G. Ladieu, and B. A. Wright. "Adjustment to Misfortune — A Study in Social Emotional Relationships Between Injured and Non-injured People." Final Report: Army Medical Research and Development Board, Office of the Surgeon General, U.S. War Department, April 1, 1948.

15. Dembo, T., G. Ladieu, and B. A. Wright. "Acceptance of Loss — Amputations," in J. F. Garrett (ed.), *Psychological Aspects of Physical Disability.* Office of Vocational Rehabilitation, Rehabilitation Service Series No. 210, 1953, pp. 80–96.

16. Dembo, T., G. Leviton, and B. A. Wright. "Adjustment to Misfortune — A Problem of Social Psychological Rehabilitation," *Artificial Limbs,* Vol. 3 (Autumn 1956), pp. 4–62.

17. Dreikurs, R. "The Socio-psychological Dynamics of Physical Disability: A Review of the Adlerian Concept," *Journal of Social Issues,* Vol. 4 (1948), pp. 39–54.

18. Fishman, Sidney. "Self-Concept and Adjustment to Leg Prosthesis." Unpublished Ph.D. dissertation, Columbia University, 1949.

19. Garrett, J. F. *Psychological Aspects of Physical Disability.* Office of Vocational Rehabilitation, Rehabilitation Service Series No. 210, U.S. Department of Health, Education, and Welfare, 1953.

20. Grayson, M. "The Concept of 'Acceptance' in Physical Rehabilitation," *Military Surgeon,* Vol. 107 (September 1950), pp. 221–226.

21. Grayson, M., "Psychiatric Aspects of Rehabilitation," *Rehabilitation Monograph II.* Bellevue Medical Center, New York: Institute of Physical Medicine and Rehabilitation, 1952.

22. *Handbook on Physical Medicine.* Sister Elizabeth Kenny Institute, Department of Physical Medicine and Rehabilitation, 1800 Chicago Avenue South, Minneapolis.

23. Kessler, H. H. *Rehabilitation of the Physically Handicapped.* New York: Columbia University Press, 1953.

24. Kessler, H. H., and A. S. Abramson. "The Rehabilitation of the Paraplegic," *New York State Journal of Medicine,* Vol. 50 (January 1950), pp. 43–47.

25. Kuhn, Manford H. "Self-Attitudes by Age, Sex, and Professional Training," *Sociological Quarterly,* Vol. 1 (January 1960), pp. 39–56.

26. Kuhn, Manford H., and Thomas S. McPartland. "An Empirical

Investigation of Self-Attitudes," *American Sociological Review*, Vol. 19 (February 1954), pp. 68–76.

27. MacGregor, Frances C. "Some Psycho-social Problems Associated with Facial Deformities," *American Sociological Review*, Vol. 16 (1951), pp. 629–638.

28. Manson, M. P. "The Concept of Rehabilitation Applied to Paraplegia," *Archives of Industrial Hygiene and Occupational Medicine*, Vol. 1 (1950), pp. 65–72.

29. Mead, George H. *Mind, Self, and Society*, ed. by Charles W. Morris. Chicago: The University of Chicago Press, 1934.

30. Mueller, A. D. "Personality Problems of the Spinal Cord Injured," *Journal of Consulting Psychology*, Vol. 14 (June 1950), pp. 189–191.

31. Mueller, A. D., and C. E. Thompson. "Psychological Aspects of the Problems in Spinal Cord Injuries," *Occupational Therapy and Rehabilitation*, Vol. 29 (1950), p. 86.

32. Myatt, M. F. "A Study of the Relationship Between Motivation and Test Performance of Patients in a Rehabilitation Ward." Unpublished Ph.D. dissertation, University of Minnesota, December 1951.

33. "Orientation Material." Department of Medicine and Surgery, Physical Medicine and Rehabilitation, U.S. Veterans Administration.

34. Reeder, Leo G., G. A. Donohue, and A. Biblarz. "Conceptions of Self and Others," *American Journal of Sociology*, Vol. 66 (September 1960), pp. 153–159.

35. Rose, Arnold M. "Generalizations in the Social Sciences," in Arnold M. Rose (ed.), *Theory and Method in the Social Sciences*. Minneapolis: University of Minnesota Press, 1954, pp. 256–272.

36. Rose, Arnold M. *Sociology: The Study of Human Relations*. New York: Alfred A. Knopf, 1956.

37. Rusk, H. A., and E. J. Taylor. "Team Approach in Rehabilitation and the Psychologist's Role," in J. F. Garrett (ed.), *Psychological Aspects of Physical Disability*. Office of Vocational Rehabilitation, Rehabilitation Service Series No. 210, 1953, pp. 33–45.

38. Schmidt, W. H. "Problems in Rehabilitation," *American Archives of Physical Medicine and Rehabilitation*, Vol. 36 (1955), pp. 687–691.

39. Schwartz, A. G. "A Study of Social Work Service to Patients

with Diagnosed Left Hemiplegia as Result of Cerebrovascular Accident." Unpublished Master of Social Work thesis, University of Minnesota, School of Social Work, June 1960.

40. Seidenfeld, M. A. "Psychological Problems of Poliomyelitis," in J. F. Garrett (ed.), *Psychological Aspects of Physical Disability*. Office of Vocational Rehabilitation, Rehabilitation Service Series No. 210, 1953, pp. 33–45.

41. Seidenfeld, M. A., and C. L. Lowman. "A Preliminary Report of the Psycho-social Effects of Poliomyelitis," *Journal of Consulting Psychology*, Vol. 11 (1947), pp. 33–45.

42. Shelsky, Irving. "The Effect of Disability on Self-Concept." Unpublished Ph.D. dissertation, Columbia University, 1957.

43. Strauss, Anselm. *The Social Psychology of George Herbert Mead*. Chicago: The University of Chicago Press, 1956.

44. Switzer, M. E. "Foreword," in J. F. Garrett (ed.), *Psychological Aspects of Physical Disability*. Office of Vocational Rehabilitation, Rehabilitation Service Series No. 210, 1953, pp. iii–iv.

45. Thom, D. A., C. F. Von Salzen, and A. Fromme. "Psychological Aspects of the Paraplegic Patient," *Medical Clinics of North America*, Vol. 30 (1946), pp. 473–480.

46. White, R. K., B. A. Wright, and T. Dembo. "Studies in Adjustment to Visible Injuries: Evaluation of Curiosity by the Injured," *Journal of Abnormal and Social Psychology*, Vol. 43 (1948), pp. 13–28.

47. Wright, B. A. *Physical Disability — A Psychological Approach*. New York: Harper & Brothers, 1960.

30

The Treatment of Tuberculosis
as a Bargaining Process

 JULIUS A. ROTH

NEW YORK SCHOOL OF SOCIAL WORK,
COLUMBIA UNIVERSITY

Interaction may be thought of as a process — a series of mutually interrelated behaviors on the part of two or more individuals or groups in which each step arises meaningfully out of the preceding steps. In Eliot Freidson's paper, we observed the interaction of doctor and patient as a conflict process. In the present essay by Julius Roth, we observe the same interaction as a process of accommodation. Unlike Sheldon Stryker and Theodor Litman, who we have seen apply traditional scientific methods to the testing of hypotheses, Professor Roth, following Herbert Blumer's argument, literally takes the role of the others he is studying.

The person in a skilled service occupation tries to keep the initiative in his relationship to his client.[1] He uses his superior

[1] The data on tuberculosis treatment on which this paper is based are drawn from systematic field notes kept while I was a patient (about one year in two hospitals), an attendant (three months in one hospital), and

specialized knowledge, his special frame of reference, and the lingo of his trade to assert his right to make decisions for the client. Even in non-professional occupations this desire to keep control is evident. The auto repair man does not want the motorist telling him "his business"; the carpenter knows better what kind of cabinets the home owner wants or needs than does the home owner himself; janitors know better when the drafts of a furnace should be opened and closed than do the residents of a building.

The ideal of a professional group is to control its own standards of service. The practitioner is to be judged only by his colleagues; clients are to accept his advice and direction as that of an expert whose competence in the area of service is far superior to their own and that of the client's family and acquaintances. The closer a professional group comes to this ideal, the more autonomous and "successful" it is.

Such autonomy can be reduced by the nature of the relationship with other professional groups (for example, the subordination of professional nurses to physicians). It can also be reduced by certain aspects of the professional person's relationship to his client. It is the latter aspect which I shall discuss in this essay.

For one thing, the goals of the professional and the client are never entirely the same. The doctor may want to keep the patient in the hospital for a long period to increase the chance that he will not have a relapse, while the patient is more willing to take his chances on leaving earlier in order to get back to his family, job, or other activities. To the physician, the patient's apparent neglect of his health will appear irrational; to the pa-

---

a sociological observer (about one and one-half years in two hospitals) in tuberculosis hospitals. In the last role I spent much of my time "hanging around" the hospital wards and offices, attending therapy conferences, making rounds of physicians, and listening to staff doctors discuss their "problems" with one another, and with their residents and nurses, conversations with staff persons at meals, in the halls, in their offices, and so on. I made a particular effort to follow up complete "incidents" over a period of time.

Some of my ideas about professional–client relationships derive from study with Everett C. Hughes at the University of Chicago. (See 8, especially Chapters 5, 6, and 7.) The work of Erving Goffman (6) stimulated my thinking about the subtleties of social interaction as a bargaining process.

tient, the doctor's apparent refusal to consider the patient's family relationships, career, and the chance to live a freer kind of life will appear inhuman. Stated more generally, the goals of the professional in his relationship to the client tend to be highly specialized (for example, the clinician is concerned primarily with arresting the infection in the patient's lungs), whereas the goals of the client include goals generated by all of his roles in addition to that of client of a given professional person.

In many lines of work the client must be educated to get him to do what the professional person thinks is best for him. But with better education, the client is also better able to judge the service and to escape from professional control. Thus, in tuberculosis hospitals the staff is faced with the constant dilemma of how to give the patient enough education about his disease and its treatment so that he can "cooperate" in that treatment, but not so much education that he thinks he knows as much as the doctor.

Even if the professional person carefully weighs the information he gives to the client, however, he may not be able to control many other sources of information to the client. Information control is the key to much of the control of decision-making and evaluation of service because the client can evaluate the service if he knows (or thinks he knows) the basis for given decisions and actions. Tuberculosis hospital patients are relatively well educated about the service they are receiving. They are surrounded by "experts" — their fellow patients — who readily pool their observations made over periods of months about their experiences with the same disease and the same forms of treatment given by the same doctors and nurses. The patient can see for himself how long patients have to wait before getting a pass, how active they can be without having a relapse, what condition they are in following a bronchoscopy, how many of what kinds of pills you should get with each meal, and so on.

With the help of such information and with goals which contradict those of the staff, patients can (and do) formulate plans for resisting the control the hospital staff tries to maintain over their lives. Again, such resistance by the clients is not unusual in professional–client relationships. All professionals experience a greater or lesser degree of such resistance to control from their clients and must in part yield to it if the relationship is to be continued. The relationship could, of course, be terminated. A patient can leave the hospital against advice in order to escape completely the control of the hospital staff, or the staff may discharge a patient whom they consider to be too "uncooperative." Most often, however, both sides succeed in continuing the relationship by compromising their goals and yielding in part to the pressure of the other party.

Thus, the treatment relationship may be conceived of as a conflict for the control of the patients' behavior, a conflict usually resolved by bargaining. The tuberculosis hospital as it exists today is the product of such long-term bargaining.

One aspect of a bargaining relationship is the relative power of the parties concerned. At one extreme are the prison and concentration camp where — at first sight — the "client" is largely helpless before those who prescribe his behavior. Even at this extreme, however, the underdog is not completely crushed and is often able to gain his goals to some degree — usually by subtle and surreptitious means (3, Chapters 7, 8, 11; 4; 7; 10). At the other extreme are cases where the professional persons feel forced to comply with the "unreasonable" demands of the clients, for example in the case of jazz musicians playing for a "square" audience. Here again, however, the professionals develop subtle means of controlling the audience without seeming to do so (1). We also have the limiting case of the client approaching colleague status, which seems to happen to some extent in the research ward reported by Fox (5). In this context the tuberculosis hospital is closer to the concentration camp, with the professionals holding most of the formal power and the clients having to rely mainly on indirect means to gain ends conflicting with those of the professionals.

Generally speaking, the patients want more and earlier privileges, more pass time, earlier discharge, and greater freedom from restrictions, and the staff want fewer and later privileges, fewer and shorter passes, longer hospitalization, and more restrictions for a longer time (for the patients). In addition, there are frequently differences between patients and staff about the need for given medicines or surgery or other forms of treatment.

A patient may believe that further hospitalization is not necessary in his case, but he is unable to leave against advice because he knows the staff can cut him off from outpatient treatment or prevent him from getting a job or refuse welfare aid to himself and his family. Such official power does not mean that the patient is helpless, however. When a patient threatens to leave against advice, the doctor is faced with the possibility that the patient's condition may deteriorate if cut off from treatment or that the patient may be a source of infection to his family and other associates. The doctor may be willing to give the patient more pass time or other privileges if these will serve to hold him in the hospital for a longer period. Thus, the patient will have used his very weakness and disability as a counter with which to bargain for greater control over his own behavior. The very regulations which are intended to strengthen the doctor's hand (cutting off the patient who leaves against advice from all treatment for a specified number of months — usually three) may thus actually cause the more conscientious doctor to give in to many of the patients' demands rather than run the risk of having the patients deprived of treatment. In fact, the more "irresponsible" patient is likely to be in a stronger position than the more conforming one because the staff member believes the former will actually carry out his threat if privileges are withheld, while the latter is more likely to be thought of as bluffing (9).[2]

It would seem at first that nurses can control the patients with regard to medicines, diet, and other aspects of the treatment carried out on the ward. Here again, however, the patients are not completely helpless. Through their observations and pooling of information patients learn which nurses are most likely to give certain drugs and nursing services and the patients ask *these* nurses whenever possible. Thus, a patient may get an aspirin or laxative from one nurse after being refused by another. He may get food outside of his diet from other patients. He may have visitors sneak in contraband medicine or food. He may fake or exaggerate symptoms to convince nurses that they should give him medicine he thinks he needs. Persistent complaining and de-

[2] One of the advantages of the bargaining concept is the fact that it provides a bridge between the Cooley and Mead theory of human interaction and some of the ways in which present-day game theory is being applied to describe and analyze human behavior.

mands over a period of time are often sufficient in themselves to get nurses to "give in" and give the patient what he wants to keep him quiet. The nurses, who usually believe that patients take too much medicine and should be discouraged from taking more,[3] make use of such tactics as stalling the patient off, trying to talk him out of his symptoms, or giving innocuous placebos. They defend their action among themselves by claiming that the patient's symptoms are "all in his head," that he might become addicted or suffer untoward reactions if given the medicine he asks for, or that he is deliberately exaggerating his complaints. At the same time, the nurse is restrained in withholding medicine and using placebos by the fact that the patient might "go over her head" and complain to the doctor that his distress is not being relieved. The nurse's bargaining position is to some degree dependent upon the readiness with which the doctor accedes to the patients' demands.[4]

Surgery is another area in which considerable bargaining goes on between the patients and staff. Patients frequently refuse surgery recommended by the physicians. Physicians may try to convince the patient of the possible dire consequences if he does not take surgery. The patient may point to the possible dire consequences (as he has observed them in other patients getting surgery) if he *does* have surgery. He may also argue that surgery is unnecessary by pointing to other patients whose cases appear similar to his and who have made a good recovery without surgery. On the other hand, some patients regard surgery as the quickest way out of the hospital or the "sure cure" and insist on having it even when the physicians are reluctant. In some cases, surgery may be considered by the physicians only because the patient has demanded it. Patients who say they want surgery and want it as soon as possible are more likely to be considered for surgery, and, if recommended, are likely to get it at an earlier time. A patient who says openly that he is against

---

[3] Specific therapeutic medicines, such as streptomycin or penicillin, are given in specific amounts at regular intervals as ordered by a physician. The kind of medicines I am discussing here are those intended to relieve distress — pain, cough, constipation, sleeplessness, difficult breathing, itching — and which are ordered to be given "when necessary."

[4] Much the same is true in the case of the attendant in mental hospitals (2, Chapters 9, 10; 11, Chapter 5).

surgery and does not want it is likely to have consideration of the possibility of surgery postponed by the medical staff and is less likely to have it recommended if it *is* brought up for consideration. A threat by the patient that he will leave against advice by a certain date if not given surgery may sometimes prompt the medical staff to move toward surgery faster than they otherwise would have.

Even an unconscious patient can bargain with a surgeon. Thus, if a pulmonary resection[5] has been planned, but the surgeon finds on entering the chest cavity that a thoracoplasty[6] seems more suitable, he may refrain from doing a thoracoplasty and simply sew the patient up again if the patient has insisted strenuously before the operation that he did not want a thoracoplasty under any circumstances.

Sometimes explicit "deals" can be made, similar to those of union–management bargaining. Patients *are* sometimes given regular and frequent passes to induce them to remain in the hospital. Patients who are threatening to walk out are sometimes offered a pass to think things over if they promise not to leave for good at this time. Patients are sometimes promised earlier conferences to reduce the chance of their leaving against advice. Patients who have left against advice have been permitted to return to the hospital after a few days, despite a ninety-day exclusion rule, on the condition that they sign up for surgery. Patients have been promised discharges within a specified period of time if they agree to take another round of gastric cultures, bronchoscopy, planigrams, and other diagnostic procedures. Patients are sometimes given an extended leave of absence to take care of what they insist is an urgent personal or family problem if they promise to return after it is over and spend at least a certain minimum period of time in the hospital.

More often, the "deal" is never explicitly stated by anyone, but is gradually worked out over a period of time as a result of pushes and pulls from either side. Thus, in a hospital where the patients had come to think of an "average" stay as about one year, the physician decided that one patient with extensively diseased lungs should stay for at least eighteen months after the

5 Excision of lung tissue.
6 Removal of ribs to partially collapse pleural cavity.

patient had refused recommended surgery. The patient, however, felt that he had been promised a discharge within a year and simply would not go along with the idea of staying a year and a half. The doctor backed down to some extent under pressure from the patient. To insist on holding him the full eighteen months, the doctor thought, might only lead to his leaving against advice immediately. The patient, at the same time, wanted to avoid leaving against advice and thus being cut off from follow-up treatment if he could manage to get a sanctioned discharge without undue delay. First the doctor thought of keeping the patient in Class 3[7] until he had been in the hospital a year and then holding him six weeks in each of Classes 4 and 5. In this way, he would get in about fifteen months of treatment, in itself a compromise over the doctor's original intentions, but yet substantially longer than the patient wanted to stay. The patient, however, wanted to be promoted immediately and spend only a month each in Classes 4 and 5 so that he could get out of the hospital in about a year. The doctor made no definite promises, but thought he would try stalling off the patient as much as possible on each promotion. The patient's continued demands and protests pushed the doctor into promoting him to Class 4 before his first year was up, but the doctor got the patient to serve most of his six-week periods in Classes 4 and 5 before he discharged him. Thus, the doctor did not keep the patient quite the full fifteen months he had hoped for after his initial compromise and the patient did not get out in the year which he had considered the "proper" length of hospitalization. On the other hand, the mutual compromise allowed the post-hospital follow-up examinations and treatment to be continued, something which both doctor and patient desired.

A bargaining ploy may have a delayed and/or disguised effect so that the person who applies the pressure cannot know for sure just how successful he has been. To the patient who assails the physician with arguments, threats, and (in the case of women) tears in an effort to get his therapy conferences, privileges, passes, and discharge sooner than the doctors want to give them, it may look as if the physician is unyielding. Yet, back in

[7] In a five-class activity classification ranging from complete bed rest in Class 1 to maximum activity in Class 5.

the conference room the medical staff take the patient's "beefs" into consideration when making their decisions about managing his case. They may well give the next privilege somewhat earlier or more readily give a discharge in a borderline case than they would have if the patient had applied no pressure. This process seems analogous to what very likely happens in baseball when a player protests an umpire's decision. Umpires never change their decisions on balls and strikes, so it may at first seem that the player is wasting his breath when he protests. If one of the subsequent pitches is doubtful, however, the umpire is more likely to call it a ball if the batter has vigorously protested a previous strike call than he would if the batter had said nothing. In this situation, if the catcher and pitcher wish to uphold *their* bargaining position, they in turn must protest a close call against them in order to place the umpire under obligation to even things up with *them*.

In most of the illustrations I have given thus far, the bargaining process has been rather open, even though the effects have been at times more or less hidden. Actually, if bargaining situations could be quantified, such obvious examples would almost certainly be in a small minority. I have relied heavily on such obvious examples simply because the bargaining process could be more easily described with them.

Most bargaining, I would guess, is a product not of overt demands and pressures, but rather of the *anticipation* by the parties involved of the likely or possible consequences of certain behavior on their part. Take the case of patients who would like to get more time out on pass than they are presently getting. The "standard" pass may, in a given hospital, be regarded as three days once a month. Some patients may push the limits somewhat by asking for a pass three weeks after the previous one or by requesting five days instead of the customary three. However, if they want as much pass time as they can get, why don't they ask for another pass after only one week or why don't they ask for ten days instead of only five? The fact is that patients believe that requesting just a little more time may result in success, but making an "unreasonable" request will only earn them the anger of the physician and perhaps a flat refusal to grant any pass at all. (Of course, how to define the limits of "reasonable" and "unreasonable" is an important question in itself.) They are in much the same position as a labor union whose members are getting two dollars an hour and want to bargain for more. They will ask for an additional thirty cents an hour (with the hope of getting fifteen, just as patients may increase their pass request from three to five days and hope to get four), but they would not think of asking for an additional two dollars an hour. Such a request would be considered grossly unreasonable by everyone concerned and would weaken their bargaining position by making negotiation impossible and alienating public support. The union in such a case is faced with the problem of deciding what are the outside limits of a "reasonable" demand which will give them a basis for negotiation. Tuberculosis patients operate in the same way when they discuss with one another how much pass time they can "reasonably" request for an occasion such as Christmas. Physicians, on the other hand, will *anticipate* whether a given patient will be unduly upset or will leave against advice if refused a pass. They will *anticipate* whether giving a "special pass" to one patient will subject them to an outburst of such requests for "special passes" from other patients. Their anticipation of such results will affect their decision about whether or not to give a pass even though no threats have been made and no overt pressure has been brought to bear.

Or a physician may *anticipate* that a given patient will "take advantage" of a promotion in activity classification and assume that he is cured and need no longer observe any rest rules. In such a case the doctor may hold up the patient's promotion beyond the time that he would for most patients in a similar condition as a means of holding down the patient's activity level. "I know Abrams is already taking more activity than most patients in Class 3 even though he's only in Class 2. He's already been in Class 2 longer than most of the other guys and he's ready for a promotion so far as his condition is concerned. But if I put him in Class 3 now, he won't stay in bed at all any more, he won't wear a mask off the ward, he'll do leather work twelve hours a day instead of only six, he'll think he's cured. The only way I can show him that he still needs some rest is to hold him in Class 2." At the same time, patients who believe they have discovered the doctor's line of reasoning may try to improve their bargaining position by making a point of appearing "cooperative" — telling the doctor how anxious they are to follow his advice, carefully hiding their violations of activity restrictions from the nurses, and so forth — on the assumption that a "good" reputation will enable them to win earlier privileges, more passes, and earlier discharge.

Patients do not actually have to threaten to leave against advice in order to get concessions toward speeding up their treatment timetable. (In fact, if the threat occurs in a covert or indirect manner, it is likely to be more successful because it does not challenge the physician's authority.) A doctor, as a result of an off-the-cuff personality diagnosis and reports from the nurses about the patient's activities, may conclude that a given patient "can't stand confinement." In order to hold on to his patient, the doctor may from time to time give him a somewhat earlier privilege to keep him feeling that he is progressing. The doctor may not originally have wanted to discharge the patient earlier than most others and may believe that he needs just as much hospital treatment as the average. But even without overt demands from the patient, the doctor may find that the logic of the timetable requires an earlier discharge in keeping with the earlier privileges granted, unless there is a very clear-cut opposing consideration, such as recent positive sputum tests or obvious changes in recent chest X-rays. "I don't think he should be released just yet, but I can't think of any good reason for holding him."

The anticipations of others' reactions are, of course, often mistaken. The staff member or patient may find that his allowances for another's reactions did not have the effect he had hoped or that allowances on one matter had unexpected effects on other matters. The doctor whom the patient decided was a "soft touch" for another pass may just have launched a "crackdown" to stem the creeping increase in pass time. The patient who seemed to accept his fate so passively may become violently angry and walk out of the hospital when the staff decides to hold him another three months. However, such unsought and unexpected effects themselves become part of the information which the doctor and patient use to decide what to do next.

Anticipation and allowances on both sides influence each other and thus form a dialectic of mutual pushes and pulls operating over periods of time. Some of the pushes and pulls are outspoken demands from staff or patients, some are talked over only within the colleague group, some operate only within the minds of the individuals. Such a dialectic cannot be meaningfully analyzed as an event or a single interchange, but only as a continuing process with an arbitrary beginning and end, as in the following oversimplified illustration.

Some patients may press for the somewhat earlier granting of a given privilege, let us say "outside privileges."[8] The doctor may resist such pressure for a time. But on one occasion a patient offers a particularly compelling argument and is granted outside privileges a month earlier than he otherwise would have been. (The doctor's anticipation of the effect on the patient of his agreement to or refusal of this request enters into his decision.) Now it becomes more difficult for the doctor to refuse similar requests from other patients because he is faced with the question of whether it is "fair" to grant the earlier privilege to one and not to others. He therefore finds himself granting the same earlier outside privileges to others with "less compelling" arguments. The more conforming patient, who would not have thought of pressing for earlier outside privileges before, now cannot see why he should not get what others get. Patients are no longer asking to be granted an "exception," but simply to be given what "everybody else" is getting.

At this point the earlier outside privileges may become stabilized at a new point in the timetable. They may even have the effect of moving forward some other privileges since the patients, and even the physician in his own mind, can argue: "If outside privileges can be taken safely a month earlier, why can't [other privileges] be taken earlier?" The doctor may feel retrospectively that he has been tricked, but he may not consider the issue important enough to fight about and lets the matter stand. On the other hand, he may decide that the changed state of affairs is not in keeping with a proper treatment regimen, or that the patients will take advantage of his leniency in this case to make inroads on the restrictions in other areas, or that the

8 Permission to go out on the hospital grounds during certain hours.

shift in outside privileges to an earlier point on the timetable damages the logic of the graduated activity program and thus threatens to destroy the program as a whole. In such a case he may wipe out the earlier outside privileges altogether, or at least firmly refuse to grant any more. The patients call such action a "crackdown." There will be a period of ill feeling while the patients accuse the doctor or reneging on his bargain and the doctor accuses the patients of having tried to put a fast deal over on him. (Such accusations may pass openly between doctor and patients or they may be passed behind each other's backs.)

For a time the patients will let up on their demands and their pressure against the limits in all directions because they believe the doctor is "not in the mood" to tolerate or give in to pressure for more freedom of action. They "lie low" in the same way as does a whorehouse operator who suspends activities temporarily when the district attorney announces a drive to "wipe out vice." The doctor, in the meantime, is keeping a sharp eye open to see that he is not "tricked" again. However, in hospitals, as in politics, such campaigns blow over. The patients dissect the doctor's words and actions, as well as pick up any information they can from the ward personnel and others, to find out when the doctor has "cooled off." Finally, a few of the more venturesome patients will tentatively renew their demands. The first efforts may be sharply rejected, proving that the patients' timing was wrong. But the time will come when the traumatic effects of the previous incident will wear off and the doctor will once again grapple with himself about just what the "fair" and "humane" way is to deal with the "needs" of the patients. (Concepts of "fairness," humanity, decency, and the like themselves become counters in the bargaining process and may bolster the bargaining position of one side or the other.) Again, he will begin to make concessions to the pressures and anticipated pressures of the patients and the cycle begins again — although things are never *quite* the same way after any cycle as they were before.

Thus, much (probably most) bargaining between persons or groups is not a matter of open threats and the deployment of power positions. It tends rather to be more a matter of A anticipating B's reaction to A's potential behavior and modifying his own behavior in an effort to control B's reaction. A's behavior then creates an image which calls for certain anticipations on B's part when B decides what response to make. This process of anticipation and modification of behavior continues so long as A and B are in communication with one another. When A or B becomes aware of this process (and there is probably always some degree of awareness of it), he may deliberately try to manipulate his own image (as seen by the other party) as a means of gaining a desired response.

References

1. Becker, Howard S. "The Professional Dance Musician and His Audience," *American Journal of Sociology*, Vol. 57 (September 1951), pp. 136–144.

2. Belknap, Ivan. *Human Problems of a State Mental Hospital.* New York: McGraw-Hill Book Company, Inc., 1956.

3. Clemmer, Donald. *The Prison Community.* New York: Rinehart & Co., Inc., 1958.

4. Cohen, Elie A. *Human Behavior in the Concentration Camp.* New York: W. W. Norton & Company, Inc., 1953.

5. Fox, Renée C. *Experiment Perilous.* Glencoe, Ill.: The Free Press, 1959.

6. Goffman, Erving. *The Presentation of Self in Everyday Life.* Garden City, N.Y.: Doubleday & Company, Inc., Anchor Books, 1959.

7. Hassler, Alfred. *Diary of a Self-Made Convict.* Chicago: Henry Regnery Co., 1954.

8. Hughes, Everett C. *Men and Their Work.* Glencoe, Ill.: The Free Press, 1958.

9. Schelling, Thomas C. "An Essay on Bargaining," *American Economic Review*, Vol. 46 (June 1956), pp. 281–306.

10. Sykes, Gresham M. *The Society of Captives.* Princeton, N.J.: Princeton University Press, 1958.

11. Taxel, Harold S. "Authority Structure in a Mental Hospital Ward." Unpublished Master's thesis, Department of Sociology, University of Chicago, 1953.

31

Marihuana Use and Social Control

HOWARD S. BECKER
COMMUNITY STUDIES, INC., KANSAS CITY

As with many other forms of deviant behavior, the use of drugs can be analyzed as the result of the breakdown of general social controls and the substitution for them of the controls of a subgroup. But Howard Becker goes further than this in his interactionist analysis of marihuana users. He considers also the possibilities for action within the subculture and the experiences which shape the individual's tendency to make use of these possibilities. Social control is seen as a product of socialization — of interaction which leads to a particular set of expectations of oneself and of others. The process of socialization involves the individual's learning to anticipate what significant others in the social environment expect of him. Becker considers the problem of how the individual in a complex society selects from among those competing normative reference groups on the basis of his own developing definition of the situation.

When deviant behavior occurs in a society — behavior which flouts its basic values and norms — one element in its coming into being is a breakdown in social controls, those mechanisms which ordinarily operate to maintain valued forms of behavior.* In complex societies, the process is somewhat more complicated since breakdowns in social control are often the consequences of the person becoming a participant in a subculture whose controls operate at cross-purposes to those of the larger society. Important factors in the genesis of deviant behavior, then, may be sought in those processes by which people are emancipated from the larger set of controls and become responsive to those of the subculture.

Social controls affect individual behavior, in the first instance, through the use of power, the application of sanctions. Valued behavior is rewarded and negatively valued behavior is punished. Control would be difficult to maintain if such enforcement were always needed, so that more subtle mechanisms performing the same function arise. Among these is the control of behavior achieved by affecting the conceptions persons have of the activity to be controlled, and of the possibility or feasibility of engaging in it. These conceptions arise in social situations in which they are communicated by persons regarded as reputable and validated in experience. Such situations may be so ordered that individuals come to conceive of the activity as distasteful, inexpedient, or immoral, and therefore do not engage in it.

Such a perspective invites us to analyze the genesis of deviant behavior in terms of events which render sanctions ineffective and experiences which shift conceptions so that the behavior becomes a conceivable possibility to the person. This paper is devoted to an analysis of this process in the instance of marihuana use. Its basic question is: what is the sequence of events and experiences by which a person comes to be able to carry on the use of marihuana, in spite of the elaborate social controls functioning to prevent such behavior?

A number of potent forces operate to control the use of mari-

* This paper is reprinted, with the publisher's permission, from *Social Problems*, Vol. 3 (July 1955), pp. 35–44. Copyright 1955 by the Society for the Study of Social Problems. The research on which the paper is based was done while I was a member of the staff of the Chicago Narcotics Survey, a project done by the Chicago Area Project, Inc., under a grant from the National Mental Health Institute. I wish to thank Eliot Freidson, Erving Goffman, Anselm Strauss, and R. Richard Wohl for reading and commenting on an earlier version.

huana in this country. The act is illegal and punishable by severe penalties. Its illegality makes access to the drug difficult, placing immediate obstacles before anyone who wishes to use it. Actual use can be dangerous, for arrest and imprisonment are always possible consequences. In addition, those who are discovered in their use of the drug by family, friends, or employers may be subject to various kinds of informal but highly effective sanctions and social punishments: ostracism, withdrawal of affection, etc. Finally, a set of traditional views has grown up, defining the practice as a violation of basic moral imperatives, as an act leading to loss of self-control, paralysis of the will, and eventual slavery to the drug. Such views are commonplace and are an effective force preventing marihuana use.

The development of marihuana-using activity in an individual may be divided into three stages, each representing a distinct shift in the person's relations to these social controls of the larger society and those of the subculture in which marihuana is found. The first stage is represented by the *beginner*, the person smoking marihuana for the first time; the second, by the *occasional user*, whose use is sporadic and dependent on chance factors; and the third, by the *regular user*, for whom use becomes a systematic daily routine.

The analysis will be pursued in terms of the processes by which the various kinds of social controls become progressively less effective as the user moves from level to level of use or, alternatively, the ways in which they prevent such movement by remaining effective. The major kinds of controls to be considered are: (*a*) control through limiting of supply and access to the drug; (*b*) control through the necessity of keeping non-users from discovering that one is a user; (*c*) control through definition of the act as immoral. The rendering ineffective of these controls, at the levels and in the combinations to be described, may be taken as an essential condition for continued and increased marihuana use.

One explanatory note is in order. It is obvious that people do not do things simply because they are not prevented from doing them. More positive motivations are necessarily present. This paper does not deal with the genesis of these positive motivations involved in the continuation and increase of marihuana use (except in passing), focusing rather on the barriers to use, and taking the motivation more or less for granted. I have described one important element in this motivation elsewhere (2). This is the knowledge that one can gain pleasure by smoking marihuana, achieved in a process of learning to smoke the drug so that definite symptoms occur, learning to recognize these effects and connect them with the use of the drug, and learning to find these effects enjoyable. This learning takes place in interaction with more experienced users who present the novice with the necessary symbols and concepts with which to organize this otherwise vague and ambiguous experience. By and large, however, the motivation to continue use will, in this discussion, be taken for granted and emphasis placed on the breakdown of deterrents to this.

The analysis is based on fifty intensive interviews with marihuana users from a variety of social backgrounds and present positions in society.[1] The interviews focused on the history of the person's experience with the drug, seeking major changes in his attitude toward it and in his actual use of it and the reasons for these changes. Generalizations stating necessary conditions for the maintenance of use at each level were developed in initial interviews, and tested against and revised in the light of each succeeding one. The stated conclusions hold true for all the cases collected and may tentatively be considered as true of all marihuana users in this society, at least until further evidence forces their revision.[2]

SUPPLY

Marihuana use is limited, in the first instance, by laws making possession or sale of drugs punishable by severe penalties. This confines its distribution to illicit sources which are not available to the ordinary person. In order for a person to begin marihuana use, he must begin participation in some group through which these sources of supply become available to him, ordinarily a

[1] Most of the interviews were done by me. I wish to thank Solomon Kobrin and Harold Finestone for allowing me to make use of interviews done by them.
[2] This is an application of the method of analytic induction described by Lindesmith (3).

group organized around values and activities opposing those of the larger conventional society.

In those unconventional circles in which marihuana is already used, it is apparently just a matter of time until a situation arises in which the newcomer is given a chance to smoke it:

> I was with these guys that I knew from school, and one had some, so they went to get high and they just figured that I did too, they never asked me, so I didn't want to be no wallflower or nothin', so I didn't say nothin' and went out in the back of this place with them. They were doing up a couple of cigarettes.

In other groups marihuana is not immediately available, but participation in the group provides connections to others in which it is:

> But the thing was, we didn't know where to get any. None of us knew where to get it or how to find out where to get it. Well, there was this one chick there . . . she had some spade girl friends and she had turned on before with them. Maybe once or twice. But she knew a little more about it than any of the rest of us. So she got hold of some, through these spade friends, and one night she brought down a couple of sticks.

In either case, such participation provides the conditions under which marihuana becomes available for first use. It also provides the conditions for the next level of *occasional use,* in which the individual smokes marihuana sporadically and irregularly. When an individual has arrived through earlier experiences at a point where he is able to use marihuana for pleasure, use tends at first to be a function of availability. The person uses the drug when he is with others who have a supply; when this is not the case his use ceases. It tends therefore to fluctuate in terms of the conditions of availability created by his participation with other users; a musician at this stage of use said:

> That's mostly when I get high, is when I play jobs. And I haven't played hardly at all lately . . . See, I'm married twelve years now, and I really haven't done much since then. I had to get a day job, you know, and I haven't been able to play much. I haven't had many gigs, so I really haven't turned on much, you see.

Like I say, the only time I really get on is if I'm working
with some cats who do, then I will too. Like I say, I haven't
been high for maybe six months. I haven't turned on in all that
time. Then, since I come on this job, that's three weeks, I've
been high every Friday and Saturday. That's the way it goes
with me.

[This man was observed over a period of weeks to be completely dependent on other members of the orchestra in which
he worked and on musicians who dropped into the tavern in
which he was playing for any marihuana he used.]

If an occasional user begins to move on toward a more regularized and systematic mode of use, he can do it only by finding
some more stable source of supply than more-or-less chance
encounters with other users, and this means establishing connections with persons who make a business of dealing in narcotics.
Although purchases in large quantities are necessary for regular
use, they are not ordinarily made with that intent; but, once
made, they do render such use possible, as it was not before.
Such purchases tend to be made as the user becomes more responsive to the controls of the drug-using group:

I was running around with this whole crowd of people who
turned on then. And they were always turning me on, you
know, until it got embarrassing. I was really embarrassed that
I never had any, that I couldn't reciprocate. . . . So I asked
around where I could get some and picked up for the first time.

Also, purchasing from a dealer is more economical, since there
are no middle-men and the purchaser of larger quantities receives,
as in the ordinary business world, a lower price.

However, in order to make these purchases, the user must have
a "connection" — know someone who makes a business of selling
drugs. These dealers operate illicitly, and in order to do business
with them one must know where to find them and be identified
to them in such a way that they will not hesitate to make a sale.
This is quite difficult for persons who are very casually involved
in drug-using groups. But as a person becomes more identified
with these groups, and is considered more trustworthy, the necessary knowledge and introductions to dealers become available to
him. In becoming defined as a member, one is also defined as a

person who can safely be trusted to buy drugs without endangering anyone else.

Even when the opportunity is made available to them, many do not make use of it. The danger of arrest latent in such an act prevents them from attempting it:

> If it were freely distributed, I think that I would probably keep it on hand all the time. But . . . (You mean if it wasn't against the law?) Yeah. (Well, so does that mean that you don't want to get involved . . .) Well, I don't want to get too involved, you know. I don't want to get too close to the people who traffic in, rather heavily in it. I've never had any difficulty much in getting any stuff. I just . . . someone usually has some and you can get it when you want it. Why, just why, I've never happened to run into those more or less direct contacts, the pushers, I suppose you'd explain it on the basis of the fact that I never felt the need for scrounging or looking up one.

Such fears operate only so long as the attempt is not made, for once it has been successfully accomplished the individual is able to use the experience to revise his estimate of the danger involved; the notion of danger no longer prevents purchase. Instead, the act is approached with a realistic caution which recognizes without overemphasizing the possibility of arrest. The purchaser feels safe so long as he observes elementary, common-sense precautions. Although many of the interviewees had made such purchases, only a few reported any difficulty of a legal kind and these attributed it to the failure to take such precautions.

For those who do establish such connections, regular use is often interrupted by the arrest or disappearance of the man from whom they purchase their supply. In such circumstances, regular use can continue only if the user is able to find a new source of supply. This young man had to give up use for a while when:

> Well, like Tom went to jail, they put him in jail. Then Cramer, how did it happen . . . Oh yeah, like I owed him some money and I didn't see him for quite a while and when I did try to see him he had moved and I couldn't find out from anyone where the cat went. So that was that connection . . . (So you just didn't know where to get it?) No. (So you stopped?) Yeah.

This instability of sources of supply is an important control over regular use, and reflects indirectly the use of legal sanctions by the community in the arrest of those trafficking in drugs. The enforcement of the law controls use by making access more difficult because of this instability of sources, rather than through its acting as a direct deterrent to users.

Each level of use, from beginning to routine, thus has its typical mode of supply, which must be present for such use to occur. In this sense, the social mechanisms which operate to limit availability of the drug limit its use. However, participation in groups in which marihuana is used creates the conditions under which these controls which limit access to it no longer operate. Such participation also involves increased sensitivity to the controls of the drug-using group, so that there are forces pressing toward use of the new sources of supply. Changes in the mode of supply in turn create the conditions for movement to a new level of use. Consequently, it may be said that changes in group participation and membership lead to changes in level of use by affecting the individual's access to marihuana under present conditions in which the drug is available only through illicit outlets.

Secrecy

Marihuana use is limited also to the extent that individuals actually find it inexpedient or believe that they will find it so. This inexpediency, real or presumed, arises from the fact or belief that if non-users discover that one uses the drug, sanctions of some important kind will be applied. The user's conception of these sanctions is vague, because few of them seem ever to have had such an experience or to have known anyone who did. Although he does not know what specifically to expect in the way of punishments, the outlines are clear: he fears repudiation by people whose respect and acceptance he requires both practically and emotionally. That is, he expects that his relationships with non-users will be disturbed and disrupted if they should find out, and limits and controls his behavior accordingly.

This kind of control breaks down in the course of the user's participation with other users and in the development of his experience with the drug, as he comes to realize that, though it might be true that sanctions would be applied if non-users found out, they need never find out. At each level of use, there is a growth in this realization which makes the new level possible.

For the beginner, these considerations are very important and must be overcome if use is to be undertaken at all. These fears are challenged by the sight of others — more experienced users — who apparently feel there is little or no danger and appear to engage in the activity with impunity. If one does "try it once," he may still his fears by observations of this kind. Participation with other users thus furnishes the beginner with the rationalizations with which first to attempt the act.

Further participation in the marihuana use of these groups allows the novice to draw the further conclusion that the act can be safe no matter how often indulged in, as long as one is careful and makes sure that non-users are not present or likely to intrude. This kind of perspective is a necessary prerequisite for occasional use, in which the drug is used when other users invite one to join them. While it permits this level of use, such a perspective does not allow regular use to occur, for the worlds of user and non-user, while separate to a degree allowing the occasional use pattern to persist, are not completely segregated. The points where these worlds meet appear dangerous to the occasional user who must, therefore, confine his use to those occasions on which such meeting does not seem likely.

Regular use, on the other hand, implies a systematic and routine use of the drug which does not take into account such possibilities and plan periods of "getting high" around them. It is a mode of use which depends on another kind of attitude toward the possibility of non-users finding out, the attitude that marihuana use can be carried on under the noses of non-users, or, alternatively, on the living of a pattern of social participation which reduces contacts with non-users almost to the zero point. Without this adjustment in attitude, participation, or both, the user is forced to remain at the level of occasional use. These adjustments take place in terms of two categories of risks involved: first, that non-users will discover marihuana in one's possession and, second, that one will be unable to hide the effects of the drug when he is "high" while with non-users.

The difficulties of the would-be regular user, in terms of possession, are illustrated in the remarks of a young man who unsuccessfully attempted regular use while living with his parents:

> I never did like to have it around the house, you know. (Why?) Well, I thought maybe my mother might find it or something like that. (What do you think she'd say?) Oh, well, you know, like . . . well, they never do mention it, you know, anything about dope addicts or anything like that but it would be a really bad thing in my case, I know, because of the big family I come from. And my sisters and brothers, they'd put me down the worst. (And you don't want that to happen?) No, I'm afraid not.

In such cases, envisioning the consequences of such a secret being discovered prevents the person from maintaining the supply essential to regular use. Use remains erratic, since it must depend on encounters with other users and cannot occur whenever the user desires.

Unless he discovers some method of overcoming this difficulty, the person can progress to regular use only when the relationship deterring use is broken. People do not ordinarily leave their homes and families in order to smoke marihuana regularly. But if they do, for whatever reason, regular use, heretofore proscribed, becomes a possibility. Confirmed regular users often take into very serious account the effect on their drug use of forming new social relationships with non-users:

> I wouldn't marry someone who would be belligerent if I do [smoke marihuana], you know. I mean, I wouldn't marry a woman who would be so untrusting as to think I would do something . . . I mean, you know, like hurt myself or try to hurt someone.

If such attachments are formed, use tends to revert to the occasional level:

> [This man had used marihuana quite intensively but his wife objected to it.] Of course, largely the reason I cut off was my wife. There were a few times when I'd feel like . . . didn't actually crave for it but would just like to have had some. [He was unable to continue using the drug except irregularly, on those occasions when he was away from his wife's presence and control.]

If the person moves almost totally into the user group, the problem ceases in many respects to exist, and it is possible for regular use to occur except when some new connection with the more conventional world is made.

If a person uses marihuana regularly and routinely it is almost inevitable — since even in urban society such roles cannot be kept completely separate — that he one day find himself "high" while in the company of non-users from whom he wishes to keep his marihuana use secret. Given the variety of symptoms the drug may produce, it is natural for the user to fear that he might reveal through his behavior that he is "high," that he might be unable to control the symptoms and thus give away his own secret. Such phenomena as difficulty in focusing one's attention and in carrying on normal conversation create a fear that everyone will know exactly why one is behaving in this way, that the behavior will be interpreted automatically as a sign of drug use.

Those who progress to regular use manage to avoid this dilemma. It may happen, as noted above, that they come to participate almost completely in the subcultural group in which the practice is carried on, so that they simply have a minimal amount of contact with non-users about whose opinions they care. Since this isolation from conventional society is seldom complete, the user must learn another method of avoiding the dilemma, one which is the most important method for those whose participation is never so completely segregated. This consists in learning to control the drug's effects while in the company of non-users, so that they can be fooled and the secret successfully kept even though one continues participation with them. If one cannot learn this, there exists some group of situations in which he dare not get "high" and regular use is not possible:

> Say, I'll tell you something that just kills me, man, I mean it's really terrible. Have you ever got high and then had to face your family? I really dread that. Like having to talk to my father or mother, or brothers, man, it's just too much. I just can't make it. I just feel like they're sitting there digging [watching] me, and they know I'm high. It's a horrible feeling. I hate it.

Most users have these feelings and move on to regular use, if

Studies in Social Process

they do, only if an experience of the following order occurs, changing their conception of the possibilities of detection:

(Were you making it much then, at first?) No, not too much. Like I said, I was a little afraid of it. But it was finally about 1948 that I really began to make it strong. (What were you afraid of?) Well, I was afraid that I would get high and not be able to op [operate], you dig, I mean I was afraid to let go and see what would happen. Especially on jobs. I couldn't trust myself when I was high. I was afraid I'd get too high, and pass out completely, or do stupid things. I didn't want to get too wigged.

(How did you ever get over that?) Well, it's just one of those things, man. One night I turned on and I just suddenly felt real great, relaxed, you know, I was really swinging with it. From then on I've just been able to smoke as much as I want without getting into any trouble with it. I can always control it.

The typical experience is one in which the user finds himself in a position where he must do something while he is "high" that he is quite sure he cannot do in that condition. To his surprise, he finds that he can do it and can hide from others the fact that he is under the drug's influence. One or more occurrences of this kind allow the user to conclude that his caution has been excessive and based on a false premise. If he desires to use the drug regularly he is no longer deterred by this fear, for he can use such an experience to justify the belief that non-users need never know:

[The suggestion was made that many users find it difficult to perform their work tasks effectively while high. The interviewee, a machinist, replied with the story of how he got over this barrier.]

It doesn't bother me that way. I had an experience once that proved that to me. I was out on a pretty rough party the night before. I got pretty high. On pot [marihuana] and lushing, too. I got so high that I was still out of my mind when I went to work the next day. And I had a very important job to work on. It had to be practically perfect — precision stuff. The boss had been priming me for it for days, explaining how to do it and everything.

[He went to work high and, as far as he could remember, must have done the job, although there was no clear memory of it since he was still quite high.]

About a quarter to four, I finally came down and I thought, "Jesus! What am I doing?" So I just cut out and went home. I didn't sleep all night hardly, worrying about whether I had f . . . . d up on that job or not. I got down the next morning, the boss puts the old "mikes" on the thing, and I had done the f . . . . . job perfectly. So after that I just didn't worry any more. I've gone down to work really out of my mind on some mornings. I don't have any trouble at all.

This problem is not equally important for all users, for there are those whose social participation is such that it cannot arise; all their associates know they use marihuana and none of them care, while their conventional contacts are few and unimportant. In addition, some persons achieve idiosyncratic solutions which allow them to act "high" and have it ignored:

They [the boys in his neighborhood] can never tell if I'm high. I usually am, but they don't know it. See, I always had the reputation, all through high school, of being kind of goofy, so no matter what I do, nobody pays much attention. So I can get away with being high practically anyplace.

In short, persons limit their use of marihuana in proportion to the degree of their fear, realistic or otherwise, that non-users who are important to them will discover that they use drugs and react in some punishing way. This kind of control breaks down as the user discovers that his fears are excessive and unrealistic, as he comes to conceive of the practice as one which can be kept secret with relative ease. Each level of use can occur only when the person has revised his conception of the dangers involved in such a way as to allow it.

MORALITY

This section discusses the role of conventional notions of morality as a means through which marihuana use is controlled. The basic moral imperatives which operate here are those which require the individual to be responsible for his own welfare and to be able to control his behavior rationally. The stereotype of the dope fiend portrays a person who violates these imperatives. A recent description of the marihuana user illustrates the principal features of this stereotype:

> In the earliest stages of intoxication the will power is destroyed and inhibitions and restraints are released; the moral barricades are broken down and often debauchery and sexuality result. Where mental instability is inherent, the behavior is generally violent. An egotist will enjoy delusions of grandeur, the timid individual will suffer anxiety, and the aggressive one often will resort to acts of violence and crime. Dormant tendencies are released and while the subject may know what is happening, he has become powerless to prevent it. Constant use produces an incapacity for work and a disorientation of purpose (1, pp. 21–22).

One must add to this, of course, the notion that the user becomes a slave to the drug, that he voluntarily surrenders himself to a habit from which there is no escape. The person who takes such a stereotype seriously is presented with a serious obstacle to drug use. Use will ordinarily be begun, maintained, and increased only when some other way of viewing the practice is accepted by the individual.

The beginner has at some time shared these views. In the course of his participation in some unconventional segment of society, however, he is likely to acquire a more "emancipated" view of the moral standards implicit in this characterization of the drug user, at least to the point that he will not reject activities out of hand simply because they are conventionally condemned. The observation of others using the drug may further tempt him to apply his rejection of conventional standards to the specific instance of marihuana use. Such participation, then, tends to provide the conditions under which these controls can be circumvented at least sufficiently for first use to be attempted.

In the course of further experience in these groups, the novice acquires a whole series of rationalizations and justifications with which he may answer objections to occasional use if he decides to engage in it. If he should raise himself the objections of conventional morality he finds ready answers available in the folklore of marihuana-using groups.

One of the most common rationalizations is that conventional persons indulge in much more harmful practices and that a comparatively minor vice like marihuana smoking cannot really be wrong when such things as the use of alcohol are so commonly accepted:

> (You don't dig [like] alcohol then?) No, I don't dig it at all. (Why not?) I don't know. I just don't. Well, see, here's the thing. Before I was at the age where kids start drinking I was already getting on [using marihuana] and I saw the advantages of getting on, you know, I mean there was no sickness and it was much cheaper. That was one of the first things I learned, man. Why do you want to drink? Drinking is dumb, you know. It's so much cheaper to get on and you don't get sick, and it's not sloppy and takes less time. And it just grew to be the thing, you know. So I got on before I drank, you know. . . .
>
> (What do you mean that's one of the first things you learned?) Well, I mean, as I say, I was just first starting to play jobs as a musician when I got on and I was also in a position to drink on the jobs, you know. And these guys just told me it was silly to drink. They didn't drink either.

Additional rationalizations enable the user to suggest to himself that the drug's effects, rather than being harmful, are in fact beneficial:

> I have had some that made me feel like . . . very invigorated and also it gives a very strong appetite. It makes you very hungry. That's probably good for some people who are underweight.

Finally, the user, at this point, is not using the drug all the time. His use is scheduled, there being times when he considers it appropriate and times when he does not. The fact of this schedule allows him to assure himself that he controls the drug, rather than the drug controlling him, and becomes a symbol of the harmlessness of the practice. He does not consider himself a slave to the drug, because he can and does abide by this schedule, regardless of the amount of use the particular schedule may allow. The fact that there are times when he does not, on principle, use the drug, can be used as proof to himself of his freedom with respect to it.

I like to get on and mostly do get on when I'm relaxing, doing something I enjoy like listening to a real good classical record or maybe like a movie or something like that or listening to a radio program. Something I enjoy doing, not participating in, like . . . I play golf during the summer, you know, and a couple of guys I play with got on, turned on while they were playing golf and I couldn't see that because, I don't know, when you're participating in something you want your mind to be on that and nothing else, and if you're . . . because I think I know it makes you relax and . . . I don't think you can make it as well.

Occasional use can occur in an individual who accepts these views, for he has reorganized his moral notions in such a way as to permit it, primarily by acquiring the conceptions that conventional moral notions about drugs do not apply to this drug and that, in any case, his use of it has not become excessive.

If use progresses to the point of becoming regular and systematic, these questions may again be raised for the user, for he begins now to look, to himself as well as others, like the uncontrolled "dope fiend" of popular mythology. He must convince himself again, if use is to continue at this level, that he has not crossed this line. The problem, and one possible resolution, are presented in this statement by a regular user:

I know it isn't habit forming but I was a little worried about how easy it would be to put down, so I tried it. I was smoking it all the time, then I just put it down for a whole week to see what would happen. Nothing happened. So I knew it was cool [all right]. Ever since then I've used it as much as I want to. Of course, I wouldn't dig being a slave to it or anything like that, but I don't think that that would happen unless I was neurotic or something, and I don't think I am, not to that extent.

The earlier rationalization with regard to the beneficial effects of the drug remain unchanged and may even undergo a considerable elaboration. But the question raised in the last quotation proves more troublesome. In view of his increased and regularized consumption of the drug, the user is not sure that he is really able to control it, that he has not possibly become the slave of a vicious habit. Tests are made — use is given up and the conse-

quences awaited — and when nothing untoward occurs, the user
is able to draw the conclusion that there is nothing to fear.

The problem is, however, more difficult for some of the more
sophisticated users who derive their moral directives not so much
from conventional thinking as from popular psychiatric "theory."
Their use troubles them, not in conventional terms, but because
of what it may indicate about their mental health. Accepting
current thinking about the causes of drug use, they reason that
no one would use drugs in any large amounts unless "something"
were "wrong" with him, unless there were some neurotic maladjustment which made drugs necessary. The fact of marihuana
smoking becomes a symbol of psychic weakness and, ultimately,
moral weakness. This prejudices the person against further regular use and causes a return to occasional use unless some new
rationale is discovered.

> Well, I wonder if the best thing is not to get on anything
> at all. That's what they tell you. Although I've heard psychia-
> trists say, "Smoke all the pot [marihuana] you want, but leave
> the horse [heroin] alone."
> (Well, that sounds reasonable.) Yeah, but how many people
> can do it? There aren't very many . . . I think that seventy-five
> per cent or maybe even a bigger per cent of the people that
> turn on have a behavior pattern that would lead them to get
> on more and more pot to get more and more away from things.
> I think I have it myself. But I think I'm aware of it so I think
> I can fight it.

The notion that to be aware of the problem is to solve it constitutes such a rationale in the above instance. Where such justifications cannot be discovered, use continues on an occasional
basis, the user explaining his reasons in terms of his conception
of psychiatric theory:

> Well, I believe that people who indulge in narcotics and
> alcohol and drinks, any stimulants of that type, on that level,
> are probably looking for an escape from a more serious condi-
> tion than the more or less occasional user. I don't feel that
> I'm escaping from anything. I think that, however, I realize
> that I have a lot of adjustment to accomplish yet . . . So I can't
> say that I have any serious neurotic condition or inefficiency
> that I'm trying to handle. But in the case of some acquaint-

ances I've made, people who are chronic alcoholics or junkies [opiate addicts] or pretty habitual smokers, I have found accompanying that condition some maladjustment in their personality, too.

Certain morally toned conceptions about the nature of drug use and drug users thus influence the marihuana user. If he is unable to explain away or ignore these conceptions, use will not occur at all, and the degree of use appears to be related to the degree to which these conceptions no longer are influential, having been replaced by rationalizations and justifications current among users.

Discussion

The extent of an individual's use of marihuana is at least partly dependent on the degree to which conventional social controls fail to prevent his engaging in the activity. Apart from other possible necessary conditions, it may be said that marihuana use can occur at the various levels described only when the necessary events and shifts in conception of the activity have removed the individual from the influence of these controls and substituted for them the controls of the subcultural group.

This kind of analysis seems to put some experiential flesh on the bare bones of the contention that the assumption of roles in a deviant subculture accounts for deviant behavior. There is, of course, a close relationship between the two. But a good deal of theoretical and practical difficulty is avoided by introducing an intervening process of change in social participation and individual conception made possible, but not inevitable, by subcultural membership, and which becomes itself the explanatory factor. In this way, the element of truth in the simpler statement is conserved while the difficulties posed by those who participate in such groups without engaging in the deviant behavior are obviated. For such membership only provides the possibility, not the necessity, of having those experiences which will produce the behavior. The analysis may be made finer by then considering those contingencies which tend to determine whether or not the member of such a group actually has the necessary experiences.

Such a view necessarily implies the general hypothesis, of some interest to students of culture and personality, that the holding of a social position, in and of itself, cannot be considered to explain an individual's behavior. Rather, the analysis of behavior must take account of social roles in a more subtle fashion, by asking what possibilities of action and what experiences which might shape the individual's appreciation and tendency to make use of those possibilities are provided by a given role. Such a viewpoint continues to insist on the analytic importance of the role concept, which calls our attention to the patterning of an individual's experience by the position which he holds in an organized social group, but adds to this an emphasis on the experience itself as it shapes conduct and the process by which this shaping occurs.

References

1. Anslinger, Harry J., and William F. Tompkins. *The Traffic in Narcotics*. New York: Funk & Wagnalls Co., 1953.
2. Becker, Howard S. "Becoming a Marihuana User," *American Journal of Sociology*, Vol. 59 (November 1953), pp. 235–242.
3. Lindesmith, Alfred R. *Opiate Addiction*. Bloomington, Ind.: Principia Press, 1947.

32

Desegregation as an Object of Sociological Study

 E. FRANKLIN FRAZIER

HOWARD UNIVERSITY

Desegregation is a process of social change affecting one of the most deep-seated feelings in our culture. This change is probably stimulated originally by the forces of industrialization, urbanization, and cosmopolitanism, and was given immediate stimulus by a U.S. Supreme Court decision in 1954. The change applied particularly to the segregated public schools of seventeen Southern and Border states and the District of Columbia. The Border states have been almost completely desegregated since 1954, and some desegregation has also occurred in the states of the upper South, thus giving sociologists considerable information about the processes of desegregation and a prognosis of the probable sequence of events when desegregation begins — as is now about to occur — in the Deep South. Professor Frazier has long been recognized as one of the outstanding students of minority groups.

A review of the relevant literature indicates that much more attention has been given to the study of the historical, political, and especially social-psychological aspects of racial desegregation than to the sociological aspects of the problem. (See 6, 22 and 26.) Outstanding among the sociological contributions to the subject is an article by Blumer in which he has presented a theoretical analysis of desegregation as a social process with special emphasis on the ecological aspects of the problem and on the role of functionaries and organized activities in the desegregation process (1). Recently greater attention has been directed to the role of the Negro community, especially the role of Negro leaders in the movement for racial desegregation.[1] But scarcely any studies have been concerned primarily with the manner in which the organization and social life of the Negro community and its interaction with the wider American community influence the nature and extent of desegregation. It is the purpose of this essay to explore and analyze this phase of the process of desegregation.[2]

In the article referred to above, Blumer has made a clear analysis of the difference between racial segregation as a natural ecological process and racial segregation resulting from conscious social policies (1). It is with the effect upon desegregation of racial segregation as an ecological process that the sociological study of desegregation should begin. Racial segregation resulting from social policies should be considered as a phase of the conflicts arising over the status of the Negro in the social organization. Racial segregation as an ecological process has been in operation almost from the time when Negroes were introduced into the American colonies. One phase of the ecological process was the concentration of Negroes who were free before the Civil War in cities and in areas outside the plantation.[3] But more important was the fact that as the cotton plantations developed,

---

[1] See, for example, Lewis M. Killian and Charles U. Smith (14).

[2] Desegregation and integration are often used interchangeably. There is some justification for this usage since desegregation and integration are correlated aspects of the same social process. Generally speaking "desegregation" refers to the process by which Negroes are being integrated into the institutional and other phases of the social life of the wider American community or American society. Unfortunately, however, the term "integration" is often used to refer to assimilation, which has a more restricted or specified denotation.

[3] See Chapter 4, "The Free Negro," in the writer's *The Negro in the United States* (11).

the concentration of Negroes in the "Black Belt" of the South provided the basis of a pattern of race relations which has persisted until the present. Although there has been a decrease in the area of the "Black Belt" and a corresponding decline in the number of Negroes in the "Black Belt," the area which comprised the old plantation South constitutes the hard core which shows the greatest resistance to desegregation.[4] In October 1960, according to the *Southern School News*, 27 per cent, or 768 of the 2,834 biracial school districts in 17 Southern and Border states, including the District of Columbia, had begun or had accomplished desegregation.[5] There were no desegregated school districts in Alabama, Georgia, Louisiana, Mississippi, and South Carolina and very few desegregated school districts in other states outside the Border states. A similar pattern in the distribution of registered Negro voters will be considered later.

The relevance of racial segregation as an ecological process for sociological analysis is not based upon the assumption that there is a mechanical relationship between the proportion of Negroes in a white community and the emergence of a system of racial segregation.[6] The sociologist is interested in human ecology because it provides the basis of divergent social orders — economic, political, and moral — which form a hierarchy. (See 21, p. 157.) In the "Black Belt" of the South, one can recognize these different systems of human interaction. The southern plantation represented, in a sense, a racial division of labor (23, p. 52). However, it should be noted that this racial division of

[4] The "Black Belt" in the South consists of those counties in which Negroes constitute 50 per cent or more of the total population. From 1900 to 1950 the number of such counties declined from 286 to 158 and the total Negro population of the "Black Belt" counties decreased from 4,057,619 to 2,078,168 (11, pp. 187–190).

[5] Vol. 7 (October 1960). In 1957, of the 3,700 biracial school districts, 684, or 18 per cent, were desegregated or had begun desegregation, Vol 3 (June 1957).

[6] This was the position of Alfred H. Stone when he stated that segregation by law was inevitable where the proportion of Negroes exceeded 10 per cent because the white man experienced an instinctive feeling of "pressure" in the presence of a mass of people of a different race (25). In St. Louis, for example, where racial desegregation of the public schools was carried out smoothly after the Supreme Court decision of May 17, 1954, 36 per cent of the school enrollment and 20 per cent of the population is Negro (*Look*, April 3, 1956).

labor was in harmony with the distribution of power. Therefore, the plantation was not only an industrial or economic institution, but it was also a political institution. In the areas
dominated by the plantation system of agriculture, there was a
paternalistic regime in which Negroes had no rights as citizens.
Since the decision of the Supreme Court of the United States
outlawing the white primary (13, p. 54), the only significant
increases in the number of Negro voters has been outside the
"Black Belt." In Mississippi, where there are 31 "Black Belt"
counties, between 1947 and 1952 the number of registered Negro
voters increased from 5,000 to less than 20,000. On the other
hand, in Texas, where there are only two "Black Belt" counties,
the number of registered Negro voters increased from 100,000
to 214,000 (24). During this same period, the number of registered Negro voters in Louisiana, where the number of "Black
Belt" counties declined during this period from 31 to 13, shot
up from 10,000 to 160,000; but subsequent political action on
the part of whites removed 40,000 Negroes from the registration
rolls.

We have noted above that as a result of the ecological process
the Negroes who were free before the Civil War were concentrated in cities and in other areas outside the plantation region.
It has been in the cities and other areas not dominated by the
plantation regime that Negroes have been able to escape from
the social controls which grew up under the plantation system.
It has been in Border states where the Negro population is
largely urbanized that school desegregation has progressed far-
thest. Even in the cities of the lower South there are movements
toward integration (3). However, it is in the cities that are least
dominated by the plantation system that Negroes are beginning
to register to vote. For it is in the matter of voting that the influence of the political system which grew up on the plantation
system makes itself most evident. For example, it is easier for
Negroes to register and vote not only in the cities but even in
the rural areas of North Carolina and in Savannah and Atlanta,
Georgia, than in Birmingham, Alabama. According to the report
of the Southern Regional Council, "Birmingham and surrounding
Jefferson County present one of the gloomiest pictures for Negroes in the South. In no other major city of the region has it

been so difficult for them to vote. Only about 7,000 of 121,500 Negroes over 21 are registered; at least that many more have been turned down." (24)

Within the cities themselves, both in the South and in the North, racial segregation has occurred as the result of an ecological process. In the larger cities of the South, there have been two types of Negro concentration (5, 82). In the older cities of the South the Negro population was widely scattered. This was due to historic factors, the most important of which was the fact that Negro settlements grew up in places close to the homes of whites in which Negroes worked. These settlements represented in a way the symbiotic relationship which exists between people on the ecological level of human relations. But this type of racial settlement should be differentiated from the racial segregation which results from the impersonal economic forces which are responsible for the ecological organization of modern industrial and commercial cities. This new type of racial segregation has appeared in the new cities of the South, or in cities where industry and commerce have determined their spatial pattern. In these newer cities there are several large concentrations of Negroes and the remainder of the Negro population is scattered lightly over a large area. These light scatterings of Negroes over a large area are generally the remnants of the historic conditions which we have indicated.

The location of the Negro communities in the Border cities tends to conform to the pattern of Southern cities though there are large concentrations of Negroes similar to those in Northern cities (11, pp. 242 ff.). It appears that neither historic nor economic factors have been solely responsible for the location of the Negro communities in the Border cities. It is perhaps because neither factor exercised a decisive influence in determining the location of the Negro population that the battles over the residential segregation of Negroes were first fought in the Border states.[7] On the other hand, it is in the large cities of the North

[7] In St. Louis the first popular vote on the residential segregation of the Negro in the United States was held in 1916. It was in the Louisville segregation case that the Supreme Court of the United States handed down the unanimous decision that it was unconstitutional to prohibit Negroes by law from buying and occupying property. The United States Supreme Court decisions of May 3, 1948, outlawing the enforcement by

that the most important studies of racial segregation as an ecological process have been carried out. The concentration of
Negroes in certain areas of Northern cities was the result of the
same economic and social processes as were responsible for the
segregation of other minority groups.[8]

Racial segregation as an ecological process is important for
sociological analysis because the spatial pattern of the community
is the basis of a moral order.[9] It is an indication of the place of
the racial group within the organization of the community and
the interactions of people within the community. At the same
time, racial segregation as an ecological process provides an index
to the absence of communication between Negroes and other
peoples and their moral isolation. The attempts to integrate Negroes into public housing projects represent an effort to break
down the moral isolation of Negroes in the urban environment.
(See 7, 18, 28.)

Despite the success of some of these efforts to develop integrated housing and break down residential segregation, the moral
isolation of the Negro has continued. It has continued not so
much because of segregation resulting from an ecological process as because of the social organization of the Negro community. The ecological process which creates segregation on the
basis of language, culture, and race brings about segregation
"based upon vocational interests, upon intelligence and personal
ambition" within the racial group (21, p. 170; 9). Because of
their isolation within American life, Negroes have developed a
community life with a set of institutions which duplicate the
institutions of the wider American community. These institu-

state or federal courts of covenants restricting the sale or rental of property to Negroes, were based upon two covenant cases from the District of
Columbia, one case from St. Louis, and a fourth case from Detroit.

[8] In a pioneer article (4, p. 105), Ernest W. Burgess stated: "The residential separation of white and Negro has almost invariably been treated
by itself as if it were a unique phenomenon of urban life. In fact, however, as recent studies already prove, this is only one case among many of
the workings of the process of segregation in the sorting and sifting of
the different elements of the population of the city. There are immigrant
colonies, the so-called Ghettoes, Little Sicilies, Chinatowns, as well as
Black Belts."

[9] See Chapter 9, "The Urban Community as a Spatial Pattern and a Moral
Order," in Park, *Human Communities* (21).

tions embody the social traditions and values which are current within the social world of the Negro. Moreover, there is an economic and social stratification of the Negro population with its different norms of behavior, different expectations, and certain vested interests. When the sociologist studies desegregation, he must take this fact into account in studying the attitudes and behavior of Negroes in regard to desegregation.

Although the Negro community is more or less isolated spatially from the wider American community and the social life of Negroes revolves around the institutions and associations of the Negro community, Negroes are, nevertheless, dependent economically upon the economic institutions of the American community. In the rural South, farm ownership among Negroes has never exceeded the 25 per cent level which was attained in 1910; and as Negroes have moved into cities their dependence upon the economic institutions of the American communities has increased. At the opening of the present century, because of the competition of white workers and discrimination in employment, some Negro leaders advocated the development of Negro businesses which would give employment to Negroes. But this proved an empty dream, for one finds that in 1960 Negro businesses, from the standpoint of Negro employment and income from capital investment, were no more important than they were in 1900. The integration of Negroes into the economic institutions of the American community has become the only hope for survival.

In the South the integration of Negroes into the economic institutions of the American community is complicated by both social and economic factors. These factors include traditional notions and attitudes concerning the status of Negroes and their fitness for certain types of work; the relationship of employers and the labor unions; the relations of Negroes and whites, especially white women, in the plants; the competition of whites and Negroes for employment in the new industries; and changing conditions of a market economy (19, pp. 179 ff.). In most of the industries in Southern cities there is a color bar which restricts Negro workers to unskilled occupations. The greatest barrier, however, to the upward mobility of Negro workers is the relative inaccessibility to them of white collar and professional occupations. Negroes in white collar and professional occupations are confined almost entirely to the Negro community.

In the North, on the other hand, Negroes have been able to break through many of the barriers to their entering white collar and professional occupations. This can be attributed partly to the absence of a deeply rooted tradition of caste. But it is also due to those changes in the organization of American life which have enabled the large industrial unions to play an increasingly important role. These industrial unions have from the beginning had a much more liberal racial policy than the older craft unions. In the South, on the other hand, the older craft unions have continued to exclude Negro workers and the political forces in Southern communities have tended to reduce the effectiveness of the industrial unions. There are other factors which should be studied by the sociologist and the most important of these is the fact that Negroes in Northern cities have political power. A large number of Negro white collar and professional workers in Northern cities are in municipal employment. This is not true in the South because the Negro does not have the right to vote. Thus, although theoretically one might assume that desegregation in economic relations would be easy, social status and political power are always involved in the economic relations of men.

Those who have been faced with the problem of the desegregation of public schools in the North as well as in the South have come up against the fact of the residential segregation of Negroes. Residential segregation, as we have seen, is partly due to an impersonal ecological process. But it is also the result of deliberate activities on the part of whites (27). Where the whites have resorted to laws and covenants in order to restrict the free movement of Negroes into areas, the sociologist will be concerned not with the ecological process but with changes in the economic organization of race relations and with the conflicts which arise in the struggle of the Negro for status (29). The conflict over status will involve the political power of Negroes most especially in Northern cities. It appears that at the present time the efforts to desegregate are directed mainly against segregation resulting from ecological factors and to a less extent against resistance on the part of whites. In the South, on the other hand, it appears that the resistance of whites to desegregation is directed mainly against the ecological process which accounts for racially mixed school districts.

When the organization of the Negro community is considered in relation to desegregation, the first fact which should be considered is the stratification of the Negro community. The stratification of the Negro community has been accelerated by the urbanization of Negroes and the resulting occupational differentiation. Increasingly, the older stratification, which consisted of a simple class system based upon social distinctions, has been effaced by a stratification based upon socio-economic classes. The process has progressed much farther in the North than in the South because of the restrictions upon the occupational mobility of Negroes in the South. In the South, the majority of the Negro population is still found in the lower class, which is composed of laborers and unskilled workers who are drawn from the rural areas. The behavior and outlook of the lower-class Negroes are largely influenced by the folk tradition of the Negro. Their family life, which lacks an institutional character, is often unstable and their children lack discipline and are poorly socialized. Above this lower class is an intermediate class which is struggling to maintain middle-class standards of life. At the top of the social pyramid is an upper class which is really a middle class according to American standards. The members of this class have broken away from the folk traditions or they are the descendants of the Negroes who were free before the Civil War or the slaves who were house servants and skilled mechanics. This new middle class, which constitutes about 13 per cent of the Negro population, is only relatively half as large as the Negro middle class in Northern cities (10, Chapter 2).

In the North, the stratification of the Negro community is based mainly upon occupation and income (8, Chapters 19, 20, 21, 22). This is the result of the fact, as we have seen, that Negroes have been able to enter most of the occupations. In the North there is a small upper class, which is becoming differentiated from an intermediate class on the basis of incomes which permit it to maintain a standard and style of life above the majority of those who derive their incomes from professional and white collar occupations. Within this upper class, which from the standpoint of income would be included in the middle class in the white American community, and the intermediate class are found about a fourth of the Negroes in the North. This new middle class in the Negro community is especially influential in determining the values and outlook of Negroes.

In studying the processes of desegregation it is important to study the interaction of the various strata in the class structure of the Negro community to the new relation of Negroes to American society. It should be pointed out that these strata represent important differences in the extent and nature of the exposure of Negroes to American culture and differences in the extent and nature of contacts with white people. The new Negro middle class, which has become increasingly important in the Negro community, has a social heritage which differentiates it from the white middle classes. In fact, the social heritage of this class is a mixture of the so-called "aristocratic" heritage of mulattoes or Negroes who were free before the Civil War and the heritage of the Negro folk who have risen to middle-class status (10, Chapter 5). Therefore, they have a style of life and set of values which do not permit them to participate easily in the social world of white middle classes. The differences in style of life and values have become evident when whites and Negroes have been brought together. If these differences are conspicuous in the case of middle-class Negroes, the class which is closest in culture and outlook to white Americans, it is hardly necessary to emphasize the difficulties involved in contacts between whites and lower-class Negroes, with their free and uninhibited behavior.

A study of the changing class structure of the Negro community is important in order to understand the social heritage and attitudes of the new strata which are rising to middle-class status and are assuming leadership in the process of desegregation. This may be seen in the movement which is being led by Reverend Martin Luther King and in the sit-ins by the Negro college students in the South. Reverend King is representative of a new leadership which is supplanting the old "accommodating" leadership. This new leadership has appeared in response to the rise of new strata to middle-class status as the result of the increasing numbers of Negroes who are attending colleges. The rise of these new strata is dramatized in the spontaneous movement on the part of Negro students who are in revolt against the former leaders (16, 17). The new strata have a different social heritage from the older leadership, who represented the "genteel tradition" of the small Negro upper class. They had become the leaders in the Negro community because they enjoyed economic and social advantages which differentiated them from the masses of Negroes. The new strata are rooted in the Negro masses, and as they have become articulate they have given a "new definition" to the problem of desegregation. In fact, it might even be said that the old "accommodating" leadership had a vested interest in segregation which the new strata do not have.

Among the institutions which have grown up among Negroes, the Negro church is the most important. The Negro church is important because it provided the earliest basis of social cohesion and cooperation among Negroes. The Negro church as an institution has a continuous history that goes back to the last quarter of the eighteenth century. This institutional form is rooted in the social traditions and the mores of Negroes and embodies their highest aspirations and peculiar outlook on life. It has been in the Negro church that the Negro has been able to give rein to his emotions and find satisfaction for his longings. Moreover, the Negro church has provided a refuge in which Negroes could find protection against a hostile white world. For a people who were isolated from the political life of the American community, the Negro church has been a political arena and provided an area of social existence in which Negroes could aspire to leadership and gain recognition. As a consequence, the Negro church continues to enlist the Negro's deepest loyalties.

These facts concerning the Negro church must be taken into account when the sociologist studies desegregation generally and especially the desegregation of the churches. From the standpoint both of the organization of the Negro community and the white community, the church offers one of the most important barriers to desegregation.[10] The Negro church organizations, like the

[10] This will sound strange to those who assert that the Christian Church should be the last place where a policy of racial exclusiveness is practiced. The Negro church is admonished that it should abandon its racial character and thus aid in the process of racial desegregation. But this shows a complete lack of an understanding of the nature of social organi-

churches in the white community, reflect the class structure of the Negro community. For the great mass of the Negro population the Baptist and Methodist churches provide emotional satisfactions and participation in a meaningful social existence, or a way of life. Upper-class and middle-class Negroes who have broken away from the traditions and way of life of the Negro masses find a more congenial religious experience in the Presbyterian, Congregational, Episcopal, and Catholic churches. Desegregation for them is not so much the desegregation of Negro churches as the desegregation of white churches. But no amount of acceptance in the white churches will bring about the dissolution of Negro churches, which are the most important cultural institutions among Negroes.[11]

In the Negro community there are, besides the Negro church, other institutions and associations which represent the peculiar traditions and special interests of Negroes. These include fraternal organizations, the Greek-letter societies, and social clubs. Then there are professional organizations among Negroes which have a long history. At the present time there are some indications that Negroes will increasingly be admitted to the local chapters of the American Medical Association. But this trend does not seem to forecast the early dissolution of the National Medical Association, the Negro professional association. The Negro professional associations, like the white, are not simply concerned with their professional interests but provide social contacts of a more or less intimate character. It is because of the intimate social contacts within professional organizations that barriers to the acceptance of Negroes in associations representing the secular interests of the community continue to exist. This is

zation. Some middle-class Negroes, in their present confusion about their racial identity and the meaning of integration, have undertaken to change the names of Negro churches. The Colored Methodist Church was changed to *Christian* Methodist Church. When a similar attempt was made to change the name of the African Methodist Church to the *American* Methodist Episcopal Church, the mass of the Negro membership revolted against the proposal (see 12).

[11] Recently the President of the National Baptist Convention, Inc. (Negro), condemned the "kneel-ins," or the attempt of Negroes to enter white churches in the following words: "If you have religion in your church, use it. Don't go kneeling in somebody else's church." (*The Pittsburgh Courier*, November 5, 1960.)

often given as the reason for not admitting Negro workers to labor unions in the South. Labor unions are important, as we have seen before, because they provide the means by which Negroes gain access to the economic institutions of the American community. Thus they are important in desegregation since they form a bridge between the Negro social world and the wider American society.

The sociologist should give attention to the integration of Negroes into sports and into the world of entertainment because it reveals certain important facts concerning both the changes in status of the Negro and the relation of desegregation to the changes in the organization of American life. Forty or fifty years ago, a Negro could neither sing a sentimental song on the American stage nor appear on the stage with whites. Within the past 25 or 30 years this has changed; however, the change has been much more radical in the North than in the South. It appears that the change is the result of two factors: first, the fact that the Negro has always been able to secure an acceptance more easily in those areas of American life which were outside of conventional society; and, secondly, the change in the organization of American life — urbanization, the growth of gigantic corporations, and the growth in power of labor unions. As a result of the change in the organization of American life, the assimilation of Negroes has become a process of assimilation in secondary groups (15; 20, pp. 204–220). The Negro is being incorporated into the institutions and associations of the metropolitan communities and he is acquiring the superficial uniformity and homogeneity of manners and fashions characteristic of cosmopolitan groups. But his loyalties and deepest attachments are still rooted in the Negro community or the social world of the Negro. Negroes may be integrated into baseball, the respectable national sport, but there is not intimate association between Negro and white players (2). The intimate social life of the Negro players is in the Negro community. It is only in Hollywood, a world removed from conventional American society, that there are signs that intimate association between whites and Negroes is becoming acceptable.

There are other aspects of desegregation which are important in the sociological study of the problem. Because of the change in the organization of American life and the change in the relation of the United States to the rest of the world, there has been a change in public policy (31). At the opposite pole of race relations is intermarriage, involving the most intimate relations of mankind. Hardly any fundamental sociological studies of the marriage of Negroes and whites have been undertaken. Most of the studies of sociologists have been no more than a priori judgments on intermarriage without empirical data to support them. The fact of primary sociological importance is that intermarrying couples should be studied in relation to their position in the organization or structure of the white and Negro communities and the interactions between these two social worlds.

By way of summary and conclusion, I shall undertake to state the important points which have been brought out in this attempt to define desegregation as an object of sociological study. First, it was shown that it was necessary to study the effect of segregation as an ecological phenomenon upon the desegregation process. Although, as Wirth has pointed out, human ecology is outside of the field of sociology, it nevertheless "provides us with one of the hitherto neglected aspects of the matrix within which social events take place." (30, p. 142) Or, as we have noted, the ecological organization of the community is the basis of the social organization. It is the relation of the desegregation process to social organization that is of primary interest to the sociologist. It has been shown that the sociologist should concern himself with the social organization of the Negro community and the social organization of the wider American community because desegregation is the result of the interaction between both the Negro and white communities, both of which are undergoing changes. Therefore, of particular interest to the sociologist are those areas of interracial contacts which are on the fringe or outside of the traditional or conventional social organization of both the white and Negro communities. It is in these "vulnerable" areas of social life that desegregation progresses most rapidly. In the final analysis, complete racial desegregation would mean the dissolution of the social organizations of the Negro community as Negroes are integrated as individuals into the institutional life of American society.

References

1. Blumer, Herbert. "Social Science and the Desegregation Process," *Annals of the American Academy of Political and Social Science,* Vol. 304 (March 1956), pp. 137–143.
2. Boyle, Robert. "The Private World of the Negro Ballplayer," *Sports Illustrated,* March 21, 1960.
3. Bullock, Henry A. "Urbanism and Race Relations," in Rupert R. Vance and Nicholas J. Demerath (eds.), *The Urban South.* Chapel Hill, N.C.: University of North Carolina Press, 1959, pp. 207–229.
4. Burgess, Ernest W. "Residential Segregation in American Cities," *Annals of the American Academy of Political and Social Science,* Vol. 140 (November 1928), pp. 105–115.
5. Demerath, Nicholas J., and Harlan W. Gilmore. "The Ecology of Southern Cities," in Rupert R. Vance and Nicholas J. Demerath (eds.), *The Urban South.* Chapel Hill, N.C.: University of North Carolina Press, 1959, pp. 242 ff.
6. *Desegregation: Some Propositions and Research Suggestions.* New York: Anti-Defamation League of B'nai B'rith, 1958.
7. Deutsch, Morton, and Mary E. Collins. *Interracial Housing: A Psychological Evaluation of a Social Experiment.* Minneapolis: University of Minnesota Press, 1951.
8. Drake, St. Clair, and Horace R. Cayton. *Black Metropolis.* New York: Harcourt, Brace and Co., 1945.
9. Frazier, E. Franklin. *The Negro Family in the United States.* Chicago: The University of Chicago Press, 1931.
10. Frazier, E. Franklin. *Black Bourgeoisie.* Glencoe, Ill.: The Free Press, 1957.
11. Frazier, E. Franklin. *The Negro in the United States,* rev. ed. New York: The Macmillan Company, 1957.
12. Frazier, E. Franklin. "The Negro Middle Class and Desegregation," *Social Problems,* Vol. 4 (April 1957), pp. 291–301.
13. Hill, Herbert, and Jack Greenberg. *Citizen's Guide to Desegregation.* Boston: Beacon Press, 1955.
14. Killian, Lewis M., and Charles U. Smith. "Negro Protest Leaders in a Southern Community," *Social Forces,* Vol. 38 (March 1960), pp. 253–257.
15. Lohman, Joseph D., and Dietrich C. Reitzes. "Note on Race

Relations in Mass Society," *American Journal of Sociology,* Vol. 58 (November 1952), pp. 240–246.

16. Lomax, Louis E. "The Negro Revolt Against 'The Negro Leaders,' " *Harper's Magazine,* June 1960, pp. 41–48.

17. Lomax, Louis E. "The Negroes Act," *Dissent,* Summer 1960.

18. Merton, Robert K. "The Social Psychology of Housing," in W. Denis (ed.), *Current Trends in Social Psychology.* Pittsburgh: University of Pittsburgh Press, 1948, pp. 163–217.

19. National Planning Association. *Selected Studies of Negro Employment in the South.* Washington, D.C.: National Planning Association.

20. Park, Robert E. *Race and Culture.* Glencoe, Ill.: The Free Press, 1950.

21. Park, Robert E. *Human Communities.* Glencoe, Ill.: The Free Press, 1952.

22. Reid, Ira DeA. (ed.). "Racial Desegregation and Integration," *Annals of the American Academy of Political and Social Science,* Vol. 304 (March 1956).

23. Reuter, Edward B. "Competition and the Racial Division of Labor," in Edgar T. Thompson (ed.), *Race Relations and the Race Problem.* Durham, N.C.: Duke University Press, 1939, pp. 46–60.

24. Southern Regional Council. "The Negro Voter in the South," *Special Report.* Atlanta, Ga., July 18, 1957.

25. Stone, Alfred H. "Is Race Friction Between Blacks and Whites in the United States Growing and Inevitable?" *American Journal of Sociology,* Vol. 13 (1907–08), pp. 677–696.

26. Tumin, Melvin M. *Desegregation: Resistance and Readiness.* Princeton, N.J.: Princeton University Press, 1958.

27. Weaver, Robert C. *The Negro Ghetto.* New York: Harcourt, Brace and Co., 1944.

28. Weaver, Robert C. "Integration in Public and Private Housing," *Annals of the American Academy of Political and Social Science,* Vol. 304 (March 1956), pp. 86–97.

29. Weaver, Robert C. "Class, Race and Urban Renewal," *Land Economics,* Vol. 36 (August 1960), pp. 235–251.

30. Wirth, Louis. "Human Ecology," in Elizabeth Wirth Marvick and Albert J. Reiss, Jr. (eds.), *Community Life and Social Policy: Selected Papers by Louis Wirth.* Chicago: The University of Chicago Press, 1956, pp. 133–142.

31. Wirth, Louis. "Race and Public Policy," in Elizabeth Wirth Marvick and Albert J. Reiss, Jr. (eds.), *Community Life and Social Policy: Selected Papers by Louis Wirth*. Chicago: The University of Chicago Press, 1956, pp. 334–353.

32. Woofter, Thomas J., Jr. *Negro Problems in Cities*. New York: Doubleday, Doran & Company, 1928.

33

Urbanism and Suburbanism as Ways of Life: A Re-evaluation of Definitions

HERBERT J. GANS

UNIVERSITY OF PENNSYLVANIA

Social scientists have noted that variations in residence — city, suburb, small town, open country — tend to be associated with different patterns of behavior. The late Louis Wirth, who undoubtedly would have contributed to this volume were he still alive, described urbanism as a way of life in a classic article published in 1938. Professor Gans now reviews Wirth's theory in the light of subsequent research. He argues that residence is less a source of variation in behavior than an index (not always useful) to other sources, that no single urban — or suburban — way of life can be identified, and that differences in ways of life between the big city and the suburb can be explained more adequately by the class and life-cycle variations of their respective inhabitants.

The contemporary sociological conception of cities and of urban life is based largely on the work of the Chicago School, and its summary statement in Louis Wirth's essay, "Urbanism as a Way of Life." (40)* In that paper, Wirth developed a "minimum sociological definition of the city" as "a relatively large, dense and permanent settlement of socially heterogeneous individuals." (40, p. 50) From these prerequisites, he then deduced the major outlines of the urban way of life. As he saw it, number, density, and heterogeneity created a social structure in which primary-group relationships were inevitably replaced by secondary contacts that were impersonal, segmental, superficial, transitory, and often predatory in nature. As a result, the city dweller became anonymous, isolated, secular, relativistic, rational, and sophisticated. In order to function in the urban society, he was forced to combine with others to organize corporations, voluntary associations, representative forms of government, and the impersonal mass media of communications (40, pp. 54–60). These replaced the primary groups and the integrated way of life found in rural and other pre-industrial settlements.

Wirth's paper has become a classic in urban sociology, and most texts have followed his definition and description faithfully (5). In recent years, however, a considerable number of studies and essays have questioned his formulations (1, 5, 13, 15, 17, 19, 20, 23, 24, 27, 28, 30, 35, 38, 41).[1] In addition, a number of changes have taken place in cities since the article was published in 1938, notably the exodus of white residents to low- and medium-priced houses in the suburbs, and the decentralization of industry. The evidence from these studies and the changes in American cities suggest that Wirth's statement must be revised.

There is yet another, and more important reason for such a revision. Despite its title and intent, Wirth's paper deals with urban-industrial society, rather than with the city. This is evident from his approach. Like other urban sociologists, Wirth based his analysis on a comparison of settlement types, but unlike his colleagues, who pursued urban–rural comparisons, Wirth contrasted the city to the folk society. Thus, he compared settlement types of pre-industrial and industrial society. This allowed

---

* I am indebted to Richard Dewey, John Dyckman, David Riesman, Melvin Webber, and Harold Wilensky for helpful comments on earlier drafts of this essay.

[1] I shall not attempt to summarize these studies, for this task has already been performed by Dewey (5), Reiss (23), Wilensky (38), and others.

him to include in his theory of urbanism the entire range of modern institutions which are not found in the folk society, even though many such groups (e.g., voluntary associations) are by no means exclusively urban. Moreover, Wirth's conception of the city dweller as depersonalized, atomized, and susceptible to mass movements suggests that his paper is based on, and contributes to, the theory of the mass society.

Many of Wirth's conclusions may be relevant to the understanding of ways of life in modern society. However, since the theory argues that all of society is now urban, *his analysis does not distinguish ways of life in the city from those in other settlements within modern society.* In Wirth's time, the comparison of urban and pre-urban settlement types was still fruitful, but today, the primary task for urban (or community) sociology seems to me to be the analysis of the similarities and differences between contemporary settlement types.

This paper is an attempt at such an analysis; it limits itself to distinguishing ways of life in the modern city and the modern suburb. A re-analysis of Wirth's conclusions from this perspective suggests that his characterization of the urban way of life applies only — and not too accurately — to the residents of the inner city. The remaining city dwellers, as well as most suburbanites, pursue a different way of life, which I shall call "quasi-primary." This proposition raises some doubt about the mutual exclusiveness of the concepts of city and suburb and leads to a yet broader question: whether settlement concepts and other ecological concepts are useful for explaining ways of life.

THE INNER CITY

Wirth argued that number, density, and heterogeneity had two social consequences which explain the major features of urban life. On the one hand, the crowding of diverse types of people into a small area led to the segregation of homogeneous types of people into separate neighborhoods (40, p. 56). On the other hand, the lack of physical distance between city dwellers resulted in social contact between them, which broke down existing social and cultural patterns and encouraged assimilation as well as acculturation — the melting pot effect (40, p. 52).

Wirth implied that the melting pot effect was far more powerful than the tendency toward segregation and concluded that, sooner or later, the pressures engendered by the dominant social, economic, and political institutions of the city would destroy the remaining pockets of primary-group relationships (40, pp. 60–62). Eventually, the social system of the city would resemble Tönnies' *Gesellschaft* — a way of life which Wirth considered undesirable.

Because Wirth had come to see the city as the prototype of mass society, and because he examined the city from the distant vantage point of the folk society — from the wrong end of the telescope, so to speak — his view of urban life is not surprising. In addition, Wirth found support for his theory in the empirical work of his Chicago colleagues. As Greer and Kube (19, p. 112) and Wilensky (38, p. 121) have pointed out, the Chicago sociologists conducted their most intensive studies in the inner city.[2] At that time, these were slums recently invaded by new waves of European immigrants and rooming house and skid row districts, as well as the habitat of Bohemians and well-to-do Gold Coast apartment dwellers. Wirth himself studied the Maxwell Street Ghetto, an inner-city Jewish neighborhood then being dispersed by the acculturation and mobility of its inhabitants (39). Some of the characteristics of urbanism which Wirth stressed in his essay abounded in these areas.

Wirth's diagnosis of the city as *Gesellschaft* must be questioned on three counts. First, the conclusions derived from a study of the inner city cannot be generalized to the entire urban area. Second, there is as yet not enough evidence to prove — nor, admittedly, to deny — that number, density, and heterogeneity result in the social consequences which Wirth proposed. Finally, even if the causal relationship could be verified, it can be shown that a significant proportion of the city's inhabitants

---

[2] By the *inner city*, I mean the transient residential areas, the Gold Coasts and the slums that generally surround the central business district, although in some communities they may continue for miles beyond that district. The *outer city* includes the stable residential areas that house the working- and middle-class tenant and owner. The *suburbs* I conceive as the latest and most modern ring of the outer city, distinguished from it only by yet lower densities, and by the often irrelevant fact of the ring's location outside the city limits.

were, and are, isolated from these consequences by social structures and cultural patterns which they either brought to the city, or developed by living in it. Wirth conceived the urban population as consisting of heterogeneous individuals, torn from past social systems, unable to develop new ones, and therefore prey to social anarchy in the city. While it is true that a not insignificant proportion of the inner city population was, and still is, made up of unattached individuals (26), Wirth's formulation ignores the fact that this population consists mainly of relatively homogeneous groups, with social and cultural moorings that shield it fairly effectively from the suggested consequences of number, density, and heterogeneity. This applies even more to the residents of the outer city, who constitute a majority of the total city population.

The social and cultural moorings of the inner city population are best described by a brief analysis of the five types of inner city residents. These are:

1. the "cosmopolites";
2. the unmarried or childless;
3. the "ethnic villagers";
4. the "deprived"; and
5. the "trapped" and downward mobile.

The "cosmopolites" include students, artists, writers, musicians, and entertainers, as well as other intellectuals and professionals. They live in the city in order to be near the special "cultural" facilities that can only be located near the center of the city. Many cosmopolites are unmarried or childless. Others rear children in the city, especially if they have the income to afford the aid of servants and governesses. The less affluent ones may move to the suburbs to raise their children, continuing to live as cosmopolites under considerable handicaps, especially in the lower-middle-class suburbs. Many of the very rich and powerful are also cosmopolites, although they are likely to have at least two residences, one of which is suburban or exurban.

The unmarried or childless must be divided into two subtypes, depending on the permanence or transience of their status. The temporarily unmarried or childless live in the inner city for only a limited time. Young adults may team up to rent an apartment away from their parents and close to job or entertainment opportunities. When they marry, they may move first to an apartment in a transient neighborhood, but if they can afford to do so, they leave for the outer city or the suburbs with the arrival of the first or second child. The permanently unmarried may stay in the inner city for the remainder of their lives, their housing depending on their income.

The "ethnic villagers" are ethnic groups which are found in such inner city neighborhoods as New York's Lower East Side, living in some ways as they did when they were peasants in European or Puerto Rican villages (15). Although they reside in the city, they isolate themselves from significant contact with most city facilities, aside from workplaces. Their way of life differs sharply from Wirth's urbanism in its emphasis on kinship and the primary group, the lack of anonymity and secondary-group contacts, the weakness of formal organizations, and the suspicion of anything and anyone outside their neighborhood.

The first two types live in the inner city by choice; the third is there partly because of necessity, partly because of tradition. The final two types are in the inner city because they have no other choice. One is the "deprived" population: the very poor; the emotionally disturbed or otherwise handicapped; broken families; and, most important, the non-white population. These urban dwellers must take the dilapidated housing and blighted neighborhoods to which the housing market relegates them, although among them are some for whom the slum is a hiding place, or a temporary stop-over to save money for a house in the outer city or the suburbs (27).

The "trapped" are the people who stay behind when a neighborhood is invaded by non-residential land uses or lower-status inmigrants, because they cannot afford to move, or are otherwise bound to their present location (27).[3] The "downward mobiles" are a related type; they may have started life in a higher class position, but have been forced down in the socio-economic hierarchy and in the quality of their accommodations. Many of them are old people, living out their existence on small pensions.

[3] The trapped are not very visible, but I suspect that they are a significant element in what Raymond Vernon has described as the "gray areas" of the city (32).

These five types all live in dense and heterogeneous surroundings, yet they have such diverse ways of life that it is hard to see how density and heterogeneity could exert a common influence. Moreover, all but the last two types are isolated or detached from their neighborhood and thus from the social consequences which Wirth described.

When people who live together have social ties based on criteria other than mere common occupancy, they can set up social barriers regardless of the physical closeness or the heterogeneity of their neighbors. The ethnic villagers are the best illustration. While a number of ethnic groups are usually found living together in the same neighborhood, they are able to *isolate* themselves from each other through a variety of social devices. Wirth himself recognized this when he wrote that "two groups can occupy a given area without losing their separate identity because each side is permitted to live its own inner life and each somehow fears or idealizes the other." (39, p. 283) Although it is true that the children in these areas were often oblivious to the social barriers set up by their parents, at least until adolescence, it is doubtful whether their acculturation can be traced to the melting pot effect as much as to the pervasive influence of the American culture that flowed into these areas from the outside.[4]

The cosmopolites, the unmarried, and the childless are *detached* from neighborhood life. The cosmopolites possess a distinct subculture which causes them to be disinterested in all but the most superficial contacts with their neighbors, somewhat like the ethnic villagers. The unmarried and childless are detached from neighborhood because of their life-cycle stage, which frees them from the routine family responsibilities that entail some relationship to the local area. In their choice of residence, the two types are therefore not concerned about their neighbors, or the availability and quality of local community facilities. Even the well-to-do can choose expensive apartments in or near poor neighborhoods, because if they have children, these are sent to special schools and summer camps which effec-

---

[4] If the melting pot has resulted from propinquity and high density, one would have expected second-generation Italians, Irish, Jews, Greeks, Slavs, etc. to have developed a single "pan-ethnic culture," consisting of a synthesis of the cultural patterns of the propinquitous national groups.

tively isolate them from neighbors. In addition, both types, but especially the childless and unmarried, are transient. Therefore, they tend to live in areas marked by high population turnover, where their own mobility and that of their neighbors creates a universal detachment from the neighborhood.[5]

The deprived and the trapped do seem to be affected by some of the consequences of number, density, and heterogeneity. The deprived population suffers considerably from overcrowding, but this is a consequence of low income, racial discrimination, and other handicaps, and cannot be considered an inevitable result of the ecological make-up of the city.[6] Because the deprived have no residential choice, they are also forced to live amid neighbors not of their own choosing, with ways of life different and even contradictory to their own. If familial defenses against the neighborhood climate are weak, as is the case among broken families and downward mobile people, parents may lose their children to the culture of "the street." The trapped are the unhappy people who remain behind when their more advantaged neighbors move on; they must endure the heterogeneity which results from neighborhood change.

Wirth's description of the urban way of life fits best the transient areas of the inner city. Such areas are typically heterogeneous in population, partly because they are inhabited by transient types who do not require homogeneous neighbors or by deprived people who have no choice, or may themselves be quite mobile. Under conditions of transience and heterogeneity, people interact only in terms of the segmental roles necessary for obtaining local services. Their social relationships thus display anonymity, impersonality, and superficiality.[7]

[5] The corporation transients (36, 38), who provide a new source of residential instability to the suburb, differ from city transients. Since they are raising families, they want to integrate themselves into neighborhood life, and are usually able to do so, mainly because they tend to move into similar types of communities wherever they go.
[6] The negative social consequences of overcrowding are a result of high room and floor density, not of the land coverage of population density which Wirth discussed. Park Avenue residents live under conditions of high land density, but do not seem to suffer visibly from overcrowding.
[7] Whether or not these social phenomena have the psychological consequences Wirth suggested depends on the people who live in the area. Those who are detached from the neighborhood by choice are probably

Urbanism and Suburbanism as Ways of Life

The social features of Wirth's concept of urbanism seem therefore to be a result of residential instability, rather than of number, density, or heterogeneity. In fact, heterogeneity is itself an effect of residential instability, resulting when the influx of transients causes landlords and realtors to stop acting as gatekeepers — that is, wardens of neighborhood homogeneity.[8] Residential instability is found in all types of settlements, and, presumably, its social consequences are everywhere similar. These consequences cannot therefore be identified with the ways of life of the city.

The Outer City and the Suburbs

The second effect which Wirth ascribed to number, density, and heterogeneity was the segregation of homogeneous people into distinct neighborhoods,[9] on the basis of "place and nature of work, income, racial and ethnic characteristics, social status, custom, habit, taste, preference and prejudice." (40, p. 56) This description fits the residential districts of the *outer city*.[10] Although these districts contain the majority of the city's inhabitants, Wirth went into little detail about them. He made it clear, however, that the socio-psychological aspects of urbanism were prevalent there as well (40, p. 56).

Because existing neighborhood studies deal primarily with the exotic sections of the inner city, very little is known about the more typical residential neighborhoods of the outer city. However, it is evident that the way of life in these areas bears little resemblance to Wirth's urbanism. Both the studies which ques-

---

immune, but those who depend on the neighborhood for their social relationships — the unattached individuals, for example — may suffer greatly from loneliness.

[8] Needless to say, residential instability must ultimately be traced back to the fact that, as Wirth pointed out, the city and its economy attract transient — and, depending on the sources of outmigration, heterogeneous — people. However, this is a characteristic of urban-industrial society, not of the city specifically.

[9] By neighborhoods or residential districts I mean areas demarcated from others by distinctive physical boundaries or by social characteristics, some of which may be perceived only by the residents. However, these areas are not necessarily socially self-sufficient or culturally distinctive.

[10] For the definition of *outer city*, see Footnote 2.

tion Wirth's formulation and my own observations suggest that the common element in the ways of life of these neighborhoods is best described as *quasi-primary*. I use this term to characterize relationships between neighbors. Whatever the intensity or frequency of these relationships, the interaction is more intimate than a secondary contact, but more guarded than a primary one.[11]

There are actually few secondary relationships, because of the isolation of residential neighborhoods from economic institutions and workplaces. Even shopkeepers, store managers, and other local functionaries who live in the area are treated as acquaintances or friends, unless they are of a vastly different social status or are forced by their corporate employers to treat their customers as economic units (30). Voluntary associations attract only a minority of the population. Moreover, much of the organizational activity is of a sociable nature, and it is often difficult to accomplish the association's "business" because of the members' preference for sociability. Thus, it would appear that interactions in organizations, or between neighbors generally, do not fit the secondary-relationship model of urban life. As anyone who has lived in these neighborhoods knows, there is little anonymity, impersonality or privacy.[12] In fact, American cities have sometimes been described as collections of small towns.[13] There is some truth to this description, especially if the city is compared to the actual small town, rather than to the romantic construct of anti-urban critics (33).

Postwar suburbia represents the most contemporary version of the quasi-primary way of life. Owing to increases in real income and the encouragement of home ownership provided by the

[11] Because neighborly relations are not quite primary, and not quite secondary, they can also become *pseudo-primary;* that is, secondary ones disguised with false affect to make them appear primary. Critics have often described suburban life in this fashion, although the actual prevalence of pseudo-primary relationships has not been studied systematically in cities or suburbs.

[12] These neighborhoods cannot, however, be considered as urban folk societies. People go out of the area for many of their friendships, and their allegiance to the neighborhood is neither intense nor all-encompassing. Janowitz has aptly described the relationship between resident and neighborhood as one of "limited liability." (20, Chapter 7)

[13] Were I not arguing that ecological concepts cannot double as sociological ones, this way of life might best be described as small-townish.

FHA, families in the lower-middle class and upper working class can now live in modern single-family homes in low-density subdivisions, an opportunity previously available only to the upper and upper-middle classes (34).

The popular literature describes the new suburbs as communities in which conformity, homogeneity, and other-direction are unusually rampant (4, 32). The implication is that the move from city to suburb initiates a new way of life which causes considerable behavior and personality change in previous urbanites. A preliminary analysis of data which I am now collecting in Levittown, New Jersey, suggests, however, that the move from the city to this predominantly lower-middle-class suburb does not result in any major behavioral changes for most people. Moreover, the changes which do occur reflect the move from the social isolation of a transient city or suburban apartment building to the quasi-primary life of a neighborhood of single-family homes. Also, many of the people whose life has changed reported that the changes were intended. They existed as aspirations before the move, or as reasons for it. In other words, the suburb itself creates few changes in ways of life. Similar conclusions have been reported by Berger in his excellent study of a working-class population newly moved to a suburban subdivision (4).

A COMPARISON OF CITY AND SUBURB

If urban and suburban areas are similar in that the way of life in both is quasi-primary, and if urban residents who move out to the suburbs do not undergo any significant changes in behavior, it would be fair to argue that the differences in ways of life between the two types of settlements have been overestimated. Yet the fact remains that a variety of physical and demographic differences exist between the city and the suburb. However, upon closer examination, many of these differences turn out to be either spurious or of little significance for the way of life of the inhabitants (34).[14]

[14] They may, of course, be significant for the welfare of the total metropolitan area.

The differences between the residential areas of cities and suburbs which have been cited most frequently are:

1. Suburbs are more likely to be dormitories.
2. They are further away from the work and play facilities of the central business districts.
3. They are newer and more modern than city residential areas and are designed for the automobile rather than for pedestrian and mass-transit forms of movement.
4. They are built up with single-family rather than multi-family structures and are therefore less dense.
5. Their populations are more homogeneous.
6. Their populations differ demographically: they are younger; more of them are married; they have higher incomes; and they hold proportionately more white collar jobs (8, p. 131).

Most urban neighborhoods are as much dormitories as the suburbs. Only in a few older inner city areas are factories and offices still located in the middle of residential blocks, and even here many of the employees do not live in the neighborhood.

The fact that the suburbs are farther from the central business district is often true only in terms of distance, not travel time. Moreover, most people make relatively little use of downtown facilities, other than workplaces (12, 21). The downtown stores seem to hold their greatest attraction for the upper-middle class (21, pp. 91–92); the same is probably true of typically urban entertainment facilities. Teen-agers and young adults may take their dates to first-run movie theaters, but the museums, concert halls, and lecture rooms attract mainly upper-middle-class ticket-buyers, many of them suburban.[15]

The suburban reliance on the train and the automobile has given rise to an imaginative folklore about the consequences of commuting on alcohol consumption, sex life, and parental duties. Many of these conclusions are, however, drawn from selected high-income suburbs and exurbs, and reflect job tensions in such hectic occupations as advertising and show business more than the effects of residence (29). It is true that the upper-middle-class housewife must become a chauffeur in order to expose her children to the proper educational facilities, but such differences

[15] A 1958 study of New York theater goers showed a median income of close to $10,000 and 35 per cent were reported as living in the suburbs (10).

as walking to the corner drug store and driving to its suburban equivalent seem to me of little emotional, social, or cultural import.[16] In addition, the continuing shrinkage in the number of mass-transit users suggests that even in the city many younger people are now living a wholly auto-based way of life.

The fact that suburbs are smaller is primarily a function of political boundaries drawn long before the communities were suburban. This affects the kinds of political issues which develop and provides somewhat greater opportunity for citizen participation. Even so, in the suburbs as in the city, the minority who participate are the professional politicians, the economically concerned businessmen, lawyers and salesmen, and the ideologically motivated middle- and upper-middle-class people with better than average education.

The social consequences of differences in density and house type also seem overrated. Single-family houses on quiet streets facilitate the supervision of children; this is one reason why middle-class women who want to keep an eye on their children move to the suburbs. House type also has some effects on relationships between neighbors, insofar as there are more opportunities for visual contact between adjacent homeowners than between people on different floors of an apartment house. However, if occupants' characteristics are also held constant, the differences in actual social contact are less marked. Homogeneity of residents turns out to be more important as a determinant of sociability than proximity. If the population is heterogeneous, there is little social contact between neighbors, either on apartment-house floors or in single-family-house blocks; if people are homogeneous, there is likely to be considerable social contact in both house types. One need only contrast the apartment house located in a transient, heterogeneous neighborhood and exactly the same structure in a neighborhood occupied by a single ethnic group. The former is a lonely, anonymous building; the latter, a bustling micro-society. I have observed similar patterns in suburban areas: on blocks where people are homogeneous, they socialize; where they are heterogeneous, they do little more than exchange polite greetings (16).

[16] I am thinking here of adults; teen-agers do suffer from the lack of informal meeting places within walking or bicycling distance.

Suburbs are usually described as being more homogeneous in house type than the city, but if they are compared to the outer city, the differences are small. Most inhabitants of the outer city, other than well-to-do homeowners, live on blocks of uniform structures as well — for example, the endless streets of rowhouses in Philadelphia and Baltimore or of two-story duplexes and six-flat apartment houses in Chicago. They differ from the new suburbs only in that they were erected through more primitive methods of mass production. Suburbs are of course more predominantly areas of owner-occupied single homes, though in the outer districts of most American cities homeownership is also extremely high.

Demographically, suburbs as a whole are clearly more homogeneous than cities as a whole, though probably not more so than outer cities. However, people do not live in cities or suburbs as a whole, but in specific neighborhoods. An analysis of ways of life would require a determination of the degree of population homogeneity within the boundaries of areas defined as neighborhoods by residents' social contacts. Such an analysis would no doubt indicate that many neighborhoods in the city as well as the suburbs are homogeneous. Neighborhood homogeneity is actually a result of factors having little or nothing to do with the house type, density, or location of the area relative to the city limits. Brand new neighborhoods are more homogeneous than older ones, because they have not yet experienced resident turnover, which frequently results in population heterogeneity. Neighborhoods of low- and medium-priced housing are usually less homogeneous than those with expensive dwellings because they attract families who have reached the peak of occupational and residential mobility, as well as young families who are just starting their climb and will eventually move to neighborhoods of higher status. The latter, being accessible only to high-income people, are therefore more homogeneous with respect to other resident characteristics as well. Moreover, such areas have the economic and political power to slow down or prevent invasion. Finally, neighborhoods located in the path of ethnic or religious group movement are likely to be extremely homogeneous.

The demographic differences between cities and suburbs cannot be questioned, especially since the suburbs have attracted a large number of middle-class child-rearing families. The differences are, however, much reduced if suburbs are compared only to the outer city. In addition, a detailed comparison of suburban and outer city residential areas would show that neighborhoods with the same kinds of people can be found in the city as well as the suburbs. Once again, the age of the area and the cost of housing are more important determinants of demographic characteristics than the location of the area with respect to the city limits.

CHARACTERISTICS, SOCIAL ORGANIZATION, AND ECOLOGY

The preceding sections of the paper may be summarized in three propositions:

1. As concerns ways of life, the inner city must be distinguished from the outer city and the suburbs; and the latter two exhibit a way of life bearing little resemblance to Wirth's urbanism.

2. Even in the inner city, ways of life resemble Wirth's description only to a limited extent. Moreover, economic condition, cultural characteristics, life-cycle stage, and residential instability explain ways of life more satisfactorily than number, density, or heterogeneity.

3. Physical and other differences between city and suburb are often spurious or without much meaning for ways of life.

These propositions suggest that the concepts urban and suburban are neither mutually exclusive, nor especially relevant for understanding ways of life. They — and number, density, and heterogeneity as well — are ecological concepts which describe human adaptation to the environment. However, they are not sufficient to explain social phenomena, because these phenomena cannot be understood solely as the consequences of ecological processes. Therefore, other explanations must be considered.

Ecological explanations of social life are most applicable if the subjects under study lack the ability to *make choices*, be they plants, animals, or human beings. Thus, if there is a housing shortage, people will live almost anywhere, and under extreme conditions of no choice, as in a disaster, married and single, old and young, middle and working class, stable and transient will be found side by side in whatever accommodations are available. At that time, their ways of life represent an almost direct adaptation to the environment. If the supply of housing and of neighborhoods is such that alternatives are available, however, people will make choices, and if the housing market is responsive, they can even make and satisfy explicit *demands*.

Choices and demands do not develop independently or at random; they are functions of the roles people play in the social system. These can best be understood in terms of the *characteristics* of the people involved; that is, characteristics can be used as indices to choices and demands made in the roles that constitute ways of life. Although many characteristics affect the choices and demands people make with respect to housing and neighborhoods, the most important ones seem to be *class* — in all its economic, social and cultural ramifications — and *life-cycle stage*.[17] If people have an opportunity to choose, these two characteristics will go far in explaining the kinds of housing and neighborhoods they will occupy and the ways of life they will try to establish within them.

Many of the previous assertions about ways of life in cities and suburbs can be analyzed in terms of class and life-cycle characteristics. Thus, in the inner city, the unmarried and childless live as they do, detached from neighborhood, because of their life-cycle stage; the cosmopolites, because of a combination of life-cycle stage and a distinctive but class-based subculture. The way of life of the deprived and trapped can be explained by low socio-economic level and related handicaps. The quasi-primary way of life is associated with the family stage of the life-cycle, and the norms of child-rearing and parental role found in the upper working class, the lower-middle class, and the non-cosmopolite portions of the upper-middle and upper classes.

The attributes of the so-called suburban way of life can also be understood largely in terms of these characteristics. The new suburbia is nothing more than a highly visible showcase for the ways of life of young, upper-working-class and lower-middle-

[17] These must be defined in dynamic terms. Thus, class includes also the process of social mobility, stage in the life-cycle, and the processes of socialization and aging.

class people. Ktsanes and Reissman have aptly described it as "new homes for old values." (22) Much of the descriptive and critical writing about suburbia assumes that as long as the new suburbanites lived in the city, they behaved like upper-middle-class cosmopolites and that suburban living has mysteriously transformed them (7; 14, pp. 154–162; 25; 36). The critics fail to see that the behavior and personality patterns ascribed to suburbia are in reality those of class and age (6). These patterns could have been found among the new suburbanites when they still lived in the city and could now be observed among their peers who still reside there — if the latter were as visible to critics and researchers as are the suburbanites.

Needless to say, the concept of "characteristics" cannot explain all aspects of ways of life, either among urban or suburban residents. Some aspects must be explained by concepts of social organization that are independent of characteristics. For example, some features of the quasi-primary way of life are independent of class and age, because they evolve from the roles and situations created by joint and adjacent occupancy of land and dwellings. Likewise, residential instability is a universal process which has a number of invariate consequences. In each case, however, the way in which people react varies with their characteristics. So it is with ecological processes. Thus, there are undoubtedly differences between ways of life in urban and suburban settlements which remain after behavior patterns based on residents' characteristics have been analyzed, and which must therefore be attributed to features of the settlement (11).

Characteristics do not explain the causes of behavior; rather, they are clues to socially created and culturally defined roles, choices, and demands. A causal analysis must trace them back to the larger social, economic, and political systems which determine the situations in which roles are played and the cultural content of choices and demands, as well as the opportunities for their achievement.[18] These systems determine income distributions, educational and occupational opportunities, and in turn, fertility patterns, child-rearing methods, as well as the entire range of

---

18 This formulation may answer some of Duncan and Schnore's objections to socio-psychological and cultural explanations of community ways of life (9).

consumer behavior. Thus, a complete analysis of the way of life of the deprived residents of the inner city cannot stop by indicating the influence of low income, lack of education, or family instability. These must be related to such conditions as the urban economy's "need" for low-wage workers, and the housing market practices which restrict residential choice. The urban economy is in turn shaped by national economic and social systems, as well as by local and regional ecological processes. Some phenomena can be explained exclusively by reference to these ecological processes. However, it must also be recognized that as man gains greater control over the natural environment, he has been able to free himself from many of the determining and limiting effects of that environment. Thus, changes in local transportation technology, the ability of industries to be footloose, and the relative affluence of American society have given ever larger numbers of people increasing amounts of residential choice. The greater the amount of choice available, the more important does the concept of characteristics become in understanding behavior.

Consequently, the study of ways of life in communities must begin with an analysis of characteristics. If characteristics are dealt with first and held constant, we may be able to discover which behavior patterns can be attributed to features of the settlement and its natural environment.[19] Only then will it be possible to discover to what extent city and suburb are independent — rather than dependent or intervening — variables in the explanation of ways of life.

This kind of analysis might help to reconcile the ecological point of view with the behavioral and cultural one, and possibly put an end to the conflict between conceptual positions which insist on one explanation or the other (9). Both explanations have some relevance, and future research and theory must clarify the role of each in the analysis of ways of life in various types of

[19] The ecologically oriented researchers who developed the Shevsky-Bell social area analysis scale have worked on the assumption that "social differences between the populations of urban neighborhoods can conveniently be summarized into differences of economic level, family characteristics and ethnicity." (3, p. 26) However, they have equated "urbanization" with a concept of life-cycle stage by using family characteristics to define the index of urbanization (3, 18, 19). In fact, Bell has identified suburbanism with familism (2).

settlement (6, p. xxii). Another important rationale for this approach is its usefulness for applied sociology — for example, city planning. The planner can recommend changes in the spatial and physical arrangements of the city. Frequently, he seeks to achieve social goals or to change social conditions through physical solutions. He has been attracted to ecological explanations because these relate behavior to phenomena which he can affect. For example, most planners tend to agree with Wirth's formulations, because they stress number and density, over which the planner has some control. If the undesirable social conditions of the inner city could be traced to these two factors, the planner could propose large-scale clearance projects which would reduce the size of the urban population, and lower residential densities. Experience with public housing projects has, however, made it apparent that low densities, new buildings, or modern site plans do not eliminate anti-social or self-destructive behavior. The analysis of characteristics will call attention to the fact that this behavior is lodged in the deprivations of low socio-economic status and racial discrimination, and that it can be changed only through the removal of these deprivations. Conversely, if such an analysis suggests residues of behavior that can be attributed to ecological processes or physical aspects of housing and neighborhoods, the planner can recommend physical changes that can really affect behavior.

A Re-evaluation of Definitions

The argument presented here has implications for the sociological definition of the city. Such a definition relates ways of life to environmental features of the city qua settlement type. But if ways of life do not coincide with settlement types, and if these ways are functions of class and life-cycle stage rather than of the ecological attributes of the settlement, a sociological definition of the city cannot be formulated.[20] Concepts such as city

20 Because of the distinctiveness of the ways of life found in the inner city, some writers propose definitions that refer only to these ways, ignoring those found in the outer city. For example, popular writers sometimes identify "urban" with "urbanity," i.e., "cosmopolitanism." However, such a definition ignores the other ways of life found in the inner city. Moreover, I have tried to show that these ways have few common elements, and

and suburb allow us to distinguish settlement types from each other physically and demographically, but the ecological processes and conditions which they synthesize have no direct or invariate consequences for ways of life. The sociologist cannot, therefore, speak of an urban or suburban way of life.

CONCLUSION

Many of the descriptive statements made here are as time-bound as Wirth's.[21] Twenty years ago, Wirth concluded that some form of urbanism would eventually predominate in all settlement types. He was, however, writing during a time of immigrant acculturation and at the end of a serious depression, an era of minimal choice. Today, it is apparent that high-density, heterogeneous surroundings are for most people a temporary place of residence; other than for the Park Avenue or Greenwich Village cosmopolites, they are a result of necessity rather than choice. As soon as they can afford to do so, most Americans head for the single-family house and the quasi-primary way of life of the low-density neighborhood, in the outer city or the suburbs.[22]

Changes in the national economy and in government housing policy can affect many of the variables that make up housing supply and demand. For example, urban sprawl may eventually outdistance the ability of present and proposed transportation systems to move workers into the city; further industrial decentralization can forestall it and alter the entire relationship between work and residence. The expansion of present urban renewal activities can perhaps lure a significant number of cosmopolites back from the suburbs, while a drastic change in renewal policy might begin to ameliorate the housing conditions of the

---

that the ecological features of the inner city have little or no influence in shaping them.

[21] Even more than Wirth's they are based on data and impressions gathered in the large Eastern and Midwestern cities of the United States.

[22] Personal discussions with European planners and sociologists suggest that many European apartment dwellers have similar preferences, although economic conditions, high building costs, and the scarcity of land make it impossible for them to achieve their desires.

deprived population. A serious depression could once again make America a nation of doubled-up tenants.

These events will affect housing supply and residential choice; they will frustrate but not suppress demands for the quasi-primary way of life. However, changes in the national economy, society, and culture can affect people's characteristics — family size, educational level, and various other concomitants of life-cycle stage and class. These in turn will stimulate changes in demands and choices. The rising number of college graduates, for example, is likely to increase the cosmopolite ranks. This might in turn create a new set of city dwellers, although it will probably do no more than encourage the development of cosmopolite facilities in some suburban areas.

The current revival of interest in urban sociology and in community studies, as well as the sociologist's increasing curiosity about city planning, suggest that data may soon be available to formulate a more adequate theory of the relationship between settlements and the ways of life within them. The speculations presented in this paper are intended to raise questions; they can only be answered by more systematic data collection and theorizing.

References

1. Axelrod, Morris. "Urban Structure and Social Participation," *American Sociological Review*, Vol. 21 (February 1956), pp. 13–18.

2. Bell, Wendell. "Social Choice, Life Styles and Suburban Residence," in William M. Dobriner (ed.), *The Suburban Community*. New York: G. P. Putnam's Sons, 1958, pp. 225–247.

3. Bell, Wendell, and Maryanne T. Force. "Urban Neighborhood Types and Participation in Formal Associations," *American Sociological Review*, Vol. 21 (February 1956), pp. 25–34.

4. Berger, Bennett. *Working Class Suburb: A Study of Auto Workers in Suburbia*. Berkeley, Calif.: University of California Press, 1960.

5. Dewey, Richard. "The Rural–Urban Continuum: Real but Rela-

tively Unimportant," *American Journal of Sociology*, Vol. 66 (July 1960), pp. 60–66.

6. Dobriner, William M. "Introduction: Theory and Research in the Sociology of the Suburbs," in William M. Dobriner (ed.), *The Suburban Community*. New York: G. P. Putnam's Sons, 1958, pp. xiii–xxviii.

7. Duhl, Leonard J. "Mental Health and Community Planning," in *Planning 1955*. Chicago: American Society of Planning Officials, 1956, pp. 31–39.

8. Duncan, Otis Dudley, and Albert J. Reiss, Jr. *Social Characteristics of Rural and Urban Communities, 1950*. New York: John Wiley & Sons, 1956.

9. Duncan, Otis Dudley, and Leo F. Schnore. "Cultural, Behavioral and Ecological Perspectives in the Study of Social Organization," *American Journal of Sociology*, Vol. 65 (September 1959), pp. 132–155.

10. Enders, John. *Profile of the Theater Market*. New York: Playbill, undated and unpaged.

11. Fava, Sylvia Fleis. "Contrasts in Neighboring: New York City and a Suburban Community," in William M. Dobriner (ed.), *The Suburban Community*. New York: G. P. Putnam's Sons, 1958, pp. 122–131.

12. Foley, Donald L. "The Use of Local Facilities in a Metropolis," in Paul Hatt and Albert J. Reiss, Jr. (eds.), *Cities and Society*. Glencoe, Ill.: The Free Press, 1957, pp. 237–247.

13. Form, William H., *et al.* "The Compatibility of Alternative Approaches to the Delimitation of Urban Sub-areas," *American Sociological Review*, Vol. 19 (August 1954), pp. 434–440.

14. Fromm, Erich. *The Sane Society*. New York: Rinehart & Co., Inc., 1955.

15. Gans, Herbert J. *The Urban Villagers: A Study of the Second Generation Italians in the West End of Boston*. Boston: Center for Community Studies, December 1959 (mimeographed).

16. Gans, Herbert J. "Planning and Social Life: An Evaluation of Friendship and Neighbor Relations in Suburban Communities," *Journal of the American Institute of Planners*, Vol. 27 (May 1961), pp. 134–140.

17. Greer, Scott. "Urbanism Reconsidered: A Comparative Study of Local Areas in a Metropolis," *American Sociological Review*, Vol. 21 (February 1956), pp. 19–25.

18. Greer, Scott. "The Social Structure and Political Process of Suburbia," *American Sociological Review*, Vol. 25 (August 1960), pp. 514–526.
19. Greer, Scott, and Ella Kube. "Urbanism and Social Structure: A Los Angeles Study," in Marvin B. Sussman (ed.), *Community Structure and Analysis*. New York: Thomas Y. Crowell Company, 1959, pp. 93–112.
20. Janowitz, Morris. *The Community Press in an Urban Setting*. Glencoe, Ill.: The Free Press, 1952.
21. Jonassen, Christen T. *The Shopping Center Versus Downtown*. Columbus, Ohio: Bureau of Business Research, Ohio State University, 1955.
22. Ktsanes, Thomas, and Leonard Reissman. "Suburbia: New Homes for Old Values," *Social Problems*, Vol. 7 (Winter 1959–60), pp. 187–194.
23. Reiss, Albert J., Jr. "An Analysis of Urban Phenomena," in Robert M. Fisher (ed.), *The Metropolis in Modern Life*. Garden City, N.Y.: Doubleday & Company, Inc., 1955, pp. 41–49.
24. Reiss, Albert J., Jr. "Rural–Urban and Status Differences in Interpersonal Contacts," *American Journal of Sociology*, Vol. 65 (September 1959), pp. 182–195.
25. Riesman, David. "The Suburban Sadness," in William M. Dobriner (ed.), *The Suburban Community*. New York: G. P. Putnam's Sons, 1958, pp. 375–408.
26. Rose, Arnold M. "Living Arrangements of Unattached Persons," *American Sociological Review*, Vol. 12 (August 1947), pp. 429–435.
27. Seeley, John R. "The Slum: Its Nature, Use and Users," *Journal of the American Institute of Planners*, Vol. 25 (February 1959), pp. 7–14.
28. Smith, Joel, William Form, and Gregory Stone. "Local Intimacy in a Middle-Sized City," *American Journal of Sociology*, Vol. 60 (November 1954), pp. 276–284.
29. Spectorsky, A. C. *The Exurbanites*. Philadelphia: J. B. Lippincott Co., 1955.
30. Stone, Gregory P. "City Shoppers and Urban Identification: Observations on the Social Psychology of City Life," *American Journal of Sociology*, Vol. 60 (July 1954), pp. 36–45.
31. Strauss, Anselm. "The Changing Imagery of American City and Suburb," *Sociological Quarterly*, Vol. 1 (January 1960), pp. 15–24.

32. Vernon, Raymond. *The Changing Economic Function of the Central City.* New York: Committee on Economic Development, Supplementary Paper No. 1, January 1959.

33. Vidich, Arthur J., and Joseph Bensman. *Small Town in Mass Society: Class, Power and Religion in a Rural Community.* Princeton, N.J.: Princeton University Press, 1958.

34. Wattell, Harold. "Levittown: A Suburban Community," in William M. Dobriner (ed.), *The Suburban Community.* New York: G. P. Putnam's Sons, 1958, pp. 287–313.

35. Whyte, William F., Jr. *Street Corner Society.* Chicago: The University of Chicago Press, 1955.

36. Whyte, William F., Jr. *The Organization Man.* New York: Simon & Schuster, 1956.

37. Wilensky, Harold L. "Life Cycle, Work, Situation and Participation in Formal Associations," in Robert W. Kleemeier, *et al.* (eds.), *Aging and Leisure: Research Perspectives on the Meaningful Use of Time.* New York: Oxford University Press, 1961, Chapter 8.

38. Wilensky, Harold L., and Charles Lebeaux. *Industrial Society and Social Welfare.* New York: Russell Sage Foundation, 1958.

39. Wirth, Louis. *The Ghetto.* Chicago: The University of Chicago Press, 1928.

40. Wirth, Louis. "Urbanism as a Way of Life," *American Journal of Sociology*, Vol. 44 (July 1938), pp. 1–24. Reprinted in Paul Hatt and Albert J. Reiss, Jr. (eds.), *Cities and Society.* Glencoe. Ill.: The Free Press, 1957, pp. 46–64. [All page references are to this reprinting of the article.]

41. Young, Michael, and Peter Willmott. *Family and Kinship in East London.* London: Routledge & Kegan Paul, Ltd., 1957.

34

Social Processes in the Metropolitan Community

WARREN A. PETERSON

COMMUNITY STUDIES, INC., KANSAS CITY

GEORGE K. ZOLLSCHAN

PURDUE UNIVERSITY

Individual behavior and community institutions are linked to the social processes operating in the metropolitan community in this final essay by Warren Peterson and George Zollschan. The authors are sociological researchers on the metropolitan community who conduct their research on its practical problems within a framework of sociological and social-psychological theory. They have found that framework most useful which views the metropolis in terms of two processes which connect the population aggregate with the institutional system — the allocation of persons to positions and the institutionalization of needs.

THE STATE OF URBAN SOCIOLOGY*

Forty-five years ago Robert E. Park introduced the city as a field of research and analysis to American sociologists (10). Park

* This essay was written while Professor Zollschan was a faculty research fellow at Community Studies, Inc.

proposed that the city be viewed in terms of two types of organization: (*a*) a social organization based on interaction and communication, culture and consensus; and (*b*) an ecological organization based on a kind of sub-social competitive cooperation or symbiosis, analogous to symbiosis in biology. Park viewed symbiosis as linking human beings together in impersonal, unintended patterns, patterns not explicable in terms of any set of rules or socially defined objectives.

For two decades following Park's "Suggestions," most American sociologists pursued urban research distinctly, although sometimes loosely, within the framework which Park had outlined. It would be justified, in our belief, to claim that Park's program was substantially fulfilled, and fulfilled with some distinction by his Chicago disciples. This program was largely one of descriptively mapping the ecological and social contours of urban life, and its fulfillment has made available a wealth of information about urban life in America which any other country would be hard put to equal.

The last two and one-half decades have been characterized by a much larger volume of research within a far wider range of conceptual schemes. The most notable advances in recent decades have been in research on social stratification, on prestige and power in the community, and (although less directly focused on the urban community) on organizations and professions. In keeping with the general fragmentation of the discipline, there has been a decline in efforts to conceptualize the urban community as an entity and an increase in structural-descriptive and structural-functional research. It is not our purpose to give a critique of such studies. Rather, this chapter is a modest effort to outline the nature of an urban or metropolitan sociology which could keep an eye on the metropolis as a dynamic system and focus on processes at various levels of the system, and especially *between* levels of the system. We take the position that urban or metropolitan sociology cannot develop from the simple addition of discrete studies of the population and economic base, social strata, ethnic groups, organizations, public attitudes and opinions, and leadership, power, and prestige. The urban community or the metropolis *exists* in the processes which connect these to one another.

Social Processes in the Metropolitan Community

The metropolis has more the form of an aquarium than of a skyscraper of building blocks. Perhaps a more appropriate metaphor is that of a deep pool in a swamp, the pool's inhabitants being affected by currents from the swamp as well as from the pool itself. Since Park's time the edges of the pool have greatly expanded and channels between pools have been dredged wider and deeper. We have greater knowledge than he did of the species of fish (and their schooling habits) but little more knowledge of the metabolism, symbiotic or otherwise, of the pool.

THE ECOLOGICAL PERSPECTIVE

The operations of the urban community have traditionally been classified as demographic, ecological, institutional, and political. In the contemporary period, there is likely to be little disagreement about the relevance of three of these. Concerning the status of the fourth, ecology, there has been considerable disagreement among sociologists, and disagreement which seems to have had the effect of immobilizing research on the metropolitan community as a community, and of directing efforts into channels which are narrower and safer. The dilemma, the ambivalent position, of ecology places sociology in a position of being highly uncomfortable with the classical formulations of Park, Burgess, and McKenzie, yet unable to proceed without dealing with the kinds of processes with which they were dealing. In effect, the baby has been thrown out with the bath.

If ecology is to be more than static description, it must deal with the processes which are in operation. Such processes are not amenable to treatment as one vast amorphous cultural system, nor in terms of symbolic interaction alone. In a simple and most obvious case, it is not possible to explain differences in the spatial patterning of large and small cities in terms of cultural differences between the inhabitants.

Among others, George Herbert Mead has been quoted by the critics of classical ecology to the effect that "the community as such creates its environment by being sensitive to it."[1] This is at least a partial distortion of Mead's view since Mead also recog-

---

[1] By Walter Firey, in a discussion of A. B. Hollingshead's "Community Research: Development and Present Condition." (2, p. 152)

nized the existence of other processes: "An economic society defines itself insofar as one individual may trade with another; and then the very processes themselves go on integrating, bringing a closer and closer relationship between communities which may be definitely opposed to each other politically." (9, p. 282)

In this passage, Mead was drawing a distinction between economic and political processes similar to that which ecologists made between ecological and social processes. Moreover, he pointed out that economic processes — "the very processes themselves" — go on integrating and profoundly influence the political.

Although Mead's chief concern was with society and the socialization of the person, he apparently recognized that it is virtually impossible to explain all human behavior by saying, "There can be no environment, apart from that which is defined into being by social and cultural processes."[2] Mead apparently agreed with Dewey's distinction between "events" — non-conscious but present and operative — and "objects" — events with social meaning and therefore subject to personal and social control (1, pp. 166–207).[3]

Ecological processes may be viewed as non-social, unsocial, or pre-social, not in the sense that the participants, if studied individually, could be found to act as non-social beings without motive or purpose, but in the sense of the participants' being unaware of or unconcerned with the effect of their action on the larger processes or the larger network of processes. It is a very complicated network of processes which constitute the metabolism of the metropolitan community.

Such a perspective on ecological processes or, rather, on processes having ecological and symbiotic character does not exclude the possibility that part of the network may be recognized and defined by some of the participants part of the time, and that all participants do interact symbolically at their point of juncture with the system. However, the meaning of acts (having a baby, occupying a house, taking a job, patronizing a bowling alley) is

[2] See Walter Firey (2, p. 152). Firey adheres to an idealistic philosophical position. For Mead's criticism of Cooley as an idealist, see "Cooley's Contribution to American Sociological Thought." (7, p. 693)
[3] See also Mead's discussion of Dewey (8, pp. 211–230).

likely to be different for the individual participants than for someone who interprets from the standpoint of the processes set in motion or kept in motion by such acts.

THE METROPOLIS AND THE SOCIETY

Despite the image conveyed by many community studies, cities are not and never have been isolated systems or closed corporations. The flow of people, goods, and services between the modern metropolis, its hinterland, and the wider society is very substantial. Immigration and emigration keep the population aggregate in flux, mass communication alters conceptions which members of the aggregate hold of needs and norms, local organizations take their cues for action from national associations. Indeed, one might almost say that the metropolis is little more than an arena through which the forces of the larger society play.

On the other hand, metropolitan communities are *the* arenas in which these forces play. The majority of the population lives in metropolitan areas and is processed by organizations located there, although many of the organizations are branches or distribution points for national concerns. In structural terms a metropolitan community is a population aggregate (with class and ethnic strata) and a set of institutions or organizations — all located within a given geographical area. It is the processes which link the population aggregate with the institutional system that constitute the critical life blood of the metropolis — and the wider society.

The population aggregate is linked to the institutional system in two ways. Historical evidence seems to indicate that the city initially emerges as a point of crystallization — a focus or convergence of forces set free by social differentiation and the division of labor *before* it becomes a dense territorial concentration of human population. It is in connection with regional needs involving defense, trade, government, and religion that cities begin, not out of some propensity of human individuals to herd together in close geographical proximity (see especially 14).

Thus, it can be said that an institutional system attracts a population, and that the need for new institutions arises from the attracted population. One set of processes is engaged in allocating persons to positions, another in the recognition, the mobilization, the institutionalization of need. A third set of processes arising from the congestion of population and organizations involves the accommodation of conflicts and interests between persons, between organizations, between classes of the population, and between the community and the larger society.

THE ALLOCATION OF PERSONS TO POSITIONS

The metropolitan community, like the pool, can be viewed as an environment in which inhabitants carry on basic life processes, including birth, growth, maturation, reproduction, aging, and death. Even without social change, such processes would go on, involving, under current practices, an allocation or distribution of persons to positions in families, homes, and neighborhoods, in educational institutions, occupations, and voluntary associations, and in ethnic groups, subcultures, and deviant segments. It includes the socialization and education of the young, the operations of the labor market, and the traditional ecological concerns with the spatial distribution of human beings in the urban environment.

Such a perspective is not new or novel. The allocation of persons to positions has long been of interest in sociology, as represented, for example, in Durkheim's concern with the division of labor and Max Weber's concern with the allocation of life chances to persons. It was basic in Robert E. Park's conceptualization of ecological process, and constitutes an important facet of the work on occupations and professions undertaken by Everett C. Hughes and his students (see especially 3).

The metropolitan community can be viewed as a vast processing mill for the allocation of persons to positions, positions which vary according to stages of the life-cycle. Much as the life-cycle itself is the vital human propellant, the allocation of persons to positions may be viewed as a fundamental process, a central social drama, of the metropolitan community.

In the most fundamental ecological sense, the allocation of persons to positions in a metropolis is dependent upon the supply of persons, the population, and the supply of positions in groups and organizations. It is also dependent upon the supply of services, of institutional services of various kinds, which have become an integral part of the allocation process. For segments of the population and for neighborhood areas, considerations of location and access are needed to explain differential allocation. Throughout the allocation process, there is a kind of ecological interdependence, such that, for example, an increased supply of positions in one segment may channel off the supply of persons, or increased access to one set of services may decrease the demand for related services. Such ecological considerations — the supply of persons, the supply of positions in groups and organizations, the supply of services, location, and access — constitute the basic ecological variables involved in the allocation of persons to positions.

The "allocation of persons to positions" conveys a deterministic connotation to the effect that persons are being channeled by the system. This is an ecological perspective on the process, a perspective which probably explains more, and explains it more economically, than any other — if one sets about to relate a massive aggregate population to a system as large and complex as a metropolis. Indeed, even on the social-psychological level, such a perspective has considerable validity, since most people most of the time either accommodate to the system, without questioning it, or feel that their course is being determined for them.

However, research on the allocation of persons to positions in the metropolitan community need not and should not be confined to the ecological perspective. The allocation network in any phase of the life-cycle or in any institutional sphere clearly involves cultural attitudes, norms, and rules which may be viewed as integral parts of the system. The study of the movement of persons through the system may most properly be called career research, the problem of career research being that of discovering and explaining the status sequences which characteristically occur for persons through the life-cycle, through any phase of the life-cycle, and in any institutional system.

The metropolitan allocation process, like other aspects of metropolitan life, is affiliated with the larger society. Migration operates to supplement deficiencies of persons in a metropolitan community and to export surpluses. There are established dominance and hinterland systems by which certain specialists are educated and/or apprenticed in certain regions and subsequently allocated elsewhere. These are the "allocation" counterparts of the itinerant career. For some time metropolitan areas have drawn, and drawn differently, on surplus rural populations.[4] More immediately within a metropolitan area, the allocation process may be viewed as including the various patterns and consequences of residential mobility — suburbanization, centralization, concentration, segregation, invasion, and succession. Considerable research on the allocation of persons to residential positions within the metropolis has been done in a framework which included ecological considerations about the supply of persons, the supply of positions (dwelling units), the supply of services (real estate organizations), location, and access (including organized and aggregate segregation devices). In general, it seems unfortunate that the ecological perspective has tended to be confined to explaining the geographical pattern of the city and that research on the allocation of persons to residential positions has not involved broader considerations of allocation to work careers, family environments, and subcultures.[5]

Actually, an ecological perspective is explicit in Gestalt psychology and implicitly involved in what might be called the "osmosis" approach to acculturation. A perspective much closer to our "allocation" approach is involved in the concepts of differential association and differential anticipatory socialization. The metropolis does not have a market for the socialization of

[4] Rural–urban, inter-urban, and inter-regional allocation occurs differentially according to socio-economic status and educational achievement and differentially for various phases of the life-cycle. For an account of post-high school urban migration, see Pihlblad and Gregory (13).

A thorough account of rural–urban migration during an occupational career is given in Warren Peterson's study of public school teachers. For Kansas City teachers, occupational mobility was the central stage for rural–urban mobility, this being facilitated by the definition of similar occupational roles in school systems which are geographically and politically separate. In the regional educational community, of which Kansas City is a part, there seemed to be considerable consensus, both in the city and the hinterland, that certain teachers, at certain career and age junctions, were entitled and might be urged to enter the city system (12).

[5] The recent rash of study and commentary on life in the suburbs and the "exurbs" includes the notion that persons are being drawn into subcultural patterns when they move to certain types of residential neighborhoods.

children in the same sense as it has a labor market or a housing market, yet there may be tolerance limits, and, perhaps, processes which allocate a certain proportion of gangs to be delinquent and a certain proportion of young people to delinquent gangs. More clearly, a school system is an elaborate machine for the differential allocation of children to positions on career routes — although its allocation mechanism may not always be in gear with other institutional systems. Similarly, the rating and dating complex may be viewed as a system of allocating to marriage and family positions.

In a more general sense, the allocation process, or processes, channel persons to positions in social strata or classes; they effect differential social mobility. Research on social stratification has amply demonstrated that status characteristics are intercorrelated with one another and has provided substantial clues to the patterns of differential association and differential educational and occupational allocation involved in social mobility (see, for example, 6, 16).

Persons through the life process, especially in phases of growth and maturation, are allocated to different social strata with different life styles — through differential allocation to positions in families and neighborhoods, schools and occupations, residential areas and voluntary associations. The pattern of social stratification is the synthetic cumulative product of several institutionally differentiated but interdependent systems.

A Perspective on the Institutionalization of Needs

The differentiation of processes involving the allocation of persons and those involving the institutionalization of need is, in some respects, comparable to examining two sides of the same coin. The essential difference lies in the difference between persons and needs. Persons participate in institutions; institutions serve needs, or provide services to persons. From the standpoint of institutions serving needs, persons are treated as customers, clients, patients, or students, with emphasis on the immediate function at hand rather than the broader social stratification, life career, and metropolitan pattern implications of the allocation perspective. That institutions or organizations serve the *needs* of persons, is, in one sense, basically symbolic of the impersonalization of urban life deriving from technical specialization and role differentiation.

Allocation processes have a substantially ecological character in the sense that most of the participants most of the time are unaware or unconcerned about the effect of their action on the system as a whole and also in the sense that the processes set in motion by individual acts — the very processes themselves — proceed with an effect that is cumulative for the person and for the system. The servicing of needs, on the other hand, has much more the character of social action in Max Weber's sense and of symbolic interaction in George Herbert Mead's sense. Needs are prominent in the public vocabulary, used both as verbs and as nouns, and are prevalent, sometimes central, in the repertoire of collective deliberation within organizations and in community groups. Moreover, the question of need satisfaction is overt and central in transactions between organizations and customers or clients. Organizations are aware that they are serving needs, although the awareness often becomes routinized and habitual on both sides. In this sense, the serving of needs is the central overt drama of the metropolitan community; the allocation of persons is the central covert drama.

The "institutionalization of need is a process" which inherently embodies social interaction and the defining of situations, the incubation and activation of need from a substratum of exigencies. The concept "need" is currently very much out of fashion in sociology. Some such term is clearly required in process analysis. "Need," as we are employing it, has similarities to "demand" as used by economists, to "motive" as used in psychology, to "attitude," as used by some symbolic interactionists, as a tendency to act. In the analysis of institutional process, "need" appears to be preferable because it is prominent in the public vocabulary and because it conveys more clearly the idea that the person feels a requirement for resources or services which he does not himself command.

However, the recognition and institutionalization of need also involves ecological considerations, of a somewhat different character from those involved in the allocation of persons. Needs gestate in the substratum of exigencies in the general population or some portion of it. They are typically delivered into public consciousness by opinion leaders and subsequently molded into various forms by the peculiar manipulations of organizations and community committees.

When need-servicing processes are established, these processes tend to go on functioning with unanticipated consequences of an ecological nature — consequences for the allocation of persons (new positions for service personnel), consequences for other organizations or institutional systems (diverting or augmenting clientele).

The institutionalization of need can be employed to describe this entire process or constellation of processes. Even where the pattern is relatively routinized, the system is dependent upon repetitive arousal and definition of needs in the population, and upon the socialization of subsequent generations of clients. Need-serving organizations may be dependent upon retaining and re-enforcing clients, as well as adapting to the life-cycle.

At one extreme, given current technology and values, needs are clearly and rapidly articulated with the onset of an occurrence. Severe illness or injury call out a need for hospitalization, a new residential area requires water and sewage disposal facilities, and a dead body must be disposed of (and ordinarily provided a funeral). At the other extreme, the undercurrent exigencies are vague and undefined, and the process of articulation and definition of need is subject to great variation, including manipulation by opinion leaders or chance exposure to need-serving organizations. With progressive secularization, the decline of Puritanism, and related trends, for example, the middle class seems to be in a state of insecurity about child-rearing practices and subject to various forms of institutionalization in relation to these practices (see 15).

The "substratum of exigencies," the incubation bed of needs, is, and will probably remain, a somewhat mysterious territory, especially in connection with such phenomena as public restlessness about child-rearing practices. In the case of population increase, births, deaths, morbidity, and other recurrent vital statistics, the point of origin of needs can be pointed to with greater ease and precision. The substratum from which incentives for social action arise is very important, and, incidently, appears to be least recognized by the structural-functionalists. David Lockwood, among others, has pointed out that "Parsons' array of concepts is heavily weighted by assumptions and categories which relate to the normative elements in social action. On the other hand, what may be called the *substratum* of social action tends to be ignored as a general determinant of the dynamics of social systems." (5, p. 136)

States of exigency are likely to occur in a population when there is a radical change in numbers or composition, a change in the incidence of life events, a change in values, or a change in the prevailing institutional pattern of processing needs. Changes in the prevailing pattern of processing needs may occur, for example, through internal routinization of organizations, or through the mobility of professions away from their original clients. Conversely, an organization may, as in the case of the National Polio Foundation, resolve need to the point where the organization is left without function and must, if it is to remain intact, make connection with other needs. In the processes of institutionalization, a variety of perceived needs and activated efforts to satisfy needs become interlaced in the operations of organizations and community committees.

Among the variety of problems which perplex modern metropolitan communities, there are some which arise from the substratum of life and death contingencies — the high birth rate which began at the end of World War II, and the extension of the average life span through advances in medicine and other technologies. The increase in children and in older persons has called out the need for an expansion of service organizations and seems also to have had the effect of calling into question the adequacy of existing organizations in processing needs. It is seldom that organizations "simply" expand. There are very interesting questions arising out of shortages of services; when services have become limited in relation to the clientele, the institutional routine is broken. The clientele and various interest groups come to question the system, or significant aspects of it.

It is abundantly clear that the needs arising from the higher birth rate and greater longevity do not become perceived by everyone in the community simultaneously. Relative proximity to the locus of the exigency on which the need is based translates itself into salience of the need for the persons involved, and into consciousness of its existence. Recognition of the need will spread when those who are aware of it interact with others, but consciousness of need in the community at large, and particularly among those who are not affected by the need, will often depend upon the publicity given it by the communications media. In a very real sense these have a "needs-disseminating" as well as a news-disseminating function.

This brings up the question of needs arising out of conflicting interests. The accommodation of interests may itself be considered as a variety of institutionalization — an "institutionalization of conflict." Professions such as that of "arbitrator" and, of course, agencies such as community councils and metropolitan planning bodies are examples of collectivities formed to deal with the institutionalization of needs where several organizations and the interests of the wider community become involved. Diverse and often conflicting interests are pervasive throughout the whole web and tissue of institutionalization processes, and organizations as well as professions have built-in mechanisms of conflict resolution and control.

The problems of education and aging are good examples of the professionalization of "need arousal" and the institutionalization of conflict. They are also forceful illustrations that the metropolis is not a closed corporation. Among other things, a local metropolis is part of the hinterland of national organizations of diverse character with varying degrees of power — federal bureaus, business corporations, voluntary associations. There are, we suggest, common processes through which national organizations participate in and exert influence on local affairs, processes which are intimately related to the ecology and the "symbiotic balance" of the local metropolis. National organizations are likely to initiate, promote, or support local change when they come to recognize need, potential demand, or demand in a local population. This is clearest in the economics of marketing; in a basic sense it also applies in such areas as public health, welfare problems, intergroup relations, and urban renewal.

The local metropolis is not only a part of the hinterland of national organizations but it is also involved in the network of opinion and attitude movements. Members of the population aggregate, with varying speed and intensity, undergo changes in conceptions of needs and norms.

Mass opinion of this kind may be mobilized by national organizations interested in promoting change, or mass opinion may give rise to pressure groups on the local level who may seek help from national organizations, or who may innovate locally. In any case, a vital and fundamental process, "the institutionalization of need," is in operation.

THE ACCOMMODATION OF INTERESTS

The political processes of the metropolis take the form of interaction among organizations and interest groups, usually concerning means of satisfying expected or anticipated needs in the population or segments of the population. Inasmuch as most of the organizations have formal or informal national affiliations and are autonomous from one another on the local level, urban political processes often have a "United Nations" quality.[6]

As Park (11), Hughes (4), and others have amply demonstrated, the urban community — in fact all of Western society — functions as a vast processing mill for the movement of ethnic, pre-urban, lower-class peoples into the dominant stream of middle-class life. This is a vital part of processes involved in the allocation of persons to positions; it enters the institutionalization of need in many ways, especially for such non-profit public service institutions as city government, the public schools, and health and welfare agencies.

There is, of course, a wide area of inter-class interaction which is essentially ecological in character, involving the allocation of persons, the allocation of resources, and the institutionalization of need in the economic sphere. This is most evident in the division of labor, in the field of consumption, and in the urban spatial pattern as expressed in such indices as land values. However, these are no longer, if they ever were, entirely taken for granted. The labor movement has placed a considerable portion

6 Even on the level of city government (which deals with a relatively small portion of the affairs of the metropolis), there are relatively few two-party systems (even in large cities). Most of the decisions are made within a dominant party or political machine and involve the accommodation of interests between factions.

of inter-class allocation processes on a conscious level so that more favorable allocation practices come to be defined in the realm of need. Similarly, city planning and more localized zoning and exclusion practices have some effect on the "natural" course of allocation of persons to residential positions.

Apart from the provision of such basic services as water and sewers and streets to the population at large, most metropolitan community issues involve inter-class problems, and most public or quasi-public institutions have to deal with inter-class differences in the prevalence and intensity of need. The negotiation or accommodation of such differences is continuous and, to a considerable extent, reduced to bureaucratic routine. It is embodied in the need-processing functions of basic institutions but, at the same time, remains unsettled and subject to change.

The public school system is an interesting example of an institution which self-consciously deals with the problem of allocating persons to positions, and, indeed, of allocating lower-class children to higher positions than their parents held.[7] Yet, internally, an urban school system has great difficulty in providing equal opportunity for lower-class children, as better teachers ask for and receive transfers out of slum schools and as the administration yields to pressures to furnish better equipment and better supplies to middle- and upper-middle-class schools. More important, perhaps, teachers and administrators tend to routinize and particularize the need-processing functions, while minority-group and labor leaders are more likely to view educational needs in terms of the allocation of persons.[8] On the other hand, the schools at the present time are also confronted with pressures to upgrade the lower-middle-class quality of public school education — to allocate scientists and other leaders to the society of the future.

Like education, social work is confronted with conflicting definitions of need from class levels. As the voluntary agencies

[7] If there were no concern about the lower classes, the public schools might not have been established, since the middle and upper classes, without public school taxes, could manage to secure private schooling for their children.
[8] This is a part of what is involved in school desegregation disputes. In St. Louis and other metropolitan communities labor is leading a drive to secure public low-tuition college opportunities.

have become dependent upon the Community Chest as a system of informally taxing the general population, they become subject to need-defining pressures from labor and minority groups. On the other hand, the mobility of the social work profession and amorphous anxiety of the middle class concerning child-rearing practices and other personal adjustment problems has instigated new definitions of need and new service techniques. Health and welfare councils are simultaneously groping with problems of the "hard to reach client" and problems of how to service suburban families. Whereas in social work and public education the overt expression of need differences among social classes tends to be dampened with discussions of services to children, to the aged, and to the handicapped, in the arena of city government politics the issues are more overtly and dramatically expressed.[9]

Class-conflict issues are most clearly polarized in the dialectic between city-manager and city-machine forms of government. There are pronounced differences in definitions of the importance of certain needs and services. The middle and upper classes are more concerned about efficient trafficways, good police protection, and attracting industry. The lower classes show more con-

[9] We are especially aware of this in Kansas City because of a recent city election campaign which brought about the return of the Democratic Party, under that name, to power for the first time since the fall of Pendergast in 1940. This seems to have occurred in part because the supposedly non-partisan Citizen's Party and the highly professional City Manager's administration had become identified, in the minds of the working class, with the interests of business, *The Kansas City Star*, and the upper-middle and upper classes. At any rate, the Democratic coalition overtly waged a class-conflict campaign and won, mellowed only by the traditional pledges of parties out-of-power for more economy, less waste, and lower taxes.

The city administration was chastised for charging fees at the city general hospital and for not volunteering staff to distribute surplus commodities to the unemployed and the needy. The financial support of the Citizen's Party was traced as deriving from "the much-touted Country Club and Plaza districts, the wealthiest section of the city," and from "plush-plush Mission Hills and Prairie Village, Kansas . . . not even allowed to vote in Missouri, much less in Kansas City. . . . How many wage earners and lunch box carriers live in Mission Hills, in the Country Club, or on the Plaza? How can these real estate barons, with their multitudinous enterprises, understand the political thinking of Mr. Average Kansas Citizen?" (*The Kansas City News Press*, March 27, 1959)

What is more interesting, the City Manager and the Department heads were attacked as high-paid professionals, as imported from outside, as agents of business interests, with the implication that such professionals are cold, aloof, and without feeling for the man with the dinner pail.

cern about health and welfare needs of the indigent. An even deeper difference involves patronage, the conscious or intended allocation of persons; the lower classes feel that city government can, among other things, serve their needs for upward mobility.

If the metropolitan community is like a deep pool in a swamp, it is a very lively pool indeed. As a means of clarifying the complex currents, we have suggested that the metropolis be viewed in terms of the processes which connect the population aggregate with the institutional system — the allocation of persons to positions and the institutionalization of needs. Both of these processes affect the pattern of social stratification.

The realities of social stratification at any given time are associated with differential needs and differential definitions of need on the part of interest groups and opinion leaders representing different segments of the population. The major service institutions of the metropolis, in diverse ways, serve to accommodate inter-class differences and serve as upward mobility routes in the allocation of persons. Metropolitan politics are played in terms of inter-organizational and interest-group differences over definitions of needs and means of serving needs. Among other things, social process analysis has prospects for rescuing the study of power and politics from such narrow perspectives as "the community power structure."

References

1. Dewey, John. *Experience and Nature*. Chicago: Open Court Publishing Co., 1925.
2. Firey, Walter. "Discussion" of A. B. Hollingshead, "Community Research: Development and Present Condition," *American Sociological Review*, Vol. 13 (1948).
3. Hughes, Everett C. "Personality Types and the Division of Labor," *American Journal of Sociology*, Vol. 33 (1928), pp. 754–768.
4. Hughes, Everett C., and Helen McGill Hughes. *Where Peoples Meet*. Glencoe, Ill.: The Free Press, 1952.
5. Lockwood, David. "Some Remarks on 'The Social System,'" *British Journal of Sociology*, Vol. 7 (1956), pp. 134–146.

6. McGuire, Carson. "Social Stratification and Mobility Patterns," *American Sociological Review*, Vol. 15 (1950), pp. 195–204.

7. Mead, George Herbert. "Cooley's Contribution to American Sociological Thought," *American Journal of Sociology*, Vol. 35 (March 1930), pp. 693–706.

8. Mead, George Herbert. "The Philosophies of Royce, James, and Dewey in Their American Setting," *International Journal of Ethics*, Vol. 40 (1930).

9. Mead, George Herbert. *Mind, Self, and Society*, ed. by Charles W. Morris. Chicago: The University of Chicago Press, 1934.

10. Park, Robert E. "The City: Suggestions for the Investigation of Human Behavior in the Urban Environment," *American Journal of Sociology*, Vol. 20 (1916), pp. 577–612.

11. Park, Robert E. *Race and Culture*. Glencoe, Ill.: The Free Press, 1952.

12. Peterson, Warren A. "Career Stages and Inter-age Relationships: The Public School Teacher in Kansas City." Unpublished Ph.D. dissertation, Department of Sociology, University of Chicago, 1956.

13. Pihlblad, C. T., and C. L. Gregory. "Selective Aspects of Migration Among Missouri High School Graduates," *American Sociological Review*, Vol. 19 (June 1954), pp. 314–334.

14. Pirenne, Henri. *Mediaeval Cities*. Princeton, N.J.: Princeton University Press, 1952.

15. Seeley, John R., R. Alexander Sim, and Elizabeth W. Loosely. *Crestwood Heights: A Study of the Culture of Suburban Life*. New York: Basic Books, Inc., 1956.

16. Warner, W. Lloyd, and James C. Abegglen. *Occupational Mobility in American Business and Industry*. Minneapolis: University of Minnesota Press, 1952.

Index of Names

Index of Names

Cavan, Ruth: on adjustment in old age, 526–536; on adult socialization, 64n; on family cycle, 507

Cellini, Benvenuto, on doctors, 208

Churchill, Allen, on new generation, 363

Churchill, Winston, on status, 316n

Clark, Margaret, on doctor–patient relationship, 208

Cleckley, Hervey M., on irresistible impulses, 450

Cloward, Richard, on opportunity systems, 474

Conant, James, on scientific theory, 438

Cooley, Charles H.: on children, 105; and game theory, 579n; as an idealist, 652n; on looking-glass self, 540; on others, 120; on perspective, 154, 526; on the self, 92–93, 110; on self-conception, 559; on self theory, 556; on significant others, 141; as social interactionist, 3, 180; on sympathy, 19n

Cressey, Donald R.: on behavior systems, 474; on crime and social learning, 440; on crime statistics, 471n; on differential-association theory, 430; on embezzlement, 550; on role theory and compulsive crimes, 443–467

Cronbach, L. J., on empathy, 46n

Dahrendorf, Ralf, on politics and stratification, 317n

Dalton, Melville, on labor-management cooperation, 267–284

Davidoff, Eugene, on melancholia, 543

Davis, Fred, on poliomyelitis, 553

Davis, Kingsley, on roles, 25

Dembo, T.: on rehabilitation, 553; on self-feelings, 556

Deutscher, Irwin: on adult socialization, 64n; on delinquency research, 468–481; on postparental socialization, 506–525

Dewey, John: on communication, 134; on events and objects, 652; instrumentalism of, 403; on "others," 120, 472n; as social interactionist, 3, 180; on thinking, 150, 153; on truncated act, 100

Dewey, Richard, on urbanism, 626n

DiPrima, Diane, quoted, 370

Donohue, G. A., on the self, 557

Dubin, Robert: on central life interests of workers, 247–266; on retirement, 528n

Duncan, Otis Dudley, on community theory, 641n

Durkheim, Emile: on *anomie*, 362; on collective representations, 30; on division of labor, 654; on egoistic suicide, 541; on organic solidarity, 261

Dymond, R. F., on symbolic interactionist concepts, 46n

Edwards, Allen L., on conflicts of perspective, 139

Emery, Frederick E., on communication, 144

Erikson, Erik: on developmental stages, 64; on identity, 78, 81, 82

Eulau, Heinz, on class and voting behavior, 132

Fallers, L. A., on social stratification, 313n

Farber, Bernard, on family types, 285–306

Faris, Ellsworth: on "others," 120; on the social act, 195; as social interactionist, 180

Ferri, Enrico, on economics and crime, 426

Festinger, Leon: on conflicts of perspective, 140; on sects, 327

Finestone, Harold, on heroin use, 369n

Firey, Walter, as an idealist, 652n

Fishman, Sidney, on rehabilitation, 555–556

Fitch, Robert, on bohemianism, 364

Flynn, Frank T., on delinquency trends, 470

Foote, Nelson N.: on human action, 451; on identification, 89n, 154; on role theory, 42n; on status, 79

Fortune, Reo, on Dobuans, 407

Fox, Renée, on client–professional relations, 578

Index of Names

Frank, Philipp, on scientific theory, 437–438

Frazier, E. Franklin, on desegregation, 608–624

Freidson, Eliot, on doctor–patient relationship, 207–224

Freud, Caroline, on beatniks, 372n

Freud, Sigmund: on the social act, 204; theory of development of, 63–64

Gage, N. L., on empathy, 46n

Gans, Herbert J., on urbanism and suburbanism, 625–648

Gault, Robert H.: on psychopathic personality, 454–455; on sexual symbolism, 458

Ginsberg, Allen: and beat generation, 363, 370; quoted, 364, 365

Glaser, Daniel, on differential-association theory of crime, 425–442

Glick, Clarence, on status, 120

Glick, Paul C., on family cycle, 507

Glueck, Sheldon, on differential-association theory of crime, 432–433

Goddard, Henry H., on delinquency, 382

Goffman, Erving: on adaptation to failure, 482–505; on adult socialization, 64n; on appearances, 87n, 91n; on identity, 93; on interaction as bargaining, 576n; on the self, 226; on the social act, 196

Gold, Herbert: on beatniks, 368; quoting Kerouac, 371n

Goldstein, Bernard, on self-conceptions, 132

Gorer, Geoffrey, encapsulated mother hypothesis of, 106

Gouldner, Alvin W., on career lines, 137

Grayson, Morris, on paraplegia, 551

Greer, Scott, on inner city, 628

Gross, Neal, on roles, 29

Grunwald, Ernest, on sociology of knowledge, 361

Habenstein, Robert W., on sociology of the funeral director, 225–246

Hall, Jerome, on kleptomania, 457n

Hastorf, A. H., on empathy, 46n

Havighurst, Robert J., on retirement, 528n

Healy, William, on delinquency, 382, 426

Herbart, J. F., on apperceptive mass, 17

Herberg, Will, on schisms in unions, 273

Hewitt, Lester E., on deviant behavior, 474n

Hill, Reuben, on interdependence of roles, 35

Hobbes, Thomas, on social disorganization, 315

Hofstadter, Richard, on bohemianism, 363

Hollingshead, August B., on physicians, 220

Holmes, John Clellon: on the beat generation, 364, 365, 368; on the Negro, 370n

Howes, E. L., on definition of the situation, 152n

Hughes, Everett C.: on adaptation to failure, 483, 487n; on allocation of professions, 654; on client-professional relations, 576n; on middle class, 662; on the "other," 119–127; on social organization, 225; on work and the self, 226, 241–244

Huizinga, Jan, on play, 109–110

Hunt, David, on delinquency, 478n

Hyman, Herbert, on reference groups, 128, 154

Jacobson, Don, on Allen Ginsberg, 365

James, William: on conflict of roles, 140; on conversion, 354; on others, 120; on self-definition, 472n; on selves, 11; as social interactionist, 180; on test of truth, 403

Janis, Irving L., on fear, 347

Jenkins, Richard L., on deviant behavior, 474n

Jenne, William C., on family, 300n

Jung, Carl, on "loss of significance," 540–541

Kallen, Horace, on development, 65–66

Index of Names

Kardiner, Abram, on Alorese, 407

Karpman, Benjamin, on kleptomania, 457n

Katz, Elihu, on communication channels, 144

Keller, Suzanne, on reference groups, 133

Kerouac, Jack: on addiction, 370n; and beat generation, 362, 364; on Negro, 370; quoted, 371; on Zen Buddhism, 370n

Kessler, H. H.: on inferiority feelings, 555; on rehabilitation, 553

Killian, Lewis M.: on conflicts of perspective, 139–140; on collective behavior, 342; on fad and fashion, 469n; on multiple group membership, 349; on Negro leaders, 609n

Kindelsperger, Kenneth W., on delinquency rates, 471n

Kirkpatrick, Clifford, on family dilemmas, 287n

Kolb, William L., on values, 371n

Koos, Earl London, on doctor-patient relationships, 208

Korn, Richard R., on differential commitment, 431

Kornhauser, William, on liberals and radicals, 321–339

Ktsanes, Thomas, on suburbia, 641

Kube, Ella, on the inner city, 628

Kuhn, Manford: on the interview, 193–206; on self theory, 540, 557

Kvaraceus, William C., on deviant behavior, 474n

Landgrebe, Ludwig, on perspectives, 144

Lang, Gladys Engel, on collective behavior, 340–359

Lang, Kurt, on collective behavior, 340–359

LaPiere, Richard T., on fad and fashion, 469n

Latif, I. L., on communication, 105

Lazarsfeld, Paul F., on communication channels, 144

LeBon, Gustav, on the crowd, 341

Lemert, Edwin M., on tolerance quotient, 472n

Lewin, Kurt, 20

Lindesmith, Alfred R.: on addiction, 550; on analytic induction, 429, 592n; on the self, 103

Linton, Ralph: on psychotics, 406; on role theory, 21, 23; on the self-concept, 164–165

Lipset, Seymour M.: on politics and stratification, 317n; on schisms in unions, 273

Lipton, Lawrence, on marihuana, 369n

Litman, Theodor J., on self-conception and physical rehabilitation, 550–574

Lockwood, David, on norms in Parsons, 660

Lombroso, Cesare, on criminology, 382

Lubell, Samuel, on the middle class, 310

Lynd, Helen, on identity, 97, 98

Lynd, Robert, 309

Maccoby, Eleanor E., on role and interview, 194

Maccoby, Nathan, on role and interview, 194

MacCurdy, John T., on demoralization, 348

MacGregor, Frances C., on disfigurement, 553

Mannheim, Karl: compared to Riesman, 371; on perspectives, 144; on sociology of knowledge, 360–361

Marx, Karl, as sociologist of knowledge, 360–361

Matza, David, on delinquency, 469, 470

Maurer, David W., on con game, 483

McCarthy, Mary, on the beatniks, 366

McCorkle, Lloyd W., on differential commitment, 431

McDougall, William, on the group mind, 10

McGinnis, W., on definition of the situation, 152n

McKay, Henry D., on ecology, 384, 427

McKenzie, Robert D., on the city, 651

670

Index of Names

Rosen, Hjalmar, on pressures on business agents, 275

Rosen, R. A. Hudson, on pressures on business agents, 275

Roth, Julius A., on treatment of tuberculosis as a bargaining process, 575–588

Royce, Josiah, on "others," 10

SAPIR, EDWARD, on communication, 134

Sarbin, Theodore R., on role theory, 42n

Saunders, Lyle W., on doctor–patient relationships, 208

Schmidt, W. H., on rehabilitation, 554

Schneider, B. H., on definition of the situation, 152n

Schnore, Leo F., on community theory, 641n

Schwartz, A. G., on left hemiplegia, 553

Schwitz, Heinrich, on customs as safety valves, 352n

Seidenfeld, M. A., on poliomyelitis, 553

Shaw, Clifford R.: on ecological method, 384, 427; on experimental research, 396

Shelsky, Irving, on the self-concept, 556

Sherif, Muzafer, on reference groups, 154

Shibutani, Tomatsu, on reference groups and social control, 128–147

Short, James F., Jr., on differential association, 437

Sighele, Scipio, on the crowd, 341

Simmel, Georg: on confidence, 213; on perspectives, 139; as social interactionist, 3; on urbanism, 625

Sirjamaki, John, on new roles, 509

Smith, Adam, on emulation, 120

Smith, Charles U., on Negro leaders, 609n

Solomon, R. L., on definition of the situation, 152n

Staub, Hugo: on kleptomania, 457; on the unconscious in crime, 454

Stern, Eric, on reference groups, 133

Stone, Alfred H., on segregation, 610n

Stone, Gregory P., on appearance and the self, 86–118

Strauss, Anselm: on identification, 154; on the self, 103; on transformations of identity, 63–85

Strauss, George, on pressures on business agents, 275

Streib, Gordon F., on retirement, 528n

Stryker, Sheldon, on role-taking, 41–62

Sullivan, Harry Stack: on development theory, 63–64; as early social interactionist, 6; on parataxic communication, 112–113; on role theory, 42n; on the self, 92–93; on significant others, 141, 154; on syntaxis, 114

Sumner, William Graham, on mores, 389

Sussman, Marvin B., on new roles, 509

Sutherland, Edwin H.: on behavior systems, 404; on confidence games, 483; on crime statistics, 471n; on interactionist theory, 425, 427–440; on learning process in crime, 476; on white collar criminals, 411

Switzer, Mary E., on rehabilitation, 552

TARDE, GABRIEL: on crime, 426; on the crowd, 341

Tawney, Richard H., on work, 248

Teeters, Negley K., on delinquency, 469, 470

Thom, D. A., on spinal cord injuries, 553

Thomas, W. I.: on definition of the situation, 130, 433; as early symbolic interactionist, 3, 180; on "others," 120; on the social act, 188

Tönnies, Ferdinand, on *Gesellschaft*, 628

Thrasher, Frederick H., on gangs, 427

Toby, Jackson, on deviant behavior, 474n

D E F G H I J — R — 7 3 2 1 0 / 6 9 8 7 6

Index of Subjects

ACCOMMODATION of interests, 662–665. *See also* Conflict; Cooperation; Social process

Act, social: and attitudes, 100; as continuous process, 321; defined, 57, 194–196; the interview as, 196–197. *See also* Action, social

Action, social: relation of, to research, 393–399; and servicing of needs, 658–660; systems of, 401–424; theoretical bases of, 403–404. *See also* Act, social

Adolescent, and delinquency, 468–481

Adult, socialization of: 63–85, 114–117, 506–525, 643; in retirement, 526–536

Affective ties, defined, 346

Allocation of persons to positions, 654–657. *See also* Class; Status; Stratification

Anomie: and beatniks, 372; defined, 361–362. *See also* Durkheim, Emile; Merton, Robert

Appearance, 86–118; defined, 89–90; and the self, 101–104

Apperceptive mass, defined, 17. *See also* Definition of the situation; Gestalt school; Perception; Perspective

Attitude: ambiguity of term, 100n; and expectation, 153; and the role of the other, 42, 45, 45n; in social process, 153

BARGAINING as a form of interaction, 575–588

Beat generation, 360–377; defined, 363–364

Black Belt, 610–611

Bohemianism: after 1920, 363, 364n; and the beatnik, 366–367

CAREERS: and gratification, 290; life, 506–507; new roles for, 544–546,

and orientation of family members, 288–289. *See also* Life cycle

Causation, pluralistic, 427–428, 439–440, 538

Change, social, 381–400; as a culture value, 510–511; and desegregation, 608–624. *See also* Transformation

Child: relation of, to grandparents, 533–535; relation of, to parents, 285–306. *See also* Adolescent

Childless, in city, 629–630

City: comparison of, with suburbs, 635–639; defined, 626; inner, 627–633; outer, 633–635; as a social action system, 413–421; *See also* Urbanism

Class: in client-professional relations, 200, 220; conflict, 664–665; effect of, on attitudes, 154; effect of, on housing, 640; and *laissez-faire* doctrine, 409–410; lower, 663; middle, 662; non-acting, 187; and the political order, 307–320; as result of allocation, 657. *See also* Class consciousness; Status; Stratification

Class consciousness, research on, 132, 307–320

Client: ambivalence of, 244–246; relation of, to professional, 199–200

Cognitive definitions, 346

Collective behavior, 340–359

Collective defense: defined, 344; discussion of, 350–352

Collective redefinition: definition of, 344; discussion of, 352–353

Commitment: defined, 321–322; differential, 431; to family, 289–290; termination of, 330

Communication: channels of, 134–135, 144; parataxic, 112; and society, 134

Community: *laissez-faire*, 409–413; relation of liberals to, 333; social processes in metropolitan, 649–666; universal, 57; urban, 413–421

Index of Subjects

Index of Subjects

Index of Subjects